THE QUEEN'S SCOTLAND

THE EASTERN COUNTIES

Already published in this series:

THE HEARTLAND: CLACKMANNANSHIRE,
PERTHSHIRE AND STIRLINGSHIRE

THE QUEEN'S SCOTLAND

THE EASTERN COUNTIES

ABERDEENSHIRE ANGUS AND KINCARDINESHIRE

By

NIGEL TRANTER

HODDER AND STOUGHTON
LONDON SYDNEY AUCKLAND TORONTO

TOWNS AND VILLAGES

A key to the towns, villages and natural features of Aberdeenshire, Angus and Kincardineshire shown on the map and mentioned in the text.

Aberdeen	N8	Carmylie	J16	Ferryden	L14
Aberdour	M1	Carnoustie	J17	Fetterangus	O3
Abergeldie	E10	Castle Fraser	K8	Fettercairn	K12
Aberlemno	H15	Catterline	M12	Fetteresso	M11
Aboyne	H9	Chapel of Garioch	K6	Feughside	J10
Airlie	F15	Clashindarroch	G5	Fiddes	M11
Aldbar	H14	Clatt	H6	Finavon	H14
Alford	J7	Clola	O4	Findon	N9
Arbirlot	J16	Clova	F12	Fintray	N7
Arbroath	K16	Cluny	K8	Forbes	H8
Arbuthnott	M12	Cock Bridge	E8	Fordoun	L12
Arnage	N5	Collieston	O6	Forfar	G15
Auchenblae	L12	Colpy	J5	Forgue	J4
Auchindoir	G6	Corgarff	E8	Forter	D13
Auchleven	J6	Corrennie	J8	Forvie	O6
Auchnagatt	N4	Cortachy	G14	Fowlis Easter	F17
Auchterhouse	F17	Coull	H9	Foveran	O6
Auchterless	K4	Cove	N9	Fraserburgh	O1
		Craig	G6	Frendraught	K4
Balbegno	J13	Craigievar	H8	Friockheim	J15
Balgavies	H15	Craigo	K13	Fyvie	L5
Ballater	F10	Craigston	L2		
Balmedie	N7	Craigton	F15	Gairnsheil	E9
Balmoral	E10	Crathie	E10	Garmond	L3
Balnaboth	F13	Crimond	O2	Gartly	H5
Balnamoon	J14	Cruden Bay	P5	Garvock	L13
Banchory	K10	Culsalmond	K5	Gellan	K10
Banchory-Devenick	N9	Cults	N9	Gight	M5
Barra	L6	Cuminestown	L3	Glamis	F16
Barras	M12			Glass	G4
Barry	H17	Daviot	L6	Glasslaw	M2
Barthol Chapel	L5	Dess	H9	Glenbervie	L11
Belhelvie	N7	Dinnet	G9	Glenbuchat	F7
Benholm	M13	Douglastown	G16	Glen Clova	F13
Benvie	F18	Dronley	F17	Glen Doll	E12
Birse	J10	Drum	L9	Glen Esk	H12
Blackburn	M8	Drumblade	J4	Glengairn	E9
Boddam	P4	Drumlithie	L11	Glenisla	D14
Bognie	J4	Drumoak	L9	Glen Lethnot	H13
Bourtie	L6	Drumtochty	K12	Glen Muick	F11
Braemar	D10	Dun	K14	Glenogil	G13
Brechin	J14	Dundee	G18	Glentanar	H10
Bridge of Brewlands	D14	Dunecht	L8	Glen Prosen	E13
Bridge of Don	N8	Dunnichen	H15	Greystone	H16
Bridge of Dye	K11	Dunnideer	J6	Guthrie	J15
Bridgend	H13	Dunnottar	M11	Gourdon	M13
Broughty Ferry	H18	Durris	L10		
Brucklay	N3	Dyce	M8	Haddo	M5
Buchan Ness	P4	Dykehead	F14	Hatton	O5
Bucksburn	N8			Huntly	H4
Buddon	H17	Eassie	F16		
		Echt	L8	Innermarkie	G4
Cairn Catto	O4	Edzell	J13	Insch	J6
Cairn o' Mount	K11	Ellon	N5	Inverallochy	O1
The Cairngorms	B10	Essie	G6	Inverarity	G16
Cairnbulg	O1	Ethie	K16	Inverbervie	M12
Cairnie	L8			Inverey	C11
Cambus o' May	G9	Farnell	J15	Invergowrie	F18
Careston	H14	Fern	H14	Inverkeilor	K15

v

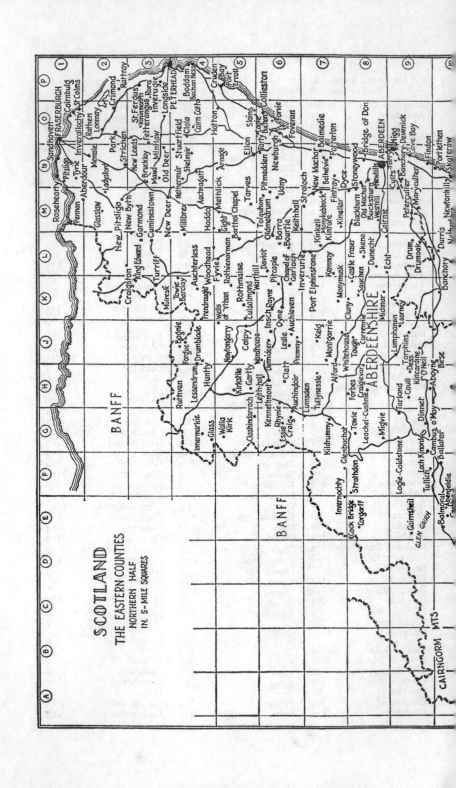

SCOTLAND

THE EASTERN COUNTIES

IN 5-MILE SQUARES

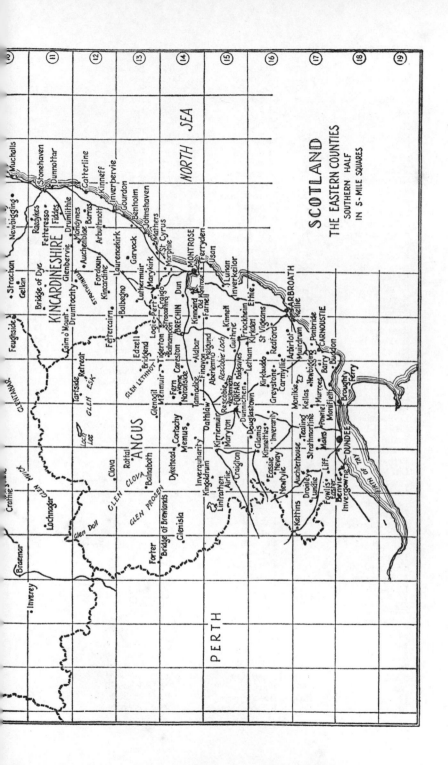

SCOTLAND
THE EASTERN COUNTIES
SOUTHERN HALF
IN 5-MILE SQUARES

LIST OF ILLUSTRATIONS

ACKNOWLEDGMENTS

Planair: plates 1, 26, 41, 43, 45, 46, 49
National Monuments Record of Scotland: plates 2, 3, 4, 5, 7, 9, 10, 15, 17, 19, 21, 22, 23, 42, 44
Department of the Environment, Edinburgh: plates 6, 13, 14, 16, 20, 24, 25, 34
The Scottish Tourist Board: plates 8, 12, 38
Brian Long: plates 11, 18, 23, 27, 28, 29, 32, 35, 36, 37, 39, 40, 47, 48
Spanphoto: plates 30, 31
Town Planning Department, Dundee: plate 33

ABERDEENSHIRE

In many ways Aberdeenshire is outstanding—not least in that it forms the great hunched shoulder of Scotland, thrusting out into the North Sea many miles farther eastwards than any other point. But more important is the fact that it contains the greatest single mass of farming and agricultural settled land anywhere north of the three counties of Yorkshire. It is only fifth in acreage of Scotland's counties —but the other four comprise, in the main, vast empty tracts of mountain and moor. Aberdeenshire's 1,252,267 acres does contain part of the Cairngorm Mountains; but this is only a comparatively small proportion of the whole. For the sheer extent of its farmlands this county cannot be rivalled. It is claimed that there are 10,000 farms in Aberdeenshire, and this, for anyone who has examined the area parish by parish, would seem like an underestimate. There are, in fact, 85 parishes in the county—with Braemar and Crathie parish itself covering over 200,000 acres, larger than nine other Scottish *counties*. Parishes are a pretty good yardstick to measure the importance of agricultural and rural areas, and in Scotland only Perthshire comes near it, with 78 parishes. Few, even knowledgeable, people, in the writer's experience, realise just how large, important and interesting an entity is Aberdeenshire—for its age-old fertility and fine pastureland has meant that always it was an area fairly highly populated, even in prehistoric times, much sought-after, cherished and, in its own way, rich. The fact that it lies, as it were, out on a limb, and not on the road to anywhere else, has caused it to be by-passed frequently by travellers down the ages—and still does— which is not altogether a bad thing, perhaps. In consequence, it represents *terra incognita* for the mass of the Scottish population, its enormous extent, multifarious interest and great scenic attractions— for it is far from the bleak and windswept expanse many consider it— little appreciated. Thus it has become something of a world on its own, an almost self-contained and self-sufficient land. Not that it is in the least inward-looking or insular; the reverse actually, as any consideration of the number of national-scope research institutes and experimental establishments will reveal. Aberdeen city, with its great and world-famous University, leading in many aspects of knowledge and investigation, not least in medical matters, has always faced outwards, not inwards—yet nevertheless epitomises its great county hinterland. And with the recent discovery and exploitation of North Sea oil and gas, off the Aberdeenshire coast, the entire area is destined for further great advances—and will seize such with both hands, undoubtedly. For it is a vigorous, masculine sort of place, and no backwater.

All this has represented a very major challenge to the present writer—inevitably—in the sheer size of it, if nothing else. The tackling of this challenge has been an education.

Anciently the mighty land-mass used to be divided into provinces which more or less coincided with the mormaorships and thanedoms of old, themselves developing into the medieval earldoms and lordships of Mar, Formartine, Garioch, Buchan and Strathbogie—and these are still fairly valid divisions. They have their own subdivisions—Mar, for instance, consists of Braemar, Cromar and Midmar. The great rivers inevitably play an important part in dividing up the land, the Dee, Don, Ury, Ythan, Ugie and Deveron; but to a large extent these can be equated with the aforementioned provinces. Apart from Aberdeen itself, there are no large towns, but a great many small ones, and villages innumerable. Only Peterhead and Fraserburgh (12,497 and 10,462 population respectively) both Buchan fishing-ports, with Inverurie (5152), are over 5000 population. Yet this is a populous land, with nothing of emptiness about it. It is the villages, and more important the farms, which still hold the people—and as kindly and friendly a people as you will find anywhere, warm-hearted as they are straightforward.

With agriculture, more especially stock-rearing—Aberdeen-Angus cattle, of course, represent the hall-mark of stock-farming—as the dominant interest, all is geared to this vastly productive industry, and the land is well farmed and quietly prosperous, with the landscapes, especially at harvest-time, an amazing sea of gold out of which arise the swelling islands of cattle-dotted green—for it is a country of low hills, low at least for Northern Scotland. Distances are vast, and *look* vast, the prospects tending to be breath-taking, with 50-mile views normal. And strangely, from almost everywhere in this huge county, the unmistakable, shapely and romantic peak of Benachie stands out on the horizon, an ever-present joy. Surely seldom was any land so cherished and presided over—never dominated—by a single hill. Benachie has always been beloved by the folk of the North-East, and deservedly so.

All the concentrated stock-raising and corn-growing brings its subsidiary industries, but these are country-based and do not tend to spoil the scene—milling, food-processing, distilling, auction-marts, fertilisers, seeds, agricultural-machinery depots and so on. Along the lengthy coastline fishing and its dependent products predominate, for Aberdeen, Peterhead, Fraserburgh, Rosehearty and the like are amongst the most important fishing-ports in the country, and from Aberdeen the fish-trains rumble nightly on the long haul to the South and London. To the north-west of the county especially, forestry is becoming ever more important, some of the forests, such as Clashindarroch, Bin, Benachie and Deer, being quite enormous. And granite quarrying, though less important than once it was, is still to the fore; many of the most famous buildings in the United Kingdom, and beyond it, are built on Aberdeen granite.

Tourism as an industry, however, is as yet little developed—

though it should be, for there is so much here for the visitor to enjoy. Royal Deeside and the eastern approaches to the Cairngorms are well known of course, also Aberdeen city itself. But the rest is largely untapped as a reservoir of attractions for the discerning traveller and holiday-maker. The scenery, without being dramatic, is fairly consistently excellent and unspoiled. Nowhere else in Scotland are there quite so many fine castles and fortified houses— for though they were much needed against internecine feuding and Highland caterans, they were not in the paths of invading armies, to be "dinged doun". Old churches are legion, even though mostly in ruin and replaced by the severely practical early 19th century "preaching-kirks" beloved by a stern race of wordy religionists and metaphysicians. These are leavened, however, by a great many Episcopal churches, even in the most rural situations, for this was a great and enduring centre of Episcopacy. Stone-circles are every-where—never was there an area with so many, even though, especially in Buchan, great numbers have been swept away in the interests of agriculture. And Pictish symbol-stones are widespread, with more of the early pagan variety than the cross-slabs, as in Angus. Other proto- and prehistoric remains are equally plentiful, though the Romans did not make much impact up here. For lovers of history and the historic atmosphere, Aberdeenshire is a delight, for here the great clans of Gordon and Forbes fought it out over the centuries, the Frasers and Hays and Urquharts assisting; here Bruce —who was himself hereditary Lord of Garioch—fought, and his brother Edward punished the Comyn province of Buchan in a "herrying" which is spoken of yet; here Mary Queen of Scots made her only venture into the North, to bring down the power of Gordon, however unwillingly; and here Montrose conducted his brilliant campaigns.

But for those to whom all this appeals little, there are other interests. The rivers, in especial, splendid streams which are an angler's paradise, and which also provide magnificent scenery in linns and waterfalls and ravines. There are the mountains, the Cairngorms, Lochnagar and the lesser-known mounths of the Forest of Birse, the Firmounth, the White Mounth, the Ladder Hills and others; and the glorious Caledonian pine-forests of upper Deeside, for climbers and lovers of scenery and the wild. And for skiers, there are the slopes above the Cairnwell Pass and Glen Shee. The enormous attractions of the coast are still less known. From Aber-deen northwards is the longest single stretch of sandy beaches, backed by dunes, in all Scotland, possibly in the United Kingdom—30 miles of golden strands, with an intervening stretch of fine cliff scenery at Slains and Collieston, the Bullers of Buchan and north of Fraser-burgh. Moreover the Ythan estuary and the nature reserve of the Sands of Forvie are a bird-watcher's joy, as is the Loch of Strathbeg and the Rattray coast farther north.

Aberdeenshire is, in fact, a country on its own, with infinite variety and enormous potential for the visitor and for its own folk, who perhaps scarcely know it as well as it deserves. Few areas of these islands are more worth discovering.

Aberdeen has always been rich in the production of ballads and songs; and in these days of the revival of folk music, the Aberdeen Bothy Ballads, and their presenting groups, are notably to the fore.

A final, small and way-out tribute. Aberdeenshire County Council is to be congratulated on at least two quite important aspects of countryside amenity—the maintaining, modernisation and pleasing identification of innumerable small rural schools; and its excellent grass-cutting and tidying-up service for the host of parish churches and their kirkyards, which make of these a model for other counties. But—why confine this only to the parish churches? Do not the poor Episcopalians, and the other non-parish churches, also pay their rates?

Aberdeen. Aberdeen is a most satisfying city. It is the right size, at 185,000 of population not too large to be comprehended comfortably, and not so small that it need lack any amenity. It is full of character, bursting with it, indeed. It is probably the cleanest-looking city in the world, thanks to its famous white granite buildings and fresh sea breezes. Its people are notable for their warm-heartedness and friendliness. It is far enough away from any other large centre of population to be entirely distinctive, the obvious metropolis for a great area. And it has a long, resounding and exciting history.

The name's derivation has been much argued over. The most reasonable claim is that it comes from *aber dubh abhainn*, meaning at the mouth of the dark water. The fact that both Dee and Don reach the sea here complicates the issue—though the Dee must have priority. The Romans Latinised its name to Diva or Deva, and called its Pictish city Devana; though some authorities hold that Devana was fully 30 miles inland, up Dee, near Loch Davan, between Aboyne and Ballater. Be that as it may, a city was bound to grow up at the mouth of this, one of the great rivers of Scotland; and when the Don, only a little less majestic, comes in only a couple of miles to the north, then the area between these two could not fail to be of the utmost importance. Especially when, as hinterland, is the greatest lowland land-mass in the country, a farming and pasture land of a magnitude such as is frequently not realised even by the normally well informed. There are said to be more than 10,000 farms in Aberdeenshire—and no one who has traversed this enormous territory in the widest part of Scotland would doubt it for a moment. Aberdeen, then, was ordained to greatness.

It is the third city of Scotland—but only just. And it is fair to admit that it lacks the magnificent scenic site of Dundee, a city of comparable size, and in so many aspects its rival. It has not the lofty eminences and skylines. On the other hand, it has not the same problems of lack of space and steeply climbing streets. Accordingly, it is very much more compact than Dundee; and though it inevitably spreads itself ever wider, today, it is still mainly contained within a recognisable perimeter of about three miles square.

Boece, a frequently somewhat fanciful historian, declares that Aberdeen was erected to the status of city by Pope Gregory, about the year 893; but of this there is no true record. The earliest extant charter, proudly preserved in the Town House in Union Street, is of 1179, and granted to the Royal Burgh of Aberdeen by William the Lion. This, of course, was *Old* Aberdeen, for there are two distinct cities, with the older to the north, nearer the Don—even though New Aberdeen, which comprises most of the present city, is of far from recent foundation. This charter of 1179 confirms the burgesses in all the municipal and trading privileges enjoyed by their forefathers under the king's grandfather, David I (1124–53); so we move back in time. We read, too, in the Icelandic saga *Heimskringla*, dated 1153, that a Norse kinglet, Eysteinn, "brought his ships to Apardion, where he killed many people and wasted the city". No doubt he came via the Orkney and Shetland Isles. Aberdeen has always had strong links with the Orcades. William the Lion, as well as granting the charter, built a palace here, and set up a mint; and his son Alexander II spent Christmas here in 1222, and founded the Black-friars Monastery. From then onwards the history of the city is stirring. Edward I, Hammer of the Scots, came here in 1296 and Wallace came thereafter, allegedly burning 100 ships in the harbour —which is probably one of Blind Harry's exaggerations. Bruce, too, had much to do with Aberdeen, holding a council here in 1308, the first major council of his reign, after his severe illness at Inverurie near by and the battle he won there, sick as he was. The then provost was valiant thereafter in support of the king; indeed he and his townsfolk distinguished themselves notably by actually attacking and forcing the surrender of the English garrison of the castle, or citadel, here—almost a unique triumph for citizenry. It was for this stout feat that Bruce gave Aberdeen the arms it still bears, three towers two and one, within a double tressure, and the motto *BON ACCORD*. Bruce also conveyed to the town the royal forest of Stocket, with valuable fishings in Dee and Don, and other privileges. He built the Brig o' Balgownie, over the Don, a very lovely single Gothic arch, of 67 feet span, 35 feet above the river, referred to by Byron in his *Don Juan*; he had been much impressed as a boy whenever he crossed this, for there was an ancient prophecy:

> *Brig o' Balgownie, though wight be your wa'*
> *Wi' a wife's ae son, and a meer's ae foal,*
> *Down ye shall fa'!*

Byron, who was half a Gordon and brought up hereabouts, was himself his widowed mother's only son, and was intrigued. Balgownie Bridge still stands, however, one of Aberdeen's treasures; and the fund Bruce left to build and maintain it has been so well administered over the centuries that 17 other bridges have been erected from

5

it, all over the town. Aberdeen, then, is much indebted to Robert Bruce. Although the Stocket Forest is now largely built up, the small Stocket Park, in the neighbourhood of the Royal Infirmary, still keeps the name, as do sundry streets and avenues.

Strangely enough, a century after this, another valiant and militant provost, Sir Robert Davidson, got himself killed while leading a contingent of citizens to the fatal field of Harlaw, not very far away, when the then Lord of the Isles made his bid to change the history of Scotland. Aberdeen was so upset about this, and its attendant inconveniences, that the Town Council thereupon passed a measure prohibiting all future chief magistrates from leaving the city bounds in their official capacity—a canny decision. Provost Sir Robert lies buried in St. Nicholas Church.

In the interim, English Edward III had burned Old Aberdeen with grim thoroughness, in 1336, in the Edward Baliol usurpation during Bruce's son's minority; and it was then that the completely new city was built, to the south.

With the rise in power of the great Clan Gordon hereafter, Aberdeen came in for a long period of domination by that turbulent and warlike race. Oddly enough, although they are often looked upon as Highlanders, largely because of the famous regiment so called, the Gordons were a very Lowland lot. Sir Adam Gordon, from Gordon in Berwickshire, a supporter of Bruce, was introduced into the North-East by that monarch and given great Comyn lands here. His line ended in an heiress a century later, who married Sir Alexander Seton, another typical southerner from East Lothian, who adopted the name and was indeed created Lord Gordon in 1429. It was thereafter that the clan began really to make a nuisance of themselves hereabouts. The son of this marriage was created 1st Earl of Huntly; and from then on the Huntly Gordons and all their ramifications dominated Aberdeen and a vast area of Northern Scotland, becoming in fact hereditary Lieutenants of the North. Undoubtedly they were prouder of their nickname of Cocks o' the North than of the earldom, marquisate and dukedom to which they climbed. No true understanding of Aberdeen's story is possible without some recognition of the continuing influence and power of the Gordons thereupon. One of them, of course, the 4th Earl of Aberdeen, became Prime Minister of Great Britain at the time of the Crimean War—but possibly the less said about him the better. In 1462 the magistrates were forced to enter into a self-preserving 10 years bond with the Earl of Huntly, giving him and his followers the freedom of Aberdeen to do more or less what they would—which was practically a recognition of a *fait accompli* anyway—in return for protection of the city from all others save only the king. A case of a devil that you know, and must put up with . . . !

This is no place to chronicle the ongoings of the Gordons in and around Aberdeen; but in all the causes which tore Scotland in the centuries that followed, the city had to play a more vivid and painful part than it would otherwise have done because of the Gordon

6

Aberdeen and the mouth of the Dee: port, fish markets, city, Deeside—and mountain background

Aberdeen. Provost Ross's House in the Shiprow, dating from 1593

involvement. The fact that, at the Reformation, Huntly and his successors chose to remain Catholic did not help in the process, and endless trouble ensued for the citizenry. Here, of course, came Mary Queen of Scots on her only expedition into the North, in 1562, to pull down the power of the Catholic Gordons, at the behest of her half-brother Moray—although herself a Catholic—when the important Battle of Corrichie was fought 15 miles to the west and Huntly died of apoplexy on the field. Thereafter, she was forced to witness the execution of his second son, Sir John Gordon of Findlater, a handsome, dashing and unscrupulous young man to whom she was said to be much attracted, and who was even alleged to have designs on her hand. Certainly, on previous form, he was quite capable of it. But this brief set-back by no means depressed the Gordons, and only nine years later they were fighting the private Battle of the Craibstone, within the modern city boundaries, when they routed an army of Forbeses and their allies with the loss of only 30 men against 300 slain. And so on. Montrose's many campaigns in and about Aberdeen were mainly concerned with the problem of Gordon allegiance to one side or the other—although Aberdeen's strongly Episcopal bias during this Covenanting period much complicated the issue. It has been suggested that this entrenched Espiscopalian attitude was concerned less with the worth of bishops and liturgies than with the simple fact that the rival universities of St. Andrews and Glasgow had come out very much on the side of the Presbyterians, and Aberdeen had to proclaim its independence of all such. Be that as it may, its stand cost the city dear—even though Montrose's famous Sack of Aberdeen in 1644 was not nearly so terrible a business as has been popularly supposed, in spite of the fact that it was the harshest deed that otherwise noble commander ever sanctioned.

If Aberdeen had little cause to love Montrose, it came to love the opposition less; for Cromwell sent General Monk here, and his troops occupied the city for several years while Monk was Governor of Scotland. So Aberdeen hailed the Restoration with relief, and Charles II, who had lodged for a day or two in a merchant's house just opposite the Tolbooth in 1650, without much joy on either side, was accepted as saviour. But by 1715 there was not much fervour when the Earl Marischal proclaimed Charles's nephew James VIII, at the Cross of Aberdeen—which still stands near the said Tolbooth. At the Forty-Five the Duke of Gordon's chamberlain proclaimed James VIII again, and Lord Lewis Gordon occupied the city in his name from November till February—when the Jacobites evacuated it, in the face of the Duke of Cumberland's army. The duke spent six weeks here.

This was the end of Aberdeen's warlike excitements. But there was no lack of other kinds—plague, kidnapping for colonial service, famine and riot. Of the last there was a sorry business on the occasion of the king's birthday in 1802, when four citizens were shot by the military who had become intoxicated while drinking the king's health. Even more humiliating, perhaps, in 1817 it was discovered that the city was actually insolvent, the magnificent and ambitious development of Union Street, one of the most famous streets in the land, having drained away all the municipal resources. Aberdeen was in debt to the tune of £225,000, and bankrupt. Trustees had to be appointed, and in due course the trouble was overcome, the shame forgotten—and Union Street remains.

Any description of Aberdeen almost inevitably starts with Union Street, one of the world's great thoroughfares. If it is less renowned than Edinburgh's Princes Street, this is only because the latter is one-sided, with its superb open southerly prospect of the Castle and Old Town. The architecture of Union Street is infinitely superior—although there has been modern vandalism here also. The street was conceived as a homogeneous whole in 1800, a masterpiece of early planning, a mile long, straight as a die and flanked by fairly consistently good granite façades. What is not always realised is that, as well as incorporating Telford's fine Union Bridge, the street is in fact built on a succession of bridges, for the level of the land varies greatly. This was part of the trouble, financially, for an entire hill and a vast number of what were then alleged to be "undistinguished hovels" had to be cleared away for this great conception—destroying inevitably much of the city's heritage of ancient housing in the process. Now the great street and renowned shopping-centre is the axis round which modern Aberdeen revolves. But much that is ancient is still incorporated near by.

At the north-east end, where Castle Street is an extension—the area of the early citadel's site—stand the Municipal Buildings, their tall turreted clock-tower one of the dominant features of the scene. This is a complex of buildings housing the Old Tolbooth, the Sheriff Court, the Town House and the Town and County Hall—the latter an unusual chamber designed to meet the joint needs of city and county councils, containing a great many portraits of past notables, one by Kneller and another by Lawrence, and the battle-worn flags of the Gordon Highlanders and others. The Town Hall next door is also a notable chamber, its timber ceiling carved and painted with the coats-of-arms of no fewer than 84 eminent men connected with the city's past. From this depend some magnificent candelabra, of Waterford glass, from the earlier Town House, the central one purchased in London about 1750 for £60—and alleged to have cost £2000 to clean recently. In the Committee Room near by are more portraits, some by Allan Ramsay and Naysmith. Above, on the top floor, is the Charter Room, where are proudly preserved the priceless charters of William the Lion (1179), Robert Bruce (1319) and Charles I (1638) along with Montrose's letter to the city in 1644, with copy of reply, early seals of the town, the Meikle Kist, or Town Chest, and other treasures. The stairway of this building is highly unusual in that neither steps nor landings have any under-support. It rises from a vestibule containing a Sicilian marble statue of Queen

8

Victoria, unveiled by her son Edward when Prince of Wales, which formerly stood at the corner of Union and St. Nicholas Streets but was brought here in 1888 to avoid deterioration.

To the north adjoins the Tolbooth, altered externally but containing within much of the 1615 jail and court-house, and possibly some of the original 1394 building. In 1704 considerable additions were made, and it is difficult to date all the various features. There are a series of small vaulted cells, one above another, ill-lit and ventilated, served by a narrow turnpike stair. Interesting but grim is the condemned cell, with its gad, or bar, across with an iron ring running on it for the chain, the shackles and jougs—probably the only such cell remaining in Scotland. Another cell was reserved for burgesses and guild-brothers imprisoned for debt. Into such small, black holes were crammed large numbers of Quakers, as many as 40 to a cell, in the late 17th century; and here were incarcerated scores of children and young people dragged from their homes, between 1740 and 1746, awaiting transportation to the plantations of America, in the aforementioned shameful kidnapping scandals. Outside the building, on the street, is marked the site of the former scaffold—from which the local saying arose that so-and-so "will be looking up Marischal Street", that being the direction in which the gallows pointed.

There is a huge, indeed enormous, new concrete and glass sky-scraper municipal building not far to the west of the older Castle Street complex, in Broad Street, facing across to Marischal College, called St. Nicholas House. This is no doubt an excellent and convenient edifice, incorporating all modern improvements, and highly necessary for the city's administration. But, like all other skyscraper-blocks, it has the effect of throwing out of proportion all around it, and when its vicinity includes the so carefully planned Union Street, the effect is unfortunate. And that it should seem in some measure to dwarf Marischal College, opposite, is worse. Here is the City Information Bureau.

Marischal is truly one of the great buildings of this, or any, country, and most justly renowned. The college was founded by George Keith, 5th Earl Marischal in 1593; but in 1860 was united with the older King's College, to form Aberdeen University. The original building was renewed in 1844, and its famous thrusting spires and soaring buttresses added in 1906. This was on the site of the former Franciscan Friary. The sheer excellence of its perpendicular white granite lines and perfect proportions, is a joy to behold. With its great quadrangle, with heraldic gateway, usually alive with young people, and its central position at the very heart of the city, it is an enormous asset to Aberdeen. At its east end, in the same style of building and incorporated in the overall design, is the handsome, reconstructed ancient church of the Greyfriars, with a fine panelled door dated 1674. In the college are many treasures, including a large number of fine pictures, several by Aberdeen's own great artist George Jameson, died 1644 and often called "the

9

Scottish Van Dyck". Here is also the Anthropological Museum, open to the public.

Also dwarfed by St. Nicholas House, just to the north, is Provost Skene's House, now islanded on one side of a granite-paved square. A very large 17th century town mansion, restored and now used for museum and display purposes, unfortunately its roof-level and pitch has been altered somewhat, causing the high stair-turrets to extrude awkwardly. It was here Butcher Cumberland stayed in 1746. There are good painted and plaster ceilings, and other interesting features.

Another provost's house, Ross's, is somewhat older, and not far away, across Union Street and a little way down Shiprow. This is a fine building, if more modest in scope, dating from 1593 and so the third-oldest house in the city. It was saved from demolition and rebuilt by the National Trust for Scotland, in 1952. It is open to the public, and is the headquarters of the British Council in Northern Scotland. Its open aspect, and the sudden prospect of the great dock area from here, is pleasing. Aberdeen's docks, like Dundee's, are in fact, remarkably close to the city centre: salt water is only 200 yards from Union Street.

Centrally in Castle Street, near the Town House, stands the Mercat Cross, a highly unusual example, with arcaded base and tall, elaborately carved shaft surmounted by a painted unicorn. Carved stone panels of Scots monarchs enhance the parapet. The arcaded base was formerly used as a post-office, strangely.

Near by, to the west, is another of the city's treasures, St. Nicholas, the mother-church of Aberdeen, standing in two acres of ancient graveyard separated from busy Union Street by a striking Ionic pillared façade and gateway. The table-stones of the kirkyard are a favourite place to sit. We read, in a Bull of Pope Adrian IV, of the Church of St. Nicholas of Abbirdone, in 1157. Nicholas was the patron of sailors. This was the original parish church, as distinct from the bishop's cathedral of St. Machar. It was the largest such in Scotland, 245 feet long, a collegiate foundation with provost and 30 chaplains. Christian, Countess of Mar, Bruce's sister, gave it a silver chalice. Being the people's own kirk, it suffered less than most at the Reformation. An unofficial General Assembly was held here in 1605, against royal commands. It was then divided into two parish churches, east and west, with the transept used as a vestibule. This is now the Drum and Collieston Aisle, the oldest remaining part, a bare and rather gloomy place called after two lairds whose effigies lie therein. A nine-bayed nave was to the left—the West Church; and a seven-bayed choir, the East Church. Little of all that remains, for the church suffered many vicissitudes of demolition and fire. Happily still surviving, and restored, is the highly unusual under-croft, not a crypt but a lower-level Chapel of St. Mary, Our Lady of Pity, comparatively small, 15th century, with rib-vaulting, built in memory of Elizabeth, the aforementioned heiress of Gordon who married Sir Alexander Seton. The panelling is notable, saved from the burned church above. Here is buried Sir John Gordon of Findlater, executed after Corrichie. After the Reformation, the Presbytery used to meet herein. The East Church above is the least interesting, the ancient medieval choir being demolished in 1834 "because it was old", and the rebuilt Gothic successor burned in 1874, when the original oaken spire with its eight bells collapsed. A granite spire weighing 2000 tons was then erected, with the largest carillon of bells in Britain, 48 of them, weighing 12½ tons—which however demanded much alteration and recasting before Aberdeen was satisfied with them. The East Church was again rebuilt in 1878. The West Church suffered less. It was dilapidated, and rebuilt in 1751, to designs given gratis by James Gibbs, the Aberdeen architect of St. Martin-in-the-Fields, London, the Radcliffe Library, Oxford, and the Senate House, Cambridge. Some of the original features survived, however, including ancient tombs, notably those of Provost Davidson who fell at Harlaw, and Provost Menzies who died in 1641. The "official" town church, here is a handsome Provost and Magistrates Gallery, canopied by a magnificent baldachin, and other places reserved for the seven Incorporated Trades representatives, and those of Robert Gordon's College. There is a fine 17th century monumental brass to Dr. Duncan Liddell, a noted scholar and benefactor. At the west end of the church are four large and splendidly colourful tapestries, believed to be the work of Mary Jameson, the artist's sister. Though one represents Pharaoh's daughter finding Moses, the river involved is spanned by the Bridge of Dee!

Behind St. Nicholas is Schoolhill, from which opens the grass-lawned quadrangle of Robert Gordon's College, Aberdeen's famous school for boys. Dating from 1732, this is an impressive, dignified building in Grecian style, with a tall central pavilion topped by a spire and flanked by lower and extensive wings, the entire concept with an air of space and light. Robert Gordon, born in Aberdeen in 1688, was a Danzig merchant who died a miser, but left £10,300 to endow "the building of a Hospital for Maintenance, Aliment, Entertainment and Education of young Boys"—an interesting order of priorities. Further to have priority were boys of the name of Gordon! Later bequests have enabled the school to expand down the years, and now it is a fine, modern academy, fee-paying, with a proud reputation.

Aberdeen Grammar School or Rubislaw Academy, is still older, dating from at least the 15th century. It also used to be sited on Schoolhill, where had stood the Dominican Friary; but was moved to Skene Street, to the west, in 1863, for lack of space. At that time its rector was the twenty-fifth in succession. It is now a very large establishment in a Scottish baronial pile, with a great tradition. Lord Byron was a pupil here for three years, and his statue enhances the frontage. The former Aberdeen Academy is now housed in a fine new million-pound building on the western fringes of the city, and renamed Hazlehead Academy.

These are both boys' schools; but there are the High School for

Girls, and also Albyn and St. Margaret's Schools for Girls. Needless to say, Aberdeen is rich in large and fine secondary schools, such as Hilton, Powis and Summerhill.

On the site of the old grammar school in Schoolhill was built the Art Gallery—notable for its collection of 20th century British paintings—Cowdray Hall, James McBey Memorial Art Library and Regional Museum—the latter mainly concerned with ships and allied marine items. At the west end of this fine building is the city's memorial for the two wars, a most handsome but restrained conception. Externally there is a great bay of white granite fronting the street, within which stands a noble lion on a plinth, simple and striking; and internally is a white circular hall with high domed ceiling, hung with flags and containing only the Books of Remembrance, dignified but with its own peace and beauty.

Schoolhill runs into Rosemount Viaduct, where tower side by side the City Library, His Majesty's Theatre and the South Church. And just behind, to the north, rises the gentle Woolmanhill, on the western slopes of which was founded, in 1740, the original Royal Infirmary, a Grecian three-storeyed edifice. The tradition of healing had been centred in this area, for here was the ancient medieval Well of Spa, an iron spring renowned for medicinal properties, the building to house which was repaired by George Jameson the artist. Spa Street still marks the site. Six years after its opening, the patients of the Infirmary were rudely turned out, at Cumberland's command, to accommodate his sick and wounded soldiers after Culloden. Aberdeen cannot have been greatly enamoured of the royal victor, for the citizens being somewhat backward at illuminating their windows in his honour, his officers ordered their men to break them instead—for which, after some trouble, the officers were fined £60. The Infirmary was removed in recent times to a 150-acre site in the high area of Stocket-hill and Forester-hill, a mile to the north-west, and is still being extended, the new teaching hospital here winning an award for fine building.

Still near the Union Street axis, are the two cathedrals of the Episcopal and Roman Catholic Churches. St. Andrew's Episcopal stands in King Street, and is a handsome if somewhat ornate edifice internally, built in 1817 to replace the small chapel in Longacre (where the extension of Marischal College now stands) which had had to serve Aberdeen Espiscopalians since the 1792 repeal of the Disabilities Act "outlawing" them. St. Andrew's was greatly enlarged in 1880, and again considerably altered in 1912 and 1935–48. Its lofty white walls and groined ceiling give it a great feeling of light and space, to counter the over-elaboration of the chancel. There are strong links here with the Episcopal Church of America. The first bishop of that Church, Samuel Seabury, refused consecration by the Archbishop of Canterbury and English bishops in 1784— because the United States had broken away from the British connection—came to Scotland and was consecrated in Bishop John Skinner's house at Longacre. Therefore from Aberdeen stemmed the great expansion of the Anglican Communion throughout America, and indeed the world. St. Andrew's can claim to be the mother-church of American Episcopalians, and a place of pilgrimage. Amongst items of interest here are a marble statue of Bishop John Skinner (1743–1816) and a jewelled chalice presented by the Diocese of Connecticut.

The Cathedral of St. Mary of the Assumption is a larger, white granite edifice in Huntly Street, off Union Street, in Second Pointed style, built in 1860, and modernised internally in an excellently austere fashion for a great Roman Catholic shrine, very lofty and with fine lines. The graceful spire is 200 feet high, with a peal of nine bells. There is an interesting series of large mosaic pictures along the interior west wall, and rich stained glass.

There are a great many other important buildings, of course, in or near Union Street and in the city generally, of which space forbids description. Mention might be made of the great Salvation Army Citadel; the Music Hall, near the access to Golden Square where more than music is provided—boxing and wrestling, for instance; the Civic Arts Centre, in a converted church in King Street; the Society of Advocates' (solicitors in Aberdeen, not barristers) Hall; the new Trades Hall in Holburn Street, replacing one in Union Street, with portraits by Jameson and much heraldry, centre for the city guilds which date from 1398 (bakers) to 1534 (fleshers); the towering nine-storey modern College of Commerce, also in Holburn Street; and a vast number more. Special mention should un-doubtedly be made of the so-called Wallace Tower, a fine Z-planned 16th century town mansion which formerly stood in Nether Kirkgate below the present St. Nicholas House, and which a few years ago was removed stone by stone and erected again on a prominent open site on the Mote Hill, Tillydrone Road, near Seaton Park and the Don, where it now forms a splendid landmark. Its true name was the Benholm Lodging.

As a shopping-centre the city is renowned, some of its emporia and stores being deservedly famous. Union Street dominates in this respect, of course; but all around are other fine thoroughfares with excellent facilities too numerous to recount. It is the commercial centre for a larger area than any other in Scotland, probably, save for Inverness.

The harbour district of Aberdeen is, and has always been, vitally important in the life of the city, one of the main reasons for its existence. Like the town itself it is really remarkably compact, comprising three westwards-probing forks from the mouth of Dee and the Tidal Harbour. There is the Victoria Dock to the north, with its inner extension, the Upper Dock, Regent Bridge between, and the shipbuilding yards of Footdee seaward; the Albert Basin in the centre, headquarters of the great fishing fleet; and to the south the Dee mouth itself, with Torry Docks and harbour. Along the central quay between Victoria Dock and Albert Basin is the famous Fish Market, three-quarters of a mile long, one of the most stirring

places in Scotland of a morning, and a favoured venue for energeti-
cally minded visitors. The proximity of the great North Sea fishing-
grounds made Aberdeen into one of the largest fishing-ports of the
world; and the advent of the long-range trawler and ice-preserving
era with its exploitation of the far northern and semi-Arctic fishings,
ensured that this most northerly great port became the white-fish
metropolis. From here the longfish-trains race, day and night,
to all the cities of the south, not least to London. And around the
docks arise the kippering-sheds, fish-meal and processing mills and
fertiliser works, while boat, net, rope and similar yards, fish-box
factories and ice-plants are natural adjuncts. The great engineers
Smeaton (late 18th century) and Telford (early 19th) were largely
responsible for the docks as they are now planned; but as far back as
the 14th century there were harbour works, and in 1610 a notable
hazard to navigation, a rock called Craig Metellan, was removed by
a famous citizen known as *Davie do a' Thing*, David Anderson of
Finzeauch.

Footdee, or Futtie as it is pronounced—and often spelt—locally, is
a fascinating suburb, a community all to itself occupying the narrow
peninsula at the north side of the Dee's mouth built round St.
Clement's Church, the site of a pre-Reformation chapel. Its squares
and lanes of small houses have long been the homes of seafaring and
shipbuilding men. There was a shipbuilding dock here before 1661.
Here are Hall-Russell's well-known yards. In the days of the fast
tea-clippers, Hall's Clipper Bows were renowned. Naturally, deep-
sea trawlers have been produced in large numbers in later days.

With its vast agricultural hinterland, cattle and farm-produce
markets are highly important, and between 4000 and 5000 cattle
pass through these weekly.

It is impossible here to give any indication of the scope of Aberdeen's general industrial output, highly important for centuries and
now modernising itself in a big way. Paper-making, brewing, animal
products, woollens, flax, and engineering have all been important.
Indeed the famous Scots hosiery trade could be said to have commenced in Aberdeen, with the African Company in 1695 contracting
for a vast consignment of woollen stockings—which seems a strange
requirement for Africa. We read that, a century later, the production
was running at 70,000 dozen pairs per annum, mainly for export to
the Low Countries. Special mention must be made, however, of the
granite-stone quarrying, cutting and polishing industry, which has
had such an influence on the face of the city, as well as on its reputation
for almost four centuries. At one time there were no fewer than 53
granite-polishing yards. And even in these days of high costs and
reluctance to build in natural stone, the trade continues. A visit to
the well-known Rubislaw Quarries, out on the Queen's Road near
Hazlehead Park, is an exciting experience. Here the visitor may
look down into a quite terrifying man-made abyss, 400 feet deep, out
of which the granite has been extracted.

Hazlehead, just mentioned, a large estate of 400 acres in the western suburbs near the A944 road, is one of many splendid "lungs" for the city, the most spacious and well endowed with amenities. Here, amongst fine gardens and extensive woodlands, is a small zoo, with a delightful free-flight area for birds, the largest in Scotland, in which visitors may walk. There is a large restaurant, a riding-school and tracks, golf course and tennis courts, and other facilities. Seaton Park, to the north, on the banks of the Don, is also large, attractive, with the advantages of Old Aberdeen's dramatic skyline close by, and the great river flowing through. Aberdeen is rich in parks and gardens, with Stewart, Springhill, Westburn, Victoria and Duthie the last on the southern outskirts by the Dee, and containing an outstanding Winter Garden, under glass, with ponds, running streams, benches, a profusion of flowers, sub-tropical trees and bushes, with budgerigars flying around. There is Johnston, Union Terrace and the Botanic Gardens, and others. The sea-front amenities are not to be forgotten, for the city is enormously fortunate in having a great length of sandy beach only a few hundred yards from its centre, with an esplanade two miles long and a well-stocked Beach Amusements Park, with ballroom, pools, playgrounds and links. Aberdeen beach on a summer day is a sight worth seeing, Red-coat guards on duty—and for those who prefer more individual delights there are miles and miles of sands stretching northwards into Buchan. Few great cities can have such a waterfront as this. The sea-wall here cost one and a quarter million pounds.

Old Aberdeen is still a sufficiently self-contained entity to merit separate treatment. Due north of the city proper, and linked by the two-mile-long King Street, it is to some extent islanded by the Old Town or King's Links golf course on the seaward side, the Seaton Park and playing-fields on the north or Don side, the still fairly open ground of Tillydrone, the Botanic Gardens and Glebe Hill to the west. Moreover, the Old Town itself, though with its narrow streets and lanes, is remarkably green, leafy and spacious. It is also called Old Machar, from the name of the parish—as distinct from New Machar to the north across Don—St. Machar's, of course, being the name of Aberdeen's splendid cathedral here.

The Cathedral Church of St. Machar is deservedly one of the most famous buildings in Scotland, and the only granite cathedral in the world. Its beauty, outside and in, is a joy to behold, its fine setting, mellow stonework, lovely lines and notable decoration and monuments, alike of infinite satisfaction. It is small as cathedrals go, only 126 feet long, with twin western towers; for really what is left is only the late 14th century and later nave. The choir and the transepts are gone, and the great central tower likewise. So, lovely as SS. Mary and Machar—to give it its full title—is today, it is a mere shadow of its former self.

St. Machar was a Celtic saint, one of Columba's aides, whose exceptional gifts seem to have aroused jealousy in some of his Iona colleagues. According to a 14th century source, Columba, for peace's sake, sent him off to the east, to look for the sign of a bishop's crozier, where his life's work would lie. The Don, just before it reaches the sea, bends in just such a shape; and here Machar built his church, about 580. Nothing of this now remains save a single incised Celtic Cross, found at Seaton. In 1136, David I made this the seat of a Romish bishopric, and a Norman cathedral was built. Nothing of this remains either, except a single piece of a square pier, preserved in the Charter Room. In 1285, Bishop Chiene pulled down the Norman choir and began a new one, completed by his successor. Not much of this remains either, and, strangely enough, it was built of red sandstone, not granite. The east gable enshrines this oldest work. By the Reformation, 26 bishops had held the see, and contributed to the building—including the famous Bishop Elphinstone; and the edifice comprised a five-bayed nave, an aisle-less choir, transepts, a great central tower 150 feet high, with 14 bells—Elphinstone's work—and the two remaining octagonal steeples 113 feet high. Then came the debacle and the Reforming mobs. The choir was totally demolished in 1560; and in 1688 the transepts were crushed by the fall of the weakened central tower, in a storm. Much in the nave, which became the parish church, was despoiled and mutilated. It is remarkable that so much beauty survives.

This is mainly Bishop Lichton's work, and in granite. The magnificent six-mullioned west window, over a fine, low-browed doorway, lights up the dignified, if plain, interior of massive rounded piers dividing off the aisles, and surmounted by a simple clerestory, all enhanced and enriched by a quite superb timber ceiling of brilliantly painted heraldry, created by Bishop Gavin Dunbar in 1520, and showing the 48 shields of Pope Leo X, the Emperor, St. Margaret, the kings and princes of Christendom and the bishops and earls of Scotland. That the Pope's arms escaped the ire of the Reformers is strange; perhaps they did not recognise them. At any rate, generations of good Protestants have since worshipped under them, unconcerned. The fact that this Pope was none other than the infamous Giovanni de Medici, created cardinal at the age of 14, is the more amusing. Bishop Dunbar, as well as providing this ceiling, instituted a hospital for 12 poor bedesmen, required to work about the cathedral and be diligent in prayer. Twelve bedesmen still receive payment from his fund—and a salmon from the Don!

No justice may here be attempted towards the interior and monuments. There is some splendid stained glass. There are recumbent effigies—one to Walter Idill, Official of Aberdeen (15th century), is one of the finest in Britain; and another to an unknown canon, showing a special eucharistic vestment called an almuce, little known elsewhere. There is an elaborate 17th century monument to Bishop Scoughall; and another to Simon Dodds, one of Elphinstone's administrators. There is a fine war memorial in Italian marble, and an interesting Charter Room with many wonderful records. And a star on the graveyard walling, at the south-east corner, marks the spot where the patriot Wallace's arm was buried, after being sent here, for exposure, by Edward I.

St. Machar's is surrounded by the delightful precincts called the Chanonry, the former residences of the cathedral canons. Nowadays the atmosphere is academic rather than ecclesiastical, for the University, founded by Bishop Elphinstone, is all around; but the peace and charm of the Chanonry remains.

King's College, the heart and centre of the University, stands a little south of the cathedral, a very lovely building under its famed Crown Tower. Bishop Elphinstone obtained the necessary papal bull from Alexander Borgia in 1494 to found the college, and by 1505 the building was completed and called after his friend and monarch James IV, who was almost as much involved as himself in the idea of a new university. Of the original work remain only the noble chapel and the Crown Tower—which had to be restored in 1633, after a fall. Other ancient parts are the Round Tower of 1525, defensive, with a gunloop; and the Cromwell Tower (1658)— though with nothing to do with Oliver Cromwell himself. The remainder of the building is 19th century, but in harmony. The chapel exterior, again in granite, is delightful and strangely modest in appearance, only two storeys high, with mullioned windows, buttresses and heraldic panels. There is a graceful slender spirelet crowning the roof, dating from Charles I's time. But the great Crown Tower, of course, dominates all—a very special crown this, that of Charlemagne, the *Kaiserkrone* of the Empire, indicative that the University was indeed universal to Christendom, not national— a notable conception. In the central courtyard, near the ancient well, is a handsome bronze statue to Bishop Elphinstone. Internally the chapel is very fine, with white walls and a lightsome air, with a timber vaulted roof and a gilded ribbing. The wooden pulpit is dated 1627, defaced probably by the Covenanters, and restored, brought from the Cathedral. In front of it is all that remains of Elphinstone's tomb, largely destroyed at the Reformation. The west end of the chapel is now screened off as a very lovely, wood-panelled war memorial for the University. The library is on the right of the chapel, founded in 1494 but the building is mainly of 1870, with half a million volumes, a few given by Elphinstone himself, and innumerable precious manuscripts. Worth quoting, as we leave King's College, is the following inscription on a brass panel:

Here one may, without much molestation, be thinking, what he is, whence he came, what he has done and to what the King has called him.

The University buildings proliferate all around, some old, some new, amongst gardens and old closes. The two colleges of King's and Marischal remained separate and independent for 250 years—a rather extraordinary situation, though they were united for a little in King Charles I's time. King's of course was senior, and originally was very much biassed in favour of theological studies. The principal had to be a theologian. The first was the famous Hector Boece, who

17

had been lecturing in Paris University; indeed the entire establishment was based on Paris. There were to be 10 other senior masters, and all but one had to be ecclesiastics—that one being a medico. Inevitably it suffered greatly at the Reformation. But Aberdeen maintained a fierce independence, theologically, and "the Aberdeen Doctors" were something of a thorn in the flesh to the covenanters of the 17th century.

In the attractive University area are many items of interest. The Snow Kirk, or St. Mary ad Nives, Our Lady of the Snows, was founded by Bishop Elphinstone in 1497, and was intended as the parish church. It did not survive the Reformation, and St. Machar's became the parish kirk. The present church is modern therefore, but the old burial-ground is still there, tucked in behind houses, with a built-up arched gateway in a wall surmounted by Elphinstone's arms. The Town House of Old Aberdeen is a lofty and unusual Georgian building with a clock and belfry, on an island site in Don Street. The Mercat Cross, renewed, small and modest, with a peculiar cap-like finial, still exists though removed to the west side of the High Street from in front of the Town House. The old grammar school was a short distance to the east.

Altogether Old Aberdeen is a place of charm and delight; also of vitality, for it teems with students. The proximity of the tree-decked Seaton Park and the River Don is a decided enhancement.

Bruce's old Brig o' Balgownie has been mentioned. It crosses the river half a mile north of here, at a point where there had been a ford from earliest times, and is deservedly a magnet for the visitor, the photographer and the artist. It was probably designed by Richard Cementarius, or the Mason, an early provost of Aberdeen. The hamlet of old houses that flanks the bridge, with their trees, is picturesque also. The part to the south, on a steep bend, is known as the Black Nook Brae, from a river pool of that name, and here is what is called the Chapter House, formerly Cruickshank's Lodging, dated 1655 and now being restored by the Town Council. The row of cottages on the north side, Cot-town of Balgownie, has also been restored. Although Bruce provided the money for Balgownie, thanks must also go to Sir Alexander Hay of Whytburgh, who in the early 17th century made provision for its maintenance.

To refer to another and even finer ancient bridge, we return three miles southwards across the modern city, to the Bridge of Dee. This dates from 1527, endowed by the good Bishop Elphinstone and actually erected by his successor, Bishop Dunbar. After being skilfully widened in 1841, from 14 to 26 feet, it still carries the weight of modern traffic. It consists of seven ribbed and vaulted arches, each of 50 feet. On the piers below the parapet are a series of heraldic panels and inscriptions; and at the south end, by a stairway, is a sundial. Originally there was a gateway or port at the north or city end, where also once was an oratory, for pilgrims and travellers to give thanks for the crossing—and possibly make a donation!—in pre-Reformation times. This chapel contained a statue of the Virgin, known as Our Lady of Good Success—and, strangely enough, rejected at the Reformation, this somehow found its way to Brussels, where it is now enshrined in the Church of Notre Dame de Finisterre. There is another ancient but lesser bridge near by, called the Pack Brig, over the Ruthrieston Burn to the east, which formerly carried the main road. Originally of timber, it was replaced in 1693 by stone, with Provost Cruickshank's arms—later being removed farther to the east and given parapets in 1923. Near by, to the north-west, has recently been opened a great new superstore, at Garthdee, well-removed from built-up areas, with its own large car-parking facilities and great variety of merchandise under one roof.

From the end of Bridge of Dee starts the attractive and very useful Anderson Drive by-pass, which skirts Aberdeen to the west—or once did, though now the city has grown west of it in a big way. Unlike Dundee's Kingsway, which has a similar scope, this fine road has on the whole not been used for industrial development, but climbs and dips through fair residential areas—although the Mastrick district, towards the north, has been developed as an industrial estate with factories and high flats. Towards the south end of the Drive is Mannofield, formerly a hamlet built by a wealthy Quaker, Robert Balmanno, in the 18th century, on derelict ground known as Foul Moor. His efforts turned the property into a thriving estate of gardens, notable for fruit, especially strawberries, where there grew up a market called Mannofield Tryst. The pleasant mansion this good man built for himself remains, and is still called Friendville.

These western suburbs of Aberdeen are spacious, with trees and gardens. The Anderson Drive threads the Ruthrieston, Rubislaw, Rosemount, Mastrick, Northfield and Woodside areas, wherein are many establishments of note, too numerous even to list. It must be remembered that there is not another city north of this in 150 miles— and none beyond. Anderson Drive goes on to join the Great North Road in the less attractive Bucksburn district, near the Don, on the way to Aberdeen Airport at Dyce, three miles to the north.

Before leaving this great city, mention must be made of the many notable research establishments here, some of world-wide renown. There is the Rowett Research Institute, for animal nutrition, founded in 1914 with funds gifted by Dr. John Quiller Rowett. The famous Lord Boyd-Orr was director here. It has the Duthie Experimental Stock Farm of 250 acres, the Commonwealth Bureau of Animal Nutrition, and a residential hall for overseas students called Strath-cona House. Equally well-known is the Macaulay Institute for Soil Research, founded in 1930 by the late Dr. T. B. Macaulay, a descendant of the famous historian. At Torry, just south of the Dee, is a positive galaxy of such places. There is the Torry Research Station, a governmental institute concerned with the handling and preservation of fish as food, with its own trawler, quick-freezing plant and laboratories. The Marine Laboratory, also governmental, helps the fishing industry in the exploitation of sea fisheries and conservation, having no fewer than four ships of its own, including

the large ocean research vessel *Explorer*. And there is the private
Unilever Research Establishment and Food Development Unit at
Torry likewise. Not far away to the south, in the Nigg area, newly
"won" from Kincardineshire, are the industrial estates of East and
West Tullos. A new Fishery College is now proposed.

One very interesting development is the proliferation, in the
Aberdeen dock area, of the bases for the North Sea oil search and
drilling. Already almost 40 companies have opened offices or other
premises; and more than 300 jobs directly connected with the oil
boom have been created in and around the city. How much greater
these developments will grow remains to be seen; but Aberdeen is
magnificently placed to benefit from and contribute to this exciting
new activity.

The inadequacy of this survey is all too evident to the author. Of
education, science, entertainment, sport, public facilities, manufactures, trade, markets, transport, local government and many
other vital aspects, little or nothing has been said. Even of prehistory of which there are relics, like the Langstanes. But all this can
be read up in the many publications available. This brief intro-
duction is intended to be only that, an appetiser. None who decide
to taste further need fear disappointment. Aberdeen never dis-
appoints—quite the reverse. And it lives up to its motto of *Bon
Accord*—for friendlier folk than the denizens of this fair city you will
not meet in this land, or other.

Aberdour and Pennan. As Aberdeenshire reaches Banffshire, in
the Buchan area, the change of scenery and character in the land is
rather extraordinary. The long, rolling, bare landscapes of Buchan
quite suddenly give way, not so much to actual major hills, but to a
high and broken plateau cut by deep and dramatic valleys and
ravines. Down one of these, the Tore or Toar of Troup, runs the
Banff border, with Troup Head and its great cliffs towering behind.
And it is here that Aberdour lies, the final northernmost parish of
Aberdeenshire, 16,500 acres of very atypical Buchan. There are
two villages, New Aberdour and Pennan, the latter probably the most
spectacularly sited in the county.

New Aberdour, which is now the kirkton of the parish, is a less
attractive village than its surroundings warrant perhaps. It was
founded in 1798 by William Gordon of Aberdour, to replace the old
kirkton down near the iron-bound shore, in certainly a more practical
position, on ground 300 feet higher and nearly a mile inland. It
consists of two streets, in the form of an L, with the present parish
church at the northern extremity, the hall near by. The church is a
large, plain, harled building of 1818, with a small belfry, a typical
preaching-kirk with galleries, externally with few concessions to
architectural beauty. The graveyard, of course, is not old. There is
a good new school. Fairs used to be held here.

The old ruined church stands in its ancient kirkyard, on a shelf
above the ravine of the Dour Burn and the shore, almost a mile to the

north, attractive and sequestered—although in a northerly gale highly exposed. It is of high antiquity, founded by Columba himself, as the *Book of Deer* records: "With Drostam his pupil he came from Hi [Iona] as God had shown him, unto Abbordoboir, and Bede the Cruithnach [Pict] was Mormaor of Buchan before him; and it was he that gave them that *cathair* in freedom for ever from Mormaor and Toisach." The roofless building is now divided into burial-aisles for various lairdly families. The south aisle is shared by the Leslies of Coburty and the Bairds of Auchmeddan, with a memorial to the latter's laird forfeited in the Forty-Five. These Bairds, chief of their name, have a handsome red-stone heraldic and inscribed panel, dated 1642, inserted in an earlier arched recess, possibly an Easter Sepulchre. There are two very ancient dated stones, of 1593, one to George Baird, a noted mathematician; another to John Whyte of Ardlawhill, a sort of lay preacher of the 16th century. The west aisle is the tomb of the Gordons of Aberdour, roofed still. There is a very unusual early font, tall and jar-shaped. The former manse close by, rather picturesque, is now a small hotel. It has a tiny pyramidal doocot at the gate. Farther down the steeply winding cliff-road, St. Drostan's Well still flows, at the shore, now from a canopy of 1884, memorial to Andrew Findlater, once headmaster of Robert Gordon's College and editor of Chambers's *Encyclopaedia*. This beach is popular with holiday-makers, being highly picturesque, with many caves in the cliffs.

Almost a mile to the east, reached by a side-road, is the spectacularly placed Dundarg Castle. The present house was built on the old site in 1938, but the foundations of the original, on its extraordinary narrow and thrusting promontory high above the waves, are still to be seen. It was a fortified site, Dun Dearg, the Red Fort, long before medieval times, and indeed appears to have been the *cathair* of Columba and Drostan aforementioned, who no doubt took over a Pictish fort. There has been considerable excavation here, by the late Dr. Douglas Simpson, and a fascinating story is revealed, with more to be discovered. After the Celtic monastery, the site was fortified again, strangely by an Englishman, Henry de Beaumont who had married the daughter of the Bruce-forfeited Comyn Earl of Buchan. He was a supporter of Edward Baliol; and Sir Andrew Moray, Regent of Scotland during Bruce's infant son's minority, took and destroyed Dundarg. But it was again fortified in the 16th century. The arched gateway to the inner bailey, and three of the ditches which protect it to landward, along with extensive grass-grown foundations, still remain. It seems to have been a timber castle on stone foundations.

Over a mile south-east, on the higher ground, is the old House of Aberdour, now a large farmery, formerly a lairdship of the Gordons. The house is a tall, harled structure mainly of the late 17th century, with wings flanking, only two tiny windows on the north side, but with a gablet and regular fenestration to the sheltered south, facing the old walled garden, a place with much character. Another former lairdship near by, to the east, is Coburty or Cowburdie, also a farm, once a Leslie property on which were sited sundry burial-cairns. The only remaining feature is a little garden-house.

The road from New Aberdour to the parish's other village, Pennan, is a delight, after the Buchan levels, rising and falling through hills and wooded dens, by whinny, broomy, brackeny braes, almost Highland in aspect, and becoming quite spectacular nearing Pennan, with sharp bends and steep gradients—the portion down to the village itself, hidden under the cliffs, being scarcely for the nervous motorist in bad weather conditions. Pennan is highly picturesque and quite large, a row of cottages shouldering into the precipices as though against the onset of the waves, many brightly painted, cheerful, some holiday-homes now. There is a harbour, which once supported 40 boats, and a boat-building yard. Inshore fishing is still carried on, but on a much reduced scale. On the hillside to the south are many squares of allotments, as detached gardens. Pennan, deservedly a favourite with visitors, was once a great haunt of smugglers, and their Quayman's Cave had its own landing-facilities. To the west are the evocatively named Hell's Lum, Devil's Dining-room and Needle's Eye rock features. Elsewhere are the Piper's Cave, with its ghostly story, and various natural arches. Cullykhan Bay is just west of Pennan Bay, and here archaeological excavations are uncovering interesting finds of the Bronze Age, as well as later periods. On the high ground above the village is Auchmeddan Church, with its elaborate granite frontage, in a bare position, built as a chapel-of-ease. There is no mansion of Auchmeddan nowadays. The Bairds were granted these lands by William the Lion. One was created Lord Doveran but died before the patent was sealed. They were forfeited as Jacobites. The famous Sir David, hero of Seringa-patam, was of this line.

Inland, up the steep and deep ravine of the Tore of Troup, two miles, is the site of a pre-Reformation chapel and holy well, at Chapelden. And on the farm of Hindstones, behind New Aberdour a mile or so, weems or souterrains have been found. The former mill-stone quarries of Aberdour were famous. Altogether it is an exciting district.

Aboyne. The conjoint Deeside parish of Aboyne and Glentanar is very large, covering 37,000 acres of hills and woodlands, as well as the level terrain flanking the river, and it will be convenient to deal with Glentanar separately. It is all heavily forested and picturesque country, deservedly popular as a holiday area. The large village, or small town, of Aboyne lies near the north bank of Dee fairly centrally, and should be known as Charlestown of Aboyne, called after Charles Gordon, 1st Earl of Aboyne; previously it had rejoiced in the name of Bunty—*boinne* meaning rippling water, and *tigh*, a house.

Charlestown, a burgh of barony, is a wide-scattered place, open and spacious, grouped around a large green or common, whereon are held the famous Aboyne Highland Games. Fortunately many of

Aberdeen. The classical lines of the Music Hall of 1820–1859

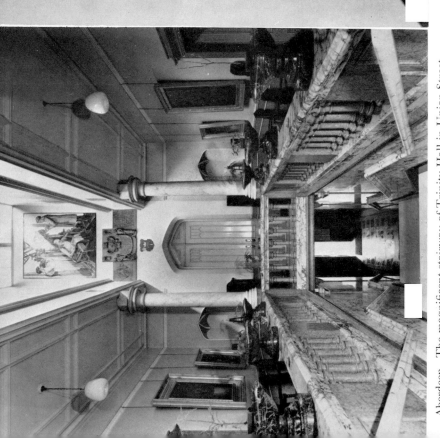

Aberdeen. The magnificent stairway of Trinity Hall in Union Street

Aberdeen. One of the most famous bridges in the land—the Brig o' Balgownie, traditionally built by Robert the Bruce in 1320

Old kirk of Auchindoir

the old Scots pines have been allowed to remain within the built-up area, to the enhancement of the amenity. There are many shops, hotels, banks, tradesmen's establishments, and a hospital. The wide yard of the former railway-station makes a second shopping-centre, with antique and tourist shops prominent. The cattle-pens of the auction-marts are near by. There are many large granite villas to the west, and some very modern and less attractive housing to the east. Also to the west lie the very up-to-date premises of Aboyne Academy, amongst trees, with the original buildings near the green. The parish church of St. Machar's, neo-Gothic, dates from 1842, and is sizeable in a fairly modern kirkyard. An interesting war memorial and Victory Hall, erected by the 2nd Lord Glentanar, stands on the north side of the green, arcaded in granite, its woodwork all from the Scots pines of Glentanar Forest. It comprises the memorial alcove, with stained glass, on the left hand, and behind, a village hall with stage and other facilities, part of which is now used as a play-school.

Aboyne Castle stands in a large estate to the north, the seat of the Marquis of Huntly—who is also Earl of Aboyne—although the castle itself is now empty and abandoned, the Marquis and his family occupying lesser houses on the estate. It is a huge pile, impressive rather than attractive, with an ancient nucleus but dating in the main from 1671, 1801 and 1869. The north-western portion was rebuilt by the 1st Earl of Aboyne, uncle of the 1st Duke of Gordon. The extensive building is grouped around a tall five-storey tower, circular but corbelled out to a square at the top and crowned with a classical balustrade instead of the usual parapet. There are slender stair-turrets in the re-entrants capped with ogee-roofs. Once belonging to the Knights Templar, the Gordons gained possession by the early 15th century. George, 5th Earl of Aboyne, succeeded the last Duke of Gordon in 1836 as head of the Gordons, 9th Marquis of Huntly, and Cock o' the North. The castle was involved in much stirring activity during the Civil Wars and Covenanting period. The walled gardens lie to the west and close to these, at West Lodge, stand two interesting sculptured stones. One appears to be about one quarter of a large Pictish cross-slab, showing the base of the cross with interlaced carving, plus mirror-and-comb symbols. It also has considerable Ogham inscriptions. Beside it lies a small, simple incised cross, which is probably a consecration-cross from the old Formaston Church. In a wood, quarter of a mile to the east, within the policies, is a small stone-circle of five uprights, four grey and one pink granite. Some of these appear to have been moved slightly, contracting the circle.

To the east of the village is the golf course, reaching to the Loch of Aboyne, an attractive wood-girt sheet of 32 acres with artificial wooded islets. Here water-skiing is pursued, and curling in winter. East of the loch, well back from the main A93 road, lies the sequestered kirkyard and foundations of the former parish church, known as Formaston Kirk, a pleasant spot. Only green banks remain of the pre-Reformation church, from which, no doubt, the

C   23 aforementioned consecration-cross came. There are a number of old gravestones, including an early heraldic one of the Innes family of Balnacraig, across Dee.

A short distance east of Formaston, an unmetalled side-road strikes off northwards over the former railway-line to the farm of Boddamend. To the left of this is a row of a dozen cottages, erected as bede-houses for the poor, and now converted into holiday chalets in this pleasing setting. This was the lairdship of Tillphoudie, the laird's house for which stood on the higher ground of the Little Hill, to the north, where the farmhouse still has the same name. There is a banked enclosure, Pictish no doubt, on this hill. Farther still on the very rough little road, is the farm of Hirnley, from which Peter Williamson was kidnapped in the 18th century, giving R.L.S. the notion for his novels *Kidnapped* and *Catriona*—or so it is said. Little Hill is a spur of Mortlich (1248 feet) a conical hill on which was a Pictish fort, and where is a monument to the 10th Marquis of Huntly.

The Deeside Gliding Club has an airfield, between the A93 and the Dee west of Aboyne. Nearing Dinnet, dealt with separately, on the edge of the parish, a large granite block was erected, in 1963, by the Deeside Field Club, with the legend: "You are now in the Highlands." To the north of the road, on the rising ground of Balnagown Hill, above Dykehead farm, is St. Machar's Cross, a monolith with an incised Maltese-type cross. Near by is a notable Long Cairn, 230 feet in length.

Alford. This is a large village, almost a little town, and also a parish of 9000 acres, lying pleasantly in the wide and fertile Vale or Howe of Alford, in the middle Don area, 30 miles north-west of Aberdeen, an important centre for a large agricultural community. Here was fought, in 1645, one of the great Montrose's famous victories. Many old and notable estates are in the vicinity. The Howe is some nine miles long, from Kirkton of Forbes to Bridge of Keig. The L in the name is not usually pronounced.

The village is lengthy, its centre clustered round a complicated road junction of the A944, with many shops, banks, hotel and two churches. Yet the parish church stands almost two miles away, the old village having lain to the west in pre-railway days. Cattle markets are held here. The school, recently extended, has risen to the status of Alford Academy. There is an unbeauteous well and horse-trough as central monument, set up by tenants and feuars of Farquharson of Haughton in 1890. Haughton estate, now a Roman Catholic establishment, lies immediately to the north, on the Don haughlands, a tall, massive and somewhat stark 18th century granite building. These Farquharsons were a branch from Breda, whose estate lies to the west near the parish church, and originally called Broadhaugh. It is modern Scots Baronial, on an ancient site, with an old beech avenue and a mausoleum. The first Farquharson of this line was known as the Meikle Factor o' Invercauld. The local poet Charles Murray lived in the house now called Murrayfield, on the Montgarrie Road, with a small public park in his memory.

The parish church, at the hamlet now called Alford West, is smallish and plain, with an unusual rounded wing to the north. It dates from 1804 and 1826, replacing one of 1603, itself succeeding a pre-Reformation church dedicated to St. Andrew. It is a typical preaching-kirk, fresh and bright within. There are a number of old gravestones, and built into the west gable a most interesting and elaborate 18th century Balfluig Memorial, displaying grotesque stone figures seemingly with bellyache, relating to the Forbes of Balfluig daughter Mary who married the Gordon minister here and died 1728. Another memorial close by is to Master Gilbert Melville, minister, dated 1678. A little farther on this road is the hamlet of Muir of Alford, with a smithy, where the Leochel Burn comes down to join Don.

Near by, to the east, is the site of the Battle of Alford, the low eminence of the Gallowhill being the position chosen by Montrose to stand in his long retiral before General Baillie after the Battle of Auldearn in Nairnshire. He allowed Baillie, with a much larger Covenant army, to cross Don at Boat of Forbes, now Bridge of Alford—and, hemming him in between the river and the Leochel Burn, defeated him with great slaughter. Here his friend, the Lord Gordon, was slain. Bridge of Alford was built in 1810 to replace the ford and ferry-boat. It is a graceful three-arched structure, with a pleasantly placed waterside inn at the far side, a quite important place in coaching days. Angling is now the attraction.

Over a mile south of the kirk, on a side-road from the A980, is the attractive 18th century house of Asloun, recently restored, and in its pleasant grounds the remains of Asloun Castle, where Montrose spent the night before the battle. The castle has been of the 16th century, on the Z-plan, but only the tall north-east circular tower survives, with a fragment of north walling. It is of handsome workmanship, with stringcourse, gunloops and three empty panel-spaces for heraldry. The ceiling of the main stair-head was a domed vault, very unusual. A charter exists referring to John Cowdell de Asslowne 1563, of the Calder family, which was later succeeded by Forbeses.

At the other side of the parish a mile east of the village stands Balfluig Castle, recently splendidly restored from ruin. It is a fine example of a tall and fairly simple L-planned tower-house of the mid 16th century, its stair-wing rising a storey higher than the main block to end in a little watch-chamber with its own fireplace. There are vaulted basement chambers, one a guard-room for the door, a prison under the stair, both splayed gunloops and circular shot-holes, and other typical features. It now makes a most handsome house, an example for other restorers. The Forbeses were a branch of Corsindae, and held the barony of Alford.

Auchterless and Towie-Barclay. Auchterless is a large rural parish of 18,000 acres on the upper Ythan, some five miles south of Turriff, with only a small village but a great many farms and old estates. Towie-Barclay is a formerly important property and castle on the main A947, seat of a family which made history.

The kirkton is fairly central, in the Howe of Auchterless, threaded by the B992, a scattered village with a school and post-office, not particularly attractive. The parish church is large, with a steeple, fairly modern and without any rural aspect, replacing an older one in the kirkyard, now fragmentary, with a crowstepped gable and belfry with bell. In one fragment is an ancient aumbry. The original church was dedicated to St. Donan, who died in 640, and the gift of the church to the Bishop of Aberdeen was confirmed by the Pope in 1157, the rector being chantor of St. Machar's Cathedral. St. Donan's Fair used to be held at Auchterless each April. The building was restored in 1780. It is now the burial-place of the Duffs of Hatton. The large kirkyard is still in use, and has some old graves, including those of Barclays of Knockleith, cadets of Towie, 1696 and 1734. Near the church is the Moat-head, no doubt site of a one-time motte-and-bailey castle, for the baronial courts used to be held here, with a Gallow-hill in the vicinity.

The old property of Hatton of Auchterless, now called Hatton Manor, was an early Duff purchase when that up-and-coming family was rising towards its earldom and eventual dukedom. It lies half a mile west of the kirkton, but has long been a farmhouse, a large L-shaped early 18th century house, harled, in poor state now but having character. It was from here that Garden Duff moved in 1820 to rebuild Balquhollie Castle six miles to the north-east, and to change its name to Hatton Castle. On Mains of Hatton, the next farm westwards, is a stone-circle with all the stones now fallen and a water-cistern superimposed. The story is that these stones were removed to form gateposts for the farm, but no horses would go through them, so they were replaced. There was a St. Donan's Well here. Over a mile north-east of the kirkton is Chapel of Seggat, now a large farm, with only a fragment of the chapel walling remaining, but a famous well, dedicated to the Virgin Mary and visited by James IV in 1504, still in good order. A mile the other side of Kirkton, southwards, is the alleged former Templar property of Templand, where there is now a disused Free church.

Towie-Barclay Castle, so called to distinguish it from Towie in Strathdon, stands two miles north-east of the kirkton, near the junction of the B992 and the B947. It is highly interesting, in trees beside the large farmhouse. Unfortunately it has been lowered by two storeys, which much changes its aspect, L-planned with a modern parapet and flat roof. Internally however it is splendid, with three basement chambers and vestibule having ribbed and groined vaulting and stone carving. There is an oratory or minstrels' gallery and other notable features. It probably dates from the 15th century—the two dates of 1136 and 1593 on one panel are both misleading. The Barclays of Tolly or Towie flourished here for 600 years; the first, a son of the Gloucestershire Lord Berkeley, coming north with Canmore's Queen Margaret, the most famous probably being Prince Michael Barclay de Tolly, the Russian general of the Napoleonic Wars. The castle is now being restored, happily.

Three miles north-east again is Hatton Castle, aforementioned, in its great wooded estate. This was Balquhollie before the Duffs' time, and has been a fairly large courtyard-type castle, probably of the 15th century, so altered at the 1820 rebuilding as to leave little of the original aspect. But the four large circular flanking-towers of the courtyard were incorporated, some with their very thick walls, vaulting and wide gunloops remaining. It was a seat of the Mowat or Monte Alto family from the 13th century till 1723, when Alexander Duff bought it. The Duffs are still there. Lendrum farm, just to the south, is the scene of the famed Turra Coo incident, mentioned under Turriff.

The west side of the parish has its own interest. There are standing-stones on the farm of Westerton, two miles west of Towie. Then four miles to the south-west, at Upper Third, are two more massive stones at the roadside. More than a mile west of this, on the north side of Kirk Hill, is the feature known as Cumine's Trench, a whin-covered grassy embankment on the valley edge, alleged to have been the Comyn Earl of Buchan's camp-site before the Battle of Barra. It may have been, but is obviously a much earlier native fortification. The Roman camp of Glenmellan, the Castra Aestiva of Agricola, covers 130 acres a mile away on the south side of the same hill, with a stone-circle of three concentric rings, and a single great monolith still upright, overlooking it. The scattered hamlet of Wells of Ythan, isolated from main roads on a fairly high and bleak plateau situation, lies a mile to the west, with quite large harled 19th century church, a chapel-of-ease, plain within and without, a school, and a cemetery, a highly remote little community.

Gordonstown, another straggling hamlet, lies at the extreme south-eastern corner of the parish, near the Rothie district of Fyvie, near the crossroads of the B992 and the B9001. And a mile to the west lies Badenscoth, another hamlet, with school, in a country of banks and braes. Badenscoth Mains is now a large farm, once an old Gordon lairdship, with interesting features. The fine, mellow, walled garden survives, with attractive garden pavilions. One has a lintel with heraldic panel and the names James Gordon and Grace Hay, and a sundial. The farmhouse has an old nucleus, and also a detached wing dating from the 17th century, much altered but with a still older moulded window-surround and good chimney-copes. It is not vaulted, but the upper chamber has a good coved ceiling and an Adam mantelpiece. The flooring of this chamber caught fire some years ago, and pulling it up it was found that the space between it and the ceiling below was packed with moss, still green though old, as a form of deadening and insulation. The first Gordon of Badenscoth was third son of the third Gordon of Terpersie, acquiring the property in 1603 from a Meldrum.

27

Ballater, Tullich and Glengairn. This comprises the northern sector of the huge civil parish of Glenmuick, Tullich and Glengairn, and includes the well-known burgh of Ballater, all north of Dee. It lies approximately mid-way between Aboyne and Braemar, with the former parish of Tullich to the north-east, that of Glengairn to the north-west.

Ballater is a pleasant little town, fairly regularly planned about a central green or square, and dominated by the steep hills of Craigendarrach to the north and Craigcoilich to the south. It has a population of only 1000, greatly swelled in the holiday season, for which it caters with many hotels, guest-houses, and bed-and-breakfast establishments. It is now a burgh, but was only established in 1770, by an enterprising Farquharson laird, mainly to cater for the flood of health-seekers who flocked here on the discovery of the mineral-wells at Pannanich, two miles to the south-east. It is still very largely a holiday-centre, though not now for mineral-water drinkers. The Pannanich Wells Hotel, however, is still there and one or two wells remain extant. Here are the renowned Dinnie Stones, two boulders with a combined weight of almost 800 lbs, carried across Potarch Bridge by the athlete, Donald Dinnie.

This is, in effect, the kirkton for the huge parish of 89,000 acres, and the parish church in the central Church Square is large, bright and granite Gothic, of 1798 rebuilt in 1875, without a kirkyard. The bell is old, of 1688, and came from St. Machar's, Aberdeen. There are also an Episcopal church of St. Kentigern, and a St. Nathalan's Roman Catholic church. Other public buildings are the Albert Memorial Hall, above the Library, and the Victoria Hall near by, both in Station Square—although the railway-station itself is now a restaurant. There are three banks and many shops. Substantial villa residences lie to the west, and there is an attractive small modern housing complex to the south-east. A youth hostel is in Deebank Road, there are caravan and camping sites, an 18-hole golf course, and other sporting facilities, and the Monaltrie Park to the northeast, the site of the annual Ballater Highland Games, established in 1864. Pony-trekking, and fishing are available, and there are many fine walks of varying lengths, notably one by the Old Line, a projected route of the Ballater–Braemar section of the Deeside Railway, never completed. Also the Craigendarrach and Seven Bridges walk. Monaltrie House, formerly the seat of an important branch of the Farquharsons, lies to the north-east, a low and long two-storeyed house of the 18th century, now looking rather dejected. It was the laird hereof, known as the Baron Ban, who founded the village.

Behind the steep wooded hill of Craigendarroch, the Crag of the Oaks, lies the Pass of Ballater, a deep rocky defile of dramatic dimensions, threaded by the B972 road. In the days before good drainage, when the haughlands of Dee were waterlogged, this pass would command Deeside. As is to be expected, there was a castle at its western end, near Bridge of Gairn, a Farquharson stronghold, sometimes called Whitehouse, sometimes Glengairn. Only the foundations are visible, 300 yards left of the farm-road to Balmenach, north of the B972. Bridge of Gairn, where the B road rejoins the main Deeside highway, after its detour through modern Ballater, is a scatter of houses, with a shop, where the Gairn comes in from the north, largest tributary of Dee. Below the bridge, behind the farm, is the ruined former parish church of Glengairn, dedicated to St. Kentigern, within its old graveyard. Only a gable of what appears to be a 17th century building remains, with a little walling, but the dyke around it was repaired by "friends" in 1832 according to a plaque at the gate. There are many old and rough tombstones, some coffin-shaped. The B972 strikes northwards hereafter up Glen Gairn for nearly six miles to join the old military road, now the A939, at Gairnshiel. It makes an attractive run through woodlands, following the winding river, with the road in process of improvement. At Gairnshiel itself, with a gaunt and tall lodge, no doubt based on a former inn, at the aforementioned road-junction, the A973, which has climbed over the high heather slopes from Crathie, crosses the Gairn by a lofty and graceful single-arch bridge of 1751. Thereafter the road twists to the right amongst the pine-woods, and here, at the waterside, is a delightful little shiel, or picnic-house, of the royal family, once a small school. On a shelf of the hillside across the road, is the long, low ruined chapel of Kirkstyle, apparently once vaulted at the east end, now in a bad state. And a little farther east, down in the pines, is the tiny modern whitewashed church of Glengairn, created a *quod sacra* parish again in 1863, and still in use, a pleasant place. The successor of the earlier school is near by, now however a private house. The military road climbs on thereafter high into the empty hills en route for Strathdon. In the other direction, just a mile westwards of Gairnshiel Lodge, is the farm of Renatton, a former remote lairdship, with traces of a ruined castle, in a small sideglen.

Back on the main North Deeside road, the stretch for two miles west of Bridge of Gairn is very picturesque, running through birch-woods, with many picnic and camping sites provided. Coillecreich Inn here was a staging-place for coaches in the old days "where excellent whisky may be had at any time for 15/- a gallon" we read!

At the other side of the Pass of Ballater, eastwards, lies the former parish of Tullich where a battle was fought in 1654 between Cromwell's troops and Royalists. Tullich Lodge, near the pass, is a modern mansion, now a large hotel, prominent on the wooded landscape. Milton of Tullich is the scattered hamlet half a mile east on the A972 and below the road here is the ancient parish church of St. Nathalan, now roofless, in its kirkyard, still in use. The oldest part is said to date from the 14th century, and certainly there is a fine Gothic arched doorway, now built up. The rest of the apertures are chamfered, and appear to date from the 17th century. There are no features within. Part is used as the Farquharson burial enclosure. Most interesting here, however, is the collection of a dozen Pictish sculptured stones outside the church near the arch. The tallest is a symbol-stone with double disc and Z-rod, serpent and Z-rod and mirror. Others of varying sizes show incised crosses. There is also a very large stone font with drain-hole. There are many old tombstones in the graveyard. Four hundred yards south-east of this, in the field below the railway-line, is a good weem or souterrain, its entrance marked by a heap of stones.

Belhelvie, Balmedie and Potterton. Belhelvie is a quite large parish and district of 12,600 acres, lying about eight miles north of Aberdeen, with a sizeable quarrying village of the same name set fairly central therein. Balmedie is another village, on the main A92 road, a mile east of Belhelvie. And Potterton is a growing community two miles to the south, off the main road. The parish is fairly low-lying, but has a central spine of green eminences, with the moorlands of Harestone and Red Moss behind; and, of course, the notable coastline of nearly six miles of uninterrupted sands, backed by dunes and links, these running together but named Blackdog, Millden, Eigie, Drumside and Menie Links. There is a coastguard station at Menie Links.

The Gothic-style parish church, dating from 1878, is quite large and stands on the rising ground at an isolated road-fork half a mile north-west of Balmedie, with graveyard, all fairly modern and unexceptional. The old church, consisting now only of a gable and a detached fragment used as a burial-vault, lies about a mile to the north-east below the A92, overlooking the seaboard. A tablet on the internal wall commemorates the family of Orrock of that Ilk; and there is a large heraldic panel of the Innes family on the south face of the detached fragment. The graveyard is well-kept and contains a mort-house; and there are many table-stones of the early 18th century.

Across the main road to the west and prominent therefrom, is the tall and rather starkly handsome 18th century laird's house of Orrock, on an eminence, its farmery near by. Almost an equal distance to the north-east, below the A92 is Menie House, large, of more decorative architecture and belonging to the 1840s—although the estate is an ancient one.

Belhelvie village, two miles to the south-west, has grown on account of the large granite quarry here—although the Statistical Account of 1840 declares that there are no quarries in the parish, nor anything geological worthy of notice. Belhelvie Lodge near by, in woodland, is not ancient. The Hare Cairn, a burial mound within a ring of trees, rises in a field half a mile to the east, in the direction of Balmedie. It is the sole survivor of many cairns, stone-circles and other relics of prehistory in the parish. A gold armlet was discovered here, now in the Museum of Antiquities, Edinburgh. At Belhelvie was born, in 1769, Alexander Forsyth, inventor of the percussion-lock, which he sold to the British Government after declining £20,000 for it from Napoleon.

Balmedie village lies along the main road, with school and post-office. Balmedie House, in wooded grounds to the north, like

Belhelvie, was formerly a Lumsden lairdship, and is now a Church of
Scotland Eventide Home. The beaches here are very popular.

In the southern part of the parish is Potterton, not a village so
much as a scattered but growing community, with a number of
modern houses, a school, a farm, a mill, and an estate which is the
home of Lord and Lady Tweedsmuir. Also a former Free church, of
1843, no longer in use. All this in undulating country around the
wooded den of the Potterton Burn. A mile to the east, on the same
burn, at Hatton of Millden, is only the site of a pre-Reformation
chapel and burial-ground, now gone. Also on this farm is a semi-
subterranean ice-house, for the storage of fish from a one-time
salmon fishery established at the burnmouth.

The western portion of Belhelvie district rises to low hills around
350 feet, with former moorland and moss, dotted with small farms,
very different from the flat links which flank the beach for so lengthy
a stretch. So level are these links that they were used in 1817 as the
base-line for the Ordnance Survey, a line five miles and 100 yards
long.

Birse and Feughside. Birse is a curious place, with no very
clearly defined entity. There is a hamlet of Birse marked on the map
nearly three miles south-east of Aboyne, across the Dee. But this is
a tiny place, really only the kirkton of the parish church. There is a
larger and growing community of more modern housing in the
woodlands near the mouth of Glen Tanar, two miles west. There is a
Birse Castle which lies remotely up at the head of the Water of
Feugh, five miles from both of these, as the crow flies, and three
times that by road. There is a great Forest of Birse, flanking
Feughside, and far beyond, with its own church, the castle being its
shooting-lodge. And there is Birse parish, comprising all this and
much more, an enormous tract of territory south of the mid-Dee
valley, 31,000 acres in extent, and this includes areas with their own
identity, such as Ballogie, Finzean and Feughside itself.

The parish church, in a somewhat isolated rural position in the
low-lying northern part, near Aboyne, dates from 1779, built of
grey granite, long and plain, but quite attractive, with a fine
stained-glass window above the communion-table, and an old
painted heraldic panel formerly attached to the front of the Farquharson gallery. In the vestibule is a most interesting inscribed stone,
six feet high, carved with a two-handed sword, battleaxe and
Maltese cross, probably of the late 12th or early 13th century, and
perhaps relating to Alan Durward of Coul, who had been on crusade
—hence the Maltese cross. It is called the Crusader Stone today,
and was found in 1799 in the foundations of the original church. This
was the seat of the pre-Reformation chancellors of the Diocese of
Aberdeen. The manse is large, near by. A mile to the south is the
estate of Balfour, where the famous Bishop Skinner of Aberdeen was
born.

Two miles east of the church, where the Burn of Cattie comes

31

down out of the Forest of Birse to join Dee, is Ballogie and Marywell. Ballogie is a large estate, formerly of the Inneses and Farquharsons, with a modern mansion and a Roman Catholic chapel of St. Michael; also a scattered hamlet and post-office. Marywell is now a farm, formerly an inn, no doubt taking its name from a holy well. To the north, over a mile, is Balnacraig House, a notable example of early 18th century laird's house on the E-plan, remotely sited and picturesque, now a farmhouse. It belonged to a branch of the Innes family, ten members of which became priests, three principals of the Scots College at Paris. They were prominent Jacobites. In the same area, to the east, is the handsome Bridge of Potarch over the Dee, of three graceful arches, built in 1813 to carry the Cairn o' Mount road, which had formerly crossed Dee here by a ford. There is a hotel and an open common, or large green, now much used by campers and caravanners, formerly the site of three annual fairs. The area is richly wooded. A notorious character called Caird Young is reputed to have leapt the Dee at its narrows here.

The B976 road climbs eastwards, after Ballogie, rising to 745 feet at Corsedarder Hill, where there is a magnificent viewpoint over the forested valleys of Dee and Feugh. Here at the roadside is the Corsedarder Stone, a granite monolith, fractured by lightning but repaired, said to have been brought from the large cairn in the woodland of Finzean near by, where it marked the grave of a Pictish king or prince named Dardanus. Across the road rises the parish war memorial, massive and handsome on this fine spot.

The Finzean area of Feughside is wide-scattered, with the modern school and a few houses on the high ground east of Corsedarder, the old school close by being now an Outdoor Centre for Aberdeenshire County Council. Finzean House, still a Farquharson possession after four centuries, lies in woodland to the west, in a large estate which once covered half the parish, the mansion long, low and fairly modern-seeming but with an ancient nucleus. Boghead of Finzean hamlet lies at the road-junction a mile to the south-east. And the kirkton of Finzean, or Drumhead, the hamlet with the church, is on a side-road a mile to the west. The church is small but most attractive, set amongst trees. The post-office is near by.

In this area, near the Strachan end of the parish, are several items of interest. Half a mile east of Boghead lies the old laird's house of Tillyfruskie, now a farm, the late 17th century house still picturesquely enclosed within its high-walled courtyard. It was an Ochterlouny place, one of the family falling at Quebec, with Wolfe, another being Sir David Ochterlouny. Just south of Boghead is Mill of Clinter, where the water-wheel still grinds corn. And across Feugh from the mill is Easter Clune, now a small farm but once more important, sequestered amongst broomy knowes. There was a castle here, of which only a fang of masonry remains beside the steading; an 18th century small laird's house stands abandoned to the west; and there was also an Episcopal chapel and burial-ground to the east, now only a circle overgrown with broom.

The troutful Water of Feugh rises high on Mount Battock, near the Angus border, and runs for 20 miles to the Dee, most of its course in Birse parish. The section westwards from Finzean through the Forest of Birse is very attractive and of Highland character. A road runs up it through scattered woodland of pine and birch and heather for six miles, probing into the hills; whereafter the road becomes private, at Birse Castle. On this stretch of Feughside there is a small hamlet, shop and sawmill in the West Clune vicinity, and a mile on, Beckett's Mill where shrub-tubs are made. The picturesque miles beyond are a favourite picnic area. At the road-end is Forest of Birse Church, sometimes called "The Kirk of the 47 Reekin' Lums", a tiny place of worship, but most pleasing, formerly a little school, and so containing a fireplace. When it was converted to a church there were 47 families here to serve; now there are five. But services are still held once a month in summertime.

The private road beyond leads to Birse Castle. This was a typical late 16th century fortalice on the L-plan, erected by Bishop Gordon of Aberdeen. It fell into ruin, and though very little remained, it has been skilfully rebuilt in the same style, so that it is not easy to tell new work from old. It is now Lord Cowdray's shooting-lodge. Another three miles up the glen, where it ends amongst hills of over 2000 feet, is St. Colm's Hill and Well, a lofty sanctuary indeed.

Boddam and Buchan Ness. This fishing-village occupying a headland, with its peninsula and near-island of Buchan Ness, is in Peterhead parish, but deserves individual treatment. Indeed it was created a separate entity and port by Act of Parliament in 1845. It lies almost four miles south of the larger town, and quite distinct, with two sizeable bays between. Since Buchan Ness is not an actual island—even though reached by a bridge—and Keith Inch, the extremity at Peterhead is, the former ranks as the most easterly point of the mainland of Scotland. Its 130-foot-tall lighthouse, built by Robert Stevenson in 1827, with its keepers' houses, makes a challenging picture.

Boddam is a compact place of pink granite houses, old and new, the former huddled close around the large double harbour. This is still in use as a fishing-port, even though it no longer supports the 65 vessels it did a century ago. It is a not unattractive place. There is a plain, harled church of 1865, with a small belfry, formerly a chapel-of-ease. Also a large school. Prominent to the west and south is the extensive spread of buildings and associated housing which makes up the large R.A.F. establishment connected with the radar and warning-system installations which dominate the surrounding landscape, with their hilltop and futuristic-seeming contrivances. Official-secrets warning notices proliferate.

Near the entrance to this complex, on a spine between two rocky inlets of the low cliffs, just south of the village, is all that remains of a strongly placed fortalice of the Keiths of Ludquharn, probably of the 15th century, Boddam Castle. A single gable, with shot-holes flanking an arched doorway, plus extensive foundations, is all that survives. This entire coastline came to be controlled by the Earls Marischal and the Keiths, after the fall of the Comyns. Near by is the Earl's Lodge Hotel, occupying an isolated position on its small headland, once the marine villa of the Prime Minister Lord Aberdeen.

Half a mile to the south, along the cliff-bound shore, is the islet of Dundonnie once the site of salt-pans. Farther south still are the dramatic features of Cave o' Meackie, Long Haven and the Hare Craig and Cleft Stane, but these are in Cruden parish. Stirling Hill, rising abruptly south-west of Boddam, is the site of great granite quarries. The hamlet at the foot, with its inn, also rejoices in the name of Stirling.

North of Boddam lies Sandford Bay, bounded by Salthouse Head and Burnhaven, described under Peterhead. Sandford has a caravan site at the beach, for here the cliffs give way, and there is a prominent late 18th century whitewashed farmhouse.

Bourtie and Barra. This is a small rural upland parish, sequestered amongst green hills, covering 5500 acres between Inverurie and Oldmeldrum; and Barra is an old estate therein, famed as the site of Bruce's victory over the Comyn Earl of Buchan in 1308. There is no village or even hamlet, Kirkton of Bourtie being merely the church, manse and a farm. The church, rebuilt 1806, replaces a pre-Reformation chapel dedicated to St. Brandon, and is situated fairly centrally, south of the Hill of Barra. The building is not particularly beautiful either without or within, hipped-roofed and with a belfry; but it is very interesting, in its old graveyard. Built into the walling externally, high up under the eaves on the south front, is part of a Pictish symbol-stone, with crescent, double-disc, and mirror-and-comb symbols—an extraordinary place to find such a thing. In the vestibule are two stone effigies from the original church, reputed to be those of Sir Thomas de Longueville and his lady—though this seems improbable. De Longueville, also known as the Red Rover, was a famous freebooter who fought for Bruce in the Wars of Independence, to whom Bruce granted the lands of Kinfauns in Perthshire. Several of his descendants were provosts of Perth; and he is claimed to have founded the Charteris family—though this again seems doubtful. The story here, at Bourtie, is that he was fatally wounded at the Battle of Barra in 1308, and buried at this church; but though he probably did fight at Barra, he almost certainly long survived that fight—for Bruce was in no position to grant him Kinfauns until after Bannockburn six years later. The effigy is probably of some crusading knight, possibly one of the King family of Barra. Also in the vestibule is the old bell, cast by John Mowat of Old Aberdeen, in 1760, and now cracked. The interior of the small church is rather dull, with a gallery and high pulpit. There is a wooden panel hanging up inscribed *R.S. 1669*.

In a field to the west of the church is part of a stone-circle consisting of three uprights and a huge recumbent, one of the largest altar-types seen. There is another stone-circle at the farm of Shelden, a mile to the east, on an eminence. A new reservoir is being built on high ground near by, at Crombiebrae.

Barra Castle stands on the lower ground a mile north-west of the church, at the side of the A981 road to Oldmeldrum, only a mile south of that little town but in Bourtie parish. It is one of the most delightful and authentic lesser castles in the country, largely of the early 17th century but with an older nucleus. It conforms to a complicated version of the L-plan, with the wing projecting so as to form two re-entrants. It has three round towers, two with conical roofs and one corbelled out to the square to house a watch-chamber. Later extensions form three sides of a square, with courtyard. The basement is vaulted, and the hall on the first floor subdivided. There is much good panelling in Memel pine. The family of King owned Barra for 300 years from the mid-13th century, and as Bruce was Lord of Garioch, they would be vassals of his own. Barra passed to the Setons of Meldrum in 1598, with whom the Kings had been long at feud. The feud continued after the Seton acquisition, for we read that as late as 1615 Elizabeth Seton pursued at law James King "sumtyme of Barra" for the slaughter of her father "with schottis of hagbuttis and muskattis, committed upon the landis of Barra . . ." The estate passed to the Reids and then the Ramsays from whom an heiress carried Barra to the present Irvine family, cadets of Drum.

Barra Hill, which rises behind to 634 feet, is crowned by a Pictish fort three acres in extent and circular. It is known as Comyn's Camp, and allegedly was where John Comyn, Earl of Buchan, Bruce's enemy, passed the night before the Battle of Barra, which was fought to the north, between here and Oldmeldrum.

The attractive small mansion of Bourtie itself stands in its estate at the southern edge of the parish. It is old without being of the fortified period, and was long the seat of the Duguids, a minor but prominent Aberdeenshire family.

Braemar and Inverey. Braemar and Crathie form a huge united civil parish, one of the largest in Scotland, of over 200,000 acres, admittedly much of it mountain, but nevertheless larger than some counties. It is convenient here to split it into two for descriptive purposes—Braemar with Inverey, and Crathie with Balmoral. Even so, each will cover a very wide area.

Braemar, with the village of that name, is of course one of the most renowned localities in the land, thanks to the royal connection and the Braemar Gathering. It lies where the River Dee, some 20 miles from its source at Wells of Dee on the summit plateau of Braeriach (4248 feet), is joined by the Clunie coming down from the heights of the Cairnwell Pass above Glen Shee, to the south, almost 60 miles west of Aberdeen, with the A93 following the Clunie. The village, picturesquely placed amongst woodlands of birch and pine, and with splendid views northwards to the Cairngorm heights, should really be called Castleton of Braemar—although the castle referred to is not the later 17th century Braemar Castle so frequently photographed, but the much earlier stronghold of Kindrochit here. This, with still-massive remains in walling and grass-grown embankments, stands on a very strong site above a linn of the Clunie, with a former mill-lade to drive the castle-mill and also to provide water for the moat. It has consisted of a great oblong keep with 10-foot-thick walls, and surrounding curtain-walls, also very massive, with subsidiary buildings within, apparently dating from the early 14th century—although there had been a royal castle on the site from Malcolm Canmore's time. It was a very strategic situation, dominating one of the great routes across the Mounth, and this vital crossing of Clunie at Dee, where there was a boat or ferry. Canmore, indeed, is credited with building the original bridge here —just above the present one—as well as the first castle. It later came to the Earls of Mar, in the 15th century, but was ruinous by 1618. It is somewhat neglected, and in this tourist-conscious area should be made much of.

The bridge which crosses the Clunie just below the castle provides an attractive viewpoint for this rocky stretch of the river, and links what are really two villages, Castleton and Auchindryne, with the latter, to the west, the larger. Below the bridge is the picturesque Mill of Clunie, beloved of artists; and just across it is the large Fife Arms Hotel. The name of Fife is prominent hereabouts, for Queen Victoria's eldest daughter, Louise, the Princess Royal, married in 1889 the 6th Duff Earl of Fife, who was duly created Duke thereof; and Mar Lodge near by became their Scottish home. The fine Memorial Park here, to the couple, is the site of the famed annual Braemar Games, so regularly attended by royalty, just to the south of the old village of Auchindryne. This is attractively grouped around a small green, and like the rest of Braemar community is well supplied with tourist shops, deer-horn works, and the like. At the east side, Castleton proper, there is another large hotel, the Invercauld Arms, erected on the actual mound where the standard was raised in Mar's Jacobite Rising of 1715. Across the road is a converted church, now the Invercauld Festival Theatre, where much enterprise has been shown and many well-known personalities have performed. At the roadside here is a monolith erected by the Deeside Field Club to mark the "Coronation of Elizabeth Queen of Scots", a nice touch. Another large building near by has been converted into the Invercauld Galleries, for exhibitions and crafts. Across from it is the house where R. L. Stevenson spent the summer of 1881 and wrote much of *Treasure Island*, with a plaque to mark it. The very large Episcopal church of St. Margaret, 1880, stands close by. Obviously there was a vast amount of development here around 1870–80. The parish church now stands on the Auchindryne side, near the castle, a modern building of 1870, quite large also, with a spire 112 feet high, with clock, replacing the earlier St. Andrew's parish church, which still retains the graveyard, almost a mile to the east.

This early church at the roadside, in the haugh of Dee, is now represented only by the mausoleum of the Farquharsons of Invercauld, erected on the site. There are some old gravestones in the kirkyard, a few very primitive with no sign of inscriptions. Just a little to the east stands Braemar Castle, amongst trees. This well-known building is frequently considered to be only a sham castle, because of its unsightly English-style crenellations and falsely battlemented upper works. But if the upper third of the building is ignored, it is seen to be a typical L-planned Scots tower-house, with two-storeyed angle-turrets and a circular stair-tower in the re-entrant. It dates from 1628, built by the 18th Earl of Mar as a barrier against the rising power of the Farquharsons. It was indeed burned by the Black Colonel, John Farquharson of Inverey, in 1689, at which time Mar was not a Jacobite. It was again burned after the failure of the 1715 and 1745 Risings, this time by the government, who thereafter turned it into a garrison-post and were responsible for the unsuitable top-hamper and the angled and loopholed outer walling we see today. It is interesting that the architect for this nonsense was John Adam, less renowned son and brother of Robert and William. The castle now belongs to the near-by Invercauld estate, and is maintained furnished as something of a showpiece. It has a grim pit or prison beneath the floor of its vaulted basement, and contains many treasures—including the world's largest Cairngorm stone, of 52 pounds.

The large and impressive, though conglomerate, mansion of Invercauld lies in its huge forested estate across Dee two miles to the east, still the seat of the chiefs of Farquharson, or Clan Finlay. Unfortunately, although it has some authentic ancient work still remaining, it has been so added to and altered as to show little external signs of age. In it the Earl of Mar planned his Rising of 1715, and here "Colonel Anne" Farquharson, married to The Mackintosh, called out the clan 30 years later for Prince Charlie. Though not a large clan, the Farquharsons have always played a notable part in Scotland's story. They derive from Farquhar, fourth son of the third Shaw of Rothiemurchus, who married the Stewart heiress of Invercauld. Their son was the famous Finlay Mor, royal standard-bearer, who fell at Pinkie in 1547. As near neighbours of the royal family at Balmoral, the Farquharsons tend to appear frequently in the royal company.

The high and beetling rocky bluffs which flank the road hereabouts to the south are a notable feature, at Craig Choinnich—called after Kenneth II who had a hunting-seat here—and the Lion's Face. At Invercauld Bridge, where the A93 crosses Dee, the old military bridge built in 1752, and a favourite with artists, can be seen to the south, six-arched and graceful. Eastwards of this is better described under Crathie and Balmoral.

West of Castleton of Braemar the road follows the wide haughs of Dee for some five miles, to Inverey, a very lovely stretch through the birch-woods and pines, always with the high hills unfolding ahead.

The Linn of Corriemulzie is reached after three miles, where a high bridge carries the road across a very narrow and deep chasm, with the foaming burn falling in a long cascade below, though somewhat hidden by leafage from above. In another mile is a lodge-house, and a white-painted iron bridge leading across Dee to the drive to Mar Lodge. This enormous house was actually designed by the Princess Royal herself, in a sort of overgrown chalet style not very suitable for the surroundings. The estate used to be called Dalmore, and was granted to a Mackenzie of Kintail by James IV, but was sold in 1720 and later acquired by the Duffs. The Lodge has for some time been used as a rather special hotel, but the estate still belongs to a descendant of the Princess, Captain Ramsay of Mar.

Inverey, another mile on, is really two villages, Meikle and Little Inverey, strung out along one side of the road, with wide gaps between the houses, an old-fashioned place still, with the forest encroaching close. The remains of its Farquharson castle still stand behind one of the houses towards the west end. The walls are not thick, and the site is not a particularly strong one. It was the home of the famous Black Colonel, third laird, a huge and colourful character who used to summon his servant, at table, by shooting a pistol in the air. The gallows tree of the Farquharsons still stands near by. Glen Ey, reaching southwards for six miles or so, is one of the loveliest valleys of the entire area. About a mile up is The Colonel's Bed, a natural cavity carved out below overhanging rocks, where the laird hid after Killiecrankie. He is said to have watched the burning of his castle from an eminence near by. Higher up the glen are the Falls of Connie, where that stream comes rushing down to join Ey. Opposite the cottages of Inverey is a granite memorial to one John Lamont, born at Corriemulzie in 1805, who made his name in the world, oddly enough, as Johann von Lamont, Astronomer-Royal of Bavaria, and a scientist of some repute, dying in 1879. There was a chapel to the north-west here, now gone. Inverey school is now an Outdoor Activities Centre of Aberdeenshire Education Authority, and there is a small Youth Hostel near by.

The road stops about two miles byond Inverey, in dark woodland, at the renowned Linn of Dee—at least it probes no farther westwards but does swing round across the Victorian Gothic bridge and turns back along the north side of Dee for over three miles, to end at Linn of Quoich. The Linn of Dee is a spectacular narrowing where the river boils and surges through a deep natural conduit with enormous force, especially in spates. That this deep gorge can be dangerous is exemplified by the memorial here to two people drowned in it in 1927. The forest hereabouts is very lovely, and is visited annually by thousands. A most picturesque camping site is found amongst the pines on the north side of the river. Beyond Linn of Dee, the walkers take over. Here starts the famous track which follows the Dee onward to its source 20 miles away—or at least to the Pools of Dee in the daunting Lairig Ghru pass, though the Wells of Dee, more than 1000 feet higher on Braeriarch, are a different story. The track, an obstacle-course here only for the toughest, continues on to Rothie-murchus and the Spey at Aviemore. Some five miles above Linn of Dee is the feature known as Chest of Dee, well worth seeing, where the waters roar and thunder in steps and stairs amongst masses of rock. White Bridge is beyond, where the tracks fork, one for the Dee and the Lairig, the other for the wild hills at the head of Glen Tilt, and so down southwards into Atholl. From this one another forks westwards, after a mile, for the pass between Glen Geldie and the head of Glen Feshie, and so to Spey at Loch Insh. It must be emphasised that these tracks are enormously long, rough, and only for the toughest walkers.

Also from Linn of Dee private roads, but available to walkers, strike northwards to the famed and beautiful glens of Lui and Derry, amongst the pine-clad slopes of the Cairngorms, renowned approaches to the mountains and amongst the finest scenery in the land. Ben Macdhui, at 4296 feet the highest of the Cairngorm or Monadh Ruadh Mountains, and the second highest in Britain, rears beyond, along with Ben a Bourd, Ben Avon or A'an, and the rest of the giants, a mountaineers' paradise.

The road on to Glen Quoich is very attractive, through Mar Forest, passing close to the back of Mar Lodge and ending at Allanaquoich, where the Quoich comes down from the north, its waters remarkably clear. Near its foot is another exciting linn, with falls and cascades flowing through a rocky, tree-lined defile. Here the action of the water has hollowed out smooth cavities, in one of which the Earl of Mar is said to have treated his supporters to a vast brew of punch to toast his Rising of 1715. It is still known as The Earl of Mar's Punch-bowl.

In this brief survey it only remains to mention the area south of Braemar, the approach of many to the area, via the A93 from Blairgowrie by Glen Shee and down Glen Clunie. The long descent through the heather from the Cairnwell Pass, with the heights of the White Mount and Lochnagar on the right, gives an everwidening vista of the Cairngorm Mountains opening ahead. Fraser's Brig, of 1750, over the Clunie, is four miles from Braemar, a double-arched, humpbacked military bridge, relic of the "pacification" of the Highlands, still in open wild country. Soon thereafter, at Auchalleter, the rock-bound Calleter comes in from the east, giving here little impression of the long and picturesque Glen Calleter, where slates used to be quarried, and extending for some seven miles up into the White Mounth massif, with the mile-long Loch Calleter four miles up, at 1600 feet. Queen Victoria's "last expedition" with her beloved Albert was to this hidden, wild valley, in October 1861. Below Auchalleter soon appears the fine 18-hole Braemar golf course, surely one of the most spectacularly sited in the land.

The Cairngorms. Because they are most unusually approached from the Aviemore area of Speyside, probably the Cairngorm Mountains are generally assumed to be in Inverness-shire. Part of the range is so, of course; but the greater part is in Aberdeenshire, with another large portion in Banffshire. The highest summit, Ben Macdhui (4296 feet) with its legend of the spectral and gigantic Grey Man of Ben Macdhui, is in Aberdeenshire, as is Cairntoul (4241 feet); and the county boundary runs along the summit ridge of Braeriach (4248 feet). So that of the four major peaks above 4000 feet, only Cairngorm itself (4048 feet) is in Inverness-shire. And of the three great rivers of the massif, the Dee and Don run wholly through Aberdeenshire, the Avon through Banffshire, and none through Inverness-shire. The acreage in Aberdeenshire is greater than that in the other two counties.

Here is no place for any description of this famous and fascinating range of mountains, nowadays possibly the most written-about and visited in Scotland, indeed the highest group of summits in these islands. But some reference should be made to their part on the over-all Aberdeenshire scene. The county is huge, and much of it low-lying, comparatively. But never, even in Buchan, is the presence of the hills and mountains wholly lost. Always, on the western horizon, the blue peaks and ridges tend to appear, if not the Cairngorms themselves, their outliers and foothills.

Oddly enough, their so unsuitable name is Aberdeen-slanted; for it was the Cairngorm Club, an Aberdeen-based mountaineering club, and which took its name from that mountain, which pioneered this area as a climbing and walking paradise, and so gradually transferred its own title to them. The true name of the great range is the Monadh Ruadh, the Red Mountains—in contradistinction to the Monadh Liath, the Grey Mountains of Badenoch.

Reverting to the physical dominance of the mountains, and the fact that the two great rivers which so largely mould Aberdeenshire emanate therefrom, it is strange that the traditional reaction to them on the part of the local folk was always one of fear rather than regard or affection. This was partly on account of the normal lowland dread of high and barren places; but more specifically in that from the Monadh Ruadh, or the Mounth as it was generally termed, was apt to come trouble—or not actually from the mountains themselves, for these were empty, but through their passes. The impact of the caterans on Aberdeenshire—as on Angus and Kincardineshire likewise—is insufficiently appreciated, caterans being the name given to the wild Highland clansmen and raiders. Up to a comparatively recent period the local records are full of them, their depredations, the measures taken to counter them, their constant threat. The Highlanders were, indeed, more or less equivalent to the Devil, and no good thing could come from their territories.

There were four main passes through the great mountains barrier, by which the raiders from Badenoch and Lochaber could descend upon the comparatively rich and settled low country, and quickly escape again without risk of successful pursuit—the Glen Feshie–Glen Geldie gap to the south; the Lairig Ghru in the south-centre; the Lairig an Laoigh, or Lui, The Pass of the Calves, in the north-centre; and the Avon valley to the north. These are still the access routes for walkers and climbers. Add to these what are still known as the Mounth passes through the foothills, from which more localised raiding was apt to erupt—as well as the more ambitious strategic inroads of conventional armies—and some understanding of the general attitude to the mountains may be gained. Folk memory and ingrained attitudes are both strong; and it might not be unfair to say that, to the great majority of the inhabitants of lowland Aberdeenshire still, the mountain mass which makes up so sizeable a proportion of the county's area, is not only *terra incognita* but something almost to turn the back upon. Appreciation ends with the pine and birch forested loveliness of upper Deeside.

Which is, of course, a pity. For the area is splendid, magnificent, unique in the British Isles, some 300 square miles of beauty, grandeur and stark savage wilderness, lonely, challenging—but dangerous. Each season, people die there—and not mainly from falling down its lofty crags and beetling precipices. They die, as a rule, from sheer exhaustion, and from numbing cold. For these high wastes are not so much Alpine in character as Arctic, their basic feature not a number of spectacular peaks but a tremendous plateau area at around the 3500-foot level, widespread, enormous, a wild and windswept tundra which makes its own weather and obeys no normal climatic rules. There is no other area in Britain remotely like it, and conditions are just outwith the experience of those who do not know it. It *can* be roasting hot up there, admittedly; but more often it is a wild playground of sudden storms, of blanketing white and freezing mists, of a chill which can quickly sap even the will to live. Often it is the sheer distances which are the fatal factor. For, because these mountains are not exciting-looking and impressive peaks, but ranges and ridges of this stupendous plateau, they tend to look much smaller than in fact they are, the impression of distance correspondingly lessened. Many a pointed 2000-foot peak elsewhere can look infinitely more daunting than these 4000-foot giants. Dimensions— and proper clothing—are the essentials to remember in the Cairngorms. And a compass, plus a good inch-to-the-mile Ordnance map.

These simple precautions, and a duly respectful attitude, make this area one of the most rewarding in the land for the adventurous, the athletic, the riser to challenge and the lover of nature. The Cairngorm National Nature Reserve covers over 100 square miles of this terrain to the south, offering an extraordinary range and variety of scenery, fauna and flora, as well as climatic conditions, with great scope for geology also. Go and enjoy it all—but do not expect to be spoon-fed, molly-coddled, or for that matter, rescued. Too many do.

Cairnie and Ruthven. Cairnie is a rural parish of 12,000 acres amongst the hills north-west of Huntly, flanking the Banffshire border, and Ruthven is one of its formerly independent constituent parishes. Others were Botary and Drumdelgie, but these are now only districts. There is quite a large modern village at Cairnie, grown up because of its proximity to the great Forestry Commission plantations of the Bin Hill.

The church is here, under the Bin Hill (1027 feet), above the ravine of the Cairnie Burn. It is fairly large, oldish and plain, with a big belfry, standing in an old kirkyard. Part of an earlier church, dedicated to St. Martin, remains in the shape of the Pitlurg aisle, burial-place of the Gordons of Pitlurg and Botary. An extraordinary effigy survives at the rear of the arch of this, with an antique inscription beginning *SIR JOHN GORDONE OF PITLURGE, KNYCHT, CAUST BIG THIS ILE . . . 1597*. There are some old gravestones. The village is pleasantly sited on a side-road from the main A96 Keith road, with a fair-sized school and War Memorial Hall. The Bin Forest, to the east, covers about five square miles.

Ruthven lies two miles to the north-east, an attractive small village in a sequestered position, notable as being the seat of the famous Tam o' Ruthven, brother of Jock o' Scurdargue, representatives of the main stem of Gordon after the marriage of their half-sister heiress with Sir Alexander Seton in 1408. Sir Thomas de Gordon of Ruthven lies buried in the kirkyard here, a recumbent effigy of a knight in full armour, in an arched recess in the walling, marking the spot. It was once within the church, which is now represented only by a gable, oddly crow-stepped only on one side, and with notably wide steps and a massive belfry. At the gateway is a weatherworn Pictish cross-slab. There are many old tombstones. The old-fashioned village has a small school, village hall and some modern houses. There are quarry workings to the east. No sign of the Ruthven castle remains.

Half a mile south-west, however, is the most interesting smallish fortalice of Achanachie, now a farmhouse. It is whitewashed, unusual in style, dating from the late 16th and 17th centuries, with developments from the original tall and small-roomed tower, all apparently somewhat reduced in height. Features are the circular stair-tower with the series of squared shot-holes up under the eaves, and the prominent projecting chimneystack of the 17th century extension. Over the door is inscribed *FROM OVR ENEMIES DEFENDE VSOCHRIST 1594*. The vaulted basement is carved with the arms of Gordon, Fraser and Campbell. Achanachie was the house of the eldest sons of Gordon of Avochie—and strangely, larger than was old Avochie itself. The Banff border is only a mile away from Ruthven.

Two miles south of Cairnie is the district of Drumdelgie, once a parish. Its church was called Peter Kirk, or the Brunt Kirk, being accidentally burned down in the 16th century. It lies in an ancient kirkyard with old gravestones, very ruinous, by the Deveron near Cairnborrow in Glass parish. Drumdelgie itself is now a high-set farm on Hill of Milleath. There is a stone-circle on the northern slopes here.

Cairnie parish extends a long way westwards of the village. The former parish of Botary lies just over a mile away, on A96, where a side-road strikes off to follow the south bank of the Cairnie Burn to Davidston. Botary consists of a hamlet, with farms, a former Free church, disused, post-office and mill. It was once another Gordon lairdship, linked with Pitlurg. Pitlurg, now a farm three miles on along the A96, has a substantial flanking tower, circular, of a court-yard castle with extensive foundations, built on a rock. The tower still rises about 30 feet, with squared gunloops and a domed base-ment vault, the upper part fitted as a doocot. The Pitlurg Gordons descended from Jock o' Scurdargue. The lands belonged to the Church until 1539 when the Gordons got them, and the castle would be built. They retained them until 1724. A later representative, General Gordon, in 1815 gained the estate of Leask and Birness, in Buchan, and gave the name Pitlurg to this.

In the valley of the Davidston Burn about two miles farther west, stands Davidston House, an interesting fortalice of the 17th century which fell on evil days and became a workers' tenement. However it is now most happily restored. The name is thought to derive from David de Strathbogie, earl of Atholl, who fought against Bruce, and on whose fall the Gordons rose. The house is L-planned, with two angle-turrets, the corbelling of which is very unusual, being built up of very small stones instead of the normal freestone tiers—presumably owing to lack of suitable local stone. A grinning mask under the north-eastern turret is dated 1678 and inscribed *I.G. AND T.A. BUILDED THIS HOUSE*. The T.A. refers to the Abercrombie wife of the Gordon laird. There is another mask, and a built-up square shot-hole window with weatherworn initials. It is good to see this fine house saved.

The portrait-painter William Aikman (1682–1731) was a native of Cairnie.

Chapel of Garioch and Pitcaple. This large upland parish of 13,000 acres lies directly under, and indeed contains part of the shapely hill of Benachie, so prominent a landmark for almost all Aberdeenshire. Chapel of Garioch parish lies north-west of Inverurie, very irregularly shaped. Its ancient name was Logie Durno, and originally there were three places of worship—Logie Durno in the north, Fetternear six miles to the south, and the Capella Beatae Maria Virginis de Garryoch, on the central high ground—where the present church now stands. The scenery throughout is very fine, with settled rich countryside contrasting with the soaring heather slopes. Pitcaple is the largest centre of population, a fairly modern village and an old estate, to the north.

The small village of Chapel of Garioch itself, really the kirkton, stands high, near the 500-foot contour, just over two miles north-east of the Mither Tap of Benachie, with magnificent views, at a junction of side-roads. The parish church is quite large and rather fine inside, dating from 1813. It has two side galleries and colourful stained-glass war memorial windows, with a mosaic memorial of highly unusual design, to Sir Robert Workman-Smith of Crow-mallie. The bell, of 1742, hangs at the wall of the interior, and has come from Logie Durno. There are some stone fragments from the original church, one dated 1600. In the graveyard are many old tombstones, and the walled burial-enclosure of the Erskines of Pittodrie. The old arched gateway to the early church and yard survives, with a roll-moulding, empty panel-space and the date 1626. A large and unsightly modern hall adjoins. A holy well, also dedicated to St. Mary, was sited in a field to the east but cannot now be traced.

A mile east of the kirkton, downhill, lies ruined Balquhain Castle with its large modern farmhouse, a picturesque spot. The castle remains consist of a lofty and massive east wall of the keep, complete almost to the wallhead, with part of a later circular flanking-tower to the west, the rest merely foundations. It has been a large and strong fortalice, set above a small ravine, and the principal seat of the Aberdeenshire Leslies from 1340 until it was burned by Cumberland in 1746 on his way to Culloden. Mary Queen of Scots spent a night here on her northern progress in 1562. Here was born the famous Bishop John Leslie, who died in 1671. There is a fine echo at Balquhain. A stone-circle stands on Balquhain lands, half a mile to the north-east, consisting of seven uprights plus a single white quartz monolith which stands outside the circle like a dramatic sentinel.

Another spectacular monolith is the Maiden Stone which stands at the roadside just over a mile north-west of the kirkton, on the way to Oyne. This is a notable example of Pictish Christian monument of the 8th or 9th century, of red granite, very high, with large symbols, its cross much weather-worn. Depicted are a centaur, a goat-like creature, rectangle and Z-rod, Celtic beast or "elephant", and the mirror-and-comb symbols. It is one of the finest extant, though with a fragment broken off. South of this, in its wooded hillside estate, is Pittodrie House, a large mansion partly modern but with an ancient nucleus consisting of a tall L-planned fortalice of 1605, with truncated square stair-tower with circular stair within. Another stair-tower rises to its conical roof at an angle of the wing. There are two more ancient gunloops in a detached vaulted building to the north. Sir Thomas Erskine of Halton, who was secretary to the youthful James V, in 1525 got these lands and probably built the first castle. John Erskine of Pittodrie was bailie for the Earl of Mar in 1635. His sixth descendant, an heiress, carried the property to Colonel Henry Knight, who took the name of Erskine. But Pittodrie has now passed from that family.

Northwards the parish drops to the Urie valley. Here is much of interest, including the original parish centre of Logie Durno, and the ancient houses of Logie-Elphinstone and Pitcaple, with the latter's modern village, all near the main A96 road to Huntly. Logie-Elphinstone is now a hotel, a large whitewashed mansion of various periods. At the front it looks to be a typical Georgian house but at the rear it shows a picturesque 17th century frontage, within a courtyard with circular stair-tower and heraldry. The former curtain-walling is pierced by an arched gateway surmounted by more armorial devices. This rear should be made more of. Elphinstones of the Glack family gained the property about 1670, one being created baronet in 1701. He built much of the additions. His heiress carried the estate to one of the Dalrymples of North Berwick. The family were Jacobites, and the famous fugitive Lord Pitsligo was frequently a secret guest here. The Dalrymple-Horn-Elphinstones sold Logie in 1903. Near the house, on the path to the walled gardens, are three Pictish stones, brought from elsewhere, all comparatively small. One displays the crescent and double-disc symbols; one a Celtic beast and crescent; the third also a crescent and double disc. Curiously, there has been an earlier double-disc and Z-rod on this stone, seemingly erased by the sculptor in favour of the superimposed symbols. There are Ogham ciphers also. A fourth stone is said to have been used as a hearthstone, and lost.

North-west of Logie-Elphinstone, half a mile, is the ruined former church of Logie Durno, within a well-kept graveyard. Only ivy-grown foundations remain amongst old and new gravestones. The burial-enclosure of the Elphinstone family is here.

Westwards of the gate-lodge to Logie-Elphinstone, on the main A96 road, an attractive picnic area has been established. Part of the extensive Benachie planted forest is on this Logie estate.

Pitcaple lies a mile to the east, with the post-office and some older cottages on the main road and quite extensive development of modern housing just off to the north. There is a large quarry here. The estate is wooded and attractive, and contains the fine castle, still occupied by the Lumsden family who gained it by marriage with a Leslie heiress in 1757. It is an interesting, tall, whitewashed fortalice on the Z-plan, mainly of the early 17th century but with older nucleus. Notable are the tall circular stair-towers and many angle-turrets with the rather peculiar lines of their roofing, an 1830 copy of Continental castellated style. The basement is vaulted, there are gunloops and shot-holes, and the castle was formerly surrounded by a moat with drawbridge. James IV visited here, as did Mary Queen of Scots, who planted a thorn-tree which survived until 1856. It was replaced in 1923 by a red maple, planted by the then Queen Mary. Charles II spent a night here in 1650, after his landing from exile in Holland. And here the great Montrose was brought, on his way to execution at Edinburgh. Near Pitcaple, to the north by the Urie, is the site of a small Roman camp, allegedly of Lollius Urbicus.

The southern part of the parish is less interesting, but with its attractions. A mile or so south of Pittodrie, on the skirts of Benachie, is the farm of Tullos, where there are the scanty remains of a 17th century fortalice in the steading. South-east of this another mile, on the farm of Broadseat, are the ruins of a very ancient pre-Reformation chapel in a walled enclosure now overgrown with trees. No features survive.

The Fetternear area, two or three miles still farther south, seems as though it should belong to near-by Kemnay rather than to Chapel of Garioch; the Don flowing between accounts for the division. Here is a large estate, formerly of the Leslies, the great mansion of which is now a ruined shell in mellow sandstone, appearing to date from the late 17th and early 18th centuries with some excellent heraldic decoration. Until the Reformation the property belonged to the bishops of Aberdeen who had a summer palace here. The Leslies got it at the carve-up of the Church lands, and made it their chief seat when Balquhain became uninhabitable. Still within the estate, but well over a mile from the house, on the bank of Don, is the ruined church of Fetternear in an old and neglected graveyard. Most of the remains are of a comparatively modern building, although on the old site, amidst a scene of desolation. St. Ninian's Well springs between church and river. The chapelry was established as early as 1109. A modern Roman Catholic Church of St. John still functions within the estate, near the stableyard.

Two miles north-west of Fetternear is the church of Blairdaff, founded as a much-needed chapel-of-ease in 1839 for the convenience of worshippers at this southern end of the parish. It is a very typical plain preaching-church, somewhat severe, with high central pulpit, some boxed-in pews and gallery. Innumerable such were built in the North-East in the first half of the 19th century.

The Benachie range, which so vehemently but attractively presides over all this countryside, is interesting in itself. The Mither Tap (1698 feet) which because of its dramatic shape—the word Benachie means mountain of the pap—seems to be the highest point, in fact is not. There are three other summits, Oxen Craig (1733 feet) the loftiest, with Watch Craig (1619 feet) and Craig Shannoch (1600 feet). A subsidiary summit, Millstone Hill (1340 feet), where in fact mill-stones were quarried for a wide area, rises two miles to the south. The lower slopes are heavily forested, Benachie Forest being enormous. It all forms a very distinct, as well as picturesque, barrier between North-West Aberdeenshire and the rest, so that the well-known song 'At the Back o' Benachie', has very real meaning.

A final note to a large and interesting parish. Although near Iverurie, the site of the Battle of Harlaw, in 1411, is within its bounds, one of the most significant conflicts of our "domestic" history, and the end of a possible Highland domination of Scotland.

Clatt. The word Clatt derives from *cleith*, meaning concealed, and well applies to this village, tucked into a fold of the Gadie valley under the Correen Hills of the Garioch—although its parish of 8000 acres spreads open and high enough up into the said hills, reaching 1588 feet. The lower ground is an attractive undulating area of farmlands, with little wood save on Knockespoch estate, and with no village other than the kirkton of Clatt.

This is not large, but is pleasingly sited on both banks of the Gadie, and was actually created a burgh of barony by James IV in 1501, for the ancient lairdship of the Knockespoch Gordons—the gallows-knowe for which stood at the "suburb" of Hardgate, to the south-east. The parish church occupies a knoll north of the Gadie, a plain, narrow, harled structure of 1799, replacing the pre-Reformation church whose piscina, tabernacle and coloured Crucifixion panel have not survived though they have been described. There is a tiny, high laird's gallery, and an old stone font. In the porch is a plaque stating: *Will Archbald, sometime in Miln of Clate, left 50 marks to helpe to build this loft for the use of the poor. 1738.* There are many old flat tombstones in the kirkyard. There was a Pictish symbol-stone near by, built into the wall of the schoolhouse—but this is now removed to Knockespoch garden.

Knockespoch is a large wooded estate on the lower skirts of the Correen Hills. The rambling mansion stands on a terraced site facing northwards, with an attractive lochan almost at the front door. The house dates from many periods, but the nucleus is a typical late 16th century laird's house, part of which can be seen at the back or south side, showing gable, stair-tower and other features. Its vaulted basement is now the wine-cellar, its gunloops built-up. The Fellowes-Gordon family are still in possession, after many generations. The fine Pictish stone aforementioned now stands in a re-entrant to the east, a monolith with double and triple disc-and-rod symbols. In the library at Knockespoch is built in a small arrow-slit window from Terpersie Castle, which belonged to the same family.

The Battle of Tillyangus, between the Gordons and the Forbeses, was fought near here in 1571, Mains of Tillyangus lying a mile to the north-west. On the higher ground of White Hill to the south-west are a large number of burial-cairn mounds, said to be the resting-places of the many dead in this bloody encounter, in which Black Arthur, brother of the Lord Forbes, was slain. But some would say that they are of earlier, prehistoric origin. The dramatic side-road to Alford, over the Correen Hills, passes the Knockespoch gates and climbs vigorously 600 feet in just over a mile, to 1281 feet—though the surface is good. The great burial-cairn on Suie Hill is well seen from the summit here, amongst the wide heather slopes dotted with Caledonian pines—a highly scenic area with superb views. Serpentine rock is found here. The road drops down near Terpersie Castle, another ruined Gordon stronghold, and on to Tullynessle. The Knockespoch gates on the main Clatt–Leslie road are enhanced by a lofty tower-like gatehouse, impressive but fairly modern.

North of Clatt village half a mile are the farms of Percylieu and Bankhead. A Pictish stone with horseshoe-and-fish symbol has been removed from Percylieu to the Leith-hall gardens, Kennethmont; and a single standing-stone is on Bankhead.

Cluny, Sauchen and Castle Fraser. This quite large rural parish of 9700 acres lies 21 miles west of Aberdeen, mainly on the ridge separating the Dee and Don valleys, with most of its drainage towards the latter river. There is no town or large community, but the village of Sauchen, lying fairly centrally and off the main A944 road, is more than a hamlet. The parish is unusual in having three major castles, although one is now a ruin and another grievously spoiled by Victorian "improvements".

The parish church stands in an isolated position a little way west of Cluny Castle, minus a kirkton, obviously sited for the convenience of the laird. It is unusual in having its kirkyard detached, on a similar grassy mound some distance to the north—presumably because of insufficient room for both on one. The church is commodious and plain, but attractively placed, with the parish war memorial in front. The graveyard, old and new and tree-girt, has many old stones, one very early and coffin-shaped; and no fewer than four mortsafes, giving the impression that it was a bad area for body-snatchers. There is an ambitious Grecian circular mausoleum for the Castle Fraser family; and another private burial-vault, unnamed but no doubt for the Cluny family of Gordon.

Cluny Castle, within its estate walls, is in clear view from the graveyard, a lofty, granite sham-castle in enthusiastic Victorian Gothic, which nevertheless does contain the ancient and authentic tower-house. This was perpetrated between 1840–72, and was described at that time as "characterised by chaste workmanship". Drawings of the original show a fine and typical 15th and 16th century fortalice. The castle was founded by a Sir Archibald Gordon, of the Huntly family, and descendants are still in possession. It is said that the double iron yett which barred the original doorway weighed four tons; and there was a water-filled moat. There is a large stableyard and farmery, in the same Victorian style, at the Home Farm, on the public road to the south-west. In the park is the Cunningar Wood, indicative of the days when rabbit-warrens were established on estates as carefully-managed sources of food. A pinetum was formed here in 1869, with some 400 varieties of tree and shrub.

A mile south-east of the castle is Sauchen, a scattered village in what has been rather bare moorland, with school, former Free church, inn and a very rural-looking bank. Its school, recently enlarged, stands some distance to the north, at Drumnahoy cross-roads, where there is also an attractive 18th century farmhouse, renovated. The fairly modern Linton House estate is near by, to the south.

Along the A944, to the west, is the Tillycairn area, of green slopes and small farms, with a hamlet, all tucked in below the tree-clad hills. There is an old mill here, at Ordhead, now disused as such but with water-wheel still *in situ*. Tillycairn Castle stands on a side-road half a mile northwards, ruinous beside a farm, but complete to the wall-head. It has been a handsome fortalice on the L-plan, with sundry refinements, the walls massive, the lower courses constructed of great unhewn boulders. The gables are surmounted by angle-turrets on elaborate corbelling, and there is a short parapet and walk at the wall-head on the west side of the wing, an unusual feature. There are numerous gunloops, some having cross-shaped slits above to improve aiming. There is a laird's-lug, or listening device, between the hall and a secret closet above the fireplace. Despite its warlike appearance, Tillycairn does not seem to have featured in any stirring history. Its only claim to fame is that it belonged to Matthew Lumsden, who died in 1580, author of *A Genealogical History of the House of Forbes*, a very early example of this type of work.

The most splendid as well as the best-known of Cluny's castles, however, is Castle Fraser, undoubtedly one of the finest in all Scotland. It stands in a large estate four miles north-east of Tilly-cairn and three miles south of Kemnay, and is still intact and well-maintained. It is one of that fine group which includes Midmar, Crathes, Craigievar and Fyvie, possibly the best of all. It looks largely of a piece, but is not, the main block having as nucleus a simple 15th century keep. But the general aspect is of a great and tall Z-planned fortalice of the late 16th century, with five-storey main block and angle-turrets, a gabled square tower to the north-west and a notable seven-storey round tower with flat balustraded roof to the south-east. Also two lower and parallel 17th century wings, built by one of the famous Bell family of master-masons, reaching northwards, the whole liberally supplied with gunloops, shot-holes, corbelling, stringcourses and heraldry. Here also is a laird's-lug device, installed this time in a window embrasure, connecting with a wall-closet in a bedroom above. These Aberdeenshire lairds were evidently inveterate eavesdroppers. Originally the great castle was known as Muchalls-in-Mar, to distinguish it from Muchalls Castle in Kincardineshire, also then a Fraser house. The Frasers came here in 1454, from Stirlingshire; and Andrew Fraser married Isobel, daughter of the then Lord Forbes, engaging to pay Forbes, at the high altar of Cluny, the curious tocher of 500 merks and a green apron. In 1633, another Andrew Fraser of Muchalls-in-Mar was created Lord Fraser by Charles I. Despite this, he took the Covenanting side in the wars that followed, and Castle Fraser was "spoiled" by Montrose in 1644 in consequence. The title became dormant at the death of the 4th lord in 1720, the Frasers of Inverallochy who succeeded being Jacobites and refusing to claim the peerage. The son of Inverallochy led the Frasers at Culloden and was slain. Collateral descendants still own the estate.

Outside the policies, to the south, is Courtcairn farm, which name commemorates the baronial jurisdiction of the lairds. On the summit of the wooded hill above is an obelisk called the Hanging Stone, not ancient, with a ball on top, which marks the site of the gallows-hill. There is a good stone-circle of nine uprights and one recumbent, 57 feet in diameter with a cairn at the centre, in a field half a mile north of the obelisk; and in another part of the same field, nearer the estate wall, are two more standing-stones, one five feet high. Still another single stone rises in an isolated position on

Woodend farm, in the low ground almost another mile to the north, a fine pillar monolith almost 10 feet high. There are others in the Leylodge vicinity, to the east.

This entire area is picturesque, with fine vistas, sheltered by the Corrennie Hills, with Benachie dominating all from the north.

Collieston, Slains and Forvie. Collieston is the favoured Buchan fishing haven and holiday resort; Forvie is a great area of sandhills, once a parish and now a nature reserve; and Slains is the coastal parish in which they are situated, some 15 miles north of Aberdeen and five east of Ellon.

Collieston, picturesque on a cliff-top, rims a deep rocky bay called St. Catherine's Dub. Here is the first good harbour north of Aberdeen, for in between stretches a long, sandy, shelving coast and links, with only one gap three miles to the south, at the Ythan estuary, where there is a tidal harbour at Newburgh. Popular with holiday-makers, Collieston has many of its fishermen's houses converted or restored. One, known as the Captain's Cabin, is formed out of a ship's deckhouse. There is a coastguard establishment; as well there might be. This rockbound coast has always been famed for its fishing. Speldings are a local specialty, haddocks dried on rock. Renowned also as a smuggling centre, the many caves and creeks of this shore gave Collieston distinct advantages in "the Trade". One cave, called Hell's Lum, is 200 feet long; and the Dropping Cave of Slains is notable for its stalactites and stalagmites. The bay itself is famous, for here, close inshore, was wrecked the *St. Catherine* galleon. The usual story is that it was one of the Spanish Armada, of 1588; but this is a mistake. It was a Flemish ship sent from the Spanish Netherlands with arms and ammunition to aid the rising of the Catholic earls of Erroll and Huntly, in 1594. Various relics have been recovered, and modern skin-divers still make attempts on the wreck.

A little north of village and harbour is Kirkton of Slains, where a rather gaunt parish church of 1800 stands on a hill in a very crowded graveyard. Here is the burial-place of the Hays of Erroll, whose castle of Old Slains lies a mile to the north. Buried here also is the victim of a fight between smugglers and excisemen.

A tall corner of the great keep of Old Slains Castle still stands on an incredibly exposed situation, on a cliff-top headland, 120 feet above the seething tide; and here the present Countess of Erroll, High Constable of Scotland and 31st chief of Clan Hay, has built a small modern house on the site of her ancestors' courtyard—a quite astonishing gesture. Gilbert Hay, 3rd baron of Erroll, in the Carse of Gowrie, married the daughter of William Comyn, Earl of Buchan and Constable of Scotland, in the 13th century, and so gained these lands. Bruce made his friend Sir Gilbert Hay, 5th baron, High Constable when the Comyns were forfeited. The stern castle must have been impregnable before advanced artillery was invented; but after the rising of the Catholic earls aforementioned, James VI came in person to blow up this stronghold. Thereafter the Earls of Erroll built up the Tower of Bowness, called New Slains, five miles to the north, at Cruden Bay. There is still a hamlet of fishermen's cottages landward here, known as Old Castle. Two cannon flank the castle ruin, one a falcon raised from the *St. Catherine*, with a plaque giving information. From here rode William, 4th Earl of Erroll, in 1514, to die with 87 gentlemen of the name of Hay, on the fatal field of Flodden. The countess, as Constable, still has her own herald, called Slains Pursuivant.

Inland from Slains lie a number of small lochs, unusual in Buchan. The largest, half a mile long, called Meikle Loch, lies behind the so-called Kippet Hills, the highest of which is 50 or 60 feet above the water! Cotehill and Sand Lochs lie to the south, smaller, and have been formed by sand barriers blown from Forvie.

This great expanse of sand dunes lies immediately south of Collieston extending to the mouth of the Ythan, three miles long and covering 1774 acres, a famous haunt of wildfowl, and now a national nature reserve under the Nature Conservancy. Here is the largest concentration of breeding eider-duck in Britain, and large colonies of terns, kittiwakes and fulmars. Shelduck and other species are also prevalent, and the plant communities of the fixed dune systems are interesting. Visitors are welcome, but asked to obey a 10-point code of behaviour and to keep away during the breeding-season, April to July, from the south end. Oddly enough this great area was once the rural parish of Forvie, overwhelmed with blown sand in a nine-days' gale at an unspecified date, after the fashion of the better-known Culbin area in Moray. The lonely ruins of the old parish church of Forvie are still visible amongst the heather and bents which have overgrown the sands, about 200 yards from the shore mid-way down the reserve. It is very small, some 30 by 12 feet, with an aumbry and signs of a rood-screen—obviously pre-Reformation. No other relics are evident.

Another pre-Reformation chapel, more ambitious, is that of St. Adamnan, set in a few trees in the Leask area, three miles north of Collieston. This has been a larger building, and the east gable still contains a good pointed arched window, though all is now very neglected. A cell is said to have been established here in the early 7th century, by Adamnan, a follower of Columba; but these remains are many centuries later than that. Near by, to the west, is the ruin of the former mansion of Leask, picturesque in an old walled garden, though the surviving masonry is not ancient. The estate was once the seat of the Leasks of that Ilk, but passed to the Gordons of Parkhill, one of whom built the house, whose ruins remain, about 1827. There is a rather good square doocot. Madam Leask of Leask has now repurchased the site.

Coull. Although quite extensive, covering 9000 acres in the fertile Howe of Cromar and its surrounding hills, this parish is a minor one in that it has no village and little entity. The large village of Tarland is near by, north-west, and Aboyne an equal distance southwards. Yet this used to be the most important centre of a wide area. For Coull Castle was the principal seat of the Durwards, and of their great barony of Onele or Oneil, the powerful family, who, though fairly briefly, ruled so much of south Aberdeenshire and Kincardineshire in the 13th and 14th centuries, the hereditary Door-wards of Scotland, keepers of the royal castle of Kincardine. Their original family name was de Lundin, from Fife—whence is the resort known as Lundin Links. Alan Durward, Lord of Coull, was regent and practically uncrowned king of Scotland during the minority of Alexander III, whose illegitimate sister he had married. Earlier they had acquired a large part of the earldom of Mar through marriage with an heiress.

The castle lies in what was formerly an extensive marsh, known as Bogmore, now drained by the Tarland Burn, 200 yards south of the parish church, the grass-grown remains being widespread and impressive. It belongs to the early 13th century, and had only a comparatively short life—for, being held by the English during the Wars of Independence, Wallace first demolished much of it, and later, Bruce had the restored edifice again pulled down. So it has been a ruin for a very long time. An ambitious excavation was carried out in 1923 by Drs. Douglas Simpson and Marshall Mackenzie, of Aberdeen, details of which may be read in Volume 48 of the *Proceedings of the Society of Antiquaries*. Tradition has it that when one of the Durwards died the church bell rang of its own accord.

The castle was a large establishment, five-sided, with five circular towers flanking high curtain-walls enclosing a courtyard. Twin drum-towers, with a pit or prison between their entry passage, guarded the entrance to the north; and a massive circular donjon-tower projected to the westward on a rocky bluff above the burn's ravine. The hall and living quarters were along the south side of the courtyard. There were protective moats and fosses. Much of this can still be discerned. It was built by Thomas de Lundin, the Door-ward or *Hostiarius*, of Scotland, whose mother was a daughter of a Countess of Mar in her own right. He also erected a bridge over the Dee at Kincardine O'Neil. His son, Colin, Lord Oneil, succeeded about 1231 and was followed by his more famous brother Alan, regent of the realm. Dying in 1268 *he* left only three daughters, and the barony of Oneil reverted to the Crown and was given to the Earl of Fife. The Fife earls took the English side in the Wars of Independence—hence the demolitions of the castle.

The parish church is pleasantly situated, quite attractive, with an old belfry and a bell of Dutch casting dated 1642, though the present kirk itself belongs only to 1792, restored 1876. Its predecessor, one of the most ancient places of worship in Aberdeenshire, was not only dedicated to but founded by St. Nathalan, along with the churches of Tullich and Bethelnie. He died in 678. William the Lion granted the church of Cul to his new abbey of Arbroath. There are some old stones in the kirkyard.

Two miles west of the church, at the roadside of the B9094, is the eminence of Tomnaverie whereon is a good example of stone-circle, well cared for by the Department of the Environment. And a similar distance both north-east and south-west of the church, on the high ground of Craiglich (1563 feet) and the Scar Hill of Tillyduke (984 feet), are large groups of burial-cairns, in clusters, on the borders of Lumphanan and Aboyne parishes respectively.

Coull House, a mile to the south-east in a wooded estate, is not old. The entire parish is much afforested, natural and planted. The Corse area to the north used to be in Coull parish but was attached to Leochel Cushnie in the 17th century, for the convenience of the Forbes lairds.

Crathie and Balmoral. This is the eastern section of the huge 200,000-acre joint parish of Braemar and Crathie, notable for containing within it the royal family's Highland home of Balmoral Castle—as well as innumerable other items of interest. It is, naturally, a mecca for visitors and in consequence is perhaps a little over-popular. But the area is scenically very lovely, a wide valley of pine and birch woodland, a little too trim in parts for every taste, all under the shadow of the great hills, Lochnagar itself dominating from the south. A notable feature is the large number of com-memorative cairns crowning many of the subsidiary heights, to various members of the royal family.

Balmoral Castle stands in a large wooded estate within a great bend of the Dee, half a mile west of Crathie Church and about eight miles east of Braemar, its Forest reaching up into the foothills of Lochnagar. It is actually an old estate of the Gordons, first leased by Queen Victoria and then bought in 1848. In 1853 the old house, a typical fortalice with extensions, was pulled down and the great Scottish Baronial edifice so frequently photographed, designed by William Smith of Aberdeen, built at a cost of £100,000. Later properties adjoining were added as time went on. A feature of the royal lands is the number of shiels, or picnic cottages, dotted over the wide area, beloved of the family, such as those of Glas-allt, Allt-na-guibhsaich, Danzig Shiel, Gelder Shiel, Gairn Shiel and so on. Further elaboration upon Balmoral, so well-known, is un-necessary here.

Easter Balmoral is a sequestered estate-village all to itself, off a back-road from the south Deeside A973 opposite Crathie Church—strangely, with a distillery behind it. There is a small general store displaying by Royal Appointment—as do many other shops in the Deeside area. The Royal Lochnagar Distillery of Messrs. John Begg hides in a fold of the land to the south, and is the successor of a famed private still at Mill of Balmoral, of one Charles Robertson who died in 1812. There is a small private golf course near by. A mile or so farther east, off the A973, is the site of St. Columba's pre-Reformation chapel, on a mound in a field at the scattered community of Balnacroft, with no remains surviving.

Near here, in the river's haugh, is Abergeldie Castle, another Gordon fortalice long in the hands of the royal family but now resumed by its Gordon owners and being refurbished. It is an attractive tower-house apparently of the 16th century, oblong in plan with a semi-circular stair-tower corbelled out to the square at the top to support a balustraded platform roof with ogee belfry-cum-caphouse. An unsuitable clock features below. Otherwise it is fairly typical, with angle-turrets, crowstepped gables, vaulted basements and so on. There is a standing-stone in the garden. The lands have been in Gordon hands since the late 15th century, the first laird, a son of Huntly, dying in 1504, his grandson slain at Pinkie and *his* grandson at Glenlivet. The parish boundary with Ballater lies a short distance to the east.

Crathie Church, where royalty has worshipped for so long, is in fact the fifth building to act as parish church. The first, dedicated to St. Manire, stood two miles to the east near the farm of Rinabaich, the site identifiable by a standing-stone near by. Then it was removed to the present graveyard site, by the riverside below the terrace on which stands today's building. In 1806 a new kirk was built up here, very plain, but it was demolished in 1893, and a timber building took its place temporarily while the present one was going up, designed by Marshall Mackenzie of Aberdeen. It is of grey granite but with rather unsuitable red tiles, cruciform in style with a square tower. Internally it has considerably more elaboration than the average country parish kirk, in marble and woodwork, but nevertheless, it is rather dark and just faintly shabby. Much of the stained glass was the gift of Victoria, and her bust, with those of George V and Edward VIII, decorate the nave. The royal aisle, with carved oak panels, occupies the south transept and faces across to that of the heritors on the north decorated with the emblems of regiments which have formed the guard-of-honour at Balmoral. A pleasing modern school is near by, also the post-office and shop.

Comparatively few of the great numbers who visit Crathie Church go down the 400 yards to its predecessor by the waterside, with its old kirkyard and manse adjoining. Roofless and more or less featureless now, the old thick-walled kirk is filled with graves. There are many old tombstones outside, some very primitive and one dated 1698. Here is buried the famous John Brown, Victoria's so-favoured servant. Also there is a memorial to the less-known James Bowman, gamekeeper inscribed *Placed here by the Queen whom he served faithfully for 17 years. Died 1885*. The east end of the kirk forms the burial-enclosure of the Farquharsons of Monaltrie—which oddly enough is in Ballater parish.

The hill-slopes flanking the Dee and Balmoral are, naturally, kept very private. Half a mile west of Crathie, the former military road, now the A939, branches off northwards from the A93 to climb over the hills to Gairnshiel and on to Cock Bridge, reaching 1738 feet in the process. Gairnshiel is described under Ballater in which parish it is. Two miles west of Crathie, in the pass below Craig

Benachie, the shapely and isolated peak which presides over so much of central Aberdeenshire, seen here from Balquhain Castle three miles to the east

The bridge amongst the pine-woods at Linn of Dee, Braemar

Cairnie. Achanachie Castle, a small Gordon fortalice

Cluny. Castle Fraser, one of the finest in the land

Nordie, is Carn na Cuihne, the Cairn of Remembrance, a former
Clan Farquharson mustering-place, where each man laid a stone on
the cairn on departure to the fray, and picked one up on return—
the remainder indicating the casualties! A monolith was erected
near by in 1953 by the Deeside Field Club.

Across Dee, here, stretches the great Ballochbuie Forest, one of the
most attractive relics of the old Caledonian forest in the land, now
part of Balmoral estate. It covers a wide acreage, the ancient pines
scattered and rising out of heather—though natural regeneration
takes place, so that there are trees of all ages. Deer are numerous.
The Garbh-allt or Danzig Shiel is in the midst, with the Falls near by,
spanned at their head by an ornate iron bridge, a favoured spot of
Victoria and Albert—and also of their son King Edward VII, who
was not a lover of Balmoral. The story is that Ballochbuie was
handed over by its original owners, MacGregors, to a Farquharson,
for a single woollen plaid. When Victoria bought it in 1878, she
called it "the bonniest plaid in Scotland".

Crimond and Rattray. Today this may be a comparatively
unimportant rural parish of 7400 acres, small for Buchan, somewhat
bleak of aspect and with no large community therein; but once it
was an area of some consequence, Rattray in fact having been a
royal burgh, with the Comyn Earls of Buchan having an important
castle here. We read, in 1627, of a court at which three bailies of the
Burgh of Rattray presided with a jury of 13. Now Rattray shows no
sign of this other than a ruined chapel. Crimond, three miles inland,
is a village with a parish church. It lies almost mid-way between
Peterhead and Fraserburgh. The parish includes half of the large
Loch of Strathbeg.

Crimond village, lying athwart the A952, is a fair-sized community,
and growing, with much new housing and a large school, in open
flat country. The parish church is a plain, harled building of 1812,
with steeple, belfry and clock, the latter with the ominous legend
THE HOUR IS COMING. Internally the church is of some distinc-
tion, with pillars. Its pre-Reformation predecessor stands within its
old graveyard, half a mile northwards. The gate-piers have
heraldic panels built in, one weatherworn with a coronet, the other
inscribed *W. HAY OF URY 1617*. Only one wall of the old church
survives, with a rope-moulded window and an arched doorway. The
former has heraldic panels inserted in both ingoings, and another
above dated 1652. The Crimond estate long belonged to the Hays,
Earls of Erroll. There is a tall obelisk to the Bannerman baronets of
Elsick, who latterly owned Crimonmogate and Logie estates locally.
There are many old gravestones. Near by to the east is a huge
deserted war-time airfield on which the Ministry of Defence have
designs to build a large R.A.F. radio-station with a 900-foot mast—
which does not please either amenity lovers or the ornithologists
interested in the wildfowl of Strathbeg Loch—and a bomb-testing
station, which is worse.

A mile due west of Crimond village is the estate of Logie, a former Gordon lairdship whose mansion is now demolished. It was the scene of the Jacobite ballad 'Logie o' Buchan'. At Netherton of Logie farm is a fine stone-circle of 11 uprights and three fallen, with a large recumbent, all within a walled enclosure with trees near the steading.

The Rattray area is coastal and distinct, at the other side of the airfield. Here the large Strathbeg Loch stretches over some 700 acres, shallow and bare, only separated from the sea by a half-mile-wide sand dune area called the Back Bar. The south end is in this parish, the rest in Lonmay. At this south-west foot is the old laird's house of Haddo, now a farmhouse, a fine, tall, T-shaped mansion of the late 17th century, with good features, eaves-course, steep roofs, chamfered windows, and much good woodwork within. A skewputt shows the initials A.B. and M.C., the B probably for Bisset—though there is record of a William Watson of Haddo, bailie of Rattray in 1675. Near by at Mill of Haddo, is the spot called Battle Faulds, where is the grave of Sir James the Rose, hero of the ballad, slain in mortal combat for the hand of the Earl of Buchan's daughter by Sir John the Graham. The site of the Burgh of Rattray lies east of Haddo House; and just a little farther is the ruined chapel of St. Mary within its kirkyard in an exposed position at the loch-foot, where the wildfowl flight. It has been a fine building, in First Pointed style, with a good triple-window to the east. There are a few old gravestones. It is said to have been founded in 911. Again a little farther east, on the farm of Old Rattray, is the green motte-hill of the former Comyn castle, destroyed like so many another in Edward Bruce's famous herrying of Buchan in 1307. Rattray House, a Georgian mansion now, lies in trees about a mile to the south, where a branch of the great Comyn family survives.

Finally eastwards stretches Rattray Head, one of the most easterly points of Scotland, where a rocky reef and series of skerries project seawards for over a mile from the otherwise flat, sandy coastline, scene of innumerable wrecks. There is a well-known lighthouse here; also a coastguard station in the sandhills. On either side, the dunes and sandy beaches stretch to infinity.

Cruden Bay, Port Erroll and Hatton. The good folk of Cruden Bay and district, 24 miles north of Aberdeen, must be well aware of the impermanence of human plans and aspirations. For surely few places have had such ups and downs and seen so seemingly important and imperishable institutions pass away. The village, or small town, itself is modern—in 1840 the only villages in the large parish of Cruden were Bullers-Buchan, the Ward, Hatton and Whinnyfold—and with Port Erroll, its fishing haven, has a population of almost 2000. But this fluctuates wildly between summer and winter, for this is a holiday resort and a renowned golfing centre. Even so, its best days seem past, unless the North Sea oil boom dictates otherwise.

Cruden Bay is a fine sickle of sands two miles long, flanked by links, in an otherwise rocky and spectacular seaboard, 10 miles south of Peterhead, with Cruden Skares, or skerries, reefs of jagged rocks and islets jutting seaward at the south end. Here Malcolm II is reputed to have defeated the Danish Canute in 1012. The old centre of the parish of Cruden was at Hatton, or the Hall-town, three miles inland; and only a tiny fishing hamlet of Ward of Cruden, under the shadow of the great Erroll castle of New Slains, was here at the head of the bay. Then, because the haven at Ward was dangerous in all but calm seas, the 19th Earl of Erroll, at the parish minister's urging, built a new and large harbour in a more sheltered location, where the Cruden Water now enters the bay, and called it Port Erroll. Here a sizeable fishing village sprang up, with some coasting trade; this is now esteemed for its picturesque cottages, many of which have been taken over and developed attractively as holiday homes, with others built. A fine 18-hole golf course was established on the long links. Then, in 1899, the Great North of Scotland Railway Company opened a line, and built a vast palatial hotel here, in pink Peterhead granite, an enormous place which stood out strangely in the bare and windswept landscape, and quickly became the haunt of the rich and fashionable. For exactly 40 years this oddity for Buchan flourished, and lesser hotels and guest-houses grew up in its shade, for golfers in especial and bathers and holiday-makers in general. Then came the wars, and in 1939 Cruden Bay Hotel was taken over by the army. It was the kiss of death. When it was released, nobody could be found to buy it; it was demolished in 1947. The lesser hotels and boarding-houses remain, however, and the Golf Club is as popular as ever. Chalets and caravans proliferate.

Like most of Buchan the district is bare, although an extensive oak forest flourished here once, and there are still relics of it along the old course of the Cruden Water. This is crossed by the Bishop's and Ladies' Bridges, the latter a footbridge nearer the sea giving access to the links and erected at the expense of the village ladies in 1922; the former by Bishop James Drummond, ousted from his see in 1659, when he came to live at New Slains with the earl, and became concerned with the dangers of crossing the river when in spate. Once there were thread-mills in the area, but today, apart from catering and the holiday industry, the largest employers of labour are the brick and tile works and kilns. Fishing is now greatly reduced. Oddly enough, Cruden Bay can claim a literary link, for Bram Stoker gained the inspiration for his well-known book *Dracula* here.

In 1597 the 9th Earl of Erroll began to extend the small Tower of Bowness, at the north horn of the bay, after James VI had blown up Old Slains Castle five miles to the south. Part of the older stronghold is still to be discerned in the south-east corner of the great ruined pile, seeming to grow out of the solid rock of the cliff-top. A huge palace developed, over the generations, so that when Dr. Johnson and Boswell came to spend a night in 1773, the former declared the site at least the noblest he had ever seen. Here the Errolls kept up semi-regal state, until in 1916 the place was sold to Sir John Ellerman, the shipowner, who dismantled it in 1925. Of pink granite, its mighty ruins soar and extend along the cliff-tops, and from its gaping windows one peers straight down to the breakers on the rocks far below. Boswell, we read, could not sleep for the roar of the waves and for fear of the beheaded Jacobite Earl of Kilmarnock's ghost, one of this family. So this palace is gone for ever also, though more remains of it than of the hotel.

More enduring are the standing-stones in the field to the south-west. And the burial-cairn on a low ridge two miles farther south-west, readily seen from both the A975 and the lesser coast-road to Whinnyfold. This last is a former fishing village at the south horn of the great bay, in the Sandford vicinity where the cliffs resume.

Two miles north of Cruden Bay is the famous Bullers of Buchan—the name is thought to be merely a corruption of boiler. This is reached from an attractive little cluster of cottages at the roadside, and then by a cliff-top footpath. It is a 200-foot-deep amphitheatre in the tremendous granite cliffs, where the sea rushes in through a tunnel to form something like a vast well, open to the sky. In rough seas this can be a daunting place. Dr. Johnson was much impressed and described it vividly, as did Scott—who also brought the islet of Dunbuy, the Yellow Rock, detached from the cliff half a mile to the south, into *The Antiquary*.

On the main Peterhead road two miles north of the Bullers, is Long Haven, a road-side hamlet with school and post-office, with inland the great R.A.F. radar and warning installations which dominate the area. Long Haven takes its name from the deep inlet of the cliffs which probes here close to the main road. To the south rises the tall rock pinnacle of Hare Craig, and to the north the Cave o' Meackie. Other dramatic features proliferate on this cliff-girt seaboard.

Inland the 18,000 acres of Cruden parish are less exciting, typical and rather dull Buchan landscape, with many mosses and low ridges. It was highly populated in prehistoric times and there are many cairns, burial-mounds and earthworks, particularly a notable cluster in the Cairn Catto district. There is a standing-stone in a field behind Greenhill farm two miles north-by-west of Bullers of Buchan. The farm of Standingstones is on the main A952 near Hatton village, but its stones have been pulled down and incorporated in the steading.

Hatton of Cruden village, three miles west of Cruden Bay just off the main road, is a fair-sized place, with bank, hotel, hall, a mill now disused and a quite large biscuit-factory. The former Free church at the upper, west, end is now used as the parish church, a fairly bare preaching-kirk with small steeple and clock, dated 1884. Near by is the school and an attractive modern housing group. Auchiries, a farm, a house or two and another little school, lies on the main road two miles north-east. This area has recently been scheduled for mineral exploitation by a large London-based company. With the North Sea oil developments and the projected booster-station, there look like being notable changes on the scene hereabouts.

Almost two miles south-east of Hatton is Chapel Hill, where a large Episcopal church on a prominent ridge site forms a well-known landmark, its spire seen for miles around. It was built in 1765 by one of the Earls of Erroll. And remotely set on the high moorland three miles north of Hatton is the former laird's house of Aldie, with a white quartz standing-stone in its rather dejected walled garden. The tall, gableted early 18th century house is now a farm-workers' tenement, with a ruined chapel of no great age adjoining.

Culsalmond and Colpy. Here is a smallish parish of the Garioch district, of 7000 acres, to the south and east of the Foudland Hills, and threaded by the A96 from Inverurie to Huntly. There is no real village, and the Kirkton of Culsalmond is a scattered place hardly to be called a hamlet. The parish slopes up from the Urie valley to the hills of Skares (1078 feet) and Tillymorgan (1250 feet), in gentle south-facing braes. Colpy is a little trim hamlet on the main road, at a junction just north of Williamston House; and Pitmachie is another, four miles south on the A96—but it has become a sort of suburb of Old Rayne across the Urie.

The present parish church was the former Free kirk, a large building of 1866, with a tall steeple and a modern graveyard, standing isolated with its manse. It is on the B9000 Oldmeldrum road, half a mile east of the A96, with a very modern school nearer the main highway. The old church stands higher, up a side-road to the north, now roofless in its ancient sloping kirkyard, with splendid views to Benachie, though fairly featureless save for an elaborate belfry seemingly of the 17th century, but no bell. An outside fore-stair for the minister remains. A still older pre-Reformation church is represented only by a piece of walling in which is a panel commemorating the Gordons of Cults. There are many old tombstones, and an interesting mort-house, two-storeyed, the lower, semi-subterranean vaulted chamber, with an iron inner door, for containing corpses for six weeks until unfit for the purposes of "the resurrectionists", when they could be buried in safety. This was a facility in great demand, being used for bodies as far away as Buchan. The upper room was used as a Sunday-school—but was, not unnaturally, less than popular with the children. This kirkyard was on the site of a stone-circle of a dozen uprights, many of the stones still said to be buried amongst the graves. Just south of the road-end to it is the farm of Pulwhite, unusual in having below part of it a subterranean moss up to eight feet in depth, overlaid by later glacial soil and deposit.

Colpy hamlet with post-office and sawmill lies about a mile to the west. There were two stone-circles here also, now gone. The farm of St. Sairs lies half a mile farther west, its name commemorating the famed St. Sairs Fair, allegedly one of the oldest in the county. And at the adjoining farm of Jericho to the north was formerly an old-established distillery, now merely part of the farm-buildings.

Tillymorgan Hill, rising behind the Kirkton, with its wooded lower slopes, used to be the scene of extensive blue-slate quarrying. Ironstone was also quarried in this parish, and sent to the Carron Iron Works—a far cry. On the northern flanks of Tillymorgan is the site of a Pictish camp with double entrenchments. The Cadgers' Road runs from the Kirkton over the eastern shoulder of the hill, no doubt an access to the well-known fairs at St. Sairs, and St. Lawrence of Old Rayne.

To the south of the parish, near the Rayne boundary, is the fine wooded estate of Newton, with its splendid gardens, meticulously kept and frequently open to the public. The mansion is a tall, dignified and substantial building of the early 18th century, full of character, on a terrace site above the Urie meadows, a former Gordon property. In the garden just east of the mansion are preserved two notable Pictish sculptured stones, about seven feet tall. One is enhanced with Oghams and a form of lettering, very unusual; the other shows the double-disc symbol with serpent and Z-rod.

Formerly there were three sacred wells in Culsalmond parish: St. Mary's, Colpy; St. Michael's, on Gateside farm on the B922; and one allegedly beneficial for scrofulous complaints, on Sauchenloan farm. There were also a number of prehistoric burial-cairns, which have not survived.

Daviot. Not to be confused with the Daviot just south of Inverness—the name is a corruption of *davoch*, meaning land sufficient to produce 48 bolls of grain—this is a small rural Aberdeenshire parish of 4400 acres lying in mainly fairly level land just west of Oldmeldrum, and, like so many others, under the shadow of Benachie. The village of Daviot stands on a low ridge, fairly centrally, with splendid and wideflung prospects of rich farming country, backed by the hills. The parish church dates from 1798, standing above the old village and below the new—for there is considerable modern housing here. It is a neat, modestly-sized granite building within a large kirkyard wherein are the usual tombstones, old and new. Internally the church has recently been renovated and remodelled, with excellent results, giving a light and cheerful, yet dignified, atmosphere. The former church-bell, a very small one cast by John Mowat of Old Aberdeen in 1752, hangs internally against the west gable, with close by, a highly modern hanging-font of unusual design. In the kirkyard are two lairds' burial-enclosures side by side on the slight eminence which was presumably the site of the original church, that to the east pertaining to the Setons of Mounie. There used to be a stone-circle retained within the kirkyard, but the stones were removed in the early 19th century.

There are two other stone-circles near by, one very fine. This is at Loanhead of Daviot, half a mile north-west of the village, in woodland to the right of the road. Here, on a slight ridge, and under the care of the Department of Environment, is a circle of 10 uprights and a double, or split, recumbent, very unusual, with an associated cairn and urn-burial. The views from here are extensive, looking across the verdant howe to Core Hill (804 feet) with its lofty B.B.C. mast. The second stone-circle is now reduced to three uprights and a large recumbent, on the edge of a copse above New Craig farm half a mile north of the previous site and easily seen from the same road.

At the other southern and western side of Daviot village lies the wooded estate of Glack, now the site of a large hospital for mental disorders, the former extensive Scottish Baronial mansion of 1875, with its towers and turrets, supplemented by an elaborate complex of buildings. On Glack was dug up, in 1833, an iron battleaxe, presumed to have been used at the Battle of Harlaw, three miles to the south, in 1411.

To the east, over a mile from the village, lies Mounie Castle, in wooded grounds south of the road to Oldmeldrum. It is an attractive small fortalice of the early 17th century on the T-plan, with a three-storey main block and projecting circular stair-tower corbelled out to a watch-chamber at the top, and reached by a small turret stair. The basement is vaulted, with the kitchen having the usual wide arched fireplace and a stone basin near by. Mounie was a possession of a cadet branch of the Setons of Fyvie, of whom came the famous Earl of Dunfermline, Chancellor of Scotland in the 17th century. Pitmeddan near by was another Seton seat, and George Seton of Mounie was second son of Lord Pitmeddan of Session. Beneath an ancient yew-tree near by stands the Newton Stone, removed here from the vicinity of Newton of Mounie farm, a small, round-headed Pictish upright, carved in relief with mirror-and-comb symbols and, most unusual, two crescents, one with V-rod and one without.

Dinnet, Cambus o' May and Kinord. Dinnet is a small village, a large estate, and a district at the eastern extremity of Glenmuick and Tullich parish; Cambus o' May is a former railway-station and hamlet three miles farther west; and Lochs Kinord and Davan lie to the north, partly in Aboyne parish, all in mid-Deeside.

Dinnet lies athwart the main A93 North Deeside road, where the B9119 coming from the south A973 road crosses it and proceeds northwards across the Moor of Dinnet to Logie Coldstone and eventually Strathdon. The position is pleasing, in pine-woodlands, after the rather bare stretch from Aboyne, where the Deeside Gliding Club has its airfield. There is a *quod sacra* parish church of 1875, near the gates to Dinnet House, but no graveyard. The building is very plain within, but the setting attractive. The estate stretches along the north side of Dee, the mansion is fairly modern. There is a hotel and shop at the village, a garage, a caravan site in the woodland, and St. James's Deeside Gallery, displaying paintings, pottery, glass, tweeds.

More than a mile to the west on the main road, at a lovely stretch of scrub birchwoods, the road flanks the southern shore of Loch

Kinord, and here, at Meikle Kinord, at the shore, is a craft workshop specialising in enamelled-work based on Celtic designs. There is also a former small private chapel, not ancient, with a highly unusual larch-wood roof, and semi-precious stones amongst the masonry, all now used as a straw-shed. Cambus o' May hamlet, with a hotel, lies just over a mile farther on, where the A97 strikes off northwards by Loch Davan. Cambus o' May Halt railway-station of course no longer functions, but it is amusing to note how the former River Inn here has a corner sliced off to allow the trains to pass. The old-fashioned hamlet is in two sections, quarter of a mile apart, with gardens climbing notably sharply behind. This is a very attractive stretch of Dee, with a suspension-bridge over the river.

Lochs Kinord and Davan are large and delightfully set amongst heather, pines and birchwoods, with the great Hill of Culblean (1983 feet) rising behind. Kinord is the southernmost and larger, and is notable for having a crannog, or artificial island, towards the east end, and a castle-site on a larger natural island to the west. This was an important stronghold, allegedly first built by Malcolm Canmore, but certainly occupied by James IV in 1505—for items in the Lord Treasurer's Accounts testify it. Covenanting troops captured it in 1645, and soon afterwards it was demolished. On the spit of land between Kinord and Davan was once a Pictish town of some size, thought to have been Devana—hence the name Davan. Many remains have been uncovered, hut circles and weems and enclosures, and relics have been dredged from the loch. This community seems to have been linked with the groups of cairns on Mullach Hill and the cluster of blue cairns some distance to the east. Today, the most obvious evidence of this settlement is the Pictish symbol-stone which stands on a knoll above the lochside to the north, between Old and New Kinord, reachable by a long dirt-track. It is a fine cross-slab, six feet high, with typical Celtic interlacing decoration, the symbols too weatherworn to distinguish, standing within a railed enclosure. This relic has moved about, for having stood near by originally, it was removed to the policies of Aboyne Castle at one stage but restored to this site by the present Marquis of Huntly.

The crossroads hamlet of Ordie is near by, but this is in Logie-Coldstone parish. At the western head of Loch Davan, on the A97, is a scatter of houses called Lochhead, attractive amongst woodland. A mile to the south-west, at the roadside, is a high monolith erected in 1956, by the Deeside Field Club, to commemorate the Battle of Culblean, the final battle of the second War of Independence, fought in 1335, six years after Bruce's death, during the Edward Baliol usurpation. Sir Andrew Moray, who had married Bruce's sister Christian and was guardian of Scotland for the child David II, soundly defeated David, Earl of Atholl, in revolt. An erratic boulder known as the Great Stane, on the side of Culblean Hill near the feature called the Vat, was where Atholl made his last stand, stating that it would flee as soon as he—an incident immortalised by Walter Scott. The earl was slain here.

The Vat itself is a fascinating natural cauldron in the deep ravine of the Vat Burn just to the south-west, and reachable by a rough track from the main road at Burn o' Vat—and well worth the trouble. It is a huge and most spectacular double cavern, open to the sky, excavated by the stream—which must have been vastly larger once to do so—with only a narrow crack in the rocks as entrance. Here Gilderoy MacGregor, the noted freebooter, made his lair in the early 17th century, terrorising the Cromar neighbourhood therefrom.

Drum, Drumoak and Park. Drum is one of the most famous castles in the land; Drumoak is the misnamed Deeside parish in which it stands—although with other items of interest than the one; and Park is the roadside village and fine estate, with its own separate history.

The Forest of Drum was a favourite royal hunting-ground, and the ancient tower which is the dominant feature of the present castle dates from about 1286, being built probably by Richard Cementarius, or the Mason, for Alexander III. It stands in a great estate, which Robert the Bruce gave to his faithful armour-bearer Sir William Irvine, a son of Irvine of Bonshaw in Annandale, in a charter dated 1323, at Berwick. The keep is massive and tall, with a crenellated parapet enclosing a flat roof, which however would originally contain a gabled garret-storey. The walls reach 12 feet in thickness, with ground, first and second floors vaulted. The remainder of the castle dates from the early 17th century, forming two sides of a square, the other two comprising a more modern gatehouse-wing, with entrance-pend, and high curtain-walling, all highly picturesque. The history of the Irvines of Drum is full of incident and colour, the lairds ever taking a prominent part in national affairs, and innumerable are the stories told of them. I mention only one. Sir Alexander was one of the Lowland leaders at Red Harlaw and especially distinguished himself on that field of so much heroism by challenging to individual combat the famous opposing champion, Red Hector of the Battles, Maclean of Duart, son-in-law and chief lieutenant of Donald of the Isles who led the Highland host. Apparently, even in the midst of such a holocaust, these two paladins were allowed to fight it out between them undisturbed—an interesting side-light on the times—which they did to such good effect that they succeeded in slaying each the other. Sir Alexander Irvine was buried on the field, where the Drum's Cairn was raised to mark the spot. The present 24th Irvine of Drum is the hero's brother's descendant.

When Bruce gave the Forest of Drum to Irvine, he retained the Park of Drum in the royal possession, that is the low-lying grazing lands near the Dee. So Park has remained a separate entity down the centuries, though the Irvines did gain it. David II, Bruce's son, gave Park to one Walter Moigne, and in 1348 John Moigne conveyed it to the then Irvine of Drum. In 1737 the Irvines sold Park to a neighbour, Duff of Culter, and thereafter this estate passed through many hands. It is a fine wooded property, with a long and valuable stretch of Dee fishings. The mansion is most attractive, built in the Grecian style, white, long and low, by the famous Aberdeen architect Archibald Simpson, designer of Marischal College, in 1822. Not far from the house, in the grounds, is preserved a Pictish symbol-stone, much weatherworn but mounted on a concrete base on which the symbols are repeated, displaying crescent and V-rod, half-moon, comb-and-mirror, etc. This originally stood at Keith's Muir, to the east, site of a great battle between the Irvines and the Keiths—though the stone of course pre-dates the fight by many centuries. It was brought for better keeping to the Hawk-hillock in Park estate, and then to its present site.

The hamlet of Park lies athwart the busy North Deeside road, the A93. There was formerly a railway-station. The parish church stands beside the school in a somewhat isolated site half a mile away on the rising ground to the north-east, a rather pretentious Gothic-style building of 1836, with graveyard around, neat but suburban-looking. This certainly cannot be said of its predecessor, a highly picturesque, ancient, ruinous pre-Reformation building down at the waterside, more than a mile to the south-east. This is St. Moluag's Church of Dalmaik—Maik being a corruption of Moluag, a Celtic missionary. The original name of the parish was Dalmaik, and somehow, with the importance of the Drum property, this changed itself to Drumaik, then Drumoak. The church is roofless but entire to the wall-head, the masonry having been restored somewhat in 1941. It served as parish church from 1062 to 1836, when its successor was built. The old bell still hangs in the belfry. The building is typically long and low, its doors on the south front and west gable having deep slots for draw-bars. That to the west has a panel-space over, and the lintel of the south door is inscribed but indecipherable. A holy-water stoup is just within and there are corbels projecting internally at the west end to support a gallery, this having been reached by a forestair against the north wall. A window at the east end of the south front has a good triple moulding; and near by in the east gable are steps up to a narrow and later door, no doubt for the Reformed minister to reach his pulpit. There are many gravestones, moss-grown and unreadable. The old font from here now lies in the steading of Cobblestocks farm at Peterculter. The fine former manse, probably of the late 17th century, stands immediately north of the church, now derelict but still with a roof with coped chimneystacks and pleasing lines. It could and should be saved. St Maik's Well is still a spring to the north-east, at the foot of a green bank. The little farmhouse is to the west, on the river-bank, and the whole makes a most attractive group. Professor James Gregory, F.R.S. (1638–75), "the greatest philosopher of the age, after Newton", inventor of the reflecting telescope, was born son of the minister here, and married the daughter of George Jameson, the Scottish Van Dyck.

There is much planted forest to the east of the parish. Rising out of it, on Belskavie Hill, is a stone tower sometimes thought locally to be ancient but in fact a 19th century folly built as a gamekeeper's cottage. It looks southwards over the Roman camp of Norman-dykes. The site, however, was a beacon-point in warlike days. The Dee Valley Caravan Park lies nearer Park village.

North-west of Park lay the former Loch of Park, or Drum, now largely drained but still marshy. In a stone-walled enclosure at its north-east end was the King's Well, of just what royal significance is not now known. There is much moss and moorland to the north of Drum parish's 7400 acres, now also mainly drained, the local names perpetuating the theme—Red Moss, Lochmuir, Rashenlochy, Quartains Moss and so on.

Drumblade and Lessendrum. This is a parish of Strathbogie lying south and east of Huntly, extending to 9000 acres of pleasant, hilly country north of the Foudland Hills, but having no village, though threaded by the main A96 Aberdeen–Huntly highway. The parish church stands in a sequestered valley, remote from main roads, about five miles east of Huntly, a long, harled building of 1773 and 1829, with an old belfry, plain within and without, with a gallery. It replaced the original chapel, allegedly of 1110, dedicated to St. Hilary whose well used to be near by, and was a dependent of Kinkell Collegiate church. In the kirkyard are some old tombstones, and the burial-place of the Bissets of Lessendrum since the 16th century. There is a former large Free church, with small belfry, kept tidy but now disused, at Brideswell a mile to the south-west, where also is the school, post-office and war memorial.

Chapelton, the site of an early pre-Reformation chapel, is now only a farm, lying on a narrow side-road two miles south of the kirkton. The chapel's position was in a wood at the roadside, and near by, below the farmhouse, is an excellent spring still in its neat stone recess, known as the Chapel Well. The curving minor roads here-abouts are not for speeding, but the prospects on all hands are very fine, over a lovely countryside. At the farm of Stonywood, adjoining to the north-east, is a stone-circle in a field, eight stones with only two still upright.

At the other side of the kirkton, a mile east, is Corse hamlet, a pleasant quiet place with a school and a rather attractive Georgian small mansion.

North-westwards two miles lies the ancient estate of Lessendrum, on hilly ground near the A97 road to Banff—indeed the Banffshire border is not far off. The mansion was destroyed by fire in com-paratively recent times, but was mainly of 1837, though with an older nucleus. The property is interesting in that it is still the home of the Bissets of Lessendrum, who are probably the oldest-established line in all Aberdeenshire. They were Normans who came north with William the Lion, and settled here—and elsewhere, at Aboyne, Lovat, Beauly and so on—so that they were old-established at

Lessendrum by the Wars of Independence. Twenty-seven generations at least have held the lands since then, the present laird farming
the old estate with highly modern methods including a computer.
The only antiquity, however, appears to be a circular doocot at the
farm of Meikleton.

South-west of Lessendrum, a mile, is Newtongarry Hill (671 feet)
with a burial-cairn at the top. Another cairn stands in a field at
Nether Brunstone farm, just off the main A97 two miles west. In
this vicinity was fought in 1307 the Battle of Slioch, where Robert
the Bruce, despite his sickness, defeated the Comyns of Buchan.
Robin's Height near by, where he is reputed to have camped the
night, is also said to have been a Roman fort—but was more
probably Pictish. Many large stones, sculptured and with inscriptions, are reported to have been broken up and carted away. Torra
Duncan is an earthwork mound in this vicinity, of uncertain origins.

The large farm of Cocklarachie, formerly a notable Gordon lairdship of a line springing from Scurdargue, lies on the side of Ba Hill
two miles south of Huntly, but in this parish. The house is a pleasant
late 17th century building, with an old walled garden. It has
chamfered windows and Adam mantelpieces within. At the other,
north-east, side of the same hill is the farm of Corsiestane, where
there is a cup-marked stone, beside a dyke between fields.

Dyce. Dyce, probably best known today as the site of Aberdeen's
airport and also of Lawson's large sausage and pork factory, has
however other claims to fame. It is an ancient Donside parish of
5300 acres which, although almost suburban at its southern end,
manages to retain a very rural atmosphere elsewhere. It is flanked
by the Don to the east and north, and by the high ground of Tyrebagger Hill, heavily forested, to the west.

The modern village, grown out of that of Gordon Place, lines the
A947 road to Oldmeldrum and is not particularly interesting,
although the woodlands of Stoneywood help to keep it separate from
the Bucksburn and Bankhead suburbs of Aberdeen. There is a long
main street, somewhat undistinguished, and much modern housing.
A riding-school flanks the approach on the east and the airport on
the west. Lawson's great red-brick establishment lies at the north
end, near the bridge over Don leading into New Machar parish. The
old bridge of 1803 was wooden, replaced by a graceful, double-
arched structure of 1845, which unfortunately has given place to the
modern steel and concrete. The farm of Mains of Dyce, here, is on
the site of a mansion of the Skene family, who had a private burial-
ground on the property.

But there are still remaining relics of the past to complement all
the modern developments. The original pre-Reformation church of
St. Fergus still stands in a lovely site at a bend of the Don almost two
miles to the north, although now a roofless shell in a well-kept
graveyard. It was once a vicarage of Kinkell. It is a typical gabled
building, with two good doorways built up, and a broken stone font

at the entrance. Built into the east gable, and under the care of the Department of the Environment, are four Pictish stones. One is a sculptured cross with double-disc and Z-rod, crescent and V-rod and mirror-and-comb symbols; another has the Celtic beast and double-discs; and the two others are small, with simple incised cross and a wheel-cross. Some fragments are also preserved. The site is in strangely wild-seeming country to be so near the city—although the great granite quarries and gravel-pits near by have to be passed to reach it. The graveyard has a mort-house. Not far away to the west is a square, pyramidal-topped monument of the 17th century to Dr. Duncan Liddell, inscribed in Latin. He was a native of Aberdeen who gained fame and fortune at universities abroad, returned to purchase the estate of Pitmeddan here—not to be confused with the better-known Pitmeddan at Udny—and bequeathed it to purchase bursaries for students at Aberdeen University when he died in 1613. He was the author of several books. Pitmeddan mansion, which lies in woodland half a mile to the south-west is not ancient, and has a tall square look-out tower. Near by is the disused Pitmeddan railway-station. There is a hillside hamlet at Kirkton farm and Overton, to the south. Presumably there was another church hereabouts once, for it is over a mile from both the ancient kirk and that at Meikle Dyce.

This Meikle Dyce is oddly named, for it is anything but meikle, being merely an abandoned Victorian church and former manse, with a factory near by, half a mile north-west of Dyce proper. The church, amongst high old trees, is something of a landmark, now gutted and used only as a store. It was built as parish church about 1865. The graveyard is still used and cared for.

Above the airfield, at present being upgraded in status, and a new BEA Helicopter headquarters—described as formerly a bleak and worthless moor—rises Tyrebagger Hill (821 feet) now largely covered with the conifers of Kirkhill Forest. The western slopes are in Kinellar parish, the eastern in Dyce. There are a number of burial-cairns amongst the high woodlands, and a large granite block called the Gouk Stane north-east of the Caskieben property. On the farm of Standingstones, immediately above the airfield, is a magnificent stone-circle crowning a subsidiary summit, amongst wind-blown trees and with far-flung prospects. There are nine uprights, one 11 feet high, and a huge recumbent. A lofty radio pylon shares the hilltop with these monuments of our early ancestors. It is a site distinctly worth a visit.

Dyce is an example of the rise and fall of transport systems. The road here was ancient. Then came the Aberdeen–Inverurie Canal of 1807, demolished 1850 when superseded by the railway, which itself is now gone, and the aeroplane takes over. The standing-stones have seen them all come and go, and will no doubt continue to do so.

Echt and Dunecht. The large rural parish of Echt, of about 12,000 acres, lies at the eastern foot of the Hill of Fare, some five miles north of the Dee and 13 miles west of Aberdeen, in a rich agricultural area—rich also in archaeological relics. It contains the two sizeable villages of Echt and Dunecht, and the large estate of the latter name. The Howe of Echt is the shallow fertile vale of the Burn of Echt. The isolated, wooded hill of the Barmekin, 900 feet, with the Hill of Fare to the south, dominates the landscape.

Echt village and kirkton stands around a crossroads of the A974 and B977, in the Howe, with church, hotel and hall. The present kirk, with its unusual clock, is comparatively modern, like its grave-yard. The earlier church stood a quarter-mile to the south, but this has completely gone, though its old kirkyard remains, with many time-worn tombstones, one very old at the south-east corner. No fewer than 13 fairs used to be held annually at Echt, for hiring, cattle and horses, indication of the fine quality of the land. The parish boasted 35 grain-mills.

There is some similarity about Dunecht village, less than three miles to the north, on what amounts to another crossroads of the same B977 this time with the A944; though on the north side, where there is a burn, bridge and little haugh, it is more picturesque. More properly called Waterton of Dunecht, this is a typically neat estate village for the great Dunecht House, with fine hall, sawmill, estates-office and substantial cottages, with modern heraldry, which has grown up round the old farm of Nether Corskie. There was once a sculptured symbol-stone at Nether Corskie, but this has been removed—where I have not been able to discover. Not removed are two handsome standing-stones in the field a few hundred yards to the north-west, one very high.

Dunecht House, standing in wide wooded policies to the south-east, is huge and less than beautiful architecturally, however ambitious, with observatory and private chapel. Originally in the Grecian style, it was greatly added to in 1877–81, by the 25th Earl of Crawford. Its splendid surroundings were not always so fertile, for on this estate no less than 2000 acres of waste land was reclaimed be-tween 1820 and 1840, by the then proprietor, William Forbes, a great improver. Later passing to the Crawfords, strangely enough the earl's body was stolen from the burial-vault of the private chapel in 1881. The estate is now the property of Lord Cowdray. The mansion can be seen from the "back road", north of Meanecht farm, where there is a small standing-stone in the field to the south of the road. Two larger standing-stones are in mid-field nearer the farm itself. There is a handsome main gateway to Dunecht House on the B977 a mile south of Dunecht village; and a more extraordinary couple of huge gatehouse-lodges at the extreme east of the estate, near the Loch of Skene which here rims the property. These have been built in grey granite to resemble twin tall Scots tower-houses, highly impressive however bogus, rising from the flat land, and notably catch the eye of the traveller on the main A944 road.

There are many other relics of antiquity in this parish. At Wester Echt farm, on high ground near the foot of Barmekin Hill, mid-way between the villages, are three large standing-stones on a field ridge.

Barmekin itself is crowned by a large, circular Pictish fort, with ramparts and entrenchments, five in all, covering six and a half acres, obviously a place of great strength. More standing-stones surround a large cairn on Calton Hill (572 feet) due south of Barmekin. There are also a number of stones and circles to the south-west, but these are described under Midmar parish. Part of the Hill of Fare is in Echt parish; but since its highest ground is in Banchory parish, Kincardineshire, it is better dealt with there.

Moving three miles to the south-east, on the farm of Tillyorn, there is said to be a hollow in the shape of a horse-shoe, large and given the odd name of Fusee. Search and enquiry failed to locate this; but almost certainly it will be a Pictish souterrain or weem. Its site should be rediscovered. What are known as The Standing-Stones of Echt—strange, when there are so many others—make a fine and easily accessible monument three miles north-east of Tillyorn, at the extreme east of the parish. These stand to the east of the side-road near Standingstones Farm. There are eight upright stones in a circle, and eight small cairns within, two containing pits and the others cists. It is good to see this Bronze Age relic so well maintained by the Department of the Environment.

Ellon. This small town, with a population of about 1800, is proud to be called the Capital of Buchan, much smaller as it is than either Peterhead or Fraserburgh. It was created a burgh in 1893, but in early days had been the seat of jurisdiction of the Comyn earls of Buchan, and the Mormaors before them, the Moot-hill, site of the Norman-type castle, now bearing a public convenience and bus shelter, in Market Street, opposite the New Inn. Ellon is also the centre for a large parish of 18,500 acres. It stands on the north bank of the Ythan just where the river ceases to be tidal, and where it is crossed by a handsome three-arched bridge, successor to one of 1793 which accelerated the growth of the town. So it was an important place when the Comyns of Buchan were the most powerful single family in Scotland—until the Bruce put paid to that account, and his brother Edward's herrying of Buchan is still remembered, when Ellon was amongst the many places burned.

It is now a pleasant little town, though with the incessant traffic of the A92 pouring through it. Part of it flanks the riverside, facing southwards; but to the north is a complex of narrow streets. A sort of square lies to the east, and here is the parish church, the site of the Tolbooth, and the war memorial. The church is large and very bright, having been tastefully restored in 1968, with some good modern stained glass, a gallery and pipe organ; also a fine war memorial alcove on the south wall. The present building really dates from 1777, replacing a pre-Reformation church of St. Mary, which was gifted to Kinloss Abbey by David I. The place indeed used to be called Kinloss-Ellon—to add to the confusion of former names, for it also was called Kermucks and the barony of Ardgith. There is a fine modern hall-complex attached to the church, and the crowded kirkyard around contains many old flat stones, also a handsome heraldic tomb of the Annand of Auchterellon family, in 17th century brown sandstone, part of the earlier church wall.

The Tolbooth is now gone, but was a good granite structure with outside stone stair, like that of Kintore. A panel with the Gordon arms therefrom is built into the gable of a shop which approximately occupies the site. There is a small and neat Town Hall in Station Road; and the large Ellon Academy, elevated to that status in 1950, is in Bridge Street, rebuilt in 1939 and extended 1956. The burgh has two parks, the Gordon Park of nine acres, with children's playground, at the riverside, and the wooded MacDonald Park and nine-hole golf course to the north. There is much modern housing, including two large private schemes, partly geared to the needs of Aberdeen commuters, one at Auchterellon to the west, and one south, over the Ythan at Craighall, with over 300 houses. In this area also is the large Episcopal church of St. Mary on the Rock, on a mound at the southern entrance to the town, designed by George Street R.A., the architect of the Law Courts in London. There is also an old toll-house here. In Union Street is a small Roman Catholic church. There are industries here, geared to the agricultural needs of the large farming area, including a tractor firm and farm-building contractors. Ellon Show, held each August in the Deer Park of Ellon Castle estate, is notable for its livestock classes.

Ellon Castle, in its wooded policies just north and east of the town, was formerly the barony of Ardgith. The ruin of its fortalice stands tall and impressive on a terrace site west of the present mansion. It consists now only of a high circular tower and portion of ivy-clad walling. This was the seat of the hereditary constables of Aberdeen Castle, the Kennedies of Kermucks. Kennedy of Ardgith slew a neighbouring laird, Forbes of Waterton in 1652 and was forfeited, the lands of Ellon, Kermucks and/or Ardgith passing eventually to Sir John Forbes of Waterton. Later, in 1752, they were acquired by the Gordon 3rd Earl of Aberdeen. He it was who built the more modern part of the castle, incorporating the old tower. Bailie William Gordon, a prosperous incomer, later purchased the estate. The mansion was rebuilt in 1851. This again is no more, and a modern successor was contrived out of the 18th century domestic offices.

Waterton, aforementioned, is an old lairdship, now a large farm, lying a mile east of Ellon, north of Ythan, headquarters of the Buchan Poultry Products Company. A portion of the old Forbes castle survives on a waterside mound to the east, oblong on plan, with remains of three vaulted basements and a heraldic panel. Beneath this is the date 1630/1770, referring to the tenure of the Forbes lairds, cadets of Tolquhon. Early Knights Templar lands, Waterton passed to the Bannermans before the Forbeses. Earlier still they had belonged, like Ellon, to the abbots of Kinloss, and the Abbots-hall was on the site of Waterton Mains farm. The Abbot's Well and part of the Abbot's garden-wall survive west of the farm.

The Buchan fishing-village of Collieston, now a favourite holiday resort

The Crathie area. A typical Upper Deeside scene

Daviot. Loanhead Stone-circle—note the great recumbent "altar stone"

Ruins of the Abbey of Deer at Old Deer, Buchan: a 13th century Cistercian establishment which superseded the famous Celtic monastery whence came the renowned Book of Deer of the 9th century

There was a ferry here, called Boat of Logie—Logie-Buchan being just across the river. There is still a boat and jetty.

Ellon has on occasion suffered from its proximity to the Ythan. In 1642 the tide rose so high as to extinguish kitchen-fires here. Pearl-mussels used to be fished for.

Less than two miles west of Ellon is the large Gordon estate of Esslemont, with a great granite mansion of 1868. The old castle, however, still stands in a ruinous state at the roadside, on the B9004, near the Mains thereof, a typical L-planned fortalice of the late 16th century, with a stair-tower in the angle corbelled out to the square to form a watch-chamber. Only the basement of this tower is vaulted, which is unusual. The ruins are much neglected. The estate belonged to the Cheynes, who also owned Arnage and Straloch, from 1381. The tenth Cheyne laird died in 1631 and Esslemont passed through Forbes and Hay hands till in 1729 Robert Gordon of Hallhead bought it. The present laird is the twenty-first of Hallhead and tenth of Esslemont.

Two miles north of Ellon, on a long, dead-end farm-road, is the former mansion of Nether Ardgrain, now a farmhouse, a tall, crowstep-gabled house of the late 17th century, T-planned but without defensive features. Over the doorway are the royal arms of Charles II dated 1664. It was the seat of a barony, erected in 1528 by royal charter and purchased by the Kennedies of Ardgith in 1629—a modest and attractive building. A mile to the west, as only a crow could fly, is the farm of Hilton, or Hiltown, once a barony also, of the Rose family, but sold in 1693 to John Turner, a wealthy Danzig merchant. Six more Turner lairds followed him, and built a large mansion which they called Turnerhall. Then this was demolished in 1933 and the estate sold. Now the farm remains on its high eminence—site of the original barony—with a very unusual feature, a windmill surmounting it, though its sails have gone. This used to grind corn and is one of the very few hereabouts.

A mile farther along the same A948 road to New Deer, is the farm of Cairndailly, on the left, where a burial-cairn on a hilltop can be plainly seen. Arnage Castle lies a mile north-west, in its wooded estate, an interesting late 16th century fortalice on the Z-plan, with rather fancy modern additions. The old portion has stair-turrets in both re-entrant angles, and another tiny turret-stair to provide access to the garret storey. The basement is vaulted, and the walls well supplied with both gunloops and triple-set shot-holes. The castle well survives to the east. The Cheyne family acquired Arnage by marriage in the late 14th century, and retained it until 1643. One of them, James, was rector of the Scots college at Douay, dying in 1602. In 1702 Provost John Ross of Aberdeen bought Arnage for 40,000 merks. His successors retained the estate until recent times.

South-west of Arnage was the barony of Drumwhindle, now a farming district, with an isolated school. In a field west of this is the Candle Stone, a 10-foot-high monolith, remains of a stone-circle, with magnificent prospects around. A mile or so south-west of

F

Drumwhindle, on the B9005 near the Ythan, is the scattered community of Michael Muir, with post-office and gravel-pit workings, very isolated.

In another remote position at the opposite, north-eastern corner of the parish, five miles from Ellon, is the Dudwick area, around Dudwick Hill (571 feet)—no great height but prominent in this level Buchan terrain. Here was formerly an important property and attractive fortalice of 1636, demolished 1865. The barony belonged to the Mitchells, who once had been called St. Michael, but was bought by General James King, of the Barra family, a Swedish wars' veteran who fought for Charles I in the Civil War and was created Lord Eythan (Ythan). He built the demolished castle, pictures of which are still extant.

Fintray and Disblair. The lower Donside parish of Fintray, of 7000 acres, lies on the north bank of the river immediately east of Kintore and Keithhall parishes and west of New Machar. Considering that its village of Hatton of Fintray is only six miles or so north-west of Aberdeen's centre, it has remained remarkably rural and unspoiled, the scenery pleasant and undulating, with much woodland. Disblair is a district and estate to the north-east of the parish.

The village of Hatton lies just north of the Don bridge carrying the B979 from Kinaldie, at Boat of Hatton—which was, of course, a ferry. It is a tree-girt little community which once aspired to higher dignity, and indeed was the scene of three annual fairs. Part of its ancient Tolbooth survives as a single arch of vaulting, just behind the post-office. The parish church, of 1821, stands on a terrace site amongst more trees to the north of the village, above the attractive kirkyard. It is a typical preaching-church with central pulpit and galleried on three sides, large-windowed and bright. It has some fine solid silver chalices—which are kept at the bank for safety—one, of 1632, is said to be made from the melted-down silver of an image of St. Meddan. This image had been reputed to have healing powers and was carried round the parish on feastdays. The brass-plate of the former Pulpit Bible of 1821 was discovered while digging the foundations of Lawson's factory at Dyce, and returned here. In the graveyard below, with no very old stones—it being a successor to ancient St. Meddan's—there is a ruined vault of great strength and with an iron door, which seems more ancient than it is, having in fact been built by the parishioners in the early 19th century to foil the activities of body-snatchers. The corpses were kept therein for three months or more, until unfit for the anatomists' purposes, and then properly interred.

There was once a small abbey dedicated to St. Giles at Fintray, an offshoot of Lindores, in Fife, and known as the Northern Abbey. Here the abbot of Lindores had a summer seat. Its site was within the policies of Fintray House, to the east, where a cottage also marks the site of a holy well. Fintray House was a large, granite Tudor-style mansion, now demolished. It was the seat of the Lords Sempill, of the Forbes-Sempill family. Forbes of Craigievar obtained the estate in 1610, after the Reformation suppression of the abbeys.

Two miles east of Hatton, and still at the riverside, is the original pre-Reformation parish church of St. Meddan's in an attractive graveyard amongst old trees at Little Fintray or Cothall. Only bare walls remain, with a crucifix-sculptured aumbry and some carved heraldic stones, this now being the Forbes-Sempill burial-enclosure. There are many old tombstones in the kirkyard, in particular three slender uprights, featureless but very interesting, probably 13th or 14th century. A slightly older crusading-type stone, with cross and sword, is near by. This was the parish church until 1703.

The hamlet of Cothall, or Little Fintray, on a terrace site, has a post-office and some restored housing. There used to be a quite large woollen factory here, employing over 100 hands, powered first by water then by steam.

The Disblair area, with its own school but no village, lies three miles to the north-east of Hatton, on much higher ground around the 450-foot contour, amidst open farmland, not far west of Newmachar village. There is a small wooded estate with cottage-style mansion and a number of farms.

Forgue, Bognie and Frendraught. This is a large parish of 17,300 acres on the edge of Banffshire just east of Huntly, of undulating and pleasant country, pierced by the quite deep cleft of Glen Dronach and crossed by the A97, Huntly to Banff, and B9001 roads. Bognie is a road-junction area where these two highways meet; and Frendraught, famous in history, is a district to the south, on the way to Wells of Ythan. It is all a water-shed area, with streams flowing to the Ury, the Ythan and the Deveron.

Forgue village is largely modern, in the Howe of Forgue a mile east of Bogniebrae road-junction on the B9001. As well as the parish church there is an inn, the Scott Hall, a school and a large Episcopal church, all pleasingly set in the green vale. The parish church, on a mound above a burn, is a plain large building of 1819 in an old kirkyard. Its predecessor was called Eccles de Forg, was dedicated to St. Margaret, and its vicar is mentioned in 1296. A silver communion-cup has been reckoned to be the oldest extant in Scotland, dating from 1567; other silver is also old. The kirkyard, which has many early gravestones, has the burial-aisle of the Morrisons of Bognie and an ancient tomb to Alexander Garden, or Gordon, with heraldry. The Episcopal church, with a tall spire, is set in trees and an overgrown graveyard, still in use, on the other side of the Howe, successor of the Chapel of Parkdargue, heather-thatched in 1716. Just over a mile down the road southwards is the large Glendronach Distillery, founded 1826, still thriving and providing employment for this remote neighbourhood. The Scott Hall in the village was provided by the owning family in 1885. On the farm of Riach, half a mile uphill to the west, is a regrouped circle of 10 stones in a field.

A mile north of Forgue is Bognie district. Here in a field is the ruin of Bognie Castle, tall and gaunt, seemingly a 17th century building of the late fortified period with fairly thin walling, a Morrison house, related to that of Frendraught. There is an old-established inn at the hamlet of Bogniebrae; and at the farm of Yonder Bognie to the north there is a stone-circle with six stones standing and one large recumbent. A mile south-west of Bogniebrae on the A97 is Cairnton, with the remains of another circle in mid-field, one stone upright, one recumbent. Half a mile farther, on the slopes of Fourman Hill (1128 feet) a shapely peak-like eminence exactly on the Banffshire border, which Mary Queen of Scots crossed in 1562 by what is still called the Queen's Road, lies the estate of Cobairdy. Its pleasant whitewashed mansion is set on a terraced site amongst trees, built out of the stones of a former castle here, now completely gone. It was a Murray then a Burnett estate.

At the other side of the parish, to the south-east, lies the once highly important estate of Frendraught, former seat of a viscountcy. A fragment of the castle thereof is still there, beside the more modern mansion, the scene of the tragedy of 1630, when the building was burned in the feuding between the Crichtons thereof and the Gordons. Lord Aboyne, second son of the Marquis of Huntly, the Gordon Laird of Rothiemay and four others died, and the Gordons blamed Crichton himself, although a trial exonerated him and another was executed. The feud grew the more bitter in consequence. Crichton's son was created Viscount of Frendraught in 1642, and was a strong Covenanter, but fought on Montrose's side at Carbisdale. The title expired in 1698 with the 4th Viscount. His wife was a Morrison of Bognie, and the lands later passed to them. A quarter-mile to the east is the hamlet of Templeland, obviously a former Knights Templar property, where there is a school and a former cottage-hospital, now reverted to private ownership, presented to the district in 1874 by Morrison of Bognie with a monument to him in the garden. There is a large and gaunt Free church at the Auchaber crossroads beyond. Aucharnie is an extensive farming community here.

Forgue, once known as the Kingdom of Forgue, presumably because of the powerful Frendraught influence, was given the status of a burgh of barony in 1612—but owing to the fall of the Crichtons, this came to nothing.

Fraserburgh. Fraserburgh, the important fishing-port and industrial burgh and resort, near the northern edge of Aberdeenshire and at the very tip of the thrusting shoulder of Scotland, with its parish of 9000 acres, suffers from a plethora of names. The parish was originally called Philorth, and the village on which the burgh was founded was named Faithlie. Locally, however, the place is usually known as The Broch, while the point of land on which it grew is Kinnaird's Head, described even by Ptolemy. It is a busy, thriving place—it claims to be the second most important fishing-port in

Scotland, after Aberdeen—and may well be more so, as the North Sea oil developments offshore advance; but not quite so important as it might have been. For there was almost a university established here. Sir Alexander Fraser of Philorth, an estate lying two miles to the south, founded the place in 1569, five years after receiving a charter from Mary Queen of Scots for a burgh of barony. He had another castle at Kinnaird's Head, which is still there. In 1592 he obtained a charter to found a university here. And in 1601, Faithlie was promoted to "the free port, burgh of barony and free regality, to be called in all time coming the Burgh and Regality of Fraserburgh". University building began, but the scheme fell through—although it was in fact *used* as a university for a little while in 1647, when plague struck Aberdeen and King's College came here.

Today Fraserburgh is a fairly regularly built town of 10,900 population, occupying its headland position with bays at either side, rocky to the north, sandy to the south, with five major roads leading in, the A92, 98 and 981, and the B9031 and 9033. It has a complex group of harbours, named Faithlie, Outer, Inner and Balaclava, with all the boat-building, warehousing, fish-processing, cold-storage and other facilities necessary, as well as timber, grain, fertiliser, coal and other industries based on the port. Kinnaird's Head Castle, now oddly enough a lighthouse, is dominant on the seaward side, amongst the warehouses, with the Lifeboat Station—with its tragic memories —and Coastguard Station near by. The castle is a massive, white-washed keep, said to be of 1570 but probably older, with six-foot-thick walling, and a parapet and wall-walk with open rounds, four storeys in height. A flat roof has been created, and the caphouse for the turnpike stair built up into the lighthouse lamp chamber. The basement is vaulted. Another strange feature is the presence of another smaller fortified building, only 50 yards or so away, lower on the promontory, called the Wine Tower, for no explained reason; it is of very rough masonry, three storeys high, all being vaulted, with no internal stair, trap-doors being the only communication, yet well supplied with triple shot-holes. The top floor has three finely carved heraldic pendants, with the Fraser and Royal Arms, and the inscription *THE GLORY OF THE HONORABLE IS TO FEIR GOD*. This tower stands above a cavern known as the Selches (seals) Hole. Kinnaird's Head is the most northerly point of Aberdeenshire and the fine grassy headland here, provided with seats, makes a notable viewpoint.

The oldest part of the town lies nearest the harbour, and here is Saltoun Square, the main centre, with a Mercat Cross, re-erected on a high base in 1850, displaying the Royal and Fraser arms and *L.A.S. 1736*, for Lord Alexander Saltoun. Just to the north stands the parish church of 1802 and later restored, a large plain building but with some character, with hipped roof and granite steeple and a clock. At the south side, externally, is the Fraser mausoleum, pyramidal in style, with heraldry. There is no kirkyard here, this remaining at the earlier and ruinous kirk's site, near Cairnbulg, a mile to the south. There is a Town House of 1855, Grecian in style, in Saltoun Square, with a high domed tower over a statue of a Lord Saltoun. The ground floor used to serve as marketplace and the town maintains an Information Centre here. There are, of course, other churches, many hotels, banks, offices, good shopping facilities and a large hospital. Fraserburgh Academy, founded by John Park, merchant, in 1872 and formerly in Mid Street, has moved to larger modern premises. Although the university came to nothing, a large new Buchan Technical College is to be built here, at a cost of £500,000, on a seven-acre site at Lochpots to the south. Ample facilities, entertainments and sports amenities, including an indoor swimming-pool, are provided for visitors and residents. There are many bed-and-breakfast establishments, two municipal caravan-parks and other permanent sites. A good 18-hole golf course on the sandy links to the south flanks the fine three-mile-long beach of Fraserburgh Bay. At the north end of this is Kirkton, where is the aforementioned kirkyard and site of the original parish church, now with a large modern cemetery attached. Only an old moulded archway remains, with an ivy-covered brick-vaulted burial-chamber and another pyramidal mausoleum similar to that in Saltoun Square, all again for the Frasers of Philorth and Saltoun. Many old gravestones are built into the walling or are still on the ground. The sand dunes rise near by. Cairnbulg Castle, the seat of the present Lord Saltoun, towers a mile away, but this is described under Rathen parish.

West by north of the town the parish of Pitsligo soon intervenes, with Rosehearty and Sandhaven villages therein. But before the rocky Phingask Shore thereto is a small industrial estate, at Broadsea. And inland half a mile is Watermill, where there was formerly a brewery, now converted into an oatmeal-mill. There is still a modern Watermill Bar here.

The southern and western outskirts of Fraserburgh are not very attractive. But farther out, southwards, in the Philorth and Sinclair Hills area, where the land is undulating and wooded, it is very pleasant. The old mansion of Philorth, which in 1666 replaced ruined Cairnbulg Castle (now restored) as a seat of the barony, was burned in 1915 but the estate remains. The famous Sir Alexander Fraser, Bruce's companion, who married his sister Mary, acquired Comyn lands in the north, at Durris. A grandson married a daughter of the Earl of Ross, and thus gained Philorth in 1375, with its great castle of Cairnbulg. It was the 8th Fraser of Philorth who founded Fraserburgh, and his grandson who inherited the Saltoun peerage through his mother. The present laird is the 19th lord. A mile to the west of Philorth are the wooded so-called Sinclair Hills, though they reach only 166 feet. But they aid the flattish Buchan landscape. At the hamlet of Gash of Philorth, here, on a slight ridge, is a prominent doocot, in the form of a five-sided tower, built apparently as something of a folly, on the site of a prehistoric cairn or circle. Not far west of this is the Red Loch, quite large, embosomed in woodland. The Memsie area, all under the shadow of the Hill of Mormond, is near by—but this again is in Rathen parish.

The writer has acquired no convincing reason for calling Fraserburgh The Broch. There does not appear to have been any broch in the area. But just south of Faichlie Harbour is Bioch Head, a minor promontory, and it is just possible that the name is a corruption thereof.

Fyvie, Woodhead, Millbrex and Rothienorman. Fyvie is a famous name in Scotland, its castle renowned, Montrose's Battle of Fyvie only a minor one but dramatic, its lords taking a prominent part in national affairs, the area celebrated in ballad. It is a large village, once actually a royal burgh, and a huge parish of 30,000 acres in the valley of the upper Ythan. Woodhead is a smaller village two miles to the east; and Millbrex, now a separate *quod sacra* parish, lies remotely six miles to the north-east.

Fyvie village, set picturesquely on rising ground to the east of the Ythan, is an interesting place with a fine parish church, large modern school and considerable recent housing development. There is a Mercat Cross, a pillar on a three-stepped base and surmounted by a cross, but this is a replacement. A large lump of white quartz here is the Buchan Stone, marking the boundary of that great province. Another cross, erected in 1868, stands in a field to the south, marking the site of the priory of St. Mary, now gone. This was a seminary, the property given by William the Lion to the abbey of Arbroath in 1179. Some of the long-dead students thereof would scarcely mourn it, or its prior, Thomas Cranno, of the mid-14th century, who wrote that the students ". . . if obstreperous . . . once out of sound of the secular world, should be soundly flogged".

The parish church, rebuilt 1808, is set on a mound south-east of the village in a very ancient kirkyard, the successor of a church dedicated to St. Peter. It is large and commodious, with a double belfry and bells, one Dutch and dating from 1609. Internally it is very interesting, with a handsome Castle Pew, a laird's loft or low gallery to the right of the chancel, with elaborate carved timber frontage; also a small stained-glass window, memorial to a son of the laird of Fyvie who died in 1909, featuring St. George, the face a likeness of the young man, Percy Forbes-Leith. There are other splendid stained-glass windows, the work of Tiffany of New York. To the left of the chancel is a stone from the earlier church inscribed *Pray for the soul of Thomas Cranno, who lies here.*—the aforementioned flogging prior. There is a painted wooden heraldic panel to Alexander Seton, Lord Fyvie, dating from 1603. Built into the east gable of the exterior are four Pictish stones. One shows a Celtic beast, with crescent and V-rod; another an eagle, with mirror-and-comb symbols; a third, a clover-leaf design within a circle, representing the Trinity in Unity. The fourth is a cross-shaft with typical Celtic interlacing. These stones came from the local schoolhouse, and from Rothiebrisbane.

In the graveyard are many ancient tombs, including a good Gordon heraldic stone of 1686. Also the graves of Lord Byron's Gordon ancestors from Gight; and that of Tifty's Annie, renowned in ballad. Another local ballad is 'The Bonnie Lass O' Fyvie', mentioned under New Machar.

Fyvie Castle stands a mile to the north, in a large wooded estate, a great and noble house which certainly cannot be done justice to here. It occupies a strong position on a wide terrace above a long, narrow loch and the river and now forms a huge L, 147 feet by 136, with its handsome double drum-tower entrance known as the Seton Tower, facing south and dating from the early 17th century, rich in corbelling, turrets and heraldic decoration. There are also the Preston, Meldrum and Gordon Towers, each similar in style but differing in date and detail. The building is complex, replete with every development of authentic Scottish castellated architecture, decoration and enrichment, its interior as magnificent as the exterior, the groined vaults, stairway, plaster ceilings and tempera paintwork particularly notable. William the Lion and Alexander II held court here; and Edward I visited "Fyvin Chastel" in 1296. Montrose was trapped here in 1644, the ditches of his entrenched camp still to be seen. Although greatly outnumbered, he managed to give a good account of himself and safely made a brilliant get-away. Later Cromwell garrisoned the castle. From being a royal seat, it passed to the Lindsays, Prestons, Meldrums, Setons, Gordons, and is now the seat of the Forbes-Leith baronets.

Mill of Tifty, whence came Mill O' Tifty's Annie of the ballad, Agnes Smith, who died 1678, lies a mile north-east of the castle. The former hospital at Fyvie is now used for a Guides' establishment.

The one-time royal burgh, with its tolbooth and cross, is thought to have been at Woodhead, the separate and smaller village lying on higher ground a mile to the east, on the B9005 road. It is a scattered place, now seemingly "over-churched", with a large established church with high tower, porch and elaborate arched entrance to the graveyard; an Episcopal church of All Saints, of 1849; and a disused Free church now a farm-store. Fairs used to be held here. Just south of the village the Ythan commences its picturesque course through the series of deep, winding dens, flanked by the Braes of Minnonie and the Braes of Gight. Gight Castle lies in the easternmost of these—but is dealt with under Methlick. St. John's Wells farm across the den, a mile south of Woodhead, has the site of two former holy wells, St. John's and St. Catherine's. No doubt there was a chapel also. At Cairnchedly here, the excavation of a burial-cairn unearthed a number of urns.

Millbrex *quod sacra* parish lies in higher moorland country, remote on side-roads, six miles to the north-east, an area of small farms and few trees but having extensive prospects, Benachie showing its kenspeckle head far to the west. There is no village, but a post-office, school, very modern hall strange to find in such surroundings and a tall, rather gaunt red-stone church in its graveyard on a gentle ridge. This was built in 1833 as a chapel-of-ease, and enlarged three years later. Evidently the population of this bare, windswept area was greater then.

At the extreme opposite end of this huge parish lies Rothienorman, three miles south-west of Fyvie, where there is a small village and church, and the Rothie and Kinbroon estates of the Leslies. Two miles south is Folla Rule, a school and large Episcopal church of St. George's, with graveyard, on a wooded hillside overlooking moorland, ambitious as to style, dating from 1897, with tall red campanile tower and much stained glass, though now somewhat shabby—an unlikely establishment to find in rural remoteness. There was a chapel of St. Rule established here in 1376. A mile further to the south-east is Cross of Jackston, a small hamlet with a former church of St. Mary's, now a straw-store at a road-junction.

Gartly. This parish, once partly in Banffshire, though small to-day in importance, extends to 12,000 acres of upland Strathbogie, north of Rhynie and Kennethmont and south of Huntly. Its village of Gartly is set deep in the narrows of the Bogie valley, north-east of the Noth range and west of Hill of Corskie, where the eastern portion of the great Clashindarroch Forest spreads over the hills. It is a place of hill-farms, with much cattle in evidence. The village itself is not large, and evidently sprang up here largely because of the railway-line and former station, and of the now disused granite quarries on the hills on either side. Despite this run-down, there is quite a lot of recent housing, forestry having come to the rescue.

The parish church is a long way off, at Kirkstyle, on a side-road two miles to the north. It is quite large, considering the remote area, a Gothic edifice of 1879 with a big organ and 82 pews, now just a little shabby inside with the population falling off. Its predecessor was dedicated to St. Andrew, and is represented by a fine old belfry on a projecting wing. This has an elaborate finish and the curious inscription *YLSIS/BETHE BULT 1621*, with another small panel dated 1621 inset under it. This is the only occasion the author can recollect of a woman's name appearing on such a place. Presumably the lady was an Elizabeth Barclay of Gartly. There are a number of old flat tombstones in the kirkyard.

Half a mile south-west, on the farm of Millhill, some cairns formerly stood, said to be the burial-place of men slain in a skirmish after the Battle of Harlaw, presumably fleeing Highlanders. And a mile to the north, where the church's side-road crosses the Bogie to join the A97, the former school is now a farm-store. Another mile north-west, on the slopes of Clashmach Hill, is the farm of Braelandknowes, where once was an ancient chapel and burial-ground, now gone. There were three other pre-Reformation chapels in this Braes of Gartly area—indication of a once quite large population.

The old supernatural ballad, 'The Baronne O' Gairtly', begins:

Twas in abut nicht's weerty hour
Nae meen nor stars gae licht,
Quhen Gairtly's baul and beirly Baronne,
Red hemward thro the nicht.

The barons of Gartly were Barclays, and important, hereditary sheriffs of Banffshire from the 12th to the 16th century, and potent enough to have this portion of Aberdeenshire incorporated in Banffshire for long. This area was indeed known as the Barony, to differentiate from the rest of Strathbogie, which was of course Gordon territory. Their old castle of Gartly still has a few tumbled remains, neglected behind the steading of Gartly Mains farm. Mary Queen of Scots spent a night here in 1562, on her expedition to put down the power of the Gordons, which ended in the Battle of Corrichie.

Glass and Innermarkie. Glass is a hilly and entirely rural parish of 12,000 acres in the Strathbogie area, west of Huntly— although not in Strathbogie itself, lying in the valley of the upper Deveron, indeed partly in Banffshire. It comprises the fairly narrow and wooded river-valley and the flanking hillsides. There is no real village, but a scattered community at Haugh of Glass and Innermarkie, about eight miles west of Huntly. Parts of the great Clashindarroch Forest clothe the hills to south and east.

The parish church stands in its graveyard, in a secluded terraced situation amongst wooded braes, at Torry, above the Deveron a mile north-east of Haugh of Glass. It is quite a large T-shaped church of 1782, harled and with an old belfry and a sundial on the wall. There is considerable stained and coloured glass, of mixed quality, and the organ was presented by Sir Frederick Bridge, of Cairnborrow Lodge, a former organist of Westminster Abbey. Near by is the mansion of Blairmore, now a preparatory school for boys, in a pleasant wooded estate.

Cairnborrow, with the Lodge its mansion, is a distinct district two miles to the east, at the edge of the parish, under the whin-clad Newton Hill (981 feet) whereon are a number of burial-cairns. The area is known as the Daugh of Cairnborrow—*daugh*, or *davoch*, being a division of land capable of producing 48 bolls, or 288 bushels of grain, a term formerly much in use in the North-East. The ancient St. Peter's Kirk is near here—but this is in Cairnie parish. Cairnborrow was a Gordon lairdship.

The school and hall of Glass, with a mill, are at Innermarkie, almost a mile due west of the church, also in wooded braes, where the Markie Water comes in to join Deveron, under the Market Hill —though whether this name is a corruption of the same, or a place where markets were held, is uncertain. Innermarkie was an important lairdship of the Innes family from 1486, when a second son of the eleventh chief of Innes gained it. They were hereditary constables of Redcastle, or Edradour, in Ross, and the fourth was beheaded in 1595 for his share in the murder of the Bonnie Earl of Moray. The baronetcies of Balveny and Coxton descend from the Innermarkie line, as did the late Sir Thomas Innes of Learney, Lord Lyon King of Arms. The castle was dismantled in the 17th century and is completely gone. Innermarkie Lodge was built in 1705 by the Duffs to replace it, and has been much extended as a shooting-lodge.

The Burn of Edinglassie comes to join Deveron just half a mile west, and the consequent opening up of the valley by these two major tributaries is known as the Haugh of Glass. Edinglassie was a Gordon property and also had a castle, now only a site, for it was burned in 1688 by General Mackay in the early Jacobite struggles. The remains of a 17th century doocot survive at the large farmsteading. It must have been a somewhat delicate position to have two castles, of differing and spirited families, so close together. Edinglassie was, in fact, to have been a burgh of barony with tolbooth. There is now a modern mansion. The road up the valley forks here, and the eastern fork crosses Deveron by an attractive 17th century bridge, widened two centuries later, built by Sir George Gordon of Edinglassie in 1655.

This eastern road climbs to a T-junction, the right-hand, dead-end road leading only to the hill-farm and one-time lairdship of Succoth. The left returns along the south bank of Deveron, to Cairnborrow. Half-way is another haugh, that of Aswanley, and here is a very interesting former laird's house of the early 17th century, now a farmhouse. It is an L-planned structure, lengthy but apparently lowered in height, with a circular stair-tower projecting to the north and a courtyard with arched entrance to the south, this dated 1692, with initials for Calder and Skene of Skene. The walls are harled, yellow-washed and supplied with shot-holes. The stair-tower has a later ogival roof. The interior is not vaulted and has been largely gutted; but the arch of a large kitchen fireplace may be traced. Elizabeth Cruikshanks of Aswanley was the mother of the famous pair of Gordons, Jock o'Scurdargue and Tam o' Ruthven. In 1440 Hugh Calder gained Aswanley from the Gordons, the last Calder laird dying in 1768 in debt to the Duff ancestor of the Earls and Dukes of Fife—who thus obtained the estate.

The main road onwards from Edinglassie reaches the interesting area under Hill of Dunmeth, or Dumeath, in just over a mile. Here, at Nether Dunmeth farm, is the remains of a stone-circle. And below the road is the Wallakirk, or church of St. Wallach, a Pictish missionary, where is St. Wallach's Well and his Bath—in the Deveron, no doubt a baptising-place. Little remains of the church, but an old broken font lies in the burial-enclosure which marks the site. The kirkyard is still used and in good order, picturesque at the riverside, with a wooden bridge across. St. Wallach allegedly died in 733, but the church is claimed to date from the 12th century. St Wallach's Fair used to be held at Haugh of Glass.

Near by is Beldorney Castle, a fine Z-planned fortalice of the late 16th or early 17th century, still occupied. It has circular and square towers at opposite ends of the tall, harled main block, with two slender stair-turrets. The circular tower has a peculiar rounded gable finish, with stringcourses. The basement is vaulted and there is much good pine-panelling and Gordon heraldry. A more modern extension is attached. The Beldorney Gordons, later of Wardhouse, stemmed from Adam, Dean of Caithness, third son of the 1st Earl of Huntly—and so presumably were illegitimate. Beldorney was sold in 1807.

Two miles above this is the Banffshire border. Glass is a very lovely parish, remote as it is interesting, embosomed in the hills.

Glenbuchat and Invernochty. A gallant Gordon laird of the Jacobite risings has made the name of Glenbuchat—also spelt Glenbucket—renowned; and Invernochty is known almost entirely for its Doune. Glen Buchat is a side glen of upper Strathdon, and also a mountainous parish of 11,000 acres amongst the Ladder Hills, which rise towards the Cabrach. It has a ruined castle and a remote kirkton, all highly attractive. The area is conveniently served by a good circular side-road which branches off the A97 at Bridge of Buchat. This was formerly a high, old, single-arched bridge, which has been replaced. The road probes north-westwards into the hills for six miles, before swinging southwards, climbing to 1344 feet, and so down to Don again at Invernochty, about 11 miles in all. The hills rise to over 2000 feet here, and there is a track northwards across them to the kirkton of Cabrach, about 10 rough miles.

The castle of Glenbuchat stands down near the bridge on an eminence above the confluence of Buchat and Don, a handsome late 16th century fortalice on the Z-plan, long roofless but complete to the wall-head and in the care of the Department of the Environment. It is unusual in having two large stair-turrets corbelled out in the re-entrant angles of the Z, each supported on squinch-arches. The outer corners are crowned by angle-turrets, two circular and two squared and gabled. There are many shot-holes, some for downward shooting. The basement is vaulted. Over the entrance is inscribed: *NOTHING ON ARTH REMAINS BOT FAME. JOHN GORDONE —HELEN CARNEGIE 1590*. These Gordons were descended from Jock o' Scurdargue, of the original line; and the best-known laird was Prince Charlie's brigadier-general, "out" in both Fifteen and Forty-five Risings. He led the Gordons and Farquharsons at Culloden, and escaped to France—to the marked distress of his unacknowledged monarch, German George, who used to awake in the night sweating and trying to pronounce Glenbuchat's terrible name. His estates were forfeited, and bought by the shrewd Duffs. They built the attractive white Glenbuchat Lodge, up at the head of the glen, on the site of a former chapel, near Badenyon. The farm of that name, the scene of the ballad, 'John o' Badenyon', is now derelict.

Kirkton of Glenbuchat lies in the valley two miles above the castle, in a pleasing setting. The old church, dedicated to St. Peter, is only very occasionally used, being remotely set, and with a more conveniently placed former Free kirk down at the hamlet. It is white-washed and plain, with a bell, its box-pews unpainted, many with enclosed little tables. There is a central pulpit, and the gallery at one end has a fine coloured heraldic panel in front. The graveyard is still in use, with many old stones, but the manse adjoining is now abandoned. Scattered old Caledonian pines behind enhance the scene. The later church, beside post-office and shop, is small and bright within. There are a number of limekilns in this glen. High above the Moss Road on the hillside to the north is the famed Garnet Stone, a large boulder from which garnets may be chipped.

Proceeding beyond Badenyon and Glenbuchat Lodge, the road rises steeply into the heather, eventually to dip down into the valley of the Water of Nochty. Here there is much planted forest, that of Tornashean, on the hillsides flanking the Nochty. At Auchernach here a tall tower-like doocot rises prominently above the trees. Lower down, where Nochty joins Don, is the famous Doune of Invernochty, the motte of a 12th century motte-and-bailey castle, presumably of the early Earls of Mar. It is flat-topped, partly moraine, partly artificial, and surrounded by a moat, traces of summit building remaining. Bellabeg hamlet is alongside, but this is in Strathdon parish—which almost encloses Glenbuchat, and ought to be read in conjunction. Formerly there was a small woollen mill at Inverbuchat.

Glen Muick and Lochnagar. This is the southern section of the great united civil parish of Glenmuick, Tullich and Glengairn, 89,000 acres, which includes the burgh of Ballater and is too large to describe conveniently in one article. This, therefore, covers the area south of the Dee, and is quite sufficiently extensive, including Glen Muick itself, part of Glen Girnock—whose stream forms the boundary with Braemar and Crathie—part of Glentanar Forest and valley, the mountain range of the White and Capel Mounths, with Lochnagar, and much else besides.

Glen Muick opens almost directly south of Ballater, the Muick joining Dee at Bridgend hamlet. Here was the old church, when Glenmuick was a parish of its own, now only a graveyard, small but picturesque, with many rough stones, one dated 1598 and many others of the early 18th century, with the burial-enclosure of the Gordons of Abergeldie—which lies six miles to the west, in Crathie parish. Near by is the site of ancient Brackley Castle, scene of the ballad 'The Baron of Brackley', and the slaying of Gordon of Brackley by Farquharson of Inverey in 1666. Brackley House was rebuilt in 1898 for Sir Alan Mackenzie fo Glenmuick. Glenmuick House itself is now demolished, a great sham-Tudor edifice, and no loss. Near Bridgend is a cairn at the roadside built in 1902 to mark the spot where Queen Victoria met the Gordon Highlanders on a famous occasion.

A mile to the west, below the A973 on the wooded slopes of The Knock, is the ruined Knock Castle, a small but tall and sturdily impressive tower of the early 17th century, successor of an older fortalice, roofless but complete to the wall-head. It is oblong, with two angle-turrets and a gabled watch-chamber, with shot-holes. The basement vault has fallen in, but the building could still be restored. There was originally a courtyard to the north. It was a Gordon hold, like so much else hereabouts, and usually held by a close relative of Huntly because of its strategic situation. Soon after the present building was finished the Forbeses surprised the laird's seven sons out digging peats near by, and slew them all. So overcome was the father that he fell down his own stairway and broke his neck. Forbes of Strathgirnock was summarily executed for this by Gordon of Abergeldie, as representing his chief, Huntly, Justiciar of the North. There is a standing-stone near by called the Scurry Stane. Strathgirnock itself, now a farm, lies off the A972 just a mile to the west, with Littlemill at the mouth of Glen Girnock a short distance farther, the latter a very attractive hamlet by a burnside amongst woodland.

Glen Muick itself is a major feature, a deep glen striking off southwards into the mountains for about 13 miles, with a public road running up it for nine of them. It is handsomely wooded with Scots pines in the lower reaches. Two side-roads enter it from the A973, on either side of the Muick, joining less than two miles up. On the western is the royal property of Birkhall, a pleasant and comparatively modest mansion of 1715, built by the Gordons of Abergeldie and now the Deeside residence of the Queen Mother, the fifteenth Gordon laird of Abergeldie having sold it to Prince Albert in 1849. Florence Nightingale was amongst the many distinguished visitors who have stayed here.

The road up Glen Muick is a pleasant winding one, though narrow for the traffic of visitors' cars. Three miles above the aforementioned junction at the bridge hamlet of Mill of Sterin—Sterin was the original name of Birkhall, from *stairean*, meaning stepping-stones—the waterfall of Linn of Muick is readily seen from the road, a fine cascade amongst pine-clad rocks. Soon after this the woodlands are left behind, and open heather holds sway, with fine prospects of the mountains. The public road ends at a car-park near the foot of two-miles-long Loch Muick, at Spittal of Glenmuick, where once there was a travellers' hospice. A private road leads to Allt-na-Guibhsaich Lodge, to the west, a royal shooting-lodge, where the footpath for Lochnagar starts. This lodge, which means the burn of the fir-wood, has been associated in recent years with Princess Marina, Duchess of Kent, and her family. Queen Victoria called it The Hut. Near the head of Loch Muick, which can at times be very beautiful, or very bleak, is another royal shiel, or lodge, the Glasallt Shiel nestling amongst planted pines, a great favourite of Victoria, with a waterfall on its burn half a mile up on the side of Lochnagar, considered by many to be the finest on all Deeside.

Lochnagar (3552 feet) is undoubtedly one of the great mountains of Scotland, and a climbers' favourite, offering, as well as an easy route up, many differing and testing ascents to its cliff-girt plateau.

The Ladder, the Red Spout, the Black Spout—these called after Cairngorm-stones found therein—are just some of the climbs, chutes for experts. Climbers have died on this mountain, so harsh can be the weather conditions and the ice; but it remains a favourite with the devotees. Tom Patey wrote of his ascents in the Himalayas:

> Masherbrun, Gasherbrun, Distegal Sar,
> They're very good training for Dark Lochnagar!

Lochnagar's real name is Beinn Chiochean, the Mountain of the Paps, Lochnagar being actually a smallish lochan in a corrie beneath the Meikle Pap.

Dubh Loch lies another two miles beyond the head of Muick, a lost water less than a mile long below the frowning sides of the White Mounth and Cairn Bannoch (3314 feet). Loch Callater and its glen lies five tough miles away over a high coll.

East of the mouth of Glen Muick the A973 runs through attractive woodlands flanking Dee and after three miles reaches Pannanich. Here chalybeate springs with strong iron content were discovered in 1760, and brought many health-seekers to the spa which grew up. An inn was established, and this is now the Pannanich Wells Hotel, on a fine terrace site overlooking Dee, some of the wells still extant behind. Queen Victoria was very interested in this; indeed it was the reason for the rise of what became the burgh of Ballater, to house the visitors. Ballaterich, a large modern farm two miles farther east, has an attractive group of houses by the burnside at the road-end. This was a place associated with the childhood of Lord Byron. The site of Deecastle, or Kinacoul, is at a farm a mile still farther east, but nothing is left. A Roman Catholic chapel, with priest's house above. was erected here, but it is now a private house.

The Aboyne border adjoins.

Glentanar. This former large Deeside parish was united with Aboyne at an unknown date; but being on the opposite, south side of the river, and largely comprising the great estate of the same name, it very much retains its own identity, and deserves separate treatment.

The fast-flowing Water of Tanar comes down out of the high mountains around Mount Keen, on the Angus border, a major tributary of the Dee, joining that river just west of Aboyne. Its last seven miles are thickly wooded with Scots pines, part of the ancient Caledonian Forest, highly picturesque and covering about 6000 acres. This Glentanar Forest is all within the estate, which reaches up to the summits of Cockcairn (2387 feet), Hill of Cat (2435 feet) and Gannoch (2396 feet), whereon is the remote St. Colm's Well. This huge property was the seat of the late 2nd Lord Glentanar, of the Coats thread family of Paisley, well-known for good works. The mansion is a rambling Victorian edifice in shooting-box style, set in delightful grounds, heavily wooded. Near by is a former ruined laird's-house, converted in 1871 into the small Episcopal church of St. Lesmo. Also within the estate is the graceful, single-arch ancient bridge, almost two miles up from the main A973 road, carrying the public footpath to the Firmounth across the Tanar. At the main road, at Bridge of Ess, attractive amongst the woodlands, is the entrance to the property, with its lofty pseudo-baronial tower gatehouse. All this A973 road along the south side of Dee is very lovely, with birch and pine forest and woodland heather.

Two miles west of Bridge of Ess, between the road and river, are the remains of the original parish church of Glentanar, known as the Black Chapel of the Moor, because it was formerly thatched with heather. All that survives are the crow-stepped west gable and green foundations amidst an old graveyard which is, however, still in use and well cared for. Amongst the memorials is a simple wooden one merely inscribed *Mother*.

Huntly. This famous little town of nearly 4000 people, capital of Strathbogie and of the Clan Gordon, stands in a strategically important position in an amphitheatre of wooded hills where the Bogie meets the Deveron, and where the Aberdeen–Elgin road, the A96, meets the Donside–Banff, the A97. Originally called the Raws o' Strathbogie, and really the castleton of the great Gordon fortalice here, it was erected into a burgh of barony in 1545. It is strange that it should have received the name of Huntly rather than Strathbogie —for Huntly is in Berwickshire; as, of course, is Gordon, from where the founders of this great semi-Highland clan came north with Bruce to take over the defeated Comyn lands, and in due course to become earls and marquises of Huntly, and dukes of Gordon. The community was here a long time before that, however—as is witnessed to by the two standing-stones which still rise in the central square—a highly unusual burghal feature. One is alleged to show weatherworn markings of the Pictish horse-shoe symbol—but this the present writer could not discern. This square is at the junction of Castle and Gordon Streets, and here also rises a statue to the 5th Duke of Richmond and Gordon. The ruined Huntly Castle stands half a mile to the north. There is also a parish of Huntly, formed in 1727 out of a union of Dunbennan and Kinnoir, of 12,500 acres.

The town is attractive, regularly laid out, with hills, rivers and woodland surrounding, though the streets are narrow and now partly one-way, for traffic. There are many noteworthy features: most prominent probably are the Gordon Schools, founded in 1839 by the Duchess of Gordon in memory of her husband the 5th Duke, on the site of the gate-towers for the castle. Here is the imposing original entrance complex, with clock-tower and pend, and great modern extension to the west, for this is the academy for the town, all reached by a magnificent tree-lined avenue from the town centre. To the right of this is the fine Lundin Community Centre, with an indoor swimming-pool adjoining. The Cricket Club is pleasingly sited to the right of the drive to the castle. The parish church, in Church Street, is large, square and solid-seeming, with hall behind, and dates from 1805, with sittings for no fewer than 1800. There is no kirkyard here, the cemetery being at the north-western extremity of the town—and kirkyards at its former component kirks. There are also the formerly Free Strathbogie church of 1840, an Episcopal Christ Church of 1850, and a Roman Catholic St. Margaret's of 1834, with a crown-topped tower, and other places of worship. Scott's Hospital, now an old folk's home, is a handsome and extensive building of 1854 on the southern outskirts. There is a Stewart's Hall, a Scottish Baronial edifice of 1874, with clock-tower and public hall. Clearly Huntley took a giant step forward in the mid-19th century—like so many another place. The Brander Library and Museum building flanks the square, the latter devoted to local antiquities. A fine triple-arched bridge carries the A97 southwards across Bogie, and here are the extensive auction-marts, scene of frequent cattle-sales for this great stock-rearing country; also an oatmeal-mill, and a camp-site and park for touring caravans. At the other side of the road, along the waterside haugh northwards, is the picturesque if neglected site of an old distillery, just across Bogie from the good 18-hole golf course.

There is a variety of industry centred in the town, generally connected with agriculture, although the Jaegar Knitwear factory is otherwise.

Huntly Castle, one of the most celebrated castles in the land, with one of the stormiest histories, deserves a volume to itself. Its ruins are still impressive, set in a strong position above the junction of Bogie and Deveron, with the green circular mound of the earlier motte-and-bailey castle of the Comyns near by to the west. This was burned in 1452 by the Douglas Earl of Moray, and the present building's earliest part started soon thereafter. It is now in the care of the Department of the Environment. The principal feature is, of course, the great central oblong keep of six storeys, with its circular tower at one angle, and magnificent early 17th century ashlar work of oriels, dormer-pediments, heraldry and stone lettering at eaves-level on the south front. A large courtyard and subsidiary buildings lay to the north and east. This great edifice was erected by descendants of the heiress Elizabeth Gordon who, in 1408 married Sir Alexander Seton, who was created Lord Gordon in 1436, and their son 1st Earl of Huntly. No space here to chronicle or hint at the tides of war, violence, intrigue as well as splendour and pathos, which surged around this fine stronghold. Let the picture of James VI, in 1594 after the Battle of Glenlivet, hacking away personally at the great walls with a hammer, in his hate, suffice. The castle was in time deserted for Bog of Gight Castle, near Fochabers, as the ducal seat, and decayed. Huntly Lodge, built as a shooting-lodge and extended in 1832 by the Duke of Gordon, is a large and rather ugly building half a mile to the north, across Deveron, now a hotel.

West of Huntly the A96 crosses Deveron for Cairnie and the north. A fork, the B9014, follows the south side of the river westwards, and a mile along this is Dunbennan, now a farm, with the site of the former parish church thereof, in its kirkyard back from the road on a grass-grown carriageway under pine-clad Dunbennan Hill, very attractive. There is nothing left of the church, but many 18th century gravestones. A little farther, at the other side of the road, is the ruined small laird's house of Arnhall, an E-shaped mansion of the 18th century, amongst trees, in picturesque desolation.

Kinnoir, the other suppressed parish to make up Huntly, lies four miles to the north, beyond the great Bin Forest which covers the Bin Hill (1027 feet) and Ordiquhill (817 feet), with the Deveron flowing at its eastern base. Kinnoir is a district of small farms, with a school, on the east side of Deveron and near the Banff border. Avochie Castle, an old Gordon estate, lies at the riverside to the north, a modern castellated mansion, pleasingly situated, with the old castle just a fragment near by. Nearer Huntly, on the south side of the Bin Hill, on the B9022, through a sort of wooded pass, is Upper Robieston farm, where there are the remains of a stone-circle.

Insch and Dunnideer. Insch is a large village or small town, which was actually a burgh of barony, situated on the southern slopes of the Foudland Hills, on the northern edge of the Garioch, 10 miles north-west of Inverurie and immediately east of Kennethmont parish, with its own parish of 8000 acres. Dunnideer is a prominent green hill, of 876 feet, to the west, with both a vitrified fort and the remains of a medieval castle on top, a noted landmark.

Insch is quite a sophisticated little town to find in this remote rural area, with good shops, banks, a large former meal-mill now used as a grain-drying store, and villas as well as cottages. The parish church is in the centre, quite large and dating from 1883, with clock-tower, gallery, four stained-glass windows and a pipe-organ, but no graveyard. Its predecessor has the kirkyard, at the earlier part of the village to the north-east, opposite a pleasing modern housing development. The old church is now no more than a gable with an empty belfry, representing a post-Reformation kirk of 1613, succeeding a chapel dedicated to St. Drostan. At the gable base is a very ancient stone with hieroglyphics and a small wheel-cross, alleged to date from 1199, but possibly earlier. And beside it, part of the torso of a recumbent effigy, defaced. There are many old tombstones in the kirkyard.

There is an Episcopal church of St. Drostan, perpetuating the old name, in the village, a large school, playing-fields and an air of rurally based prosperity. Rothney, the southern "suburb" of Insch, nearer the main A979 road, is actually in the civil parish of Premnay, a rather ridiculous situation.

Dunnideer is quite a famous spot, its isolated conical hill with the fang of castle crowning it, long involved in history. The vitrified fort here is alleged to have been built by the semi-legendary Grig, king of the Picts. It is oblong and measures 220 feet by 90, with a well and outer works, its secondary ramparts part-way down the hillside, obviously a very strong place. The later castle is said to have been erected by David, Earl of Huntingdon, brother of William the Lion.

This may be so, but it was one of the two chief strongholds of the Garioch lordship, and in 1260 was the seat of Sir Joscelyn de Baliol, brother of the founder of Baliol (Balliol) College. It has been an unvaulted square tower, with pointed arched windows, and was mainly built from the stones of the fort. No doubt added to and modified, it was occupied by the Tyrie family as late as 1724. Dunnideer, in its Pictish period, has been linked with the Arthurian legend.

Facing Dunnideer to the south, across the gut of the Shevoch Burn, is the higher Hill of Christ's Kirk (1021 feet) with a modern sepulture on the summit. This is actually in Kennethmont parish, but so near to Insch it should be described here. Christ's Kirk on the Green was once a pre-Reformation parish of its own, later joined to Kennethmont. On the south slopes of the hill are two farms, one called Christskirk and the other Sleepytown. At the first is the site of the ancient church and graveyard, now neglected behind the steading, with some tumbled masonry and one or two fallen gravestones, one dated 1757. It was quite a famous place, thought to have been the scene of King James I's poem *Chryst's Kirk on the Grene*. Its parish was also called Rathmuriel, or the Haugh of Moreal. On the green here, now gone, was held annually on a night in May, Christ's Fair, or the Sleepy Market. Just why this fair was held at night is not explained, but the farm of Sleepytown just to the north-east commemorates. There is a stone-circle in a field still farther to the east, two stones remaining, easily seen from the road to Insch.

North of Insch a mile, on Inschfield farm, off the side-road to Largie, is another stone-circle on a low ridge, three stones remaining upright. A mile away northwards on a still less important road, near Myreton farm, is the Picardy Stone, within an enclosure in a field, in the care of the Department of the Environment. It is a fine early Pictish symbol-stone, seven feet tall, featuring double-disc and Z-rod and mirror symbols. Farther to the north, on the skirts of the Foudland braes at the 700-foot contour, is the isolated hamlet of Largie, rather decayed, its school no more, but the land still farmed right up the hillsides. Above this used to be large granite quarries. Candle Hill, to the west, has another stone-circle—as have a number of Candle Hills in Aberdeenshire—but it is hidden in woodland. The word is said to derive from these being the places where the monks of old kept their bees to provide wax for the votive candles.

Inverurie and Port Elphinstone. The royal burgh of Inverurie, where the Urie joins the Don, with its industries and population of over 5000, is the capital of the Garioch area of Aberdeenshire, and one of the most important towns of this great county. Its parish covers another 5000 acres of pleasing Donside countryside. Port Elphinstone, across the larger river, and actually in Kintore parish, is something of an industrial suburb.

The town has a long history. The first burgh charter is alleged to have been granted by William the Lion, but this has gone; and the oldest remaining *novodamus* charter, by Mary Queen of Scots, is dated 1558. But long before that it was the head burgh of the Garioch lordship in the great earldom of Mar. Robert the Bruce inherited this lordship, and knew Inverurie well. It was suitable, therefore, that one of his early victories was fought just to the north, the Battle of Barra in 1308, where he defeated the Earl of Buchan and the Comyns, although rising from his sick-bed at Inverurie to do so. The famous Bass of Inverurie, a lofty, conical mound to the south-east of the town, was the site of the early motte-and-bailey castle. There was a constable of this as early as 1180.

The pre-Reformation church stood at the foot of this mound and the graveyard is still there and in use, in a delightful situation amongst the riverside meadows. Here are preserved, amongst the tombstones, four Pictish symbol-stones of various sizes. One, recumbent, bears the crescent and V-rod, mirror-and-comb, serpent, and double-disc symbols; another has a most lively carving of a trotting horse; a third has a double-disc and Z-rod; and the fourth is merely a decorated fragment. There is also a heraldic tombstone dated 1616, to one Walter Innes, with extraordinary angels as supporters, from the interior of the old church; and two other recumbent stones, probably from a stone-circle. They all make up an important group.

The town is built of grey granite, and though scarcely beautiful has considerable character. The long High Street widens towards the north to a sort of square wherein is the Grecian-style Town Hall of 1863, with clock, on an island site, where the A96 and A981 fork. At the back is the Library and Museum, wherein, amongst other relics, is the Inverurie Dagger, a bronze weapon of 1500 B.C., the only one of its class ever found in Scotland. The parish church of St. Andrew stands about half-way up the west side of the High Street, a granite "Gothic" edifice of 1840, replacing a predecessor of 1775. It is large and has been splendidly restored within, in 1965, to make a delightful, bright and simply dignified place of worship. The new woodwork of the war memorial communion-table, pulpit, lectern and pews, is of a high order, and mosaics of the Christian symbols of lamb, dove, fish and pelican enhance the chancel floor. This could be a model for the improvement of many rather dull 19th century parish churches. There are some old bibles in a show-case in the vestibule, including a Breeches Bible of 1599. There are five other churches in the town.

There is an Inverurie Academy, opened in 1909 but with fine modern premises—though the first school of the burgh dated from 1607. A large hospital lies to the south-west, facing the Don, with, behind it, a tree-girt pleasure-park and sports ground. To the east of this, within the town, rises the Cuning Hill, a small and probably artificial eminence now grown with Scots pines, off Barclay Street. Although the name suggests a cunninghar or rabbit-warren—a common enough medieval amenity—this hillock is alleged to be the burial-place of King Aodh or Eth, slain by his own people here in 881. Urns were unearthed.

There is a small industrial estate to the north of the town, and considerable industry elsewhere. The well-known Inverurie Locomotive Works are now gone, but the extensive premises are used for boiler and engineering establishments. Auction-marts, cattle-slaughtering and meat-marketing are important in this centre for a large pastoral and agricultural area. There is much modern housing, not all of it lovely; and a golf course to the west, with the Burgh Muir near by. Just north of the latter is Brandsbutt farm, where there is a massive Pictish symbol-stone, in the care of the Department of the Environment, displaying a large carving of serpent and Z-rod, with crescent and V-rod, plus an Ogham inscription.

Across the modern Bridge of Don, which carries the A96 to Aberdeen and which replaced a fine three-arched bridge of 1791, is Port Elphinstone. This suburb got its name by being the northern terminus of the 18-miles-long Aberdeen–Inverurie Canal, a development, largely on the initiative of James Elphinstone, which greatly increased the burgh's prosperity, built in 1807. The railway in due course superseded the canal; and now, in turn, is itself gone. But the mills and works remain. The large Broomend and Crichie paper-mills dominate the area. There is an Eventide Home here, and much modern housing. Near by, east of the road, is the henge or prehistoric temple of Crichie, where there remain three standing-stones within a wide, ditched circle, one with a Celtic beast and crescent and V-rod symbols. Another monolith stands about 200 yards to the south. Farther west of Crichie, over a mile, is the area known as Bruce's Camp, where the hero-king's forces were encamped prior to the Battle of Barra—but this is in Kintore parish likewise.

The landward area of Inverurie parish is interesting. A mile to the west, on the north side of Don, is Ardtannies, an ancient lairdship at a picturesque stretch of the river, now a farm. There is a cave in the precipitous bank opposite, used as a refuge by sundry fugitives in the past. A mile farther up-river on the estate of Manar, is the ruined pre-Reformation chapel of St. Apolinaris, who was allegedly a disciple of Peter. It lies well below the road, above the river-bank, in a walled enclosure overgrown with trees, the interior of the chapel site used as burial-place for the former Gordons of Manar. This ancient place of worship has given name to the St. Polinar's Fair, which used to be held at Inverurie; and also to the farm of Polander near by. Manar House is a large Georgian mansion.

The house of Aquhorthies, near the sequestered hamlet of Burn-hervie, stands on a fine terraced site in a wooded estate two miles farther west, near the parish boundary. It is a handsome and substantial laird's house of 1720, a former dower-house of the Leslies of Balquhain and Fetternear. On the high ground behind it, half a mile to the north-east, is a fine stone-circle consisting of 11 uprights and one huge recumbent, with quite magnificent views around. Two miles away, to the east, on the farm of Dubston, was another henge monument; but this has disappeared, its presence only discovered by aerial photography.

North of Inverurie the A96 follows the open valley of Urie. On the farm of Conglas is a single pyramidal standing-stone in a field, all that is left of a circle. Across the valley from here, on the ridge of Harlaw to the east, was fought in 1411 the bloody Battle of Harlaw, between the Regent Albany's nephew, Alexander, Earl of Mar, and Donald of the Isles, a most famous and significant affair. A tall, pinnacle-like monument marks the spot. A mile farther on, where a side-road forks from the A96, at the entrance to the farm of Drimmies, is another Pictish symbol-stone, rather roughly incised with mirror-and-comb and an unusual shallow S-symbol. This stands right at the roadside, but is probably noticed by few travellers. The next farm on the main road, Inveramsay, was once a quite important lairdship, formerly called Peelwalls, indicative of the castle built thereon, now gone. It was granted in 1357 to Sir Robert Erskine, and was occupied, after the Forty-Five, by Charles Hackett, a well-known Jacobite. Seen from here, on the hillside to the left, is an unusual stone-circle with a white quartz outlying monolith—but this is properly described under Balquhain, in Chapel of Garioch parish.

Brief mention should perhaps be made of William Thom, the Inverurie weaver-poet (1798–1848) who for a time became a feted celebrity, even in London.

Keig. On the north-eastern slopes of the Howe of Alford lies Keig, a small parish, very rural, of 8000 acres, with a pleasant and fairly modern little village of mainly estate houses, and the large and important property of Castle Forbes. The village lies just off the B992 road to Insch, three miles up from Whitehouse, on a terraced site facing southwards, and has a pretty tree-lined approach, crossing the Don at a fine stretch of the river by a high 100-foot, single-arched, graceful bridge built in 1817. The parish church stands back on higher ground, in the Gothic style and dating from 1835 in a graveyard with no very old stones. It is high and bright within, with a single gallery at the west end. Its predecessor stands in the castle grounds. West of the village a mile is the farm of Old Keig, and here, above the steading, is a stone-circle 66 feet in diameter, with trees. On the high ground to the north, at 930 feet, is the Barmekin, a circular hill-top fort 220 feet in diameter.

Not far east of the village is the large wooded estate of Castle Forbes, once called Putachie, the seat of the Lords Forbes, premier barons of Scotland. The present mansion stands on a wooded shelf high above the river, built in the early 19th century by the well-known Archibald Simpson of Aberdeen in the so-called castellated style, in granite, and scarcely beautiful, though the setting is fine. No doubt it replaced a perfectly good and authentic Scots tower-house of Putachie. Internally it has many treasures, not the least the extraordinary black sculptured bear's head, in stone and presumably Pictish, which projects from above the dining-room fireplace. This famous relic is alleged to represent the monstrous bear traditionally slain by the founder of the family, Ochonachar, and from which the Forbeses took their heraldic emblem. Probably it is much older. Beneath it is the great two-handed sword of Black Arthur, a brother of the 8th Lord Forbes, who was killed in the clan battle at Tillyangus between the Gordons and the Forbeses in 1576. The hill of Lord Arthur's Cairn, in Tullynessle and Forbes parish, perhaps refers to this encounter, only a few miles south of Tillyangus. The Forbes progenitor, Ochonachar is supposed to have come from Ireland to help the Scots king subdue the Picts. The first recorded Forbes had a charter of Forbes lands from Alexander I, who died 1124. One of his descendants was created 1st lord about 1440, and his successors took a prominent part in the affairs of the North and nationally. The present lord is the 23rd, and a former Minister of State. Druminnor Castle in Rhynie parish, eight miles to the northwest, used to be the seat of the family.

Below the mansion, southwards, near the riverside but still in the policies, is the site of the original parish church dedicated to St. Diaconianus, mentioned as early as 1202. It stands within its old graveyard, but the remains represent a roofless 17th century post-Reformation church, as indicated by its chamfered windows and doorways and its skews. It is now the Forbes family burial-place. There are also some fairly old tombstones in the long grass. It is a pleasant situation.

A little north of Keig and the castle gates, a side-road strikes off to the east. In the planted forest above Mill farm, is a fine stone-circle of eight remaining uprights, two over 10 feet high, and a huge recumbent. Farther along this road a mile is the amusingly-named wooded pass of My Lord's Throat. Half a mile farther northwards on the B992, to the left, is the farm of Balgown, once a separate lairdship, and is still a small estate of four farms belonging to the Roman Catholic Church.

Keithhall and Kinkell. This is a conjoint rural parish of 7700 acres, united in 1754, situated just east of Inverurie in the lower Don valley. Keithhall is also a large and famous estate, seat of the Earls of Kintore. The parish centre is now at Kirkton of Keithhall; which is rather sad for ruined Kinkell Kirk, for this was once a very important church, ecclesiastical master of the neighbourhood. It is not entirely abandoned, however, for the Department of the Environment now has it in charge as an ancient monument.

Keithhall is unusual in having not only a split personality but a history of name-changing. The parish was formerly called Montkeigie, and the estate Caskieben. This was when the ancient baronet family of Johnston were the lairds. Then in 1662 Sir John Keith, third son of the 6th earl Marischal, bought the property—and the Johnstons removed to Kinellar, where they called their new and smaller estate Caskieben. Keith had greatly increased in fortune over the well-known Honours of Scotland business at Dunnottar and Kinneff, for which he was presently created Earl of Kintore. He changed the name of his purchase to Keithhall. The parish decided, by 1700, that it might as well be called Keithhall too. Sir John did more than change the name; he built an entirely new and impressive mansion—not however demolishing the old one but tacking the new in front. So we have this remarkable two-faced building, Caskieben, at the back, a fairly typical late 16th century Z-planned fortalice, tall, with circular stair-towers in the re-entrants; and at the front, the stately, regularly planned façade of 1665–1700, with its great heraldic achievement over the central doorway, surmounted by coronet, suitable to the dignity of the new earl.

This is not the only interest of the large mansion. On a circular motte-hill slightly to the north, near the stableyard, which was the site of the earliest Caskieben Castle, is a Pictish symbol-stone of early type, a rough monolith inscribed with a fish plus double-disc and Z-rod. This is said to have been recovered from the Don, near Inverurie. And to the east of the house, a low garden wall has a most interesting coping, carved with coach and horses, thistle, lion and other weatherworn representations. There is a similar carved coping at Inverugie Castle, Peterhead, also a Keith place.

In the large and attractive estate, with its loch and many remarkable old trees, is the former parish church of Montkeigie some way to the east on a green mound. Here are many old gravestones. There is still another burial-ground on the property, private to the Kintore family and of later date, on higher ground just within the east driveway. Outside, but near by, are the present parish church, school, and Kirkton hamlet, with a mellow old manse and walled garden farther to the north. The church dates from 1772, the old church of Kinkell having been unroofed to provide materials for its building. It was renewed in 1875, and is plain and rather dull. The hamlet is very isolated.

Kinkell Church lies down in the haughs of Don, near a farm-steading and directly across the river from the large paper-works at Broomend, Inverurie. It is now a shattered ruin but is particularly interesting, typically long and narrow, and dating substantially from the early 16th century, although with older foundations, the builder being Master Alexander Galloway, its rector, but himself architect of the first Bridge of Dee at Aberdeen and the Aberdeen Chartulary. There are a number of special features. Notable is the yellow stone grave-slab of Gilbert de Greenlaw, who fell at Harlaw in 1411, showing a fine representation of an armoured knight, very waisted as to cut, with sword, dirk and heraldry—one of the few of this period in Scotland. Oddly, the back of the slab has been utilised to serve as memorial for a member of the Forbes family, inscribed *I.F. 1592*. There is a handsome sculptured aumbry of 1528, for the Reservation of the Sacraments, and a curious early metal panel of the crucifixion, with Galloway's initials, *A.G. 1525*. It was the Reformation, of course, which brought down St. Michael's of Kinkell. Its rector was a prebendary of St. Machar's Cathedral, and had under him the vicarages of Montkeigie, Kintore, Kinellar, Kemnay, Drumblade and Dyce. To have its own parish incorporated in Montkeigie and to have its roof stripped off to cover that humdrum little kirk, was the ultimate indignity. The Michael Fair used to be held here, with important sales.

Two miles east of Kinkell, remotely set in a quiet valley, is Balbithan House, a highly attractive and interesting laird's-house of the early 17th century. Balbithan has been called the last of the tower-houses, but this is a mistake, perpetuated by writers who take the date 1679 on a metal sundial attached to an angle-turret as dating the building, and knowing that there was an earlier castle elsewhere. The story is that the Chalmers laird thereof decided that he was too close to Hallforest Castle, across Don, for comfort, and in the interests of privacy built a new house in this remote spot. But there are references in the Register of the Great Seal to the *Newbigging* of Balbithan as early as 1600, and a charter of the *novo loco de Balbithan* in 1635. Moreover, the two wings of the L-planned house are obviously of different periods, the south wing and the stair-tower being considerably older. There are angle-turrets at the corners of both wings, but the corbelling supporting them is not the same. Unfortunately the roofline has been lowered at some period, slightly detracting from the appearance of an otherwise most charming building, and it makes rather a nonsense of the angle-turrets which now cannot be entered. There are no visible shot-holes or gunloops, but the harling could cover such, in the older part. Altogether Balbithan is a delightful challenge to all interested in such places, and has been lovingly restored by the present owner. The great Montrose made it a rendezvous during his campaigning in the Covenant wars. Balbithan Island lies down in the Don, a low green enclave of the coiling river, where presumably was the site of the original castle. Mid-way between them are the two farms of Balbithan, east and west; so that the area of the name is strangely scattered.

A mile north-east is the pleasant hillside village of Kinmuck, again remote from anywhere. Possibly it was its remoteness which commended it to the Quakers who settled here in the troubled 17th century. Their Friends' Meeting House is still there, now a private house, but retaining its good late 17th century features of crow-stepped gables, fine chimney-copes, and chamfered window-jambs. There is also a louping-on stone for the ladies to mount pillion behind their menfolk. The Quaker cemetery is just down the road, all the gravestones identical, marshalled in neat if crowded ranks. The Quakers were industrious folk, and set up a woollen-mill half a mile to the south-east, by a burnside, which is now an attractive ruin. It is interesting that it was from here that one of the Quaker families went south to Hawick to help set up the woollen and hosiery industry which has made that Border town world-famous, through the firm of Wilson & Glennie. South of the village a mile, a standing-stone is to be found two fields back from the road, on the west. At Neilsbrae, another mile south, is an old packhorse-bridge, now disused.

North of Kirkton of Keithhall a mile there is a burial-cairn on the top of an eminence. And up on the moor-like lands over two miles to the north-east is the Kendal district, where, at Old Kendal farm, was once the Burnet castle of Ardiherauld, now gone, from whence came Gilbert Burnet, bishop of Salisbury, historian, author and professor of divinity, allegedly the only churchman whom Charles II could stand.

Kemnay. Kemnay is a large village or small town, on the Don, four miles west of Kintore, famous for its granite quarries; and also a small parish of some 5000 acres. It is not a particularly attractive place, but the surrounding scenery is pleasing, and the quarries lie well to north and east. The name is thought to derive from Kaims, the line of low moraine hillocks, glacial deposits, which here flank the Don. There is a farm of Kaimhill. Once a ferry-boat plied here across the river.

The town, on the B993, is of roughly triangular shape, with the apex to the south. Here, to the right of the main Aberdeen road, stands the parish church in its kirkyard, surrounded by modern housing. It is plain and not very old, although on an ancient site, replacing one of 1632, which itself replaced the pre-Reformation chapel of St. Anne, reputed to be the mother of the Virgin Mary. The interior is quite attractive, with two galleries. There are many old flat gravestones in the yard, and the burial-vault of the Burnetts of Kemnay, from 1720.

Kemnay House is interesting, and stands in its grounds half a mile to the south. Although much of the mansion is unbeautiful and of later date, its nucleus is a tall, L-planned tower-house of the early 17th century, the wings of which have been extended, that to the north at an early date. The original aspect is best seen from the back, with the door in defendable position in the re-entrant, and a stair-turret projecting above second-floor level. The basement is vaulted, and there has been a curtain-walled courtyard at this side. Kemnay was Church land and passed to the Douglases of Glenbervie at the Reformation; and from them to Sir Thomas Crombie who built the mansion. Thomas Burnett, a strong Hanoverian of the Leys family, bought the property in 1688. In the 1790s Burnett of Kemnay was a noted agriculturalist, said to be the first in Aberdeenshire to grow turnips in fields.

The huge granite quarries of Kemnay, still worked by the founders, John Fyfe Ltd., now specialise in making the ground-up rock into pre-cast blocks. Stone from here was used in the construction of the Forth Bridge (railway) and the Thames Embankment.

Andrew Stevenson, a schoolmaster, started a highly modern-sounding Adventure School at Kemnay. Although not a university graduate, he was appointed parish schoolmaster in 1820, and he commenced this project. He also began, in 1831, to take in boarders from various parts of the kingdom to vary the "class structure" and by ten years later had 30 boarders and 160 day-pupils. As well as academic subjects, his pupils went in for gardening, making furniture, musical instruments—indeed built up an orchestra. His establishment got the unofficial title of Kemnay Academy, and was famous enough to have an article to itself in *Chambers Journal*, No. 468.

A mile south-west of Kemnay is the hamlet of Craigearn, attractive by a burn-side. Here is what is known as the Lang Stane of Craigearn, a single standing-stone, near a modern bungalow, 12 feet high and without any distinguishing marks. Despite its prominence on Ordnance Survey maps, it appears to have no greater significance than innumerable other standing-stones in this area—though it is taller than most.

A mile west of Kemnay, in the direction of Benachie, is a croft called Greatstone—and well-named. In the field near by is an enormous erratic boulder, 20 by 12 feet, and 10 feet high, an extraordinary mass to have been carried into these level lands by ice. Further west along this road is Blairdaff, where there is a Free church of 1839 and a hamlet, just outside Kemnay parish, in Chapel of Garioch.

Also in Chapel of Garioch is the ancient estate and chapelry of Fetternear. But since it is six miles from that parish centre and only a mile north-west of Kemnay, across Don, it is better described here. The lands were long Church property, the ruined chapel here having been founded in the 12th century. Then in 1329 the first house was built as a summer residence of the bishops of Aberdeen. At the Reformation the last bishop conveyed the property to Leslie of Balquhain, in the same parish, and the ancient mansion was enlarged and remodelled. Unfortunately it was burned down in comparatively recent times. Much of its mellow stone walls still stands however, decorated with heraldry, revealing a mixture of styles and periods. The surrounding estate is large, and the owners now occupy a smaller modern house. There is also a more modern Roman Catholic church, granite-built in 1859, and a more ancient chapel and burial-ground.

Kennethmont, Leith-hall and Wardhouse.

As might be anticipated, there is the story that this parish takes its name from being the burial-place of one of the early Scots Kings Kenneth, but this can be discounted. The name almost certainly derives from *ceann*, or kin and *moine*, the head of the moor or moss. It is a parish of 8000 acres at the extreme north-western end of the Garioch, at the head of Strathbogie, with a quite large village of the same name. Leith-hall is the famous estate to the north, now a showplace of the National Trust. Wardhouse is a large estate to the east, with a former railway-station and hamlet.

Kennethmont is a pleasant open village strung out along about a mile of the A979 Inverurie to Huntly road eight miles south of the latter town. There is much modern housing set back behind gardens, some of it for old folks. The present parish church stands to the east some distance, at a road-fork, plain and quite large, in grey granite, dating from 1812 restored 1910. Near by is the school, also sizeable, and the ambitiously designed Rannes Public Hall of 1909, with its twin conical-roofed towers. Half a mile farther east is the large Ardmore Distillery of Messrs. Teacher, quite a community with its own houses and spreading bonded warehouses. This was always a noted area for distilling spirits, with considerable "private enter-prise" in the matter at one time if all tales are to be believed. The railway-line still passes this way en route for Elgin and Inverness.

The original parish church stands in its still-used graveyard in a very remote position almost half a mile north of the village—the full name of which is Kirkhill of Kennethmont. It is reached only by a dirt road across the fields, but is very attractive once reached, looking across the valley to Leith-hall. Unfortunately only the presently used part of the kirkyard is kept in order, that to the east, the older part, being badly neglected. Therein stands the ruins of the pre-Reformation kirk dedicated to St. Rule, or Regulus. This is where King Kenneth is alleged to be buried. There are many old stones, but none of real antiquity. The Leith-Hay burial-enclosure is at the east end of the ruin, and near by is a table-stone erected by General Alexander Hay in 1805 to commemorate an old soldier, Andrew Mathieson, who died aged 100, with the intention that this might be the place of interment for other such old soldiers "as may chuse it". The manse at Kirkhill stands isolated behind the village in old trees, a tall gaunt old house.

Leith-hall, in its large wooded estate, lies almost a mile to the north, and is a deservedly popular place to visit. The house is unusual and has much character, consisting of four wings grouped round a wholly enclosed courtyard entered only by a pend. The north wing can be identified as the original fortalice of 1650—al-though the south wing was constructed in the late 18th century to match, even to the provision of angle-turrets, so that to the uninitiated all may seem of an age. The original was a simple rectangular block, rough-cast, of four storeys, with turrets at all corners. The basement is vaulted, the hall as usual on the first floor. Contained is a notable collection of Jacobite relics and family heirlooms. Part of the house is open to the public from May to September, the rest provides accommodation for selected tenants, with quarters kept available for the family. The property was called Pielside once, allegedly with a Piell Castle. James Leith, formerly of Leslie, came in 1650, and built this house. His descendants included many famous soldiers, one of whom, the aforementioned General Alexander, raised the Royal Aberdeenshire Regiment and distinguished himself in the Napoleonic Wars. He succeeded his uncle, Hay of Rannes, and adopted the name of Leith-Hay of Rannes. The last of the direct line was killed in the late war aged 21, and in 1945 Mrs. Leith-Hay presented Leith-hall to the National Trust for Scotland. The circu-lar, whitewashed stableyard to the north is interesting and attrac-tive. In the beautiful and extensive walled gardens behind this, well worth visiting, is kept a collection of stones gathered from various places. Here is the Tod Steen, from Newbigging of Clatt, a broken Pictish stone with a wolf and mirror symbol. Another, the Salmon Stone, from Percylieu, also in Clatt, shows the horse-shoe and fish symbols.

North of Leith-hall a mile, just east of the main A979, is the steeply-climbing hanging valley of Cults, reaching up into a corrie of Knockandy Hill (1426 feet). There is reputed to be both a ruined castle and a stone-circle somewhere up here, but inspection and enquiry failed to discover either, though there are a few small hill-farms clinging to the braesides. Clashindarroch Forest covers a vast area of the high ground to the north and east with planted conifers. The name means the stone in the oakwood, so perhaps there *is* a stone-circle lost therein somewhere.

Wardhouse, sometimes spelt Wardis, lies two miles eastwards of this, on the southern slopes of the same hill. The great mansion is now a gaunt ruin, roof removed and partly demolished, but is still impressive on its remote hillside. It was the seat of a branch of the Gordons, with Spanish connections. More than two miles farther to the east are the green earthworks of an early motte-and-bailey castle, easily seen across the Shevock Burn from the A979. This was the Castle of Meikle Wardhouse, garrisoned for King Charles in 1647. It was in that part of Kennethmont which formerly was the separate pre-Reformation parish of Christ's Kirk on the Green—which itself is two miles to the south-east; but this being so near Insch, it is better described thereunder.

A mile south-east of Kirkhill of Kennethmont itself are the farms of Ardlair and Holywell. A good stone-circle crowns the green ridge between these two, at 700 feet, with only two uprights remaining but six fallen. Apt to be unobserved in the next field eastwards 400 yards and slightly lower, are two smaller individual standing-stones, the westernmost of which is a Pictish symbol-stone with Celtic beast and rectangle designs, much weatherworn. The other is plain. At Holywell, a short distance east of the steading, is the former well, now only a hollow in the corner of the field.

Kildrummy. This is a famous name in Scotland, the site of one of the greatest castles in the land, though now very ruinous, main seat of the ancient earldom of Mar and the place where Bruce's brother Nigel was betrayed, and captured, with the queen, his sisters and the Princess Marjory in 1306. As well as the castle there is an unusual and highly interesting parish church, and other features of note. The parish occupies a higher valley west of the Don, and extends to 10,000 acres of hilly land.

The castle, set on one of the great mounth north–south routes, deserves a volume to itself, architecturally and historically, but can only have a few lines here. It is a notable fortress of enceinte, dating from the 13th century, much altered in the 14th. It consists of an extensive shield-shaped enclosure within high curtain-walls, on the

edge of a deep ravine, with wide flanking ditches to protect it elsewhere and a moat. There are twin drum-towers to the gatehouse,
unusual in northern castles and the work of English Edward I, and
five circular flanking-towers, that to the north-west being the donjon
or Snow Tower and very large, with a well in its floor, and five
domed vaults one above another, each having a gap in its crown
through which water from the well could be hoisted. There are
internal buildings to the north, beside the Warden's Tower, with
postern-gate, including a lofty chapel with handsome triple window
to the east. The central courtyard, rising from south to north, is
cobbled and large. Much of the building is now reduced to foundations, but there are lofty sections remaining, especially overlooking
the ravine to the north. Gartnait, Earl of Mar, married Bruce's
sister Christian, and Kildrummy was an obvious refuge for the new
king's womenfolk to flee to, under care of the Lord Nigel, after the
defeats at Methven and Dall Righ, while Bruce was a fugitive in the
Highlands. But the treachery of the castle blacksmith allowed the
English pursuers in, and terrible was the resultant savagery inflicted
on the occupants. The castle was thereafter dismantled, but rebuilt
before 1333, when Lady Christian was again defending it during the
Baliol usurpation. It was a magnet for stirring events. The Wolf of
Badenoch, for instance, here seized the Mar heiress and forcibly
married her, gaining the earldom for himself—a rogue who was yet
a brilliant soldier, and the victor of Red Harlaw. James III's unfortunate favourite, Cochrane the architect, was given the earldom
and Kildrummy—and finished up hanging over Lauder Brig. The
first Lord Elphinstone was granted the castle in 1507, and his
descendants managed to retain it until 1626, when the Erskine Earls
of Mar got it back. It was garrisoned by the Royalists in 1654, but
captured for Cromwell. Dundee's troops set it afire, and it was
involved in the Rising of 1715, Mar's Rebellion. On the collapse of
that effort, however, it finally was dismantled. The ruins are now in
the care of the Department of the Environment. There is a collection
of carved stones kept here, including a broken Celtic cross. Allegedly
a vaulted tunnel, high enough for a horse and rider, ran from castle
to burnside.

Across the ravine is the later Kildrummy House, now a hotel, a
handsome mansion of no great age on a terrace site, with notable
climbing and rock gardens open to the public. The bridge carrying
the drive across the stream is a replica of the famous Brig o' Balgownie. The A97 road here runs down the wooded Den of Kildrummy in very attractive country. There is no real village, but an
inn on the main road, and off to the east, down near the river, more
of a community at Nether Kildrummy and the Milltown. Just north
of these is the farm of Templeton, once also an inn, a former property of the Knights Templar. At the Gallow-hillock here flints
found have indicated the site of a "factory" for Stone-Age implements.

A short distance farther along the A97, a short side-road leads off to the parish church, isolated on a green mound amongst the meadows—indeed it used to be called the Chapel of the Lochs, before the surroundings were drained. The present church dates from 1805, with a hipped roof and unusual in appearance, said to be the original "you can make a kirk or mill of it", plain internally with a three-sided gallery. There is an ancient font from the pre-Reformation kirk above, cast out by the Protestants, taken to Marischal College, and eventually returned here. Its Presbyterian successor is a modest pewter bowl—which, however, was taken and held as security for half a year's stipend for the minister who had dedicated the standard of revolt in 1715. There is a small wooden cross, made in 1967, hanging above the pulpit, made from part of the last of the Bell-trees, whereon the church-bell was formerly hung near by. There is a small wheel-cross with shears, in the entrance. The ancient church dedicated to St. Bride crowns the hillock, amongst the crowded gravestones, only parts remaining. Below it was the burial-vault of the Earls of Mar, where Christian Bruce is thought to lie. The Elphinstone Aisle, crowstepped and still roofed, dates from 1605 and contains the tombs of some of that family. Within a protected stone alcove is an interesting large flat tombstone of a knight and lady, built into this Easter Sepulchre—referring to a 16th century Forbes of Brux laird. There are other interesting tombstones.

On the higher ground west of the main road, on a sort of shelf between hills and Donside haughland, is an interesting area prehistorically. Here, at Muirs of Kildrummy farm, in trees west of the side-road, are two Pictish weems or earth-houses, still intact. Querns from these are kept in the church. Some distance east of the same road is Lulach's Stone, a standing-stone nine feet high, in moorland —one of the many so-called, allegedly marking the site of the slaying the stepson of MacBeth by MacDuff in 1057.

Farther along the A97 northwards, where the Mossat Burn comes in near the junction with the A944, is Mossat Toll and the very popular roadside Mossat Store, renowned for selling almost everything, a highly unusual establishment for a remote area. Turning back south-eastwards, about a mile down the A944, where it joins the Don again, is Macharshaugh, where a little way up is the site of a very early church dedicated to St. Macarius, a Pictish missionary, in a lovely riverside setting. Near by, at Invermossat, is a large granite quarry, still working. Also Brux Lodge, the Forbes seat. At Clova, just in this parish to the north-west two miles, was an early monastery dedicated to St. Moluag—but Clova is better described under Lumsden, Auchindoir and Kearn.

Kincardine O'Neil and Dess. The name of this large mid-Deeside parish of 18,000 acres causes much comment, with its Irish flavour. The apostrophe in the O'Neil, however, is a modernism. There was a barony of Onele, and the present village was once a burgh of a barony. There are many Kincardines in Scotland, which can be translated as merely the head of the hill. The Statistical

Account of 1842 refers to a Burn of Neal or Neil here. The parish, which includes the small town of Torphins and district of Learney, which are dealt with separately, rises from the riverside to much high ground, and is flanked by Banchory, Lumphannan and Aboyne parishes.

The village of Kincardine O'Neil was once important, for here the vital Cairn-o'-Mount road crossed Dee, the principal communication between Strathmore and Moray. The line of this road is still to be seen just west of the kirkyard. Here Thomas the Durward built a bridge in the early 13th century; and here his more famous son, Alan, erected a church and hospice for the relief of wayfarers crossing the Mounth. The church, now roofless, is still there in the parish grave-yard, a very fine building with architectural ambitions, buttresses and a notably lovely Gothic doorway to the north, now built up. There are further foundations to the east, with the present east gable obviously formerly an internal wall, in which are aumbries and built-up windows. It looks as though this was formerly the choir of the pre-Reformation church, with the hospice dormitory above. Despite the architectural worth, the building had a thatched roof, which was burned in 1733 by a young man shooting pigeons upon it—presumably with a flintlock gun. The interior has been used as the burial-place of the Davidsons of Dess. There are old gravestones in the kirkyard, including an oddly knobbly one in-scribed with a curious incision resembling a double H. In the 18th century markets used to be held herein, using the table-stones as stalls.

The present parish church dates only from 1865, set in trees across the road to the east, and is plain and rather bleak within. Nearer the old kirk is an attractive little backwater of lanes by the burnside, where there is a house designated a female school, of 1856, in memory of one Morrice. A well near by, renewed, is dedicated to St. Erchan or Erchard, a Celtic saint of the 10th century. The village has a fairly wide street, with hotels and houses catering for visitors, this being a renowned holiday area, all in granite. There is a pretty Episcopal church at the west end, pleasing within. Kincar-dine House, on high ground to the east, is a large modern Scottish Baronial mansion. From the Durwards, the property passed to the Strachans and then the Forbeses and Gordons. There was a Mill of Kincardine to the north. The Bridge of Potarch, described under Birse across the Dee, stands nearly two miles to the east, a graceful three-arch structure of 1812.

The Dess area lies some two miles west of the village, where the Dess Burn comes in from Muir of Dess, in a wooded ravine. Dess House occupies a terraced position in woodland to the east, and contains some old work. A road to Lumphannan runs up the burn-side; and just west of the road-end, on the A93, is the Gallows Stone, a reminder of the baronial powers, found on the Gallows Hillock near by and erected here by the Deeside Field Club in 1962. There is a picturesque little waterfall known as the Sloc o' Dess in the

Huntly. The Gordon Schools,
founded by the Duchess of Gordon
in 1840 in memory of the 5th duke

Huntly Castle of the Gordons—
"the most splendid heraldic doorway in the British Isles". Note
that the upper religious imagery
was defaced by the Reformers

Inverurie. Balbithan House, lovingly restored

Park House, Lower Deeside—properly Park of Drum—built in 1822 by
Archibald Simpson, architect of Marischal College

wooded ravine half a mile up. Higher, emerging on to the open Muir of Dess, was the former Dess railway-station.

Kinellar and Blackburn. Kinellar is one of the smallest parishes of Aberdeenshire, of only 4250 acres set 10 miles west-north-west of the city and just south of Kintore; and Blackburn is a main-road village on the A96, just beyond the wooded slopes of Tyrebag-ger Hill. This is the only village, although a mile farther on, near the parish boundary, on the edge of the heathy moorland before Kin-tore, is the oddly named Glasgoforest hamlet. This name has an echo in Glasgoego, which was the old name for the estate whose modern mansion is called Kinellar House. *Glas*, of course, merely means greyish.

Blackburn village was originally called Broadford of Glasgo, and grew up round a distillery established here in 1821—which however failed. It is quite a large community, with school, inn, shops, post-office and caravan-site, also a decayed Free church. The situation is pleasing. Immediately to the north above, on the wooded hillside, is the small estate of Caskieben, which acquired this name in 1662 when the Johnstons of the real Caskieben, now Keithhall near Inverurie, had to sell that large and ancient property to the Keiths, and came here.

The parish church is grievously isolated from the population, being sited one and a half miles to the north, in a remote high position, with only the Kirkton farm for company, replacing a pre-Reforma-tion chapel that was a vicarage of Kinkell. It is a not unattractive small building of 1801, with modern dormer windows which help to make it very bright and pleasant within, a gallery round three sides, and a bell of 1615. Also an old pre-Reformation font lying outside the door. Less obvious, if more exciting, built into the wall of the north vestibule is a Pictish symbol-stone of unusual type, having a large targe-like design with three smaller circles within, plus crescent and V-rod below, all rather floriate. This is not the only intimation that here was a very early and pre-Christian seat of worship, for the church is built on the site of a stone-circle, and two of the monoliths are built into the kirkyard walling to the south, while another is in the yard partly below the grass. There are some old gravestones, one dated 1651, for John Keith, bailie of Aquhorsk, grandson of the Earl Marischal. And here is buried the Reverend John Row, princi-pal of King's College, Aberdeen 1652–60, author of a history of the Kirk of Scotland. The manse near by is old and tall, and over the garden-entrance is the date 1615 and initials J.W. for the Reverend John White.

Half a mile to the south, in a field west of the road near Cairn-tradlin, is a single standing-stone. Kinaldie lies almost a mile to the north-east, down on the low ground of the Don, almost opposite Hatton of Fintray, with another tall standing-stone prominent on a ridge. There was a railway-station here, and an estate whose mod-ern mansion is built on an ancient artificial mound. A bridge near

H

by carries the B979 across where there used to be a ferry called the Boat of Hatton.

South of Blackburn and the main A96 is a low-lying area—where farms rejoice in the names of Wogle and Nether Wogle—which thereafter rises to more green and wooded slopes. Here is the estate of Tertowie, its large Scottish Baronial mansion replacing an early house, and now an educational establishment. There is a standing-stone near Mains of Tertowie, and three concentric-ringed cairns. Many relics have been found hereabouts. Farther south, close to the Skene border, is the Drum Stone (described under Skene) and the Assembly Cairn near by, on the hilltop of Auchronie, a notable viewpoint. A Roman road crossed this area, from Normandykes at Peterculter to the camp at Kintore. On the Kinellar Muir to the west, actually in Kintore parish, are a great cluster of cairns and tumuli stretching for two miles, indication of much early occupation. As usual, this is put down to a great battle with the Danes—who are blamed for most of the tumuli and burial-cairns of the North-East!

King Edward, New Byth and Craigston. The ridiculous corruption of Kineddar into King Edward seems to date from the late 18th century, that sad "North British" period in Scots history. It was known as Kineddar always before that, Kinedor in the 10th century, when St. Gervadius, an Irish anchorite, built an oratory here; valiant if pathetic efforts have consequently been made to try to link Edward of England with the place. It is a large Deveron-side parish of 18,500 acres at the northern extremity of Aberdeenshire, the Banff boundary one of its borders. New Byth is its only real village, at its south-east corner; and Craigston an old estate and castle, with hamlet, to the west.

The parish church is by no means central, lying at the north-west corner, on the A947. There is a very scattered hamlet here, with school and post-office as well as the church. This, standing in a fairly modern graveyard at a crossroads, is a medium-sized so-called Early English edifice of 1848, bright and pleasant within, with three galleries and a high pulpit. Its predecessor half a mile below in the valley, however, in its ancient kirkyard, is more interesting. It is entered by a fine moulded arched gateway, with panel above inscribed *1621 I.V. and E.S.*, with the motto "I Hope" and two tiny stone masks. The ruined church gable has a decorative belfry and old bell, and another arched doorway with shield above and the initials *M.W.G.* and a worn date. There is still another arched door to the south, built up. The gable skews are heraldically decorated. The south transept, or Craigston Aisle, has still another roll-moulded arch, surmounted by Urquhart heraldry. The body of the church is now the Duff family burial-place. Standing isolated, part probably of a still earlier church, is an arched Easter Sepulchre recess with weatherworn Latin inscription and very beautiful thistle and leaf carving. Other carved stones are built into walling. There are many, 18th century table-stones in the kirkyard. The large former manse dated 1767, stands near by. It is all a lovely and secluded spot. Fragments of Pictish symbol-stones are said to have been found here.

Ruined Kineddar Castle is sited at Castleton farm a mile to the south, with the main A947 curving round the thrusting mass of masonry—which many will mistake for a small cliff. This was a strong and important 13th century stronghold of the Comyns, Earls of Buchan, overlooking a stream from what is now a pine-clad eminence. There are many massive fragments and fangs of masonry and traces of the moat. Bruce destroyed it after his defeat of the Comyns. Below is an attractive bridge of 1771 over the lower ravine.

A mile south-east is the large farm of Strocherie, its 18th century farmhouse having two splendid coved ceilings and other decorative work of a high order, built in an extension by the Duke of Fife for his own use. Another mile south and east is the farm of Gairnieston, which was a barony once. There was a castle here belonging to the Dalgarno family, its site now marked only by an isolated tree west of the southern approach.

This brings us to the Craigston area, with its Den, farms and hamlet at Mill of Craigston. Craigston Castle stands in wooded policies, but may be glimpsed from the B9105 road, a highly unusual fortalice of 1607, still in the hands of the Urquhart family who built it. Lofty and commodious, it is built on the E-plan, with the two projecting wings linked in interesting fashion at fourth-floor level by an archway supporting an ornate balcony with parapet. Square angle-turrets appear to have been planned but never completed. Heraldic panels declare: *THIS VARK FOUNDIT YE FOURTENE OF MARCH ANE THOUSAND SEX HOUNDER FOUR YEIRIS AND ENDIT YE 8 OF DECEMBER 1607*. John Urquhart, tutor of Cromarty, uncle and guardian of the young chief of the family, and grandfather of the famous Sir Thomas, the Cavalier translater of *Rabelais*, who claimed to chronicle his descent from Adam, built it. Internally the house is very fine, with vaulted basements, a splendid hall, much excellent woodwork and other treasures, including a notable library.

Four miles east of Craigston on the A98 was Byth House, once seat of another branch of the Urquharts, now a farmhouse. Some heraldry and walling only remain of the castle of 1593, built by a Forbes. James Urquhart, second of Byth, founded New Byth village in 1764, two miles to the south. This is quite a large community, on a gentle slope overlooking the shallow vale of the Monquhitter Burn. It consists of a long main street with a "leg" at the south end, where stands the former chapel-of-ease, a plain red-stone church of 1851 which replaced a former converted weaving-shed of 1792. It is interesting within, for the galleries have been closed off, lowering the ceiling and giving an attractive coved effect which light paintwork enhances. There is a handsome heraldic memorial plaque in Derbyshire alabaster to Major Colclough Beauchamp Urquhart, who died a hero's death fighting the Dervishes in 1898, his last words "Go on, lads—never mind me!" The village, in rather bare but now fertile country with wide vistas, has a former charity-school and two shops. There was a distillery here once, and though a weaving village it was also famed for shoe-making. Newbyth in East Lothian was called after it by a cadet, Sir John, Lord Newbyth. On the low ridge of Auchnagorth to the north-east can be seen a stone-circle, of 10 stones, three upright, beside a water-cistern. Crudie is a roadside hamlet on the A98 near by, with school.

Three miles north is the Crofts of Clochforbie area of Fisherie, with Hill of Fisherie (748 feet). There is the Muckle or Grey Stane of Clochforbie, a noted landmark, recumbent stone of a circle, 12 feet long, with a story, like so many. It is said a treasure was buried beneath—a recurring theme—and when an attempt was made to dig this up a voice from below ordered "Let be!"—which effectively halted the excavation. Fisherie was once a barony, with its castle-site at the Mains, but this is gone. Here the 4th Duff Earl of Fife settled, in about 100 crofts, Highland crofters evicted from their holdings in the early 19th century Clearances—a pleasing gesture. At Mill of Fisherie is an artificial mound readily seen just east of the hamlet and school, a chambered-cairn.

At the very north-west of this large parish, and indeed of Aberdeenshire, where Deveron makes a great bend, are Eden Castle and House, above the river. The castle stands isolated at a road-junction, a tall ruin but with many features surviving—which just conceivably might yet be restored. It is L-planned, of the late 16th century, with a corbelled stair-turret in the re-entrant and many gunloops and shot-holes. The basement is vaulted, and on one window lintel the date 1577, on another a crescent. The east gable has collapsed. It was a fortalice of the Meldrums, passing to the Leslies.

Both sides of the Kineddar Burn's long ravine display a former raised beach for some miles. Marine shells have been found here.

Kintore. The grey royal burgh of Kintore sits doucely in the green valley of the Don, 12 miles north-west of Aberdeen, on the A96, and only four miles south of the other royal burgh of Inverurie. It is a pleasant little town, despite its lofty status only of village size, with a population of 750; but it has a fine Town House of 1737–47 to help uphold its dignity, on an island site, handsome with curving forestairs and a clock-tower—and a shop tucked out of sight round the back. The clock was a gift of the Earl of Kintore in 1772. Like so many another, there is some doubt as to the exact date of the royal burgh charter. It can display a charter of James IV, in 1506; it is officially said to have had one of William the Lion; but claims that actually it goes back to Kenneth II—only unfortunately that charter is lost. Sadly, however, in 1833, a Government Commissioner declared that it "was in the most impoverished condition of any town in Scotland". It certainly does not give that impression today.

Kintore is also quite a large parish, of 9000 acres, and the parish church stands in the town almost opposite the Town House, at a complicated road-junction. The present building is the third on the site, and dates from 1819, being quite large. It was originally a vicarage from Kinkell, one of six; but in 1754 the situation was reversed when part of Kinkell parish was annexed to Kintore. At the kirkyard gate are two exceedingly interesting stones. One is a fairly rough Pictish monument of early type, with Celtic beast and crescent and V-rod symbol on one side, and a fish plus triple-disc and crossbar symbol on the reverse. The other is simpler but very un-usual, a large circular stone with an incised wheel-cross. There are some old gravestones in the kirkyard.

Kintore has its Burgh Muir to the west, with the site of a Roman Camp close by. The name of Deer-dykes has been used for this area, but probably the dykes refer to the camp's embankments. The Burgh Muir area, extending almost two miles to the west on rising ground, is becoming a popular place to build away-from-it-all houses, amongst the whins, scattered pines and birches. Croft-type houses have long been established here.

Just to the south of this, but reached from the lower B994 road, is the impressive ruin of Hallforest Castle, standing on low ground which would formerly be marshy and defensible. It is a tall 14th or early 15th century keep, still in part complete to the parapet corbels, four storeys high, with lower and upper floors vaulted. It is alleged to have been built by Bruce; but in fact he was against building castles, on principle, knowing the danger they could be in wrong hands. The building is probably considerably later than his date. But Bruce did give the lands in 1324, part of his inherited Lordship of the Garioch, to Sir Robert Keith, the Knight Marischal, who had aided him in his campaigns. The Keiths retain the property, for the Earls of Kintore are named Keith-Falconer. Hallforest was a resi-dence of the Earls Marischal until 1639. It was much involved in the Civil and Covenant Wars period. There is a modern hamlet growing up at the crossroads to the south. Still farther south, more than a mile, at the Kintore end of the moorland stretch called the Muir of Kinellar and at the west side of the A96 near a modern house, is a curious rock formation called the King's Chair. It is seemingly natural, by the side of a small burn amongst marshy scrub birch-land, rather in the shape of a throne. Across the main road from here is the extensive concentration of burial-cairns mentioned under Kinellar.

Stone is very much in evidence at Kintore, one way or another, there being much granite quarrying in the area, the Ratch-hill quarries, two miles to the north-west, being enormous. North of Ratch-hill, across the valley in higher ground, is the great split boulder known as the Cloven Stone, near the farm of that name. This, strangely enough, was where the court of the royal burgh of Kintore was held; and here, in 1596, poor Isobel Cockie was con-demned to be burned for witchcraft, she having allegedly "rossen to death" a man who, however, miraculously recovered by drinking from a holy well!

North of Clovenstone a mile is Thainston, an estate with a hand-some mansion, not old, which was the seat of Sir Andrew Mitchell, British ambassador to Prussia in the time of Frederick the Great, a notable man. At the side of the by-road opposite the mansion, to the south, is the spot called Chapelyard, alleged to be the site of a pre-Reformation chapel and burial-ground. It may be, but gives the impression of a much earlier and typical circular burial-cairn within a retaining wall, now tree-grown. The Camus Stone, giving its name to Camiestane Farm, is said to be near by, but could not be discovered. At the other side of Thainston estate, to the north-west, is the encampment known as Bruce's Camp, where the hero-king is said to have spent the night before the Battle of Barra.

There is a single standing-stone in a field to the east of the main A96 at Fullerton, half-way to Inverurie. And in another mile, still in Kintore parish, are the large paper-mills at Broomend and the Pictish monuments at Crichie; but these, along with Port Elphin-stone, being so close to Inverurie, are dealt with thereunder.

Leochel-Cushnie, Craigievar and Lynturk. This central Don-side parish in the Succoth Hills was united in 1795, and extends to 12,800 acres, large and lacking any clear outline. It lies south-west of Alford, flanked by the A980 on the east but otherwise untouched by main roads. The Leochel Burn—pronounced Luchle—has the Cushnie as one of its tributaries, flowing down the picturesque and remote Howe of Cushnie. Most of the parish is hillside above 1300 feet. Craigievar is the famous castle of the Forbes family, at the extreme east of the parish, above the Leochel; and Lynturk is an area in a projection to the north-east thrusting into Tough parish.

The present parish church lies roughly central, in the Howe of Cushnie, half a mile south-east of Milton of Cushnie hamlet, in pretty countryside of farmland and hills. The church stands back from the road on a slight mound, approached through trees, and is plain and harled, with a granite porch, dating from 1797. Bright within, it is lit by gas-lighting and has a gallery. The Lords Sempill, from Craigievar, are buried here. The old church of Leochel was very much more remote, on the farm of Kirkton almost two miles to the west by farm-roads, tucked into a dead-end valley. It was dedicated to St. Bride, and the adjoining farm of Brideswell still has the spring of St. Bride on its high ground to the south. The former church, with its 17th century aisle built by Sir William Forbes of Craigievar, is now very ruinous and the kirkyard overgrown. There are many old gravestones, mostly of the early 18th century.

Milton of Cushnie is a scattered hamlet with post-office. To the east, half a mile, where the Howe narrows in amongst woodlands, stand the ruins of modern Cushnie House, demolished, and the Old Place of Cushnie. The latter is now unoccupied, the windows boarded up and not in good condition; but it could and should be restored, an attractively crowstepped-gabled L-planned laird's house of the late 17th century, just outwith the fortified period. It obviously has an older nucleus to the west, and the doorway in the re-entrant has a roll moulding of earlier date, though this has been heightened in unsightly fashion. There are two heraldic panels, one early and excellent, displaying the Lumsden arms. The windows have mainly been enlarged. Here is a house worth saving. The lands were Leslie property until the early 15th century when they were acquired by the Lumsdens.

Three miles north-west of Milton, over the hills, near the Don again, is Mains of Cairncoullie, where there were a number of weems or souterrains. Of these only one remains identifiable, 400 yards or so west of the farm at a field entrance near the Smiddy Croft. Stones cleared from the fields have been dumped here, but the underground Pictish storehouse may still be traced. A single standing-stone rises in a field across the valley, readily discerned, on Sinnahard farm.

Three miles in the other direction from the Milton, south-east, Craigievar Castle stands splendidly on a wooded hillside above the Leochel and the A980. It is one of the most renowned Scottish castles, some claim the finest of its kind, and now the property of the National Trust. Despite its elaboration of turrets, corbelling and decoration, it is basically a simple L-planned tower-house of the early 17th century, tall and almost graceful, with a squared stair-tower in the angle culminating in a balustraded parapet. All the elaboration is above third-floor level. The angle-turrets are two-storeyed, and the stair-tower rises three more storeys above main roof-level. Internally it is equally interesting, the Great Hall a magnificent apartment with plastered vaulted ceiling, highly un-usual. No fewer than five turret stairways serve the upper chambers. The surrounding courtyard walls are gone, but one of the flanking-towers remains as a circular doocot. The Mortimers owned this property from 1457, but William Forbes, second son of Corse near by bought it "by his diligent merchandising in Denmark", and finished building this fine house in 1626. His son was created a baronet in 1630, and his great-grandson married the eldest daughter of the 12th Lord Sempill, *their* grandson succeeding eventually as 17th lord.

Corse Castle, whence these Forbeses sprang, lies two miles to the south-west, just off the A974 road to Tarland. The old castle is now a tall and picturesque ruin beside a pretty pond, but enough survives to show its fine style, with angle-turrets, round tower and many gunloops, a Z-planned fortalice dated 1581, unusual in having only part of its basement vaulted. Patrick, first of Corse, was a brother of the 1st Lord Forbes, dying 1448. His successor, whose house had been plundered by Highland caterans, vowed "If God spares my life I shall build a house at which thieves will knock ere they enter!" This castle is the result. His son was the famous Patrick, bishop of Aberdeen and chancellor of King's College, a brother of the builder of Craigievar. The modern mansion of Corse lies to the west, in a wooded estate. Up the same side-road half a mile is the site of the ancient Terry or Turry Chapel and burial-ground, now only a wooded circle in a field. This area was originally in Coull parish.

Still another fortalice in Leochel-Cushnie is Hallhead, the early seat of the Gordons of Esslemont, now a farmhouse. It is remotely situated at the end of a long farm-track, on high ground two miles due south of Milton, not readily reached from any main road. It is a smallish T-planned laird's-house of the late 17th century, with a crudely corbelled-out stair-turret in the re-entrant giving access to a watch-chamber at the head of the stair-wing. The building is not vaulted, and parts of the surrounding courtyard remain, with the date 1703 on a former coach-house. The present house, which is not the first, was built by the 9th Gordon laird in 1686. These were a branch of the "Jock and Tam Gordons", descending from Sir Thomas Gordon of Ruthven. Descendants retain possession.

The Lynturk area six miles to the east is an almost detached portion of the parish which seems as though it should belong to Tough. It is wide-scattered along a side-road between Kirkton of Tough and Muir of Fowlis. The castle of Lynturk was a strength of the Strachan family, and was listed in 1612 as amongst the strongholds of Mar. It was ruined by 1792, but still with a deep and broad fosse around it. A later small laird's-house, now itself abandoned, rises on the site, at Castleknowe of Lynturk farm, and near the steading is a fragment of the former Chapel of Lynturk, with a lintel dated 1762. The successor of this church stands over two miles to the west, near Muir of Fowlis hamlet, a plain, grey-granite edifice with no graveyard, amongst trees beside a pleasant manse. Muggarthaugh Inn, now a hotel, and the corn-mill of Ladymill are near by. There is a Linn of Lynturk, in a ravine with a small waterfall, nearer Tough, said to be haunted by a green lady—of a fierce disposition apparently, for she attacked the Leslie laird of Kincraigie, who was only saved by his dog, one dark night—or that was his story.

Leslie. Westwards of Premnay, in the low green hills that enclose the Gadie valley, lies the sequestered small parish of Leslie, of 4500 acres only, under the forested heights of Knock Saul (1355 feet) and Suie Hill (1362 feet) with its burial-cairn in the Whitehaugh Forest. There is a small Kirkton of Leslie village at the waterside, about four miles south of Insch, with the ruined Leslie Castle near by; and the tiny hamlet of Duncanston two miles to the north-west. There is no other centre of population.

Leslie village is pleasingly set in its valley, at a little crossroads, with its church and school. The parish kirk stands back up a tree-lined lane, a rather severe, rectangular building of 1815, with an elaborate belfry. It is very plain inside also, with a small gallery, but bright. There is an old graveyard above the burn, where amongst the tombstones the Forbes builder of the castle lies buried.

Farther along this same lane half a mile, is the farm of Chapelton, where once was the pre-Reformation church, now only a site in a field, its former font accidentally buried under new farm-building.

The height called Four Lords' Seat behind, marked the meeting-place of four estates. Half-way along this lane, near its highest point, may be seen at a distance the remains of a stone-circle, actually on Loanend of Leslie farm, to the east, two uprights remaining, one of them enormous.

Leslie Castle is a very picturesque ruin, with the main features surviving and which might yet be saved by a determined restorer. It stands in a field, with old trees, a short distance east of the village, a lofty and commodious house clearly illustrating the late date at which defensive fortalices were being built in Aberdeenshire, for it dates only from 1661, though many of its features are more typical of a century earlier. It is L-planned, with a square stair-tower in the re-entrant angle—admittedly a late feature; but with the usual circular angle-turrets, liberally sprinkled with shot-holes, and gun-loops guarding the doorway. The basement is vaulted, and the kitchen contains a wide arched fireplace; there is an unusual vaulted strongroom on the first floor of the wing, next to the large hall. There is heraldic decoration. Bertolf, a Fleming, gained these lands of Lesselyn in the Garioch in the 12th century and adopted the name. So this is where the Leslies sprang from, not Leslie in Fife—which was called Fettykil previously. The last Leslie of Leslie died in debt in the early 17th century, and his widow married the creditor, William Forbes of Monymusk, whose son built Leslie Castle in 1661. It is interesting that the heir of the indebted Leslie had managed previously to buy Lickleyhead, from the Leiths, in Premnay near by, and built that castle in 1629. The Leiths in turn bought Leslie from the Forbeses, so that there was a general switching of properties. There is a disused Free church of 1876 at the roadside half a mile east of the castle.

Mill of Leslie, with the school, is a short distance west of the village; and half a mile beyond is Johnston, now a farm, whence came the Aberdeenshire family of that name, whose son, Arthur Johnston, wrote the well-known ballad 'Gin I Were Where Gadie Rins, at the Back o' Benachie'. The Ringing Stone—which incidentally does not ring—is a single upright monolith about six feet high, a quarter-mile east of the steading.

On higher ground north of the Gadie valley are some features of interest. Nearly a mile north of the village near Old Leslie farm, is Braehead, and on the crest of a green ridge here is a large recumbent standing-stone. Duncanston hamlet lies secluded amongst the fair green braes almost two miles on, with a Congregational church. Newbigging farm, north-east of Old Leslie on the Insch road, had a Pictish stone, broken, depicting a wolf and mirror symbol, the Tod Steen, but this has been removed to the gardens of Leith-hall, Kennethmont.

Logie-Buchan and Tarty. This is a small parish lying on both sides of the Ythan near its attractive estuary, just east of the little town of Ellon, a quiet, rural, low-lying place much dominated by water and wildfowl. The Ythan here widens rapidly, and even the Tarty Burn to the south develops a sizeable estuary. The part of the parish north of the river is slightly higher, though even here the loftiest point is only 234 feet. There is now no village, and nine-tenths of the area is farmland, with some wood on the ancient estate of Auchmacoy, to the north, and much tidal foreshore. The great Sands of Forvie, now a nature reserve, lie just across the estuary, but are in Slains parish—see Collieston. The Ythan is the Ituna of Ptolemy.

The parish centre is at the kirkton on the south bank two miles east of Ellon, with only the church and manse now, although once there was a sizeable community connected with the important ferry which here carried the main road to the north. Indeed markets were held here, and in the 17th century the Presbytery had to take steps to suppress the holding of markets at the kirk on the Lord's Day—also wrestling-matches and football! Now there is a slender bridge, erected as a war memorial to two wars, carrying a side-road north-wards. The rather plain church dates only from 1787, set on an ancient site in a graveyard with some old stones. One of its earliest post-Reformation incumbents was the Reverend Alexander Arbuth-nott, nephew of Baron Arbuthnott, appointed here in 1568, who became principal of King's College, Aberdeen, the following year. He retained the charge of Logie-Buchan however, indeed adding to it that of Arbuthnott in the Mearns "provyding he administrat the sacraments of Jesus Christ or ellis travell in some other als necessar vocation to the utility of the Kirk and approved by the samen". Something of a pluralist, in fact, despite his stern reforming ten-dencies. He aided John Knox to revise the Second Book of Disci-pline, and was a notable mathematician, jurist, physician and poet, as well as divine and administrator. He died at the age of 46 in 1583—so he was only 32 when he became principal.

The Tarty district lies two miles to the south, where there are a hamlet, school and sundry farms. Prominent near by is the ruined castle of Knockhall—but this is described under Newburgh and Foveran. In 1644 there was an incident in the Civil War when the Covenant Committee at Aberdeen sent a body of men to assail the lands of non-Covenanting lairds hereabouts, and they were defeated at Tarty, disarmed and sent ignominiously home by the locals aided by certain Gordon lairds—to the great alarm of Aberdeen, which took urgent measures to defend the city against this small adversary.

North of the Ythan lies Auchmacoy estate, held by the Buchan family from before 1318. They took a prominent part in local and often national affairs. Major-General Thomas Buchan of Auch-macoy became commander of King James's forces in Scotland after the fall of Dundee at Killiecrankie. He was defeated next year at Cromdale, but fought again at Sheriffmuir. The present turreted mansion dates only from 1835, but there is an older hall-house type of building on the property, possibly of the late 17th century. Most interesting is the very unusual doocot to the north, near Mill of Auchmacoy, standing in an open field. This is tall and circular, with two stringcourses, and corbelled out to the square to make possible a crowstepped-gabled roof. It dates from 1638. There was one rather similar at Leuchars, in Moray.

There is a notable echo where the Ythan flows from Ellon parish into Logie, through a rock barrier. The river here was famous for its pearl-mussels; the large pearl in the Scottish crown is said to come from here.

Logie-Coldstone. This quite large but scarcely important parish lies on the northern verge of mid-Deeside, in the Cromar district, but partly in Donside, for the high ground is drained into both rivers. It extends to 13,500 acres, much of it heather and hill, including the summit of the shapely and prominent Morvern (2862 feet) celebrated in a poem by Byron, and with the most superb views. The lower part of the parish, which appears once to have been the bed of a large loch, lies to the east south of Migvie and west of Tarland, nowhere falling to below 500 feet. There is no major centre of population, Newkirk or the Kirkton of Logie-Coldstone itself being only a scattered small crossroads community amongst forested country, and Ordie another hamlet at crossroads to the south. Nevertheless there are a number of items of interest.

There were originally two parishes, Logie-Mar and Coldstone, united in 1618. The present parish church at Newkirk was built in 1780 and rebuilt 1876, a rather unattractive gaunt building at the roadside, without kirkyard. Near by are the school and post-office, and a few houses and small farms. The position is very attractive, however, amongst old woodlands, with Morvern presiding to the west. Near by is the farm of Mill of Newton, built into the steading of which, it is alleged, is a Pictish stone bearing the crescent and rectangle symbols—but this the author failed to discover, nor does the farmer know of it. The disused Free church of Braes, now a store, lies amongst lovely pine and heather forest at the end of a pleasant path half a mile to the south-west.

Logie old church is to be found remotely sited near the farm of Galton, off the main A97, a mile to the south. At the end of a cart-track is a small graveyard amongst trees, the site of the pre-Reformation church, now the Farquharson burial-enclosure. There are a number of old tombstones and near the gate, outside the wall, is a large flat-faced standing-stone. This also is alleged to be a Pictish sculptured stone, but if so the carving is so weatherworn as to be indiscernible. It is called the Walloch Stone. The early church was dedicated to St. Walloch, the Earl of Mar giving the revenues thereof to St. Andrews in 1153.

Half a mile north-east is Blelack House in its wooded estate, now a hotel. Its nucleus was a tall, old, E-planned house of the Gordons, probably late 17th century, but nothing of antiquity is now visible. West of the house was the chalybeate medicinal well known as Poll Dubh, meaning the dark pit or hole. Nearly two miles to the south, beyond the crossing of the A97 and the A974, lies the tiny hamlet of

Ordie, in moorland and scrub country with some planted forest, rather pretty. Loch Davan, a small part of which is in this parish lies a mile to the south-west but is better dealt with under Dinnet and Kinnord.

The ancient church of the original Coldstone parish stood on a picturesque terrace site a mile north of Newkirk, on the verge of Migvie parish, the church itself now gone but the graveyard still in use and well kept, overlooking a sequestered green valley, with the former manse below now called Kirklands. A fragment of burial-vault is all that remains of the church, but this has an elliptical stone built in, with a cross in relief, within an oval ring, unusual and an early sculpture. Lying on the bank to the east is a medieval grave-slab with a long cross in relief. There are a number of 18th century flat gravestones.

The A97 climbs over to Donside immediately beyond, reaching 1213 feet in the process.

Longside and Mintlaw. The Peterhead area of Buchan has a vast hinterland of fairly level agricultural parishes, in barish, treeless country, with quite large villages. Longside is one of these, of 10,000 acres, six miles to the west, in the valley—if that it can be called—of the South Ugie Water. And Mintlaw is another sizeable village, still further west. Clola is a hamlet to the south.

Longside village, containing the parish church, is quite attractive, large, grouped at the centre of a network of roads but basically on the A950. Although it is six miles from the coast, it is only 80 feet above sea-level. It is fairly compact, with quite a lot of modern housing; but many of the older streets and lanes retain quaint names. The church is central, large, seated for 1350, and plain, dating from 1835, with a steeple. It stands in a crowded kirkyard, which is entered by an interesting lych-gate dated 1706, one of the few authentic in Scotland, with recesses in the ingoings. The earlier church, roofless, stands near by, dating from 1620, and once claimed to have ten doors—though this is not now apparent. It has a fine old belfry, typical 17th century skew-putts, and less typical roll-moulded windows which seem earlier. In the kirkyard are many old tombstones. One, erected only in 1861, is to the famous Jamie Fleeman, or Fleming, (1713–78) "the Laird of Udny's Fool", who pleaded "Dinna bury me like a beast." Another commemorates the renowned clergyman, John Skinner, who died in 1807 aged 86, in the arms of his son, Bishop Skinner, equally well known. He was Episcopal minister of this parish for 64 years, author of *Tullochgorum* and other songs, and of *The Ecclesiastical History of Scotland*, and a correspondent of Robert Burns. There is an old recessed and arched tomb in the kirkyard wall to the east, bearing the Gordon arms.

The school stands on a pleasant south-facing terrace site near by; but the former Free church is now derelict. The Episcopal church of St. John's, however, standing isolated to the east of the village, is interesting, large and handsome, within and without, in First

Pointed style, built 1853 to replace the church at Tiffery not far away burned by the Hanoverian troops in 1746. It is indeed largely a monument to John Skinner, and contains a museum-case with his Prayer-book of 1637—that of King Charles, which precipitated the National Covenant; also his pewter communion-vessels, and records, with some silver spoons. Skinner's cottage at Linshart still stands, where he preached from the window after his Tiffery church was burned. At Linshart, too, was a mill for grinding the jawbones of whales, for fertiliser—from the Peterhead whaling-ships.

Longside grew rapidly in the early 19th century, with the establishment of a woollen factory at Millbank, now gone. The Cairngall granite quarries, to the east and opened in 1808, are famous, stone from these being used to build the foundations of the Bell Rock Lighthouse, the Houses of Parliament, Covent Garden Market, etc. There was a distillery at Crookedneuk, the Glenugie, on the way to Mintlaw, also no more.

Mintlaw village lies three miles west of Longside, on the edge of Old Deer parish, at the junction of the A92 and the A950, a busy place for traffic, with the large central roundabout rather dominating it all, though it has the appearance of the former village green, with grass and bushes and a central war memorial. There is a large modern school. It is a fairly recent community; founded only at the beginning of the 19th century, and is well served with banks, shops and so on. Monthly fairs used to be held here.

The rural areas of the parish have their own interest. North of Longside is the Rora district, with its great Moss. To the east lie the lands of Buthlaw, a Gordon lairdship, now two farms. The modern property of Willowbank near by is now a training centre for the mentally handicapped. There is a large disused airfield to east and south, at the parish boundary; and due south of Buthlaw another ancient lairdship, now a farm, of Faichfield, where the fine old fortalice of the early 17th century has only recently been demolished—a great loss. Two miles due south of Longside village is the Ludquharn area, where there was a castle of the Keiths, and near it the widespread lands of Nether Kinmundy, a former Gordon estate, with hamlet and school.

Kinmundy House itself, now a ruin, and a Ferguson property, lies two miles to the west near Clola, actually in Old Deer parish, on the A92 four miles directly south of Mintlaw. Clola is hardly a hamlet, more a scattered community, with Shannas, between them rising to a Free church of 1863, no longer used for worship, a mill, a former smiddy, and cottages and farms. The large farm of Inverquhomery, formerly an estate of the Bruce family, now belonging to the great London firm of Sainsbury, stands half-way between Clola and Longside.

In the extreme south-east of Longside parish is the Cairn Catto site, with a notable group of cairns and a burial-chamber, on hilly ground. To the west of this is a very large and detached portion of the Forest of Deer, above the Moss of Cruden.

Ardallie is a district not far from Dudwick, two miles west of the aforementioned forest, near the junction of the parishes of Longside, Cruden and Old Deer—indeed it is a *quod sacra* parish formed to serve outlying worshippers of all these parishes, with that of Ellon to the south. It has an isolated church and manse, but no grouped community other than a school near by, on the A92 mid-way between Ellon and Mintlaw.

Lonmay, St. Colms and Kininmonth. The Buchan coastal parish of Lonmay, of 12,000 acres, lying south of Fraserburgh, including its *quod sacra* parish of Kininmonth, used to be called St. Colms; and the fishing village of that name is the largest centre of population. The parish has a long sandy coastline of over five miles, bordered by dunes, and includes half of the Loch of Strathbeg, at 550 acres one of the largest sheets of inland water in Aberdeenshire.

St. Colms, standing at the northern tip, is a typical fishing village except that, like Inverallochy and Cairnbulg to the north, it has no harbour. But at least it has a sandy beach for drawing up the boats. The usual huddle of low-browed cottages hunch their gable-ends to the narrow streets, as though against the North Sea winds. At the northern end is the "suburb" of Charlestown, for some reason in Rathen parish. Inverallochy Castle ruin, also in Rathen, stands inland a mile. There is a school and a former railway-station. Also an ancient ruined church in a crowded little graveyard right out on the sand dunes, only a scrap of masonry remaining with no real features but many old tombstones. It was dedicated to St. Columba, and abandoned in 1607 when a successor was built three miles inland. Two miles south of St. Colms, on the farm of Netherton, near the sandhills north of Strathbeg Loch, is the site of the former Fraser castle of Lonmay, now completely gone.

Strathbeg Loch, two and a half miles long and half a mile wide, formed by the drifting sands blocking the mouth of its burn, is shallow, bare and windswept, a great haunt of wildfowl. Unsuccessful attempts have been made to drain it. Half is in Crimond and Rattray parish. The sandhill area between it and the sea, half a mile wide, is called Back Bar. The coastline here is utterly deserted for miles.

The parish church stands isolated from any village, near the large Gordon estate of Cairness—presumably moved here for the convenience of the laird! The present building dates from 1787, plain and unremarkable, in a not ancient graveyard. Near by to the north, in the same lane beside the Cairness policies wall, is the ruin of the church built in 1607, removed from St. Colms, in an older kirkyard. There are heraldic panels on the gate-pillars, but only a scrap of masonry of the church, with a renewed panel which declares that this house was built for the worship of God by Lonmay parish in 1607. There are many old gravestones. A former Episcopal church of St. Columba, of 1797, stands at a small crossroads to the south, now a farm-store, and the school near by is no longer in use—though

there is a hall still. Cairness House is a large granite Grecian mansion, built by Playfair in 1799 for the Gordons of Buthlaw and Cairness, with Ionic pillars and carved cornices. There is a ruined
observatory to the north. These Gordons are descended from Lesmoir, and one of them distinguished himself as a general in the Greek
War of Independence, writing its history about 1832.

A mile to the south is the large wooded estate of Crimonmogate,
with its small loch. This was formerly a seat of the Bannerman
baronets of Elsick. The late 18th century mansion is also somewhat
Grecian in design, with a hexastyle granite portico. Another mile
south is the farm of Newark on which is a good stone-circle with two
upright stones and a recumbent, plus others fallen, within a wide
ring of lesser stones, with trees.

Kininmonth, three miles more southwards, at the bottom of this
long parish, has an estate which once gave name to a family of that
Ilk. Only in 1874 was this area constituted a *quod sacra* parish of its
own, although after long agitation its church was built about 1837 to
serve the worshippers at this end of Lonmay, six miles from the parish
kirk. There is a scattered hamlet here.

Lumphanan. This modest parish of the Mar area of Southern
Aberdeenshire is best known for being the place where MacDuff
slew MacBeth in 1056. But it has had other impacts on Scotland's
story. Edward I of England stayed at the Peel here, in 1296. And it
featured too prominently in the disgraceful witch-trials of James VI's
reign, when the parish minister appears to have been a man as
lacking in human charity as he abounded in imagination.

Today Lumphanan is a pleasant place amongst the green hills, its
village on the A980 road from Banchory to Alford, the parish extending to 8750 acres, and once part of the great barony of Onele of the
Durwards. Alan Durward gave the patronage of the church of
Lonfanan to the hospice he founded at Kincardine O'Neil in 1233.

His castle at the Peel Bog is now represented by a large artificial
motte, situated in the low ground—and formerly defended by marshland—less than a mile south-west of the village, called the Peel of
Lumphanan, reached from the side-road to Dess. It is a large and
notable example of its kind, on which formerly a typical timber
castle would rise, this covered by clay to prevent attackers firing it,
the whole surrounded by deep ditch or moat. The traces of masonry
which remain on the top would not be of this early castle, but of the
hall-house which succeeded it, and which was there until 1782. The
Durwards—hereditary Door-wards of the royal castle of Kincardine
in the Mearns—had many strongholds in this area, Coull the principal, and another near by at Maud.

The parish church is situated on the same side-road, near the Peel
and well south of the village, very much a former appendage of the
castle. Indeed its one-time manse, which shares with it the hillock in
otherwise swampy ground, has a distinctly fortified air about it, with
an ancient nucleus, of which a relieving arch is still visible externally.

It is now restored as a private residence, and with its grouped out-buildings makes an interesting complex. The church itself dates from 1762, enlarged 1851, but even so is small and plain, in an old kirkyard with some early gravestones. Internally it is bright, with a gallery on three sides. Its predecessor was dedicated to St. Finan. It is possible that the name Lumphanan is a corruption of Llan-Finan.

Near by, and still south of the village, is the farm of Cairnbeathie, whereon is both MacBeth's Stone and MacBeth's Well. Then there is MacBeth's Cairn, to the north of the village. The story is that when the usurper King MacBeth—who may not have been so black as Shakespeare painted him—was pursued by Malcolm Canmore, son of the King Duncan he had slain, he got as far as Lumphanan and made his last stand here, where the Earl MacDuff slew him. Allegedly he drank from the Well, which is close to the former railway-bridge, and fell beside the Stone. Thereafter his body was buried at the Cairn to the north, before being dug up and taken to Iona for re-interment amongst the ancient kings. How accurate these traditions may be is anybody's guess. The Stone is probably a prehistoric standing-stone; and the Cairn, surrounded by a ring of trees, easily seen from the main road across a dip to the east, is obviously a much more ancient and typical burial-cairn—though it might well be considered a suitable spot to bury the slain monarch temporarily.

The village itself is attractive, on a south-facing slope, not large, but with some modern housing development. High on the hillside above it is the impressively placed former United Free church, with its tall steeple, and a steeply terraced more modern graveyard which must have its problems. It certainly has excellent views.

Some two miles south and south-west are two places of interest. The first is Auchlossan, now a farm at the Dess roadside. This was a lairdship of the Rose or Ross family. The old mansion dates from the 17th century, rectangular and very plain, with its roof-level lowered and crowstepped gables gone. But it retains shot-holes guarding the door—which is obscured by a modern porch—and over it a heraldic panel with the Rose arms. A series of eight corbels project at eaves-level, for what purpose is not now clear. A second son of Sir William Rose of Kilravock, in Nairnshire, obtained Auchlossan in 1363. The 8th Rose laird was killed at Malplaquet in 1709. The name had been changed to Ross, and of this family came the Provost Ross of Aberdeen whose restored house is now so famous there.

The other item is the ruins of Auchenhove Castle, a mile across country to the west, and some distance south of the present mansion of Auchenhove. The remains are scanty, in a remote position amongst wind-blown trees overlooking the wide Muir of Dess. It was a Duguid stronghold, and in 1634 the family were declared to have held their lands for 200 years. The Lady of Auchenhove featured in one of the witch-trials. The castle was burned by Cumberland's troops after Culloden, the laird being "out" with

Midmar Castle

Kildrummy Castle—"noblest of northern castles"—
chief seat of the great earldom of Mar

Monymusk. The Priory Church of St. Mary

Strichen, Buchan. Interior of a typical preaching-kirk (1790)— note the dominant of the pulpit, the boxed pews, gallery and general stern lines

Prince Charles. He is said to have watched the flames from a spot on Corse Hill, to the west.

There is a cluster of ancient burial-cairns on the high ground on the Hill of Millmaud, an outlier of Corse Hill, at the 1000-foot level, two miles north of the village. Also a much larger group on Corse Hill itself, partly in Coull parish.

Lumsden, Auchindoir and Kearn. Lumsden is a pleasant and remotely-placed quite large village just north of the Don at Kildrummy, in the Correen Hills area, on the A97 road to Huntly; and Auchindoir and Kearn is its joint parish of 19,000 acres, united in 1811—although the Kearn part of it has more or less sunk without trace. The area is a watershed, the Water of Bogie's headstreams rising here and flowing northwards to Deveron, and the Mossat Burn flowing southwards to Don.

Lumsden is a regularly planned place, built as late as 1840 by one of the Lumsden lairds of Clova, around a grassy square, with school, hotel, modern village hall and considerable recent housing, also the former Free church, of 1843 and 1889, now used as the parish church as more convenient for the population. The village stands high, at 745 feet, with the Buck of Cabrach (2368 feet) to the west and Brux Hill (1558 feet) to the east. Clova estate lies to the west, large, with its rambling and composite mansion amongst woodland, still a Lumsden possession. It was granted by Lumsden of Tillycairn near Monymusk, to his brother in 1588. There was an ancient parish of Clova dedicated to St. Moluag, which did not survive the Reformation—hence the Lumsdens.

The former parish churches, two of them and both roofless, stand two miles north of Lumsden, off the main A97, on the B9002 at Craig. The church of 1811 is unremarkable and now a gaunt shell above the road-junction. But its predecessor half a mile to the west, in the wooded Den of Craig, is highly attractive, in mellow old stone, on a mound above the ravine amongst old trees and dedicated to St. Mary. It is a typical long, low-gabled building, with a belfry of 1664 to the west, and a splendid arched and moulded early doorway near by on the south front with dog-tooth ornamentation. Over the later squared and roll-moulded door is an ogee-headed panel inscribed *M.A.S. 1658*. There are small, pointed, narrow windows on the north side, and the north-east skew is dated 1638 with initials and crest. Internally there is a magnificent decorated aumbry for the reservation of the sacrament, surmounted by an incised cross, a holy-water stoup, and two old Gordon of Craig heraldic stones, dated 1557. There are many old tombstones in the kirkyard. All in all, a delightful place of peace. The motte of the "Castrum Auchindoriae" of Boece, a more ancient motte-and-bailey stronghold than the present Craig Castle, rises a short distance to the east of the old kirk, oval and 25 feet high. This was known as Cummin's Craig, and was presumably a Comyn stronghold.

Craig Castle, more properly Craig of Auchindoir, stands farther

I

up the Den, a most interesting and unusual fortalice in an ancient estate, with more modern mansion attached. The castle has the peculiar feature of a gabled roof superimposed above and flush with the former parapet and walk, a later and probably 17th century alteration, when the angle-turret was added. The building is essentially a massive L-planned fortalice of the early 16th century, however. The rough-cast walls, seven feet thick, are well supplied with wide-splayed gunloops, and notable heraldic panels; Gordon shields flanking the royal arms, in colour, surmount the arched doorway, with a good example of iron grilled window above, and the date 1548. The door is reinforced internally with an iron yett, and the basement is vaulted, with a pit or prison in the thickness of the walling. The hall on the first floor has had a mural chapel or minstrels' gallery above, so that priest—or entertainers—could be observed from the room beneath. There is a finely panelled chamber at this level. A handsome entrance arch admits to the courtyard, dating from 1726. The first Gordon of Craig was a grandson of the famous Jock o' Scurdargue, and probably built the castle soon after 1510. He died at Flodden three years later. *His* grandson was slain at Pinkie, and the next laird involved in the murder of the bonnie Earl of Moray at Donibristle in 1592. And so it went on. The lands were sold in 1892 to the present family. The countryside around is most attractive, hill, valley and woodland, the Den actually anciently landscaped and renowned in poetry.

In a field west of the farmhouse of Cuttieburn, half a mile to the north-west, is a large boulder with numerous cup-markings.

Wheedlemont Hill (1152 feet) rises another half-mile to the north, and on the summit is an oval earthwork enclosure measuring 180 feet by 90, with a ditch and outer rampart. And on the farm of Wheedlemont below is the remains of a stone-circle, with one upright and one recumbent. At Upper Ord farm a mile north-east and lower, near Rhynie although in Auchindoir parish, is another stone-circle consisting now of only two uprights.

Druminnor Castle is in this parish, also, to the north-west; but being so very much closer to Rhynie, it is better described thereunder. There were a number of souterrains in this parish, which do not seem to have survived—they are an inevitable menace to cattle, and farmers can scarcely be blamed for filling them in.

Meldrum and Oldmeldrum. Meldrum is a parish of 8000 acres in the Garioch area of Aberdeenshire, called Bethelnie until 1684; and Oldmeldrum is its small town, which lies on a ridge to the south of the parish—*meall druim* meaning a lumpish ridge. The district is pleasantly hilly but fertile, and with fine views.

Oldmeldrum is an attractive, old-fashioned little burgh of much character, clustered round a small square which contains the Town Hall of 1877, with Urquhart heraldic decoration, an old inn, and shops and banks. The streets and lanes are irregular and quaint, but there is modern housing also, notably the Westbank Old People's

Home, a pleasing establishment with fine prospects. The parish church stands a little way to the east, on higher ground, and is an agreeable T-shaped harled building, established here on removal from Bethelnie in 1672, enlarged 1767 and remodelled 1954. Internally it is bright and prepossessing, with white walls, two small galleries and some good stained glass. There are old stones in the graveyard. St. Matthew's Episcopal church stands to the north, near the gates of Meldrum House. There are other churches.

Glengarioch Distillery still functions, at the north side of Oldmeldrum; but the former brewery, more central, is now an antique saleroom. There is a golf course to the east, beyond the parish church, with a very modern small clubhouse. And on a fairway is the Groaning Stone, a simple erratic pyramidal boulder. How it got its name is not clear.

The parish area has a number of interesting features. Meldrum House lies in a large wooded estate just north of the town. It is now a rather special hotel, but still the home of the family of Duff-Urquhart which has owned it for centuries. From the Meldrums of that Ilk, who held it from 1236, an heiress carried it to William Seton, brother of the 1st Earl of Huntly, in the mid-15th century. The Setons retained possession until another heiress delivered it to a son of Urquhart of Cromarty in 1670. The house has an old nucleus, but this is lost in an admixture of styles.

Less than a mile to the north is the now abandoned farm of Chapelhouses, where once was a pre-Reformation chapel and burial-ground, of which no sign now remains. There was a Lady Well here also. A Pictish weem or earth-house was discovered here in the early 19th century, but this too is lost. The original parish church of Bethelnie, however, dedicated to St. Nathalan, is still to be found, at the farm of Oldkirk, two miles north-west of the town—although it is something of a walk from the road. Here, in a neglected graveyard overgrown with nettles, are the foundations of the church, part of which has been used as a burial-aisle for the Meldrum House families. Over the doorway a granite panel states: *Beneath this building rest the remains of many members of the Meldrums Setons and Urquharts of Meldrum A.D. 1236 to 1863.* St. Nathalan, a Celtic missionary, is alleged to have preserved the parish from the plague by crawling around its perimeter on his knees. An alleged Roman camp was at Bethelnie, but the site has been ploughed up.

There is a picturesque old mill, with wheel still intact, by the burnside at Ladyleys, on the parish boundary to the east.

William Forsyth, the eminent arboriculturalist (1737–1804), after whom the shrub Forsythia was called, was born here. So was Sir Patrick Manson, in 1844, famous for research in tropical medicine.

The Battle of Barra was fought just south of Oldmeldrum, in 1308, between Bruce and the Comyns under the Earl of Buchan—but this is in Bourtie parish.

Methlick, Haddo and Gight. This Ythan valley area lies

north-west of Ellon on the edge of Buchan, Methlick being an extensive parish of 15,000 acres with a large village, Haddo House being the famous estate of the Earls of Aberdeen and Haddo, and Gight another important lordship of the old Gordons. It is actually in Fyvie parish, but is more conveniently dealt with under Methlick—as is Shivas in Tarves parish.

Methlick is an unusual village for Aberdeenshire, in a valley facing north across the Ythan, built on one side of the road only, its buildings rather more pretentious than is normal for so rural an area. There are a large school, banks, hotel, shops, playing-fields, the Beaton public hall of 1908, and a handsome Gothic parish church of 1866 with lofty gabled clock-tower in a pleasant green with planted trees. The earlier church, now roofless, stands in its kirkyard to the north, dedicated to St. Devenick, its belfry with the old bell still intact. The kirkyard has a frieze of old gravestones built into its walling. The large open burial-enclosure of the Gordon Earls of Aberdeen is here, with a very lengthy list of names inscribed on the coping, all restored by the 7th earl in 1901. The Free church, now disused, stands on the hill across the river.

Haddo House in its extensive wooded estate of more than 1000 acres, partly in Tarves parish, lies to the south-east, a renowned place. This has been the home of the Gordons of Haddo for five centuries, Patrick Gordon thereof being slain at the Battle of Arbroath in 1446. They claim to represent the main male line of the great clan. Sir George, Lord Chancellor, was created Earl of Aberdeen in 1682. The 4th Earl was a not very effective Prime Minister, however good a laird. The present laird has recently succeeded to the Marquisate of Aberdeen, his former courtesy title being Earl of Haddo. The Palladian mansion, built in 1732 to designs by William Adam, with terraced gardens, is an impressive classical building, one of the great houses of Scotland, full of treasures and fine pictures, open to the public at intervals; Gladstone once spoke from the head of the steps at the front. It has become doubly famous as the headquarters of the Haddo House Choral Society which, against all trends, has succeeded in drawing music-lovers from far and near to this corner of rural Aberdeenshire. The Countess of Haddo is a trained musician, and the Earl and she founded this Society after they took over the estate from the 7th Earl and 1st Marquis—of the renowned "We Twa" partnership—who had built the wooden hall to seat 600 as a community centre for the tenantry, in itself an extraordinary gesture. Since 1948 the Society has gone, deservedly, from strength to strength, the choir now numbering about 180 drawn from the surrounding area and from the city of Aberdeen. The most distinguished soloists and musicians are glad to attend the concerts, operatic and dramatic performances. The original castle of the estate was called the Place of Kelly, and was beside one of the lochs on the property. It was a strong place, but attacked by 6000 Covenanters under Argyll, in 1644, it fell after a three-day siege, and Sir John Gordon, 1st baronet, was taken to Edinburgh and beheaded, as a supporter of Montrose and King

Charles. An obelisk to Sir Alexander Gordon, who fell at Waterloo, rises on the property.

Just to the north-east of the estate is Chapelton, over the Tang-landford bridge across the Ythan—which commemorates the purely mythical St. Englatium, of Tarves—on the edge of the heathery and widespread Bellmuir with its croft-type farms. Here there was a pre-Reformation church, now gone. A mile farther to the north-east is the House of Shivas, a highly interesting fortalice of the late 16th century, gutted by fire in 1900 but restored as the seat of Lord Catto. It is a tall L-planned building, with a circular stair-tower and a stair-turret in the re-entrant. The walls are well guarded with triple shot-holes, the basement is vaulted, and the hall on the first floor has a large fireplace, garderobe and aumbries. The courtyard is a modern replacement. There was a Shivas of that Ilk family, from whom the notorious Archbishop Shivas, James III's astrologer Primate descended, but at an early date the property passed into other hands, coming eventually to George, Lord Gordon in 1467. By the end of the next century, however, the Grays were established as lairds, and the renowned Mary Gray plane tree grows near by. It all makes a delightful establishment. A standing-stone is built into a wall at the road-end here; and there was a stone-circle above the road near Old Mill of Shivas.

Cairnorrie hamlet lies due north of Methlick three miles, on the A981, with its school and post-office, in rather bleak country but with magnificent views. The Ardo area of small farms lies to the west of it, dissected by the deep and wooded Den of Ardo, the side-road from Cairnorrie to Gight crossing the stream beside a disused but picturesque single-arched bridge half-way. Near by, to the south, is the Well of St. Devenick. A couple of miles to the south-west, reached from a farm-road off the B9005 to Fyvie, is the ancient ruined stronghold of Gight Castle—pronounced Gicht, and actually in Fyvie parish but much nearer Methlick. It is picturesquely situated in old parkland on a green shelf above the den of the Ythan, with the Braes of Gight opposite. The remains are substantial, indeed from the northern approach the place seems almost to be complete to the wall-head; but the south and west sides are much shattered. It has been an L-planned strength within a courtyard, probably of the 15th and 16th centuries, with many gunloops and keyhole windows, a range of three basement cellars and a kitchen, all vaulted, and an ogee-headed empty panel-space above the entrance. There has been later building to the east, all in a strong position at the edge of the den. Not to be confused with Bog o' Gight Castle near Fochabers, later Gordon Castle, this fortalice belonged to the Maitlands until 1479 when it became the property of William Gordon, third son of the 2nd Earl of Huntly. The last of the Gordons was the heiress Catherine, who married the profligate Hon. John Byron. Gight therefore would have passed to their son, the poet Lord Byron, had it not been sold, to pay his father's debts, to the Earl of Aberdeen in 1787. The castle was much involved in the Montrose campaigns.

The Gight area is pleasing near the river and its dens, but elsewhere rather barren, with small farms.

Midmar. The parish and district of Midmar is a rewarding one. Lying on the northern skirts of the Hill of Fare, it is a delightful area of forested hills and green dens, six miles north of Banchory and three west of Echt. There is no real centre of population, no actual village, and only one or two hamlets. But there are two castles, one notably fine; two ancient churches and an attractive later one; a motte and moot-hill; two magnificent stone-circles; and sundry other items of interest, all set in highly attractive scenery, which includes the large planted Midmar Forest to the south.

Undoubtedly the best-known feature is Midmar Castle, which stands on a terrace of the wooded hillside a mile south-east of the kirkton. It is one of the finest examples of 16th century tower-house in the land, one of that splendid group in this area which includes Castle Fraser, Crathes and Craigievar. It is built on the Z-plan, with a wealth of turrets and an unusual circular tower of six storeys, with crenellated parapet and ogee-roofed caphouse. The building, although now unoccupied, is maintained by the owners, Gordons of the Cluny family. The Gordons gained the property in 1422, but it passed to the Forbeses, Grants, Davidsons, Elphinstones and Mansfields, before being bought back by Colonel Gordon of Cluny in 1842. Under all these ownerships it was variously called Ballogie and Grantfield as well as Midmar. All a somewhat pedestrian history for so fine a fortalice.

The old church of Midmar stands on a mound in the wooded den of a burn, to the north-west. It is a typical, early, long, low building, now roofless and with its interior divided into burial-enclosures for the lairdly families of Midmar, Corsindae and Kebbaty. There has been a handsome four-light mullion window to the east, but otherwise the windows are notably small. There are 17th century skewputts at the gables; and one of the doorway lintels is inscribed *A.? and I.F.* The roof has been extraordinarily steep. There are many old gravestones. Near by, to the west, is the green motte known as Cunninghar—meaning of course, a rabbit-warren. It is obviously artificial, and may once have been crowned by an early timber castle.

The present church stands on high ground a quarter-mile to the north, in trees. Most suitably, it has been erected beside a very much earlier place of worship, a very fine stone-circle, which now shares the kirkyard with all the gravestones—a splendid example of continuity. It has seven upright stones and one huge recumbent, all kept in good order. The church is said to date from 1787, though it looks later. Oddly, there is a single small red-granite standing-stone isolated in the field to the west of the church, appearing to have no connection with the rest.

Another and even larger stone-circle stands above the delightfully named farm of Sunhoney a mile to the east. This is a huge group, 70 feet in diameter, 11 great uprights and one enormous recumbent 17 feet long, with cup-marks—the latter being grey granite, the uprights pink. In a land of such features, this one is remarkable. Another circle lies at Balblair, a mile to the north; and still another three miles to the west, in the Bankhead area.

On a side-road two miles north-west of the kirkton is the picturesquely-sited hamlet of Comers, with the post-office in the foot of a grassy den with steep banks. A mile to the north of this is the former small lairdship of Kebbaty, with a modest but good 18th century house, derelict but about to be restored. Avenues of old trees lead up to it, in most pleasant country. There were Davidsons here before the Gordons purchased the property.

In sight, a mile to the east, is the whitewashed mansion of Corsindae, consisting of a small but tall tower-house of the 16th century, with still older nucleus and modern additions. This modern work has been erected in the same style, and all harled and whitewashed, so that to the uninitiated the division may not be apparent—although the larger windows give it away. The circular stair-tower to the left is the old one—although even that is not so old as the gable alongside. There are two vaulted basement chambers. Corsindae was a Forbes lairdship. In 1605, Irvine of Drum apprehended John Forbes of Corsindae, one of "the insolent society of boyis denounced for slaughter and other enormities". The Privy Council had to order a strong armed guard to escort him all the way to Edinburgh for fear of reprisals from Clan Forbes.

At the extreme north-east of the parish—indeed once a parish on its own—is Old Kinnernie, where are foundations of an ancient church in a still-used graveyard with many old stones. It has two mort-safes for the protection of corpses from body-snatchers. There are wide-open prospects here, but a great quarry in the forested Broomhill near by provides employment but hardly amenity. In 1743, Kinnernie parish was suppressed, the southern half added to Midmar and the northern to Cluny. The minister here, Ross by name, being a supporter of episcopacy was in time promoted to be archbishop of St. Andrews under Charles II. A later incumbent, moved by the meagre stipend and poor state of Kinnernie, approached the great man for aid. The archbishop, however, read him a lecture on economy and declared that when *he* was minister of Kinnernie he managed very well on such stipend, and ate roast fowl for Sunday dinners. Bowing out, the suppliant declared: "It would have been no great loss to the Church of Scotland though Your Grace had yet been eating roasted hens at Kinnernie!"

Monquhitter, Cuminestown and Garmond. On the western edge of Buchan, east of Turriff, Monquhitter is a large but rather empty parish of 17,500 acres of largely moorish land, crossed by the shallow Vale of Idoch to the north, where are the villages of Cuminestown and Garmond close together, the former quite large. The parish was disjoined from Turriff in 1649. The estate of Auchry, near Cuminestown, was much involved in the history of the area.

The parish church is at Cuminestown, which is really the kirkton overgrown, with Auchry policies lying just to the north across the Water of Idoch. Provost William Cumine, or Comyn, of Elgin bought Auchry in 1670; and in 1763 his descendant Joseph Cumine thereof, a noted agriculturalist and linen manufacturer, founded the large village of Cuminestown close to the parish church which his predecessor had built. The village consists of a very long main street, along something of a ridge, with a northerly extension at the west end, and is quite attractive on its slope above the Idoch. There are a school, hall, bank and shops. The parish church stands somewhat isolated at the north side, in its kirkyard, to which a modern cemetery has been added. It is large, seating 1000, plain, of red stone, and the present building dating from 1764 enlarged later, is bright within, with three galleries and some stained glass. Its bell is of 1689. In the kirkyard is a good heraldic memorial to William Cumine, who died in 1707, and many old table-stones. The village also has a small St. Luke's Episcopal Church in its own graveyard. This was always a notable Episcopal area.

Auchry estate is wooded, to the north. A mile to the west is the farm of Castle of Auchry, where the earlier fortalice was sited. One of its dormer pediments is built into the farmhouse gable, a quartered Comyn shield with the initials *P.C.* and *M.C.* and the motto *CONSTANT AND KYND.* Joseph Cumine's son sold the estate in 1830. Trysts, or cattle fairs were held in Cuminestown each April.

It is unusual, in a scantily populated rural parish to find two villages so close together as are Cuminestown and Garmond. The latter is very much the small brother, born slightly later, lying in open, almost moorland country just over a mile to the north, consisting only of a long but gapped single street, with a former school and no church. Why it was considered necessary to establish another of these weaving-crofting communities here is not obvious.

Two miles south of Cuminestown is the oddly named Waggle Cairn, on the northern flank of Waggle Hill, a very slight eminence of only 585 feet. There are other Waggles and Woggles in Aberdeenshire, presumably a corruption of some Gaelic word. This burial-cairn rises amongst the mosses in which this parish abounds, an almost treeless area. Near by to the south-west is the Howe of Teuchar—which perhaps gives the impression of a deeper and fairer valley than is fact. Here is a school and a few houses. Lendrum, the farm of the Turra Coo, is near by, in this parish—see Turriff.

Monymusk. This is one of the most interesting areas of Aberdeenshire, although it is only a medium-sized village, a great estate and a large parish. It lies in the mid-Don valley just south of the abruptly towering Benachie, three miles west of Kemnay, in very pleasant countryside. Monymusk House and Church vie with each other in interest; but probably the palm should go to the latter, for it is the older, and the early importance of Monymusk was ecclesiastic. We read that a chapel hereabouts, now gone, was one of the earliest seats of the Culdee missionaries in the North of Scotland; and that in 1078 Malcolm Canmore paused here on an expedition against rebels in Moray, and vowed that if given the victory he would present his Crown barony to Holy Church, even allegedly marking out with his spear the ground for the base of the tower—a picturesque touch. Be that as it may, in 1170 Gilchrist, Earl of Mar, built a priory here, forcing the Culdees—who still seem to have clung on, despite Malcolm and Margaret's determined Romanisation of the Celtic Church—to turn Augustinians. The priory continued until the Reformation, although latterly in some decline, the second-last prior, John Elphinstone, not helping matters by being convicted of murder. The Forbeses of Corsindae gained the lands at that great carve-up, and the priory chapel was turned into the parish church—which it still remains, and still dedicated to St. Mary.

It is a handsome building, of pinkish granite with dressings of Kildrummy sandstone, having a massive square tower with flat crenellated roof—though this had a spire once—at the west end. There have of course been many alterations, but with the major renovation of 1932 much of the interior was restored to its original state. Two Norman arches were uncovered, with other features, and the old choir, which had been used as a coal-cellar, given pride of place again. The interior is now highly attractive. The choir is enhanced by a fine modern stained-glass window in the Strachan tradition, unusual in representing a local scene, with Benachie in the background, and a Culdee missionary, with Celtic front tonsure, and the sculptured-stone now at Monymusk House. Another window, in the tower, is the gift of the Presbyterian Church of Oklahoma. There are two Pictish incised stones at the foot of the nave arch, one with wheel-cross and the other with pagan swastika. A panel dated 1583 commemorates the Forbeses, first Reformed proprietors— actually one of the priors and four of the ministers have been Forbeses. There is some excellent modern wrought ironwork by the local blacksmith; and old collection-ladles and part of the jougs remain in the vestibule.

Externally, there are many old gravestones in the kirkyard, including one small wheel-cross stone of great antiquity. Traces of the early monastic buildings and gardens remain to the north. In the manse garden, to the south, a burn running through used to serve the monks' fish-pond, which was in the sunken ground before the house. Indoors are preserved the parish records, dating from 1678; also fine William and Mary silver cups, dated 1671; and a silver bowl for baptisms, of 1772. While on the subject of treasures and relics, mention should be made of the famous Monymusk Reliquary. This exquisite 7th century casket is now in the Museum of Antiquities, Edinburgh, but it came from this priory and was long kept at Monymusk House. It contained a bone of St. Columba, and was a much-prized object in old Scotland, being known as the

Brecbennoch of St. Columba, and was indeed carried before the Bruce's host at Bannockburn. It is probably the most precious surviving relic of the ancient Celtic Church.

Monymusk House lies a few hundred yards north-east of the church and village, on the bank of Don. It is a large rough-cast and yellow-washed pile, clustered round a lofty and massive central keep, which William Forbes built in 1587—although there may well have been an earlier monkish nucleus. The tower is L-shaped and now of five storeys; but the two upper storeys are an 18th century addition, and detract from the appearance of the house. The corbelling for the former parapet and walk is still evident on the east front, and that for the angle-turrets on the west. A tiny semi-turret projects in the south-west re-entrant at third-floor level. Internally there are many fine features and treasures; but pride of place must be given to the notable Pictish sculptured stone, which is built into the walling of one of the downstairs apartments. It is a cross-slab, seven feet high, with symbols and decoration. It was brought here from the roadside a mile to the east, for preservation, having been found in a field about 1800, and saved by Sir Archibald Grant. It is perhaps a pity that it has been thus built in, however, since it hides the obverse, which may have highly interesting symbols.

Sir Francis Grant, Lord Cullen of Session, bought Monymusk from Sir William Forbes in 1712 for £116,000 Scots. His son, Sir Alexander, is reputed to have planted more trees than anyone else in Britain, 50 million in 50 years, permitting his son and grandson to sell timber to the value of £20,000 sterling—more than their great-grandfather paid for the entire property. Lord Cullen's second son was an even more celebrated lawyer, Lord Advocate William Grant, later Lord Justice-Clerk Prestongrange, who features so prominently in Stevenson's *Catriona*. The Grants are still at Monymusk.

The village was almost entirely rebuilt in the early 19th century. It is grouped round a small green, very neat and tidy. On the east side some building, now used as a hall, was formerly Lord Cullen's School, endowed by that laird for the benefit of his tenants. There used to be a distillery and a pottery, using local clay, at Monymusk, but these are no more. Sawmilling, naturally, was always an important industry. There used to be three annual fairs.

A short distance north of the village, in a planted strip just west of the road, are three small standing-stones in an eight-foot triangle, by the burnside. And a mile on the other side, east of the village, is an unusual milestone inscribed with the date 1754, declaring it to be one mile from the bridge, with the name Young and sundry other letters, probably a relic of Marshal Wade's road-building gangs. A stone cist was uncovered at the farm of Nether Mains near here, with human remains, two of the teeth of which are preserved at the Manse.

Just over a mile north-west of Monymusk, the ruined castle of Pitfichie stands at the roadside. This is now in a bad state, particularly the north front; but the remaining sides are fairly complete to the wall-head, and the building could still be saved. It was an interesting late 16th century fortalice, rectangular, with a large round tower, unusual in that its massive chimneystacks are curved to match the tower walling. The angle-turret at the opposite corner is square, not circular as is normal. A semi-circular stair-turret rose in the eastern re-entrant, corbelled out to form a gabled caphouse at summit. Pitfichie belonged to the small and little-known family of Urrie or Hurry, of which came the famed General Hurry of the Civil War period, who fought both for and against Montrose. We read that in 1650 William Urrie of Pitfichie, and others, raided tenants' houses of Forbes, maltreating wives and actually seeking to burn alive babes "lyand in thair creddillis"—for which he was duly outlawed. Thereafter Pitfichie passed to the Monymusk Forbeses, and being so close to the larger house, was allowed to decay.

A mile still farther north along this road lies the entrance to Paradise Wood or Garden, a timbered pleasure-ground laid out in 1719 by Lord Cullen, with a great many fine and ancient trees, some over 100 feet high—spruces, larches and oaks, all most picturesque.

Newburgh and Foveran. Newburgh is a large village at the mouth of the Ythan, 13 miles north of Aberdeen; and Foveran is its parish area, of 10,000 acres, with an old estate of that name but no village, in wide-spreading farmlands fairly bare of trees, typical of the Buchan area, with its part of the magnificent sandy beach which stretches from Aberdeen almost to Collieston. Because of its position on the wildfowl-haunted Ythan estuary, with the vast Sands of Forvie Nature Conservancy Reserve across the river-mouth, Newburgh has become an important place for naturalists.

The village is not unattractive, save for the eyesore of the large and partly abandoned warehouse and mill at the northern end, with its quay, which rather dominates the flat landscape. There is a church in the village, not the parish church. It was founded as a chapel-of-ease in 1882, called the Holy Rood—which was the name of the pre-Reformation chapel near by, founded by the Comyn Earl of Buchan in the time of Alexander III and sometimes known as the Red Chapel of Buchan, the old graveyard of which, still in use, lies out at a little point called the Inches, thrusting into the estuary. All that remains of this early chapel is now the Udny family burial-vault. There are some old tombstones in this place of wild birds and winds. The village has a modern school, the Udny Arms Hotel, and a camp-site near the high sand dunes of the shore to the south. Here is an old vaulted icehouse for the storage of fish, for Newburgh was a fishing-port once; more than that, the port of Ellon, and salmon-fishing, by net and line, still continues. The Port of Newburgh even had a Newburgh Shipmasters' Friendly Society. There was a lifeboat-station, now superseded. Foveran Links stretch in sandhills to the south, and there is a golf course seawards of the village. To the north, opposite the aforementioned warehouse, is Culterty Field Station, of Aberdeen University, a highly interesting establishment for research in ornithology, zoology and biology which has grown out of one man's great interest in birds and wildfowl here, and linked with the nature reserve. There are several ponds, with a great variety of fowl.

The Old Statistical Account of 1793 says of Newburgh that it is "a dirty place in pleasant and commodious situation, with six or seven alehouses". Its population was then under 200!

Half a mile north-west of Culterty, on a slight ridge which makes it a landmark in this flat terrain, rises the ruined castle of Knockhall, of the Udnys, beside its tall whitewashed successor amongst wind-blown trees. The castle is lofty and plain, a fortalice of the late 16th century, added to slightly later, roofless but entire to the wall-head and capable yet of being restored. It has an unusual plan, being an L with a square tower projecting mid-way along one front. There are no turrets, but the walls are well supplied with gunloops. The doorway in the main re-entrant has a lintel dated 1565, and two empty panel-spaces above and the door has been secured by a draw-bar with slot. The basement is vaulted. There is part of a circular flanking-tower for the courtyard surviving. Knockhall was built by the 3rd Lord Sinclair of Newburgh, a great Reformer, but sold in 1633 to a son of Udny of that Ilk, with which family it still remains. It was involved in the Covenant wars, but accidentally burned in 1734 when the famous Laird of Udny's Fool, Jamie Fleeman, or Fleming, saved the family from death. The small white mansion of 1775 which succeeded it is attractive, despite the somewhat bare position.

Foveran parish church stands in its graveyard a mile south-west of Newburgh beside the Foveran House gates, a plain edifice of 1794, with a central pulpit and gallery and a pipe-organ. There are a few oldish stones in the kirkyard and a two-storeyed mort-house. Foveran House itself is old and commodious without being ancient or beautiful, with a tall sham tower at the back, successor of an early castle of which no trace survives. This was the Turing's Tower of which Thomas the Rhymer prophesied in the 13th century:

When Turing's Tower falls to the land,
Gladsmuir shall be near at hand . . .

The tower fell about 1720. The Gladsmuir reference is difficult to identify—unless it refers to the Battle of Gladsmuir of 1745, nowa-days known as the Battle of Prestonpans. The Turings were the original proprietors, a family which seems to have died out entirely—although there is a bust of Judge Turing, of the Charles I period, on record. This was the seat of Sir Samuel Forbes, born 1653, author of *A Description of Aberdeenshire*, a cadet of Tolquhon.

The oddly-named places of Tillery, Tipperty and Tarty are in this parish and area. Tillery is a small Grecian-type mansion far to the west of the parish, near Udny Station; Tipperty, on the main A92 road, is a burnside hamlet with a tile-works and a school; and Tarty is a district near by, at the Logie-Buchan boundary, where was fought a minor battle between Covenanters and royalists in 1644.

New Deer and Maud. The large Buchan parish of New Deer covers 27,000 acres of that undulating, fairly bare but fertile area west of Peterhead, with a large village of the name, roughly central. Maud is another large village three miles to the east, between New and Old Deer. There are hamlets at Savoch and Auchnagatt, to the south.

New Deer village, at a crossroads of the A948 and A981, is a long-strung-out place climbing a ridge for the best part of a mile, with its old name of Auchreddie perpetuated at the foot, around the cross-roads. The parish church stands on a terrace site above, something of a landmark, a Gothic Third Pointed edifice rebuilt in 1865 with a square clock-tower, replacing one of 1622 itself the successor of a chapel dedicated to St. Kane. The kirkyard is across the street, with many old flat stones, and the burial-enclosure of the Dingwalls of Brucklay. The lengthy village thereafter is really only one street thick, with two other churches, former Free and United Presbyter-ian, in its length. There are banks, hotels and many shops, to serve a large agricultural community. At the top of the village the road forks, the left branch leading to a tall and eye-catching steeple-like monument crowning the Hill of Culsh (529 feet) in memory of William Dingwall Fordyce of Brucklay, M.P., erected by tenants in 1875. A modern cemetery is near by.

Brucklay estate, in a land short of trees its woodlands welcome, lies two miles to the east, the large Scottish Baronial so-called castle now in ruins, but the property still maintained, with modern Bruck-lay House a mile to the south. A mile to the west, in a field west of the A981, rise the gaunt ruins of Fedderate Castle, two tall fangs of pink granite, all that remains of a six-storey keep, vaulted and strong, which was sited in a moss and approached by a causeway and drawbridge. It was a hold of the Irvines of Drum, later passing to the Gordons, and was occupied by the Jacobites after Killiecrankie but taken by King William's troops. There is a Water of Fedderate, indeed a district of the name.

A mile west of New Deer is Bruce-hill, where Edward Bruce, the king's brother, is said to have passed the night before his defeat of the Comyns at Aikey Brae, in 1308. Two miles south of this is Slacks of Cairnbanno hamlet, with school. The old lairdship of Cairnbanno is now a tall old farmhouse.

East of Cairnbanno and south of New Deer two miles, is the Muckle Stane of Auchmaliddle, marked Standing Stones on the Ordnance map but actually formerly one of those peculiar rocking-stones which, unfortunately, our forebears insisted on casting down for some reason. This one is of white quartz, now in three fragments. It must have been enormous. Still farther east by south, two miles, is Nethermuir House, a former Gordon lairdship, now a roofless ruin in a ravaged estate, used as a hay-store. The remains are not old. This is on the A948, and three miles south of it is the modern crossroads hamlet of Auchnagatt, with a hotel and hall, on the railway-line. And another mile south is the older hamlet of Savoch, or Savoch of

Deer, made a *quod sacra* parish in 1834, where, across the railway and up a hill, is the plain church, with belfry and graveyard, and the former school. The church was put here as a chapel-of-ease to serve worshippers of this remote area from five parishes—New and Old Deer, Ellon, Tarves and Methlick.

Three miles east of New Deer, on the boundary with Old Deer, is the large railway-junction village of Maud, with many streets, cut up by the railway and its bridges, in the valley of the South Ugie Water. It is not a notably attractive place, but has many services. Cattle marts are held here. There is a small, neat church, and a rather gaunt and quite large hospital for geriatrics. To the south-east of Maud—sometimes called New Maud to differentiate from the farms of Old Maud, where once was a castle—is the large farm of Clack-riach on the east-facing slope of a long hill, actually in Old Deer parish. Here, in a wood across the farm-road, are the scanty remains of Clackriach Castle, a former Keith stronghold, consisting of a corner of gable about 20 feet high with a circular mural chamber in the first-floor angle. The countryside hereabouts is more picturesque than the Buchan usual, with rolling banks and braes and some trees, but wide vistas.

Newhills, Bucksburn and Stoneywood. This civil parish of 10,000 acres is now very largely suburban and partly engulfed in the city of Aberdeen. But its high-lying and western portions are still very much countryside, and deserve treatment separate from the city. Newhills lies mainly on the high ridge of land between Dee and Don, west and north of Rubislaw and Hazlehead, while Bucksburn lies south of Don on the lower ground and Stoneywood north of it, bounding Dyce parish.

The word hills comes into much of the nomenclature here; Kepplehills, Kirkhill, Brimmond Hill, Elrick Hill, Tyrebagger Hill, and so on—for the area, though only four miles from the coast, lies around the 500-foot contour, with higher points. There is no real parish centre, for Newhills has no village; and the city has spread its housing schemes into the Bucksburn area especially, in a big way. But there is still an authentic village at Kingswells, at the south-east side, near the boundary with Peterculter and Cults.

Newhills parish church stands high, on Kirkhill ridge overlooking the encroaching city, but still isolated, detached, under the bare Brimmond Hill, a quite large building, plain and wide, with a small belfry, and dating from 1830. Its predecessor stands still higher, near Kepplestone farm on the site of the original chapel or capella—hence the name. Here is the ruined 17th century church in its kirkyard, built in 1663 through the efforts and generosity of George Davidson of Pettens, an Aberdeen burgess who gave money and lands to erect the church and pay the minister for a separate parish—hitherto this had been a far-out part of Old Machar. The remains have few features. Inserted in a window embrasure is a stone in memory of two brothers, ministers, named Howe, who died 1765 and 1768.

Oddly, a monkey-puzzle tree presides solitary over this windswept spot. Newhills House is near by, amongst trees—which are in short supply hereabouts—now an Old People's Home. There is a feature known as the Newhills Cross—but this is really on the side of Tyrebagger Hill, two miles north-west, a great boundary-mark in the shape of a cross of turf and stones, marking the bishop of Aberdeen's episcopal lands, now largely covered by planted forest, east of Bishopton farm. Nearer, on Brimmond Hill, are a number of burial-cairns. The large Brimmondside housing-scheme spreads below Newhills churches, with its roadhouse, modern school and other features.

A more unusual cairn, the Long Cairn, lies two miles south-west on the other face of the ridge, beside a pylon, one of the very large unchambered cairns, originally 108 feet long but now extended with stone-clearance from the fields, and much dilapidated. Nevertheless it is an important prehistoric monument and should be better cared for. Not far east of here, just off the A944, is Kingswells, where there is quite a large and growing village on the south-facing slope, an inn known as the Four-Mile House—that distance from Aberdeen—and the little plain, former Free church at the crossroads, with a hall. Also the picturesque old mansion of 1666, in its small wooded estate to the west. Kingswells House, a former possession of 12 generations of the Jaffrey family from 1587, is E-shaped with crow-stepped gables; and a stone in front declares: *O-LORD-MAK-VSL-YVELLYE-STONIS-OF-THY-ETERNAL-BVILDING. DEO-GLORIA. 1688.* Near by to the north is a Quaker burial-ground, with trees, with no names but a numbered plan. The Jaffreys were Quakers, and Alexander Jaffrey of Kingswells, provost of Aberdeen during the Civil Wars period and Member of Parliament, was one of the Scots Commissioners sent to invite Charles II to return from exile in 1650. Behind Kingswells still farther north is a fine example of what is known hereabouts as a consumption-dyke, a very wide wall made up of stones gathered from the fields, a way of disposing of such in stony country. This one is 30 feet wide, with a walk along the top, and 1500 feet long. Two miles east of Kingswells, at the city-edge, is Oldmill, formerly a reformatory of 1857 and now a hospital, a very large and ornate building with a high tower and clock. Opposite is the huge new Hazlehead Academy. Hazlehead Park and golf course are here also—but these are described under Aberdeen.

At the other side of the ridge, northwards, Bucksburn is altogether too built-up now to describe distinct from the city. But reference might be made perhaps to the fine new library, and the modern police buildings. Bankhead, which is a western extension, has an academy, with beyond it the two well-known research establishments of the Rowett Institute, on the right of the A96, and the North of Scotland College of Agriculture at Craibstone, on the left, the latter in a large estate—named after the battle fought hereabouts in the Civil War—and formerly a property of the Sandilands family, whose rather ugly Georgian mansion has not been improved by conversion into offices. Elrick Hill rises still farther west, its Den famed as being the hide-out of a notorious robber-gang, who used a long cave in the hillside as base—now closed up. Elrick's quarries have provided much granite—as have the famous Dancing Cairns quarries at Bucksburn. Bankhead, Bucksburn, Auchmill and Stoneywood were all former villages, now engulfed.

Stoneywood lies across Don from the rest, and the old bridge thereto was built by the same George Davidson who provided the parish church in 1663. The river here is grievously polluted by industry, which is a great pity, for the stretch eastwards of Bucksburn, in the wooded defile of Persley Den, is very lovely with its quiet and sequestered walks amongst the beech trees for a long way along the north bank, but spoiled by the filthy water. The Stoneywood area to north and west is notable for the huge and old-established paper-works here, founded 1770, and now part of the Wiggins, Teape empire, its ramifications widespread. Stoneywood House, large and rambling in its pleasant grounds, with a lake, is incorporated. Waterton House near by, however, remains private, an attractive old mansion. The trees and parkland of these two properties help to make the area pleasing, despite the industry. Stoneywood formerly was called Craigharr, and belonged to the Moir family, well known in Aberdeen. The name Craigharr is still perpetuated in street-names. A chapel-of-ease was founded here in 1879, now the *quod sacra* parish church.

New Machar, Monykebbock and Straloch. The parish of New Machar, originally part of the deanery of St. Machar's—indeed once called Upper St. Machar's—was detached as a separate parish at the Reformation period. It covers 9000 acres of moorland, farmland and undulating country north of Aberdeen and east of Dyce, with a large village of its own name. Monycaboc, or Monykebbock, was the former parish religious centre; and Straloch a large and famous estate to the north-west.

Newmachar village is situated on the A947 road to Oldmeldrum, about 10 miles north-north-west of Aberdeen, at a road-junction, towards the north of its parish. It is a growing place, not unconnected with the large mental hospital near by at Kingseat, with almost 100 new houses added since 1953, a large school, hall, hotel, bowling-green and other amenities, less than picturesque perhaps but with wide prospects over quite pleasant country, Benachie in the distance. It has absorbed the kirkton, once called Summerhill, and the parish church is here, dating only from 1791, although its predecessor was moved here from Monycaboc in 1639. It contains some good stained glass by Douglas Strachan, the Crombie Memorial window commemorating the ancient links of New Machar parish with the bishops of Aberdeen and the deanery of St. Machar's. There are some fairly old gravestones in the kirkyard.

Monykebbock, once a barony, is now a farm with associated

cottages, lying just off the B979 road to Fintray, a mile to the south-west. In a field to the east are the circular walled graveyard and foundations of the ancient pre-Reformation chapel of St. Colm, with its plaque indicating it as a place of worship from 1256 to 1609. Colm was one of St. Drostan's missionary helpers, in Pictish times. There are older gravestones here. Half a mile to the north-west, on an eminence in another field of the same farm, is a single slender standing-stone, six feet tall, rising out of a circular cairn. Another smaller individual stone stands half a mile due west, on Chapel of Elrick farm, south of the road. A flat one, no doubt from its former stone-circle, is built into a dyke near by.

Elrick House stands in woodland just a little farther east, an attractive, smallish but substantial mansion of the Adam period, with many interesting features. It was an old estate of the Strachans, but came to a branch of the Burnett family in the mid-17th century, the first Burnett of Elrick marrying Mary, the painter George Jameson's sister. They remained in possession until comparatively recent times, and therefore built this house. The circular doocot of its predecessor, probably of the 16th century, stands to the north, with its many stone nesting-boxes. There is much good Adam decoration and fittings in the house, including fine chimneypieces, also panelling brought from Hilton House, Aberdeen. In the gardens, which have been landscaped at one time to frame the picturesque Elrick Burn and parkland, grows the famous Fassifern Rose, a plant brought from Prince Charles Edward's villa in Rome, cuttings from which grace the royal garden at Balmoral.

Straloch House was built by John Ramsay of Barra in 1760, a fine mansion, tall and dignified, with flanking pavilions. It lies in an extensive wooded estate two miles north-west of Newmachar village, and is famous as the seat of Robert Gordon of Straloch (1580–1661), the noted geographer, mapmaker and scientist, first graduate of Marischal College and founder of Robert Gordon's College, Aberdeen. Previously Straloch had belonged to the Cheyne family, once so powerful in the North-East. Possibly this is why, oddly enough, the estate was at one time a detached portion of the far-away county of Banff, where the Cheynes were particularly prominent. The lands later passed to the Ramsays of Barra, and they still belong to the Irvines of Barra Castle. In the grounds is the site of the former St. Mary's Chapel, now a pleasant garden amongst yew-trees, with the holy well close by. Built into the outer gateway of the walled garden are two heraldic panels, evidently dormer pediments from the earlier Gordon house demolished by the Ramsays.

There was still another pre-Reformation chapel in the parish, at Clubsgoval, the old name for the estate of Parkhill, six miles to the south-east. This was also dedicated to St. Mary. At Parkhill was found, in 1864, a silver chain engraved with Pictish symbols, now in the Museum of Antiquities, Edinburgh. The large 18th century mansion, built by Skene of Dyce, has been demolished recently, replaced by a smaller modern house. Although the name of Clubsgoval has gone, Goval itself is still to the fore. Near the road-end to Old Goval farm, a mile north on the A947, is a massive standing-stone six feet high, in the field, legend linking it with the Captain in 'The Bonny Lass o' Fyvie'. Another interesting prehistoric feature here, on the moorland north of Goval farm, is the remains of a chambered cairn, still recognisable.

The word Goval is the same as in Loch Goul, or the Bishop's Loch, which lies a mile to the east of Parkhill, via the pretty Den, with the Lily Loch and Corby Loch farther east still. It gets the second name because the bishops of Aberdeen maintained a small palace on an islet therein, reached by a drawbridge—although the representation thereof shown in the aforementioned stained-glass window at New-machar shows a permanent timber-bridge. The energetic Bishop de Bernham is said to have been burned to death within its walls in 1282. Lily Loch is smaller; and Corby Loch largely in Old Machar parish.

Just north of these lochs is the extensive area of the Red Moss, where the moorland reaches 330 feet. The sea, however, is only three miles away. And northwards beyond Red Moss is the large mental hospital of Kingseat. It took its name from the estate here, whereon was a stone on which Malcolm Canmore is said to have sat, weary, and called for water from the near by well, called Betteral Well—which local ingenuity, needless to say, has contrived to turn into Better-than-Ale Well.

At the very northern boundary of the parish, with Udny, is the hamlet of Whiterashes, still on A947, with post-office, school and Episcopal church.

Old Deer, Stuartfield and Fetterangus. Old Deer is a justly famous name, for from its ancient Celtic monastery, founded by Columba himself in the 6th century, came the renowned Book of Deer, a Latin manuscript of the 9th century incorporating the first-known example of Gaelic script, a volume now in the library of Cambridge University. Old Deer is also a village and a Buchan parish of 27,000 acres. Stuartfield is another village a mile to the south; and Fetterangus still another two miles to the north.

Old Deer village lies in the valley of the South Ugie Water 10 miles west of Peterhead, perhaps the most pleasing of the Buchan villages, amongst the trees of the Aden and Pitfour estates. It is of only medium size, with an air of age about it, the main street dominated by two large churches, the parish and the Episcopal St. Drostan's. The former, in its tree-girt kirkyard, with its pre-decessor behind it, seats 1000 and dates from 1788, restored 1881, with a clock-tower and spire 103 feet high. Oddly, it was built to house a library in its basement. The earlier church, roofless and altered, has a Norman arch within, an Easter Sepulchre recess, a holy-water stoup and a piscina. There are a number of heraldic panels on the outer walls, badly weatherworn, and one to the north, undated, to an Earl of Mar. East of the former chancel is the burial-place of the Fergusons of Kinmundy and Pitfour.

The Episcopal church near by, also sizeable, has a children's chapel and also some stained-glass windows with unusual ascriptions, one to Bonnie Dundee and one to Queen Margaret, wife of Malcolm Canmore, bracketed with a more modern lady. St. Drostan's is also the name of an old folk's home farther up the street. There is an old inn, and there was formerly a woollen-mill. A small factory makes tractor trailers. And at Biffie, half a mile to the southwest, was an old-established brewery, later a distillery, but now only a farm with some oldish buildings and part of a vault.

East of the village nearly a mile, on the north bank of Ugie, are the ruins of the Abbey of St. Mary of Deer, now in the care of the Department of the Environment—but unfortunately only open in the summer season. This is not identical with the Columban monastery of St. Drostan, although obviously the two overlap. The Celtic and Culdee foundation flourished until at least the reign of David I, whereas the abbey, a Romish Cistercian establishment was founded in 1218 by William Comyn, Earl of Buchan. The last of the Commendator Abbots, Robert Keith, second son of the Earl Marischal, arranged it so that he hung on to the property, and got it erected into a temporal lordship of Altrie in 1587. The remains are of reddish sandstone, Early English in style, with not a great deal left of the cruciform church 150 feet by 90, with five-bayed nave. A Pictish symbol-stone is said to be built into the walling somewhere here, but this could not be confirmed. Fine garden walls surround the ruins, but these are of later date. Near by is an attractive 17th century three-arched bridge over the Ugie.

Just a little farther west, on the other side of the southern B9029 road, is the Aikey Fair stance, where is held a famous fair each July. Near by was fought, in 1308, the Battle of Aikey Brae, when Edward Bruce, later King of Ireland, defeated the Comyn Earl of Buchan, on his brother Robert's behalf, which victory was followed by the notorious herrying of Buchan. On Parkhouse Hill above is a good stone-circle with five erect stones and five fallen. The site of a Pictish village was discovered on the northern slopes of this hill, also.

Immediately north of Old Deer lies the large Pitfour estate, its mansion now demolished though the stableyard and lodges survive. Also a large chapel standing high on a bare ridge, a landmark though a tattered one, with a clock-tower, used as a cowshed. The estate embosoms a fine artificial loch of 45 acres, with a good shallow-arched bridge at one end and a Grecian pillared temple at the other, all in somewhat attractive decay. It should be attractive, for a century ago the then laird, Admiral Ferguson, spent £80,000 beautifying it all. The high ground behind is now heavily forested, the Forest of Deer including Loudon Wood, White Cow Wood and Drinnie's Wood, rather engulfing stone-circles at the first two and an earthwork or Pictish weem at the third.

Near the last, almost two miles north of Old Deer and half a mile west of the village of Fetterangus, is the ruined ancient church of that name, in its isolated graveyard, with a war memorial gateway thereto.

There is not much of the old building left, badly overgrown with ivy, built on the site of a stone-circle. But a Pictish stone is still inset in the kirkyard wall, weatherworn but alleged to show a design of circles—which the present writer could not discern. There are many old gravestones placed in and around the ruin, as well as modern tombs, and an old font is preserved. To the north, almost a mile, on the farm of Goval is a single standing-stone. Fetterangus itself is a not very attractive village of the late 18th century, with a plain church, a Chalmers Institute Hall, a square of a sort, older cottages and modern housing at the back.

At the other side of Old Deer, a mile to the south is Stuartfield, a village of about the same size and age as Fetterangus, at a crossroads on the B9030, regularly built, also with a square or central green, a former Free church, and a mill at the south end now producing animal feeding-stuffs. At the north end is a "suburb" rejoicing in the name of Quartalehouse, where is an abandoned church of 1843 and hall, making a distinctly seedy approach. The village was founded in the late 18th century and originally called Crichie. Crichie itself is a small estate less than a mile farther south, with a single remaining stone of a circle at the edge of the driveway, known as the White Cow Stone. There was a St. Drostan's Well at Mains of Crichie.

Old Machar and Bridge of Don. It is strange that the parishes of Old and New Machar, for which St. Machar's Cathedral in Old Aberdeen was the ecclesiastical focal-point—if hardly the centre— should lie at the other side of Don, and still seem so much detached from the modern city—even though there has been a certain amount of "infiltration" in the Balgownie and Bridge of Don area. The city is very much in evidence, of course, its multi-storey buildings towering on the southern skyline; but the parishes are not yet suburban. Originally Old and New Machar and Newhills chapelries comprised the Deanery of St. Machar's. New Machar was made a separate parish at the Reformation, and Newhills about a century later. This left Old Machar truncated as the "metropolitan" parish, but it was still large, at 12,500 acres, lying between Dyce and the sea.

The main A92 road crosses the Bridge of Don about two miles north of Aberdeen city centre, and a third of a mile east of the famous Old Brig o' Balgownie, that handsome and attractive Gothic-arched monument to a distant past, dealt with under Aberdeen. A picturesque group of cottages with rose-gardens flank the tree-clad riverside here, known as the Cot Town, favourites with photographers. There is considerable modern development hereabouts, inevitably, with even a Bridge of Don Industrial Estate—and opposite this, on the east side of the A92, the large Scottish Infantry Depot barracks; nevertheless, there is still an atmosphere of detachment from the near-by city. The Bridge of Don itself, with five arches, was built in 1831, but has been modernised since, to make a fine access to Aberdeen from the north. Seawards of the bridge is Robert Gordon's Institute of Technology Radar Station, beside the coastguard station, and close by, access to the extraordinary stretch of sands and links, which extends northwards for a dozen miles to the Ythan estuary and beyond—where the name *machar*, Gaelic for flat sandy coastal links, comes from. These beaches, backed by sand-dunes, and then the succession of links—Balgownie, Blackdog, Mill-den, Eigie, Drumside, Pettens, Menie, Drums and Foveran Links, make up a seaboard that few cities can rival. Needless to say, their use for golf courses is not overlooked. Nearly three miles up, the solitary and oddly shaped rock called Black Dog, prominent in all this sand, marks the parish boundary. At high water its top looks like a dog's head. There is an army firing-range here. There is also an entertainments centre and restaurant called The Range.

Inland the parish quickly rises to moorland, surprising to be so near the city. The majority of the parish area has this moorland flavour, with scrub-birch, whins and even heather, though nowhere does it rise above 330 feet. There are many sand and gravel pits working, but no real villages, and of course no kirkton. The hamlet of Newton of Murcar lies at a fork of the A92 about two miles up, with the Murcar Golf Club to seaward. The school, however, is called Denmore, which is a sort of alternative name for the district, Murcar and Denmore inextricably interwoven. Dubford, another hamlet a mile to the north-west, has a single standing-stone a little south of Hillhead farm.

Three miles to the west of this, across the Perwinnes and Grand-home Mosses, is the very different area of Grandhome or Grand-holm, where the land drops again to the Don and the mills prolifer-ate—for development has tended to follow the river. Grandholm Works are large and old-established woollen-mills. Grandholm House near by is an attractive late 17th century mansion on the E-plan, pleasingly sited above the waterside, of two storeys, with heraldry above the central doorway. A small gabled doocot stands to the east.

To the north of the parish, but central between the Don and the sea, is the quite large Corby Loch, the largest of a group of three, Bishop's and Lily Lochs being in New Machar parish.

Much of the old civil parish of Old Machar is now within the city of Aberdeen, and does not require to be dealt with here.

Oyne. Oyne is a parish in the Benachie area between Don and Urie just west of Chapel of Garioch, small in importance and popu-lation but extending to 10,000 acres, more than half of which com-prises the Benachie range, so prominent an Aberdeenshire feature. Its village, incorporating Old Westhall, flanks the A979 road four miles west of Pitcaple, in the Urie valley, not a particularly attractive spot although the surroundings are fine, "at the back o' Benachie". There was a railway-station here formerly, which accounts for its position—the actual kirkton of Oyne being almost a mile to the east, on higher ground. There are three interesting castellated structures in this parish.

The old kirk of Oyne, dated 1807, stands out on a small hilltop as a notable landmark. But closer investigation reveals a sad story. It is now a farm-store, its surroundings a dump for old cars and rubbish. Its graveyard, because of the rocky site, is a quarter-mile away, at the roadside; and this is in good order, with some old tombstones. The famous bishop, John Leslie, the historian, was parson of Oyne in 1559. The former Free church, nearer Oyne village, is now the parish church, with its own manse behind. In the field above is the Gowk Stane, a single massive standing-stone seven feet high. There was another standing-stone at Mill of Carden a mile to the east, at the junction of the A96 and the A979, but this has gone. Possibly it is one of the Pictish symbol-stones now collected beside the garden of Logie-Elphinstone, in Chapel of Garioch parish. Still remaining, however is the important stone-circle on the whin-covered hilltop at Hatton of Ardoyne farm a mile north-west of Oyne village. An interesting story is told of this. Many years ago two of the stones were removed to form gateposts for a field, but horses could hardly be induced to pass through the gate so formed. Eventually the farmer decided to replace the stones in the circle—and it was noted that whereas it had taken two horses all their time to haul the stones *down* the hill, one horse took them back uphill quite easily!

North of Oyne village lies the wooded estate of Westhall, with its small but most interesting castle of the 16th century, a more modern mansion attached. It is an L-shaped, parapeted tower, extended to the east in the 17th century, with a conical-roofed stair-tower on this wing. An elaborately corbelled stair-turret rises in the re-entrant, over a squinch arch. The walls are massive and the windows small, the basement being vaulted. Westhall was a property of the bishops of Aberdeen, and came at the Reformation to a branch of the Gordons. Gordon of Westhall was Collector of Cess in 1649. James Horn, vicar of Elgin, bought the property in 1681, marrying a daughter of the 7th Leslie laird of Pitcaple. An heiress carried Westhall to the Dalrymple-Elphinstones of near by Logie-Elphinstone, who added Horn to their name.

In the low ground of a pleasant green howe south-east of the kirkton stands the impressive ruin of Harthill Castle, a most delightful place which has not gone so far that it might not be saved. It is an excellent example of a Z-planned fortalice of the early 17th century, unusual in that its gatehouse (for the former curtain-walled enclosure) has largely survived, one of the very few to do so. The castle is tall, with square and circular towers and angle-turrets, the moulded doorway still having its deep socket for a draw-bar. There are many other interesting features. It was allegedly built by Patrick Leith, a cadet of Leithhall, in 1638, but its appearance suggests a slightly earlier date. The first Leith laird had a charter of Harthill in 1531. Young Harthill was a noted supporter of the great Montrose, and was executed for it in 1647. The brother who succeeded was a different type, and quarrelsome. He came to blows with the provost of Aberdeen, in church there, to the effusion of blood, declaring that the worthy provost was "a doitted cock and ane ass!" Imprisoned, he tried to set fire to the jail. Four generations later the last laird burned Harthill deliberately behind him and went off to London, to die a pauper.

Oyne parish has still another fortified house, the Place of Tilly-four, situated five miles south of Oyne village beyond the barrier of Benachie. Picturesquely set by the Don where it winds through the wooded hills four miles north-west of Monymusk, it is an interesting small fortalice of the late 16th century, on an older site, which has been greatly restored and extended in 1884 after falling into semi-ruin. The additions and alterations, done in the same style of architecture, make it difficult to tell what is old and what new, particularly as the roof-level of the original house was altered. The old part is sturdy, almost squat, L-planned, with a short stair-turret corbelled out in the re-entrant supported on a squinch. The courtyard to the south has been entered by an arched gateway. A renewed panel over the door is dated 1626. Tillyfour originally belonged to the Earls of Mar, as a hunting-seat. The lands passed to the Leslies in 1508 and Sir John Leslie of Tillyfour was created a baronet in 1628. But the Leslies have been long gone.

The dramatic range of Benachie should really be described under Oyne parish, but it is more convenient to do so under Chapel of Garioch, at the other side of the hill.

Peterculter. Although now more or less an extension of Aberdeen city, almost a superior residential suburb, Peterculter is in fact an interesting place in its own right, not yet having altogether lost its independent identity. It is a large Deeside parish, as well as an overgrown village, covering some 16 square miles, with much unspoiled and as yet undeveloped country to the north, away from the main river and roadside area. The busy A93 North Deeside highway does detract from the character of that lower section, however much it brings in material benefit. The Milltimber and Murtle areas of the parish, to the east, are partly dealt with under Banchory-Devenick and Cults, in Kincardineshire, into which they merge. There are claims, as at Maryculter across the Dee, that the original name was Petra-cultura, which sounds romantic; but more likely the culter part, pronounced cooter, stems from *cuil-tir*, Gaelic for the back-land.

The main street and shopping area, with hotels, guest-houses and large villas, demands no description other than that it is clean, neat and the road broad and busy. There is more interest below the road, in the haughlands of the Dee. Here stands the parish church, granite-built in 1779, with a small belfry, and dedicated as was its predecessor to St. Peter. The older church stood immediately to the south. There are many old flat gravestones in the kirkyard, one dated 1678, but because these are face-up they are largely indecipherable from weather-wear. There is a mort-house for guarding against body-snatchers; and a most attractive modern memorial-enclosure, planted with heather, for the ashes of those cremated, something which might well be copied elsewhere. St. Peter's Well lay at the foot of the kirkyard, now filled in.

The Gormack and Leuchars Burns, from the higher ground, unite to form the Culter Burn, which flows into the Dee here, and gave water-power for a number of mills. Of these the great Culter Paper Mills founded 1750, are very prominent, at the west end of the village, although no longer relying on water-power. This is the main employer of labour hereabouts, fortunately tucked away discreetly in its wooded den and so spoiling no prospects. Farther down are the meal-mills of Kinnerty; and still lower the rather picturesque Gavin's former snuff-mill, dated 1840, once producing three hundred-weight of snuff a week, now being converted into a dwelling-house. The low-lying area due east of this, and actually on the other side of the river, is known as Inch of Culter and was once an island in the Dee.

The A93 crosses the den of the Culter Burn by a high bridge, and here is a feature worth halting to see. The sides of the den are deep, rocky and precipitous; and, standing on a ledge of the north face near by, is the brightly painted statue of Rob Roy MacGregor, high above the weir, striking amongst Scots pines. The original may have been a ship's figurehead, which has required renewal. Rob Roy visited his kinsman Dr. James Gregory hereabouts in 1714, and is alleged to have leapt the Culter Burn, in some pursuit; but most assuredly he did not leap it here, for the precipice is perhaps 100 feet high. At the other, west end of the bridge, is a high knuckle of wooded knoll wedged between two bends of the burn, a most strong defensive site. At the summit of this is, not the remains of a castle, as might be looked for, but Peterculter's tower-like war memorial. The view therefrom is good. Farther up the stream, above a reservoir for the paper-mill, were carding and sawmills.

Still on the low ground, but crowning a gentle green eminence of fields a mile to the south-west, is the site of the Roman marching-camp of Normandykes, 938 by 543 yards, covering 48 acres, supposed to have been constructed by Lollius Urbicus, of Antonine Wall fame, and at one time thought to be the Devana of Ptolemy. Only a trace of ditch and rampart remain. A cistern and well here were filled in after accidents, in recent times. At the small farm of Cobblestock to the east, in the steading, is an ancient font said to have been brought from the pre-Reformation church of Dalmaik, in Drumoak parish.

The land rises fairly steeply above the main road, and most of the parish lies on this high ground, reaching 706 feet at Kingshill. Terraced housing, even with much modern development, only climbs a short distance, whereafter the countryside is remarkably rural and unspoiled considering its proximity to the city, with heather, birch-scrub, old pines and much modern planting. Culter House stands within a wooded property half a mile to the north, now a boarding-house for St. Margaret's School for Girls. It is large, but has as nucleus a late 17th century ha' hoose. It shows the arms of Cumming of Culter, descended from the Comyns who acquired the lands at the end of the 13th century and retained them until 1726. Countesswells is another old mansion, also of the late 17th century, in this parish, mentioned under Cults. And at the small estate of Binghill, between these two, there is a stone-circle in the grounds.

Peterhead and Inverugie. This burgh, famous for its granite quarries and its great convict prison, is not nearly so grim a place as might be thought, having much character and an interesting history, as well as quite a spectacular situation. The town, with a population of 12,700, is the largest north of Aberdeen until Inverness is reached; and there is a parish of 9000 acres. It was called Peter Ugie until the late 16th century, its pre-Reformation church being dedicated to St. Peter, and the then village lying just south of the Ugie estuary. Inverugie community, with its castle, lies two miles to the north-west. Peterhead is often locally called the Blue Town, the town of the "blue Mogganers". This refers to the long blue stockings the fisherman used to wear, *mogan* being Gaelic for boot-stockings.

Peterhead, which prior to the Reformation belonged to the Abbey of Deer, was acquired by the Keiths, Earls Marischal, in 1560; and George, 5th Earl, founded the village in 1593, it being created a burgh of barony. This was on Keith Inch, the low-lying rocky islet which lies just off the headland, and is now part of the harbour area, reached by a swing-bridge. There was a tall T-planned castle of the period here, now completely gone. Indeed practically all of the original village and warehouses is now demolished or derelict, and the site has been used for a rubbish-dump; but this unhappy state of affairs is scheduled to improve, for here are to be the depots and service facilities for great new North Sea oil and gas developments, which are going to make such an impact on Peterhead. This Keith Inch plays a valuable part in providing a breakwater for the large triple harbour contrived by the renowned engineers Smeaton (1773) and Telford (1818). Petitions had been constantly presented to Parliament for the creation of a great harbour of refuge here—no fewer than 30 insurance establishments, shipping companies and other bodies signing it—for the stormy nature of this area of the North Sea has always been notorious, a state of affairs which the advent of the oil-rigs will much publicise in future. This is the most easterly point of Scotland. The fine harbour facilities, for long so greatly appreciated by seafarers, are now the main seat of the inshore fishing-fleets, since the deep-sea trawlers have so largely monopolised Aberdeen. And they are just what the oil-men require.

Oddly enough, after the forfeiture of the Earls Marischal for their share in the Jacobite Risings, the superiority of the town was purchased, in 1728, by a girls' school, in the shape of the Merchant Maidens' Hospital, of Edinburgh—the well-known Mary Erskine, or Queen Street, School—a strange situation for so masculine a place.

The burgh soon moved on to the mainland from Keith Inch, and became a self-governing authority in 1774 and a parliamentary burgh in 1833. The old Town House of 1788 stands at the top end of Broad Street—which is something of a marketplace—but has been demoted from its original function, and indeed its appearance spoiled by the removal of its twin forestairs to the former door at first-floor level. It has a spire of 125 feet. In front, on an elevated and stepped forecourt, is a statue to Field-Marshal Keith, a brother of the Earl Marischal, forfeited after the 1715 Rising, who rose high in the service of Prussia and was killed in 1758. The statue, a copy of one in Germany, was presented to Peterhead by William I, King of Prussia, in 1868. Near by in the centre of Broad Street, rises the tall granite pillar of the Mercat Cross, surmounted by the Marischal arms, erected 1832. And at the foot of this wide street is the handsome Arbuthnot House, of the Georgian period, former home of the Arbuthnot family long prominent locally. It is now the Town House, retaining much excellent period decoration, although extended.

The parish church, or Muckle Kirk, stands at the south-west end of the town, a large and quite impressive building of 1803 seating 1800, with a spire of 118 feet, but no kirkyard—which is still at the site of the original St. Peter's church a little to the west, at the southern entry to the town proper, where it climbs a bank, with many old gravestones. Here is a pyramidal-roofed bell-tower, to the west, with a Dutch bell of 1647; and to the east the remains of chancel and arch of the pre-Reformation chapel. Near by, to the east, are the Kirkburn tweed and blanket mills, with a modern showroom, and in the same vicinity the large processed-food factory of Crosse & Blackwell, major employers of labour. A fairly modern hospital is in the same Kirktown area.

Amongst other features of the town are the academy, founded in 1846 "for affording the means of a liberal education for all classes of the inhabitants"; the Episcopal church of St. Peter, in Merchant Street, of 1814; the museum and library at the corner of Queen Street, with interesting items of old Peterhead, including the former Town House bell cast for George, Earl Marischal of Scotland in 1725. The coastguard-station lies to the north of the harbour area, and the lifeboat-station to the south. Near the latter is the site of the former pavilioned Wine Well, demolished 1936, the most celebrated of the many mineral wells—Peterhead in 1793 advertising itself as a spa. Many of the old streets and lanes remain, in the compact town on its thrusting promontory, seeming to huddle together closely against the North Sea winds—such as Love Lane, Maiden Street, Tolbooth Wynd and Uphill Lane. In contrast, an interesting block of very modern but traditional-style five-storey flats rises opposite the Muckle Kirk.

There are three named "suburbs" of the main town—Roanheads to the north, former fishermen's quarters; Buchanhaven once an independent fishing-village, with its own jetty and sandy beach, now incorporated in Peterhead but retaining its old parts unspoiled although the new housing area on the higher ground, with its large new school, is less than distinguished; and Cairntrodlie to the west, where is most of the modern development

Strangely enough, the two features which many people are apt to associate with Peterhead, are not really at the town at all. The great prison is actually at the village of Burnhaven, a mile to the south beyond Peterhead Bay with its park flanking the beach. Two long breakwaters stretch from north to south across the mouth of this bay, creating a huge sheltered area, that to the south built by convict labour. The prison buildings do not unduly dominate. Nevertheless Burnhaven is not the most attractive part of Peterhead area. On its Meet-hill to the west—a former moot-hill or seat of baronial justice—rises a tall tower-like monument celebrating the repeal of the Corn Laws. The Glenugie Distillery, makers of the popular Long John whisky, lies at Invernettie just at the south end of Burnhaven. The famed Peterhead granite quarries are, in fact, in the Boddam area still farther south.

North of Peterhead the Ugie enters the sea by a narrow estuary, which the A92 crosses some two miles up, near Inverugie. The river valley is pleasant here, with some of the woodland so scarce in Buchan. Here is Inverugie Castle, actually in St. Fergus parish, but conveniently described here, former seat of the Earls Marischal, now badly collapsed although comparatively intact not so long ago. It was a courtyard-type castle of the late 16th and 17th centuries, with two large round towers linked by an oblong main block, an unusual plan. Four storeys high, the towers rose a storey higher, with a lower 17th century wing projecting northwards at the west end. There is still an arched gateway to the courtyard, but the wall coping to the side has gone, with its coach-and-horses carvings, dated 1670, similar to those at Keithhall, Inverurie. Anciently there was a Cheyne motte-and-bailey castle near by, of which the Keiths married the heiress. They then built an earlier stone castle here in 1380. Here was born the famous Field-Marshal Keith.

There are quite a number of modern houses going up in the pleasing vicinity, around the former hamlet and modern mill. There is a picturesque old three-arch bridge crossing the Ugie amongst the meadows.

Strangely, there is another large castle less than a mile away to the north-west up this valley, Ravenscraig, originally called Craig of Inverugie. It is an older structure, with walls of up to 11 feet thick, on the L-plan; and though very ruinous, much more remains standing, amongst old trees, than at Inverugie. The basement is vaulted, and a mural straight stair rises to first-floor level, above which a turnpike continues, to develop into a circular tower at top, highly unusual. There was an oratory or chapel in the thickness of the west wall. This also was a Cheyne stronghold which passed to the Keiths. James VI was here for "the Laird of Craig of Inverugie's daughter's marriage". It was the seat of the barony of Torthorston.

James VIII, sometimes called the Old Pretender, landed for his ill-fated bid to regain the Stewart throne at Peterhead, in December 1715, a non-heroic figure who cost the Keiths and Peterhead dear. Earlier, in 1642, the town was granted a supernatural manifestation and warning: " . . . in a seamanis house at Peterheid there was hard, upone the night, beatting of drums, uther tymes sounding of trumpettis, playing of pifferis and ringing of bellis, to the astoneishment of the heireris. Trubles follouit."

Pitsligo, Rosehearty and Sandhaven. Pitsligo parish, of 5000 acres, lies along the coast west of Fraserburgh, the most northerly parish of Aberdeenshire. Rosehearty is its largest village and the northernmost point. And Sandhaven is another fishing village two miles to the east. There is a hamlet called Peathill, with the parish church, inland a mile. The countryside here begins to change from the typical flat and bare Buchan landscape to the hills and cliffs of the Banffshire border.

Rosehearty has its own sturdy character, with the old fishing village at its west end not unattractive, its low-browed cottages gable-end to the streets, many brightly painted. There is a large harbour, now less used than once, when there were 88 boats working from here. A modern swimming-pool adjoins. The Square is at the east end, with shops and a bank, and open to the north. Just round the eastern corner is the only remaining ancient building, the former Dower House of Pitsligo, dating from 1573, but with a dormer pediment built in of only 1766, all now only a roofless shell. The streets follow a regular pattern and the village, with a population of 1140, is large enough to be a small burgh. Indeed it was created a burgh of barony for Lord Pitsligo in 1681. It had been founded, allegedly, in the 14th century, partly by a company of shipwrecked Danes. A large school lies to the south, as does the rather gaunt former Free church on the brae (1844) now an Established congregation. On the hillside above the village are two prominent tower-like monuments, one a war memorial, the other a former look-out. The coastline here is sandy to the east, on the links of which was once a chapel, now gone, and rocky with low cliffs to the west, where is the cave of Cowshaven, where the fugitive Lord Pitsligo hid after the Forty-Five.

Behind Rosehearty, half a mile and a mile south-east respectively, are two ruined castles, Pitsligo and Pittullie, both originally belonging to the Frasers of Philorth, oddly close together and sharing the same bare ridge. Pitsligo is the older, and Rosehearty is really its castleton. It is now very ruinous, but sufficient remains to show that it has been a powerful and impressive establishment, developing from a massive 15th century keep into a major courtyard castle, with flanking drum-tower, gunlooped curtain-walls and considerable subsidiary buildings. All has been enclosed within a pleasance and orchard, with high walls and an arched gateway with heraldry, to the west. The courtyard doorway is surmounted by the royal arms of Scotland and James VI's initials, dated 1577. James was only 11 then, but it is an indication that the lands were held direct of the Crown. Pitsligo passed from the Frasers to the Forbeses of Druminnor, by marriage, in the 15th century. Alexander Forbes was created Lord Pitsligo in 1633—and it was his grandson who became famous for his wanderings as a fugitive after 1745. It is sad that this fine castle is so poorly cherished.

Pittullie, to the east, has unusual features. Dating from the very end of the 16th century, and later, it has a long and comparatively low main block, with a taller stair-tower at the west end, provided with strange turret-like windows at the angles and a stair-turret, in the re-entrant, rising high above. There are other turrets, and empty panel-spaces. The basement is not vaulted. The Frasers held these lands from the 14th century, but eventually they passed to the Cumine family. Although now also very ruinous, it is said to have been occupied as recently as 1850.

Sandhaven village lies a mile north-east of Pittullie Castle, and is smaller than Rosehearty and less attractive. It has much modern housing, two churches, and a small new school. There is a boat-building yard at its harbour. This west end of the village is called Pittullie, more pleasing of aspect, retaining the character of a typical Buchan fishermen's community. A rocky beach lies eastward called the Phingask Shore.

South of Rosehearty a mile, beyond Pitsligo Castle, stands the parish church in an isolated position 170 feet higher than the village, and from its prominence sometimes known as the Visible Kirk. The building is modern but stands in the old kirkyard with the ruin of its predecessor of 1633 near by. The parish was disjoined from Aberdour, to the west, that year, and its first minister was the famous Andrew Cant, the Covenant leader. The old building has an elaborate belfry of that date, and considerable heraldry, with a panel dated 1634 and *A.L.P.* for Alexander, Lord Pitsligo, the builder, with skull, crossbones and hour-glass. Inside, the south wing is the Pitsligo Aisle, with the family burial-vault beneath, the floor of the aisle being four feet higher than that of the church. There has been much good woodwork here, now gone, a moulded stone arch and a pointed arched window. In the vault are interred generations of the Forbeses, from the first lord, 1636, to Charles Forbes-Trefusis, died 1893. There are many old gravestones of the 17th century and later, in the kirkyard.

Half a mile to the west, prominent on an eminence, is a tall and decorative doocot of the 19th century, on the farm of Smithyhillock, and seaward of this, the former lairdship of Braco Park, now a farm, with its own small square 18th century doocot and remains of a high old wall for the garden. The views from this hillside, to Troup Head and the cliff-bound coastline to the west, are very fine. There is a small crossroads hamlet of farms at Mid Ardlaw, two miles to the south.

Premnay and Auchleven. Premnay is a small, hilly parish of

5000 acres picturesquely set under the towering western slopes of the Benachie range, in the valley of the Gadie Water "at the back o' Benachie". Auchleven is its village, at a crossroads on the B992 and a side-road to Leslie. The civil parish boundary runs right up to the larger village of Insch, two miles to the north, and Rothney, a "suburb" thereof is really in Premnay parish—a rather ridiculous situation.

Auchleven is a pleasant, medium-sized village, with some new housing and a hotel, on the Gadie Water. Formerly it boasted a woollen and a meal-mill, but these are no more. There are no special features, and the one-time St. James's Chapel here is now not known. Half a mile to the south-east is the seat of the Premnay estate, Lickleyhead Castle, a tall and attractive L-planned fortalice dated 1629, although it almost certainly contains an older nucleus. It has typical Aberdeenshire two-storeyed angle-turrets, with tiny round upper windows, as at Castle Fraser, and also a long narrow stair-turret in the re-entrant, corbelled out to the square at top to give access to the gabled watch-chamber in the wing. The basement is vaulted, and the hall on first floor a fine apartment. It was originally a seat of the Leith family, and there was a Patrick Leith of Lickleyhead in 1574; but it was sold in 1624 to the heir of Leslie Castle near by, who presumably built the castle as it now is. It has passed through a number of hands since then.

The parish church of Premnay is not at Auchleven but more than a mile north-east, beside a farm on a side-road. The building is small and neat, in granite, dating from 1792, with an apparently old bell. The graveyard is across the road, alongside the manse, a peaceful and lovely place, with some old flat tombstones but no trace of the original church, which no doubt stood in the midst. Half a mile to the north-east is the large farm of Overhall, formerly the seat of a branch of the Leiths, also the Gordons, its large farmhouse still showing signs of its late 17th century origins. Edingarioch, just south-west of Auchleven, was another Leith estate now a farm. Two miles south of Auchleven, east of the B992 road to Keig, is the deserted farm of Druidstone, on the lower slopes of Black Hill, and here is a small stone-circle of four uprights in a group of trees.

The countryside of Premnay parish is pleasantly scenic, mainly cattle-pasture with not much arable and many rough and whinny patches. The great Whitehaugh planted forest covers the low hills to the west, and to the east the heights of Hermit Seat (1564 feet) and Watch Craig (1619 feet) enclose the view, the latter with a prehistoric settlement site high on its northern shoulder.

Rathen, Inverallochy and Cairnbulg. Rathen parish of 10,000 acres lies south and east of Fraserburgh, with the twin fishing villages of Inverallochy and Cairnbulg at its north-east corner. Much of the well-known landmark of Mormond Hill comes into this parish.

Rathen's kirkton lies towards the south, just off the A92 from

Aberdeen, a scattered hamlet in pleasant country, with school and parish church. Oddly enough Rathen post-office is almost two miles away, near the former railway-station, in a rather bare area of small farms. The church is quite large, Gothic in style, of 1870, with a steeple, and stands apart. Its predecessor is a little to the east, in an ancient kirkyard, an ivy-clad ruin, with an arched entrance inscribed *ALEXANDER FRASER OF PHILORTH PATRON*, with heraldry. Internally there is an ogee-headed piscina and aumbry. This pre-Reformation part communicates with a 17th century extension by a wide chamfered archway. The older part was dedicated to St. Ethernan, and the later aisle was added by Fraser of Memsie in 1646. Though the belfry is dated 1782, its bell is of 1643. In the old church, in 1644, occurred a renowned supernatural happening: "about tyme of morneying prayer for diverse dayes togither, hard in the church a queire of musicke, both of woces, organes and other instrumentes." The sound came from the upper loft "where the people used to heare service, but they could sie nothing".

Mormond House, a former Gordon lairdship, with classical mansion, lies under Mormond Hill (768 feet) to the south, a great whaleback crowned now by the futuristic-looking installations of the R.A.F. Signal Station.

Memsie crossroads hamlet, where the B9032 crosses the A981, lies two miles to the north-west of Rathen; and at a lesser crossroads half a mile to the east, where is the school, is the remarkable Memsie Cairn, a large and well-preserved example of a round burial-cairn of stones, 15 feet high and 60 in circumference, now in care of the Department of the Environment. A beaker and broken leaf-shaped sword were found here. A sand and gravel-pit workings is near by, on Cairnmuir. Almost a mile to the south is the late 17th and 18th century mansion of Memsie, a tall and attractive house with good coped chimneystacks, central gablet and two small linked pavilions. It belonged to a branch of the Philorth Frasers for three centuries, latterly becoming a farmhouse but again being improved.

Another half-mile south is House of Auchiries, which fell on evil days. Now roofless and grievously covered in ivy, it has been an E-planned and commodious laird's-house of the 17th century, within a walled garden to east and north. The two wings stretch westwards, with the doorway between protected by two shot-holes. Internally the unvaulted kitchen has a wide arched fireplace, though the hall's, above, is roll-moulded. A later wing is to the rear. The overgrowth of ivy blankets all external features, but the house appears complete to the wall-head and might yet be saved. The domestic offices to the west are being restored. Auchiries was a lairdship of the Ogilvie family, and here the famous fugitive Lord Pitsligo hid for a time in 1756 and died here in 1762.

Two miles the other side of Rathen, almost on the Lonmay border, is another large burial-cairn, at Concraigs, in less good condition than Memsie. Due north, past the former railway-station nearly three miles, is Cairnbulg Castle, the magnificent restored seat of

Lord Saltoun. It is an impressive towering stronghold of the 14th, 15th and 16th centuries, with later additions and restorations, basically a tall and massive keep, with parapet and gabled caphouse, and a circular flanking-tower of the courtyard, now linked to the main house. The walls are very thick, with mural chambers, and also a pit within the walling for prisoners. The present building appears to date from after 1375 when Sir Alexander Fraser, grandson of Bruce's brother-in-law, married a daughter of the Earl of Ross and obtained these lands. The 8th laird founded Fraserburgh in 1569, and the 10th succeeded, through his mother, to the peerage of Saltoun. For long the castle was in ruins, when the family seat was Philorth House to the south-west, but this was burned in 1915, and Lord Saltoun is back in the restored Cairnbulg.

Rather strangely, only two miles to the east rise the tall ruins of another strong castle, Inverallochy, in a field flanking the B9033. This has been a fortalice of some importance, now in a crumbling state but impressive still, with a lofty north-east tower and broken curtain-walling 30 feet high in places. A gunloop faces north. This was a Comyn stronghold and allegedly a stone bearing their arms remained above the entrance until comparatively recent times, inscribed *I, JORDAN CUMING, GAT THIS HOUSE AND LAND FOR BIGGING THE ABBEY OF DEER.*

Just as there are twin castles of Cairnbulg and Inverallochy, so there are twin villages—or rather, the joint village of Inverallochy-Cairnbulg, lying on the rocky coast over a mile northwards, across the disused and littered airfield. Inverallochy lies east of the B9107 and Cairnbulg west. There is little to choose from between them, both typical fishing villages with close-set rows of low cottages huddled gable-ended to the narrow streets and lanes. Oddly, there is no harbour at either, boat-shores on the shingle being the former landing-places—though nowadays the fishermen work out from Fraserburgh three miles west. There is a large modern school and a very plain *quod sacra* church.

The Jacobite ballad of 'Logie o' Buchan' was written by George Hacket, the Rathen schoolmaster in 1736. He was deposed.

Rayne, Warthill and Rothmaise. Rayne is a Urieside parish of 8000 acres lying north of the river immediately above Oyne, with the A96 Aberdeen to Huntly road skirting its southern boundary. Warthill, or Wartle, is an old estate and large hamlet to the northwest of the parish; and Rothmaise a district farther north still. The main centre of population is the village of Old Rayne, down beside the Urie and the main road.

Old Rayne was once a burgh of barony, for the barony of Westhall (in Oyne parish). It still has its 17th century mercat cross, a 10-foot shaft of pink granite based on a five-step plinth and surmounted by a saltire weathervane. The bishops of Aberdeen used to have a residence on an eminence in the centre of the village, of which no trace survives. Old Rayne is quite large, and attractively set above the

Airlie. Reekie Linn waterfalls at the mouth of Glen Isla

Broughty Ferry. Claypotts Castle, a seat of the Grahams of Claverhouse

Arbroath Abbey, scene of the signing of the Declaration of Independence

Urie meadows, with considerable modern housing. There is a hotel boasting an outdoor swimming-pool complete with chute and high dive, also a small caravan-park. The St. Laurence Fair used to be held here—locally called Lowran—a famous cattle and horse market, discontinued about 1935. There is quite a large school.

Half a mile east of the village, on the crest of a low hill to Broombrae farm, is a circle of seven stones, only one still upright. This no doubt was the Standing Stones of Rayne where, in 1349, a court was held to settle a dispute between the bishop and one William of St. Michael over the ownership of lands.

The parish church is not at Old Rayne but at the Kirkton, a remote hamlet amongst the fields two miles north-east. The church, known as the White, or Fite Kirk of Rayne, plain but pleasing and with a very lovely outlook over open country, dates from 1789 although the ornate belfry belongs to 1619. There is a large kirkyard, with a manse dating from the 17th century near by. Internally the church is attractive, lit by large windows although the woodwork is dark, with a small gallery and some good stained glass. A huge old key is preserved, and pewter plate, also a stool of repentance. There are memorials to the Leslie lairds of Warthill, 13 of them, from 1513 to 1956. About a quarter-mile west is the Bowman Stone, really only a group of massive flat outcrops, with the foundations of a cottage, alleged to have been the scene of archery contests. The famous John Barbour, author of Barbour's *Bruce*, was parson of Rayne, dying in 1395. Rayne North School lies a mile north of the hamlet, isolated, at a crossroads.

A mile west is the large estate of Warthill, held by the Leslies for so long, and still owned by descendants. An ancient fortalice was replaced by a large Scottish Baronial mansion in 1845, some of which is presently being demolished. An old heraldic panel is built into the south front, under glass, with the Leslie arms and the date 1686; and another, very defaced, is at the rear of the house. Meikle Wartle is a quite picturesque large hamlet with a former inn, lying at a junction of side-roads half a mile to the south-west. William Leslie, second son of the 5th laird, born 1657, schoolmaster at Chapel of Garioch, was persuaded by Count Leslie to go to Rome in 1684, where he embraced the Catholic faith and became professor of theology at Padua, bishop of Laybach and a prince of the Holy Roman Empire.

The Rothmaise area lies along the B9000 road from Oldmeldrum to Culsalmond—and which presumably follows the direct line of the Roman road which is said to traverse the parish. There is no village or hamlet, and the former lairdly establishment is now the farm of Rothmaise Mains, with only a single weatherworn stone, let into a gable, to show for past glories. On the slopes of Rothmaise Hill (854 feet) to the north-east is the site of the former Chapel of the Virgin and St. Mary's Well. And above, on the skyline, is the Black Cairn, an ancient burial-mound. The Crichton and Fedderate Stones, now allegedly badly dilapidated, are said to lie hereabouts,

but could not be traced. A duel was fought here between representatives of these two lairdly families.

Rhynie and Essie. This is a large parish of 13,000 hilly acres,
united in 1760, in the heartland of the Gordons, on the Water of
Bogie under the towering peak of Tap o' Noth. Rhynie is also a large
village, situated on the Moor of Rhynie. It surrounds a railed-in
green, or small central park, with shops, school, hotel and modern
parish church, its hospital now a children's home. Fairs used to be
held here. The green is interesting in that it boasts four small
standing-stones, two at the west gate, two at the east, presumably the
remains of a stone-circle here. The present parish church, to the
west of the green, with a tower of 1889, is commodious and bright
within, with a gallery. There is a slightly broken 12th century font
at the entrance. A small Episcopal church of St. Mary's stands
quarter of a mile off, on the side-road to Druminnor, a pretty little
building inside and out.

The old parish church of Rhynie stood down in the haugh of the
Bogie half a mile to the south, on its own side-road past the hospital.
The graveyard is still here, in a sequestered position amongst old
trees. There are many old tombstones, some leaning against the
walling. Notably, there is a deep stone coffin lying beside a pointed-
arched canopy, relic of the former church, the recess now containing
a Gordon gravestone of 1668. Against the wall externally, at the
gate, are two fine Pictish symbol-stones. The larger depicts an
unusual dog-like creature, cut off at the middle, with double-disc and
Z-rod, and mirror-and-comb symbols; the other, a crescent and
V-rod with mirror.

There is another Pictish sculpture near by, the Craw or Cro
Stone, standing isolated in a field between the graveyard and the
main A97, not far from the road. It shows a spirited rendering of the
Celtic beast and a fish symbol. There is alleged to be another symbol-stone somewhere in the vicinity, depicting a man carrying a rod,
but this could not be traced.

Altogether Rhynie is a notable area for pre- and proto-historic
relics. The Tap o' Noth itself sports a vitrified fort of considerable
size, with a kiln and burial-cairns to the west. Also on the summit is
Clochmaloo, the Stone of St. Moluag, famous Celtic missionary.
Below at the farm of Upper Ord, actually in Auchindoir parish but
near Rhynie, are the remains of a stone-circle. And on the neighbouring farm of Wheedlemont is another, with an earthwork on
Wheedlemont Hill. At Old Noth farm, three miles to the north on
the A97, is alleged to be a monolith called the Drumel Stone, which
could not be traced. The story is that it was removed to form the
lintel of a steading-door, but the door thereafter was so often found
open and the animals strayed, that the stone was eventually taken
back—and the trouble ceased. Then, near Druminnor Castle to the
south-east of Rhynie, on the Mains farm, is the Corse Stane, in a
wood behind the steading. Despite its singular name, there are

three stones here, one seven feet high, one a recumbent, the other fallen. Lastly, on the slopes of the Correen Hills more than a mile to the south, again at Auchindoir parish, is the site of a native fort, at Cairnmore, near where the Battle of Tillyangus was fought (Clatt parish). So Rhynie is something of an archaeologist's paradise.

Essie, a parish since 1227, came badly out of the parish union. The site of its church is three miles to the west, on the Dufftown A941 road, where there is still a graveyard with many old stones but no sign of the kirk. A mile to the east is the site of the formerly great Gordon castle of Lesmoir, now completely gone save for a few green banks amongst roadside trees, with pigs in possession. This was an important branch of the Gordon clan and it was demolished by General David Leslie in 1647, who hanged 27 Highlanders, royalists. A relic does survive of this castle, strangely enough, over three miles away, in unexpected situation. On the farm of Milton of Noth, a lairdship of the youngest son of the first Gordon of Craig, north of Rhynie, is the former steading of Lochrie, in some trees below the road. Built into the gable of the cottage here, now abandoned, is a moulded stone fireplace of the 16th century, surmounted by a large heraldic panel in red sandstone, with the arms of Gordon of Lesmoir, with supporters and a defaced Latin inscription. Why this came to be built-in here is not clear.

An even more significant link with the Gordons, in this parish, is Scurdargue now only a farm, near Lesmoir. Probably, in fact Lesmoir was the seat of the famous Jock o' Scurdargue, who, with his brother, Tam o' Ruthven, maintained the old line of the true Gordons after their heiress cousin of Strathbogie married Sir William Seton and carried the chiefship to the Huntly line. Scurdargue is merely *sgurr dearg*, the red pointed hill, the Gaelic name for Tap o' Noth. The renowned Jock was interred in the kirkyard of Essie.

The enormous Clashindarroch planted forest covers a great area of the hilly ground to the north and west of Rhynie, one of the largest in Aberdeenshire.

Druminnor Castle, though in Auchindoir parish is near Rhynie village, a highly interesting place, the original Castle Forbes, seat of the chiefs of that great clan before they removed to Keig parish. Undoubtedly they were just too near the Gordons, here, for any comfort. Druminnor, after long neglect, was gallantly repurchased by a member of the clan a few years ago, the Hon. Margaret Forbes-Sempill, daughter of Lord Sempill, and restored, largely by her own hands. She made an excellent job of it—but unhappily died before its fullest completion. It is an unusual and attractive fortalice of the late 16th century, incorporating a stronghold of 1440, built on the L-plan, with the wing circular at base and corbelled out to the square above to form a gabled watch-chamber. There is a stair-turret in the re-entrant, many wide gunloops, and three notable heraldic panels above the door. Because of the steeply sloping site, there are two storeys more on the south front, making it look very tall here. These semi-subterranean basements are vaulted, and the kitchen has a great arched fireplace. In the vaulted chamber next to it the fireplace lintel has the delightful inscription *A HAPPY ROOM 144?. I.R.*—presumably for King James II. Fifteen Gordons are reputed to have found Druminnor less happy, being slain in the hall above, at a banquet. To even list the stirring events connected with this castle, and the Forbeses, would almost entail cataloguing the story of north-east Scotland.

St. Fergus and Rora. Probably comparatively few know of the existence of St. Fergus, or could place it on the map. It is one of those rural Buchan parishes, medium-sized, of 9000 acres, but with no very important or outstanding features. Yet it has its interests. What place in Scotland does not?

St. Fergus, originally called Inverugie parish, and then Langley, lies along the sandy coast between Peterhead and Rattray Head, its southern boundary the River Ugie, its northern a vague line across the open mosses and sandhills. It has a village of the name—or rather, two, for they lie separate about half a mile, one the Kirktown. For the rest, it is farms, bare treeless fields, wide vistas, mosses and long sandy links and beaches, six miles of the last, the highest point being only 164 feet above sea-level. Inverugie Castle is in this parish, just, on the north bank of Ugie; but this is much more conveniently described under Peterhead, along with the neighbouring Ravenscraig Castle on the south bank. But the remote hamlet of Rora, although actually in Longside parish, is nearer St. Fergus, and better dealt with here. Strangely, St. Fergus was for long a detached part of Banffshire—this because the Cheyne lords of Inverugie were also hereditary sheriffs of Banff.

Five miles north of Peterhead, the A92 passes the roadside village of St. Fergus, on its way to Fraserburgh. Most of the village lies back from the road, and this part is quite attractive, with some trees—always precious in Buchan. There is a former Free church. A side-road climbs slightly inland to the Kirktown, with post-office, which stretches along a gentle ridge for some distance. A little apart, at the east end, is the quite large parish church of 1763, renewed 1869, harled and with a small belfry. On the east gable is an inserted stone dated *1616 L.V.K.* Inside it is commodious, a preaching-kirk with a gallery, brightly painted. The manse near by is large, dating from 1766. There is a ruined two-storeyed building, with fireplaces, just outside the kirkyard wall, with apparently 17th century skews—possibly the original school? The kirkyard has no very old stones, these being at the site of its predecessor.

Old St. Fergus Church, dedicated to that Irish 8th century missionary, lies remotely out on the level sandy links almost two miles from the village, beyond North Kirkton farm, but perfectly accessible, the graveyard still in use. Here are many ancient stones. The remains of the pre-Reformation chapel, abandoned 1616, consist of two walls, largely built up with old tombstones, one still containing an aumbry in the former chancel. Buried here is a town clerk of Edinburgh, one Henderson, who died in 1760. There is a mort-house. Along the landward wall of the kirkyard is a row of curly iron hooks to which to tie horses.

The scattered hamlet of Rora lies two miles west of the Kirktown, on the edge of the extensive Rora Moss, and with St. Fergus Moss to the north, a remote and out-of-this-world spot, with small crofts around, its school now abandoned, but still with post-office and hall. Stacks of peat are still to be seen outside the houses, and one of the cottages retains its thatched roof, held down by a network of rope. There were granite quarries here.

Skene and Westhill. Skene is an extensive rural parish of south Aberdeenshire, of about 10,000 acres, nine miles west of Aberdeen, with a large loch and two old villages, Kirkton and Lyne of Skene. And now there is in addition a new community springing up, to the east, called Westhill. There is an ancient estate of Skene, from which an old Scots family takes its name. The area was once fairly bleak moorland, but 19th century planting changed that.

Skene House is a huge, gaunt, pile, set in extensive wooded policies in the western corner of the parish, three miles from the kirkton. There is much old work in the building, its nucleus a typical tall Scots tower-house; but it has been so cluttered up with additions and alterations in the "Gothic" style as to leave little authentic externally. Bruce erected the lands and loch into a barony for his faithful servant Robert Skene, in 1318; so there were Skenes here before that. The last and 28th Skene of that Ilk died in 1827. The Hamiltons bought Skene in 1880, and remain.

The oval Loch of Skene, almost a mile long, of 312 acres, lies in level ground to the south-east, prominent from the A944, with Dunecht woodlands coming close, and tall modern castellated gate-houses therefor near by. It is only 12 feet deep, and a haunt of wild-fowl.

The Kirkton is a sizeable village and growing, half a mile north of the A944, on the B979, and quite attractive. The parish church of 1801 replaces an earlier building dedicated to St. Bride, once belonging to St. Leonard's College, St. Andrews. It is plain, harled and rather squat, but its high windows make the modernised interior bright. There are many old gravestones in the kirkyard, and a mort-safe; also two ancient stone fonts. Near by, in the drive-way to Kirkville House, is an unusual high and slender squared doocot, probably of the early 18th century.

The other old village, Lyne of Skene, lies three miles to the north-east, at the junction of the B972 and the B9126, a less settled-looking place and smaller, more scattered and higher set, but with wide prospects northwards. The former school here has been converted into a community centre. The new community of Westhill is more remarkable, however, for here, just over a mile east of Kirkton, on the old Alford road north of the A944, a large "garden-city" develop-ment is planned, eventually to comprise 2000 houses—mainly for

Aberdeen commuters, of course—of which some 120 have already been built. Westhill will be very carefully laid out, with open parkland, gardens, amenity areas and so on, with houses of varying design. There will be a shopping-centre, schools and recreational facilities. The Arnhall Moss near by, notable for its botany, will be preserved as garden and boating-pond. Westhill was only a hamlet of 90 souls in 1961—though it was larger once, with its own Congregational church and manse and hall, both church and hall now converted into private houses. This new development will make an enormous difference to Skene parish inevitably, especially to the Kirkton near by—where 50 new houses have also been built recently. The rural atmosphere will not be easy to maintain. Just a little east of Westhill is Brodiach farm, originally the Six Mile House, an inn on this old coaching-road. In the stackyard across the road is a huge sundial dated 1790, formed out of a great granite boulder, and inscribed *JOS. ALLAN*. Proctor's Orphanage lies nearer the Kirkton, and dates from 1890, nowadays a family home for seven children run by a small Trust.

There is another community in this parish, Garlogie, three miles to the south-west, south of the loch, on the A974. It is fairly far-flung, with Roadside, Milton and Netherton of Garlogie, as well as the hamlet. An Aberdeen firm established a spinning-mill here in the early 19th century, employing over 100 people to make yarn for its carpet-works, with a school in connection, but all this is gone. There is still an inn. The area is heavily afforested, and in the woodland north of the hamlet are the remains of an ancient fort and some burial-cairns.

All Skene vicinity is rich in archaeological relics, especially stone-circles and standing-stones. A mile north-east of Roadside, on Springhill farm, are two standing-stones, with another 300 yards north of the main A974 near Cairnie. At Cairnie itself is a walled cairn on a mound above the road. A mile north-east of Kirkton is the pine- and whin-clad hill of Keir on which is a circular fort, once thought to be Roman but probably Pictish. And a mile north-west of this, on rising ground, is a single standing-stone to the left of the road: and so on, all around.

There is a particularly interesting stone in an exposed position on the ridge a mile north-west of the last. This is the Drum Stone, where Sir Alexander Irvine of Drum paused on his way to the fatal field of Harlaw and looked back, the last point from which he could see Drum Castle. He told his brother Robert that if he did not return, Robert was to change his name to Alexander and take his new wife—the marriage was not yet consummated—and raise up heirs to Drum in his stead. He died in spectacular fashion in slaying the famous Red Hector of the Battles, chief of the Macleans. His brother carried out instructions to the letter, and all subsequent Irvines of Drum descend from him. The stone stands within walling, carefully preserved, inscribed *DRUM STONE 1411 HARLAW*.

There are two enormous erratic boulders in a sloping field near

South Fornet farm, to the north-west; and more standing-stones near by. Obviously this was a highly significant area in the worship-rites of our Bronze Age forebears.

Strathdon and Corgarff. The name implies the wide valley of the Don; but Strathdon is nowadays accepted to refer to a large parish of 47,700 acres lying near the head of that great river, and its kirkton area—although this is really the hamlet of Bellabeg. The parish was anciently called Invernochty, the Nochty joining Don at Bellabeg. Corgarff is a *quod sacra* parish seven miles farther up the valley, with its well-known castle at Cock Bridge, where the Lecht road to Tomintoul starts its dramatic climb. This all was, and still is, Forbes country, and of much interest as well as fine scenery.

The parish church stands to the east end, on the south side of Don, a large and over-elaborate granite Gothic building of 1853, with a lofty spire. Its crowded graveyard has many old flat stones—and the interior boasts over 30 marble commemorative tablets! There is an enormous memorial to one David Mitchell, outside.

Bellabeg, just across the river, acts as the kirkton village, a pleasant scattered community amongst trees, on the B973, which would be better called Invernochty. The Doune of Invernochty lies just to the west; but this is in Glenbuchat parish, and described thereunder. Bellabeg is where the former Donside coaches used to make their terminus, and has shops, post-office, school and so on. The Lonach Highland Gathering and Games are held here anually. This meeting has a rather different origin from most such games, the Lonach Highland and Friendly Society being formed in 1825 "for the preservation of the Highland garb and language". The Society's hall is at Culquhonnie, half a mile down the road. Here too is a hotel on a terrace site, where markets used to be held; and beside it the ruins of Culquhonnie Castle. This was a stronghold of the Forbeses of Towie, and the tradition is that it was never completed. It is ivy-clad and very ruinous today but certain features survive despite neglect, showing it to have been a typical L-planned fortalice of the 16th century, with vaulted basements, including a pit or prison, and another vaulted chamber on the first floor, which is unusual. There are slit windows and gunloops.

Castle Newe—pronounced Nyowe—estate lies to the east, a Forbes property still although the mansion has been demolished. It was a large granite edifice built by the famous Archibald Simpson in 1831, engulfing an old fortalice of 1604—but both are now gone, the laird living at Allargue near Corgarff. About four miles east-wards, with a stretch of Glenbuchat parish intervening, is the Glen-kindie estate and hamlet; but this is described under Towie, which it adjoins. The Deskry Water, an important tributary of Don, comes in from the south between Newe and Glenkindie; and on the hill of Clachcurr above are two prehistoric burial cairns.

Half a mile west of Strathdon Church is the picturesque bridge of Poldullie, carrying a side-road across Don, 70 feet high, narrow and single-arched, built in 1765, with the Pot of Poldullie below—a wide pool in woodland at a bend of the river, very attractive. A little farther west the main road threads the hamlet of Roughpark, with a former steep-roofed church, shop, garage and sawmill, amongst trees. A series of old estates then flank the river to the north. The first is Candacraig, with a large modern mansion replacing the early house of ten generations of Anderson lairds. Then there is a fine E-shaped, probably early 18th century, house at Edinglassie, with later extensions, on a pleasant terrace site almost a mile up from the main road, with later extensions, built by the Forbeses; as was Inverernan at the mouth of small Glen Ernan a little farther west, also E-shaped and of 1764 date. And another mile on is the former old mansion of Skellater, again E-shaped and probably of the late 17th century, a modestly fine place now unfortunately abandoned and used as a straw-barn. This house might still be saved. General John Forbes of Skellater married a princess of Portugal and became a field-marshal of that country, dying in 1809.

A mile beyond Skellater, the old military road, now the A939, strikes south to climb over to Deeside, reaching 1738 feet in the process. A quarter-mile along it, south of Don, is the interesting tiny Roman Catholic chapel of Tornahaish, still functioning. It has pleasing features, in a delightful situation, and boasts a beautiful communion-chalice. There is an attractively restored private cottage-residence attached. Sometimes the little chapel is packed, in the holiday season. The former old inn at West Tornahaish still shows its rows of bunk-beds for travellers. There is a youth hostel in the neighbourhood.

The Corgarff area is now reached, with the main Donside road rising to 1280 feet. Here there is a scattered community with school, and a small church amongst trees, a preaching-kirk of 1834, built by Sir Charles Forbes of Castle Newe—as was the school. There are five heraldic panels fronting the gallery.

Almost two miles onward is Cock Bridge, near the small eminence known as The Cock, where the road turns sharply northwards to climb very steeply, by the famous Lecht route to Tomintoul, notably one of the first to be blocked by snow in winter. There is a hotel here, at Allargue, at the foot of the hill. And near by is Allargue House, another E-planned mansion with later extensions, on a fine terrace site with splendid views, now the seat of the Forbes baronets of Newe, representing the ancient line of the Lords Pitsligo. Within its estate, to the west, is the dower-house of Auchmore, a small, old white-washed house of 1650, much altered in the 18th and 19th centuries, plain but pleasing.

Corgarff Castle rises bold and stark across the valley to the south, a dramatic stronghold with a dramatic history, recently restored. It is a tall, plain tower of four storeys and a gabled caphouse, built in the 16th century and altered after the Forty-Five as a military fort to dominate this Jacobite area for the government. It still has the loopholed curtain-wall of that period surrounding. There is a machicolated projection above the doorway for the casting down of missiles. The basement is vaulted. Cargarff belonged to the earldom of Mar but was annexed to the Crown in 1435, and given to the Elphinstones—one of whom presumably built the present castle. The Earl of Mar recovered it in 1626; but after the failure of Mar's Rising of 1715 it passed to the Forbeses. Not that the Forbeses, so prominent locally, had not already taken an interest in it, for we read of an Elphinstone complaint to the Privy Council in 1607 that Alexander Forbes of Towie, and others, came to his fortalice of "Torgarffa and with grite geistis, foir-hammeris" and other instruments forcibly broke in and fortified it as a house of war, assisted by "Highland thieves and limmers". It was burned by the Jacobites in 1689 to deny it to the Government forces, and again by the Government in 1716 to deny it to the Jacobites. In 1571 it had been burned also, the scene of the tragedy of Edom o' Gordon and the deaths of Lady Forbes and her family—rather than Towie Castle, sometimes alleged as the scene.

Just north of Allargue and Corgarff lies the Banffshire border.

Strathdon altogether is a highly interesting area, well worth exploring, its side-glens and hill walks offering a great variety of attractions—especially when Glenbuchat is included. Five weems or Pictish souterrains have been discovered in the parish, but these have not been maintained. There were also holy wells and springs at various points.

Strichen. This is a small town and Buchan parish, at the south-western foot of Mormond Hill (768 feet), 10 miles south by west of Fraserburgh, the town or large village with a population of 1700, the parish of 10,000 acres. Mormond Hill is well known nowadays for its great R.A.F. Signal Station, radar and early-warning installations, which stand out hugely on the crest, a noted landmark; also for the White Horse cut on its south-western slopes, and the Stag on the south-eastern. The first was the work of a somewhat eccentric Laird of Strichen, Captain Fraser, who entertained Dr. Samuel Johnson. He also erected a building on the summit, its ruin still there, known as Rob Gibb's Hunting Lodge. And he founded the village of New Leeds, four miles east of Strichen, which was intended to rival the great Yorkshire city of that name, but which languished rather and is now not much more than a hamlet. The Stag on Mormond Hill was cut later, in 1870. Both these figures are picked out in white quartz rock in the turf, and catch the eye from afar.

Strichen, which was originally the village of Mormond, was laid out in 1764 by Lord Strichen of Session, father of the aforementioned laird, at the period when so many Aberdeenshire lairds were improving their estates and seeking to create employment and better accommodation for their tenantry. His lofty aims were "to promote the Arts and Manufactures of this country, and for the accommodation of Tradesmen of all Denominations, Manufacturers and other industrious people to settle within the same". It is a regularly planned place, not unattractive—much more so than, say, New Pitsligo or New Byth, of the same period. Moreover its surroundings are more undulating, wooded and picturesque than most of central Buchan. Perhaps it never quite reached the heights Lord Strichen envisaged. But it has a town house of 1816, with steeple, churches, banks, hotels, schools and an excellent library, though its hospital is now a fish-net factory. Alas, though the town still flourishes, the great mansion of Strichen House is now a gaunt shell, a Grecian pile with Doric pillars, in the wooded and landscaped grounds laid out by Gilpin. This mansion replaced the old fortalice, and was built by the Bairds of Gartsherrie, ironmasters, who bought the estate from the Frasers—who, having succeeded to the peerage of Lovat, moved north to those great properties.

The church position is involved. What is now the parish church, at the north end of the town, without kirkyard, was formerly the Free kirk, large, with a steeple, and bright within. It was much more conveniently placed than its predecessor, which stands in its old kirkyard almost a mile to the south, on a slight ridge in open country. This is still intact, though unused, a large and high building of 1790, a preaching-church with three-sided gallery. Lord Strichen is buried here—he was one of the judges in the famous Douglas Cause. And in the graveyard is *its* predecessor of 1620, erected by the judge's great-grandfather Thomas Fraser, the parish, formerly part of Fraserburgh, being constituted independent in 1627. This is now a tall ivy-clad ruin with an outside stairway, its features so overgrown as to be indiscernible. Its bell, cast in the Low Countries and dated 1633, is now in use in the present kirk. There are many old gravestones here. The modern cemetery is attached. In the town are also Episcopal and Roman Catholic churches. The notable Anderson and Woodman Library should be mentioned, in a pleasingly converted linen-mill, its librarian and custodian a fount of local knowledge. In its garden is a dormer-pediment from the original Strichen fortalice, dated 1580 with initials *T.F.* There is some industry at Strichen, notably quarrying, concrete-slab-making and sawmilling.

Strichen estate, to the south, is still extant though the mansion is down, and has one or two interesting features. A stone-circle stands on a little ridge across from the mansion-site. Dr. Johnson asked to see this, when he visited Strichen, but made the typical unmannerly comment that he thought some of the trees more worthy of notice. Near by is a doocot of the earlier house; and the circular foundations of the former Tolbooth have been made into a hermitage or chapel.

Tarland and Migvie. This is a conjoint parish in the picturesque Howe of Cromar, just north of mid-Deeside, united about 1700, and comprising 17,400 acres of undulating to hilly country on the southern slopes of the Succoth Hills. Tarland is quite a large village and one-time burgh of barony; and Migvie a hamlet with a tiny old church in a pleasant valley three miles to the north-west.

Tarland is a modestly busy place, "capital" of Cromar, one of the divisions of the ancient earldom of Mar, and centre of a wide agricultural area—especially on the day of the annual August Tarland Show. There used to be seven annual markets held here, as well as weekly fairs, and even a small-debt court. These are no more; but it still has banks, shops, tradesmen, considerable recent housing, and moreover the headquarters of the well-known Mac-Robert Farms of Douneside near by. The parish church is large and modern, a handsome granite edifice dedicated to St. Moluag, built in 1870 to replace the old kirk which still stands roofless in its crowded graveyard near the little village Square. This, only a shell now, seems to be basically of the 17th century, altered 1762 and with an earlier belfry. There are some old gravestones, and outside, flanking the Square, a memorial to Peter Milne, violinist and composer of Scottish music. In front is a modern Celtic-decorated well, commemorating one Francis Donaldson, 1913. The predecessor of the old kirk was dedicated allegedly to St. Mathulock—which may be the same as Moluag—and given by the Earl of Mar in 1153 to the priory of St. Andrews. There is an abandoned United Free Church a little way west of the village. A popular golf course stretches to the east.

The House of Cromar, formerly the well-known seat of the renowned Marquis and Marchioness of Aberdeen, "We Twa", lies to the north-east in wooded policies, and is now the equally well-known R.A.F. Rest Centre for flying personnel, known as Alastrean House, established in memory of the three sons of Sir Alexander and Lady MacRobert, killed in the Second World War. All around stretch the wide farmlands of the experimental and well-managed MacRobert Douneside Farms organisation, the tall silos of the Alamein Training Centre, for instance, prominent on the rising landscape a mile to the north-east. Near by, on the roadside of the A974, is the farm of Culsh, at which is a fine example of Pictish souterrain or weem, an underground stone-lined storehouse, now in the care of the Department of the Environment, quite long, horse-shoe-shaped and high enough to stand up in. A mile farther up the road eastwards, at Slack, which means *slochd* or throat, where the road emerges from a little pass in the hills, is a splendid viewpoint for Cromar and the Dee valley. The Deeside Field Club erected a useful indicator here in 1970.

At the other, western, side of Tarland, half a mile, is a single standing-stone in a field, and an equal distance beyond, in the wooded grounds of Mclgam Lodge, a stone-circle. South of this, less than a mile, on rising ground on the estate of Corrachree, is said to be one of the four Pictish sculptured stones of this parish—but the writer was unable to trace this, with the mansion temporarily shut up. Another two of the stones are at Migvie, three miles farther to the north-west. On the way, in a field at the roadside, near Mill of Migvie, is another souterrain or weem, this one in a poor condition. Migvie itself is a pretty hamlet sequestered in attractive country. Its church, on a grassy eminence, formerly dedicated to St. Finan or Finnian, dates from 1777, tiny and cottage-like but still in occasional use. In the graveyard, amongst the many old tombstones, is a fine Pictish symbol-stone, with a spirited rendering of a horse and rider on one side, and a Celtic cross on the other. The second incised stone is a small consecration wheel-cross of somewhat later date, lying on the ground at the church wall. Above the adjoining farm of Kirkhill, to the south, are the very scanty remains of the former castle of Migvie, once a minor seat of the Earls of Mar.

Still farther up this secluded and quite steeply rising valley is the estate of Tillypronie, extensive on a wooded hillside. On a terraced site at over the 1000-foot contour, is the modern mansion, with magnificent views over Cromar and Deeside. Here, at the gravel approach, is the fourth Pictish stone, smallish, displaying the symbols of a two-legged rectangle and crescent with V-rod.

To add to this wealth of proto-historic relics of the neighbourhood, there is a good stone-circle at Tomnaverie, just one mile south of Tarland—but this is in Coull parish.

Tarves and Barthol Chapel. Tarves is one of those large but entirely rural Formartine parishes on the edge of Buchan, of 16,000 acres of undulating country. It lies between Ellon and Oldmeldrum, with a quite large central village, Barthol Chapel being a picturesque hamlet situated five miles to the north-west. The area is not high, but open with wide vistas, being very little wooded except on the great estate of Haddo House to the north-east, most of which is in Methlick parish.

Tarves village is set on a slight ridge, its centre clustering round a former small green which has, unfortunately, been covered in tarmac to form a car-park, amenity sacrificed to convenience. There are a number of shops, a Melvin Hall with rooms gifted by Andrew Carnegie for library purposes and a Queen's Room commemorating Victoria. Some attractive side-streets branch off to the north. The parish church stands at the eastern end of the village, on an eminence in an ancient graveyard which contains some interesting features. Most notable is the Tolquhon Tomb, part of the Tolquhon Aisle of the original pre-Reformation church of St. Englatius, a purely mythical saint, the real founder of the church here being the Irish missionary to the Picts, Muirdebar, an odd circumstance. The imaginary saint's name persists in Tanglandford and Tanglan's Well. The tomb was built for himself in 1589 by Sir William Forbes of Tolquhon, 7th laird, a man of culture and enlightenment who founded and endowed a bedehouse for paupers in Tarves. Bedehouse Croft perpetuates the fact. The Renaissance memorial is imaginatively decorative, heraldic, with an arched recess below an embattled cornice, in red sandstone. Featured, as well as beruffed little figures of the laird and his lady, is a fox with goose in mouth and a hound pursuing a hare. Presumably Tolquhon Castle, now in Udny parish to the south, and described thereunder, was then in

Tarves. There are some old gravestones of the late 16th and early 17th centuries, in especial those to two members of the Craig family, both heralds. Also one inscribed *M.R.1613*, actually built into the walling of the church at ground level. The present church was erected in 1798 and rebuilt 1825. It is a typical preaching-church, a little gloomy within. This is one other site for the alleged burial of Sir Thomas de Longueville, the Red Rover, of Bruce's and Wallace's time, who is locally claimed to have died at Ythsie hereabouts.

The Ythsie district, pronounced approximately Icy, lies over a mile to the east, comprising a hill and a number of farms. On South Ythsie there is a stone-circle, unusual in that it is set in a hollow and not readily seen from the farm-road, consisting of six uprights around a central cairn. On Ythsie Hill, at 390 feet the highest point around, is a monument known locally as The Prop, erected on the site of an ancient cairn, by tenants, to the memory of the Prime Minister 4th Earl of Aberdeen, of near-by Haddo House. A mile to the north is the former old farming estate of Shethin, once a property of the family of Hoddeston or Ogston, its castle gone, demolished in 1644 on the orders of the Covenant leaders, by which time it was in Seton hands. The present small mansion dates from the early 19th century and has some items of interest. There was also a chapel of St. John, now no more, its font thought to be at Ellon Castle. A Roman camp is likewise claimed for the vicinity. Still remaining is a small stone-circle, again not readily seen from any road, in fields to the north-west.

At the other side of Tarves, a mile to the north-west, is the farm of Tillyhilt, off the B999. On the edge of a ravine, on its higher ground, is the site of Tillyhilt Castle, a former Gordon stronghold of which only grass-grown foundations remain. Farther along the same road, a mile, is Mains of Keithfield, now a Haddo farm but once a separate barony of Tillygonie. Traces of the 17th century laird's-house, with a chamfered window, remain in the garden walling; and near by is a good circular doocot of earlier date, with two stringcourses, now in poor condition. At Courtstane farm in the same area, no doubt the site of the barony court, is the remains of a stone-circle.

A side-road strikes off due westwards from the major road-junction here, and a mile along is the quite attractive little milling hamlet of Fochel, its mill still producing animal feeding-stuffs. And another mile farther is Barthol Chapel, a larger hamlet, very remotely situated, with a *quod sacra* parish church which is something of a landmark, with its detached graveyard on a separate hillock, and a fine modern school. Barthol is merely a shortening of St. Bartholemew, and this was the scene of an annual and old-established sheep and cattle fair. The place was originally called Futhcul (obviously the same as Fochel) and the chapel dedicated to St. Bartholemew.

Almost four miles to the south-east—for this is a far-flung parish— is another remote hamlet amid the spreading pastures and fields,

Craigdam, once called Craig-doune, with a school and a former church of a Secession congregation, indeed the mother-kirk of many such congregations in the North-East. The breakaway dated from 1752, but this church was built in 1806, a cairn in the garden commemorating the fact. It was reunited with Tarves congregation, in 1958, and the building is now a house. A mile south-west of the same side-road is one more farm called Aquhorthies, on which is the site of a pre-Reformation chapel of St. John's, with its walled grave-yard in a field. This was turned into a Quaker burial-place by its Forbes lairds, the only remaining gravestones being to Forbes of Blackford, 1786, and Admiral Leith of Leith-hall, 1788, and their ancestors.

The House of Shivas stands in the extreme north-east corner of this parish almost eight miles from here, with the huge estate of Haddo House intervening. Since the latter is in Methlick parish, and Shivas is much nearer Methlick than Tarves, it is dealt with thereunder.

Torphins and Learney. Torphins is a large village, or a small town, attractively sited on a terraced position above the mid-Dee valley seven miles north-west of Banchory, and in Kincardine O'Neil parish. It is a quietly thriving place of nearly 600 population, and a noted holiday-resort, and deservedly so, especially for the more mature visitor, with many hotels and guest-houses, but otherwise almost entirely residential. It gives no impression of antiquity, however—which is not to be wondered at, for it has developed from a mere hamlet only since the railway came to the area in 1859—which line is now closed again. But Torphins is securely popular, amongst its woodlands, with fine views over Deeside.

The A980 threads its main street, wherein is the former South Church, now the Church Hall, the large Learney Arms Hotel and the Learney Hall. Learney is an estate and 17th century barony, of which was the famous and recent Lord Lyon King of Arms, Sir Thomas Innes, a tower of strength in things traditional. It lies two miles to the north, on the rising ground of Learney Hill.

Torphins is more attractive off the main street, as is not uncommon. The aforementioned Learney Hall thereon is large, almost over-ambitious for so rural an area, in grey granite, and erected by Colonel Francis Innes in 1898 in memory of his parents' sixtieth wedding anniversary—a pleasing notion. Down a side-street to the south is a good modern development of eight two-roomed houses for old folk. Also in this direction is a small row of former almshouses converted into one residence by Sir Thomas Innes, who left his son to laird it up at Learney House. On a circular little tower-like porch, added, are the Innes arms.

Notably the most picturesque part of Torphins is unseen from the main road, on higher ground amongst trees to the north-east—no doubt the knoll which gave the place its name, *tor-fionn* meaning the light-coloured knowe. Here is a sylvan setting indeed for a bank, as for another hotel, the War Memorial Hospital, villas and the very unusual established church. This last is large, built on a wooded eminence in 1875, in a sort of Bavarian style of architecture, quite pleasing within and without, with lattice-paned windows and many timbered gablets. It was planned by Colonel Thomas Innes, father of Colonel Francis, as for both Episcopal and Presbyterian worship, an early example of ecumenical endeavour which, unfortunately, did not eventuate. There is no graveyard, the actual parish church being at Kincardine O'Neil.

Torphins has a large school which has recently lost its junior secondary status under the comprehensive reorganisation. Also a very scenic golf course to the north-west.

The road beyond the church, the B993, passes near Learney House amongst the wooded foothills. This is a large mansion, with a 17th century nucleus which has been greatly altered down the generations, especially after a fire in 1837. It is on the E-plan, with a courtyard, in grey granite like all else hereabouts. This part of the great Durward barony of Onele was granted to Irvine of Drum in 1446. That family remained in possession until 1696, and so built the earliest part of the existing house. It then passed to the Forbeses of Craigievar and then to the Brebners in 1747, from whom the Inneses, of the Raemoir family, gained it by marriage. It was formerly called Largeny.

Almost two miles south-east of Learney is the Craigmyle estate, the mansion of which has been demolished. A much more ancient relic survives, however, in the Pictish Craigmyle Stone. This stands on high ground, at Cothill, a spine of land with glorious prospects in all directions, close to a pleasant converted cottage. It is a tall mono-lith, seven feet high by four broad, with weatherworn symbols of a serpent and two-legged rectangle. There was a Pictish camp at Campfield to the south.

At the other side of Torphins, due south, near the farm of Cock-ardie, on the moorland of Moss Maud above the valley of the Beltie Burn, is the remotely sited Castle Maud, an early stronghold possibly of the late 13th or early 14th century, a seat of the Durward barony of Onele. The foundations of a keep some 30 feet square stand to a height of eight feet centrally amongst grass-grown banks and ditches in scrub-woodland. What may be either a domed well-cavity or an oven remains in a corner of the walling, together with an aumbry and arrow-slit window. The Durwards were, of course, the powerful family who arose as hereditary Door-wards or Keepers of the royal castle of Kincardine in the Mearns.

The large granite quarry of Craiglash is half a mile to the south. In this vicinity is the Warlock Stone, an undistinguished boulder on the hillside, presumably with witchcraft associations.

Tough, Whitehouse and Corrennie. Tough is a Donside parish of 7000 acres lying south of the Howe of Alford, under the shadow of the Corrennie Hills; and Whitehouse is a small village and estate to the north of it, lying on the main A944 road. The area is undulating but basically slanting from south to north, the parish boundary running along the Corrennie ridge, 1621 feet at Benquhallie, its highest point, sinking to 474 feet at Whitehouse.

Nineteen miles from Aberdeen, the Corrennie area is reached first, on the A944, at the quarrying hamlet of Tillyfourie—not to be confused with Tillyfour and also Tillyfoure, both not far away. Here, in a sort of pass through the wooded hills, are two great red-granite quarries, just outwith the parish. The Corrennie planted forest is extensive, reaching into the adjoining parishes of Cluny and Monymusk. The Tough boundary runs north-eastwards from here along the summit ridge, and on one of the eminences, Green Hill (1307 feet) rises Luath's Stone, a 12-foot monolith allegedly marking the grave of Lulach or Luath, Lady MacBeth's son—although it is probably of prehistoric origin. There were a number of stone-circles on these heights.

Two miles on from Tillyfourie, a side-road strikes off on the left to Kirkton of Tough. At the junction is the former inn of Whiteley, now pleasingly restored as a private house. The Kirkton, a sequestered hamlet by a burnside, lies a mile westwards, with school, shop, church and manse. The parish church stands on a knoll, and dates from 1838, stark grey granite and plain, but in a pleasant setting, brown-painted within, a typical galleried preaching-kirk with high raised pulpit dominating. There are some old gravestones in the kirkyard, and a very elementary iron mort-safe. On walling near by is the date 1732. Traditionally the Auld Kirk o' Tough is a stone-circle, in a remote position on the high ground —interesting confirmation of a theory the author has evolved that the original Celtic Church missionaries utilised the stone-circles of the sun-worshipping Picts before they started building actual churches. Many later churches continued to be built in stone-circles. It would also account for the many elaborate Pictish cross-slabs, with their pagan symbols, as marking outdoor places of worship in the 8th and 9th centuries. In this connection it is notable that the famous Nine Maidens, daughters of St. Donevald (from Glen Ogilvie in Angus) lived here in the 8th century—the time of the Christianising of the Picts—digging the soil with their own hands, and much revered by the Picts.

In the howe below the Kirkton stand the gaunt ruined walls of the former mansion of Tonley. Although the remains are almost wholly of the 19th century, there was an ancient nucleus. It belonged to a family called Byres, one of whom was a noted antiquary, who actually lectured on antiquities in Rome. Near by is the farm of Kincraigie, once a lairdship of the Leslies.

Whitehouse, partly in the parish of Keig, lies at a road-junction a mile to the north-east, not notably attractive. It formerly had importance as a railway-station, succeeding the service of a stage-coach which called here daily on its way from Aberdeen to Strathdon. The mansion near by is modern, on a terraced site commanding

Arbroath. Auchmithie fishing-village and the geometrical pattern of the Angus fields

Brechin. The new High School

Forfar. Guide-dogs for the Blind Training School

fine views of the Howe of Alford, and was the seat of a branch of the Farquharson family, commemorated in the parish church.

Remotely situated three miles away on high ground to the south-west is Tillyfour, a farm with a large 18th century house and garden, on a ridge amongst trees. This was the home of William McCombie (1805–80) known as the "King of Graziers", a pioneer of the Aberdeen-Angus breed of cattle, whose fame brought Queen Victoria here to visit him in 1866. He sat as Liberal M.P. for West Aberdeenshire, the first tenant-farmer ever to be elected from Scotland.

This upland area now shows many abandoned farm-places, owing to the amalgamation into larger establishments; but the land itself offers no signs of neglect.

Towie. The Donside parish of Towie is well-named, for Tuath means north-facing, and most of the parish lies on the south side of Don looking across to the great hills. But the parish was once called Kilbartha. It extends to 12,000 acres and has only the one small village, at a junction of side-roads down near the riverside. Here, at the kirkton of Towie, as well as the church are the school, post-office and a cluster of houses. The castle of Towie, which has recently been demolished by the new proprietor, stood here formerly. It was only a ruined shell, and was in fact never completed it is said; but it was a picturesque addition to the scene, with some good corbelling and other features. It was a Forbes place, dating from the late 16th century, and its predecessor is frequently alleged to have been the scene of the notorious savagery enacted by Captain Ker, on the orders of Gordon of Auchinduin, brother of Huntly—the Edom o' Gordon ballad—where Lady Forbes and her children and retainers, 27 in all, were burned to death after the Craibstone fight of 1571. The tragedy is also claimed for Corgarff Castle and other places, however.

The parish church dates from 1803, is low, plain and harled, with a small belfry and a gallery. There are a number of old tombstones in the kirkyard, also an iron mort-safe. There is alleged to be, or to have been, a Pictish sculptured stone here, but enquiries and inspection failed to discover it. On the higher ground to the south, at the farm of Nether Towie, was the site of a pre-Reformation chapel, where, it is claimed, the aforementioned Lady Forbes was buried. The position is still pointed out, but is overgrown and featureless. There was another pre-Reformation chapel at Kinbattock farm a mile to the west, remotely situated. This presumably was the original parish church of St. Bartha, Kinbattock believed to be merely a corruption of Kilbartha. There is also the site of a motte for a timber castle here. At the farm of Rippachie, at the parish boundary, above the 1000-foot contour another mile to the west, are two little old humpbacked bridges, in bare moorland country. Below this, southwards on the Deskry Water, is the isolated old inn of Boultenstone, which must have been a welcome refuge on many an occasion.

To the north of kirkton of Towie, just across Don, where the side-road joins the main A97 Donside road, is a pyramidal standing-stone, unhewn, near a house, beneath which, allegedly, is a bull's hide filled with gold. On the main road here is the hamlet of Glenkindie, with store and inn and a large estate. The fine and extensive mansion of the Leith family had ancient beginnings, built by the Strachans in 1595, but this is largely lost in the later work. The Kindie Burn comes in from the north in a picturesque little valley threaded by a dead-end road. Two miles up this, where Glen Guie joins, is the farm of Chapelton, where was the site of the pre-Reformation chapel of St. Ronan, now incorporated in the steading. There is no remaining feature. St. Ronan's Well is still pointed out, a spring in boggy land near by.

Two miles east of Glenkindie, on a side-road flanking the north bank of Don, is the Peel of Fichlie, a fine artificial motte-hill, 60 feet high, with fosse and some masonry on top. Presumably there was a motte-and-bailey castle here—although one well-known expert declared that nothing of the sort existed. It may just have been an earlier proto-historic fortification on the site. On Ghlascul Hill (1178 feet) to the north, is Cairn Fichlie, an ancient round cairn easily discernible on green rising ground, where one of those peculiar Pictish carved stone balls was found. There are other tumuli in the area, claimed to represent the burial-places of the slain in one of Bruce's battles, with David de Strathbogie, Earl of Atholl, but these are almost certainly prehistoric sites. One is in a field south of the road beyond Peel of Fichlie, on Ley farm. There was a weem, or souterrain, on the farm of New Morlich, off the A97 a mile west of Ghlascul Hill, on the way to Kildrummy, but this has been filled in as a danger to cattle. At Sinnahard, a farm south of Don at the parish's eastern extremity, is a single standing-stone in a field, mentioned under Leochel-Cushnie. There was a pre-Reformation chapel here. The later church, on a mound, is now disused. The views between here and Milton of Towie, are magnificent.

Tullynessle, Forbes and Montgarrie. The Donside joint-parish of Tullynessle and Forbes lies across the river immediately north of Alford, with the village of Montgarrie almost a suburb thereof, connected by a bridge. The parishes were united in 1808, and together cover 11,000 acres of pleasing rural countryside, green hills and riverside plain, the heartland of the great clan of Forbes.

The present parish church is at Tullynessle, lying some three miles up an attractive green glen probing the Correen Hills, from Alford, on a winding side-road to Clatt and Kennethmont. There is no real kirkton hamlet, but a large and modern community hall for the area stands at the crossroads near the school. The church is large and somewhat gaunt, grey granite, dating from 1840, the worst period, doing less than justice to its pleasing surroundings. The old belfry of its predecessor, dated 1604, has been re-erected in the kirkyard. There are some old gravestones. The stableyard across the road is interesting, reminder of the times when such was a necessary feature of the rural church. This one has additional interest, with a window to the north-east with moulded and chamfered jambs, and a lintel dated 1673. The manse is near by.

The castle of Terpersie stands in the throat of a side-valley a mile to the north-west, now unfortunately in very dilapidated condition. It has been a good Z-planned fortalice, of the late 16th century, with large circular towers diagonally flanking the gabled main block, well supplied with gunloops and shot-holes, and a corbelled stair-turret in an angle, dated 1561. The basement is vaulted, with small octagonal vaulted chambers in the base of each round tower. A 17th century addition rises to the east. William Gordon, the builder, was a son of Lesmoir, fought at the Battle of Corrichie and was responsible for the killing of Black Arthur Forbes, brother of the Lord Forbes and champion of his clan. General Baillie burned Terpersie before the Battle of Alford. The last laird was revealed to the Hanoverian troops, hiding after Culloden, by shouts of "Daddy" from his children, the last victim to be executed after the Forty-Five Rising.

Montgarrie is a pleasant village around a crossroads down in the Don levels. Baillie camped here in 1645. A large meal-mill here still works by water-power; but a former woollen blanket-mill is defunct. At the farm of Druidsfield, just to the south, two standing-stones rise in a field above the long driveway to the mansion of Whitehaugh. This estate, from 1584, was a possession of a branch of the Forbes-Leith family. The house is extensive, enlarged in 1838, and in the Grecian style, with massive pillared portico. A mausoleum lies to the north-west. Fields here called Temple Close and St. John's Close commemorate the ancient holding of these lands by the Knights Templar. At the other, western side of Montgarrie, is Syllavethy, where there were formerly granite quarries.

The former parish of Forbes lies to the westwards, up Don, with the kirkton three miles on. What is now called Bridge of Alford was formerly Boat of Forbes, where were the ferry and fords, the latter used by Baillie in 1645. There is an attractive riverside hamlet here, with its hotel once a coaching inn, and cottages amongst trees. The three-arched bridge was built in 1810. The stretch of Don in the Vale here is quietly sylvan after its constriction in the hills and emergence at Brux and Littlewood. Directly above it, northwards, rises Lord Arthur's Cairn (1699 feet) of the Correen Hills, named after the aforementioned Black Arthur Forbes. The erstwhile parish church of Forbes lies down at the waterside, not on the usual mound, at a wide bend of river and road. It stands roofless but with the walls entire, in an old graveyard, well cared for, with many old flat stones, a lovely and sequestered spot. The walls are thick and there is an aumbry and recess, possibly for an effigy; but the building appears to date from the 17th century rather than pre-Reformation, with later alterations. The near-by estate of Littlewood was formerly a Forbes place, as is Brux, two miles on, both with modern mansions. Forbes of Brux, "out" in the Forty-Five, escaped the fate of Gordon of

Terpersie by working as a stone-dyker. These properties are, however, just outwith the parish.

Turriff. The busy little red-stone burgh of Turriff, notable in history, lies in undulating foothill country in the Deveron valley, at the northern edge of Aberdeenshire, indeed only 11 miles south of Banff. It has a population of only 2750, but this is little indication of its importance. There are many industries and services based here to cater for the great agricultural and stock-raising area, including foodstuffs processing, fertilisers, seed-warehouses. Markets are held. There are a number of hotels, many banks, offices and shops, and a cottage hospital. The parish of Turriff covers 18,500 acres.

The town is built on something of a ridge above the haughs of the Idoch Water, and has an embryo central square, with the streets fairly regularly planned. A burgh of barony under Holy Church since 1511, it became a police burgh in 1874. It has a very long history, not all of it capable of authentication. Allegedly Lathmon, a Pictish prince, had his capital here, and the name Dorlaithers—now a farm and formerly a Gordon lairdship to the south-west—is said to refer, Dun-Lathmon. "Wander with the blue-eyed Cutha in the vales of Dunlathmon." The ancient church is claimed to have been founded by St. Congan, a Pictish missionary, whose Cowan's Fair has long been held here. Malcolm Canmore is said to have built a church at Turriff; and in 1214 the Celtic heiress Countess of Buchan gave it to Arbroath Abbey. In 1272 her son, Alexander Comyn, Earl of Buchan, created an almshouse, the Maison Dieu Hospice, for 13 poor husbandmen; and this was later endowed by Bruce, in memory of his brother Nigel. There is a mercat cross, referred to in 1557, 20 feet high, re-erected 1865. The Earl of Erroll's Town Lodging, a large and composite building in a poor state and threatened with demolition, stands at the street corner near by. The Hays of Erroll, who had a seat at Delgatie Castle, were for 350 years superiors of Turriff. At the other side of the street here, a dormer pediment with monogram and date 167? is built in above a shop, probably from the church.

The ancient church stands badly neglected in its old graveyard, behind a good moulded, arched gateway with pilasters, to the west, It is a very historic spot, in more than masonry and gravestones. For here the great Montrose held the town against Huntly in 1639, the first action in the First Bishops' War, an occasion which sparked off the enmity between these two which was to cost them both so dear. This bloodless victory was called the Raid of Turriff. And three months later another Gordon-versus-Covenanter encounter here, where the fortunes were reversed, was called the Trot of Turriff. The old church, of which only the choir remains, is roofed in only at the east end, where there is a gable with elaborate double belfry dated 1635, with a bell dated 1557, with heraldry, and a clock below. The full building was 120 feet long. There are many interesting panels and memorials of the 16th and 17th centuries, to the Hays,

Barclays of Towie, Gordons of Dorlaithers, Forbeses and others. One to a Barclay, 1636, bears six Latin elegiacs. An old pre-Reformation stone font is built into a window-embrasure. The whole complex ought to be a show-piece for Turriff.

The later parish church, a plain but commodious edifice on rising ground to the north, was built in 1794 and enlarged to seat 1650 in 1830. It has some good old silver communion-plate. There is an Episcopal church of St. Congan, of 1867, with spire, partly a memorial to Bishop Alexander Jolly (1755–1838) whose ministry commenced here. There are other churches. Turriff Academy, large and modern, replaces the earlier grammar school. The town has many sporting facilities, parks and playing-fields, notably the Upper and Lower Haughs, and the Den Park and Brodie's Braes at the southern side of the town. There is a nine-hole golf course at Rosehall to the west, where also is industrial expansion.

The Turra Coo incident is almost nationally famous. In 1913 a Turriff farmer, Robert Paterson, Lendrum, refused to pay the new insurance stamps for workers which Lloyd George had instituted, and had one of his beasts, a white cow, taken by the sheriff-officer to Turriff Square, to sell to pay the dues. The local farmers, however, not only would not buy, but created a riot and in it the cow escaped and found its way back to Lendrum. A cairn is being built at the farm, where the cow was eventually buried, to commemorate.

The parish area has much of interest. Delgatie Castle and estate lie two miles to the east, above a narrow loch and valley, a tall and imposing keep of six storeys with parapet and walk, of the 15th century, plus an equally tall gabled extension of a century later, walls harled and whitewashed and supplied with gunloops. The interior is interesting, with ribbed and groined vaulting and tempera painting. A wide fireplace lintel is dated 1570, inscribed *MY HOYP IS IN YE LORD*. Long a Hay of Erroll seat, it passed like so many another into Duff hands; but once again it has a Hay laird, commissioner to the Countess of Erroll, High Constable.

Most of the parish lies west and south of Turriff—for the Banff-shire border lies close, to the north. The valley of the Deveron is attractive here, with a graceful, three-arched bridge of 1826 near the town. Muiresk is a small estate with a pleasing E-shaped mansion of the 18th century, with an earlier nucleus and the Royal Arms of Scotland on a panel on the east front. There is a hamlet of Milton of Muiresk, with a school. The Laithers area lies two miles farther west, with its House, Hill, Mill, Bogs and so on, belonging of old to the Dempsters of Auchterless, the mansion not old. The Dorlaithers Gordons bought the property in 1722, it having been Dempsters' also, previously. Alexander Gordon, the buyer, of the Cocklarachie branch, was a general in the Russian army.

The Turriff area is rich in mineral springs, not a few of these having been exploited by the old Church, St. John's, St. Mary's, etc. There was a renowned Physic Well in the immediate vicinity of the town.

Tyrie and New Pitsligo. The great lands of Buchan, the north-eastern sector of Aberdeenshire, are scarcely beautiful in any conventional way, bare and treeless with no real hills to diversify the scene. But they have their own strong character, and the vast skies, and far-flung vistas and feeling of space are notable. Tyrie is not a large parish for Buchan, 11,000 acres of one-time moss and moorlike land, now well developed agriculturally; and New Pitsligo—oddly named, for it is about eight miles from Pitsligo itself and not even in the same parish—is its only real village.

New Pitsligo is hardly beautiful either—indeed rather resembling a Lanarkshire or Stirlingshire village—although its surroundings are pleasantly wooded, unusual hereabouts. It is almost a small town, and a *quod sacra* parish of its own, founded in 1787 by Sir William Forbes of Pitsligo. Formerly there was a hamlet here called Old Caik, or Cavoch—allegedly a haunt of smugglers and illegal distillers. Weaving was to replace this, of course, the linen trade then being on the advance. Pitsligo lace is still made here. Granite quarries were established near by. Today it is a mile-long village of neat grey houses in two parallel streets with intersections, with a population of 1400, and banking, hotel and shopping facilities. There is a large school, public hall and library. The established church is large, seating 1000. It stands in the higher part of the village, in a kirkyard, and dates from 1798, renewed 1853, a typical preaching-church with prominent pulpit but rather dull within. There is an Episcopal church of St. John the Evangelist, 1871, rather fine, with its own graveyard, indication that this was a strong Episcopalian area. It is down on the main street.

The civil parish of Tyrie stretches mainly north-eastwards for about six miles. The parish church stands isolated at the northern extremity, in the shallow valley of the Water of Tyrie, not far from the little community of Boyndlie. Its predecessor was known as the White Kirk of Buchan and dedicated to St. Andrew. It is a small, plain building of 1800, built on a sloping site within an old kirkyard, back from the A98 Fraserburgh road, simple and bright within, very pleasing with a small gallery. In the porch is the important feature known as the Raven Stone, a Pictish symbol-stone dug up in the kirkyard. It is now built into the walling, so that only one side is visible, and the symbols are picked out in black, showing a large bird—though hardly a raven—and rectangle and Z-rod. There are some old gravestones, including the Forbes of Boyndlie tomb. The manse near by is a building of 1763, of some character. In the vicinity was formerly a mound, known as the Moat, no doubt the site of an ancient motte-and-bailey castle. At the Mains here was a later castle of the Frasers, now gone, its only relic a red carved stone let in above the farmhouse back-door. There are quarries and sandpit workings in the neighbourhood.

Boyndlie estate and scattered community, with a pleasantly sited school in the low ground of a little valley, lie to the south-west a mile. The mansion is not old but the estate is, established by a scion of the Forbes of Pitsligo family who was killed at the Craibstone battle with the Gordons in 1571. A descendent laird was taken prisoner by Montrose in 1644. The Forbeses are still at Boyndlie. To the west is the farm of Craigmurnan, where, in a natural amphitheatre, is a spring known as the Murnan or Mourning Well. There were a number of weems in the area, now gone.

A mile farther west, along the A98, is the crossroads area of Ladysford where there is a former school, now a hall, gifted by a Forbes laird of Boyndlie. The farm here was once a small laird's mansion. The Law Cairn, a burial-cairn, stands isolated a mile west, in the Craigmaud area.

Udny, Pitmedden and Tolquhon. Udny is a large parish of 11,000 acres in the Formartine area of Aberdeenshire, on the verge of Buchan, west of Ellon and east of Meldrum, an agricultural and pastoral district, fairly low-lying and without any notable hills. There are two very differently sized villages, comparatively close together, Udny and Pitmedden, each with a famous estate near by of the same name. There are also the hamlets of Udny Station and Logierieve, which grew up because of the railway, well to the east. Whiterashes is nearer, a not particularly interesting roadside hamlet on the main A947, to the south-west.

Udny village occupies a pleasant sloping site on an open village green, with some modern development—especially interesting is the attractive group of old people's houses, Academy Court, on the site of the old academy west of the green, with their garden precinct at the rear. The parish church stands on the north side, a dignified granite building with square tower, dating from 1821, in Gothic style and with a clock. The parish was created in 1597, and the original church, built between 1600 and 1605, called Christ's Kirk of Udny replacing a pre-Reformation chapel, lay south of the green, where still is the graveyard and an interesting round mort-house to foil body-snatchers, complete with turntable for the coffins. The sloping kirkyard, with its prospects over the far-flung farmlands, contains many old gravestones, and the burial-enclosure of the Seton lairds of Pitmedden. A fine modern school has been erected to the north, replacing the academy founded first in 1786 by the parish schoolmaster as a boarding establishment. It attracted the sons of the gentry and became quite famous. The founder's son became headmaster thereof at the age of 17, and four years later became minister of Bourtie! To the south of the green is the hall, erected in memory of Dr. Alexander Spence D.D., who ministered here for 47 years.

The gates of Udny Castle estate are near by. The castle has been in the hands of the same family for six centuries, and is a magnificent lofty keep dating from the early 15th century, heightened in the 16th and enhanced with angle-turrets in the 17th. There were until recently large Victorian and other extensions, but these have been cleared away, leaving the tall old fortalice to rise sheerly from its green lawns, whitewashed and highly attractive, a landmark for miles around. There are five storeys and a garret, with parapet and walk, small windows, splayed gunloops and elaborate corbelling. The interior has been most tastefully and imaginatively restored by the present laird and his wife—she was the Hon. Margaret Udny-Hamilton, daughter of Lord Belhaven, who had inherited Udny at the death of the last laird in the direct line. Most interesting use is made of the many little mural chambers, and even the pit within the thickness of the walling, as extra sleeping accomodation. Over a hall doorway is the legend: *LET NO ONE BEAR BEFORE THIS THRESHOLD HENCE, WORDS HEARD HERE IN FRIENDLY CONFIDENCE*—an admirable injunction. The entire castle is a model of restoration. The first recorded Ranald of Uldney had a charter from David II, Bruce's son. The twelfth of the line employed the renowned James Fleeman, or Fleming, "the Laird of Udny's Fool", a sort of licensed jester, who was instrumental in saving the family from fire at their other castle of Knockhall, in 1734.

Pitmeddan village, which lies only a mile north-east of Udny on the B9000, is much larger, with some agricultural industrial plant, but rather less attractive in appearance. There is considerable modern housing, some of it an admirable reconstruction of older buildings. St. Meddan's Terrace is set behind green lawns, an asset to any village. The former Free kirk is now united with the established parish church at Udny, services being held in both each Sunday.

Pitmedden, however, is best-known for its famous late 17th century garden, now in the care of the National Trust. The estate lies half a mile north-west of the village, the mansion-house itself not being particularly interesting, having been burned in 1818 and rebuilt. But the formal gardens are a delight, splendidly kept and full of interest. The sunken Great Garden contains an elaborate pattern of floral designs, with sundials, horologes and fountains. It is flanked by two ogee-roofed two-storeyed pavilions of 1675, summer-houses of a sort, one having a bath-house beneath. The creator was Sir Alexander Seton, Lord Pitmedden of Session, created a baronet in 1683. A son, Bonnie John Seton, died at the Battle of Brig o' Dee in 1639, and his bleeding heart forms part of the family coat of arms. The Setons gained Pitmedden in marriage with the Panton family heiress.

A mile north-west of Pitmedden House, in a remote situation on a side-road, stands the highly interesting and handsome ruined castle of Tolquhon, in the care of the Department of the Environment. It is now a courtyard castle, with a splendid drum-tower gatehouse and inner and outer courts, though the original was a simple 15th century keep erected by the Lothian family of Preston of Craigmillar. This is largely gone, but the Forbes range of 1584 is complete to the wall-head, though roofless, a main block and circular and square towers, plus flanking extensions, with many gunloops, iron yetts, vaulting and a secret chamber. The gatehouse pend is surmounted by a fine heraldic panel inscribed: *AL THIS WARKE EXCEP THE AULD TOUR WAS BEGVN BE WILLIAM FORBES 15 APRIL 1584 AND ENDIT BE HIM 20 OCTOBER 1589.* The brother of the 1st Lord Forbes gained Tolquhon by marriage with the Preston heiress in 1420. James VI was entertained here in 1589 on his campaign against the Catholic Gordons—with whom the Forbeses were always at feud. The 10th Forbes laird saved Charles II's life at the Battle of Worcester in 1651, and was knighted. The name Tolquhon applies to a number of farms in this highest part of the parish.

There was still another castle in this parish, at Dumbreck Mains nearly two miles to the east, the seat of an ancient family of Dumbreck of that Ilk. Nothing of the castle remains save an unusually-shaped 16th century shot-hole built into the steading-wall, with another curiously decorated stone near by. Philip de Dumbreck was sheriff of Aberdeen in 1348. The family retained possession until 1564, the Meldrums succeeding. There was a chapel, with burial-ground, on the ridge to the north, but only the site remains. On Mill of Torry to the south-east there were weems or Pictish souterrains, but these also are gone.

At the other side of the parish, near Whiterashes and its caravan-park on the A947 to Oldmeldrum, the ruined mansion of Pittrichie can be seen on a slope to the east, near Kingoodie, an ancient estate of the Maitlands from Thirlstane in Lauderdale, here from 1400 to 1813, and given a baronetcy. A good circular doocot of earlier date survives, the mansion itself dating only from 1819. Near by, on the low ground at Bogfechal farm, was another weem or underground earth-house; but this also cannot be traced.

At Tillygreig, a farm two miles south-east of Whiterashes, was formerly a pre-Reformation chapel dedicated to St. Michael. But like so much else hereabouts, nothing but the name remains. A mile or so east of Tillygreig is the estate of Tillycorthie, now an experimental farm for Aberdeen University, its mansion a students' residence.

ANGUS

Although it is only tenth in size and eleventh in population of the counties of Scotland, Angus has always been one of the most important, in its influence and its history. The fact that it contained Dundee—before this became a county in itself—the fourth city of the land, helped of course; but Angus was important before Dundee was. From the earliest recorded times this was a vital area of the country, the centre of the main Pictish power; and though, with the growing supremacy of the Scottish monarchy, neighbouring Perthshire tended to become the focus of government, largely for strategic reasons, at Forteviot, Abernethy and Scone, nevertheless Angus remained of major status right down our story, its mormaorship and later earldom always amongst the most influential; and when agriculture, industry and fisheries superseded these earlier manifestations of power and authority, it was still to the fore.

Covering some 540,000 acres and with a population of about 95,000, Angus lies between the Grampians and the sea, a fair sample of Scotland in miniature, in any aspect of the word fair, having within it every feature of the country at large—a level seaboard plain, fertile farmlands, undulating pastures and woodlands, foothill country and upland, deep glens and the true mountains of rock and heather rising to 3500 feet, with over 60 peaks topping the 2000-foot contour. Moreover there is a corresponding variety of man-made features, industry partnering agriculture and fisheries, city, industrial community, country town, village, hamlet, landed estate, and forest planted and natural. Castles, mansions and old churches abound, as do more ancient relics of the past, Pictish symbol-stones and cross-slabs in especial, with their weems or souterrains more frequent here than anywhere else south of Caithness. Stone-circles and standing-stones are legion—but then so are fine holiday resorts, golf courses, sandy beaches, attractive fishing-villages, cliffs, splendid fishing rivers, and fair prospects everywhere. For this is the joy of Angus—it is largely unspoiled, its varying scenery a delight. The county is no backwater, however, with industrial estates, multi-storey flats, great concrete and glass schools, modern distilleries, large quarries, even services for off-shore oil-exploration; but these do not seem to have defaced the countryside and scene in any major way. Angus retains its very varied attractiveness.

The county is alleged to have got its name from a brother of Kenneth II, who died in 995; or alternatively, from a modest hill near Aberlemno, so called long before Kenneth's day, and important as a place of meeting. Certainly Aberlemno, with its renowned group of Pictish sculptured stones, obviously featured with importance in our early history.

Angus is divided into four distinct sections, laterally. There is the coastal plain, sandy shores backed by links and then gently sloping fields—although north of Arbroath the sands give place to lofty cliffs culminating in Red Head, one of the proudest forelands on the east coast. This division is roughly 37 miles long, with an average width of some five miles. Then there is the green range of the Sidlaw Hills, highest and widest to the south but extending north-eastwards to peter out in detached green hogbacks in the Aberlemno area—although technically these are hardly Sidlaw summits. This belt, with its associated moorland, never reaching 1500 feet, extends for over 20 miles, between three and seven miles wide. The next layer is the great and fertile vale of Strathmore, one of the major topographical features of Scotland, rich as it is lovely, reaching north-eastwards from the Perth area to the sea, its northern end known as the Howe of the Mearns. The Angus section, central, is about 30 miles long, again averaging some five miles across. Lastly, there is the lofty upland region, the Grampian heights and their foothill country, covering more than a third of the entire county, generally known as the Braes of Angus, and pierced by the fine northern-probing glens of Isla, Prosen, Clova, Ogil, Lethnot and Esk, with their subsidiaries, famous as they are picturesque, a land of their own. Some of these reach 20 miles in length, their rivers noble. The proud, unbroken, shadow-slashed and often snow-streaked barrier of these mountains is the constant background to the rest of Angus, in especial of Strathmore, a presence lovely, serene, brooding or challenging, but never to be ignored or forgotten.

The county, which for a time was called Forfarshire, after the county town but which has happily reverted to its original name, is notable for many things—its distinctive medium-sized towns, such as Forfar itself, Brechin, Arbroath, Montrose, Kirriemuir, Carnoustie; its ancient aristocratic families and their castles; its fine bridges; its champion-class golf courses; its salmon-fishing; its world-famous cattle; its fruit-growing; its prehistoric remains; its Arbroath Abbey, scene of the signing of the famous Declaration of Independence. All these and much more are dealt with hereafter, however inadequately, They add up to something quite splendid and unique.

Aberlemno, Aldbar and Melgund. Many more people should visit Aberlemno than do so. It stands on the high B9134 road from Forfar to Brechin, equidistant, an attractive route with fine vistas. Aberlemno is a rural parish of 9000 acres, lying on the east side of Finavon Hill; Aldbar was once a parish of its own, to the north, with a large and ancient estate; and Melgund was an important barony, with a ruined castle of some fame.

Aberlemno is most famous, and properly, for its magnificent group of Pictish symbol-stones. There are four of these, three standing by the roadside near the farm-cottages of Crosston; and one in the kirkyard of the parish church to the south. Of the three, two are cross-slabs, one eight feet tall, with wheel-cross and bowed angels, and on the reverse horsemen and dogs, all with intricate Celtic

decoration. The smaller has the usual symbols. The third stone is of
an earlier class, a rude monolith unhewn, inscribed with a serpent,
double-disc and Z-rod and mirror-and-comb symbols. That in the
churchyard is very handsome, seven feet high, with cross and interlaced beasts on one side, and horsemen, hunters and warriors on the
other, with notched rectangle and Z-rod, and triple-discs. This slab
has a hole pierced through one of the cross-cavities, possibly of later
date. The group, *in situ* better than in any museum, constitutes a
splendid item of Scotland's Pictish heritage.

Aberlemno Church stands down near the burnside, off a side-
road, and is largely a 1722 reconstruction of an earlier building,
pleasantly antiquated in appearance. The interior is galleried on
three sides, small as it is, and brightly painted, with some old box-
pews. There are three pewter communion-cups of 1779. Many old
tombstones grace the small kirkyard, a row of 17th century ones
lying against the manse walling. The large pre-Reformation font,
with rope-moulding, is now in the manse garden. Also built into the
garden wall is a small and attractive gabled doocot.

Oddly, the parish name is quite unsuitable. There *is* a Lemno
Burn—but not that which the parish flanks. It rises near Carsegownie, two miles to the west, and flows westwards away from
Aberlemno, eventually curving round the west flank of Finavon Hill
actually north-west of Forfar, and returning eastwards to fall into
the South Esk at Finavon Castle, after a course of nine miles, but
only two from its source, though on the other side of the hill. However, *leumnach* means leaping, so that Aber-leumnach could mean the
confluence of the leaping burn—which might well apply to the other
stream, which flows from a near-by source but in the other direction.
Carsegownie, just mentioned, is a large farm, formerly an old
lairdship. The farmhouse is E-shaped and creamwashed, on a shelf
of Finavon Hill, with over the door the date 1680 and initials *A.C.*
and *E.C.* It has had most of its early features modernised. There is a
larch-grown burial-cairn with concentric rings near the roadside.

A mile north of the church, on the north-facing flank of Finavon
Hill, is the farm of Woodrae or Woodwray. This was once a quite
important barony, with its own castle. Only the 17th century lean-
to type doocot remains. But under the kitchen floor, when the castle
was being demolished, was found another Pictish symbol-stone
cross-slab, now in the Museum of Antiquities, Edinburgh, displaying
animals around the cross, horsemen and a bull and double-discs.
Also Jonah being swallowed by a very odd-looking whale. This
stone was for a while in the care of Sir Walter Scott, at Abbotsford.

Quite near Aberlemno Church, to the north-east, is Flemington,
with its ruined castle, now mainly roofless, ivy-clad and in a bad
state beside the farmhouse. But the main features survive, of an
early 17th century fortalice on an L-plan variation, of three storeys,
with unusual stair-turrets in angles and many gunloops and shot-
holes. The basement is vaulted, and the kitchen has a wide arched
fireplace. Robert III granted Flemington to Sir William Dishington,

whereafter I have discovered no history until the 18th century. Reverend John Ochterlony, former Episcopal clergyman of the parish, ejected repeatedly from the church, continued to minister to the faithful from the even then abandoned castle—his single-minded determination being in due course rewarded by the bishopric of Brechin, in 1742.

A mile and a half east of Flemington is the more famous castle of Melgund, set above a steep small den, an extensive and impressive ruin of rose-red masonry, very fine. Although appearing to be a typical 15th century keep with 16th century additions, it was all in fact built as a piece by David Beaton, the renowned cardinal, archbishop and chancellor of Scotland. The keep is L-shaped, with six-foot-thick walling, four storeys high to a parapet and walk, with unusual caphouse above. The magnificent great hall in the eastern extension must have been one of the finest apartments in the land. The initials of Beaton and Margaret Ogilvy his "chief lewd", for whom he built this palatial home, are on the building, and this "marriage-stone" treatment lends credence to the theory that the couple were in fact married, although the lady had to be reduced to the status of mistress when Beaton took holy orders in order to succeed his uncle as archbishop and chancellor. She was a daughter of the 1st Lord Ogilvy of Airlie. The Beaton descendants continued to live here until, in the 17th century, it passed to a Marquis of Huntly. Eventually Melgund came by inheritance to the Elliots of Minto, and the Earl of Minto's heir still bears the title of Viscount Melgund.

South of Melgund is the great Montreathmont Moor and Forest, a vast area, partly in this parish, partly in Farnell, always wild and wooded and now largely planted forest. At its south-west corner is the Pitkennedy area, with a scattering of houses and a small school, an estate that belonged to the Chalmers of Aldbar.

Aldbar itself lies well to the north-east of Aberlemno, four miles, and has very much its own entity, even though unhappily its large castle has comparatively recently been demolished. It stood above the deep wooded Den of Aldbar, in which is a waterfall, only two miles south-west of Brechin, where the high ground of the Aberlemno ridge drops suddenly to the Esk valley. It was an unusual building of the late 16th century, with parapeted stair-tower and angle-turrets, erected by Sir Thomas Lyon, treasurer of Scotland and a harsh and vigorous man, brother to the 8th Lord Glamis. He was one of the kidnappers of the young James VI at the Ruthven Raid. He left no heir and Aldbar passed first to Sir Peter Young, a tutor of the king, and then in the 1740s to the Chalmers of Balnacraig in Aberdeenshire—who still retain possession, now using one of the estate-houses as dwelling. There is a chapel, modernised in the 19th century, deep in the Den, long only a mausoleum and burial-ground of the lairds but once the pre-Reformation chapel and then the parish church, until its parish was suppressed in the 17th century. Another Pictish cross-slab used to be kept here. It was removed to the castle, and when that was demolished, sent to Brechin Cathedral. Another later stone is now in the Museum of Antiquities, Edinburgh, a small medieval tombstone incised with cross and knight's sword, probably of the 13th century. Half a mile south of the castle site, on higher ground, is the artificial mound of the Court Law, prominent in open country, where the barony courts would be held in the pre-Lyon times when this was a lordship of the Cramond family, from the mid-15th century.

Airlie and Lintrathen. Airlie is a famous name, because of its renowned family and their castle; but there were Ogilvys of Lintrathen before they reached the peerage with the Airlie title. The two places are side by side, where Glen Isla opens on to Strathmore, two distinct parishes in fact, in the highly attractive Grampian foothills country between Alyth and Kirriemuir. Neither are populous—indeed they do not contain a large village between them —but they are both interesting and picturesque.

Airlie, or Errolly as once it was, is much the smaller, only 9000 acres, to the south and west, on the very border of Perthshire, the fine River Isla its dominant feature. The famous castle stands at the end of a 100-foot-high spine, above the junction of Isla and Melgam Water, in a very strong defensive site. Nevertheless it was not impregnable, and probably its greatest renown springs from the well-known occasion when it fell to the Covenanting Marquis of Argyll, in 1640, and which gave rise to the ballad, 'The Bonnie Hoose o' Airlie'. Argyll, in his hot hate against a hereditary foe, did a thorough job of demolition, "taking hammer in hand and knocking down the hewed work of doors and windows till he did sweat for heat at his work". So that not a great deal is left of the original 15th century castle save only the great and long frontal façade of high curtain-wall and northern tower, which had been somewhat altered in the late 16th and early 17th century. Behind is the pleasing but later house, reconstructed after the débâcle. Despite the song, however, the incident of turning out the Lady Airlie into the hills by Argyll did not take place here, but at Forter Castle, a more remote stronghold high up Glen Isla. The Earl of Airlie was away with King Charles in England at the time.

In 1432 Sir Walter Ogilvy of Lintrathen, treasurer of Scotland, descendant of the Ogilvys of that Ilk near by, and of the Celtic earls and mormaors of Angus, received a licence to fortify his Tower of Eroly from James I. His grandson was created Lord Ogilvy of Airlie, and the 8th lord made Earl of Airlie in 1639—a year before the Argyll incident. The Ogilvys were always the staunchest of king's men, and it is fitting that in recent times a son of the house, the Hon. Angus Ogilvy, son of the 9th Earl, should have married Princess Alexandra.

Below the castle, the Isla runs for a mile through a most picturesque wooded gorge called the Den of Airlie, famous botanically. The road from Alyth crosses this by a high bridge offering fine prospects, east of the farm of Bruceton, the river here being the county boundary. Although Bruceton therefore is in Perthshire, it is convenient to mention here the Pictish symbol-stone which stands in a field below the road and the farmhouse, much weatherworn but still with certain of the carvings discernible. Only half a mile away, but on the high ground above the road at Shanzie, is another standing-stone, this time a plain monolith.

The hamlet of Kirkton of Airlie lies over a mile south-east of the castle, in the deep hollow of a burn. The parish church and kirkyard occupy a knoll above the stream with its little bridge, an attractive situation. The church dates from 1781 but has a pre-Reformation nucleus; and a very interesting red-stone aumbry showing the Five Wounds of Christ is built into the east vestibule. The interior is plain but pleasing. On the sill of a south window is the date 1781 and initials. There is a fine double burial-enclosure detached to the south, with moulded gateway, dated 1609, to Mr. William Malcolm, minister, and family. There are many old recumbent gravestones, one dated 1596. Between Kirkton and castle, two weems or souterrains were discovered, one on Barns farm, 70 feet long.

A mile to the south, on the A926 Alyth to Kirriemuir road, is the pleasant strung-out village of Craigton, on the south-facing oak-wooded slope. There is a great deal of oak-wood in this area, and a particularly fine avenue flanks this road near the gates of Lindertis. This estate, seat of the Munro baronet family, is well known for its prize cattle. The Gothic mansion was rebuilt in 1813. To the south-east of it, near Lendrick Lodge, in an open field, is a six-foot-high standing-stone on a ridge above marshland. Farther east still, at the edge of the parish, in the area of the farms of Reedie and Auchindorie, there was a Roman encampment of which no trace is now evident. Three miles westwards along this same side-road is a small disused church, dated 1813, with former manse. There was once a castle at the farm of Baikie, a mile to the west, but this is wholly gone. Two miles or so farther west, in the very corner of the parish, is another and well-known Roman encampment and site of fort, at Cardean. Again no traces are obvious in the fields. Another standing-stone of six feet surmounts a small rise south of the A926, between the little school at Baitland road-end and Craigton village.

Lintrathen is a much larger parish, of 23,000 acres, largely mountainous, dominated this time by the great Loch of Lintrathen, a most picturesque, wood-girt sheet of water almost two miles long, under the steep Knock of Formal (1158 feet). It is now one of Dundee's major water supplies. Near the centre of its south side, the Melgam Water flows out; and at the bridge here is the parish church and an attractive scattered hamlet called Bridgend of Lintrathen. The church itself is small and plain, dating from 1803, and still lit by oil lamps, with ancient recumbent stones in the kirkyard and a small Pictish stone built in near the door. The manse near by is notably large and fine. To the east is a prominent green hillock with a burial-cairn on top. The Melgam, a little lower, has a series of cascades in the area of Clintlaw and Shanally farms.

These pale to insignificance, however, in comparison with the magnificent feature known as Reekie Linn, on the larger Isla, farther west in this parish. Just below the B954, at Bridge of Craigisla and Kilry post-office, the river is constricted by narrow rocky walls in a wooded defile, and thereafter plunges over in a great waterfall, with such force that the spray rises like smoke, to account for the name. It is all most spectacular, and easily reached by a public footpath. The fall and whirlpool below has carved a great cavern out of the cliff, all known as the Black Dub, and with ancient legends attached. There is another fine fall, less accessible and well-known, over a mile downstream, called the Slug of Achrannie, less high but still more narrowly compressed; also with a cauldron below. The parish is well named *Linn-an-t-Abhainn*, rapids of the river.

To the north of the parish and the loch are two large valleys branching off into the high hills, some of which reach the 2000 feet mark. These are the glens of Back Water, or the upper Melgam, to the north-west, and of the Quharity Burn. Up the first, half a mile north of the loch and above the B951, at Pitmudie, are three great standing-stones in a wood, one a magnificent massive obelisk 11 feet high; another, similar, has fallen; and the third may never have been upright. They make an impressive and eerie group in the hush of the plantation. There are three burial-cairns in this neighbourhood. A side-road leads for some three miles up from the B951, to Backwater Reservoir, opened by the Queen in 1969, which has flooded two miles of the upper part of this glen. The easterly valley, of the Quharity, is wider and open, presided over by the towering modern Balintore Castle, a great brown-stone Scottish Baronial pile, seen for miles. Braes of Coul lies below, with a small loch near by. There is another group of standing-stones on the farm of Knowhead, to the east.

North of Bridge of Craigisla, a side-road follows the Burn of Kilry upwards, climbing high, to the 1300-foot contour and down into Glen Isla again at Bridge of Brewlands, a scenic route. More prosaically, the B954 climbs up over the shoulder of Knock of Formal, the main route up Glen Isla. A mile up is Fornethy House, now a residential school of Glasgow Corporation for convalescent and other children in need of a holiday, an excellent establishment in lovely surroundings.

Glen Isla is separately dealt with.

Arbirlot and Kellie. The rural parish of 6700 acres and small village of the same name should really be called Aberelliot; but the name has been corrupted. It stands two miles west of Arbroath—which of course should be Aberbrothack—where the Elliot Water is joined by the Rottenraw Burn, and then enters the sea a mile on.

The village is delightfully set in the river's den, beside an old bridge, a modest scattered place though once considerably larger, indeed having its own annual cattle-fair. The Elliot was a good stream for driving mills, and there were no fewer than five here, four for meal and one for flax—though it was claimed that the dams and lades spoiled the fishing. Arbirlot seems to have been quite a place once, for controversy. Smuggling was a favourite pastime strangely enough—though this seems to have died away because "the foreign merchants did not receive very regular remittences": a moral, here.

The parish church stands picturesquely in an old graveyard above a waterfall of the wooded Kellie Den. The church was ancient, but rebuilt in 1832. Apparently there were some heart-burnings about this rebuilding, for it is recorded "The old church was seated at the expense of the farmers, and its seats being used for the new one, the farmers . . . charged a rent for the same. The aisle, which contains most of the additional sittings . . . was built at the expense of the Kirk Session, who have found it a very profitable investment . . ." The Church Mercantile! One gathers that old Arbirlot had its eye pretty firmly on the main chance, for such a picturesquely seques-tered nook. There are many old gravestones in the kirkyard, and a war memorial window in the church. George Gledstanes, arch-bishop of St. Andrews was minister here in 1597; as also was the famous Dr. Guthrie, from 1830 to 1837.

Just to the south, seaward, is Kellie Castle, a most handsome and interesting fortalice of the 16th and 17th centuries. It consists of a tall, five-storeyed L-planned tower-house, with later and lower wings, all enclosed in a curtain-walled courtyard with pend, gate-house and protective circular flanking-tower. There are gunloops and shot-holes, angle-turrets, dormers and crowstepped-gables, all highly attractive. The house was deserted and almost in ruins a century ago, but the Maule-Ramsay family restored it most authentically. It is still their property and a much-prized resi-dence.

Kellie was acquired by the Ochterlonys, from Ochterlony in Dunnichen parish, in 1402, who changed its name to Ochterlony so that they might continue to be called "of that Ilk". Sir William sold the property to Sir William Irvine of the Drum family and went to Guynd in Carmylie parish in 1634. It was bought by the 3rd Earl of Panmure in 1679 for £11,000 Scots, on account of debts contracted by the Irvines on the king's behalf in the Civil War, and given to his second son, Harry Maule, deputy Lord Lyon and a noted leader of Mar's Rising of 1715—Mar being his brother-in-law. At the collapse of the Rising, Harry Maule of Kellie and his brother the 4th Earl fled to Holland and were forfeited. But Kellie was eventually bought back, and Harry's son created Lord Panmure. This title in due course merged with that of the Maule-Ramsay Earls of Dalhousie, who retain possession.

There was formerly a village at Bonnyton, or Bonnington, over two miles to the west—not to be confused with the better-known Bonnyton near Montrose, whose lairds, the Woods, were influential in old Scotland. Bonnyton here was a possession of the Earls of

Crawford, passing to the Fotheringhams in mid-16th century. Now only a few houses remain. Kellie Moor lies just to the north, around the 350-foot contour, with Pitlivie Moor stretching to the west, strangely bare and bleak country to be so near the sea in a Lowland county.

Arbroath. The royal burgh of Arbroath prides itself on being the smallest Large Burgh in Scotland. But prides itself, and deservedly, on much else. Its renown will never fade, of course, as the place where, in 1320, was drawn up and subscribed the famous Scots Declaration of Independence, accepted as one of the most stirring and significant affirmations of freedom the world has known. This took place in the abbey established in 1178 by William the Lion, in memory of his friend Thomas à Beckett, which became one of the most powerful institutions in Scotland. The community which grew up around it, at the mouth of the Brothock Burn, 17 miles north-east of Dundee—Aber-brothock, or Arbroath—developed into the burgh of the mitred abbot, with its abbot's harbour of 1394, and in due course was made a royal burgh, just when is not clear, though King James VI gave it a charter of *novodamus* in 1599. It has always been a thriving, vigorous and go-ahead town, good at meeting challenges, very much a coastal community getting much of its livelihood from the sea, but with a rich agricultural hinterland. Now it has a population of 21,000, and combines a resounding past with a lively appreciation of the present and great ambitions for the future, both as an industrial centre and a holiday resort. One can feel that Arbroath typifies the well-doing, no-nonsense yet history-conscious Lowland Scot at his sturdiest.

The abbey, where it all started, crowns an eminence north-east of the old town centre, now surrounded by green lawns and gardens; and though ruinous, has sufficient of its red-stone magnificence remaining impressively to dominate all. It has been a very large establishment, its great cruciform church to the north and east almost 300 feet long, and formerly with a tall central tower and steeple at the transepts crossing and two lesser but still massive towers at the west end, parts of which remain. The central tower is wholly gone, but the south transept is well represented, and the sacristy aisle, called St. Mary's, of late 15th century date, remains more or less intact, a fine, lofty, double vaulted building with much good stonework, aumbry, double piscina and decorative windows. Before the high altar at the choir's east end was buried William the Lion himself, whose headless effigy has been removed to the museum in the abbot's house. The complex range of conventual buildings lie mainly to the south—cloister, frater, chapter-house, warming-house and dorter, kitchens and so on—now reduced largely to foundations but with the tall abbot's house, late 15th century imposed on a splendid 12th century vaulted sub-croft with large fireplace, still intact although it has undergone much alteration, being occupied as a dwelling-house until comparatively recently. Its museum contains many treasures. To the extreme west of all is the projecting gate-house range, the first part most visitors see, with its square flanking-tower jutting into the High Street, and its fine vaulted pend, through which a public street passes, defended by machicolated parapet and portcullis. This portcullis now features as the emblem of the town's arms. The entire complex, best seen probably from the open ground to the east, is imposing and exciting, a magnificent monument to the colourful past. Some of the colour not so long past, either, for here, in April 1951, was secretly brought the Stone of Destiny, abstracted from Westminster Abbey by young Scots patriots the previous Christmas Eve, so that it might be brought to light again in dignified fashion, with a secret promise that it would remain in Scotland for a month, "while tempers cooled". Unhappily this promise was ignored by the Scotland Yard detectives, who promptly, and as secretly, whisked it away back to London in the back of their car, the same night—setting Scotland in an uproar thereby. The present author was not uninvolved in this final episode.

Bernard de Linton, Bruce's secretary and chaplain, was abbot here, and chancellor of Scotland; and he it was who, under the hero-king's guidance, drew up the great Declaration of Arbroath, as a letter to the Pope, subscribed here by the barons of Scotland. And here many another ruler of Scotland presided, for the mitred abbots of Arbroath were apt to be amongst the most influential men in the kingdom. Perhaps the most famous was Cardinal David Beaton, who remained abbot even after he became Archbishop of St. Andrews, primate and chancellor of Scotland, and whose traces are so thick on the ground in surrounding Angus. At the Reformation, the abbey and its vast lands went to the king's Hamilton relatives, and included the patronage of 34 parish churches, no less.

The parish churchyard still lies around and to the north of the abbey, with a great many ancient stones. One particularly interesting appears to have been built into walling of a former church extension, and depicts a ruffed lady and gentleman, he holding a Bible, well executed, with the initials *M.I.P.* and *M.G.*, and the Graham arms. This would be an early Reformed minister, the M standing for Magister or Master of Arts. It is dated 1674.

Close to the abbey, to the south, is the present Old Parish Church, in Kirk Square off the High Street, a not very impressive or exciting building, though large, dating mainly from 1764, with steeple and clock. Its parish was created in 1560. In 1797, another large church was established as a chapel-of-ease, called the Abbey Church, close by. There are a great number of churches in the town—13 in all. But just in case it is felt that Arbroath overdoes it in this respect, it is recorded that in 1831 there were no fewer than 85 alehouses here, one to every 18 families!

The High Street is long, running northwards from the harbour to the abbey, and broadening in the centre. There is rather a fine Town House in restrained Classical architecture, erected 1803, containing many valuable documents, charters and so on in the Council Chamber. Adjoining to the north is the Guild Hall, of 1728 rebuilt in too ornate fashion in 1881, where the Guildry Incorporation still meets. This Incorporation dates from 1592. Interesting is the large figure 4 on the shield above the doorway, indicative of the original four royal burghs of Scotland—of which, however, Arbroath was not one! On the other side of the Town House is the quietly distinguished Sheriff Court building, formerly the Mechanics' Institute. And behind the Town House, reached by a quaint pend, is the large and quite impressive Corn Exchange building, which has been used as a cinema and is now partly deserted. Farther down the High Street, towards the harbour, is the large and highly modern Webster Memorial Theatre and Arts Centre opened by Princess Margaret, with seating for 633.

Arbroath, as befits a holiday centre which reckons to entertain 70,000 visitors per season, is good at providing facilities for leisure activities. There is a fine modern community and sports centre in Marketgate, with a very wide floor-space geared to various indoor sports and which can be seated to hold 600. Next door is the indoor swimming-baths; while some distance to the south-west, on the way to the West Sands, is one of the largest open-air swimming-pools in the country. Around this latter, reached from a fine esplanade road called Queen's Drive, are many other facilities, including paddling-pool and miniature railway and bus features for the children, tennis and putting and so on. Gayfield, the Arbroath Football Club's ground, is to the east; and flanking the West Sands beach is the 18-hole golf course. A very commodious caravan site adjoins.

By no means all the attractions cluster in this vicinity. Out on the Cairnie Road, to the north-west, near the West Cemetery, is the huge indoor bowling stadium, of which Arbroath is justly proud, erected in 1966 by a private company, which caters for bowling enthusiasts from a very wide area, with no fewer than 1500 members of its club. There is quite an extraordinarily expansive "floor", measuring 126 feet square, of eight rinks, covered in green Acriturf, also excellent supporting social facilities. Then, to the north-east of the town, flanking the beach which leads to the famous cliffs, is another large recreational area, starting from the attractive Springfield Park behind the fire station, with its old walled garden with rose-bushes and open-air bandstand enclosure, and children's playground. From the high ground of its eminence, there are splendid views up and down the coast. From this the very long Victoria Park extends eastwards, with promenade, a delightful "lung" for the town, at the far end of which commence the cliffs, with their fine cliff-top walk, extending for miles. Where park yields to cliffs, at Whiting Ness, is the site of the former chapel of St. Ninian, now gone, although its St. Ninian's Well is still there, and maintained, with another wishing well close by. A cliffs nature trail, established in 1971 by the Scottish Wildlife Trust, commences here.

The cliff-walk deserves especial praise, and is one of the town's greatest assets for visitors. In rich red stone, honeycombed with caves and inlets, diversified by tall stacks and thrusting headlands, it stretches for three miles northwards to the picturesque fishing village of Auchmithie, with features all the way to entice the explorer on. The names themselves entice—Stalactite Cave, Elephant's Foot, Needle's E'e, Blow Hole, Dickmont's Den, De'il's Heid, Forbidden Cave and so on. The Needle's E'e is a natural arch on the cliff-face; and Dickmont's Den the longest of the inlets, deep and narrow with an island stack in its mouth; while the De'il's Heid is an extraordinary bulbous-topped pillar. Half-way along, there is a slight lessening of the cliffs to form the wide, rock-ribbed Carlinheugh Bay. There are points where a descent to the rocky shore may be made, from which caves can be reached. Wild flowers cling to the ledges and sea-birds circle and cry. The slender column of the Bell Rock Lighthouse, which guides shipping into the Tay estuary, can be seen on a clear day 12 miles away, on a reef which used to be considered the most dangerous spot on the Scottish east coast. The present 120-foot-high pillar is the 1808 successor of the original warning bell fixed here by an abbot of Arbroath.

The Bell Rock Lighthouse has its shore establishment at Arbroath. Just south of the harbour is a quadrangle of substantial houses within a gateway, rather like a little fort, with a tall, circular crenellated signal-tower. The harbour itself is quite large, taking ships of up to 1000 tons, but mainly a fishing-haven. There are two busy boat-building yards, long-established. Here is the lifeboat station, with the coastguard station to the north. The area between the harbour and the abbey is the oldest part of Arbroath, known as the Fit o' the Toon, an extensive and quite attractive fisherman's quarter, with narrow streets and long rows of cottages. This is the home of that well-known delicacy the Arbroath smokie; and unlike so many ancient and traditional home industries this one is still flourishing. Almost every second house seems to hang a sign indicating smokies for sale, and behind the cottages are the little yards where the haddocks are cured with smoke from hardwood chips and sawdust, locally obtained. To stand to windward of Arbroath is to be immediately aware of the pervading scent of woodsmoke. There are some quite good Georgian houses with pillastered doorways facing the harbour and elsewhere, and one excellent late 17th century red-stone house of some size in West Newgate Street. Through this part of the town the Brochock Burn winds its way to the sea; and where it actually reaches salt water, just north of the harbour, is a pleasant little stretch of beach, with some sand. The main sand area is, however, well to the south, flanking the golf course.

Arbroath, however, is proud of its image as a modern, go-ahead commercial town, eager to attract new industry. Its industrial estate at Elliot lies to south and west on the skirts of the former West Common, and on the green rise here are the up-to-date factories of such well-known firms as Braemar Knitwear, Metal Box, Panmure Tool, Giddings & Lewis Engineering, and so on. The traditional industry of sail-making and canvas still flourishes—though not to the extent of employing 500 weavers as once it did—with Messrs. Webster to the fore. It is satisfying to see the engineering firm of Keith Blackman still with attractive old-style offices in the middle of the High Street. The large and highly modern Moray Firth maltings plant, costing £600,000, was opened in 1971. Undoubtedly North Sea oil developments will play their part here.

New housing developments are spectacular, partly to the south of the harbour area, opposite Inchcape Park, but mainly inland to west and east. The new Westway by-pass flanks a large and very modernistic complex, in the centre of which is the equally modern Timmergreens Primary School, all very bright and cheerful. Arbroath does well educationally, with both a high school and an academy as large senior secondary schools of some renown. The former stands in its own grounds in a lofty open position in the Keptie Road suburb, with impressive buildings. Behind it is a green eminence, part of Keptie Park with its boating-loch and island; and crowning this eminence is an extraordinary large castle-like edifice, red-stone, with crenellated tower and parapets—although this is, in fact, no more than a notably disguised water-tower. Opposite the high school, utilising its former north wing, is the Angus Technical College, also with highly modern and pleasant premises to the rear. Arbroath Academy, a well-known establishment founded in 1821 has now moved out to the northern suburbs, housed in a great concrete and glass building off the Seaton Road. In this same new-housing area is the Eastern Cemetery, large and pleasing, most interesting in having not only uncovered a weem or Pictish souterrain at its highest point, but in having preserved this, amongst the graves, with a little box-hedge encircling it, a crescent-shaped formerly underground storehouse, 15 feet long.

There is also an outstanding feature in the other, Western Cemetery, a mile away. This is the quite extraordinary Patrick Allan-Fraser Memorial Chapel, a huge, overgrown edifice in a jumble of architectural styles, which is nevertheless quite impressive in its sheer bulk and contrasts, erected by the last laird of Hospitalfield as a mausoleum, and completed 1884. With its two towers, clock, elaborate sundials, balconies, numerous apartments and passages, this is unique as a memorial, however flamboyant.

Hospitalfield itself is half a mile to the south, reached from the Westway by-pass, almost as elaborate and overdone architecturally although enshrining an ancient mansion of which odd traces remain —including its typical 17th century doocot at the farm-steading across the road. The great house still stands in part of its estate—it was once a hospital connected with the abbey, having its own chapel of John the Baptist. It is now a residential college for students on courses from the four art colleges of Scotland, and is full of treasures and museum-pieces left by Patrick Allan-Fraser. The music room, for instance, has two rare 17th century tapestries, as well as fine instruments and a notable carved-wood ceiling.

Special mention must be made of Arbroath's eight parks, which cover no less than 200 acres, and are well maintained and supplied with many facilities. The burgh common-lands have helped in this, and the connection is preserved in such names as Low, West and Cricket Commons. The Victoria Park to the north-east, commemorating that queen's Jubilee, is the largest, flanking the shore for almost a mile, along which cars may drive. Here is held annually the Angus Show.

Arbroath is a parish as well as a burgh, and this has a small landward area of almost 1000 acres. But it is inextricably mixed up with St. Vigeans parish, so full of interest, wherein are the Royal Marine Commando Group Station, with its 200 Admiralty houses, the renowned ancient church, and the Pictish stones museum—all dealt with separately. Auchmithie actually is in St. Vigeans parish, but is best described here since it tends to be linked with Arbroath, for obvious reasons. It is a most picturesque cliff-top fishing-village after the Mearns fashion, three miles north of the town, and renowned as the Musselcrag of Scott's *Antiquary*, a popular haunt of visitors, with its steep cliffs and boat-strand haven seeming to contra-indicate any fishing development and to make talk of smuggling distinctly more credible. The coastline here is full of interest. One of the most spectacular items is the Gaylet or Geary Pot, a huge pit, 120 feet deep and 150 in diameter, opening in a field 200 yards from the sea and half a mile south of the village, just beyond Laverock Den, into which the tide surges through a cavern. The Forbidden Cave lies farther south with prehistoric links. Auchmithie is reachable by bus. With excellent private initiative, the Auchmithie Housing Association was founded in 1970 to save the character of the old village, restore cottages , and harmonise the quite large new housing development. Inland, to the south-west, is Dickmontlaw, the highest point in the parish at 323 feet, with an artificial mound crowning it. Near by is Seaton House, comparatively modern in a pleasant wooded estate. There was a castle of Easter Seaton near by, built in 1583 by Sir Peter Young, which stood near the present farmhouse. Sir Peter was a great man in 16th century Scot and, tutor to James VI, and later ambassador to Denmark, amongst other offices.

No history of Arbroath is possible here, although inevitably it took a major part in the nation's affairs. Highlights, apart from the parliament Bruce held when the Declaration was signed, were the battle in 1445 between the Lindsays and the Ogilvys, in which the leaders of both clans fell with 500 others; and the raid of the French privateer *Fearnought* under Captain Fall, in 1781, when both shots and letters were exchanged with the town, the latter making amusing reading. No damage was done by either.

Auchterhouse and Dronley. This historic area was renowned in the days of Wallace and the Wars of Independence, when its laird, Sir John Ramsay, was one of the hero's comparatively few aristocratic supporters:

Good Sir John Ramsay and the Ruthven true,
Barclay and Bisset with men not a few:
Do Wallace meet—all canty, keen and crouse;
And with 300 march to Ochterhouse.

It is a small parish of 5448 acres, lying due north of Dundee five miles, on the fairly steeply rising Sidlaws flanks, today an attractive and favoured district for adventurous commuters and others appreciative of a high and dramatic housing situation. There are three main communities, the central Kirkton village; the Bonnyton area to the west, with the mansion's hamlet itself on the main road; and the rapidly growing Dronley area on the lower ground to the south.

The baronial mansion of Auchterhouse is highly unusual, a mainly late 16th and early 17th century house, approximating to no typical style of the period, but most pleasing, with its long three-storey main block, offset gabling, steep roofs and massive projecting chimney-stack. Internally also it is very fine, with a splendid 17th century plaster ceiling in the drawing-room, and a heraldically decorated fireplace. The oldest part of the house seems to have been built by the Buchans. Sir John Stewart, son of the Black Knight of Lorn who had married James I's widow, Queen Joan Beaufort, was created Lord Auchterhouse and Earl of Buchan, himself having wed the heiress daughter of Sir Alexander Ogilvy of Auchterhouse. By 1648 the 3rd Earl of Kinghorne, laird of Glamis, was in possession, he who had the title changed to Earl of Strathmore. Later the lands came back to the Ogilvys, Earls of Airlie. Near by are the ruins of an earlier fortalice of the Ramsays, which has come to be known as Wallace's Tower, merely because the hero sheltered there. On the property also are examples of the souterrains or weems for which this area is notable, early Pictish underground refuges. The main A927 road to Alyth passes through the quite picturesque hamlet with its former mill.

The Kirkton is much larger, and still growing, set high in the lap of the hills, a pleasant place with wide prospects. The parish church, standing on an intermediate ridge, has developed from ancient origins, and dates now in the main from 1775, incorporating work of 1630. An old doorway is built up in the south front, there is a bell-tower at the west end, and fragments of early window tracery are set in walling and gateways. Internally the church is very attractive and bright, with good stained glass and a chancel arch still retained, the choir itself pleasingly panelled with the old wood of former pew-backs. There is an ancient stone font still in use, and many old stones in the kirkyard.

To the north, beyond a dip of agricultural land, Auchterhouse Hill rises steeply to 1399 feet. At the foot nestles the delightfully placed Sidlaw Hospital, 44 beds, on a terrace site looking south. Somewhere near by is said to be a stone-circle lost amongst the heather. Another stood on the farm of Templelands (sign of a Knights Templar establishment) to the south-east, demolished when the railway was built. Tradition has it that a great battle was fought hereabouts in Pictish times. A mile east of the Kirkton is the small estate of Balbeuchly, with a Georgian mansion. A Pope's Bull of the mid-11th century specifically alienated this property from the bishops of Dunkeld, and gave it to the parish of Caputh—an extraordinary proceeding which no doubt enshrines some murky story. It long had the strange effect of excluding Balbeuchly from any of the services and benefits of Auchterhouse church near by—a sort of Papal pariah.

Dronley is an area rather than a village, there being Dronley old hamlet itself, set centrally in the wide valley of the Dronley Burn; North Dronley near the main road, a thriving residential development; South Dronley, a tiny farmtoun hamlet with a double-arched bridge amongst burnside meadows; and Dronley Wood, a large acreage of pleasant old woodland and new planting. The Dronley Burn joins with the Fallows Burn near Kirkton of Strathmartine, to the east, to form the Dichty.

Barry and Buddon. Barry is a village and small coastal parish lying at the base of the great Buddon Point peninsula, between Monifieth and Carnoustie, nine miles east of Dundee. The parish used to extend to 5300 acres, but Carnoustie, which was part of it, is now a burgh on its own. To be so near a great city, therefore, Barry is a strangely non-populous area, for there are no other villages.

The village itself is divided into two distinct parts, however, Barry proper and Barry Links Station, on the railway-line a half-mile to the south, where almost as large a community has grown up. The old part of the kirkton of Barry lies in the den of the Pitairlie Burn which here cuts its way through the very distinct bank of the former coastline to find its way to the sea thereafter across the wide flats and links of Buddon. This part of the village is attractive, with the former church, ancient and enlarged in 1818, but now roofless, standing in its well-kept graveyard high on the west bank, and a former mill and its cottages in the den by the waterside. There are many old gravestones in the yard, and in the ruined church itself a renewed heraldic panel dated 1664, to Grizel Durham and David Alexander of Pitskellie. Pitskelly is now a farm to the north. The modern parish church of Barry stands at the extreme east end of the village, on the bank, and was formerly the Free church.

A side-road goes southwards to Barry Links Station, and ends there so far as public travel is concerned, for beyond stretch the extensive army firing-ranges of Barry Camp and Buddon Ness, where access is restricted to walkers, and only when the red flags are not flying. This large triangular area with approximately three-mile sides, is a vast sand dune and links terrain of about 10 square miles, self-reclaimed from the sea, which once came right up to the aforementioned bank. It is an interesting territory, wild and empty, where the wild geese flight and the sand-storms blow, but with its own rich fauna and flora. It is a pity that the army monopolise it, for it should be a nature reserve, so happily close to Dundee. At its tip are two disused lighthouses, called the High and the Low, set up to guide shipping into the Tay estuary channel, but presently made useless by the moving sand-banks. The Low one was actually shifted some distance intact, by engineers at one time, to a new site; but this also proving abortive, the Abertay lightship was anchored out in the estuary to replace them. This is a bad coast for wrecks, and the Broughty Ferry lifeboat itself was lost with all hands as recently as 1959, going to the aid of the lightship which had broken adrift from its moorings in a gale. Whales as well as ships come to grief here; and even in 1638 we read that an Admiralty Court held at "the Budden Sandis within the flood-mark of the sea". It was concerned with Durham of Grange, for "wrongous medling with ane quhall lyand upone the schore".

Less than half a mile inland from the kirkton is Grange of Barry, a former farm of the abbey of Arbroath, then a small estate, and now a farm again. A tumulus rises beside the farmhouse, buttressed with stone at the base, which has been scooped out to contain a water-cistern. The land here is black fertile loam, very different from the sandy wastes only a short distance to the south, below the bank. The estate of Ravensby lies across the den of the Pitairlie Burn. It belonged to the Guthries, and in 1578 William Guthrie of Ravensby slew Patrick Gardyne of that Ilk, which started off a feud that was to convulse the families for long. The estate of Woodhill lies a mile westwards, Auchinleck property from 1408, with a ruinous 17th century doocot. The house was rebuilt, by Lorimer, in 1908, panels of 1604 and later, being built in, old dormer pediments bear the initials W.A. and M.D. The last Auchinleck was provost of Dundee in 1619.

George Buchanan alleged that a great battle took place at Barry in 1010 between Malcolm II and an invading force of Danes under a Viking called Camus, who was soundly defeated and himself slain. The many tumuli in the area are said to represent the large numbers buried from this contest, which caused the burn to run red three days! This is all considered to be highly doubtful, however; as is the attribution of the so-called Camus Stone in Monikie parish, as the memorial of this Viking—for it is obviously a typical Celtic Christian cross.

Brechin. The ancient town and royal burgh of Brechin is very insistent upon its status as a city—despite the fact that its population is only 7000. But as seat of one of the oldest bishoprics in the land— even though its cathedral is no longer the said bishop's seat—it can claim at least one attribute of a city. And it was so described in various documents of the past, including a royal proclamation of 1569. It certainly has all the marks of maturity, on its climbing, riverside site by the South Esk, just where the great vale of Strathmore begins to merge with the Howe of the Mearns, 13 miles north-east of Forfar. Lying between the mountains and the sea, and 25 miles from the nearest sizeable town northward, Stonehaven, it is a red-stone community of haphazard streets and closes, many trees, steep braes and sudden prospects, with quite a lot of modern development to parallel its antiquities and air of the past. It keeps its industry mainly down on the low ground by the riverside, to the south, and so inconspicuous.

What is conspicuous is the cathedral and its renowned Celtic Round Tower, which together dominate the little town, standing at the west end and high above the river, looking across to the castle, here rather hidden by high and ancient trees. The cathedral itself dates from the 13th and 14th centuries, with later alterations and a large rebuilding in 1806, the whole being restored in 1900. There is however a Norman nucleus, itself overlaying a far earlier Culdee establishment of the Celtic Church, of which the Round Tower is the only relic. The episcopal see was established in 1153 by David I; but its first cathedral was demolished early in the 13th century to make way for the present pointed Gothic edifice, dedicated to the Holy Trinity—although the tall spired tower dates from a century later. This has been described as the completest and best remaining example of its kind in Scotland, and rises 70 feet to the crenellated parapet, with the spire of stone 58 feet higher. Here is the belfry for the "Meikle Bell", recast in 1780 but a century older, which strikes the hours still, the little bells in the spire striking the quarters. The church was originally cruciform, but in the 1806 reconstruction the north and south transepts were swept away. In 1900, however, the south transept was rebuilt; and a side chapel was added to the north in 1951.

The cathedral is comparatively small, 198 feet by 58, but is none the less attractive for that. Its main entrance, the west door, is very fine, with five orders of carving, and is surmounted by a 15th century window with four tall lights, the arched head simulating a tree and branches. The nave is fairly bare, of five bays, dimly lighted by eight clerestory windows, the timber roof being modern. The chancel has been largely restored, after post-Reformation neglect, when it was in fact barred from the rest of the church, the reconstruction being admirable. There is much fine stained glass, by Douglas Strachen and others. Flanking the chancel arch are two built-in stones. One is the head of a most unusual Northumbrian-type cross-slab, found in a garden near by, with the inscription *S MARIA MR CHR*, St. Mary Mother of Christ, dating from the 9th or 10th century and notably different from our own Pictish slabs. The other is heraldic, with crozier, thought to apply to Bishop George Shoreswood (1454–63). On the floor lies a 12th or 13th century tombstone with incised decorative cross and a pair of shears.

At the back of the nave are other interesting relics, prominent amongst which is the fine Pictish cross-slab brought here when Aldbar Castle was demolished, a tall narrowish stone with its cross flanked by ecclesiastics, and on the reverse, two more ecclesiastics, a man fighting a beast, a horseman, a harp and a donkey at the foot, the last most unusual. This could be an 8th century piece. Near by is a coped recumbent stone, possibly 10th century, with strange human face and large eyes. There are many other fragments of carving. Preserved here are the ancient font, the "Deid Bell" of the early 16th century, and much 17th century pewter and silver.

The cathedral is fine, but it is the Round Tower which rises beside it which is almost unique, for it is one of the two examples on the Scottish mainland (the other is at Abernethy, Perthshire) of this type of Celtic building—but this is superior. There are similar towers in Ireland. It is 86 feet high and only 15 in diameter at base, tapering slightly; the spire at the top rising another 20 feet is not original. It may date from around A.D. 990, and represents the Celtic Church's Culdee college here. In 971 Kenneth II gave "the great monastery of Brechin to the Lord" according to the Pictish Chronicle; so that we do not know exactly when the establishment was founded. The workmanship is superb, the tapering, in 60 courses, being admirably done, the walls three and a half feet thick at the foot and two and a half at the top, the interior diameter shrinking only slightly. The doorway is six feet above the ground, for security, the lintel enhanced by a fine representation of the crucified Christ. The tower was originally free-standing, and makes a splendid memorial to our Pictish ancestors. An interesting sidelight to this is that the occupation and office of smith was very important in Pictish days; indeed there is a theory that the famous Dunfallandy Stone at Pitlochry which shows a mounted smith, represents a priestly cult of smiths, after the Wayland the Smith tradition from Europe. And the office of smith to the lordship of Brechin was a very ancient and probably Pictish inheritance, and became hereditary in the Lindsay family, with many privileges.

There are many old gravestones in the cathedral churchyard, for its church became the parish church of Brechin after the Reformation, the episcopal bishop of Brechin's seat being now at Dundee. The bishop's palace is gone, but the bishop's close remains, and the Cathedral Manse is built on the site of the palace garden. The bishops had a country seat at Farnell Castle four miles to the south-east—which see. To the west of the cathedral is Chanonry Wynd, where the manses of the canons used to be. None survive, but several old houses and gardens maintain the sequestered atmosphere.

The family of Maule have held Brechin Castle, just across the wooded ravine of the Skinners' Burn, which here joins Esk, from time immemorial, and it is still the seat of the Maule-Ramsay Earls of Dalhousie. Sir Thomas Maule held it heroically for three weeks against the might of English Edward I in 1303, until he was killed by a missile. Nothing of that building survives today, but its successors arose on the same strong site above the ravines. Although the present house dates mainly from the late 17th and early 18th centuries, there remains the L-planned vaulted basement storey at the west end, now converted into an attractive dining-room and ante-room. This looks like 16th century work. A highly interesting feature is the subterranean ice-house to the east, dug into the steep bank, a fearsome deep dark hole for the storage of perishable food-stuffs—although perhaps originally for less domestic purposes. The castle stands in a magnificent park, and seen across the deep den of the Esk makes a spectacular picture.

The town itself has few notable buildings. The quite effective Tudor magnificence of the Mechanics' Institute, which fronts all travellers from the west and divides the main approach, was erected in 1838 at the expense of the Lord Panmure, an ancestor of the Earl of Dalhousie. The so-called City Hall, in Swan Street, is less ambitious than its name; and the town chambers are unremarkable. At the east end, on the lower ground, is the pleasing tree-girt St. Ninian's Square, with a handsome Public Library building, and an elaborate fountain erected in memory of the 11th Earl. In this lower riverside area is considerable industry, including the large Denburn jute works, the Valley Works, also jute and man-made modern fibres, and the S.C.W.S. creamery. Although much of the housing here is old but undistinguished, there is some good modern housing development. At the riverside itself, where is the Auld Brig of Brechin, is a recreation area, with putting-greens, paddling-pool and so on, with a caravan-site farther to the east. The large Maison-dieu Church in this area is modern, retaining the old name of an almshouse, hospital and chapel, founded in 1256, a single wall of which remains off Market Street, with good pointed arched door, three narrow windows and a piscina.

The higher parts of the town, to the north and west, are mainly residential, with many fine villas in large gardens—although here also are the two distilleries, the North Port and the Glencadam. Here also is the large St. Andrew's Episcopal church in pleasing surroundings, with an enormous old tree opposite, and the dignified former high school buildings near by. The new and spectacularly modern high school, opened by Princess Margaret, stands in an open and prominent position well to the north-west—where, from certain angles it stands out rather like a great factory. However, at closer range, with lots of grass and planted trees, it looks better. It traces its history to the grammar school founded in the cathedral in 1429.

Brechin, like Montrose, is notable for the number of little closes opening off its pavements, giving pleasing glimpses into a more domestic and unhurried world than the traffic-dominated main streets. This traffic problem is acute here, with the main Aberdeen highway of the A94 pouring its heavy transport through the narrow old streets, to the disadvantage of all. A by-pass is planned—and it is to be hoped that old Brechin will survive until it is in fact built. Its climbing High Street—which unfortunately has lost its mercat cross —is spared the worst of the traffic; but even this has to carry the A933 and the A935 to Arbroath and Montrose respectively. Brechin does not want to become any sort of museum-piece or backwater, nor to revert to the 19th century—although that may not have been so quiet, for there were no fewer than 60 inns or alehouses here in 1833 —but its pleasing character cannot be maintained under the full impact of today's motor-traffic.

Brechin is quite a large parish, as well as a royal burgh, extending to almost 25 square miles. Indeed there is a place called Little Brechin, two miles to the north-west, a scattered crofting-type community rather than a village, with small farms, a school and a post-office. There is a village at Trinity, one mile north of the town on the A94, pronounced Tarnty, commemorating the Holy Trinity of the see's dedication. Here great cattle, horse and sheep fairs used to be held four times a year, some of the largest in Scotland, on Trinity Muir—which is now a fine 18-hole golf course. It is interesting to note that today the fairs have degenerated into an annual visit of "the shows"—but this is still held on the original site, on the golf course, which must at times hold its problems.

Near Trinity village is the old estate and barony of Keithock, with some interesting features. The mansion is mainly of the Adam period; but within it remains the nucleus of a late 17th century house, its moulded doorway surmounted by a large panel with the Edgar arms impaling those of Forrester, and the date 1671, now enhancing the interior. There is some panelling and other traces of old work. Spanning the den's burn in the grounds is an old pack-horse-bridge, on the line of the former Edzell road. And at the farm of Little Keithock, nearer the village, is a pleasing square, white-washed doocot, with three heraldic panels built into its sides, showing the arms of Donaldson and Baillie and the date 1624. The Lindays held the barony from the 15th century until 1617 when the Edgars succeeded them. Templewood of Keithock near by belonged to the Knights Templar, and was bought at their forfeiture by Bishop Carnoth.

Just north of Keithock, at the parish boundary with Stracathro, is the site of a Roman camp, supposedly called Tina; but of this few signs remain. The Battle of Brechin, particularly bloody, was fought south of here in 1452 between the notorious Tiger Earl of Crawford and his Lindsays and the Earl of Huntly; the farm name of Huntlyhill commemorates. There was another battle in 1130, two miles to the north-west, also in Stracathro, between David I and Angus Mormaor of Moray, near the farm of Auchenreoch.

The former barony of Findowrie is to the west of this parish, with its Killievair Stone, but these are described under Menmuir, near by. Well to the south-east is the area of Arrat, once also a barony and seat of the Arrats of that Ilk from 1264 till the Reformation, now only a farm. There was an ancient chapel of St. Magdalene here, rebuilt 1429 but now gone. Ardovie, too, to the west three miles, was a former lairdship, the Speids thereof having a prominent tomb in the cathedral graveyard. They were a notable family.

Broughty Ferry and Barnhill. Broughty is an excellent example of how an ancient independent community may manage to survive, and retain its own identity, when swallowed by the spread of a great city. Lying only three miles east of the centre of Dundee, which has had to expand widely because of the constrictions of its site, it inevitably has been overtaken. The great nabobs of Juteopolis were the first to seek to take it over, finding its pleasant seaside situation admirable for building their ambitious and extravagant mansions. Most of these are now hotels or institutions; but because these rich manufacturers liked privacy as well as display, they surrounded their palaces with large gardens and high walls—which still remain and keep the more distressing forms of urban sprawl at bay. Moreover Dundee itself is now proud of having an authentic seaside resort within its boundaries, and so is concerned not to destroy its character.

And character there is, even if Broughty Ferry is no longer a burgh on its own (it was once the third largest town in Angus, though for only a short time). It is a breezy, bright place, however lacking in architectural claims of individual excellence, spreading along the coast from Dundee's Stannergate to where Barnhill joins up with Monifieth, three miles. The presence of the sea dominates Broughty; that, and its castle; and also, to some extent, the wooded mansion-dotted heights of Fort-hill or Balgillo. Two other factors which do not fail to make themselves felt are the busy A930 road threading the town; and the main railway-line to Aberdeen, which all along this coastline has, not unnaturally, chosen the easy course, hugging the sandy shore links, and tending to cut off the communities from the sea, save by a succession of bridges over and under. This gives the railway-passengers a delightful journey, but is less kind to the local residents. However, undoubtedly the railway played a large part in building up Broughty as a holiday resort, so that much of the place has been erected *after* the lines were laid.

The history of Broughty is really that of its castle, which was an important stronghold dominating the mouth of the Tay, and at times ranked as a fortress of national significance. It stands dramatically on a headland, Broughty Craig, thrusting into the sea, with the harbour tucked in at the west side—and so does indeed dominate the entire seaboard prospect for miles, a tall and massive five-storeyed tower rising proudly above gunlooped curtain-walls. It is now a double-tower, but the landward portion is of comparatively modern date—though built in approximately the same style. The authentic keep has sheer, thick walls, harled, rising to a crenellated parapet and wall-walk, with gabled roof within—although this top storey has been much altered. There are a number of machicolations at parapet level, for the dropping of unpleasantness upon unwelcome visitors below. It dates in the main from the late 15th century, although there is an older nucleus. The approach is still by the now permanent drawbridge over the former landward-side moat. It is now leased by Dundee Corporation and is used as a museum featuring natural history exhibits, arms and armour, furniture, etc.

Broughty was acquired by the 3rd Lord Gray, of near-by Foulis and

Castle Huntly, in 1490; and whatever was on the site previously, it was described by the Earl of Crawford in 1496 as "the new fortalice of Broughty". Though undoubtedly it was devised to levy toll on shipping entering the Tay, in conjunction with another Gray castle on the south side at Ferry Port on Craig, and to control the lucrative ferry between them, it was not long before it was involved in much larger excitements. During the regency of Mary of Guise, the English under Somerset invaded Scotland, to force a marriage between Henry VIII's son Edward and the infant Mary Queen of Scots; and Patrick, 4th Lord Gray commenced the career of treachery for which that family became notorious, meeting the invaders at St. Andrews and agreeing to deliver up Broughty Castle. For this he was arrested and imprisoned. The Scots Privy Council minutes of 1547 say: "Our auld ynemies of England hes, by way of deid, taken the craig and place of Broughty and ramforcat them." Also: "Our auld ynemies being in the hous of Broughty are apperandly to invaid the burc of Dundie and haill cuntrie, and to burn, herey, sla and destroy . . . etc." The Council ordered 300 men to be raised, 100 hagbutters and 100 spearmen, the half to be equipped by the superior clergy, at a levy of £600, and the rest at the charges of the citizens of Dundee, plus 100 horsemen from the counties of Perth, Angus and the Mearns. However, the English garrison numbered over 2000—not all crowded into the castle, for they built a fort on Balgillo Hill to the North—and were not dislodged for two years. The castle was then partly demolished. It was built up again, and held by the Lords of the Congregation at the Reformation, until captured in 1571 by Seton of Parbroath in the Catholic interests. During the Cromwellian interlude, General Monk captured it, and imprisoned herein old Sandy Leslie, Earl of Leven, the Covenanting commander-in-chief, and other members of the Estates, whom he had captured at the unfortunate parliament held at Alyth, before packing them all off to London. Later, in the industrial age, the castle fell on hard times, and was actually used as a railway store. But during the Crimean War it was taken over by the government and fortified as a coastal defence strongpoint. The army remained in possession until after the Second World War.

To landward of the castle is an open park called the Castle Green, with children's playground and an interesting leisure centre, a hall with stage and other facilities. To the east is the Windmill Garden, where once such feature stood. To the west, the quite large harbour, once terminus of the Fife ferry and a haven for fishermen, is now given over to pleasure craft—although the Royal Tay Yacht Club headquarters and moorings lie farther west nearer Dundee.

The sea-front at Broughty has still many low-browed but characterful former fishermen's cottages. Amongst them, looking somewhat out of place, is Beach Crescent, a short terrace of more ambitious housing, one of which has been turned into the Orchar Art Gallery, an admirable private venture, one of the few in Scotland, with a notable collection of both oil and water-colour

Dundee. The Tay estuary and the Road Bridge, with Fife in the background

Dundee. The Commercial College

Dundee. Dudhope Training Centre with a glimpse of the Tay Railway Bridge in the left background and Fife beyond

paintings, many of the 19th century Scots school; but also etchings by Whistler and others. It is open to the public. Farther west along the sea-front is the lifeboat station, with its plaque commemorating the men of the lifeboat *Mona*, lost with all hands in 1959. Near by is a typical fishing-village public barometer, dated 1859.

Still farther west, and not readily discovered behind derelict property at Chapel Lane, is the site of a former pre-Reformation chapel in an old graveyard, now barricaded off. There are many old stones, and a mort-house.

Until 1790, Broughty was a mere fishing-village in Monifieth parish, with only some 50 fishermen's cottages. So the rest of the town is comparatively modern, laid out in rectangular plan, long and fairly narrow. The main shopping-street is Brook Street, running the entire length of the town, and well-served. On the quickly rising ground to the north are the best residential areas. Here is now the Anton House Training Centre for disabled girls; also the Black Watch War Memorial Home. Up here was the English fort, with its draw-well. Broughty only became a *quod sacra* parish in 1834, so the parish church, St. Aidan's, is not ancient. Another parish was carved out, St. Stephen's, in 1875. St. Mary's Episcopal church, designed by Sir Giles Gilbert Scott, is rich in stained glass from London, Belgium and Germany.

One of Broughty's basic features of course is its beach, a magnificent stretch of golden sands, reaching on eastwards to Monifieth and Barry. There are water ski-ing facilities. The annual swim across the Tay estuary takes place from here.

A mile south-west and inland of Broughty rises the quite spectacular and interesting castle of Claypotts, sometimes spelt with only one t. It is really in Dundee parish, but conveniently described under Broughty. It stands near a busy crossroads of the A92 and the B978, in an enclave of attractive modern housing and overlooking a pond, all very eye-catching, an unusual fortalice, entire and in excellent order, in the care of the Department of the Environment. It is a late 16th century building on the Z-plan, oblong with large circular towers at two opposite corners, these corbelled out to the square at roof-level to form gabled watch-chambers, in dramatic, almost exaggerated fashion, the walls pierced by many gunloops and shot-holes. It was built by the Strachan, or Strathauchane, family about 1560, and passed to the Grahams of near-by Claverhouse in 1625. At the forfeiture of Bonnie Dundee, the Douglas family obtained the lands, the Earls of Home in due course succeeding. The great Douglas and Angus housing extensions of Dundee lie adjacent. There is a legend of a drudging brownie attached to Claypotts, one of these supernatural domestics—allegedly driven away by a jealous female servant who did not know when she was lucky.

At the east end of Broughty is Barnhill, really in Monifieth parish and formerly a separate village. No doubt its name was originally Barony Hill. Oddly enough, the only and abrupt little hill hereabouts is not so called, but known as Reres Hill Park. It was gifted by the 10th Earl of Dalhousie, and its summit makes an excellent viewpoint, especially across the water towards Tents Muir. At the roadside is a decorative Gothic arch presented by Provost J. G. Orchar in 1887, to mark Queen Victoria's jubilee. Barnhill began to be feud out by the Earl of Panmure on 99-year leases about 150 years ago, and is now a favoured residential area. One of the large houses is now the Armitstead Children's Hospital. And to the north, on higher ground, is the large Dundee School of Nursing, overlooking a highly modern and quite impressive new housing area, well laid out.

The area to north and east is described under either Monifieth or Murroes.

Careston. This small Strathmore parish of 2000 acres, one of the smallest in Angus, is pronounced Car-is-ton, allegedly taking its name from one Carald, a Danish leader who fell here fleeing from the battle at Aberlemno. It was, however, formerly called Fuirdstone, from a ford on the South Esk, and the fortalice of this name, now gone, stood on the farm of Balnabreich at the south-east corner of the parish. Careston lies mainly north of the river, four miles west of Brechin and consists of little more than the large estate of Careston Castle, there being no village or large hamlet. All most people see of it is the busy A94 highway which threads its southern extremity. It is well worth-while to turn off, for a little, to the north.

The parish church is delightful, and stands remotely off a back-road, north-west of the castle, down a lane amongst old trees. It basically dates from 1636, although it has been renewed and restored pleasingly, small but with character. Its main feature of interest is the north aisle, inside and out. This is in fact the laird's loft of the Carnegies, former owners of the castle, and is entered separately by a roll-moulded doorway with heraldic panel above displaying the Carnegie arms. It has a tall mullioned window to the north and a small moulded one to the east. Internally, this loft or aisle is highly interesting, having its opening into the kirk framed in very fine carved woodwork, with an elaborate decorative lintel and stone breast. The choir of the church is stone-slabbed, and up two steps. There are old pewter communion-cups on view, and one or two old gravestones in the yard. The back-road near by is pleasingly rural, with a small school but no kirkton.

Careston Castle is a large and rather extraordinary house, being in fact two houses, back and front. The older part, unfortunately much spoiled, lies to the north, and has been a lofty Z-planned tower-house of the late 16th century, now rising from a clutter of later building, its circular stair-tower and angle-turrets having lost their conical roofs and been finished with sham battlements. But the crowstepped gables, stringcourses and heraldic dormer pediments remain. The front of the mansion, on the other hand, facing south, is that of a tall and symmetrical laird's-house of the early 18th century, with regular and large windows and much carved stonework, with the date 1714. The building also contains a nucleus of an early 15th century castle. It was long the seat of a family called Dempster, who took their name from the office of deemster or adjudicator of the Scots Parliament, Haldane de Dempster doing homage in 1296. This line died out in the 16th century, and the Lindsays took over. Later Careston passed to Sir Alexander Carnegie, brother of the 1st Earl of Southesk. In 1707 Sir John Stewart of Grandtully purchased the estate and rebuilt the south front.

Nearly a mile west of the castle, in a sequestered and remote position far from any tarmacadamed road, is the hamlet of Marcus Mill, very picturesque in its decline, but still with four houses occupied at the leafy bank of the Noran Water. The tall old red-stone mill buildings are now used as a store. Just across the river, reachable thus only by a shaky footbridge, is the farm of Waterson, once a barony on its own, with a family of Waterson of that Ilk. Nothing now remains to remind of that period. Marcus, or Markhouse, is a small estate to the south-west.

At the other, eastern end of this small parish, is Balnabreich, just south of the A94, with a milk-bar at the road-end, now again only a farm but with a long history. Indeed here, at the junction of the Noran and Esk, is thought to have been a Roman camp commanding the aforementioned ford, which was of obvious importance. Balnabreich, or Fuirdstone, became a lairdship of the Guthries, and its Law-hill is still pointed out.

Carmylie, Redford and Greystone. Set near the centre of Angus, Carmylie is an upland parish of some 12 square miles, occupying a sort of tableland rising towards the tail-end of the Sidlaw Hills, reckoned locally to be a cold place and a little bleak. Yet it is a fine free breezy area, of wide vistas, and, like the other districts of Angus lying south of Strathmore, cut deeply by the hidden wooded dens of the various streams. It has two other villages than Milton of Carmylie, Redford and Greystone, neither large. Indeed the entire population is probably less than 1000.

The Milton, only a hamlet, lies at a crossroads a quarter-mile south of the parish church, which stands isolated on rising ground, with only the manse for company. The church dates from 1609, when the parish was formed out of portions of surrounding parishes; but it is on the site of a pre-Reformation chapel dedicated to the Virgin Mary. It is well built of warm reddish ashlar, and only slightly altered, with a raised gablet to the south. It is said that the principal heritor, responsible for building it in the 17th century, bankrupted himself in the process; admittedly the lands changed hands just after this period, the Strachan lairds then being replaced by the Ochterlonys —who still remain. There is a moulded doorway and window at the south side, typical of the period; and two stone masks form the skew-putts of the east gable. Also on this east gable is a consecration cross, difficult to discern. In the west gable is a stone dated 1670, with initials *A.O.* and *H.M.*, for Ochterlony and Maule; and another inscribed *M.I.S. 1721*, for Master James Scott, the minister. Internally there is a memorial stained-glass window suitably decorated, to the Rev. Patrick Bell, the inventor of the reaping-machine, who was minister here for 26 years. He is buried in the kirkyard, dying aged 68 in 1869. The agricultural motif is maintained amongst the tombstones, for a number, of varying ages, show an unusual representation of a plough, plus a coulter in a wedge-shaped frame, obviously not all the work of one sculptor. There are many old stones, one revealing the determined and stay-at-home pessimist:

Let marble monuments record their fame who distant lands explore,
This humble stone points out the place where sleeps a virtuous ancient race,
Their sire possessed ye neighbouring plain before Columbus crossed the main
And tho ye world may deem it strange, his sons contented seek no change,
Convinced wherever man may roam, he travels only to the Tomb.

Carmylie parish, like its neighbours of Monikie and Monifieth, was a great quarrying centre, producing the famous sandstone Arbroath paving, building stone and also slates. At one time 300 men were employed hereabouts, and the stone sent to London and even America, shipped from Arbroath. Numerous fossils have been found in the camstone beds, of reeds, other vegetation, wood and fishes. Some stone in Cologne Cathedral is said to come from here.

The parish boasts a most handsome, commodious and spectacularly modern hall, set in an even more isolated position than the church, at a roadside mid-way between the Milton and Redford village, over a mile to the north-east. A railway-line used to connect Redford to the main line at Arbroath, built privately by an Earl of Dalhousie for the transport of the stone, the main old quarry area lying immediately to the north-west, on the high ground. Between Redford and the aforementioned hall is an equally remotely-sited auction-mart, a strange thing to find set down alone at the roadside.

A mile north of this quarry area is Boath Hill, 600 feet, from which standing-stones were removed in the early 19th century. On the northern flanks of it, facing towards Strathmore, is the farm of Back Boath. Here was once a pre-Reformation chapel, stones from which are said to be built into the farm-steading. Certainly there is a roll-moulded doorway built-up here, but it seems rather later, and looks more secular than ecclesiastic. This is at the very northern edge of the parish.

A mile east of the Milton lies the ancient estate of Guynd—pronounced Gind, as in begin—still the seat of the Ochterlonys, who came here from Kellie Castle at Arbirlot in 1634. All these lands belonged originally to the abbey of Arbroath, and we read of the Abbot Malcolm, twenty-second thereof, making a preambulation of the abbey lands of Dunnichen, Guynd, Kingoldrum and Ochterlony in 1460. Archbishop James Beaton, nephew of the cardinal, as abbot of Arbroath, in 1549 granted lands of Guynd to John Beaton of

Balquharry "for the defence of the monastery against the invaders of the church liberties in these times when the Lutherans are endeavouring to invade the same". The Beatons seem to have kept the lands until 1597, when presumably the Strachans gained them. Whether by bankruptcy or not, the Ochterlonys replaced them, and took over a mansion on the brink of the Black Den. This house, so greatly altered as to be unrecognisable as belonging to the 17th century, is still on the site, but is no longer used as a mansion, the Ochterlonys having built a handsome Georgian house in parkland a little to the north. In the den of the Elliot Water, to the east, are vestiges of a Caledonian fort, or dun, sometimes erroneously referred to as a Roman camp, triangular-shaped and strongly sited, where the two dens meet.

A mile west of the Milton lies another famous place—although only a farm today. This is Carnegie, where that great family, progenitors of the Earls of Southesk and Northesk and many another notable, took its name. They came here in 1358, then calling themselves de Balinhard, Sir Walter Maule granting them the lands of Carnegie in his barony of Panmure. There was a castle here, now gone—though an old walled garden remains. The Carnegie property remained in the hands of the Southesk family until the mid-19th century, when the Panmure Maules got it back.

The village of Greystone lies on a side-road a mile north of Carnegie, a pleasantly sited place on a south-facing green slope, with a Free church now deserted and shuttered-up. No local tradition seems to be recollected as to what particular stone gave the village its name. However, in the parish of Dunnichen, four miles to the north, just north-east of the village of Letham, is a large rough boulder known as the Girdle Stone, from carvings thereon resembling a griddle. This is locally and traditionally alleged to have been carried here long ago from "the Crafts [or crofts] of Carmylie" by a witch, in her apron, the strings thereof breaking when she was passing over Letham and the stone falling here. It is almost certainly the Grey Stane referred to in a note on the marches of Dunnichen parish about 1280. So I suggest that Greystone is almost unique in being able (if it only knew) to claim a name from four miles away and with occult significance.

A large tumulus or burial cairn formerly topped Carmylie Hill near by; and two holy wells were sited somewhere on the lower slopes, known as Carmylie and Monk Mudie's Wells.

Carnoustie. The burgh of Carnoustie lies mid-way between Dundee and Arbroath, one of the "lang touns" of the Angus coast, somewhat wedged in between sea and rising ground. Most famous as a golfing mecca, it is also a favourite family holiday resort, with miles of splendid sands and many attractions. It has a population of 5650, which puts it quite high in the Angus league; but this is a very modern development, for a century ago its numbers were only 1700, and 50 years before that it was but a village in the parish of

Barry. The name, however, is ancient, and said to mean the Cairn of the Heroes, alleged to refer to the semi-legendary battle between Malcolm II and the Danes, fought hereabouts in 1010; admittedly there are many tumuli and burial-cairns in the vicinity.

The town is not distinguished architecturally or in planning; but it is a bright, clean, go-ahead place, with a long main street, sea breezes and many hotels and guest-houses. Unfortunately, the ever-present main Aberdeen railway-line runs between town and beach, which tends to lessen the essential atmosphere of a seaside resort—a handicap which all this coastline suffers under. But this is only superficial, and does not apply to West Haven fortunately; it by no means deters the devotees, and many families have holidayed here for generations. There is industry at Carnoustie also, the Panmure Works of W. G. Grant & Co., making jute goods and textiles, succeeding the four early linen-mills. Organised parties of visitors are shown round these well-equipped works.

Golf, however, is the outstanding feature here, and Carnoustie Championship Course has seen some of the most exciting scenes of international golf. Walter Hagen has called it the best course in Britain and one of the three best in the world. Four Open Championships played here have produced champions in Tommy Armour, Henry Cotton, Ben Hogan and Gary Player. The Amateur Championship has been played at Carnoustie three times, the British Ladies, the Mixed Foursomes, the British Boys and innumerable others. For less ambitious players and tyros there is the Burnside 18-hole, and a nine-hole course and three putting-greens. And the by-products of golf flourish, naturally—club-houses, golfing hotels, golf-shops and professional establishments. The town indeed is a forcing-ground for professionals, over 300 of them having gone out to teach the world the game.

There are other sports catered for also, of course—bowling, cricket, tennis, yachting, sea-fishing, pony-trekking and so on. Less active interests do not go by the board, summer and winter, and the Musical Society productions, ballroom dancing, gymkhanas and children's parades are all popular. There is a conference centre seating 500, with cafeteria, a large caravan-site in wooded parkland in the Carnoustie House grounds, and camping-sites—even a baby-sitting service. A handsome modern high school was opened by Princess Alexandra in 1971, costing one million pounds.

There is not much of antiquity to be seen here, to be sure, with even the parish church dating only from 1838, before which the parish was Barry. But the former fishing-village of West Haven, situated at the east end of the town, is attractive, with many old cottages and the air of the sea. There is no actual harbour, but a boat-shore. There is a coastguard station. The beach here is deservedly popular, safe as it is extensive, and backed to the east by dunes to offer shelter from winds. Away to the west stretch the golden miles to Buddon Point, seamed here and there with the fixed nets of the salmon-fishers.

A mile and more to the east is East Haven, another fishing-village —but this is in Panbride parish.

Carnoustie does its developing to the west, rather, towards Barry village and the great army ranges, with much modern housing. Inland lie the farmlands of Barry parish and the great estate of Panmure.

Cortachy and Inverquharity. Cortachy and Clova parishes were united in 1608; but Glen Clova is an entity in itself, and will be treated separately. Inverquharity is a famous ancient castle and district, actually in Kirriemuir parish, but being much nearer, and in the same valley as Cortachy, is dealt with here.

Cortachy parish is huge, but mainly empty hillside, for this area is very much in the lap of the Grampians, at the mouths of Glens Clova and Prosen. There is no real village, but Dykehead, half a mile north-west of the kirkton of Cortachy, is a sizeable scattered hamlet at the wooded junction of the Clova and Prosen roads, with a quite large and well-doing hotel having extraordinary modern architectural development. The kirkton, delightfully set in the wooded den of the Esk, is very much an estate hamlet, at the gates of Cortachy Castle, with Gothic parish church of 1829, built at the sole expense of an Earl of Airlie, near by. There are many old mossy gravestones in the yard, some of the 17th century, amongst which is the ornate table-stone to James Winter, inscribed *I.W. 1732*, recalling the Battle of Sauchs (described under Fern). It was set up by the other surviving leader of that notable encounter, Mackintosh in Ledenhendrie, hero of the fight. Just to the east of the church is the mausoleum of the Airlie family. In the den below is the old single-arched Bridge of Cortachy, over the South Esk, and a few yards downstream lies the great boulder known as the Devil's Stane, no doubt an erratic. The local legend is that Satan threw it in an attempt to destroy the building of the church's predecessor, but missed! The manse and the former mill, now a village hall, are in the den, at the far side of the road, all very leafy and attractive.

Cortachy Castle, seat of the Earl of Airlie, is a famous house delightfully sited within a bend of the river, in wooded grounds, with a renowned holly hedge 400 yards long. The castle is readily seen from the Memus road east of the church. Although greatly altered and enlarged down the centuries, with at least six periods of building, its nucleus was a courtyard-type castle of probably the 15th century, of which three of the flanking-towers remain, the fourth being the keep which has been incorporated in extensive later work. The south-west tower is the least altered, circular at base but corbelled out to the square above to form a watch-chamber, unfortunately given unsuitable Tudor-type chimneys by some "improver". The conical roofline of the south-east tower, with its parapet, is modern, as is much else. The castle is full of treasures and relics of this most renowned family of Ogilvy. Sir Walter Ogilvy of Auchterhouse was granted Cortachy by James III in 1473 and seems to have built the oldest part of the remaining edifice, although there was a castle here in the 14th century. Bruce is said to have used it as a hunting-lodge. Various branches of the Ogilvys have held it, the Airlie branch moving in when Airlie Castle to the west was destroyed by Argyll during the Covenant and Civil Wars. Charles II spent a night here in 1650, and the following year it was sacked by Cromwell's troops in consequence. The 1st and 2nd Earls were most notable royalists, lieutenants of Montrose; while their descendants were forfeited in turn for supporting the Stewarts in the Jacobite period. However, they are still here; and the present Earl's brother, the Hon. Angus Ogilvy, is married to Princess Alexandra. A lofty monument to David, 11th Earl, who fell at Diamond Hill in the South African War, rises on top of Tulloch Hill (1246 feet) above Dykehead, and is a prominent landmark.

Bridge of Prosen, on the B955 Kirriemuir road a mile south of Cortachy, is another old single-arch spanning an attractive stretch of that river, with deep tree-lined den, rocky bed and broken water. This entire area is richly wooded; indeed what is alleged to have been the largest oak-tree in Scotland was dug out of a marsh near here, containing 1000 cubic feet of timber.

Inverquharity is a still older Ogilvy barony, having belonged to 14 generations of the family, from 1420 until the late 18th century, when they lost it—although the Nova Scotia baronetcy conferred in 1626, and still held by the head of the family, is "of Inverquharity". The castle is deservedly renowned, a tall and massive red-stone 15th century fortalice on the L-plan, which, after being in a state of semi-ruin for generations is now most happily being restored to form a home again.

It stands picturesquely above the Carity Burn near its junction with the Esk, with very thick walls faced with good ashlar, rising to a parapet and wall-walk. A notable feature is the caphouse and watch-chamber at the stair-head, provided with its own little fireplace and chimney for the guard. The building is being most lovingly restored. During the process a deep well was discovered in the wing basement, now rehabilitated. Amongst the many other interesting features is the great iron yett that guards the doorway, the licence for which is still preserved, granted by James II in 1444. It reads:

"Rex—A licence be the King to Al. Ogilvy of Inercarity to fortify his house and put ane iron yet therein."

Sir John, third son of Sir Walter Ogilvy of Auchterhouse, gained these lands in 1420. One of his descendants was beheaded after Philiphaugh, fighting with Montrose. The family has taken a prominent share in the nation's history.

There is an Inverquharity farm and also a mill of the name, survivor of at least two others near the castle, traces of the lade for which remain. Farther downstream a mile was another castle, Shielhill, belonging to cadets of Ogilvy, on a crag above the Esk, now gone though there is a modern mansion. A chapel also stood near by, and St. Colm's Well. Shielhill Bridge, high over the river, is picturesque, narrow and old—although whether the famous water-kelpie aided in its construction, as alleged, is not proven. This was the scene of the lexicographer Dr. John Jamieson's ballad of that name.

Douglastown and Kinnettles. These are a village and a parish in south-west Angus, just east of Glamis. Kinnettles—which is said to mean the Head of the Bog, and its kirkton known locally as The Bog—is a very small parish of under 3000 acres. This bogginess is not now very evident, in a quite attractive wooded hill-and-valley area flanking the Arity or Kerbet Water.

Douglastown village lies athwart the busy A94 Perth to Forfar road, four miles south-west of the latter. It is not large, and smaller than it was, with a slightly decayed air. Nor is it old, having been founded only in 1792 as a flax-spinning centre, its mill, driven by water-power, being one of the earliest such in Scotland, established by James Ivory, a remarkable man. He was a teacher at Dundee Academy, and afterwards a famous professor internationally, and knighted by William IV. In partnership in this enterprise he was joined by the laird of Brigton near by, William Douglas, and the village was called after him. Unfortunately the venture was not a success, and in 1814 the mill was dismantled.

The bridge here was built in 1770, by subscription; but it is on the site of a Roman bridge, on their road between camps at Coupar Angus and Forfar.

Brigton estate lies just to the south, and contains an old and commodious whitewashed mansion, amongst fine woodland on the banks of the Kerbet, with an unusual tall doocot to the rear, seemingly of the 18th century. It was an ancient Strachan property, acquired by the Lyon of Glamis family in 1615 and held till 1762, when the Douglases of Glenbervie purchased it, descended from the 5th Earl of Angus. Brigton Hill (543 feet) is a detached, flat-topped summit to the east, with extensive views.

Kinnettles House, near by, is modern, an enormous Scottish Baronial pile built in 1867. It was also anciently a Strachan property, passing to the Lindsays, the last of whom was Archbishop Thomas Lindsay, primate of Ireland, who died in 1713. A 17th century lean-to doocot, with stringcourses, is all that remains of the old establishment.

The kirkton of Kinnettles lies at the riverside half a mile farther south-east, on the B9127, in a pretty position and with a pleasant row of cottages but displaying a very gaunt and unattractive church. This dates from 1812, and a pre-Reformation kirk was pulled down to accommodate it in the ancient graveyard. There are many old stones here, some as early as the 1620s, a great row of them leaning against the east wall of the yard. The manse is notably large. It is sad that so many of our forefathers, at this period, should have been so lacking in any sense of beauty in their ideas of worship. One stone in the kirkyard refers to a Colonel William Paterson, son of a gardener at Brigton, who rose to be Lieutenant-Governor of New South Wales, a Fellow of the Royal Society, and an explorer, dying in 1810.

Another old estate and district, a mile to the east, is that of Invereighty, on the edge of Inverarity parish, a property acquired by Sir James Young, son of the more famous Sir Peter, and Gentleman of the Bedchamber to James VI. The house was vastly altered in 1872 by Baxter of Kincaldrum.

Due west of Invereighty a mile is the farm of Foffarty, which once was a place of some consequence. As an estate it belonged to the bishops of Dunkeld, and because of this was not in Kinnettles parish at all, but in far-away Caputh near Dunkeld, until annexed by the General Assembly in 1773. At the Reformation it passed into secular hands, and in 1659 the Bowers of Kincaldrum, a Catholic family, built a chapel here. It was, however, burned down by a party of dragoons in 1745.

Dun. The name of Dun and that of Erskine are almost interchangeable, so great an impact did the family of Erskine of Dun make on the Scottish scene. The estate and the parish of Dun also are all but indistinguishable, or were, set to the north-west of the great Montrose Basin. The parish is of 7700 acres, and without village or recognisable hamlet, threaded by the A935 road from Brechin to Montrose, a purely rural and little-populated area on a long, gently-rising northern slope.

The House of Dun, now a hotel, and the parish church, lie close to each other on either side of the Den of Dun, a picturesque tree-clad ravine, towards the south-centre of the parish and near the main road. The mansion is a large and elegant Adam house of 1758, on the site of the former castle. Its predecessor was famous as the home of a family extraordinarily prominent without being in the upper ranks of the aristocracy. They came from Erskine Castle in Renfrewshire—near where the new Erskine Bridge crosses Clyde—and we read:

> *Robert Stewart was made King*
> *Specially throw the helping*
> *Of gude Schir Robert Erskine.*

Be that as it may, Sir Robert bought these lands in the North-East in 1348. From him descended a long line of talented and sometimes unruly men. Four Erskines of Dun fell at Flodden, laird, brother and two sons. The best-known undoubtedly was John Erskine of Dun, the famous Superintendent of Angus, one of the leaders of the Reformation, who died in 1589. The family were inclined towards religion, but also towards controversy. They were apt to interfere powerfully in local Montrose, as well as national, politics, causing at times considerable resentment; but they also did much for the town, and founded the school which grew into the well-known academy. Their town-house is still in one of the gable-end closes off the High Street, now used as offices by the *Review* newspaper. The last in the male line died in 1812, his daughter marrying the 12th Earl of Cassillis, 1st Marquis of Ailsa.

The old parish church lay within the estate policies in its grave-yard, approached by way of the gardens, now run as a commercial establishment. Most attractively set on the lip of the green Den, there are many old tombstones, some of them Erskine although the family burial-ground is actually detached, over a wall to the north. The church is small, roofless and Gothic-ised. The parish was formed in 1583, uniting a pre-Reformation chapel here with that of Eccles-john, which was near Langleypark, a mile to the east. The present church dates from 1840, plain with a rather fancy tower, erected in memory of William Hay Kennedy Erskine "by an attached and sorrowing people"—indicating that a member of the Cassillis Kennedy family took the Erskine name and continued the lairdship, obviously to the satisfaction of at least some of the tenantry.

Bridge of Dun, particularly handsome a mile to the south, carries a side-road across the South Esk just before it enters Montrose Basin, and dates from 1785. This area is very much wildfowl-haunted marshy tidelands directly opposite Old Montrose of the Grahams. The burn which forms the Den comes out of the loch called Dish of Dun, on high but also marshy moorland, now much forested, over a mile north-west of the church. The farms are wide-scattered, with a great deal of white space on the map, green on the ground. It is noteworthy that while Mains of Dun is down near the Basin, North Mains of Dun is two miles away up on the moor-like land.

There is a garden centre established at the main roadside near the house gates.

Dundee. Until recently, Dundee was the city in Scotland that one was apt not to visit unless one had special occasion to go there—despite the fact that it is the fourth largest. Isolated on an almost peninsular site, it was quite a long way from anywhere else and not on the road to anywhere either. Now, with the building of the Tay Road Bridge, all that is changed. Instead of the 22-mile detour to the east from Perth, the main road north-eastwards from Edinburgh, via the Forth Road Bridge, debouches directly into the city; and the rest of Scotland is at last getting to know Dundee. Which is satis-factory, for this is a city with much to offer, far more attractive than many have assumed and, of course, historically important—more so, indeed, at an earlier date, than was Glasgow, or even Edinburgh. Once the centre of gravity of Scotland was considerably farther north than today, and Stirling, Perth and Dundee were vital towns when Edinburgh was "out on a limb", more like a northern offshoot of England, and Glasgow was little more than a quiet bishop's burgh; which makes it sad that Dundee seems always to have been a place for sweeping away the old, starting afresh, priding in being up to date. For instance, this is the first city in Scotland to appoint a city manager. History or none, this is not a place to visit for ancient monuments, quaint prospects, the enshrined past—or even, one must confess, civic beauty.

Yet the site rivals Edinburgh's; possibly it is the finest in Scotland. At the mouth of the Firth of Tay, where the green Sidlaws come down close to the sea at the end of the fertile Carse of Gowrie, it has a sheltered, south-facing situation in the laps of the hills, looking over to North Fife and the sea. But these same hills have ever posed a problem for the city's expansion, for there is practically no coastal plain, and the streets begin to climb almost from the funnels and masts and derricks of the dock area, with terraced building perched two-thirds of the way up the Law, with its earthworks, 571 feet high but only a mile from the shore. There are other hills and ridges, all offering an interesting background, splendid viewpoints and the open spaces so valuable for a modern city—but tending to form a highly restrictive barrier to the development of Dundee. Perhaps that is why it has been a pioneer in the high-flat development in Scotland, and the skyscraper blocks soar here as though to rival the hills. Now the city has, as it were, burst its hilly banks, and is spreading far and wide beyond into the green valleys of Strathmartine, Strathdichty and Liff, eating up the Angus countryside, towards the true Sidlaws, and along the coast eastwards to engulf Broughty Ferry and Monifieth, though not yet Carnoustie. This was no doubt inevitable.

The prevalence of Pictish symbol-stones and Celtic cross-slabs around Dundee appears to indicate that this was an important area in the Dark Ages. Indeed a great battle was fought here, at Pitalpie, between the Picts and the Scots, at which King Alpin, Kenneth's father and legendary begetter of the MacGregors was slain. Even earlier settlement was revealed by the finding of a prehistoric kitchen-midden site in the Stannergate, east of the town. The Romans were here, their forts and camps circling the city from Catter Milly to Lour. But it was as a fishing and trading community for the rich hinterland of Gowrie and Strathmore that Dundee became important in the historical era, enough to be granted the status of royal burgh by William the Lion in the 12th century. By a century later Dundee was featuring regularly in Scotland's story, for here was William Wallace brought up, and he made it his base during the early stages of the Wars of Independence. Edward, Hammer of the Scots, was here twice, wreaking his savageries on town and castle in consequence. Wallace, as guardian of Scotland, in the absence of a king, raised his supporter Alexander the Skirmisher, or Scrymgeour, to be constable of Dundee; and Bruce, when he gained the throne, made the office of standard-bearer hereditary in that family. The Earl of Dundee, James Scrymgeour-Wedderburn of Birkhill, *Mac Mhic Iain*, still holds the office. Here, at the Greyfriars Monastery in 1309, during those terrible war years, a great meeting of the clergy of Scotland made a gallant and solemn declaration of support for Robert Bruce as King of Scots, and defiance of the English, to convince the Pope and Christendom—thus pre-dating by 11 years the more famous Declaration of Arbroath by the laity. The Church was always strong here, with St. Andrews, the ecclesiastical metropolis near by, and the abbeys of Arbroath, Coupar, Balmerino, Lindores and Scone not far off. About 1482 the great bell-tower of St. Mary's was erected, a magnificent monument which happily still survives as the main landmark of the city, with its three churches huddled below it. Inevitably Dundee played a prominent part in the Reformation, with Knox and Wishart preaching here, and the famous mob setting out for Perth on its destructive mission—although this always sounds as though to be taken with a pinch of salt. By then it was the second city of Scotland. Montrose took it during his royalist campaign of 1645; and shortly after, in 1651, Cromwell captured it—and humiliatingly also captured a sitting of the Scots Parliament being held at Alyth, 20 miles away. Bonnie Dundee—James Graham of Claverhouse, Viscount Dundee—was provost of the city in 1684; and in the Jacobite Rising of 1715 the town supported the Stewarts. In the subsequent Rising of 1745, however, the city fathers prudently took the Hanoverian side—and had the humbling experience of being locked up in their own gaol by the Jacobites under Lord Ogilvy. The son of Provost Duncan so involved became the famous admiral, Hero of Camperdown. Possibly as a counter-gesture, after Culloden, the magistrates conferred the freedom of the burgh on the victorious Duke of Cumberland.

All this time trade and commerce had been expanding, and gradually the emphasis grows on matters economic and industrial. The Dundee Bank was founded in 1763, with linen and textile production the financial source of revenue. At one time most of the canvas sails of the British Navy were woven here. Then, with the growth of the East India Company, and Scots participation, jute came partly to supersede the flax industry, and Dundee became in fact the jute capital of the world. Every schoolboy in Scotland knows that Dundee is famed for the three Js—jute, jam and journalism, the last two referring to the great Keiller firm, the inventors of marmalade, and to the D. C. Thomson group of newspapers and magazines. The vast expansion of the jute industry, for sacking, packaging, floorcloth, rope, felting and so on, created enormous wealth for the few, and ever-increasing employment for the many—also problems for the city fathers, with expansion everywhere and little suitable ground for it. The palaces of the jute nabobs sprang up all around the city, with their spacious grounds, further restricting opportunities for housing the workers. So the teeming, climbing slums proliferated, the warrens of tenements replaced the more gracious architecture of less hectic days. The nabobs' mansions were excellently built, largely in bastard Scots Baronial style, and are mainly still extant, though now used as hotels and institutions; but the squalid, huddled slums are very largely demolished and the new housing estates, which spread far and wide and are such a feature of modern Dundee, are their modern and in the main admirable successors. This happened in every great city, but in Dundee the expansion was more sudden, more explosive than most, and the area more constricted. Also the contrast with great wealth and poverty was more extreme. The balance has taken a lot of rectifying.

It was not only jute and linen, of course. Whaling and sealing, shipbuilding, engineering, locomotive-building, carpet-making, bonnet-making, all played their part. There were once 66 thread-twisting mills in Dundee. Sugar-refining was important, and there were seven cotton-spinning companies. The wealth made itself was put to use, and Dundee became a dynamo of investment. Indeed this was where some of the great investment trusts, so popular today with small savers, originated.

The flood-tide of industrialisation of the 19th century brought its blessings and advancements, as well as its problems and unsightliness. The Royal Infirmary of 1798 was only the first of a great succession of fine hospitals, institutions and amenities. A university college linked with St. Andrews was founded in 1880, to become the University of Dundee only in 1967. The ancient grammar school, at which Wallace himself was a pupil, was succeeded by the academy in 1785, and this in turn developed into the Dundee High School in 1834—though at first it rejoiced under the splendid title of The Dundee Public Seminaries. The Morgan and Harris Academies followed, with many technical and commercial colleges—for this was a most typically well-doing city, with all the Scots passion for education. Despite the well-known disaster of the first Tay railway bridge in 1879, it was rebuilt soon after, one of the longest bridges in the world.

Today the city is thriving, forward-looking, and still the fastest expanding in Scotland, its industries notably diversified—though jute is still important—its industrial estates models, in the forefront of the technological age. Indeed, if Dundee has a fault, it is that in its preoccupation with the gleaming future it has sadly neglected its past, and few can rival its record in "dinging doun" its ancient and historic buildings to replace them with the latest. Few marks of antiquity survive, therefore, to the city's great loss. But it makes up for this, in some measure, by the splendours of its parks and open spaces. The Camperdown Park, for instance, covering no less than 735 acres of grass and lovely woodlands, must be amongst the largest and finest in Britain.

The city centre of Dundee, by the very nature of things, is nowhere near the centre of the city! Inevitably it is crammed down on the southern perimeter, near the Tay and the docks, so that salt water, like the northern end of the great 1.4-mile-long road bridge, is within a few hundred yards of City Square and the mercat cross. It is, in fact, for a great city, a very small centre. I know of no clear and obvious metropolitan area so tightly contracted, in a major conurbation of 183,000 population. Narrow it has to be; but it is not even very long, east to west. Nethergate and High Street run together, with short streets off to north and south; then just past the central City Square, the main street splits into two east-going thoroughfares, Seagate and Murraygate, with Commercial Street crossing them and leading up to Albert Square, with Reform Street off. And that is about it, as far as the major shopping, commercial and office centre is concerned—although the city actually extends to 12,000 acres or 19 square miles. It is strange, too, to walk only a short distance along Seagate, for instance, with its fine shops, and find oneself amongst quiet warehouses and modest old dockside lanes; just as, at the other end of the main axis, Nethergate changes from tall city-type building to substantial tree-girt villa-style housing in an equally short walk, even if this is now used mainly as offices, and the modern University buildings tower above all.

Plumb in the centre of this tight complex rises what is affectionately known as the Old Steeple, the splendid 15th century Gothic tower of St. Mary's, 160 feet high, of warm ochreous sandstone, square and massive yet well-proportioned, with lancet arched windows, parapet at the wall-head and a spire-topped caphouse for its winding turnpike stairway. This, though substantial enough, is all that remains of the great cruciform church of St. Mary—a statue to the Virgin and Child, though a replica, again stands high at its western corner, unusual in a Scots kirk building. The church had grown from a 12th century foundation by Earl David of Huntingdon, brother of William the Lion. Exactly when this was built is not known, but Earl David's daughter Margaret was married therein in 1206 to Alan, Lord of Galloway—and from this union came the renowned Devorgilla who married John de Baliol and so produced variously, Balliol College, Oxford, Sweetheart Abbey, King John Baliol and the Wars of Independence. That William Wallace was, so to speak, to set the spark to the said Wars here in Dundee also, is a strange coincidence. St. Mary's Church had a chequered history indeed, being burned, savaged, sacked and restored time and again. But even the great 15th century building is all gone save for this tower; and the three churches which cluster under its enduring guardianship date from no earlier than the mid-19th century. They are known as the City Churches, with the modern St. Mary's to the east, now the parish or High Kirk of Dundee, rebuilt 1844; St. Paul's in the centre, dating from 1847; and St. Clement's—called after a still earlier church—known usually now as the Steeple Church, at the west, under the tower itself. There are not many remaining examples of three large churches under one roof, although it was common enough in Scotland after the Reformation; St. Giles' in Edinburgh was so divided. The basement of St. Mary's Tower was used at one time as a prison for moral offenders, but later "ane new prissoun was biggit above the volt in St. Androis Iyile in the eist end of the kirk". The tower served as a fortress during General Monk's storming of Dundee in 1650, and when it fell, by the garrison being smoked out by burning wet straw, there was a massacre, and the defending General Lumsden's head was affixed to a spike on the corner of the steeple, where it remained for nearly a century and a half.

To the north of this cluster of churches, strangely but satisfyingly overshadowed by the soaring tower, is the highly modern traffic-free shopping precinct known as the Overgate Development, a typical glass and concrete multi-level complex, pleasingly lightened and diversified by judiciously planted trees and shrubs. It is convenient and practical—but scarcely remarkable in that the like can be seen in a hundred other towns and cities. At the other, south side, amongst more flowerbeds, rises the replica mercat cross, dating only from 1874 and replacing the original which stood in the Seagate near the former Tolbooth, where a bronze plaque marks the site. It was removed in the 15th century and demolished in 1777.

Across the busy Nethergate, to the south, opens the City Square, where there is an underground car-park. (The car-parking facilities is an excellent feature of this forward-looking city.) The Square is now an open space, with seats and flowerbeds, all its ancient buildings swept away. At its head rises the impressive classical façade of the Caird Hall. This is one of the largest halls in the country, erected in 1923 at a cost of £200,000, seating 2780, with accommodation also for a choir of nearly 300, or a 75-piece orchestra. A magnificent gift to the city by Sir James Caird, a magnate who also provided the Caird Park, it is not always that a hall of such dimensions is required or can be filled. The smaller Marryat Hall, however, decorated in Regency style, adjoins. Sadly, the splendid Town House, designed by William Adam in 1734, an arcaded classical building with a steeple, and known as the Pillars, was demolished in 1931, and replaced by the present city offices on the west side of the Square—a grievous mistake. Many other relics of character and antiquity were swept away from this crowded area of the Old Town, including Strathmartine's Lodging, the 1600 town house of the Duncans, ancestors of the famous admiral and Earls of Camperdown, and also the old Lion Tavern.

Flanking City Square to the east is Castle Street, now a modern shopping street, with an access to the City Arcade Market for fruit, vegetables, etc., situated under the Caird Hall. Number 8 Castle Street was the printing establishment of James Chalmers, who invented the adhesive postage-stamp; and Number 12, site of the bookshop of Robert Nicoll (1814–37) poet and politician of note despite his early death. Here was also, more recently, the site of the Whitehall Civic Theatre.

"The site of" is rather the theme-song of Dundee. Near by, to the north-east is that of the former Castle of Dundee, on Castlehill, where Wallace slew the English governor Selby's son. Here now rises, at the corner of High Street and Commercial Street, St. Paul's Episcopal cathedral (of the diocese of Brechin), a somewhat gloomy-looking building externally but handsome within, designed by Sir Giles Gilbert Scott, in cruciform, Second Pointed style, with a

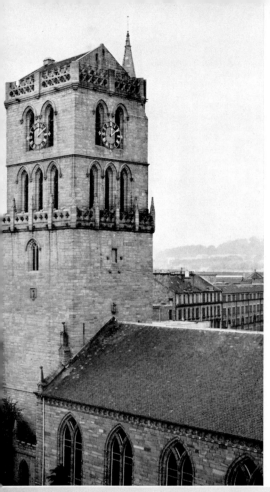

Dundee. The Old Steeple of the
city churches, with Balgay Hill
in the background

Dundee. Reform Street

Edzell Castle. The pleasaunce and 17th century lodge

Cortachy. Inverquharity Castle in process of restoration

steeple 220 feet high and a noted landmark. It cost £13,000 in 1855. Dundee, needless to say, has innumerable churches, of all denominations, many of them very fine. One of the most pleasing, St. Andrew's, in an old graveyard off the Cowgate, is the oldest actually surviving, erected in 1772, with a typical Georgian façade. Unfortunately its tall spire was recently struck by lightning and part of it fell through the main roof much damaging the fine interior. Here is no place to list the others, but mention should perhaps be made of the very modern ones erected in the ever-extending housing schemes, usually connected also with community amenities.

Some way farther east along Cowgate, amongst the dockland warehouses, stands the sole and isolated relic of the walled city—the Cowgate Port, more usually known as the Wishart Arch. This not actually very massive or impressive gateway for a city port, its crenellations modern, was where George Wishart, the early Protestant martyr, in 1545 preached for the comfort of the people during a visitation of the plague, those still hale standing in the street to the west, those pestilence-stricken outside the walls in the Sick Men's Yard, "raising up the hartes of all that heard him, that thai regarded nott death". He himself was to be burned to death at St. Andrews a month later.

Some of the streets branching off Nethergate and High Street are notable for the excellence of their quality shops—Reform Street, Whitehall Street and Commercial Street particularly. At the head of Reform and Commercial Streets, to the north at the foot of the first of the hills, lies Meadowside and Albert Square, with the central island site filled by the imposing Public Library, Art Gallery and Museum buildings. There are eleven branches, but this is the Central Library, with 120,000 volumes for lending and 74,000 for reference; also it houses city records on film and the Dundee Local Collection. The City Museum stands next door, and contains notable collections tastefully displayed. Of particular local interest are the examples of Pictish symbol-stones and Celtic cross-slabs for which this area is famed including a 5th/7th century stone from Strathmartine, with beasts and symbols; another from the same area of the 9th century, with slot for an upright cross; another beast-and-symbol stone from Aberlemno, where there are many; an 8th/9th century fragment from Tealing with Pictish fish, etc. There are models and photographs of souterrains or underground Pictish dwellings from Tealing again, Airlie, Pitcur, Carlungie and Ardestie, ancient dug-out canoes from Kinnordy and Errol, and also Roman relics—all testifying to the importance of this district in ancient times. Highly admirable also is the Mary Slessor Corner, an imaginative memorial to a splendid and vigorous character, a shoemaker's daughter from Aberdeen who came to Dundee in 1859 to work as a child-weaver, before going out to Calabar, West Africa, as a missionary in 1876, there to become a queen to the natives, but never lowering her standards of service, compassion, justice (as magistrate) and reform, making as a matter of course the most hazardous journeys alone through the wilds, and dying in harness in 1915, aged 67. Here are displayed a fascinating collection of personal relics, photographs, etc.

The Art Gallery contains many works of Dutch, Flemish, Italian and French artists, as well as British, and a large collection of more modern watercolours. At the west side of the same open area, called Barrack Street, is the Shipping and Industrial Museum, an unusual exhibition of great value to those concerned with maritime and commercial development, also ancient tools and weapons and symbols of medieval punishment. There are portraits here, too, including one of William McGonagall (1825–1902) a weaver from Step Row, whose tragi-comical effusions in both verse and prose have become known the world over. A Children's Library is housed in the same building; and the adjacent Rotunda Art Gallery is used for modern art and photographic exhibitions.

Barrack Street stands on the site of the gardens of the old Greyfriars monastery. After the Reformation, in 1564, this ground was given to the city as a burial-ground by Mary Queen of Scots, who often visited Dundee; and this cemetery oddly enough came to be used extensively as the open-air meeting place of the Incorporated Trades and craftsmen, rejoicing in the name of the Howff. It is still there, filled with ancient tombstones, though discontinued for burials in 1878. The guild-brothers of Dundee must have been hardy chiels. They even paid the Town Council £5 12s. per annum for the privilege of holding their meetings in this graveyard, until the new Trades Hall was built in 1778, in Murraygate. There are complete lists of the tombs here, the oldest being that of James Muir, a burgess who died in 1577. Near by is one erected by James Keiller to his mother, in 1813, inventor of marmalade and founder of the famous firm. The Scrymgeour constables of Dundee, and generations of provosts, magistrates and prominent—and not-so-prominent— citizens are here interred, including Provost Alexander Duncan of Lundie, of the late 17th century, who took command of the defences when Claverhouse attacked the city in 1689, and was the great-grandfather of Admiral Duncan of Camperdown fame.

In this same area to the north of Overgate is the heart of the Thomson-Leng "empire", the great publishing house which has meant so much to Dundee for long, produced so many well-known newspapers, periodicals and magazines, and been the nursery of generations of journalists. Surprising is the number of famous pressmen, far and near, who it transpires have started their careers here. In this corner are published such as the *Sunday Post*, the *People's Friend*, the *Dundee Courier*, the *Evening Telegraph*, and a large number of organs of popular reading, from specialist magazines and women's papers to comics. Also that very excellent monthly, the *Scots Magazine*, first published in 1739 and still one of the brightest ornaments of the Scottish scene.

To the west of St. Mary's Tower and the Overgate Development rises the tall new Angus Hotel, with 57 bedrooms mostly with private bathrooms, T.V. and telephones, with excellent conference and ball-room facilities accommodating up to 500. The Queen's Hotel, also in Nethergate, is a little smaller, but with fullest facilities; while the Tay Centre Hotel, recently renewed, in Whitehall Crescent facing the estuary, has 100 bedrooms and everything of the latest. There are many other smaller and family hotels, in the centre of the town and on the outskirts, catering for every variety of traveller and rectifying the one-time complaint that Dundee was sadly short of such facilities.

A little farther west, where Nethergate becomes the road to Perth, clusters the admixture of buildings of all shapes and sizes which makes up the University of Dundee, with its principal 12-storey skyscraper tower facing south and set back from this main thorough-fare. Although it only reached separate university status in 1967, it had been Queen's College of St. Andrews University since 1897. It is now a thriving and forward-looking educational institution to head up the many technical, commercial and specialist colleges of the city with, in 1969, 2394 students and residential accommodation for over 1000. It confers degrees in medicine, dentistry, law, science, education and the arts.

Dundee Commercial College, formerly housed in five schools, now occupies a splendid new £806,000 nine-storey building at the junction of Barrack and Constitution Roads, opened in 1969. Kingsway Technical College was opened four years earlier, to replace the former Trades College—as its name implies on the Kingsway by-pass road, some way to the north-east. The College of Education, with over 1000 students, has outgrown its premises, and is to be rehoused in a 26-acre site at Craigie, two miles to the east. Dundee Institute of Art and Technology, comprising the former well-known Jordanstone College of Art and the College of Technology, where architecture, town-planning, design, as well as the graphic arts, sculpture and so on, are taught, along with engineering, electrical, civil and mechanical, navigation and other courses, is another example of Dundee's passion for education.

For younger scholars, the high school already mentioned stands in Reform Street, on the north side of the former Meadows, once some-what restricted common pasture, now only a few yards from the city centre. It is a quite handsome classical building opened in 1834, and once suffered the strange handicap of having nine headmasters at the one time, each independent of the others, collecting their own fees and hiring their own assistants. It was 1883 before a single rector was appointed. The well-known Morgan Academy stands farther out, on the Forfar road north of Baxter Park. It sprang from a bequest of £70,000 left by a jute nabob, John Morgan, the ambitious, château-like building in its own grounds being erected in 1866. William Harris, another local philanthropist, gave £20,000 towards the better endowment of the high school, in 1880, on condition that another secondary school be set up with £10,000 more —the Harris Academy, some way out on the Perth road, on the way to

Invergowrie. There are 12 other secondary, 46 primary, eight nursery and four special schools, under the direction of the local authority, employing some 3200 staff and educating some 34,000 school-children and 14,000 further education students.

Before leaving the old part of Dundee, something falls to be said about Dudhope Castle, which overlooks it from high ground part-way up the Law. Now standing in a steeply-terraced public park, this was the seat of the Scrymgeours, hereditary constables of Dundee and royal standard-bearers, for 400 years. The large building has suffered greatly at the hands of time and Dundee, but at least it is not a ruin. The original fortalice was probably an oblong tower to which wings were added to form an enlarged L-plan, this now being represented by the south-east corner of the whole. As it stands it is mainly a 17th century edifice, impressive but less than beautiful, of four to five storeys but reduced in height—which always damages the appearance—with round, conical-roofed flanking towers and a pend entrance between drum-towers in the centre of the east front opening onto an inner courtyard. The belfry and gablet surmounting this is more modern. There has been a great deal of internal alteration, for the place has been used as a barracks and even as a woollen mill. Its interior is not in good condition, and the only use the city can find for it is as a store and as modest clubrooms for a number of bodies. But at least it is still there, and there are people making efforts to ensure its preservation. The history of Dudhope and of Dundee are intervolved. The early castle of Dundee, on lower ground, was demolished by the Scots to make it untenable for any further English invaders; and after Bannockburn Dudhope was built for the constables. Frequently the Scrymgeours were at logger-heads with the provost and magistrates, and Dudhope must have been the scene of lively ongoings. The 8th constable was himself provost, however, in 1528; and so was his successor—a case of joining them if you can't beat them, presumably. The eleventh also managed to get the provostship, but seems to have been less than popular, for the parish minister declared that if they must choose a provost for greatness ". . . a lord was griter nor a baron, an earl griter nor a lord, and the Devil was gritest of all!" It was the twelfth who was created Viscount of Dudhope by Charles I in 1641, and his son died from wounds received fighting for Charles at Marston Moor, while *his* son, the 14th constable fought for Charles II at Worcester. Later the castle was sold to Graham of Claverhouse, and the famous Bonnie Dundee here brought his bride, Jean Cochrane, granddaughter of the 1st Earl of Dundonald. In 1792 the castle became a mill, but only for a year, and thereafter was turned into barracks. It became the property of the town in 1893.

Behind Dudhope the Law rises ever more steeply, terraced by housing, until its green cone thrusts up at 571 feet, surmounted by Dundee's memorial cenotaph to the dead of two wars. The view from here is magnificent, with far prospects all round. There is a direction indicator identifying landmarks far and near. The summit was once the site of a prehistoric fortification, traces of earthworks surviving. A road winding spectacularly round the hill now allows cars to reach the top.

From this viewpoint the hilly nature of Dundee is dramatically demonstrated. Near by to the west rises the wooded lesser hogsback of Balgay, a gentler hill utilised partly as an attractive cemetery and partly forming the site for the Mills Observatory. In the hollow between lies Dundee's best-known early suburb, Lochee, an industrial community with no pretensions to beauty, once almost a separate town, with its own shopping and business centre. It started with the Industrial Revolution as a handloom weaving community for coarse linen fabrics, with bleaching introduced thereafter. Here the Cox family began to develop the jute processing, and prospered mightily. In 1849 they began the erection of the largest jute factory in the world, the Camperdown Linen Works. Its enormous chimney, 282 feet high and oddly ornate by modern standards, is known as Cox's Stack and is a well-known landmark. Many other mills and works for spinning, weaving, dyeing, printing and bleaching were also built. Originally a part of the parish of Liff, Lochee, with its dramatic rise in population became a *quod sacra* parish of its own in 1880. The architecture and aspect of the place is scarcely distinguished; but efforts are being made at improvement, and the sky-scraper blocks rise here as elsewhere in Dundee, and clearance of slum property proceeds.

Industry is of course dispersed all over this great city; but the actual industrial estate set up here in 1948 was a pioneer of its kind in Scotland, and highly successful as well as extensive. Indeed, it extends much of the way along the great and lengthy Kingsway by-pass which circles Dundee to the north for about six miles. Here is a vast concentration of modern industry, in spacious well-laid-out factories, producing a notable variety of goods—watches, business machines, computers, cameras, electronics, even false teeth. Some famous firms have works here, such as the National Cash Register Company—occupying over 1,000,000 square feet in eight factories, with an investment of over 10 million pounds—Ferranti Ltd., Timex, and others; besides big indigenous firms such as Bonar, Long Ltd., Malcolm, Ogilvie Ltd., Valentine (the post- and greetings-card makers) and Stewart & Son, the Cream of Barley whisky blenders and bottlers.

In the midst of all this heartening industrial development, there are still traces of stirring doings of the long-distant past, even if only in names. Just south of the centre of Kingsway are housing schemes and streets bearing the names of King's Cross and Pitalpin. These commemorate a great battle fought here A.D. 831, between Alpin, 68th king of the Scots, and the Picts. Alpin, who was the father of the more famous Kenneth I—and from whom also the MacGregors, or Clan Alpine, claim descent—was based on the Law, with the Picts to the north at Tothelbrow in Strathmartine parish. In the fearful battle which followed in the lower ground here, Alpin was

slain, and his head cut off and carried by the triumphant Picts to
Abernethy, their capital. Later of course, in 834, Kenneth Mac-
Alpine had his revenge, achieved complete victory over the Picts,
united both peoples into Scotland—and had his father's head
reunited with his body and taken to Iona where were the graves of
the royal line. A large stone, with a 10-inch-deep socket-hole, used
to stand here, alleged to have been that in which Alpin set up his
standard. It is called the King's Cross, and is now removed to
Camperdown Park, just south-west of the mansion.

This Camperdown Park is a most magnificent "lung" and playground for any city. It lies just north of West Kingsway and entered
therefrom by a long driveway, the great estate of the Duncans of
Lundie, Earls of Camperdown, and was opened as a public park by
the present queen when she was Princess Elizabeth, in 1946. Covering no less than 735 acres of woodland, grass parks, lawns and
gardens, it is utilised by the city for a great variety of amenities;
yet because of its size, undulations and trees it still retains the aspects
of a huge private demesne. Here are an 18-hole golf course, football
pitches, pitch-and-putt and tennis courts, pony-riding facilities, a
nature-trail, a small zoo and an aviary, with other attractions in
addition to the splendid walks and restful delights of ancient settled
peace and tree-clad parkland. Many of the trees here are notable,
including a large weeping wych-elm, claimed to be the original in
Scotland. The mansion-house itself, built in 1824 by Robert, son of
the famous Admiral Viscount Duncan, and created Earl of Camperdown in 1831, is a handsome Grecian-style edifice in white Killala
sandstone, with massive octostyle Ionic portico, based on the Temple
of Dionysius. Internally the building is as fine, its central hall, with
cupola, being lined with pillars of Sienna marble from Italy. The
architect was the famous William Burn. Herein is housed the
Spalding Golf Museum, containing perhaps the oldest existing
golf-club in the world, dated 1680, and many other features of
interest covering three centuries of golf. There is a restaurant in the
park.

Other than this and Caird Park (262 acres and described under
Mains and Strathmartine) there are in a city well supplied with
open spaces Riverside Park (150 acres); Baxter (37 acres); Dawson
(48 acres); Dudhope (22 acres); Stobsmuir (11 acres); Balgay Hill
(60 acres); and The Law (22 acres); with many other smaller parks
and open spaces, giving a total of 1335 acres.

The dock and estuary-side area, so important to the city, and the
first that most visitors see on arrival, extends for a considerable
distance eastwards from the old town. The Port of Dundee provides
deep-water facilities for vessels up to 12,000 tons, with the King
George V Wharf for oil-tankers up to 20,000 tons, all with modern
harbour facilities. It has been most famous as *the* jute port; but all
general cargo is handled, and there is now a large oil installation
and depot at Stannergate, with private coastal tankers' jetty 500 feet
out in the estuary, and a great "farm" of storage tanks. A Dundee

Pilotage Authority is based at Broughty Ferry. The Dundee, Perth & London Shipping Company, founded in 1826, engages in coastal, Continental and Canadian services. The North Sea oil development is affecting Dundee docks also.

The shipbuilding industry has been established here since 1874, when a yacht for the earl of Caledon initiated and gave name to the Caledon yard, which grew into a major enterprise. It can build vessels up to 560 feet in length, and has a world-wide reputation. Since 1968 it has been united with Henry Robb Ltd., of Leith, as Robb-Caledon. Much of the metal structuring for the Tay Road Bridge was manufactured here.

An outstanding feature of this dock area was the great Royal Arch in Dock Street, an enormous triumphal archway beloved of the Victorians, built in 1848 to commemorate that queen's visit to Dundee four years earlier. It had an Indian aspect, elaborately carved, as is suitable for a city so linked with the Sub-Continent. It was demolished, a casualty of the Tay Road Bridge approach complex.

Only a mile or so farther eastwards from this Stannergate and dock area, is Broughty Ferry and West Ferry. This is all now incorporated in the Dundee municipal area. But since it has always had its own very definite and independent identity and character, the author has elected to describe it separately. Items of interest, therefore, such as Claypotts and Broughty Castles, the harbour, fishermen's dwellings and art gallery, appear under Broughty.

As outstanding and eye-catching, though a deal more useful than the Royal Arch, but at quite the other end of the city, is the vast new Ninewells Hospital being erected on a 200-acre site between Invergowrie House and the great modern Menzieshill housing scheme. This tremendous project, a teaching hospital and medical school, the first planned in Britain since the last war, is to have 761 beds, and its ever-soaring costs concern the authorities, the 15-million-pound mark having long been passed. Built mainly by the Musselburgh firm of Crudens, it will be a mighty milestone on the road of medical progress.

The author recognises all too clearly how superficial a survey he has made of this great city, lack of space dictating the omission of so much. Little or nothing has been said, for instance, of the many renowned personalities whom Dundee has bred or nurtured, such as Hector Boece, the famous if somewhat fanciful philosopher and historian, born in the Overgate in 1465, who became first principal of the combined University of Aberdeen; of Robert Fergusson, the talented but unfortunate poet so greatly admired by Burns; of Ann Scott, of the house of Buccleuch, born in a 15th century house also in the Overgate, who married the ill-fated Duke of Monmouth, illegitimate son of Charles II; and of "Bloody Mackenzie", the famous Sir George Mackenzie of Rosehaugh, lord advocate and eminent literary figure, who saw the light of day here in 1636, and so on. It would have been only suitable, too, to detail the many not born in Dundee but who had lived and worked here, such as Sir

Robert Watson Watt, inventor of radar, born at Brechin but living for a time at Garland Place, Constitution Road; and Mary Wollstonecroft Godwin, the author of *Frankenstein*, who lived in a cottage near Peep-O-Day Lane, and eloped with Percy Bysshe Shelley. These, and a host of others, the interested visitor must needs seek out for himself, with the author's apologies, in fairness to this great and friendly city at the mouth of Scotland's greatest river.

Eassie and Nevay. This is one of those areas little known even to the generality of the knowledgeable. Not one in a hundred, I would imagine, could say where either of these places are. Yet they are full of interest, and Eassie at least highly accessible. Though there is no real village, these are small parishes in Strathmore, Western Angus, just west of well-known Glamis, covering only 5000 acres between them.

Eassie, now only a ruined church, farm and mill, lies on the busy A94, two miles west of Glamis. The land is rather treeless here, but with wide vistas to the Grampians and the Sidlaws. The church, roofless and ivy-clad, stands on a knoll some way back from the road, in a graveyard with some old stones, one dated 1650. The church itself is not particularly interesting, with few features; but something it contains is highly so. This is the Eassie sculptured-stone, a fine example of Pictish cross-slab and symbol-stone, long neglected, indeed lying in a burn, but now housed in a windowed shelter built in the former choir, and in the care of the Department of the Environment. It is of red sandstone, about six feet high, with the usual elaborate cross on one side, with symbols, and pictorial designs on the other, priests, animals and, oddly, a flower-pot—a rather rare representation. It is thought to date from the 8th or 9th century.

A mile west, the farm of Castleton marks the site of the one-time Castle Nairne, on an artificial mound. Coins of Edward I were found here. At the adjoining farm of Ingliston, the English army under Edward is believed to have camped in 1296—as the name indicates. A stone coffin was unearthed here.

Half a mile south of Ingliston, under green Kinpurney Hill with its tower-like observatory built by a laird of Belmont, is the hamlet called by a plethora of names—Eassie and Nevay, Balkeerie, and North and East Nevay. The present parish church and manse is here, also the school. The church, built in 1833, is not particularly interesting. There are more trees hereabouts.

Old Nevay Church lies a mile to the west, almost on the Perthshire border, in lower ground, surrounded by a picturesque and old-world, if somewhat decayed hamlet. The fact that this is called Kirkinch reveals that this low ground was once flooded and this was an island. The ruined ivy-covered building crowns a green knoll, and is rather more interesting than Eassie, being typically long and low in the pre-Reformation style, with the usual two doorways on the south front, now built up by old gravestones. One very fine stone, dated 1597, is built upside-down into this wall; and there are many more old stones in the graveyard.

To the south-east of this parish is the Sidlaw glen of Denoon, most of which lies in Glamis parish, and is more suitably dealt with there.

Sometimes reference is made to the Battle of Eassie being fought here in 1057. But this in fact took place in the Aberdeenshire Eassie or Essie, near Rhynie, where the usurping Lulach was slain by MacDuff.

Edzell. The pleasant large village, almost a little town, of Edzell lies at the north-east end of Strathmore, on the west bank of the North Esk, six miles north of Brechin, and almost at the mouth of long Glen Esk. Although itself in a notable flat area of moorland, woods and farmland—with a great military airfield near by—the hills to the north seem to dominate. The village itself gives little impression of age, the streets wide, open and set at rectangles, the buildings mainly of the 19th century. But because of its fine ruined castle, a seat of a powerful branch of the great Lindsay family, Edzell was fairly prominent in history. It is deservedly popular today, and makes an excellent touring centre for a wide area. This is the very northern tip of Angus.

Edzell is also a very large parish, extending to over 20,000 acres, not all of which is dealt with here, as much of it is in Glen Esk, which is treated separately. And any account of Edzell district must also mention the glen of Lethnot to the north-west, which demands its own description.

The present village really should not be called Edzell at all, but Slateford, its former name; for Edzell proper lies over a mile to the west, at the mouth of Glen Lethnot, where is the castle and the former parish church and burial-ground. However, with the church moved to its present position in 1818, and the castle a ruin, the name moved also. The village really began to grow in 1839, and in planned fashion, feud out on 99-year leases by Lord Panmure. Oddly enough, Edzell was a famous place for pistol-making in the 17th and 18th centuries, the names of Andrew Strachan and James Stewart being renowned; but these probably subsisted at *old* Edzell.

To travellers approaching from the south, the Memorial Arch spanning the main road catches the eye. It is similar to the Queen Victoria Jubilee Arch at Fettercairn five miles away; but in fact it is a monument to the 15th Earl of Dalhousie, who died in 1887, and whose family have owned the area since 1715. The large and over-ambitious Inglis Memorial Hall towers near by, in the Main Street; but otherwise the village is doucely unexceptional. There is some attractive modern housing in an enclave off Church Street, to the west. The present parish church, with its spidery belfry, stands in an isolated position to the north, on whin-dotted common land amongst the trees, quite large but without graveyard. Near by are the cattle-pens for the sales which have long been held here. The common land is an asset to the amenity. There is no lack of accommodation for visitors, with three hotels and other guest-houses. A good 18-hole golf course adjoins to the west, flanking the West Water, out of Lethnot.

For antiquarian interest it is necessary to take the side road to the north-west, leading to Glen Lethnot and Navar amongst the hills. Less than a mile along is the large farm of Mains of Edzell, with its fine example of late 16th or early 17th century gabled doocot. The famous castle lies in a delightful setting, back from the road a little farther, and deserves a book to itself. It is quite a complex of mellow red-stone building, guarding one of the ancient Mounth crossing routes. The great keep, oldest part, dates from the early 16th century, replacing an earlier timber castle sited down on the Castle Hillock nearer the river. It is oblong, with a slightly projecting stair-tower, five storeys in height with a parapet and open rounds, and well supplied with gunloops on all fronts. The great hall is very fine. To the east is a large L-shaped range of the late 16th century, now very ruinous, with gabled roofs and no parapet, but having a large circular flanking-tower to protect the curtain-walling which surrounded all and enclosed the courtyard. But the most exciting feature is the attractive pleasaunce, or walled garden enclosure, with is own subsidiary buildings, including the quite delightful little early 17th century lodge or summer-house, fortunately still roofed and entire, a tiny miniature castle in itself, two-storeyed, with its own stair-tower, angle-turret and shot-holes. The pleasaunce walling, 12 feet high, is unique in Scotland, with its series of splendid sculptured panels, representing the planetary deities, the liberal arts and the cardinal virtues. All this was the work of Sir David Lindsay, Lord Edzell of Session, a most notable and cultured man and a great traveller, who modelled it on designs from Nuremburg in 1604. He was a son of the 9th Earl of Crawford. The Crawford Lindsays gained Edzell by marrying the Stirling heiress of Glenesk in 1357. Here much that was important in Scotland's story took place. It was the home of the Wicked Master of Crawford whose activities still shock. Here Mary Queen of Scots held a privy council in 1562. Cromwell garrisoned it in 1651. During the Maule regime it was involved in the Jacobite campaigns. A terrible curse signalled the end of the Lindsays of Edzell, when the lord hanged two dumb brothers for poaching, and their gypsy mother declared:

"By all the demons of hell, I curse you! For you, Lady Crawford, you shall not see the sun set; you and the unborn babe you carry will both be buried in the same grave; and for you, Lord Crawford, you shall die a death that would make the boldest man ever born of woman, even to witness, shriek with fear."

Lady Crawford died that same evening, and her husband was torn to pieces by wolves a year later—tradition alleging that the wolves were the incarnate spirits of the two dumb brothers.

Farther along the Lethnot road is the picturesque kirkyard of

Edzell, with its former parish church, dedicated to St. Laurence, represented only by the Lindsay aisle. But this is highly interesting, having been the choir of the pre-Reformation chapel, with a piscina to the left and a priest's door to the right, with an arched recess for an effigy in the west gable. Below is the subterranean burial-vault of the Lindsays, reached by a trap-door. There is a consecration-cross cut on the wall outside. And preserved in the aisle are the ancient font and many stones, including an interesting Pictish sculptured slab, four feet by two, with much elaborate Celtic decoration now very weatherworn. It was discovered when the kirkyard walls were renewed in 1870, and for a time thereafter lost. It is good to see it saved. The chapel has a defensive grille in its remaining window. There are many old gravestones, though the kirkyard is still used as the district burial-place. St. Laurence's Well used to be near by. There is a water-fall in the West Water half a mile to the west.

There is much of interest in the parish in Glen Esk, including the former constituent parish of Newdosk or Neudos; but these are better treated elsewhere. The Angus-Kincardineshire border lies along the line of the Esk immediately east of Edzell. Beyond this, actually in Fettercairn parish, is the large R.A.F. establishment and airfield, where so many American airmen have been stationed. And to the west of it is the old lairdship of Arnhall, now a large farming estate, with old work incorporated in the mansion, including a panel dated 1622 with the initials *C.E.S.* It was originally a Straton property, passing to the Carnegies, like so much else. They sold it in 1796 to one John Brodie for the then enormous sum of £22,500 sterling, and the new laird much improved and reclaimed the mosses and moorland. His daughter was the famous Duchess of Gordon. A small woollen manufactory was established here.

Two miles to the north-west, Gannochy Bridge spans the Esk at the very mouth of the glen, carrying the B966 road to Fettercairn. This famous bridge was built in 1732 and widened 1796, based on two great rocks which here flank the river's deep and quite spectacular chasm. It was erected at the sole expense of a simple tenant farmer, John Black, a benefactor if ever there was one. It is a single arch 30 feet high by 52 wide. The fine woodlands of The Burn estate adjoin, with the well-known Loups of Esk falls, ravine and rapids.

To the south of the village is the large Edzell Wood, through which the main road runs, with, to the west, the Gallows Knowe of the former barony.

Farnell and Kinnaird. This is a small rural parish and a great and historic estate, the seat of the Carnegie family, Earls of Southesk. The parish, formerly called Farneval, or even Fernwell, lies east by south of Brechin, on the way to Montrose, and extends to 5750 acres. There is no real village, but a pretty estate hamlet, at the kirkton, lies just south of Kinnaird Castle policies at the attractive Den of Farnell. It is all a wooded area, with an air of settled peace.

The parish church stands in its kirkyard on a tree-clad eminence, and is a Gothic-style structure with rib-vaulted ceiling dating from 1806, simple and pleasing within though rather ornate outside. The gallery is faced with good carved panelling. This church replaced a 17th century building, although there presumably was an earlier one still, the consecration cross for which is said to be built into the kirkyard wall—although this was not traced by the writer. A late Pictish cross-slab from here, called the Farnell Stone, is now in Montrose Museum, depicting Adam and Eve, with Celtic decoration. There are many old tombstones in the kirkyard.

Near by, to the west, is Farnell Castle, a small but highly interesting fortalice, recently restored by Lord Southesk, which was formerly the country palace of the bishops of Brechin—and a modest palace indeed. Now a T-shaped building, of tall main block and small central circular wing, it nevertheless belongs to two periods, the eastern portion being the bishop's work, the western half added after the Reformation by the new secular owners, the stair-tower in centre linking. This tower is interesting in that it is corbelled out to the square at top, not to provide the usual watch-chamber but solely to facilitate the fitting of a squared, crowstepped-gabled roof—extraordinary lengths to go for such purpose. The gable of the east part is finished with the gabled crowsteps peculiar to ecclesiastical buildings; and the sacred monogram *I.M.*, for Jesu Maria, with heavenly crown above, is on the northern skew-putt. There are corbels to support an external timber gallery on the east gable, an unusual feature, and a strange buttresslike erection at ground level at the west end, for purpose unknown. Bishop Meldrum refers to it as "Palatium Nostrum" in 1512. Bishop Campbell alienated it to his kinsman, the Earl of Argyll, at the Reformation. But the Carnegies got it in due course. It fell on evil days, and became first an almshouse for old women, then a farmworkers' tenement. Now, restored and pink-washed, it is again a very attractive residence.

Kinnaird Castle in its huge deer-park is one of the finest seats in Scotland. The castle, though seeming of comparatively modern date—for it was largely rebuilt by David Bryce in French château-style between 1854 and 1860—yet contains the early nucleus, with vaulted basements and thick walling. It had been vastly extended in 1770, allegedly with 365 windows. The façade facing south across the landscaped park, 208 feet long, is particularly impressive, with its towers, long stone balconies and balustraded terracing. Internally it is a treasure-house of relics and pictures. The woodlands here are notable, many of the trees being almost 500 years old, though most were planted in the late 18th century. There is an old kirkyard in the grounds, with the foundations of the original Kinnaird parish church, formerly Cuikston, united with Farnell and dedicated to St. Rumon or Rumald. There is a knoll called Rumes' Cross, probably where the Pictish cross-slab came from. Duthac Carnegie (of Carnegie in Carmylie parish) married Mariota de Kinnaird, the heiress, in 1409, and the Carnegies proceeded to cut a very wide swathe in Angus, indeed in Scottish history. In 1616 David, head of the family, was created 1st Lord Carnegie, then in 1633 Earl of Southesk. He was the great Montrose's father-in-law—but did not always see eye-to-eye with his son-in-law. The 5th Earl was forfeited for his share in the 1715 Rising, but the estates were bought back by a kinsman and the forfeiture reversed in 1855. The present 11th Earl married as his first wife Princess Maud, daughter of the former Princess-Royal and the Duke of Fife, and their son, Lord Carnegie, has inherited, through her, the dukedom of Fife.

The parish is almost wholly covered by the estate. But there are one or two items of independent interest. The farm of Fithie, on rising ground to the south, was once the seat of a family of Fithie of that Ilk, and their small castle is said to have some remnants incorporated in a roadside cottage south of the farm—although the author could not discern any sign. Also a weem, or Pictish underground storehouse, is reputed to be on these lands, just where is uncertain. It is interesting to note that the effigy covering the alleged coffin of William the Lion at Arbroath Abbey is reputed really to be that of a Fithie of that Ilk. Fithie fell to the all-conquering Carnegies in 1549. The farm of Carcary, to the east, had the extraordinary record of having been held by the Lyell family as tenants of Carnegie, from 1663 to 1878.

The great Montreathmont Moor is partly in Farnell parish, and is now largely forested.

Fern, Noranside and Vayne. Fern, or Fearn—the Gaelic for alder—is a medium-sized parish of 8000 acres on the Braes of Angus, lying east of Tannadice and seven miles north of Forfar; Noranside is a Borstal institution and associated community, and Vayne is an ancient barony, with ruined castle and interesting features. The upper part of the parish is mountainous, reaching 1900 feet at Hill of Garbet. The lower part is threaded by the Noran Water.

The kirkton, with school, lies fairly centrally for the lower section, at a road-junction beside a sylvan ravine called Fern Den, the parish church occupying a green hillock therein. Though small, it is of very long lineage, being allegedly founded in A.D. 666 and dedicated to St. Ninian. It was rebuilt rather ornately in 1806. Its bell, dated 1506, is cracked and replaced, and now kept in the vestibule, along with the iron jougs. The interior is plain but pleasant. I could not find the Ghaist Stane, said to stand near the kirk. In the yard are many old weathered tombstones. One is notable, called the Ledenhendries stone. This commemorates one Mackintosh, farmer in Ledenhendries, who was "captain" of the parish defenders who tackled and defeated with great slaughter a raiding party of Highland caterans around the end of the 17th century, called the Battle of Sauchs, or the Raid of Fern. This hero outlived his lieutenant, James Winter, for whom he had a table-stone set up in Cortachy kirkyard in 1732.

A mile west of the kirkton lies Noranside House, once a wooded estate with an early 19th century mansion, which was converted into a tuberculosis hospital, and more recently into a large Borstal institution, with enterprising management and ideas as to re-education. There are extensive modern housing schemes for the staff, very fine, in the neighbourhood, making this much the largest community in the parish. West of one of the schemes, on the road to Memus, is a single standing-stone on the crest of a field ridge south of the road.

Near by, on a shelf of Deuchar Hill (970) to the north, is the white-washed small mansion of Deuchar. This was the home of the ancient family of Deuchar of that Ilk, one of the oldest in Angus, who were here from the 11th century until 1818, said to have received the lands as a reward for aid at the Battle of Barry in 1010. A mile to the south-east of Noranside, at a hub of roads near the Noran Water, at Wellford farm is an ancient well. Its spring still bubbles up at the south side of the road, opposite cottages; but I have been unable to ascertain to whom it was dedicated.

South-east of the kirkton is the large Redford Wood, planted forest and well-grown, covering almost two miles. To the south-east of this there are two ancient earthworks, at Hilton of Fern, now tree-clad mounds. A mile to the west is Vayne. This was the seat of the barony of Fern, granted to the Norman Montealtos, or Mowats, by William the Lion in the late 12th century. The remains of the present 16th century castle no doubt incorporate foundations of their stronghold, on its lofty eminence above the Noran Water at the edge of a field below the modern farmhouse. In 1450 the Lindsay Earls of Crawford gained the property, and no doubt built the present castle. They lost it to the Carnegies in 1594, and the 3rd Earl of Southesk added to and altered it in the 17th century. Quite a lot remains though long a crumbling ruin, vaulted, with a circular stair-tower. Stones from it are built into the farm-steading, one, weatherworn, displaying an earl's coronet, a monogram and Latin motto. Below the castle, to the east at the riverside, is a stone known as the Kelpie's Footprint, a large sandstone boulder with a deep hoof-like indentation. Vayne was an important barony in the old days. The building of the castle has been wrongly attributed to Cardinal Beaton. His daughter married the Lindsay heir. A single standing-stone, relic of a circle, rises in the field to the east.

The Cruick Water, a fine trouting stream, comes down through the parish from the mountains, rising on Mowat's Seat, last remaining reminder of the Montealtos. A footpath from the farm of Afflochie to the north probes into the hills in a big way, after seven miles reaching the lonely Waterhead at the top of Glen Lethnot and so on another eight miles over the Priest's Road to upper Glen Esk and then eventually another 15 miles to Deeside, a major journey. The back-road which leads to Afflochie through the green foothills there turns west to wind and climb picturesquely to Glen Ogil, by Auchnacree. This rambling, whitewashed mansion, with prominent heraldic decoration, dates only from 1836, but is the successor of an old laird's house, with much woodland.

Ferryden, Craig and Usan. This area forms a wide promontory between the great Lunan Bay and the almost equally large Montrose Basin, a plateau of no great elevation ending in Scurdyness and lighthouse, all very much with its own identity. Ferryden is now almost a suburb of Montrose, linked by the suspension-bridge, but successfully retaining something of its individual character as a former fishing-village. Craig is the parish, of nearly 5000 acres, recently linked with the *quod sacra* parish of Ferryden; and Usan is the southern coastal district, with its Fishtown now practically a coastguard village. There are also the Boddin Point area farther south, the central estates of Duninald and Dysart, and the higher Rossie district to the west.

Ferryden, lying along the south side of the South Esk estuary, facing across to Montrose, is a terraced village of fishermen's houses now largely restored and modernised as a pleasant residential community for the near by town, with the former large fishing-fleet almost gone—it used to employ 200 men—but salmon-fishing is still persisting. Ferryden is quite large, long though narrow, extending for the best part of a mile along the estuary, with fine views northwards, its peaceful atmosphere aided by the fact that there is no through road, and climbing lanes between the terraces. Modern housing is set on higher ground. The church is plain, with no kirkyard, and was the Free church of Craig parish formerly. Before the road bridge was built, Ferryden used to be the ferry-station for the main Aberdeen road. The bridge makes use of the island of Inchbrayock, or Rossie Island, which all but stops up the estuary like a cork for the bottle-neck of the vast landlocked Basin. *Innis Breac* was the chapel-isle of the 6th century St. Brioc, and was important enough to be a parish of its own once. It is rather unsightly now, unfortunately, nicer to look from than at, because of industrial development and detritus. Its church was ruinous by 1573, but part of it still exists, in the large and still-used graveyard, as a lairds' burial-place, with six heraldic dormer pediments built into the interior, relating to the Scotts of Rossie. There are many old gravestones around. Here, from Celtic Church times, were kept two Pictish cross-slabs, now removed to Montrose Museum.

A winding narrow road runs one mile from Ferryden to Scurdyness where, on a low headland, rises the tall, whitewashed lighthouse, with keepers' houses, a pleasant spot. The cliffs which rim the coastline to the south have died away here. The views northwards are extensive. There are many stake-nets for salmon.

The Kirkton of Craig hamlet lies a mile to the south-west of Ferryden, on the higher ground, the Gothic-type parish church being a prominent landmark. The parish was formed out of Inchbrayock and St. Skeoch, to the south, in 1618. The church, dating from 1799, seems somewhat ambitious for its rural state; but it has recently suffered the demotion of not having a minister of its own. The kirkyard is not particularly interesting. Craig House, or Castle is an exciting place, however, lying on slightly lower ground to the north, a most unusual complex, still an occupied mansion, dating from the 15th and 17th centuries and later. It retains two square parapeted flanking-towers of a 15th century courtyard castle, a fine if somewhat crumbling gatehouse entrance, and a later L-planned range dating probably from 1637, which date appears over a former doorway. Altogether the composition is most picturesque, with high curtain-walls, gunloops, parapets and crowstepped gables. Craig was a seat of the Woods or de Boscos, kinsmen of Bonnyton. Sir David Wood was comptroller of Scotland under James V. They built the original castle and soon after 1617 it was acquired by David Carnegie, 1st Earl of Southesk and given to his second son, brother-in-law of the great Montrose. Craig passed later to the Scotts of near-by Rossie.

Rossie Castle lay almost inconveniently close—less than half a mile to the south-west. The old fortalice is gone, and its great 1800 successor also has recently been demolished, only a vast pile of rubble remaining. William the Lion gave Rossie to the Norman Malherbe family and Thomas de Malherbe was sheriff of Angus in 1277. The family assumed the name of Rossie, but lost the lands to the Scotts of Logie in 1650. The Rossie area is extensive and scattered, Rossie Moor with its lochans lying three miles to the south-west. Rossie Approved School is now a very large establishment, modern and progressive, on a ridge in that area.

East of Rossie is the Dysart district, not to be confused with the town in Fife. It was a barony, and though there is now no mansion, there are three large farms of the name. It had its own church once, site unknown. It belonged to the Melvilles, one of whom fell at Harlaw, then Guthries and Lyells. Oddly enough the Lyells were until 1682, hereditary town clerks of Montrose, surely one of the most peculiar baronial appointments. Nether Dysart farm seems to have been the site of the original castle, and there are a number of relics of antiquity here. A weatherworn heraldic panel is inset over the former doorway of the farmhouse; and in the walled garden are two heraldic stones, one a dormer pediment dated 1594 with the Melville arms and initials, the other dated 1714 over a gateway lintel. Upper Dysart farm still has a lean-to 17th century doocot. Dysart used to be a detached portion of Maryton parish.

A mile north of Nether Dysart is Duninald Castle, a large castellated mansion of 1823. The original fortalice of this property was down at the coast, half a mile, rejoicing in the sinister name of Black Jack. There is only a slight projection of the cliff-face there now, but it is still so marked on the Ordnance Survey map. Scions of the Lords Gray used to roost here, and were an unruly lot—as records of the Privy Council indicate. Near by is Boddin Point, the northern horn of Lunan Bay, where there is a fishing harbour, still used as such for the salmon-netters, but little left of the hamlet. On the tip of the Point itself is an unusual limekiln, massive and almost like a castle, with corbelling and stone vaulting, as well as brick. The first kiln was built by the laird of Rossie in 1696, and extended, as now, in 1750. The lime was for fertiliser.

Easily seen from here, just up the coast, is an interesting feature
known as the Elephant Rock, a remarkable natural projection of the
cliff, with considerable resemblance to that animal, the trunk forming a natural arch. Above it, perched dizzily, is the tiny ruined
chapel and graveyard of St. Skeoch or Skay, one of the disciples of
Columba. This was the church of the ancient parish of that name, or
Duninald, united with Inchbrayock in 1618 to form Craig. The
little building on the cliff-top survives almost to the wall-head, and
there are two consecration crosses incised on the east wall. It was old
enough to be restored in 1587. In the graveyard are a number of old
stones, one to a doctor of divinity. It seems an extraordinary place
for a house of worship.

The Usan district lies immediately to the north, on the coast. The
name is a corruption of Ullishaven, or Ulyssishaven, and pronounced Oosan. There is a Georgian mansion of this name, two farms,
and the former fishing-village of Fishtown (or Fishertown) of Usan.
There is no harbour, but a boat-strand, and amongst the rocks an
ancient vaulted icehouse for the storage of fish. The fishers' houses
are almost all gone, though the old school is still inhabited. But
there is a large coastguard station here, with tower and modern
cottages. Unfortunately the old coastguard houses, a long row of
them just below, with the tall former look-out tower, have merely
been abandoned, leaving rather an unsightly scene in an attractive
spot. Usan is a famous place for gathering agates and other semi-
precious stones washed up from submarine rocks. The famous Archbishop Leighton came of the family which lairded it at Usan from
the 14th century.

Finavon and Oathlaw. This is a small parish and district lying
immediately north-east of Forfar, and traversed by the busy A94
Aberdeen highway. Finavon is the old name, as it is of a prominent
isolated hill to the east, and of an ancient estate and ruined castle
near the main road; while Oathlaw is the present parish name, and
a hamlet and church set on a side-road to the north. The parish
covers 5300 acres and is now linked with Tannadice.

Finavon was very important in old Scotland, as the principal seat
of the powerful Lindsays, Earls of Crawford. Their formerly great
castle is wholly gone, and the ruined tower which still remains within
the estate, where the Lemno Burn joins the South Esk five miles
north-east of Forfar, appears to date only from the 16th century,
though the lower storeys may contain older work. It is massive,
86 feet tall, with vaulted basements, crowstepped gables and a single
remaining angle-turret. The east front is badly riven, and the north
unusual in having no single aperture or window. The floors have
fallen in. At the tower-top, to the south-east, is said to remain the
iron hook from which the notorious Earl Beardie hanged the minstrel
who foretold his defeat at the Battle of Brechin, 1452—but this
dating seems unlikely. The history of Finavon would fill volumes,
the Lindsays coming here from Edzell in 1375. After the Battle of

Arbroath in 1446, David 3rd Earl and his brother-in-law foeman, Ogilvy of Inverquharity, were both brought here wounded. The earl died, whereupon his countess went to her own brother's sick-room and smothered him with a pillow. Her son was the potent and savage 4th Earl, called the Tiger or Beardie, whose cruelties were abnormal even for that age. There is a large modern mansion near by in the wooded estate. Near by also was the original pre-Reformation chapel, dedicated in 1380 to the Nine Maidens, and called for some reason Aitkenhauld, its kirkyard now all but obliterated. This in due course became the Reformed parish church; but falling into a poor state, the parish centre was moved to Oathlaw, a mile to the west, where there had been a chapel-of-ease. The Carnegies got Finavon, like so much else locally, in 1672, explaining the decay of the castle. There is still a roadside hamlet of Milton of Finavon, and a well-known bridge at the right-angled bend of the main road just beyond. There was a spinning-mill established here in the early 19th century. The area is heavily wooded; indeed it was all part of the royal forest of Plater or Platane.

Oathlaw is an attractive small scattered hamlet, with school, at a hub of side-roads, and sequestered. The Gothic church lies amongst old trees to the south, somewhat bare and neglected. It dates from 1815, and has a handsome silver baptismal basin dated 1742. The minister was dragged from his pulpit here in 1715 by four women, in the Jacobite troubles. There are stained-glass war memorial windows. A tall table-stone is erected against the east gable, showing a man's figure and a weatherworn Latin inscription.

A mile to the south-west of this, nearer Forfar, is the site of the large and important Roman camp of Battledykes. It is now all green farmland, with nothing to be seen, but was an establishment of 3000 by 1850 feet, large enough to accommodate 26,000 men. Suitably, overlooking this invaders' encampment from the lofty summit of Finavon Hill three miles to the east, is one of the finest native Early Iron Age vitrified forts in the land, at 663 feet. It is quite readily reached, especially from the Aberlemno side, by a pleasant winding side-road of Highland atmosphere climbing to it; and apart from the extensive remains, it is a delightful spot to visit, amongst whins and broom, with glorious views. The green ramparts, ditches and vitri-fied masonry are all very clear, measuring 500 by 120 feet, and interesting in having the necessary central well, or spring, still very evident. Excavations here in 1933-5 revealed much of interest, and evidence of metal-working, pot-making and weaving by our early ancestors. There was another rather similar fort on Turin Hill two miles to the south, called Kemp's Castle—see Rescobie. A later dun was superimposed on that site. The farm and former castle of Woodwray lie on the northern slope of Finavon Hill a mile from the fort—but this is in Aberlemno parish and better dealt with therein.

At the other end of this four-mile-long hill, actually in Rescobie parish and only two miles from Forfar, is Carsegray, an estate with a most pleasantly-sited ancient mansion, sitting on a shelf of the wooded hillside facing south. The house is E-shaped, whitewashed, and at first glance homogenous. But closer inspection reveals that the east wing represents a small T-planned early 17th century fortalice to which the 18th century house has been added. It is only two storeys and a garret, with a stair-tower corbelled out somewhat above first-floor level, and crowstepped gables. There is an empty panel-space above the door in the re-entrant, and the latter has had a shot-hole to defend it. The barony of Carse, belonging to a family named Rynd, was bought in 1741 by Charles Gray, a cadet of the Lord Gray, who changed the name to Carse Gray. It remains with his descendants.

Forfar. No one is likely ever to accuse the county town of Angus of lacking character. It is one of those places which just could not be anywhere else. Superficially its reddish-stone streets may at first glance resemble those of Brechin or Arbroath; but such impression is of the most fleeting. The cause, undoubtedly, is more the Forfar folk than the actual physical attributes of the town—though it has its significant features. The fact is that the citizens of the royal burgh are, and always have been, a highly individual lot, forceful, independent, humorous. Not to put too fine a point on it, they have a good conceit of themselves—and not without cause. The essential individuality of Forfar—which should really be spelt Farfar, as once it was, and as it is still pronounced locally—can be summed up in these two items. The jingle:

Bonnie Munross (Montrose) will be a moss, Brechin a braw burgh toun,
But Farfar will be Farfar still, when Dundee's a' dung doon!

And the story of the Forfar man who approached the London bookstall and asked for the *Dispatch*. On being asked which *Dispatch*, he answered testily, "*The Farfar Dispatch*, of course." When regretfully told that it was not available, he picked up *The Times* with a sigh, saying, "Och, weel—I'll just hae to mak do wi' your local paper."

Standing in the midst of the great and fertile vale of Strathmore, with the ranked Grampians to the north and all the lesser hills of Fotheringham, Dunnichen, Turin and Finavon cradling it, Forfar is the centre and hub of a large agricultural community, with a population of 10,000, a busy, well-doing, lively place, with an age-old history. Once it was called Angusia, and as late as 1675 a map still gave it that original name. Nevertheless its castle, which was a favourite seat of the early Scottish kings—Malcolm Canmore held his first parliament here in 1057—seems always to have been called Farfar. The site is still pointed out—though the castle itself was demolished by Bruce to prevent a second occupation by the English —on the Castle-hill, behind Castle Street, the principal shopping-street in the centre of the town, and reached by a lane off Canmore Street. It is now marked only by an octagonal tower and flagpole.

Forfar, like many another hoary burgh, is singularly lacking in ancient buildings. It seems to be in the Scottish character to sweep such away and start afresh in times of stress—which has its admirable and sad sides, both. The town has certainly always been a great place for starting again, standing on its own feet, self-help. Its present thriving state could well have been much otherwise, for it has suffered many vicissitudes, and the rise and fall of trades and industries which could have brought the burgh low: but always adaptability and sturdy individuality have triumphed. Even comparatively recently, the decline in jute manufacture, which had replaced linen to become the major employment, has not set back Forfar for long; for it has branched out with notable vigour for a comparatively small community into quite new industrial development, with the manufacture of synthetic fibres—pioneering polypropylene in Britain, for instance—tartans and tweeds, carpets, ladder-making, agricultural engineering, light iron-founding, prefabricated joinery fittings and specialities such as bagpipe-making and Strathmore honey processing—with whisky added! Strathmore is a large fruit-growing area, and canning has developed, while Forfar's nurseries are famous. Yet not so very long ago, Forfar citizens used to be called soutars—like Selkirk's—because its main industry was then shoe-making. Perhaps this trade was inherited from the Romans—who were much in evidence hereabouts—for at the camp at Kirkbuddo, not far away, were found great quantities of worn-out footwear of the legions, who presumably had established a replacement factory in this cattle-rearing area. The site of another and greater Roman camp is at Battledykes, just two miles north of Forfar, where there was accommodation for no fewer than 26,000 soldiers.

After the brief Roman interlude the Picts resumed their sway, and this neighbourhood is rich in their relics, with many examples of symbol-stones and cross-slabs and their forts and souterrains. At Restenneth, which is almost an eastern suburb of Forfar, Nechtan, king of the Picts, was baptised by St. Boniface in A.D. 710. The Romish priory which grew out of this Celtic monastery makes a delightful and highly interesting place to visit. The great Bruce is said to have buried an infant son here.

Holy Church has long been notably strong in Forfar—and it is good to know that the various branches thereof unite to hold an annual service at Restenneth where Christian worship has been offered for over 1260 years. The Chapel of Forfar seems to have been erected in 1241, probably replacing an earlier and Celtic foundation, in honour of St. James the Greater, an unusual dedication in Scotland. The present Old Parish Church rises on the site, on a tree-clad mound above East High Street. It is a large and handsome building, dating mainly from the 18th century, with a 19th century clock-tower, the bells of which are older. One, Lang Strang, cast in Sweden in 1656, was given by Robert Strang one of Gustavus Adolphus' Scots importees and brother of Forfar's provost. The interior is impressive, with two galleries and a large organ; there is much stained glass, notably three war memorial windows, two for the

First World War one for the Second, with the many, many names of the fallen all inscribed. The church has some very fine 17th century silver, with the Guthrie arms; also an old pewter dish said to be the finest in Scotland. A kirkyard, with many old tombstones, surrounds.

There are many churches in Forfar, of course. But special mention must be made of the Lowson Memorial or East Church. This is a large and splendid cruciform building, the bequest of Provost Lowson of Balgavies, a Forfar manufacturer, built in 1912–15 by Dr. Marshall Mackenzie of Aberdeen, who made skilful use of the very best in traditional Scottish church architecture with enormous success. The tower, for instance, is recognisably similar to that of St. Monan's in Fife. The internal treatment, woodwork and furnishings, are of as high an order. It is enheartening to see a modern building so excellent in all respects. The stained glass is quite exceptional, the Creation, Apocalypse or Revelation, Te Deum windows and so on, being worthy of any great cathedral. The complex, with manse, occupies two acres of a slight mound just off the Montrose road, where it forms a prominent landmark. It is recorded that the masons for this notable building remained to complete the work in the early part of the 1914–18 war, and then volunteered as a group for active service—from which many did not return.

With all this emphasis on the church, it is rather surprising that Forfar has long been noted for its almost Continental Sundays, with places of amusement, recreation-grounds, swimming-pool etc., and also certain shops, open in the afternoon and evening. This is no new development, for until 1597 even the weekly Forfar Fair was held on a Sunday. Why this tradition, so unusual in Scotland, should have developed, is a mystery. It certainly has not cramped church-growth.

There are many public buildings of note. The Municipal Buildings themselves occupy an island site at The Cross, the junction of Castle Street and High Street—cobbled streets still, by the way. Their Town and County Hall is a late 18th century edifice by Playfair, with its handsome Council Chamber also containing stained-glass war memorial windows and Book of Remembrance. As the main Forfar war memorial is a tall tower prominent on the ridge of Balmashanner, south of the town, the victims of holocaust are not likely to be forgotten here. There are pictures by Raeburn, Romney, Hoppner and Opie; also fine chandeliers. Near by, in West High Street, is the Meffan Institute, housing an excellent public library and a small museum. Amongst the latter's exhibits is one particularly unusual, interesting and apt for this area—a pictorial blanket woven by a Miss Farquhar of Pitscandly House near by, with wool from that estate, displaying accurate representations of the main Pictish symbols, mirror-and-comb, crescent and V-rod, double-discs and Z-rod, Celtic beast, etc., with typical Celtic decoration, beautifully done. At the other end of East High Street, back-set a little, is

the former manse of the Rev. Dr. John Jamieson, compiler of the
Scottish Dictionary. He was minister of the Secession Church here
from 1780 to 1796. The Sheriff Court-house and County Buildings
are at Market Street, off the Brechin road.

Forfar has a notable large hall, to seat over 800, in the Reid Hall,
Castle Street, with a rather ornate exterior, rebuilt after the late war
at a cost of over £100,000. The Forfar Academy, a well-known fee-
paying school with a resounding former-pupils' roll, is now housed in
highly modern premises on the Bankhead brae off the Brechin road,
with near by the Fyfe-Jamieson Maternity Home. There is another
large new school building erected on the Glamis road to the west.
Amongst the many other prominent establishments is the Training
Centre of the Guide-Dogs for the Blind Association, off the Dundee
road, an excellent institution whose charges may be seen learning
about traffic in Forfar's busy streets.

Forfar Loch deserves special mention. It lies west of the town, the
westernmost of the chain of lochs which ends at Balgavies, six miles
to the east. It is over a mile long, and quarter that wide, but has
been much larger. On the north side is an artificial peninsula called
The Inch, said to be the site of Queen Margaret's palace, with a
causeway thereto. Much of the surrounding marsh and mire has
been reclaimed in the past and though the present methods of re-
clamation, using the east end mire as a dump for the town's rubbish,
is scarcely an improvement to amenity, Forfar's plans for the Loch
are in fact ambitious, with it to become the town's principal recreation area, with sailing-club, angling, football, cricket, tennis, a picnic
area, caravan site and other amenities. Forfar is already rich in
parks, with the Reid, Steele, Boyle and Langlands Parks, and the
Balmashanner ridge—incidentally called "Bummy" by the locals.
Reid Park is the oldest and largest, a fine stretch of grassland and
trees rising up towards Balmashanner, gifted by Provost Peter Reid,
manufacturing confectioner, of Forfar Rock fame. There are ample
facilities for organised games in these parks. And Forfar Golf Club
has a good 18-hole course at Cunninghill, over a mile out on the
Arbroath road, where visitors are welcome—it being of a standard to
have housed the Scottish Professional Championship. Fishing is well
catered for hereabouts, in more than Forfar Loch, permits being
available for Glen Ogil Reservoir and Rescobie Loch, as well as in
many hill burns and the Lunan Water.

The Lunan Water, which flows into Lunan Bay after a fairly
straight course of some 15 miles, rises just to the east of Forfar. In
fact, the village of Lunanhead is now really a suburb, with quarrying
and pre-cast stone works, modern housing, and a tiny church built
in memory of Charles Gray, of Carsegray near by, in 1884. This is
just north of Restenneth Priory and at the beginning of the pleasant
B9134 road which leads by Pitscandly, with its Blackgate standing-
stones, and Aberlemno with its Pictish monuments, to Brechin.
There is a cairn-circle near Carsegownie on this road, larch-grown,
with concentric rings.

Forfar has another satellite village at Kingsmuir nearly two miles to the south-east on the road to Carnoustie, high-set on the rise towards Dunnichen Hill, becoming popular for modern housing away from the town. Modern housing indeed is very much in evidence at Forfar, private and council—a most energetic drive for the latter resulting in the burgh having now 1928 council-owned houses against 1850 private, with both figures growing fast, however. There are two industrial sites of over 20 acres available, one to the north near the important auction-marts and Market Muir—the principal markets of Angus.

Fowlis Easter. Here is a castle, still occupied as a farmhouse, a most excellent ancient church, a hamlet and a parish conjoined with Lundie since 1618, all situated on a ridge of the Sidlaw foothills about six miles west of Dundee, on the verge of Perthshire. To be so near the city it is all most attractively rural, detached and unspoiled. It is not to be confused with Fowlis Wester, near Crieff, where there is also an ancient church and parish but now no castle.

Very early the lands belonged to the Maules of Panmure, but came with an heiress to the Mortimers about 1190, who held them for 180 years until another heiress carried them to Sir Andrew Gray of Broxmouth, in East Lothian, thus introducing that powerful and unscrupulous house into Angus. Here, and at Castle Huntly and Broughty Castle, the Grays were seated from 1377. In 1715 they moved to the new Gray House at Liff, Fowlis being sold to the Murrays of Ochtertyre—who however never lived here. The castle was once a great and important stronghold, with curtain-walls, flanking-towers and keep. The remaining part, dating mainly from the 17th century, was formerly the Lady's Tower, or Bower, and consists of a tall rectangular building of four storeys, with a circular stair-tower to the south, and alongside it an interesting projecting chimneystack housing the flue of the great kitchen fireplace. Unsightly modern dormer-windows spoil the roofline. A later and lower wing extends to the north. It is a salutory thought that some of the worst treacheries and Machiavellian intrigues to stain Scots history were probably concocted here, and at Castle Huntly, the notorious Master of Gray especially distinguishing himself in this respect during the reigns of Mary Queen of Scots and her son. After their day the castle actually sank to the level of a village ale-house, but is now a private house again.

The church lies a few hundred yards to the north-east, at the head of the Den of Fowlis, in its ancient graveyard. It is a typical long pre-Reformation building, though somewhat larger and taller than usual, and notable for a number of features, especially its splendid paintings. Dedicated to St. Marnoch, there is a tradition that it was built in 1142 by a Lady Mortimer, as a prayer-in-stone for her husband's return from a crusade. But in fact Fowlis did not come to the Mortimers till later, and the church really dates from 1453, built by the 1st Lord Gray, son of the Sir Andrew above—although there was a much earlier church on the site prior even to 1138. It is a fine example of Scoto-Gothic 15th century architecture, of polished ashlar, with some good mullioned and tracery windows and a notable doorway in the south front, with ogee-headed arch surmounted by a handsome crested helmet, for Gray. A pair of iron jougs, for wrongdoers, still hang near by. Internally, there are two stoups for holy water at the north and south doors—the lesser entrance at the north probably being for women, who were often kept separate in church—a fine oaken 15th century rood-screen, a highly decorative aumbry, and the unique series of religious paintings on wood, one of the Crucifixion, as large as 13 feet by 5. There is also a damaged octagonal stone font, and a 15th century bronze almsdish, depicting Adam and Eve, of German origin. The eastern end of the church was used as a mausoleum for the Grays. In the kirkyard are two stones of especial interest. One is a simple and substantial plain cross, roughly dressed, probably much older than the present church the other a hog-backed recumbent gravestone, with sword and hunting-horn carving, considerably later than the cross and unconnected therewith though they are side by side.

A painted inscription in the church long mystified scholars, but Dr. Dalgety, a local historian, has deciphered it to declare, in odd Latin: "Andrew Lord Gray and his devout lady built this church to Saint Marnock; if you ask when, in 1453, the year in which he was abroad as ambassador at Rome. But thou, O Lord, have mercy upon me. Amen." Presumably written about 1550 by a provost of the then Collegiate Church of Fowlis.

To the north-west lay a former loch, known still as Piperdean, and now drained and largely a plantation, where tradition has it a piper was once drowned. Near by is a farm known as Muirloch.

Friockheim and Kinnell. The odd name of this large Angus village, almost a small town, always attracts attention, although its explanation is humdrum. It is pronounced Frickham, and was formerly in Kirkden parish, mid-way between Forfar and Arbroath. To confuse the issue, the immediately adjoining small parish of Kinnell has been linked with the *quod sacra* church in Friockheim, so that the latter is now the centre of worship for Kinnell also.

The village is comparatively modern and of an unusual triangular shape, with the apex, the church, facing west, and a broad base half a mile to the east. The name used to be the perfectly normal Gaelic one of Frioch, or *fraoch*, meaning heather, its hamlet and mill part of the barony of Gardyne. In the early 19th century the land was feud out by the laird, on the instigation of one John Andson, or Anderson, who erected a flax-spinning mill. It was then called Frioch Feus. In 1824, for some obscure reason Mr. Andson, with the consent of the laird, by public advertisement changed the name to Friockheim. Why the Germanic suffix is not evident today; it is the only such in Scotland.

Friockheim is not unattractive. It has two long main streets, that to the south, along the B965, one-sided only, and less pleasing than the older-seeming northern one, which flanks the tree-clad dip to the Lunan Water and mill-lade. The houses are very trim and neat. The flax-mill has gone, but is replaced at the waterside by a mill for making candlewick bedspreads. Adjoining is a factory for rope-soled sandals. There is also a joinery-works—so Friockheim is fairly self-supporting. The former railway-station and massive bridge, to the west, are no longer used. An ancient burial-cairn lies half a mile to the south, near a group of old quarries.

Gardyne estate, with its fine later 16th century castle, is a mile to the south-west. The original building is oblong on plan with a circular stair-tower corbelled out to form a gabled watch-chamber. There are highly unusual stone-roofed angle-turrets crowning the south gable, each with tiny dormer-windows such as I have not come across elsewhere. The walls are well supplied with gunloops, and there are machicolations for pouring boiling water or other unpleasantness on unwelcome visitors—a late flowering of this refinement. There is a large later addition. The Gardynes of that Ilk were permanently at feud with the Guthries of that Ilk, near by, each family monotonously causing the death of the chief of the other over generations, a situation which resulted in the Privy Council eventually forfeiting both. The Guthries managed to get their lands back, but Gardyne was sold in 1682 to James Lyell of Dysart (Dysart in Angus) a merchant who had made money in London. Only recently the last Lyell laird of Gardyne died, and the estate changed hands for only the second time. The Gallows Law of Gardyne rises half a mile north of the castle, a tree-covered mound in a field.

The Gardyne family, although losing Gardyne, did not disappear from the area, and are still very much present. A branch, of Lawton in neighbouring Inverkeilor parish, acquired Middleton, the adjoining estate to Gardyne on the east, early in the 18th century; and their descendants, the Bruce-Gardynes, are still there. Middleton is an attractive estate of old woodlands, with a large whitewashed mansion mainly of the 18th century but containing an earlier nucleus, as witnessed to by the 16th century roll-moulded fireplace in a ground-floor apartment. At the back is a most pleasing cobbled court; and a dormer pediment of the earlier fortalice is built into a near by gable.

Kinnell parish is rather dominated nowadays by the flat expanses of a disused wartime airfield. The kirkton is a scattered hamlet lying less than a mile north-east of Friockheim. A two-arched, humped bridge carries the side-road from the B965 over Lunan Water, with Milton farm pleasantly placed above the haugh. The church lies a little farther and higher and is now closed, though its graveyard is still used. The fairly plain building dates only from 1855, replacing a pre-Reformation rectory dedicated to St. Maelrubha. Its bell was cast by Borgerhuys in 1624. Kinnell was once a barony belonging to the Ogilvys, and its Court and Gallows Hills are near by. The former fortalice, now disappeared, was in one of the Milton fields. There are many old gravestones. More important, there is alleged

to be a Pictish symbol-stone, with serpents, at one time said to form
the lintel of a garden door of the adjoining manse. A search for this
revealed no certain trace; but there *is* an unusually massive stone
lintel built over the west gateway from kirkyard to manse-yard. No
features are evident on its face, but investigation of its underside
might possibly be rewarding, where it is mortared into the wall.
There are two 17th century panels let into the ingoing of the east, or
minister's, gateway near by, whether from the original church or the
castle is hard to say; and a stone inscribed *M.D.K. 1635* set over a
window of a manse outbuilding. The manse, no longer used as such,
has a delightful south-facing, terraced garden.

Two miles away to the east stands the castle of Wester Braikie, in
rather bare country. The building is now derelict but fairly entire
still, a tall and handsome tower-house on the L-plan, typical of the
late 16th century, with a stair-turret in the re-entrant and an angle-
turret crowning one gable. Gunloops and shot-holes proliferate and
an iron yett guards the doorway. It was built in 1581 by Thomas
Fraser, son of the 5th Lord Lovat, Bruce having granted the barony of
Kinnell to Sir Simon Fraser of Oliver, chief of the name, after
Bannockburn. So the Frasers were here before ever they moved
north to become Highland. In the mid-17th century Braikie passed
to the Grays and then the Ogilvys. It is sad that this fine castle,
which could still be saved, should further decay. *Easter* Braikie, now
also a farm half a mile away, was a separate lairdship, with its own
old castle, demolished in 1823.

Bolshan, or Balleshan, another farm two miles north-east of the
kirkton beyond the airfield, was also once an Ogilvy barony with its
own chapel. Its castle was described as "Lord Ogilvy's special residence" in 1612, but like the chapel is wholly gone. It stood on the
Hill of Bolshan.

Glamis. This is a name famous in Scotland's history, legend and
literature. The renown of its splendid castle and the celebrated Lyon
family which has owned it for so many generations, and to which the
Queen-Mother belongs, tends perhaps to overshadow the remainder
of this fine Strathmore parish 10 miles north of Dundee. This is a
pity, for there is a great deal of interest here.

Medium-sized, the parish covers 8000 acres at the foot of the
northern Sidlaw slopes and stretching out across the strath nearly to
Kirriemuir, with the great estate of the Lyon Earls of Strathmore and
Kinghorne lying centrally. This is so well-known and much written
about that only a few words are necessary. The central six-storeyed
keep of mellow reddish stone is liberally enhanced with angle-
turrets, parapets and dormers, with much heraldic decoration; and
the 3-storeyed flanking-wings and towers add to the impressive effect.
The Great Hall is a magnificent apartment measuring 54 by 21 feet,
with enormous fireplace, mural chambers and fine paintings.
Famous is the vaulted crypt or Secret Chamber, with its legends.
This castle dates from the 15th century, with great additions and

alterations in the two centuries following; but of course there was the much more ancient stronghold of the Thanes of Glamis on the site, first mentioned in 1034, and incorporated in the existing work. Robert II gave Glamis to his son-in-law, Sir John Lyon, chancellor of Scotland; and his grandson was created 1st Lord Glamis in 1445. It is still owned by their lineal descendant of about 25 generations, the 9th lord being created Earl of Kinghorne in 1606, and the 3rd Earl given the added earldom of Strathmore in 1677. The Lyons' story is almost that of Scotland itself. There is a good view of the castle from a bridge, at Bridgend, on the A928 Kirriemuir road.

The village of Glamis lies at the southern gates of the estate, a most attractive place of old houses and lanes, bowered in ancient trees, and now fortunately well by-passed by the busy A94 which used to thread it. Here, on a bank above Glamis Burn, is the parish church, somewhat plain outside though with a clock-spire, which is somewhat unusual for this period, 1793. It is delightfully restored and decorated within, bright, with excellent oak woodwork and carvings, a finely carved gallery to the west, and good stained glass. St. Fergus, a Celtic missionary, founded a cell here in 750; and the medieval church was dedicated in 1242—this edifice being demolished to build the present one. In the vestibule is a fragment of a 9th century Celtic cross-slab, with typical interlacing pattern. There is a large and crowded graveyard surrounding, with many old stones, and the rather plain Strathmore aisle, a burial-vault, is attached to the north-east end of the church. Down the bank, at the riverside near a footbridge, is the Lady Well, a former holy spring.

Of great interest is the famous Glamis Stone, a lofty and fine example of Pictish cross-slab and symbol-stone which stands in the manse garden just south of the church. This is 10 feet high, with the usual decorative cross on the south side and fish and serpent symbols on the north. Foolishly it has been called King Malcolm's Stone, because of a legend that Malcolm II was slain here, and a great and ingenious edifice of fantasy built up out of the Pictish symbols—which of course were carved in the 8th or 9th century, centuries before Malcolm. Glamis is particularly rich in these important early Celtic relics, a unique feature of the Scottish scene. There is a smaller one in a wood on the side of Hunter's Hill in the Thornton area, less than half a mile to the south-east, four feet high and much weatherworn, within a rail. This also has a cross on one side, and a serpent and other symbols on the reverse. And there is a third, known as St. Orland's or the Cossans Stone, remotely sited in an open field above marshland near the railway line two miles north of Glamis, on the farm of Haughs of Cossans. This is seven feet high and more slender, and has been broken but repaired, now in the care of the Department of the Environment. As well as an unusual high-relief cross, there are many symbols and the representation of men in a boat, such as I have not seen elsewhere. Altogether these Pictish relics make a splendid attraction for Glamis, and should be better known. There was another Lyon castle at Cossans, now vanished.

In the village is the National Trust's Angus Folk Museum, where an attractive row of 17th century cottages at Kirkwynd, with stone-slabbed roofs, has been taken over to house a collection of farm and domestic implements and furnishings. Lead used to be worked near Glamis.

There is quite a large village at Charleston, on the wooded hillside of Rochelhill a mile to the south, with many of the houses being restored and rehabilitated. This area is near enough to Dundee to attract commuters. Charleston, though settled-looking enough, was founded only in 1833, when 50 houses were built on a three-acre site. The farm of Mains of Rochelhill above, has a good lean-to 17th century doocot. The village really lies at the foot of Glen Ogilvy, the Sidlaw Hills here comprising three parallel ranges running roughly north and south, with the glens of Ogilvy and Denoon between them. The former is the shorter, reaching two miles up into the hills from the A928, a wide, green and fertile vale, in no way spectacular, with 10 farms. The name *ocel-fa* is ancient British for high plain. This is where the surname Ogilvy came from. It was bestowed on Gilbert, son of Gillebride, 3rd Celtic Earl of Angus, of a long line of mormaors, by William the Lion in 1163. This was the senior stem, the Ogilvys of that Ilk and of Powrie. From them the Ogilvys of Lintrathen descended, the third of whom was created Lord Ogilvy of Airlie in 1491, and the 8th lord created Earl of Airlie in 1639. The Ogilvys of that Ilk had their castle in the mouth of the glen, where Hatton of Ogilvy farm is now, though no trace remains. At Milton near by, where the Glamis Burn from the glen flows under the main road, the former milling hamlet is now burgeoning with many new houses. There is no church or cell in Glen Ogilvy now, but the valley had links with the Celtic St. Donevald, one of whose nine daughters was St. Findoca, after whom St. Fink near Alyth is named.

The parallel glen of Denoon lies two miles to the west, longer and more attractive. Reached from the Nevay road, its own side-road climbs through the large wood of Balgownie Muir into a wide hanging valley, very secluded. On the summit of Denoon Law, within the mouth of this, where quarrying has taken place, is a large earthwork. Its green banks have enclosed a great area, the circumference being no less than 1020 feet, thought to have been a retreat for prehistoric local folk in time of danger. There are traces of an internal building. A smallholding near by used to be known as the Pict's Mill. An Ogilvy castle stood hereabouts also, just where is not clear. Some would place it within the earthwork site; but the hill at the other side of the glen is named Castleward. The road continues another two miles up the glen, to end in a high corrie of Henderson Hill, at 1212 feet. The last farm, in the lap of the hills, is Wester Denoon, and part of the steading here has obviously been the lower storeys of a fortalice. There is a roll-moulded doorway and window to the south, and many very small windows built up. A good stepped doocot stands near by. Both probably date from the late 16th or early 17th century.

To the east of the parish, on the Thornton side-road, is the remote, high-set hamlet of Arniefoul, a few cottages and a farm now, but in 1834 with a population of 106. Hayston Hill rises behind, on which there is another earthworks site.

Glen Clova and Glen Doll. Glen Clova is reputed to be the most lovely of the Angus glens; and Glen Doll, striking off westwards near its head, certainly the wildest and most remote. Between them, they cover a vast stretch of mountain territory, storied as well as scenic.

Until 1608, when it was united with Cortachy, Clova was an independent civil parish; and it still remains very much an entity in character, and with its own *quod sacra* parish church, tiny as this is. The glen is very long. The stretch covered by the public road, the B955, from Cortachy at the mouth to Braedownie where the road ends, is about 13 miles; and the glen goes on thereafter many road-less miles towards Loch Esk, lonely amongst the mountains near the Aberdeenshire border. From this upper glen, a famous track, called the Capel Mounth, climbs over the hills to Ballater on Deeside—a route for tough walkers.

Glen Clova is entered at Dykehead, the post-office hamlet for Cortachy—which also serves as entry for the parallel glen of Prosen, described separately. The lower reaches of Clova are heavily wooded and very attractive, with patches of ancient Caledonian Forest persisting amongst whins and broom. The road remains high above the river for some miles, with the levels below well farmed. Less than four miles up the road forks, at Gella Bridge, a graceful single arch on a pleasant stretch of the South Esk, with the mountains closing in and heightening. Prongs continue up each side of the glen. Above, on the west, is Craigs of Lethnot (1608 feet) and near here was the Chapel of Lethnot, alleged to have suffered the attentions of the Devil during construction, he removing the stones by night that had been laid during the day. The church was sufficiently complete, however, to be destroyed by more mundane forces in 1746—namely the anti-Jacobite military.

Following the westward road, plantations begin to replace the natural woodland and by Wester Eggie forestry is dominant. By now the flanking hills are exceeding 2000 feet. Three miles on is Milton of Clova, a scattered hamlet at another bridge, with the river placid here. This is the centre for the glen, with church, school and hotel. Why it should be called Milton, rather than kirkton, I have not discovered, though the mill is there too, still with wheel but now used as a fish hatchery. The church is small and dates only from 1855, replacing an older and larger one, large enough to have had a gallery added in 1731—indication of the decline in population since then. The iron jougs for malefactors therefrom are now in the Museum of Antiquities, Edinburgh, for some reason. Just a little farther north, the road running only on the east side now, on a green ridge, are the scanty remains of Clova Castle, small and oblong, with a circular stair-tower. This was an Ogilvy place, inevitably, as was all else hereabouts. It is reputed to have been "spoiled" by Cromwell's troops in 1650. There was a later mansion somewhere near, but no trace remains. Presumably this was the house of a remarkable lady, the poet Dorothea Maria Ogilvy of Clova, niece of an Earl of Airlie, who died in 1895. Her epic about this area, called *Willie Wabster's Wooing and Wedding on the Grampian Mountains*, is an extraordinary *tour de force*, the authenticity and forcefulness of its Angus dialect hard to associate with a gently-born Victorian lady—even if she *had* been delving in the local Dr. Jamieson's Scottish Dictionary. As also is her expressed opinion of the Reverend Ferguson, the Glen Prosen parish minister

> *For in the river gurgling on, Will heard the voice of Ferguson,*
> *And the ramgunshoch, hellish laughter, like brattlen stanes cam'*
> *brumblen after*

Her love of Clova is forever enshrined here—although some southern readers may be less than clear as to details:

> *Oh barony o' Clova, green and grand, strinkled wi' spairgen strype and*
> *brattlen strand,*
> *The sweetest strath in a' my fatherland;*
> *Yet wi' the warld I whamle whan-a-bee, ramfeezled runt, I hirple owre*
> *the haugh;*
> *Nae worth for beef or broth or milk o' whey, a rail-e'ed, rousy,*
> *girnigo-gibbie.*

At Rottal, half-way back to Gella Bridge on the east-side road, is a farm and mansion, with pony-trekking establishment. Here, in 1833, was dug up a huge oak, 43 feet long, out of which much fine furniture was made—indication of a warmer climate than today's.

The mountains are now steep, craggy and dominant, with great scooped hanging corries ringed by cliffs. Unseen from the road there are two quite large lochs cupped in corries up there above 2000 feet, Lochs Brandy and Wharrel—though the first was called Breny formerly. This area is strong in the supernatural, and there is a witch's curse recorded that one day the cliffs above Brandy will collapse into the loch, causing such an overflow that will sweep away all life in the glen below. Alarming fissures have indeed appeared in the ground by the Witches Craig—one reputed to be 45 feet across—but so far the glen is spared. On the other side of the valley, the outlying spurs of great Dreish (3105 feet) make an exciting backcloth.

Braedownie, three miles on, where the road stops and Glen Doll opens off to the west, is most attractively set amongst woods and steep crags. Here starts the public footpath to Deeside, the Capel Mounth, by Loch Muick, leading on up the Esk until that stripling river bends away westwards towards its reputed source in Loch Esk—although the longer stream of Falfearnie seems to be the true head-waters. A mile south of Loch Esk is a fine waterfall, 60 feet high.

At Braedownie, and the mouth of Glen Doll, are two well-sited youth establishments. Nearest the road is Scott Lodge, outdoor centre for Dundee's Boys' Brigade, a pleasant timber-built house. Farther into the glen-mouth, amongst the extensive Glendoll Forest, is the Scottish Youth Hostel of Glendoll Lodge, a large whitewashed mansion. A finer recreational site for young people would be hard to imagine, not only for the scenery and the mountaineering and walking, for Clova and Doll are notable areas botanically, whither experts come from near and far: and wild life too is abundant, with blackcock, capercailzie and ptarmigan frequently seen, as well as the more common grouse, and of course, red deer. Under Red Craig, which presides over Braedownie on the east, is the Cave of Weems— something of a duplication of terms, since weem, or *uamh*, is the Gaelic for cave. This weem is unusual in that our Pictish forefathers have here used natural clefts in the rock, and improved and extended them with flat slabs of stone, after their normal souterrain architecture, with alternative entrances.

Glen Doll has a narrow, densely wooded entrance, under the towering Dreish on the south and Craig Mellon (2815 feet) on the north; and then widens out into a hidden but large basin which can be lovely or grim, according to weather conditions, but is always grand. Its sides rise steep and immensely high, with Mayar (3043 feet) partnering Dreish, and other enclosing hills almost equally high. Its river is called the White Water—as well it might be—not the Doll; and there is a lonely farm amongst sheltering trees at its centre. The renowned walkers—or climbers—track known as Jock's Road, rises from the riverside to scale and cross the heights, to Braemar, passing near Loch Esk and Broad Cairn (3268 feet), a testing route, but one full of interest and challenge. Who Jock was is not recorded. Glen Doll is noted for its alpine flora.

Glen Esk and Lochlee. Glen Esk is one of the longest of the Angus glens, probing for about 16 miles from Gannochy Bridge, near Edzell, into the Grampian massif, forming the major portion of the North Esk's course, from its formation by the junction of the Lee and Mark Waters. For the last mile or so herein, the river forms the boundary of Angus and Kincardineshire. For almost half its distance, Glen Esk is in Edzell parish; but the upper reaches are in the mountain parish of Lochlee, a vast area of 58,000 acres, remote and little populated. It is convenient to describe the Glen Esk part of Edzell parish here, to a progressive topographical pattern. A road goes up the west side of the valley only for three miles, then degenerates into an old track for a few more miles before petering out; so this is best dealt with at the end. The east-side road runs from Gannochy Bridge right up to the foot of Loch Lee itself, and indeed continues far beyond as private roads up the Lee and Mark valleys.

Immediately on turning in from the B966 Edzell to Fettercairn road at Gannochy, the large wooded estate of The Burn lies on the left. This is famous for the magnificent riverside scenery of the Esk

here, cutting through a long series of deep chasms, ravines and caul-
drons, with the Loups of Esk and the Rocks of Solitude well-known
beauty-spots. There is a two-and-a-half-mile footpath linking these,
on private property. The Rocks of Solitude however may be
reached by a short access path from the road, where it nears the
river about a mile and a half up, with gate and stile. The scenery is
spectacular. The mansion, built in 1791 by Lord Adam Gordon, is
now used as a students' hostel, but still in the proprietor's hands, who
lives in the near-by stable-block, a most attractive house. The stone
tower above the road, near the Rocks access path, is not old, but a
kind of folly.

Near this path, on the opposite side of the road, a narrow side-
road strikes off eastwards at the attractive group of cottages known
as Woodburn, leading to the hillfoots Balfour area, and serving hill-
farms. Just over a mile along, where the farm of Kirkton is marked
on the Ordnance Survey map, is an interesting feature. This is the
kirkyard of the former parish church of Newdosk, or Neudos, now
completely gone but once an independent parish, united with Edzell
in 1662. The kirk was dedicated to the Pictish St. Drostan, and is
now commemorated only by the name of Kirkton farm. But the
graveyard is still maintained, in a pretty sequestered position. There
are many old tombstones, and one red-stone monolith, unfortunately
entirely weatherworn and featureless, may well be Pictish. There is
also a recumbent humpbacked gravestone of early date. A St.
Drostan's Well was to the east. Newdosk was important enough to
be a thanedom once, the thanes being commemorated by the names
of Upper and Nether Thaneston farms, nearer Fettercairn.

Over another mile up the main glen road is the farm of Auchmull,
on the right, where the little side-glen of the Corfinnoch opens. There
was a castle here, demolished in 1773, built by the same Sir David
Lindsay, Lord Edzell who so greatly improved that larger castle, in
1601. He built it for his son—who later had the misfortune to kill his
uncle, Lord Spynie, in a street brawl in Edinburgh, and was a hunted
man in these parts for 10 years, unsuitable in a judge of Session's
son. No trace of the castle remains.

Farther on nearly three miles more, past a farm of the name of
Waggles, is another, to the right of the road, named Colmeallie,
where, on a small eminence at the steading is a fine stone-circle, of two
concentric rings with central hollow, seven uprights remaining. It was
cleared and tidied up by voluntary effort some time ago. There were
others in the district, now gone. At Millden, two miles on, is a
shooting-lodge and hamlet, where the Turret Burn joins Esk. There
are a number of hill-farms up the Turret valley, and also many
ancient burial-cairns. On the summit of the hill-shoulder of Mod-
lach, where the old road used to take a high route, is a three-storeyed
circular tower built in 1826 to guide and shelter travellers, and called
St. Andrew's Tower, the work of the glen's Freemasons.

The Retreat, a former whitewashed shooting-box on a terrace
above the road two miles on from Millden, is now a most admirable

Glamis. Angus Folk Museum

Glamis. Interior of the Angus Folk Museum showing box-bed
and period furnishings

Where Glen Doll branches off Glen Clova, Angus

folk museum and Highland Home Industries depot, with a notable collection including a great number of local relics, books, photographs and pictures, semi-precious stones, arms and tools, snuff-mulls, household-goods of every description, even a whisky-still. There are rooms furnished and equipped for various periods, with models in costume, all most authentic and attractive—even a blacksmith's shop. This fine institution arose partly out of the enthusiasm of Miss Greta Michie, and is deservedly popular with visitors—who may also appreciate the tea-room with its home baking. It is open from 2 to 6 daily.

Tarfside, only a short distance on, is the central focus of the long glen, where a number of small side-valleys come in from north and east. There are a number of houses, one on the site of the Blue Cairn, a thriving Freemasons' Lodge, a post-office and the Maule memorial church in trees at the roadside, built in 1857. Also, near the bridge, St. Drostan's Episcopal church, erected in 1880 by Lord Forbes in memory of Bishop Forbes, for 28 years bishop of Brechin. It is a fine building, looking a little forlorn these days, but still open to visitors—as the parish kirk is not. A rather pathetic notice points out that the congregation now numbers "about a dozen". This was formerly a strong Episcopal area, and the old chapel stood up on the moorland of Rowan Hill almost a mile to the west on the line of the old road, now only green banks amongst the heather, measuring 75 by 15 feet, with a tiny resthouse to one side. This little place was nevertheless the religious centre of a congregation numbering some 600 for over two centuries—until the government troops demolished it in the Jacobite troubles, its people being loyal to the Stewarts. Their minister then, the Rev. David Rose—an active pastor who preached alternately here and at Glen Lethnot, walking by the difficult mountain route between still called the Priest's Road—was arrested at the instigation of his Presbyterian colleague at Lochlee, the Rev. John Scott and removed from his charge. Three years later, Mr. Scott was thrown from his horse when passing the ruins of the Episcopal chapel, and killed. Near this remote moorland site, at the side of the former road, is the Cross Stone, a three-foot boulder carved in bold relief with a large cross on its rough face, almost certainly Celtic work. There was much proto-historical activity in this area, with a hut-circle, an ancient furnace or kiln, and many burial-cairns amongst the heather. Diagrams of this interesting site may be seen at the Retreat museum. The open strath of the Tarf and its tributaries is dotted with hill-farms; and high up behind it, at over 2000 feet, is the Hill of St. Colm and St. Colm's Well. Presumably there was a hermitage up here. Drostan, the Celtic saint who missionarised here, was a disciple of Columba. On the top of Rowan Hill is the prominent Maule Monument, oddly enough erected by Fox Maule, Earl of Dalhousie in 1866 *in memory of 7 members of his family already dead, and of himself and two others when it shall please God to call them hence.*

The new parish church of Lochlee lies four miles on from Tarfside,

Dalbrack and its single-arched bridge, and the pony-trekking station, being passed on the way. The building is small, harled and neat in its graveyard by the Burn of Branny, the interior brown-and-cream with a little gallery and canopied high pulpit. It dates from 1803. Droustie's Well (a corruption of Drostan) is near the former manse. Here the public road stops.

It is well worth the walk to continue the farther mile to the foot of Loch Lee, through the woodland. Here rises the tall and impressive tower of Invermark Castle, in a strong strategic and tactical position, to serve as an outpost for the larger Lindsay castle of Edzell. Four storeys and a garret in height, it belongs to two periods, early 16th century in the main, with the two upper storeys added in the early 17th, replacing a parapet and walk by angle-turret and gabled roof. Interesting features are the rounded corners, the two tall chimneystacks pierced by window-openings, and the door at first-floor level, formerly reached by a bridge and still guarded by its fine iron yett or grille, made of iron mined and smelted locally at Tarf-side. The Lindsays used Invermark for controlling Highland cater-ans—and it was a useful hiding-place when things got too hot else-where.

Half a mile on is Invermark Lodge, the ancient church and Kirk-ton farm, and the foot of the loch, now a reservoir of the East of Scotland Water Board. The pre-Reformation chapel of St. Drostan, formerly thatched, is now a neglected ruin, and sheep use the grave-yard. This church was "spoiled" by Montrose's troops—so sacrilege was not all on the one side. There are few old gravestones not so weatherworn as to be indecipherable. One commemorates Al Brown, with crossed spades, a mask and a wheel-cross, dated 1732. And here is buried Alexander Ross A.M., who was dominie of the little ruined school for 51 years, and a poet. He was author of 'Helenore', a saga of a Highland cateran raid, and died in 1784.

Loch Lee is over a mile long, and Glen Lee continues for another five miles, winding deep into the high hills of the deer-forest. Up here, amongst beetling crags, are the spectacular waterfalls of Unich and Damff. The land is empty now, but once was the home of a sturdy Highland people. The same applies to the almost parallel valley of Glen Mark, to the north, considerably longer. Up here are cairns. Also a former rocking-stone at Gilfumman, unhappily de-stroyed by folk who considered these relics of antiquity somehow evil. Here also is the Queen's Well, where Victoria drank on a famous expedition in 1861, with a massive granite crown-canopy erected by Lord Dalhousie who had accompanied her. Farther up is Balna-moon's Cave, refuge of the Carnegy Rebel Laird for many months after Culloden, with a large price on his head. In upper Glen Mark you are only a short distance from the Aberdeenshire border and three miles from Loch Muick.

Returning to the foot of the glen, a much less well-known and briefer foray can be made up the west side of the Esk. The tarmac road goes for only two miles, to the farm of Dalbog. Here are the remains of a stone-circle on a bank above the steading, four smallish uprights in a row, and also allegedly the site of a former castle, chapel and well, though these could not be traced. Iron was worked here once. Beyond Dalbog the hills shoulder close, and the dirt-road continues, with deteriorating surface amid pleasing birchwood and braes scenery. There is indeed a noted beauty-spot up here, at Bridge of Mooran, where the Esk is reached not far above the Rocks of Solitude on the other side, very attractive. Two miles on from Dalbog is the lonely farm of Cornescorn, set high on a terrace. And over a mile still farther the reputed castle of Forbie, rather vaguely marked on the map, which the present author searched for but failed to find amongst the steep woodlands. Whoever built a castle up here must have had an uneasy conscience.

Glenisla. This is the westernmost of the famous Glens of Angus, those picturesque valleys which probe northwards into the lofty and lonely eastern Grampian mountain mass from the wide and fertile vale of Strathmore. It is also a parish of its own, and a large one, covering over 40,000 acres. The glen is traversed by double roads for much of its length, although the upper reaches have only a minor road degenerating into a track for many miles. The total length, from the remote fastnesses where the Isla rises on the Aberdeenshire border, down to Bridge of Craigisla, is about 20 miles, with the parish centre, Kirkton of Glenisla, some six miles up.

Two good roads enter the glen from the south and south-east, the B954 from Craigisla, or Kilry post-office, just above the spectacular falls of Reekie Linn; and the B951 from Kirriemuir, following the east side of the large Lintrathen Loch and the Melgam Water. They join about three miles up, and a side-road strikes off to the right to continue up the narrowing glen of the Melgam or Back Water for a further four miles, to finish at Glenhead. Here this side-valley splits into a cartwheel of smaller glens having private roads or tracks— Glens Finlet, Taitney and Damff, and the valleys of the Hole Burn and Moss of Glanny. This remote area is known as Glenisla Forest, and is in Lintrathen parish. The Backwater Reservoir now floods much of the valley.

Glenisla proper commences a mile north of the main road-junction, near Bellaty. A short distance on is the Youth Hostel at the large mansion of Knockshannoch, a fine centre for walkers if a rather unsightly house. Just to the north, where the Newton Burn comes in, is Newton Farm, where once was the castle of that name, a seat of the Ogilvy of Airlie family, proprietors of the whole area. No trace now remains.

The Kirkton lies another mile on, a scattered place at a temporary widening of the glen. Here there are a hotel, pony-trekking facilities and a school, as well as the parish church, a plain rectangular building of 1821, bright within, with old box-pews, set in a grave-yard with some ancient stones. There is a ruined Free kirk of 1829 near by. A Lady Well used to be sited near the former manse. Sheep and cattle fairs were once held here, in September, unlikely as this now seems. An obelisk near by erected in 1872 commemorates one Patrick William Small, a well-loved local landowner.

A mile more and Bridge of Brewlands is reached, where a graceful old single-arched bridge has been superseded by a modern structure, and there are a few houses. Here is a road-junction, with a hilly side-road coming in from Kilry on the south; another striking off west-wards up the Alrick Burn valley to Blacklunans in Glen Shee, Perthshire; the main B951 crossing, to proceed up the west bank of Isla; and still another road continuing up the east side.

From now onwards the vast bulk of dark Mount Blair (2441 feet), an isolated mountain with extremely rocky, broken slopes to the east, dominates the upper glen. The B951 contours the foot of this, under steep, stony braes, for two miles more, to swing off to the west at Forter through quite a pass, reaching 1187 feet, out of Isla and into Glen Shee at Clackavoid, three miles. A lesser road continues up Isla. At Forter is a picturesquely-sited ruined castle, the scene of the Earl of Argyll's callous treatment of the Countess of Airlie in 1640, during the Covenant wars, the incident made famous in the ballad 'The Bonnie Hoose o' Airlie'. Although Argyll "masterfully brake down and destroyed" the place, spoiling all within, the walls remain entire to the roofline, in marked contrast to neighbouring Newton Castle, which has disappeared entirely. Forter is built on a variation of the L-plan, five storeys high, the basement vaulted. It has two angle-turrets, and a stair-turret within the main re-entrant.

A mile to the east, behind a ridge and so unseen from the road, lies the loch of Auchintagle, half a mile long. To the south, on the aforementioned road on the east side of Isla, are the hamlet of Folda and the rather plain 19th century mansion of Glenisla House. North of this point the road continues up the main valley another four miles to end at Tulchan Lodge. Beyond this cars may not go, but a track leads on for another four miles or so to what must be one of the most remote national nature reserves in the land, that of Caenlochan. This is probably more normally approached from upper Glen Shee, but even from there the approach is on foot and strenuous. Upper Glen Isla was always renowned for its botany, and this reserve of 9000 acres on the great hills of Monega and Glas Maol (3502 feet) is notable for its wild flowers, saxifrages in especial, which grow on the ledges of the great rocky cliffs, inaccessible to sheep and deer. These relatively base-rich rocks produce a flora rather similar to that of the better-known Ben Lawers. It is unlikely to suffer from over-satura-tion by visitors.

Glen Lethnot and Navar. This pleasant and sequestered area is hidden from the rest of Strathmore in an enclave of the hills behind the Caterthuns, and is probably, on that account, the least visited of the Angus glens, though far from the least accessible or farthest away. Indeed it starts only two miles west of Edzell, reached by the road past the castle, and is well worth a visit. There were two distinct parishes here until 1723, totalling 26,000 acres, the parish churches being only a mile apart—but on opposite sides of the West Water. The building of a bridge altered that, and the parishes were united. Today worshippers must go to Edzell.

There is nothing spectacular on the scene here, but it is all exceedingly pleasant and unspoiled, a land of hill-farms, pastures and quite fertile fields, though with the great hills always looming close. It can be approached in two other ways—by the easy road from Kirkton of Menmuir, to the south, passing a group of burial-cairns on the way; or by a narrower and steeper road with many bends and exciting prospects two miles to the east, which climbs over the coll between the White and Brown Caterthuns and drops sharply to Burnfoot. Near here it meets the Menmuir road, and a fork on the higher ground at Blairno beyond leads westwards two miles to Tillyarblet and Tillybirnie; also oddly enough to Rome and Ireland, two isolated farms far up the Paphrie Burn. Back near the fork at Lightnie farm, a track leads down across a field to a wooded enclosure, which is the kirkyard of the former parish church of Navar. This was taken down at the union, and only the belfry tower remains amidst the bushes and nettles. There are old gravestones too, amidst the neglect, and one dated 1904—which seems extraordinary, so overgrown is everything. The church-bell, dated 1655, was taken to Arbroath Museum.

The other fork at Blairno leads steeply down to Bridgend, the glen's centre. On the way down, on a mound above the twisting road, is a cairn-circle, 30 feet in diameter, with small standing-stones. Bridgend is an attractive hamlet, with a school, in the valley-floor. The 18th century bridge collapsed in a flood, and the modern replacement alongside is scarcely beautiful. The road forks here again, to the right leading eastwards to Edzell, to the left probing northwards up the winding glen for another eight miles, to end at Waterhead—although a private track goes on up the Water of Sauchs into the mountains, to the Shieling of Sauchs at the 2000-foot contour. On this upper section there is little to note, however fine the prospects. At lonely Braco farm there is a stone-circle; and three miles farther, at Tillybardine, the Priest's Road strikes off due northwards by the Clash of Wirren for Tarfside in Glen Esk—and a muscular, dedicated Episcopalean minister he must have been who commuted thus. Two hundred years ago a major road to Deeside was planned for this route.

East of Bridgend half a mile, on a mound south of the winding road, is the former parish church of Lethnot, now also a ruin and not visible from the road. The red-stone remains date from only 1827, but older work is incorporated. An early stone coffin lies at the door, unfortunately broken. Internally two 18th century memorials are the only features. The graveyard however is cared for, and here is buried James Black, the tenant farmer who built Gannochy Bridge, near Edzell, as a result, it is said, of seeing the ghosts of people drowned at the dangerous ford there three nights running—although the ghosts were, in fact, prefabricated to obtain this result; an unusual method of fund-raising. Alleged supernatural connections are strong here, for the Rev. John Row, who got the local bridge built and united the parishes, is said to have kicked the Devil in person through the earthen floor of the miller's house at Drumcairn near by. Later, unfortunately, he broke his neck, falling down the manse stairs while chasing Satan again with a fork, this time in the guise of a black cat. He lies beneath the floor of his ruined kirk, interred in 1747. The ancient pre-Reformation font of Lethnot, lost on a number of occasions, and once used as a pig-trough, is now at Edzell Church. The original church was dedicated to the Virgin Mary, and there is a St. Mary's Well near by.

There was an Episcopal meeting-house at Clochie, to the east, but it was destroyed by the same company of Argyll Highlanders who burned the chapel at Rowan Hill in Glen Esk, after the Forty-Five. The Lindsay castle of Dennyferne used to stand on the farm of Newbigging, up on the slopes of the Hill of Formal, but this has gone. Standing-stones formerly here have also been removed. A fragment of a Pictish cross, with spiral decoration and Hiberno-Saxon characters, from Lethnot, is now in the Museum of Antiquities, Edinburgh.

Glen Prosen. This is another of the beautiful Angus glens which thrust deep into the Grampian mountain-mass from the fertile vale of Strathmore, less long than its neighbour Glen Clova but almost as fair. Like the other it is entered from Dykehead of Cortachy, below the wooded Tulloch Hill (1246) with its prominent obelisk, monument to the 11th Earl of Airlie, who fell at Diamond Hill in the South African War in 1900. In typical Ogilvy fashion he was leading a charge of cavalry at the time, his last order being "Files about, *gallop*!" and his last actual words, "Moderate your language please, Sergeant!" There is another road into the glen from Kirriemuir and Kinnordy, following the west side of the Prosen, but this is less direct, and is notable for the number of steep hills between Lednathie and Spott. Prosen is about 12 miles long, its river rising on the lofty breast of Mayar (3043 feet), its upper reaches wild and lonely.

Just within the mouth of the glen, at a sharp bend in the road below the Airlie monument, is another and more modest memorial at the roadside, in the form of a well and horse-trough. This fountain was erected to commemorate the famous explorers Captain Robert Falcon Scott and Edward A. Wilson, who died at the South Pole in 1912. They had spent holidays here, as guests of a London publisher. The prospects, as the glen opens after the wooded constriction of its mouth, are very lovely.

From here on the slopes are clothed with natural birch-woods, unlike the pines of Clova. Houses and farms are far between. The flanking hills have rather odd names—The Goal (1466 feet) Long Goat (1870 feet) The High Tree (2001 feet) Craigie Thieves (2256 feet) and so on. The short Glen Cally comes in on the right.

Two miles above the Cally is the rather picturesque Bridge of Spott, where there is a large old farmhouse in woodland, and the single-arch bridge links with the west-side road. Half a mile farther, on this east side, the road ends at the attractive hamlet of Pitcarity, the only community in the glen. Here is the church—for Glen Prosen was made a *quod sacra* parish of its own in 1874, formerly having been part of Kirriemuir, 10 miles away. The church is small, whitewashed and pleasing, in a little graveyard by the burnside; and there are a school, guest-house and a few other houses. Beyond opens a long drive up to Balnaboth House in a large wooded estate, the seat of the lairds of Prosen. It is a fine old rambling E-shaped mansion, yellow-washed, with a late 17th century nucleus but mainly 18th century, long an Ogilvy property, cadets of Airlie. Of this family came Dorothea Maria Ogilvy, the poet, a lady of much character, who does not hesitate to call the minister of Glen Prosen Forky Ferguson—in one of her more polite references.

It is the west-side road which continues beyond Bridge of Spott, but it goes only another three miles or so, through country with recent planting but becoming barer and less attractive, to end at Glenprosen Lodge and the Forestry Commission. The river and a track proceed deeper into the high hills, to the lonely ruined house of Kiba, under Mayar

Back down the west road with its gradients, the small side-glen of Uig opens off at Easter Lednathie, to probe into more oddly named hills such as Tarapetmile and Clinking Cauldron. Footpaths radiate from Glen Uig over into Glen Dye and the Balintore area of Glen Isla.

Guthrie. Guthrie, as well as being a well-known surname in Scotland, is an ancient parish and barony with a famous castle. And there are other items of interest in the vicinity to attract the visitor. Guthrie lies to the north of the A932 Forfar to Arbroath road, less than two miles west of Friockheim and two miles north-east of Letham, in the open valley of the Lunan Water, a very rural area without any village of its own. Its antiquity is notable, for there was a Culdee establishment of the early Celtic Church here, called Gutherin, conveniently near to the Celtic shrine of Restenneth. William the Lion granted it to the abbey of Arbroath, at the Romanising process of the Celtic Church, in 1178. It thereafter became a quite important collegiate church. The Guthrie family have been here almost as long. The "good Squire Guthrie" was a valiant supporter of William Wallace. The famous Guthrie Celtic Bell, of the 8th century, in its little shrine, long kept at Guthrie Castle, is now in the Museum of Antiquities, Edinburgh.

The parish church stands picturesquely sited half a mile north of the main road, close to one of the gates of Guthrie Castle. It was built in 1826, replacing a very ancient building with painted ceiling, which ironically enough a commentator in 1793 described as "an elegant building which may stand for a thousand years to come".

All that remains of the latter is part of the transept, turned into the Guthrie aisle and burial-place. It adjoins to the south, and is dated 1479. This has a good moulded window, an ancient font within, and a fine ogee-arched doorway in the north wall, with stone masks supporting the lintel. The modern church is plain, with belfry, almost square within, and bright. In the vestibule is a list of its ministers going back to 1372, eight of them Guthries, one being appointed Bishop of Dunkeld in 1664. There are many old grave-stones in the kirkyard and its gateway is enhanced with the Guthrie arms and the date 1639.

The modern manse adjoins; but the remains of an older manse lie just within the gateway to the castle, now roofless and overgrown with ivy. It has been a large building. The scattered hamlet in-cludes this kirkton and, a few hundred yards to the north, further cottages called Cottown of Guthrie, at a crossroads, with Guthrie Hill rising behind to 494 feet, surmounted by an early burial-cairn. There is attractive wild birch-scrub country to the east; and to the north lies the enormous planted forest of Montreathmont Moor, thousands of acres of it, once a royal hunting-forest, amongst the glades of which lie sundry battle-cairns and an ancient well.

Guthrie Castle stands in a large and beautiful estate, the gardens of which are a notable feature, with a picturesque lochan. It is a handsome square tower of the 15th century, round which a modern mansion has grown, just a little spoiled by the too enthusiastically restored modern parapet and the too tall pyramidical-roofed cap-house for the stair. The walls are very thick, with mural lobbies and stairway. It is said to have been built, presumably on the site of an earlier stronghold, by Sir David Guthrie, Lord Treasurer and Lord Justice-General, in 1468. His son fell at Flodden, with three brothers -in-law. A grandson married a daughter of Gardyne of that Ilk near by in 1558, and their son, quarrelling with his relatives, was stabbed to death by his Gardyne cousin, thus precipitating the notorious feud which was to harass this countryside for generations and result in the downfall of both families. Though forfeited by James VI in consequence, the Guthries managed to reacquire the property, although through a junior line. The estate is still owned by descendants.

South of Guthrie estate are two others, both interesting, Pitmuies and Balmadies. These are actually in Kirkden and Rescobie parishes respectively, but being close to Guthrie are conveniently dealt with here. Pitmuies is an old and commodious whitewashed mansion of the Lyell family, in wooded parkland with a lochan, and a large and old-fashioned farmery adjoining, the whole making quite a picture. It flanks the A932 to the south. A 17th century lean-to type doocot, somewhat "improved" is in the garden. On the main roadside, in a cottage garden, is a highly interesting feature, a Pictish cross-slab symbol-stone, much weatherworn. The top is broken off, but it is about five feet high, with apparently crosses on both sides, which is very unusual. One animal is still to be discerned, and various ornamentation. It used to stand in an exposed situation at the roadside, and has been removed here for better preservation.

Balmadies estate lies immediately to the west, and used to be called Auchtermeggities. It was an Ochterlony house, passing to the Piersons, then being bought back by another branch of the Ochterlonys. The present mansion, a pleasant Georgian house, dates only from 1820; but the old fortalice on the site has left its relics. Into the western driveway's gateposts have been built two shot-hole stones. And close by, inset in the garage walling are three panels. One dated 1615, with the initials *R.B.*, showing thistle, rose and fleur-de-lys. The next dated 1657, with a Latin inscription which declared:

> *My foes keep out, O house; to friends and strangers open be;*
> *And may this ever be the will of him that holdeth thee.*

The third stone, long and narrow displays *M.A.P.* and *M.M.* with two heraldic shields much worn.

Almost a mile north-west, on a hillock of a field overlooking the Lunan Water is the ancient burial-ground of the Ochterlonys and Piersons. There was a chapel here, now gone, dedicated to St. Ninian. Over the gateway is inscribed *ANO MDCLXIX*. There are neat rows of ancient gravestones from the early 17th century onwards, to the two families; also some to the tenants. Farther along the riverside to the east is Mill of Balmadies, now derelict, with a stone dated 1687. Below it, as part of the mill-lade, is one of the few remaining examples of the eel-ark, a device for trapping the eels which for centuries have haunted these waters. Many references to these appear in old charters. This one is a wooden box about five feet by four, with a grating. It was used until quite recent times. Indicative of the importance of this fishery locally, the former railway-station of Aldbar near by used to be despatch-centre for eels for the London market.

Inverarity and Kirkbuddo. This is part of the rural area of Angus lying north of the coastal plain and south of Strathmore, Inverarity being a parish and Kirkbuddo a detached portion of Guthrie parish. There are no real villages in either, but several large estates, two or three hamlets and many farms. Most of the area is the attractive open valley of the Arity or Kerbet Water, between Fotheringham Hill on the north and Labothie Hill to the south.

The parish church stands at a road-junction north of the river, near the hamlet of Milton of Inverarity, about five miles south of Forfar, on the B9127. It is a plain but pleasing whitewashed building of 1754, with a small belfry housing a bell dated 1614. The interior is typical, with gallery and central pulpit. There are a number of old gravestones in the kirkyard—notably those leaning against the walling at the roadside—but these have been brought from the older church, which stood in what are now the grounds of Fotheringham House half a mile to the east. Of this building nothing remains, save old yews to mark the spot, beside the site of the former great mansion, also removed.

Fotheringham estate dominates Inverarity, and is still owned by the Fotheringham family, their home now a modern house on the other side of the B9127. The Fotheringhams, traditionally of Hungarian stock, came to Scotland with Queen Margaret, wife of Malcolm Canmore. Henry de Foderingeye did homage to Edward I in 1296. Thomas had lands in Kettins parish, Angus, in 1378; and possibly the same Thomas acquired Wester Powrie, near here, in 1412. They retained the name of Fotheringham of Powrie, but their growing possessions included not only Murroes and Tealing but by the early 16th century the barony of Inverarity, acquired from the Ogilvys. They gave their name to the estate and to the near by hill (822 feet). The 16th century fortalice of Fotheringham they erected on the site of the original kirkton was replaced in 1861 by a great Victorian Scottish Baronial mansion, architect David Bryce. However, this in its turn is gone, although the estate-houses remaining constitute quite a community. There is a circular pagoda-type 18th century doocot, and an attractive little water-house of the same period, near the roadside.

The Milton hamlet is pleasantly sited to the west, with single-arched bridge, old trees, school and some modern housing. A mile farther west, at a crossroads on the A929, is another hamlet, Gateside, slightly larger, with views of the Braes of Angus and the mountains. The substantial farm of Kincreich here was a separate property as early as the 12th century, and once a possession of the Knights Templar. It was a grange of Coupar Angus Abbey, and Abbot Donald Campbell thereof duly alienated it prior to the Reformation, to the laird of Kincaldrum—and his own pecuniary advantage. Kincaldrum estate lies immediately to the west, its large and unbeauteous early 19th century mansion now derelict. The Guthries acquired the property in 1446 and held it for 200 years, whereafter it passed through many hands. Kincaldrum Hill rises to 911 feet, with an ancient earthwork to the west, just over the Glamis border.

North-east of Fotheringham Hill is the district of Lour, partly also in Forfar parish but convenient to deal with here. As well as Lour estate itself, under Lour Hill, an extension of Fotheringham, there are Grange of Lour, Little Lour—which used to be a barony of its own, and is now a large farm—and Muir of Lour. Carnegie of Lour was a notable name in old Scotland—and the Carnegies are still there. Once there was a family called Lour of that Ilk, but in 1643 Sir John Carnegie of Ethie, brother of the 1st Earl of Southesk (father-in-law of the great Montrose), bought the lands. He was created Lord Lour, then Earl of Ethie, but misliking the title changed it to Earl of Northesk. The present line descends from Patrick Carnegie, a son of the 2nd Earl of Northesk who built this handsome late 17th century mansion for him. On the top of Lour Hill (761 feet) is a prominent observatory tower. The Lour area was formerly part of a separate parish of Meathie, united with Inverarity in 1612.

South of Lour is the crossroads hamlet of Kirkbuddo or Whigstreet, odd name, a modest place, its school half a mile farther south still at the prettily-sited Holemill, where there is an unusual mill with circular east gable and stone slates, on the Kerbet Water. Not far to the east is the site of a temporary Roman camp, at Haerfaulds, part of the earthworks and gateways of which may still be discerned from the B9127 road. It measured 2280 by 1080 feet, and accommodated 10,000 men. Kirkbuddo House lies beyond, a pleasant old mansion amongst trees. It has replaced an earlier fortalice, and a dormer pediment therefrom, with the initials *E.G.* for Guthrie, is built into the farm steading to the rear. Kirkbuddo is actually a misnomer. It used to be Carbuddo, and derives from Caer Buite. This was St. Boethius, an early Celtic missionary who was credited with restoring to life the daughter of King Nechtan of the Picts: and the king, in gratitude, gave him this land on which he built his dwelling and chapel. (Dunnichen, or Dun-Nechtan, parish lies just to the south, and Nechtan's Mere, a drained loch there, is alleged to be the site of the famous Battle of Nechtansmere—although others place this far away from Angus.) Boethius or Buite died in 521. His chapel was half a mile to the south of the mansion, on what is now the farm of Drowndubbs. The old burial-ground is still there, in a field by the Kerbet Water. The chapel and its manse was demolished in 1822. The Chapel Well, now roofed over, lies just to the south. A notable Celtic stone leans against an old beech-tree in the graveyard, showing a simple wheel-cross, part of the front unfortunately flaked away. This relic should be preserved. There is also an ancient broken font, and many old gravestones of the Erskine family and descendants, dating from 1615. They were cadets of Erskine of Dun, and Sir Thomas, secretary to James V, acquired Carbuddo in the early 16th century. When Colonel Francis Erskine died in 1833, it passed down the female line to the Jacksons, the present lairds.

Invergowrie. Invergowrie is an awkward place to delineate. Situated on the Tay estuary, on its own bay only four miles west of the centre of Dundee, it has become practically a suburb, yet most of it is not only not in the city, not in Angus at all, but in Perthshire. It was a parish, but was incorporated in Liff in the 17th century; yet its ancient church was at Dargie rather than Invergowrie itself and the mansion and estate of Invergowrie lie a mile away, nearer Dundee. Altogether Invergowrie is something of a non-entity, using the term in its true sense. But it is a highly interesting place, for all that.

At the extreme eastern end of the Carse of Gowrie, as its name indicates, it sits at the mouth of the Gowrie Burn, Invergowrie proper to the west, Dargie to the east. In parts this burn marks the Perth–Angus border, but the march is highly erratic hereabouts. Most of the village, if so it can be called, therefore lies outwith this county, and is not particularly attractive. The interesting features, oddly enough, nearly all lie to the east.

The ruined church, attractively sited on a green mound at the burnside—though now unfortunately all but surrounded by an old car scrapyard—is reputed to be the most ancient Christian shrine north of Tay, said to have been founded by a Romanised Celtic missionary, Kiritanus Albanus, or St. Curitan, about A.D. 710, when he landed at the mouth of this "Gowrie Burn in Pictland" on his return from Rome. However, the building is a typical long, low pre-Reformation chapel of probably the 15th century, now roofless and neglected. It is famous as the "home" of the renowned Invergowrie Stone, formerly set into a built-up window but now removed to the Museum of Antiquities, Edinburgh. This is a fine example of Pictish cross-slab, decorative Celtic cross on one side, and on the other three robed and large-headed clerics above a pair of coiled dragons, dating probably from the 8th century. In another window was built a second stone, quite different, of a horseman with circular shield, drinking from an eagle-headed horn, his tired-looking horse climbing a hill. This is sometimes called the Bullion Stone, and is also now in the Edinburgh museum. A plaster-cast is in the vestibule of Liff Church. It was dug up at Bullion House near by, and is thought to be of Norse rather than Pictish origin, representing a slain warrior climbing the traditional ascent to Valhalla. It certainly differs from the normal Pictish style. Outside the graveyard gate, at the burnside, has recently been re-erected a tall monolith of red sandstone, eight feet high, devoid of carving. Local report has it that this was merely a bridge across the burn hitherto; but while no doubt it was so used, fairly obviously it has had earlier significance. Perhaps many feet have worn away any inscriptions.

Behind Invergowrie is much of interest in its former parish. Invergowrie House, formerly a seat of the great family of Gray, still stands within its much-reduced tree-girt policies a mile to the east. Now divided into flats, it is maintained in good order, a tall old fortalice of the late 16th and early 17th centuries, much altered and added to, with original angle- and stair-turrets surviving, shot-holes and heraldic decoration. It was built by Sir Patrick Gray, brother of the 5th lord about 1568, and his arms and initials, with those of his wife Agnes "Neper" or Napier and the date 1601, are built in at the present front door. In 1615 the lands passed to Robert Clayhills of Baldovie, of an eminent Dundee burgess family, and remained with successors until recently. In the south-west corner of the grounds is an alleged burial-mound. In its former lands to the north rises the enormous new Ninewells Hospital.

Directly north of Invergowrie village, where the modern Kingsway by-pass strikes off to encircle Dundee, is Bullion House, not old and now Water Department offices. But near by, indeed now covered by the by-pass highway, is the site of Catter Milly Roman camp. Some suggest that the name is derived from the Latin *Quator Millia*, meaning 4000, a legionary numeral; though more likely it is the Gaelic *Cathair*, a fort, and *mileadh*, warriors. Excavations here, at the road-making, unearthed sundry relics—but also the above-mentioned Bullion Stone, dating probably from the 10th century, long after Roman times. Just across the road is the late 19th century mansion of Greystanes, now a hotel; and 100 yards from its front door, in a railed gap in the garden walling, is a huge boulder known as the Paddock Stone, a grey lumpish erratic, devoid of carving but having a legend as well as a name. This describes how the Devil (over in Fife, be it noted) one day perceived that Christianity had come to Pictland and Curitan's church had been built at Dargie. Much put out, he picked up two stones to hurl across Tay. One fell short, in the estuary, where it still stands out; and the other over-shot the mark and landed here, one mile north of Tay, to become the Paddock Stone.

Along the Kingsway by-pass another mile, between the industrial estate and a large housing scheme, on the former farmlands of Balgarthno, is a stone-circle of nine members, only one erect, still *in situ* though now within a playing-field.

Inverkeilor and Ethie. This is a large coastal parish of some 10,000 acres six miles north of Arbroath, notable, amongst other things, as having as its most easterly point the tremendous headland of Red Head. Ethie was a parish of its own once, united with Inverkeilor after the Reformation. Its castle and estate was also the seat of an earldom, for a short time.

The village of Inverkeilor is quite large and not really beautiful, standing on the lip of the wide deep valley of the Lunan Water two miles south-west of its outflow to the sea. The village is at a road-junction of the A92, with the Chance Inn hotel, manse, post-office, school and modern housing, its former Free church now a hall. The parish church, a little way apart on a prominent site at the head of the green brae, is interesting and unusual. It dates from the 17th century with additions of 1735 and 1830, restored and re-roofed in 1862, and is a very long narrow building, T-planned, in red stone, with a plain interior and two galleries. At the east end is the oldest part, the Northesk aisle of the Carnegie family, with roll-moulded windows and three heraldic panels, dated 1636, with the initials *I.C.* for Sir John Carnegie, 1st Earl of Northesk, and his wife. There are many old gravestones in the kirkyard, mainly of the 18th century.

Ethie estate lies two miles to the south-east, almost on the coast. The large castle is frequently said to have been built by Cardinal David Beaton, but this is a mistake. It was a place of some antiquity before he gained it, a square keep of the 15th century incorporating even older work. He lived here in 1530 and again from 1538 to 1546 and certainly added to the house. It was again greatly extended in the late 16th and 17th centuries and later, to form the present very large mansion, with its inner and outer courtyards, quite impossible to describe briefly here. The oldest part is the range to the south-west, which incorporates the lower storeys of the original keep, containing three vaulted basement chambers, that to the east being the early kitchen. The high balustraded tower, which rises above all, is modern, and the entire roofline has been altered. The property passed to Sir Robert Carnegie in 1549 after the death of Beaton and was granted in 1596 to his younger grandson, Sir John—his elder brother Sir David getting the principal seat, Kinnaird. Sir David, who was the father-in-law of the great Montrose, was created 1st Earl of Southesk in 1633; and his younger brother Earl of Ethie in 1647—but in 1662 went to the unusual length of getting the title changed to Earl of northesk and Lord Rosehill and Inglismaldie—why, is not clear. Rosehill is a farm near Ethie. The property remained with the Northesk family until comparatively recent times. It was the prototype of Knockwinnoch of Scott's *Antiquary*. There was a chapel here, of the cardinal's.

The coastline is dramatic, with high cliffs and jagged reefs culminating in Red Head, 250 feet high, to the north, a dizzy place of wheeling, screaming sea-birds, and one of the finest cliffs in Scotland. The great fields sweep up from the west to the very lip of it. At the north end, where the cliffs dip somewhat, though still high, is the remote and ruined chapel and former burial-ground of St. Murdoch, isolated far from any road, with only the east gable and foundations remaining on the edge of a den. Yet this, almost unbelievably, was once the parish church of Ethie, before being united with Inverkeilor. The farmhouse of South Mains, by whose track it is approached, is the only house in sight.

Not in sight but less than a mile away, hidden at the foot of the great cliffs, is the tiny former fishing-hamlet of Ethiehaven, most extraordinarily and romantically situated on a terrace above the waves, at the southern horn of Lunan Bay, a place which has to be discovered to be appreciated. Soon after this the cliffs dwindle to the long dune-backed sands, for miles.

Between Ethie and Inverkeilor is the hamlet of Cotton of Inchock, attractive if somewhat decayed-seeming at a burnside. Inchock was once a lairdship of its own, and relics of former status remain. On the west gable of the red-stone steading by the road-junction is built in an empty heraldic panel-space of early date and the small windows have 17th century chamfered jambs. Near by are the broken remains of a doocot, with some of the stone nesting-boxes surviving.

Inland from Inverkeilor is also much of interest. At the foot of the main-road brae north of the church, the B965 road strikes back westwards up Lunan Water, soon passing the large sand-pit workings at Balmullie Mill. Just beyond this, opposite Lunan Bank farm, is a picturesque square of cottages marooned in the field amongst old trees below the road, part-deserted. This is March of Lunan, once a small weaving community. A short distance farther, on the same side, is the pleasant red-stone 18th century Adam house of Lawton, now a farm, dignified and characterful. It was a Gardyne possession from the late 16th to the late 18th century. An ancient stone mask is built into the steading wall.

A mile on, at a parting of the ways, is the sequestered, rural hamlet of Chapelton, still with a functioning smithy. The chapel of Boysack or Whitefield, from which it takes its name, is still there, roofless now and its little kirkyard a private burial-ground for the Lindsay-Carnegie family of Boysack and Kinblethmont. Boysack itself, a mile to the north, is now just a large farm near the Lunan Water. To the north-east is Compass Hill, which is being drastically bitten into by huge quarry-workings; and to the west, at the hamlet of Leysmill, are many old former quarries, where the profitable Arbroath pavement was worked. South of Chapelton lies the farm of Templeton, with St. Germain's Well, once a property of the Knights Templar. Farther east is the large estate of Kinblethmont, still belonging to the Lindsay-Carnegies, as it has done for centuries. The present mansion is comparatively modern, set in old woodland; but the remains of the ancient castle, seemingly basically of the early 17th century, are hidden in shrubbery near by to the west. The building now stands only to first-floor level, with two vaulted basement-chambers, a shot-hole and slit windows. In the modern mansion's vestibule is a fine example of early type Pictish symbol-stone, a rude monolith upturned by the plough, incised with the typical Celtic beast and crescent-and-V-rod. Also treasured in the house are Prince Charles Edward's tartan doublet and a spare wig, left here apparently by oversight on a visit by the prince.

Kettins. A little-known name in Scotland, which ought to be much more renowned, Kettins is a village and parish of south-west Angus on the Perthshire border in Strathmore and less than two miles from Coupar Angus. It is a richly settled-looking area of old estates, good farms and much woodland on the northern flanks of the Sidlaws, picturesque and interesting; and though the A923 Dundee to Blairgowrie road crosses the parish, the village itself lies half a mile to the east, sequestered and pleasing, with an irregular green bisected by a stream with an old bridge, all enhanced by tall trees.

The parish runs to 7815 acres, its boundary also the county's for much of its length. The large estate of Hallyburton occupies a considerable portion.

The parish church, by the burnside in the village, is exceedingly interesting. The site is very old, stemming from a Culdee cell here, prior to 1249 when the Romish Ecclesia de Ketnes was established, subsidiary to Coupar Abbey. At later periods it belonged to the Hospital at Berwick-on-Tweed, the Cross Kirk Friary at Peebles, and the Red Friars of Dundee. How much old masonry may be incorporated in the present fabric is difficult to say, for in 1768 the walls were substantially heightened, much of the stone being brought from the ruins of its former "overlord", Coupar Abbey. There were further alterations and the tower was built in 1891. The handsome interior is notable in having no fewer than 16 stained-glass windows, unusual in a country church. There were once five other chapels dependent on this church—at Peatie, South Corston, Pitcur, Muiry-faulds and Denhead—none of which now remain.

There are some remarkable features here. Taking pride of place is a lofty and massive Pictish sculptured stone slab on the north side of the kirkyard, nine feet high, supported with iron rods. It was long used as a footbridge across the burn—similarly to that at Dargie, Invergowrie—so that the north face is worn completely smooth. Its south face is weatherworn only, and shows typical Celtic decoration, spiritedly-carved animals, and the Temptation of St. Anthony by women, a not uncommon theme. It is a splendid relic of our early ancestors. There is also a fragment of a Celtic cross. At the east end is an ancient stone font, set on a pedestal formed from part of the shaft of the former mercat cross, the rest of which is lost. At the other, west side, has been re-erected the former belfry, containing the ancient and historic bell. This Flemish bell has a Latin inscription, translatable "Marie Troon is my name. Master Hans Popenruider gave me. 1519". Popenruyder was a well-known gun-founder of Mechlin, and the bell obviously was made originally for the abbey of Maria Troon (or the Throned Mary) at Grobendonck, near Antwerp which was destroyed in 1578. How it reached Scotland is a mystery, but it has been at Kettins from at least 1697, when the Kirk records refer to it. It is much treasured. There are many old gravestones, including one particularly interesting one to Patrick Yoolaw or Yeulo, dated 1699, an unusual name of a family dwelling at Mill of Peatie for three centuries. The epitaph has this cryptic passage:

with Christ in glor he is gon befor follow wee most of him we wile say no more.

At the entrance to the kirkyard is an attractive lych-gate donated by a laird of Hallyburton in 1902.

This large estate, immediately to the south of the village, is an example of name transference at two removes. The original Haly-burton, or Holy Burgh-toun, was near Kelso in Roxburghshire and gave its name to an ancient family who in time became lords of Dirleton in East Lothian. Walter, second son of the 1st Lord Haly-burton of Dirleton, married the heiress of Alexander de Chisholm and so obtained Pitcur, here, in 1432. In time this branch became chief representers of the name, and when they outgrew Pitcur Castle moved to the handsome new castellated mansion which they named Hallyburton House. Later the estate passed by marriage to the Gordons of Huntly. It was bought in 1879 by Mr. Graham Menzies, of the Caledonian Distillery.

Pitcur castle stands over a mile to the south, in the lap of the Sid-laws, now ruinous within the steading of a farm. Although the roof-line has been sadly altered to give it a strange aspect, it is still in fair condition, a massive T-planned 16th century fortalice, with circular stair-tower, stringcourses and vaulted basements. Not far to the east, in a field across the main road, is a large former souterrain or earth-

Montrose. Hillside Distillery, home of Vat 69 whisky

Kirriemuir. Sir J. M. Barrie's birthplace

Lunan village, Bay and the Red Castle

house of early Pictish times. A much earlier castle than Pitcur, called Dores, alleged to have been a residence of Macbeth, crowned a hill to the south; but this is now only a site. It is recorded that from a tumulus near Pitcur 1000 loads of stones were removed! Human bones were found near the centre of this vast burial-mound.

Amongst the many other items of interest in Kettins parish, those at Lintrose House, near the hamlet of Campmuir in the south-west corner, are pre-eminent. Here, as the name suggests, was a large Roman camp, traces of which can still be discerned in rampart and ditch within Lintrose policies, a picturesque waterfall near by. This mansion itself, although not apparently ancient, was recently discovered to have as core a typical late 16th century fortalice, with circular stair-tower, wholly hidden within. This had been another Hallyburton house, formerly called Fodderance, one of its lairds being the Session judge, Lord Fodderance. To the east, in a field, are the remains of another souterrain, or weem—the Gaelic word for cave. The estate later passed to the Murrays of Ochtertyre, like Fowlis Easter not far away; and it is interesting to note that the Euphemia Murray, to whom Burns wrote the song at Ochtertyre (near Crieff), was really from Lintrose, the Flower of Strathmore.

At the other side of the parish to the east, is the Keillor district— High, Hill of, Chapel of, House of, and so on—partly in Newtyle parish. Keillor, now a large farm, was once a small lairdship of the Geekie family, like Hallyburton and Yoolaw, not a common name in Scotland. In 1713 Alexander Geekie, surgeon in London, instituted a bursary for educating boys at Kettins in memory of his brother William, of Keillor. This is not to be confused with Inverkeilor in the same country, near Arbroath; nor Keillor in Fowlis Wester parish, Perthshire. It is famous for Aberdeen-Angus cattle.

At Baldowrie, another large farm near by, at the side of the back-road to Newtyle between the farm and High Keillor, is a tall Pictish symbol-stone in a half-circle of trees. It is six and a half feet high, and is carved with a wolf or bear, typical double-disc symbols and possibly the mirror. But all is very weatherworn. It is marked on the Ordnance Survey map only as a standing-stone, but is much more important than that indicates.

A final note on this interesting area. No less than 28 acres of land at Coupar Angus formerly belonged to the poor of this parish, having been purchased by the Kirk Session therefor in the mid-18th century—an unusual land-ownership.

Kingoldrum. This is another of the Braes of Angus parishes, medium-sized but short in population, situated near the mouth of Glen Isla some three miles west of Kirriemuir. There is only the one village, and that not large, Kirkton of Kingoldrum, grouped at a road-junction and a peculiar bridge over a bend of the Cromie Burn, a quite picturesque place beneath a steep, whin-clad hillside, a strange mixture of ancient and modern. The parish church stands high, to the west, apart, in an old kirkyard, but itself dating only from 1840, replacing a pre-Reformation chapel. It is recounted in the Statistical Account that when the old church was being taken down "various stones, on which devices had been cut, were discovered imbedded in the building. Two stones on which crosses are finely carved, with accompanying hieroglyphics, may be particularly mentioned." These obviously were Pictish cross-slabs or symbol-stones. Half of one elaborately carved is in the Museum of Antiquities, Edinburgh; but the fate of the others I have not ascertained. Also in this museum is a Celtic saint's bell from Kingoldrum. The church is very plain, but pleasant and bright within, recently refurbished, with good oaken pews and panelling as memorial to a late member. The aforementioned bridge is unusual, being placed above a small waterfall and having two arches, one provided with a sluice-gate to control a former lade for the mill slightly downstream, now looking somewhat derelict.

A little to the south of the village is Balfour Castle, now a farm, said to have been built originally by Cardinal David Beaton for Margaret Ogilvy, his "chief lewd", or again, his secretly wed wife, which may be the truth of it. She was a daughter of the 1st Lord Ogilvy of Airlie. But the Ogilvys possessed Balfour before Beaton's time; and the castle was probably built by the lady's brother Walter. The Ogilvys retained it for long, until passing to the Fotheringhams of Powrie. A substantial circular tower with vaulted basement, wide gunloops and stringcourses, plus a peculiar and later lean-to roof, is all remaining of the original work—no doubt the flanking-tower of a large quadrangular castle. The modern farmhouse attached no doubt incorporates some of the earlier building. A mile to the south, on the farm of Cairnleith, is a burial-cairn, easily discerned in a field. To the east lies the large tract of Loch Kinnordy, part loch, part reedy swamp, which has always been a shallow place, from which large quantities of marl have been extracted.

Most of the parish is very hilly. Off a side-road to the west, high-set on the ridge of Shurroch Hill, is a standing-stone. Below the hill, to the south in a secluded situation in the Cromie Burn valley, is the attractive mid-18th century laird's-house of Baldovie, now a farm. On the high shoulder of Strone Hill, two miles to the north-west, is an interesting feature known as the Abbot's Cross. This is not any carved stone, but a collection of boulders placed to form a great cross, and marking the former boundary of the Arbroath Abbey lands, dating probably from the 12th century. Kingoldrum was a property of that abbey, given by William the Lion, part of his royal hunting-forest. A proclamation of Alexander III prohibits anyone from hunting or from cutting wood in the Forest of Kingoldrum without the abbot's permission.

At the Kenny area to the west, near the Lintrathen boundary, there are a series of cascades in the Melgam Water known as the Loups of Kenny.

Kirriemuir. For long it was the done thing to introduce the burgh of Kirriemuir as "Thrums", the fictional name bestowed upon it by Sir J. M. Barrie, the creator of Peter Pan, who was born here; but Barrie, like many another luminary of not so long ago, is less read and popular today, and Kirriemuir reverts to its own good name and fame—and very properly too. It is a pleasant, tight, little redstone town, of narrow streets, slopes and no recognisable plan, lying above the Gairie Burn at the foot of the Braes of Angus, with a population of some 4000. It is also a large parish of about 16,000 acres—larger once, before Glen Prosen was hived off. The name is thought to derive from *Ceathramh Mhor*, the Large Quarter, a reminder of the days when the great parish of 35,000 acres was divided up into sections, of which this was the southern. It was called Kerymore in the Arbroath Abbey Register of 1201; and also in its first charter as a burgh of barony in 1459. It became a police burgh in 1875. However, it has long been known affectionately as Kirrie, to inhabitants and all others in Angus—although the folk of near-by Forfar, with whom it has an age-old rivalry, have been known to call it otherwise. This feud began over the ownership of a small patch of ground called the Muir Moss, lying between the two burghs, which are only five miles apart; though most locals could not tell you that, despite the vigour of their self-perpetuating competition. Kirriemuir is unusual in having four satellite villages, rather than true suburbs—Southmuir, Maryton, Westmuir and Northmuir. The former royal forest of Lyffeden was near by.

Kirriemuir's parish church, renamed the Barony Kirk after 1929, is a large, spired building dating from 1786, standing in the centre of the town, near the Market Place and Town House. It rises from an old kirkyard, overlooked on all sides by houses, wherein are many ancient tombstones, some of them piled in stacks in the interests of space and convenience. One humpbacked stone is dated 1668, and there are others of the 17th century. The church, which replaced an earlier cruciform building, is large and seated for 900, galleried, with a high domed ceiling and much stained glass. Violet Jacob, the Angus poet who died in 1946, is commemorated here. This church was famed for its five Pictish sculptured stones but these have been removed to a timber, glass-fronted shelter on the high ridge of the modern cemetery on Kirriemuir Hill to the north-east, a lofty repository with splendid views—but not perhaps the place where most people may conveniently inspect them. The stones are very fine. The largest is a cross-slab about four feet high, depicting two horsemen and a stag, with symbols; a smaller one has a cross on both sides, rather unusual; another, broken, has a cross plus horseman with spear and targe; and on the wall is a fragment with an angel and Greek-key pattern. Lower down in the terraced cemetery, Barrie is buried.

The birthplace of James Matthew Barrie, born 1860, died 1937, is a two-storeyed whitewashed cottage at 9 Brechin Road, now in the care of the National Trust and open to the public. To the south of the town, at the junction of the A926 and the A928, near the South

Kirk in Southmuir, is another cottage known as A Window in Thrums, title of one of Barrie's books, in which it features. At the foot of the hill north of this runs the Gairie Burn with riverside walk and park in Gairie Den; and here are two large jute-mills, the main employers of labour in the town, established around 1870. Other industry is represented by the Angus Milling Company, producing oatmeal and animal feeding stuffs; and smaller concerns catering for the large farming community—there are 71 agricultural units in the parish, large and small. Kirriemuir is a favoured place to retire to, and deservedly, and the town and district is well served by community amenities and societies. It is also excellently placed as a centre for visitors to the Angus glens and a scenic countryside. The Webster High School, now in a large building of 1954 which cost £160,000, grew out of a seminary founded by John Webster, banker, who in 1829 left £7000 for the purpose. It is the higher education centre for eight parishes. The Airlie Arms is an old coaching inn, with typical yard.

The detached satellite villages grew up in the early 19th century, Southmuir close by but the others averaging a mile's distance. Maryton lies to the south-east of Southmuir, and is the smallest and oldest-seeming, with the raspberry-fields all around, fruit culture becoming ever more important hereabouts. Fields of daffodils and tulips also proliferate. Here is Thrums Caravan Park. Just to the south, in a cottage garden on Balmuckety, are two massive standing-stones—though they are no longer upright. Westmuir lies a mile away, on the A926 Alyth road, with some 50 houses, shop and village hall, right on the parish boundary, with near by, over in Airlie, the site of a Roman encampment on the farms of Reedie and Auchindorie. Northmuir is different, larger and a very distinct community sited on high ground behind Kirriemuir Hill, a very open village covering a large area, with fine prospects. Here are the auction marts where major cattle sales are held; also a large sawmill, park, playing-fields and Kirriemuir golf course. On the summit of Kirriemuir Hill, just to the south, is a tall standing-stone, nine feet high by six broad, amongst Scots pines and broom and magnificent views. Here also is a pony-trekking station. There used to be two rocking-stones near by, but these are gone.

There are two other hamlets in the parish, one at Roundyhill at the extreme south, with some dozen houses in a rather bleak area known as the Muir of Cabbylatch; the other, larger and two miles east, has the odd biblical name of Padanaram—although it was formerly called Ellenorton and was established in the early 19th century by the Meason family of Ballinshoe.

Ballinshoe—pronounced Benshie or Ballinshie—is now a large farm lying two miles south-east of Kirriemuir off the Forfar road. On it, near the farmhouse, is the ruin of a tiny late 16th century castle, oblong, with one angle bevelled off and a single angle-turret, mainly complete to the wall-head but in a bad state of repair. Possibly the smallest castle I have seen, it was erected by one of the

Lindsays, who gained this property in 1559. Not far to the south, just off the main road, in a field is the private burial-ground of the Fletchers, who succeeded the Lindsays in 1645. It has a wall and arched gateway, but is neglected. The farm to the west is still called Fletcherfield.

A short distance farther west is the estate of Logie, whereon is a tall, plain tower-house of the 16th century, much altered but still occupied. Oblong on plan, it has a circular stair-tower, with shot-hole and altered over-sailing roof. The re-cut date 1022 on the west gable of an 18th century extension is obviously an error. The base-ment is vaulted and there is some good 18th century panelling. Logie used to be called Logie-Wishart, and was long a property of that family, of whom came the great Montrose's chaplain, later Bishop of Edinburgh.

Another important and large estate, with some 24 farms, is Kinnordy, the mansion a mile north-west of the town. The large Loch of Kinnordy was drained in 1730 for its shell marl, and is now more marsh than loch, but a great haunt of wildfowl. There was an artificial island here, thought to have been the site of an early castle of the earls of Angus. An ancient canoe was found near by. The mansion has an early nucleus, but this is not apparent. It belonged to the Ogilvys of Inverquharity, but was sold to Charles Lyell of Gardyne in 1770. The third Charles Lyell was created a baronet in 1848, and was a famous geologist to whom Darwin dedicated his *Origin of Species*. Inverquharity Castle is itself in Kirriemuir parish, but being much nearer to Cortachy is better dealt with there.

The northern part of the parish has its own interest, its foothill countryside most pleasing. Half a mile north of Northmuir, beyond the attractive Caddam or Caldhame Wood, where blaeberries grow, is a single standing-stone at the roadside, relic of a circle; and a mile to the north-east, in a field of the farm of Auchlishie, is a weem or souterrain, at present closed up but with plans for opening it. A coracle was found here. Another similar Pictish earth-house is sited on top of Meams Hill to the north-west, 65 yards long. There is a burial-cairn at Balloch, at the extreme north-west of the parish, by the Carity Burn.

Letham, Kirkden and Dunnichen. Letham is a large village, almost a small town by Angus standards, in the parish of Dunnichen, five miles east of Forfar, in the wide valley between the Hills of Fotheringham and Dunnichen; and Kirkden is a separate rural parish lying immediately to the east, yet having its former church in the outskirts of Letham village—a curious arrangement. It is hardly possible to describe Kirkden, formerly Idvies, separately.

Letham is a neatly laid-out community, in rectangles and criss-cross streets, a planned entity covering an extensive site, south-sloping, above the dens of the Vinney Water, lying between the main A932 and A958 roads, a strangely isolated place, fairly self-contained. In 1861 it had a population of 1231 although today it is much less. It was founded about 1788 by the well-known character, "Honest George" Dempster M.P., a man of vision and initiative, laird of near-by Dunnichen estate, "for the purpose of securing a constant supply of people for the labour required on his property and a nursery of robust and healthy children". So a moor became a planned village, with gardens, and flax-spinning and weaving was encouraged, with a weekly market for the sale of the produce; two spinning-mills, a lint-mill and two plash-mills for cleaning the yarn, were set up. Then the concentration of power-mills in Dundee changed all, and Letham's busyness sank away. But it is still a pleasant populous place, airy and open, with wide prospects, a broad square and sturdy grey-stone cottages. George Dempster was a real character. In London, Dr. Johnson declared that Dempster gave him more displeasure than any man he had met for a long time—a recommendation in itself. Burns called him a true-blue Scot:

> *A title, Dempster merits it:*
> *A garter gie to Willie Pitt . . .*

He had ambitious ideas about farming, forestry and employment generally, and with a large fortune inherited from a wealthy Dundee merchant father, put them into practice in places as distant as Mull, Loch Broom, Spinningdale in Sutherland, and Skye, as well as here in Angus. Not all prospered, by any means. Honest George was a trier. He was secretary of the Order of the Thistle for no less than 52 years. He died in 1818, and is buried at Restenneth Priory, nearer Forfar. Oddly enough, despite his nickname—or perhaps because of it—he was fined £30,000 for bribing voters to elect him.

The church at Letham dates from 1845, succeeding the old kirk in the Den, to the south, where is still the graveyard. It is commodious, and bright within. A caravan-park adjoins. Many of the cottages here are being modernised and refurbished. Letham is not so far away from Dundee, Forfar and Brechin to fail to appeal as a residential area.

The two deep and green ravines lying directly to the south of the village, Vinney and Letham Dens, are assets scenically. In the former, to the west, is a disused spinning-mill and an attractive and sequestered house. In the latter, is the previous parish church of Kirkden, and its manse now a private house. The scanty remains of the church, on a knoll, have been reduced to formal walling, with the old Dutch bell, dated 1676, erected on top. The interior is used as burial-place for the Lyells of Gardyne Castle, to the east. There are a number of old stones in the graveyard, and at the gateway is built-in a former lintel inscribed:

M.M. 1739. All ye who enter at this gate, O now prepare for your last state.

Half a mile north of Letham is a very interesting feature. At the junction with the Dunnichen–Balmadies road, set flat on the ground, is the Girdle Stone. This is a large, diamond-shaped boulder, four feet by three, with incised circular symbols, of Pictish origin, placed here to mark the boundary with Rescobie parish. But the traditional story is that it came from the hamlet of Greystone, in Carmylie parish five miles to the south, being carried by a witch in her apron, which not unnaturally gave way to the strain, and the boulder fell here. It is certainly odd that Greystone should be so named, with no stone there to account for it. It would be interesting to discover the real reason for this. The stone should be set up on its end, not lying flat where rain and frost and tractor-wheels will further obliterate the symbols.

There was another and still more famous stone near by, the Dunnichen Stone, a more typical Pictish symbol-stone of the early type, massive and unhewn, with double-disc and Z-rod, mirror-and-comb, and "flower-pot" symbols. It used to stand in the walled garden of Dunnichen House, the substantial Georgian mansion of the Dempsters a mile to the west; but this has fairly recently been demolished and the stone removed to Arbroath Abbey, temporarily. However there are moves afoot to bring it back where it belongs. It might well be set up on the triangle of grass outside the parish kirk, where it would look very well.

Kirkton of Dunnichen is pleasantly sited under the wooded hill, on an open, south-facing shelf, a small, scattered hamlet. The church, a typically plain building, dates from 1802. There are old stones in the graveyard, many leaning against the west wall. Once the parish church was at Crosstoun of Dunnichen, but this may not be the same site, for there is still a farm of Crosston half a mile to the south-east. A still earlier church was on an artificial island in the former Mire of Dunnichen, or Nechtan's Mere, protected by a drawbridge and dedicated to St. Constantine, a Cornish kinglet and martyr, who came to Scotland with Columba. This name degenerated into Cowsland or Causnan, and here used to be held an ambitious annual St. Causnan's Fair, each March, which went on for days. St. Causnan's Well was near the church.

This Nechtan's Mere was, of course, the site of the great battle thereof, in A.D. 685. There are innumerable conflicting accounts of this, with different personalities involved. The generally accepted version is that it was between Ecgfrith, king of the Angles of Northumbria, and the Picts under either King Nechtan himself, King Brude, or King Loth. All these were admittedly Pictish kings, but not all at the same time, or of the same Pictish kingdoms. It seems a bit late in the day for Nechtan, who was baptised by St. Boniface at Restenneth early that century. Anyway, large numbers of burial tumuli and graves have been found in the area. The loch or mere has long been drained. Nechtan had a fort or palace on Dunnichen Hill. Another Pictish fort was on top of Dumbarrow Hill three miles to the south-east. This vies with Barry Hill, Alyth, as where King Arthur's erring Queen Guinevere, or Wanda, had her romance with a Pictish prince; and a rock on the hill is known as Arthur's Seat.

One of the many legends about Nechtan's Mere is that Arthur himself was slain thereat—all notably confusing.

A third hill, to the west, is now called Lownie. This was formerly Ochterlony where the family of that name sprang from. At the western skirts of it, near Cottown of Lownie, at the junction of the Dunnichen and A958 roads, is an ancient well in a cottage garden, now filled in. It is just possible that this was the aforementioned St. Causnan's Well, for where the artificial island of the original church would be, before the loch was drained, is uncertain.

Kirkden parish, so involved with its neighbours, lies mainly some three miles to the east, and was once called Idvies. It was an ancient thanedom, under the abbey of Arbroath from 1219 onwards. There is still an Idvies Hill, south-west of Dumbarrow, a mill and farms of the name. On the farm of Gask, and just east of Bractullo, or Bractie Law, is a prominent, green, tree-topped motte in a field, a typical law-hill, whereon once would be the motte-and-bailey timber castle of the thanedom. Skulls and relics have been found here. Four hundred yards to the north-east, in a strip of woodland, is the site of the original pre-Reformation church of Idvies, dedicated in 1243 to the Celtic St. Maelrubha or Melrua. Though the adjoining field is still named the Kirkshed, nothing of the church remains, save the old saint's well, known as Sinruie, a corruption of the name, and still used as a water-supply, roofed over in the wood. It was once assigned the usual virtues of a chalybeate spring "even after the applications of several physicians had proved ineffective". Idvies Mill is attractive below Dumbarrow's whin-covered hill.

Just to the north is the ancient estate of Gardyne, with its fine castle; but this is more conveniently described under Friockheim, as is Middleton, another historic property a mile to the east. Pitmuies, highly interesting, also in Kirkden parish, is dealt with under Guthrie, which it adjoins. As will be gathered, Kirkden, as a parish, is something of a headache to delineate.

Liff and Benvie. These two parishes have been united since 1758. They lie immediately north and west of Dundee, in the foothill country of the Sidlaws, and the city has taken great bites out of both. Indeed the industrial suburb of Lochee was formerly in Liff parish. Nevertheless, the two hamlets which name them have remained unspoiled and quite charming. Oddly enough, they are now each possibly the smallest centres of population in their respective areas, with Dundee housing schemes proliferating, and the large villages of Muirhead of Liff and Birkhill Feus ever growing.

Liff is said to derive from the Gaelic for a flood or torrent. This may seem inexplicable; but once the River Isla is said to have flowed into the Tay estuary here, and the Isla used to be spelt Ileff. Kirkton of Liff, scarcely large enough to be called a village, is delightfully situated on the 350-foot contour, at the northern verge of the Gray House estate, less than five miles from Dundee G.P.O., a scattered place amongst old trees, lanes and by-roads. It grew up very much under the shadow of the great family of the Lords Gray. With such lairds it cannot always have been a quiet place. They have gone, and their mansion stands abandoned; and the church, with its 108-foot-high steeple a noted landmark, now gently dominates.

These were church lands, given to the abbey of Scone by Alexander I, in the 12th century. The present edifice, third on the site, dates only from 1839 and stands in an attractive kirkyard with many ancient stones. It is of Gothic style, a little short for its height, but pleasing. At the door is a defaced pre-Reformation stone font. The bell, cast by Jan Burgerhuis, dates from 1696. In the vestibule is a memorial stone to the Cox family, formerly Cocks, famous in Dundee for their industrial pioneering from 1742 onwards; also a plaster-cast of the Bullion Stone, a sculptured fragment of great antiquity, seemingly of Norse rather than Pictish origin, depicting a horseman drinking from an eagle-headed horn, thought to represent a slain Norse warrior climbing towards Valhalla. The original, now in the Museum of Antiquities, Edinburgh, was dug up near Bullion House near Invergowrie. A fine kirk poor box of 1718, oak with iron bindings and two locks, stands within.

A short distance to the north-west is a most charming modern house, set in a woodland position above a joining of ravines to form the Den of Gray. It is called Hurly Hawkin, a strange name but significant to those knowledgeable in early Scots history. Hurly Hawkin was actually a game, beloved strangely enough by some of our ancient kings, consisting merely of tobogganing down a steep incline sitting on an upturned cow's skull, clinging to the horns. There is a spot on the northern slopes of Stirling Castle rock called Hurly Hawkin, where the game was played by James V and others. Says Sir David Lindsay of the Mount:

Ilk man efter their qualitie, they did solist his majestie,
Sum gart him rauell at the rackett, sum hurlit him to the hurlie-hacket.

Hurling, of course, means sliding or wheeling; and hawkie used to mean a cow. It seems that Liff was where the term originated. It was long claimed that here was the site of a palace of Alexander I; but recent excavations indicate a much older building, a circular broch-like edifice 40 feet in diameter, with massive walls 14 feet thick, and various occupation dates. This is not broch country, but there are remains of a similar building at St. Bride's Ring, at Murroes. The story is that an attempt was made on Alexander's life here, but escaping to the coast, he made a thank-offering of the lands of Liff to Scone Abbey. Probably this incident actually happened at Baledgarno in Abernyte parish, Perthshire, to the west, where *was* a royal palace.

There was a brewery at Liff in the 17th century, and later.

To the south lies the estate of Gray, its lands now worked by the Smedley canning firm. The mansion has been deserted since 1936, and is in a sad state. It has been a fine and picturesque building, of

271

1715, on a south-facing terrace, with considerable architectural excellence, ogee-roofed stair-towers, flanking pavilions and heraldic decoration, set amongst fine old trees. The Grays came here from Fowlis Castle, to the west, and from Castle Huntly at Longforgan, a notable and powerful family in old Scotland, by no means always strictly virtuous.

The Royal Dundee Liff Hospital, with 620 beds, lies half a mile to the east in its own grounds.

Muirhead of Liff is a much larger and expanding community, now almost a residential suburb of Dundee, on the open ground of the Backmuir of Liff, a mile to the north-east of the great Camperdown Park, which happily separates it from the encroaching city. It is a pleasant breezy place of wide prospects on the A923 Coupar Angus road, merging on the east with Birkhill Feus, an earlier 19th century private housing development backed by rising and fine woodlands.

Benvie lies over a mile to the south-west of Liff at the other side of the Gray estate, on the road from Invergowrie to Fowlis Easter. It is a tiny place beside a winding stream, entirely rural. Of the ancient church only part of a gable remains, with a broken font, but the graveyard in which it stands is highly interesting and well-kept. At the gateway are two inset stones, dated 1633 and 1643, with the arms of Scrymgeour, Viscount Dudhope, and Lady Isabella Kerr, daughter of the 3rd Earl of Roxburgh, once part of a sundial. More exciting, standing amongst the gravestones is a fine example of a Celtic cross-slab, still in good condition, depicting on one side the usual decorative cross and on the other two horsemen, one above another, with spears and round shields, a precious relic dating from probably the 7th century, pleasing to find still where it has always been, rather than in a museum.

Near by is the former meal-mill. It no longer works as such, but its wheel is still in place within the building, unusual in that it was driven, out of sight, by an underground lade drawn off from the burn to the west. A hundred yards to the north, at the side of the burn, is still a piped spring. This was once the renowned healing well of the White Lady of Benvie who, dying of the plague, was not allowed to be buried in consecrated ground. Her unquiet spirit haunted the place until the minister allegedly met the ghost, Bible in hand, and was assured that if he had her remains reinterred in the kirkyard, where her body had lain would spring up this well, which would be infallible as cure for the plague. So goes the story.

Benvie seems first to be mentioned in 1292. It was a possession of the Scrymgeours, constables of Dundee, from 1384 till 1654, passing later to the Grays. Here grew the famous Benvie or Autumn Pear, in the orchard of the former manse, claimed to be the original source of this type of fruit.

The former estate of Balruddery, or Balruthrie, lies a mile to the west, its early 19th century mansion now demolished, but its wooded den famed for geological and botanical interest. Amongst fossils found here was that of a gigantic lobster.

Logie-Pert and Craigo. This wide and scattered rural parish of 5800 acres lies in open undulating country at the northern rim of Angus, just south of the North Esk. It has no centre and no real village, although the modern jute-milling community has grown up at Craigo to the extreme north-east. There were two small parishes here formerly, Pert and Logie-Montrose, united in 1661, both former churches remaining, though roofless ruins, in their old burial-grounds, about four miles apart at the Esk-side.

The present parish church, dating from 1840, stands remotely, towards the middle of the parish, on the Gallery Burn, with a small hamlet and school near by, a tall and rather gaunt building, unlike its predecessors, which have been low and characterful. This, however, is a replacement of one of 1775—which would be the building wherein, three years later the 7th Lord Falconer, who was distinctly eccentric, shot a bird during divine service, which had flown in through an open window—explaining that this was to prevent the bird disturbing the minister and congregation. The Muir of Pert stretches to the south-east, towards Dun and the Montrose Basin, a wide and open, little-populated countryside, with fine prospects especially over Strathmore towards the Grampians. Here was a former airfield. Near where the Gallery Burn joins the Esk, a mile north of the church, is Gallery House, a highly attractive and interesting late 17th century laird's-house, tall and whitewashed, on the E-plan with two tower-wings and Fullerton heraldry. The weather-vanes of the towers are dated 1680, and there is a fine walled garden to the west. The estate passed from the Fullertons to the Lyall family—the former descending from Fowlers to the king at Kincardine. This is one of the finest and least altered examples of the immediately post-fortified period in Angus.

Old Pert pre-Reformation church stands above the Esk just north of North Water Bridge, beside the A94, a red-stone ivy-clad ruin which has latterly been used as a burial-place for the Lyalls of Gallery. There is a good double-pointed window to the east and a belfry to the west. The kirkyard is well maintained, and there are many old gravestones, including one to a Buchanan family, dated 1751, inscribed: *I do ring. I did ring. I once rang. I shall ring.* The North Water Bridge near by, built first in the late 16th century by the famous John Erskine of Dun, allegedly as the result of a dream, was rebuilt as a toll-bridge in 1814 and is now replaced by a modern structure to carry the busy A94. Great fairs used to be held here. At the Bridgend hamlet was born the shoemaker father of John Stuart Mill.

The other side of Gallery, two miles, lies Craigo, with its large jute-works hidden in the Esk's den, and its modern housing scheme above looking rather odd in these otherwise rural surroundings. There is a crossroads hamlet of North Craigo—which strangely enough is to the south of Craigo. This is because the original estate of Craigo lies a mile farther south, with a large Georgian mansion, long the property of a branch of the great Angus family of Carnegy.

The tumuli known as the Three Laws of Craigo lie half a mile to the west, in woodland, and were burial-mounds from which quite gigantic skeletons were exhumed along with a black ebony-like wrist-ring or bangle.

All this has been on the Pert side of the parish. Logie lies to the north-east, and its ancient church stands picturesquely at the river-side opposite Morphie on the Mearns side, where there was once an important ford—see St. Cyrus parish. The church has been most interesting, and formerly maintained as a burial-place of the Car-negy family, but is now badly neglected, though the kirkyard is kept neat. There are Carnegy and Macpherson-Grant arms over the door, dated 1857, and within, though much is of later restoration, a piscina and holy-water stoup and a good early triple-light east window. The church was dedicated to St. Martin, and St. Martin's Well, reputedly medicinal, still springs half-way up the brae to Mains of Logie farm, by which the old church is reached.

Half a mile to the east, off the road, is the former village of Logie, now only two or three cottages. One of these has been converted, with loving care, into a tiny church for a Free kirk's continuing con-gregation, modestly attractive. This despite the fact that the former Free kirk, called the Denkirk, up at the main road, stands shuttered and abandoned. The former large Mill of Logie is closed. There was a bleachfield here in 1770, and a spinning-mill established in 1810.

Lunan. Lunan is undoubtedly best known for its great Bay, three miles wide, lying between Arbroath and Montrose, with its magnifi-cent stretch of golden sands enclosed by the towering cliffs of Red Head to the south and the lesser promontory of Boddin Point to the north. But there are also a small parish of 2000 acres, formerly called Inverlunan, and the Lunan Water, which rises at Lunanhead near Forfar, and is notable for the string of lochs along its upper course—Balgavies, Restenneth, Fithie and Forfar itself.

The parish church and small kirkton lie near the outflow of the Water into the Bay, most picturesquely sited in a wide green hollow half a mile from the main A92 road and two miles north of Inver-keilor. The church itself is small but pleasant, a red-stone edifice of 1844 incorporating ancient work, in a neat kirkyard. There are two old panels built into the walling, one heraldic; but no especially interesting gravestones. Walter Mill, priest here for 40 years, was one of the last martyrs of the Reformation, being burned at St. Andrews in 1558 for turning Protestant. A tablet commemorates him. Near by is the former Georgian mansion of 1825, enlarged 1850, now an attractive-looking hotel. There is an old double-arch bridge over the Water.

Just where the Lunan Water finds its winding way through sand-hills to the Bay, rises Red Castle on a steep mound which had formerly been crowned by an early fort, its impressive ruined keep dominating the centre of the Bay. This was the seat of the barony, and was allegedly built for William the Lion by Walter de Berkeley, to counter the raids of Danish pirates. Lunan was then a royal hunting-ground. Bruce gave it to Hugh, 6th Earl of Ross, husband of his youngest sister Matilda, in 1328. None of the present castle dates from so early a period, the shell of the keep, complete almost to the wall-head at one side, seeming to be 15th century work. There is a dreadful pit or prison 25 feet deep, below. It appears to have come into Cardinal Beaton's possession—he owned near-by Ethie Castle, in Inverkeilor—and through him one of his offspring, Elizabeth Beaton, brought it to her husband, the Stewart Lord Innermeath. He was a member of Queen Mary's party in the troubles of her reign, and Red Castle was destroyed therein. The barony later passed to the Guthries. The castle, in semi-ruinous state, was last occupied by the ousted Episcopal minister, James Rait.

Later lairds still were the Blairs of Lunan House, and there is a memorial to one, colonel in the Bengal Army, an obelisk standing within an enclave of modern housing at Braehead, on high ground to the north. He died at sea on his way home to receive the honour of knighthood. Buckie Den, near by, is a romantic ravine, with waterfalls.

Lunan Sands, some of which are reputed to "sing", are renowned. The area used to be notable for smuggling, and many are the tales told of such activities. Red Head, to the south, its cliffs rising to 250 feet and the haunt of seafowl, features in Scott's *Antiquary*; but it is described under Inverkeilor. Lunan's baronial story is exemplified in the names of sundry of its farms—Court-hill, Cote-hill, and Hawk-hill. The farm of Arbikie to the south-west was once an old laird-ship. There is a long range of tumuli here alleged to be the graves of the slain in a great battle with invading Danes.

Lundie. To be so near to Dundee, only nine miles, Lundie is an extraordinarily remote place—and feels it. Set high in a re-entrant of the Sidlaws, on a dead-end road at about the 600-foot contour, crouching under the Crag of Lundie and reached by winding but picturesque ways, it is a small parish of 4296 acres, united with that of Fowlis Easter, to the south-east, as long ago as 1618. There is no real village, only the attractive little kirkton; yet the name is a not unimportant one in Scotland, with Lundie's lairds playing quite prominent parts on the national scene. This Lundie must not be confused with that other, in Fife, more commonly nowadays called Lundin; nor yet with Lundie in Golspie, Sutherland.

The parish really comprises the watershed of the Dichty Water, here called the Dronley, which flows down Strathdichty to the sea at Monifieth. It is a place of lochs cradled amongst green hills, seven of them no less, though all reduced in size by drainage. The largest, Long Loch, situated a mile north of the kirkton, is almost a mile in length, though narrow; it is said to be only a twelfth of its original size, nevertheless. Most of the parish nestles along the south face of the Sidlaws; but the Ledcrieff section, to the west, does as it were, spill over the pass into Strathmore, with pleasing views thereof. The main A923 Dundee to Coupar Angus road threads this pass, amongst old Scots pines at 758 feet.

The kirkton lies two miles east of this in the lap of the hills, a delightful spot with old church, former manse and mill, and a hamlet grouped round a tiny green and sharing a wooded mound with the kirk, village pump still *in situ*. The church, likewise, is small, but interesting, of some antiquity but restored drastically in 1847. Most features date from that not very inspired period, though a small lancet window in the north wall is ancient. A curious domed mausoleum is attached at the east end, and is now used as a vestry. The interior is lined with natural pine strip-boarding, an unusual treatment, and is modestly plain save for the stone ogee-shaped canopy of a pre-Reformation aumbry beside the pulpit. There are many old stones in the kirkyard. Particularly interesting is that of the famous Admiral Viscount Duncan, the hero of Camperdown (1797), amongst the other Duncan of Lundie graves. This renowned sailor, Adam, second son of the 3rd laird, was considered to have deserved so well of his country that, after his death in 1804, his son was created Earl of Camperdown. The 4th and last earl died in 1933. The admiral's victories over the Dutch need not be recounted here. The epitaph on the stone was written by himself. The Duncans, as well as being lairds of Lundie, were prominent Dundee merchants and often provosts of the city; and Camperdown Park there was the seat to which they removed from Lundie Castle. The mausoleum aforementioned is not that of the admiral but of Sir William Duncan, baronet, a cadet, who became physician to the king, after making a large fortune in India, and died in 1789.

Of Lundie Castle only a farm of the name remains, over a mile from the church, no traces of the fortalice surviving. Once there were two fairs annually at Lundie, in June and August; also two alehouses. Now there is not even a resident minister for this hamlet amongst a farming community.

Mains and Strathmartine. While properly these two names should be included in the Dundee article, since they nowadays lie within the city boundaries, like Broughty Ferry they have sufficient identity and character to merit separate treatment. A pity were they to get lost in the larger canvas.

These were two ancient parishes of south-west Angus, united in 1799, traversed by the Fithie and Dichty (or Dighty) Waters and comprising a number of old estates and villages. Today Dundee on its outwards march has spread over much of the area, its great housing schemes and industrial developments dramatically changing the face of this Sidlaws foothill land. But much of great interest remains, and thanks to the establishment of the great Caird Park of 262 acres, within which lies Mains Castle and Den o' Mains, some open area between it and the city proper is maintained.

The name of Mains itself is odd—for of course there are literally thousands of Mains in Scotland, since it merely means the home farm

of an estate. This parish used to be called Earl's Strathdichty, a
better name. It belonged early to the Earls of Angus; but by the
marriage of a daughter to Graham of Fintry in West Stirlingshire, in
1476, it passed to that family, and in due course they altered the
name to Fintry. There was a castle somewhere here as early as 1311,
but the present ruined building dates substantially from the 16th
century. Why *Mains* of Fintry is not clear. Perhaps this castle was
not built on the site of the original, but at its home farm. Gradually
only the word Mains became general.

The castle stands on the south side of the deep wooded ravine of
the Dichty. It is tragic that such an interesting, unusual and picturesque building, though long the property of Dundee Corporation,
should be allowed to remain in such state of utter neglect, especially
within a public park, a prey to vandals. How much longer it can
survive is doubtful; much has gone in the 10 years between my last
visits. It has been constructed to form three sides of a square, the
fourth, enclosing the courtyard from the west, being a high and
parapet-crowned curtain-wall with defended arched gateway. The
six-storey, tall and unusual stair-tower, heightened with its peculiar
four-gabled watch-chamber in 1630, stands at the north end of the
main block or north wing. The castle has been well built and is
commodious. It was mainly erected by Sir David Graham about
1562, whose wife was Margaret a daughter of Lord Ogilvy of Airlie.
His son and heir, another David, was a nephew of Cardinal Beaton,
his mother and the Cardinal's secretly married wife being sisters; and
he came to an abrupt end, like David Beaton, being executed for
treason—or, at least, for belonging to the losing side in the Reformation troubles.

Just across the ravine is the similarly neglected former church in
its overgrown ancient graveyard. Only mere fragments remain, but
the site is attractive amongst trees and fallen tombstones. And down
in the dean itself, between castle and church, is a spout of spring
water coming out of the rock-face on the south side, with its own
fame. It has the strange name of Sinavey, corruption of some saint's
name, and was renowned for its excellent quality, never known to
run dry. Upstream in this Dichty valley is the popular picnic-place
and beauty-spot of Den o' Mains.

Elsewhere in the large Caird Park, gifted by Sir James Caird, are
many sporting and amenity facilities, including golf courses of nine
and 18 holes, football, cricket, hockey and basketball pitches, and
the King George V Stadium for athletics and cycling.

Not far to the north lies the former famous estate of Claverhouse,
one-time seat of a cadet branch of the Grahams, one of whose lairds
became the famous soldier and statesman, the "bonnie" Viscount
Dundee who fell at Killiecrankie. His house has gone, but a folly, or
artificial ruin, was erected by a later proprietor, and can still be seen
from the road from Trottick to Fintry, across a little loch, swelling of
the Dichty, a red-stone pile in a field. The estate is now largely
built up, with an attractive modern private housing development

277

amongst retained old trees. The large Claverhouse Bleachworks are now a store, with modern industrial factory near by.

At the Trottick crossroads amongst the ever-growing housing schemes and soaring flats, stands the not very beautiful church of the united parish, dating from 1800 and built to be central, a plain roomy structure in a graveyard well locked up against vandals and all others. When it was built, with accommodation for 900, it was considered to be too large for the parish; it would be interesting to hear the minister's views today.

To enumerate all the great city housing extensions hereabouts would be tedious. One of them, Downfield, used to be only the largest village in the parish; there is a private golf course there now. Whitfield, one of the newest, and still building, is vast, with clean-lined multi-level housing and exciting features. It lies beyond the equally large Fintry scheme, to the east, with the attractive and unusual Longhaugh Roadhouse tucked into a leafy hollow between, beside a vast quarry. Americanmuir, oddly named but a corruption of Merrick Muir it is said, lies to the west.

All this relates mainly to Mains. Strathmartine is farther north by west, and is not as yet so built up and developed. Its former church and Kirkton stands at a complex road-junction in the Dichty valley, near where the Dronley and Fallows Burns join. The name comes from a legendary Martin, one of the many heroes declared to have killed a dragon which had devoured nine maidens. Martin's Stone still stands, a mile and a half to the north, railed off in an open field near the farm of Balkello; but this is a typical Pictish symbol-stone slab, four by two and a half feet, broken at the top, depicting a horseman in a panel, with underneath the usual Celtic beast, horse and rider, plus serpent, with Z-rod symbol. No doubt this gave rise to the legend of the dragon. It is a precious relic, however, of probably the 7th century A.D., and good to see still standing in its original setting.

Kirkton of Strathmartine is a scattered village, with the site of the old church in another locked graveyard beside the burn. As at Mains, only fragments of the building survive, but there are some interesting tombstones, including that of the Ogilvys of Inverquharity and Baldovan. There are also fragments of Pictish stones built into the walling. Baldovan itself lies a mile or so to the east, and is still an estate with a substantial mansion, to which the ancient line of Ogilvy baronets moved when the 5th baronet sold Inverquharity Castle in the 18th century, after having owned it for 14 generations, from 1420. Near by, westwards, is the great Strathmartine Hospital, with 639 beds, grown out of the former Baldovan Asylum for Children founded by Sir John and Lady Ogilvy in 1854, a fine place in pleasing surroundings.

Immediately to the south of the Kirkton is Clatto Moor, a ridge reaching 533 feet above sea-level between Strathmartine and Dundee, where a great new storage reservoir and filter station has been built at a cost of one million pounds holding six million gallons, largely to provide North Fife with an ample water-supply, to be carried in a new 24-inch main across the Tay Road Bridge.

Strathmartine Castle, which lies half a mile north of the village on a pleasant terraced site looking southwards over the vale, is not ancient or a castle, but rather a Regency-type mansion formerly belonging to the Laird family. But there was an ancient fortalice in the grounds, now removed. From here came the Strathmartine Stone, another Celtic slab, in the Dundee Museum.

Maryton and Old Montrose. Maryton is a small parish of 3700 acres to the west of the great landlocked Montrose Basin; and Old Montrose, now a farming estate, was once important indeed as the barony which gave title to the Grahams, earls, marquises and dukes of Montrose. The parish has very recently been combined with that of Ferryden and of Craig, to east and south.

As its name implies, Maryton was church lands, the abthane lands of a Culdee monastery, and at the "Romanisation" of the Celtic Church became first a vicarage of Brechin Cathedral, then gifted to the abbey of Arbroath. At the Reformation its first Protestant minister was Richard Melville, laird of Baldovie. He was an elder brother of the more famous Reformer, Andrew Melville, and father of the almost equally famous James Melville. The present parish church was built in 1792, very plain but in an attractive site with fine prospects. Its bell dates from 1642. There are some old gravestones in the kirkyard, one dated 1702 still using the old spelling of Monros(s). The kirkton has a manse, school and farm, quite picturesque. Maryton Law rises 335 feet to the south, whereon was the justice-seat of the barony of Old Montrose.

This lies out in the wide levels of the former marshlands at the head of the Basin, and indeed once must have been something of an island therein. Old Montrose is a misnomer. It should be *Alt Moine Ros*, meaning the burn of the promontory in the moss. Sir David the Graham, a supporter of Bruce, was granted these lands in 1325 in exchange for those of Cardross, on the Clyde estuary, on which the King built the residential castle in which he died. The 3rd Lord Graham was created Earl of Montrose in 1505. There is some doubt as to whether the 5th Earl, the great James Graham, later 1st Marquis, was born here or at the town house of the family in near by Montrose, in 1612. At his downfall and execution, the lands went to his enemy and former lieutenant, the notorious 1st Earl of Middleton. There is little left now of the former great establishment, demolished in 1840, with only some slight traces of old stonework in outbuildings and stableyard of the present mansion, some rollmoulding and a relieving arch, plus a monogram stone in the near-by farm-steading. Down at the shore of the vast Basin is a small pier and harbour, almost lost amongst the reed-beds, where once coal was imported and grain and potatoes exported. For generations the Lyall family farmed here notably.

Half a mile to the north-west across the flats that are now rich

T

arable and were once wildfowl-haunted marshlands, is the hamlet of Barnhead, at a little road-junction, a rather attractive if somewhat decayed spot islanded amongst trees, its disused Free church now a garage. The South Esk bounds this territory to the north and the great deer-park of Kinnaird Castle to the west. Back on the main A934 road flanking the southern edge are the two interesting old properties of Bonnyton and Fullerton, both now farms but both former lairdships. Bonnyton came to the Woods, or de Boscos, by marriage in 1493, and the family made a big impact on Angus. They were hereditary keepers of the king's forests, from Kincardine. Their castle is gone, but on a farm-steading gable at the roadside are two handsome heraldic panels therefrom, with the royal arms, those of Wood and two stone masks. The wooded Den of Bonnyton is on the south of the road. Only a mile farther east is Fullerton, originally Fowler-toun, which was the home of the king's fowlers, managing these marshlands for the royal castle of Kincardine, who took the name of Fullerton of that Ilk. It remained a separate lairdship until 1789. There is another wooded den coming in here. Fullerton Den used to be known as Ananise Den, a name coming from Ananie, as Fullerton was called before Bruce's time.

Menmuir, Tigerton and Balnamoon. Menmuir is one of the large Braes of Angus parishes (10,000 acres) lying four miles north-west of Brechin; Tigerton, pronounced Tiggerton, is a small village therein; and Balnamoon, pronounced Bonnymoon, is the large and ancient lairdship which has for long played a major part in Angus affairs. The parish, whose boundaries are confusingly involved with those of Brechin and Careston, is also notable for containing the two remarkable hills, and their Pictish forts, known as the Caterthuns.

The Kirkton hamlet and parish church lie on the southern skirts of Menmuir Hill with its cluster of burial-cairns, three miles north of the A94. The church dates from 1842, a plain building replacing one of 1767. But there has been a religious centre here from time immemorial, and before the Reformation was dedicated to St. Aidan, whose well was in the vicinity. The Picts, so strongly represented on the hills above, may also have worshipped here, for two of their symbol-stones, formerly built into the kirkyard wall, now lie in the Balnamoon burial-enclosure at the north side of the church. They are rather hidden here, behind railings and a locked gate, so that details cannot be discerned, and would be much better set up in a place where people could inspect them. They both appear to be somewhat broken, one being very small. The Balnamoon aisle, with its basement relieving arch for the vault beneath, is the oldest part of the present church, having a heraldic panel dated 1639, with the Carnegy arms. There are some fairly old gravestones in the kirk-yard. The parish school is close by. A road runs northwards from here, over the west shoulder of the White Caterthun, to Lethnot.

Tigerton is really only a hamlet also, lying about 500 yards to the east, quite attractive, with a few red-stone houses. One of the cottages was once used as an Episcopal chapel in the days of religious intolerance. Behind the houses is the green Gallows Hillock of the Balnamoon barony.

Balnamoon House stands in its large and wooded estate almost a mile to the south-east, with a typical 17th century lean-to doocot between. The mansion, although looking today as though belonging to the 1820–30 period, has an ancient nucleus dating from 1490 which forms the north-west wing and is clearly discernible—though the heraldic panel thereon is of much later date. There is quite a lot of 1680 work at the back, and built in here is a dormer pediment dated 1584, brought from the former castle of Findowrie to the south. There is a rather unusual straight stairway in the old part of the house, as effective defensively as a turnpike. Balnamoon contains a great many treasures, relics and family portraits of the Carnegy-Arbuthnott family, who are still in possession. The most exciting is one of the original sheepskins of the National Covenant of 1638, with the signature of the great Montrose, allegedly in his blood, taking pride of place. The Carnegys of Findowrie and Balnamoon were connected with Montrose, the first of this line being Sir Alexander, brother of the 1st Earl of Southesk, Montrose's father-in-law. Before the Carnegys came to Balnamoon it was a lairdship of the family of Collace, now completely died out. The later lairds took prominent part in national affairs. The Rebel Laird is probably best known, out in the Rising of 1715 and condemned to death. But his execution was set aside on some nicety of the law relating to a wrong description in the charge. A pardon in due course was signed, dated 1721, and this hangs in the house.

Findowrie lies two miles to the south, actually in Brechin parish, and now a large farm though still belonging to the Carnegy-Arbuthnotts. It was where the Arbuthnott name came from, and though no trace of the building remains, three of its dormer pediments are built in, two in the steading and one in an upper room of the farmhouse. The initials, monograms and arms of the Arbuthnotts are well displayed, with the dates 1638 and 1642. In Balnamoon is a charming little water-colour showing the castle before it was demolished in the early 19th century, a typical and pleasing L-planned fortalice with crowstepped gables and angle-turrets.

A mile south-east, still in Brechin parish but in this neighbourhood, is the Killievair Stone, a single standing-stone in the field north of the road at Barrelwell farm, four feet high but without features.

Menmuir parish is traversed from west to east by the Cruick Water, which flows into the North Esk at Stracathro, with a number of mills along its course. There was a royal hunting-forest called Kilgary here once, with a castle no trace of which remains. It had its own thane in charge until the mid-14th century. Bruce gave a grant of it to the Berwick burgess Peter Spalding who aided him in the capture of Berwick-on-Tweed in 1318. In the forest was the hermitage chapel of St. Mary, and in 1454 the hermit-in-residence was one

Hugh Cumynth. The farm of Chapelton marks the site, and there is a spring in the vicinity called Lady Well.

The Grampians all along their southern slopes send out foothill offshoots at around the 1000-foot level, often called the Braes of Angus. In this parish these stretch from Shandford Hill on the west to the Hill of Lundie on the east, with many burial-cairns near the summits and ridges. Obviously these heights were utilised by our Pictish ancestors as useful strongpoints of wide prospect. The two hills next to Lundie are the Caterthuns, a mile apart, the White (978 feet) to the west and the Brown (943 feet) to the east, a narrow side-road rising steeply but enticingly to surmount the col between and on northwards to Lethnot. The name is really Caithir or Cader Dun, meaning the Strongpoint of Worship. The fort on the White is said to be the strongest Pictish fortification known, much admired by archaeologists. It is elliptical, 600 by 400 feet, with stone ramparts and a deep outer ditch, with a further double entrenchment 200 feet farther down. The Brown fort was less important, and its remains are of turf, and grass-grown, with several concentric circles of rampart and ditch. The Brown is so called from its turf walls, the White from the gleam of its stone embankments.

Monifieth. This is the central of the three holiday resorts that stretch eastwards along the coast from Dundee and, though smaller than either Broughty Ferry or Carnoustie, is the most ancient; also it always had its own *quod civilia* parish, of which Broughty and Barnhill used to be a part, while Carnoustie was part of Barry. It is now a burgh of some 4000 population, lying six miles east of Dundee and at the western base of the great low-lying sandy peninsula of Buddon Point, as Carnoustie lies to the east. None of these places are really picturesque or beautiful, their situation hemmed in between sea and quickly rising ground causing them to be long and straggling, without any real town centres. But that situation has its own advantages in splendid sands and golf links and wide sea vistas.

Monifieth, the name said to derive from *monadh-feidh*, the hill of the deer—a stag features in the burgh arms—has inevitably become something of a dormitory suburb for Dundee. But it retains its own character—as is only suitable in a place with so long a history. For here was a Pictish town—a mile or so inland at Monifieth Laws, where King Hungus or Angus had a great stronghold, now represented by the hill-top vitrified fort. There are Pictish souterrains at near-by Ardestie and Carlungie, and symbol-stones from Monifieth are now in the Museum of Antiquities, Edinburgh. Here came Regulus, or St. Rule, with the relics of St. Andrew, Scotland's patron saint, after his landing at Kilrymont, or St. Andrews; and the cell he founded, at Balmossie a mile inland, was later succeeded by a Culdee church nearer the sea, on the site of which now stands the parish kirk of St. Rule's, the Culdees being ousted only in 1242, a very late lingering for the old Celtic Church. This is a large building, plain but with a pleasant galleried interior, rebuilt in 1813. It contains two war memorial stained-glass windows. Also a plaque relating that near by lie the remains of Patrick, Lord Ruthven, knighted on the battlefield by Gustavus Adolphus, a general also of Charles I, victor of many battles, created Earl of Forth and Brentford. He was a companion-in-arms of the great Montrose, who also had links with Monifieth. The church possesses two beautiful silver communion-chalices, dated 1638 and 1642, lost for a century but recovered; also a bell cast in the Low Countries in 1565 inscribed *Henry I am all for truth. Jacob Ser made me.* There are four old heraldic stones in the east gable, taken from the former mausoleum of the Durhams of Grange, the local great family. Old gravestones abound in the kirkyard. There is the burial-place of the Erskines of Linlathen, an estate to the north-west. One of the inscriptions is to James Paterson of Castle Huntly, who married Anna Gray, the heiress of the Lords Gray, of Broughty, Castle Huntly and Fowlis, whose son married a daughter of the Linlathen line with the unlikely name, for a woman, of David (1791–1867). Between kirk and main road is another church-like building. This is a famous Sunday School Hall, the first built in Scotland in 1882 after the American model, containing no fewer than 600 seats. Those, obviously, were the days!

The Pictish symbol-stones now in Edinburgh are: (1) a tall shaft with men carved, one playing the harp, and decoration, probably of the 10th century; (2) a small cross-slab, with fish and crescent-and-V-rod symbols, and deer-head; (3) a squared slab with spectacles, comb and Z-rod symbols, and a cross on the back.

Monifieth is unusual in having its largest industrial concern actually flanking the main street for some distance, hardly to its enhancement. This is the engineering works of James F. Low & Co., makers of textile and bakery machinery. But catering for holiday-makers has long been the town's major preoccupation and its two fine golf courses and splendid miles-long golden sands are deservedly popular. There is a playground area on the links to the north and east, and a very large car-park for the many visitors to the beach—which as elsewhere along this coast is rather cut off from the town by the railway-line and has to be reached under bridges. The great peninsula of Buddon Ness with its links and lighthouses, army camps and firing-ranges, is best described under Barry.

The parish of Monifieth is full of interest. Half a mile north of the town is the estate of Grange of Monifieth, once a farm of the abbey of Arbroath, its whitewashed mansion-house now a country club. This was the Durham seat, a powerful family for long, their castle however demolished. Here it was that the great Marquis of Montrose was housed for one night on his humiliating journey to Edinburgh and execution, after his betrayal by Macleod of Assynt in 1650. Lady Grange sought to effect his escape from his gaolers by plying the guards with drink and dressing the Marquis in women's clothing. He almost got away, but was discovered by a trooper who had been away foraging on his own, missed the drinking, and gave the alarm—

a sad mischance. The Durhams had been given the lands originally by the Bruce, and remained in possession for almost 400 years. They sent cadet branches to Pitkerro, Omachie, Ethiebeaton, Ashludie, Ardestie and Denfind. Near by, to the east, is the large modern chest-hospital of Ashludie.

A mile west of Grange, on the Dichty Water, is the aforementioned Balmossie, once called Monichi of Balmossie, which is interesting, with the parish of Monikie now lying five miles to the north. Balmossie was a former milling hamlet in the green den of the Dichty, now all but overwhelmed by modern housing. Here was where Regulus founded his chapel, of which no trace now remains amongst the raspberry-canes. Allegedly stones therefrom were built into the mill here, now derelict; but inspection revealed that this built-in masonry was not from an early chapel but from a fortified house or castle of the 16th century, and includes a good roll-moulded doorway, part of another moulding, and half a wide-splayed gunloop. Obviously therefore there was once a fortalice on this site, or close by. There was indeed a lairdship of Balmossie, and the Bruce gave a charter to one Alan Balmossie, of certain lands in Dundee. Later the property fell to the Maules of Panmure.

To the north, a mile, lies Ethiebeaton, now just a farm but once an important barony, with its own Gallows Hill near by. In 1290 Sir David de Betun thereof was sheriff of Angus. Bruce confiscated the lands, for the Beatons had supported his enemies, and gave them to his friend the High Steward. The Beatons went to Fife and are normally reckoned to be a Fife family. Thence came the famous cardinal. The notion that Cardinal Davie owned Ethiebeaton is a mistake. It was Ethie Castle near Lunan Bay which he occupied between 1538 and 1546.

Another mile to the north is the highly interesting feature known as St. Bride's Ring, of much earlier date. Crowning an abrupt little hill in woodland east of Kingennie House, here are the massive remains of a circular building. It has been described as a stone-circle, but this is nonsense. The heavy masonry, almost lost amongst trees and brambles, is about 50 feet in diameter internally, with walling seven feet in thickness. It is in a very strong position, and obviously was a fort; but not the large type of fort or encampment—more like a broch. No brochs are recorded for this area, so I hesitate so to call it. But it has that appearance. Why it got the name of St. Bride I have not discovered, although there was a pre-Reformation chapel at Kingennie dedicated to St. Bridget. But these remains are earlier and military. There was a castle at Kingennie.

The Law of Monifieth, with its great vitrified fort of King Hungus, rises prominently a mile to the east, 400 feet high, with a mansion near by. The fort measured 390 by 200 feet. Near the centre has been a circular building paved with flagstones. Many relics have been found here, including coins, iron axes, swords, a stone cup, etc. Burial cists have also been unearthed.

The two very similar earth-houses or souterrains of this parish lie to the north-east and south-east, over a mile away at Carlungie and Ardestie farms respectively. Both are in the care of the Department of the Environment. The first is in a field 100 yards from the side-road to the farm. The roofing slabs have been removed and the underground circular paved and lined corridor opened to the light. These places were used by the Picts merely as refuges and store-houses, not as residences, and date from the 1st and 2nd centuries A.D. That at Ardestie is about 400 yards north of the main A92, also in a field, is deeper and crook-shaped and associated with four small stone huts which had stood within the crook, on the surface. The names of Carlungie, and also Balhungie near Ardestie, are signifi-cantly similar to Hungus the king.

The hamlets of Drumsturdy and Omachie, immediately to the north of Monifieth Laws, were once much larger, housing workers in the great quarries of Omachie, which was once a barony on its own belonging to the Durhams. From these and surrounding quarries, which at one time employed some 300 men, came the well-known building stone called Arbroath pavement, exported far and wide, even to America. The quarries are still worked. The village of Newbigging close by, also a quarrier place, is larger, with a former United Presbyterian church—but this is in Monikie parish. The former villages of Cadgerton and Fyntrack have entirely dis-appeared.

Monikie, Craigton and Newbigging. This rural parish lies eight miles north-east of Dundee and four north of Monifieth, and is readily identified, both on the ground and on the map, by the double Monikie Reservoirs of the Dundee Waterworks, of 73 and 46 acres, which, with a third one two miles to the north at Crombie, supply some 650 million gallons. The parish is medium-sized, of about 9000 acres, and contains the villages of Craigton and Newbigging. Monikie itself consists of two hamlets, the Kirkton and that at the former railway-station a mile to the west; plus another, reduced to a scatter of houses, at Guildy farther to the east. Two small ranges of hills divide the parish into three districts of differing character, traversed by the streams and dens of Monikie, Pitairlie and Buddon Burns.

The larger Monikie hamlet at the west end of the reservoirs, is quite an attractive place, with a surprisingly large granary, formerly a seed-crushing mill, to find in such a rural site, the works of the Panmure Trading Company, which dries and stores grain from a wide area, especially barley for the distilleries. The branch-line and former railway-station are closed. Half a mile to the north-west is the highly interesting Auchinleck or Affleck Castle. This is an excellent example of the sturdy and massive free-standing tower of the late 15th century, little altered, five storeys and 60 feet high, with cor-belled parapet and two distinctly unusual square caphouses, the flat roofs of which form lofty watch-platforms. The first and second floors are vaulted, and the latter has a handsome pillared fireplace and a delightful little vaulted oratory, only seven feet square, with holy-water stoup, aumbry and pointed-arched window. Also a tiny laird's bedchamber above at half-floor level, with a private stair, and a squint-hole to look down unseen into the hall. The building is in the care of the Department of the Environment, and open to the public. The Auchinlecks or Afflecks of that Ilk were hereditary armour-bearers to the Earls of Crawford, and one did homage to Edward of England in 1306. The family provided a number of provosts for Dundee. The modern mansion stands near by, where the key is obtained. The last of the name to hold the lands disposed of them to one Robert Reid in the mid-17th century. Reid of Affleck was forfeited for his share in the Rising of 1745.

The village of Craigton is small, a scattered place but pleasant, lying at the other, east, end of the reservoirs. On the wooded Downie Hill to the south, within the large Panmure estate, are two features. One, highly obvious, is the tall chimney-like tower, 105 feet high, rising out of curious small rustic chambers at ground level. This is known as the "Live and Let Live Monument", and was erected by the tenantry of Lord Panmure in 1839, in enduring testimony to the kindness and generosity of the laird, William Ramsay Maule, created 1st Lord Panmure after the forfeiture of his ancestor, the 4th Earl of Panmure, for his Jacobite activities. Seven counties can be seen from the parapet of the monument, which is a conspicuous landmark from the sea.

Near by on the same hill, to the east, in the centre of a driveway, is the Camus Stone, or Cross, an interesting and decorative Celtic Cross six feet high, ornamented with weatherworn sculptured figures, including a man flanked by two kneeling angels, and with two sets of priestly figures below. These are on the east face, the west face being badly worn. The sides have typical interlaced Celtic decoration. This is an unusual type of Celtic monument, with none of the Pictish symbols apparently, and wholly Christian; no doubt of later date than the more usual cross-slabs. It is alleged to mark the grave of a Danish Viking chief called Camus, slain in a great battle with Malcolm II in 1010. But circumstantial as this sounds, it is improbable that a pagan invader would be thus honoured with so fine a Christian monument. Much more probably it is connected with the early Celtic Church. It is mentioned as the Cross of Cambuston in a deed of 1481; and there was a corn-mill of Cambuston in the barony of Downie, near by, in 1582. Which name is a corruption of which it is hard to say.

The Kirkton of Monikie, lying a mile to the east, has a parish church built in 1812, fairly plain. There are some old stones in the kirkyard, one dated 1656, and a mort-house. An interesting modern notice-board, beautifully carved in wood, with fine Celtic ornamentation, stands by the roadside, dated *R.M. 1962*. Built into the walling of a roadside cottage at the farm here are two dormer pediments, one dated 1587. These look as though they had come from a fortalice. Guildy lies half a mile to the north-east, a few houses, with the wooded Guildyden of the Monikie Burn to the south, part of the Panmure estate. There is much planted forestry hereabout, especially on Pitleavie Moor.

Newbigging is a larger village lying in the southern of the three divisions of the parish, erected in connection with the great quarries of this Omachie area which produced the famous Arbroath pavement stone and employed many workers. The quarries still function. Here there are a church and manse, formerly United Presbyterian. All this area was once part of the great thanedom and barony of Downie; and the farm of Old Downie, a mile to the north-east, was the site of its castle, on a green mound. It must have been an important place once, considering the number of subsidiary castles near by to support it. Duncan de Dunny is mentioned as early as 1254. Only a mile to the west is the farm of Pitairlie, where was another castle. One of its stones is built into the farm offices, dated 1631, with the initials of Alexander Lindsay. All the Downie properties were in Lindsay hands until the Maules got them in the mid-17th century. Denfind is another, half a mile to the north. Its fortalice has also disappeared. The name is alleged to have derived from the Fiend's Den near by, in which a monster or warlock, with an appetite for human flesh, is said to have dwelt, until apprehended and taken to Dundee, and burned "with his wife, bairns and family". This, with further circumstantial detail, from Lindsay of Pitscottie—but one wonders! A fourth castle in this same crowded vale of the Pitairlie Burn was at Ardestie, already mentioned under Monifieth, in connection with its Pictish weem or souterrain. This is more than a mile south of Newbigging. A number of carved stones from this castle are built into the farmhouse and cottages, one dated 1625 and another 1688. The Earls of Panmure themselves used to occupy Ardestie Castle at times. There was a chapel near by, with a well, but its site is unknown.

If all this recital of former castles seems tedious, it is an indication of the enormous number of such fortified houses formerly dotting the Scottish countryside. There are still a large number—but nothing to what must once have been the case. In the 16th and 17th centuries it was a land of castles indeed.

In the northern third of Monikie parish, with much moorland and high ground, there is less of detail—but splendid views, especially north over Strathmore. Up on Downie Moor, near Gallow Hill—this seems too far away, nearly four miles, to be the gallows-hill of Downie Castle—there is a large cairn on the farm of Harecairn, survivor of many such, it is said, connected with some major battle of early days. It is pleasingly situated, near a dirt-road which leads up to some radar-masts, and on the edge of a wild moorland area of whins, heather and scattered Scots pines, an airy and attractive scene—and one which must represent what a great deal of Scotland looked like once. A mile north-eastwards, beside the former railway and near the farm of Skichen, is the wooded artificial mound on which are the scanty remains of a very ancient strength called Hynd

Castle, history unknown. It appears once to have been an artificial motte rising out of marshland.

Montrose. Montrose is the aristocrat of Angus, different from all its other burghs, with a character all its own. Even the most superficial glance establishes that, and closer inspection and knowledge only confirms it. In fact Montrose is one of the most unusual medium-sized towns in all Scotland. It has a population of only 10,700, yet it has the air and aspect and assurance of a much greater place, more than some cities have. Its streets are wide and stylish, its buildings often ambitious and full of character, its planning orderly and spacious. Besides Montrose, Dundee might be described as *nouveau riche* and overgrown, Arbroath bustling and workaday, Forfar and Brechin small-time. Montrose folk may not actually say so—but that is the impression the town gives.

It is set in an unusual, almost islanded position, midway between Dundee and Aberdeen, on the level sandy coast between the outflows of the North and South Esk Rivers, moreover with the sea on one side and the vast landlocked bay of Montrose Basin on the other, four square miles of salt-water, which gives the town a unique atmosphere. Yet this penning-in process produces no air of cramping; on the contrary, the feeling of space and order is most apparent. One gets the impression that Montrose did not just grow, but was planned. This is not quite true, but there is an element of truth in it.

Basically Montrose's plan is simple, much more so than most towns. There is a long main street, which unfortunately has to carry the A92 highway, extending for over a mile from the suspension-bridge over the South Esk estuary to approximately level with the northern shore of the Basin. The central portion of this is the High Street, wide and open and lined with shops—although once there was a central row of houses called Rotten Row, demolished 1748. There is something special about this street, looking really more like an elongated marketplace; the original houses are all gable-end on to it. This gave the Montrose folk the nickname of "gable-enders". It is an unusual arrangement, *en masse*, as it were, and had significant consequences. Doorways not being in the gable-ends, there had to be access-ways down between houses. These are still there, innumerable narrow lanes or closes on either side of the street, with interesting back-courts. Gardens had to be included, so these too were long and narrow, usually separated from each other by very high walls. These long plots, or riggs, all were the same length, and at the foot of them the merchants, importers and lairds built their warehouses, coach-houses, stores and so on—for Montrose was a great place for the import and export trade, with a fine harbour, and most local lairds maintained town houses here. One of the excellent things about the town was that, beyond this lower eastern street that developed, an open green belt has always been maintained; so that we have a lengthy series of tree-lined parks, gardens and recreation areas stretching from one end of the town to the other. Development east of this again, nearer to the sea, has been fairly consistently planned and well laid-out. And beyond this is the four miles' long belt of grassy links, from the South to the North Esk estuaries, and the equally long golden sands of a magnificent beach.

There is much notable architecture. The Steeple dominates all, near the head of the High Street, a graceful landmark seen for miles, no less than 220 feet high, the dignified clock-tower and spire designed by Gillespie Graham in 1832. Oddly enough, though *attached* to the Old Parish Church, it is not really part of it, an after-thought. The church itself is large, and plainly impressive, seating no fewer than 2500, built in 1791 to replace a pre-Reformation church which had been in existence since the 13th century, dedicated to St. John the Evangelist. It is a very tall edifice, and very unusual in having two tiers of galleries. Within is the antique five-armed candelabra presented to the original church in 1623 by a native, Admiral Clark, one of Gustavus Adolphus' Scots, of the Swedish Navy. The church, too, conforms to the gable-end pattern, so that its kirkyard has to stretch down the riggs eastwards, long and narrow, and divided by its own close, the attractive Church Walk, with in-numerable ancient gravestones ranked amongst old trees and flowerbeds on either side.

Just north of the Steeple is the Town House, projecting into the street on the east side, an interesting construction of 1763, height-ened in 1819, with an arcaded piazza—in which is sited the Informa-tion Centre for visitors. Near by is a statue to Sir Robert Peel. Although in almost every case modern shop premises have been erected in front of the gable-end old houses, these remain, as do their closes, usually therefore entered by pends through building—and it is well worth-while to look down a number of these, to dis-cover the old-world Montrose behind, picturesque and quiet 17th and 18th century houses, good doorways, pleasant courts and hidden gardens. As has been said, amongst them were the town houses of local lords and lairds—who seem to have appreciated the delights of Montrose, even though their castles were only a mile or two away. Fine examples are, for instance, the *Montrose Review* newspaper's office in the town house of Erskine of Dun; the Retreat, that of the Ochterlonys; Straton House, a most interesting and unusual mid-18th century red-brick mansion with many excellent features; Mooran House, of the 17th century, and so on. The town house of the Earls of Montrose, south of the Steeple, in Castle Place, has been greatly altered down the years, and now serves as premises for the Department of Employment and Productivity; but parts of the ori-ginal remain, in the lower storeys and to the rear, and one basement room is pointed out as the birth-place of the great Marquis himself—although there is a school of thought which holds that he was born in 1612 at Old Montrose, the castle in Maryton parish three miles to the south-west. It seems unlikely that he would be born in a base-ment chamber, anyway—even though it has a fine moulded fire-place. This Castle Place is approximately on the site of Castlehill, or

Forthill, where was the original castle of William the Lion, wholly destroyed by Wallace in 1297, the English having held it—indeed Edward I having made it a sort of headquarters. Across the road from this is the handsome Public Library building, in red stone; and down Bridge Street, the southern section of the main artery, is the Montrose Royal Infirmary of 1837, another fine edifice.

But all the notable architecture is not centred on the main thoroughfare. To the east is a very important part of Montrose, developing later, and flanking the aforementioned green belt. Here, in Panmure Place, on part of the former Links, rises the very impressive Montrose Academy, a famous school dating back to the mid-16th century at least. The present building is in classical style, dating from 1815, with a prominent gleaming golden dome, and large modern extensions to the rear. Here Greek was taught in Scotland allegedly for the first time; and former pupils and teachers were George Wishart and Andrew and James Melville, and other Reformers; as well as a great many other luminaries, including David Lindsay, first Bishop of Edinburgh, who was involved with Jenny Geddes in the famous stool-throwing episode in St. Giles'.

Almost across the road is the Museum and Art Gallery, where there is a fine collection both of pictures, ancient and modern, and of items of interest. Notable are three Pictish stones—the Farnell Stone, a large late cross-slab with Celtic decoration and representations of Adam and Eve; the Inchbrayock Stone, removed from that kirkyard, on Inchbrayock or Rossie Island half a mile away in the mouth of the South Esk estuary, another remarkable cross-slab, of rather crude workmanship but with interesting details, showing Samson slaying a Philistine with the ass's jawbone, what might be Delilah cutting off Samson's hair, a typical hunting-scene and some odd symbols; the third one, smaller, is also from Inchbrayock, with a cross on one side and a Pictish huntsman on the other. There is also a cannon-barrel alleged to come from the French sloop which was run ashore here in 1745 during the Jacobite episode—Montrose was much involved in that Rising—but which appears to date from a much earlier period. There is a unique collection of agates and semi-precious stones, this area being rich in such. An astonishing feature of this building is the white-walled gallery upstairs for modern art, which, when the said white walls are pushed aside, reveals behind them the filled bookshelves of a great library, on cursory examination of considerable value though thus hidden away.

Also in this Panmure Place district, set amongst the small parks, is the Episcopal church of SS. Mary and Peter, unusual in standing in a graveyard with many old stones, a great number of the 18th century; the interior is very bright and handsome, with two side-chapels. Farther to the south, in Melville Gardens, is the modern Town Hall, opened by Princess Alexandra in 1963, a fine multi-purpose building of much value to the town's many social institutions. Montrose mounts an arts festival, for instance, for 10 days each summer. In this neighbourhood there is much dignified and worth-while residential architecture. The William Lamb Memorial Studio, in Market Street, contains a notable collection of the famous sculptor's works.

To the south-east is the port area, with many granaries, ware-houses, timber- and boat-building yards, Customs House and so on. Yet, though a busy trade is still carried on, especially with Scandinavia, there is not the usual rather dingy and unprepossessing dock-side aspect—on the contrary. This Continental export–import trade is of very long standing and is what made Montrose so prosperous and cosmopolitan in the old days, and the reason for so many ware-houses and wine-cellars at the bottoms of gardens, wine being a major import. Smuggling too, no doubt, was a fairly consistent preoccupation.

Despite its aristocratic atmosphere, Montrose is very much a place of industry with, as well as the dock and shipping and salmon-fishing trade, distilling, preserve-manufacture, phosphates, flax, paper, artificial fibres, the Glaxo Laboratories, and so on, also a large trade in seed-potatoes. The old-style Lochside Distillery is prominent at the roadside to the north of the town, almost opposite a peculiar and highly dignified octagonal red-stone water-tower which attracts attention. But the huge Hillside Distillery of Messrs. Sanderson, of Vat 69 fame, with its towering modern silos and hoppers and exten-sive sheds set amongst beautifully laid-out lawns and flower-gardens, lies a mile farther north in the Hillside village area. For the future, too, Montrose is scheduled to be a shore-base for the North Sea oil-drilling operations, using part of a former railway-station, with special vessels at the harbour to service the offshore rigs.

Montrose is renowned as a holiday centre, and deservedly. The beach itself is an unfailing attraction, and there are many additional amenities such as two 18-hole golf courses, one of championship standard; six public tennis courts; putting, bowling and pitch-and-putt greens, five caravan-parks, a great modern indoor swimming-pool; a childrens' adventure play ground—and of course, many hotels and guest-houses. Yachting is very prominent in the vast Basin, sea- and rock-fishing, angling, pony-trekking, bird-watching on the Basin margins and marshes, and many other pur-suits are readily available. There is the most pleasant countryside for touring, the Angus glens, Deeside, the Red Head cliffs and Lunan Bay, and other scenic areas all within easy motoring distance, with castles in abundance. The Holiday Bureau at the Town House Information Centre is there to help.

Montrose, however, is a parish of 4700 acres, as well as a royal burgh, mainly of level land and inevitably with a strong tang of the sea everywhere; probably a quarter of the land surface is sandy links. Most of the parish has to lie north and west of the town. To the north are two old estates, Charleton and Kinnaber, formerly Car-negie places, the Georgian mansion of Charleton now a maternity home, and the dignified, whitewashed late 17th century laird's-house of Kinnaber readily seen from the main road. Railway-trains used to race, by the east-coast and central routes, to be first at Kinnaber junction here, where the lines joined, and so have priority on the single line onwards to Aberdeen. Near here the parish ends at the North Esk, which is crossed by a fine eight-arched bridge of 1773, erected at local expense for £6500 but with the gracious aid of King George to the tune of £800 out of the forfeited Jacobite estates! This is declared in a panel.

The large village of Hillside, something of a detached suburb, lies a mile to the west, with the Vat 69 distillery between. It is a place of mixed aspect, very attractive at its upper area, with a green, old gardens and trees; but much less so at its lower and eastern end. The large Sunnyside Royal Mental Hospital stands in wide grounds to the north, and the red-stone mansion of Rosemount pleasing to the west, with old limekilns near by. In the low-lying area between Hillside and Montrose were former small old lairdships, relics remaining. Hedderwick House, now a crumbling ruin, has been an attractive late 17th and early 18th century E-shaped mansion, with some early roll-moulded windows, within a mellow walled garden, orchards and old trees. It was a Graham place, passing to Erskines and Scotts. Borrowfield, not far to the south-east, is also late 17th century though now a farmhouse in a walled garden, tall, L-shaped, with an odd corbelled projection on the south front and a draw-bar socket for the door. It belonged to the Gardynes, passing to the Tailyours. Here the parish boundary of Dun is near, treated separately.

Montrose has had a long and stirring story; it suffered from the Danish raids as early as 980, and according to Boece was the Celurca of the 10th century and the Solarch of the 12th. Its motto is apt— "*Mare ditat, Rosa decorat*". The Sea enriches, the Rose adorns. Montrose lives up to its motto still, a sort of small garden-city by the sea.

Murroes, Kellas and Powrie. Murroes is a small rural parish of 5000 acres lying immediately north of Broughty Ferry and northeast of Dundee, and looks as though in some danger of being encroached upon by the city, as has been so much else. The name is merely a corruption of Muirhouse; but though the area may have had some moors, it most obviously has always held rich estates, and is now fertile undulating land, drained by the Murroes, Fithie and Dichty Waters. It rises from less than 200 feet above sea-level to almost 800 in the extreme north, but without any major hills. As elsewhere in this area of Angus, the deep and sudden wooded deans, or dens, of the streams are a delightful and unexpected feature. Kellas, or Hole of Murroes, is a hamlet; and Powrie an ancient castle and property, once with its own village, at the extreme west of the parish. There is, however, quite a plethora of castles here, including Ballumbie, Pitkerro, Gagie, Murroes itself, and the site of Wedderburn.

The kirkton and castleton of Murroes is a most attractive grouping of parish church, castle and farm around a green and pleasant den spanned by an old bridge—but no village. There was a pre-Reformation church here, but it was rebuilt in 1848 over the vault of the Fotheringham family, leaving however the north aisle of 1642 still identifiable. This has a doorway with heraldic panel and that date, and iron jougs hanging beside it. Built into a gateway in the north wall of the kirkyard near by is the figure of a man wearing a ruff and displaying a heraldic shield, now weatherworn. There are many old gravestones in the kirkyard, some dating from as early as 1655 and 1660.

The castle stands only a stone's throw to the south, a small, modest but delightful fortalice of the late 16th century, in a garden not an estate. It is still entire, occupied and well cared for, although it at one time served only as a farm bothy. It is unusual in a number of ways, consisting of a long narrow main block of only two storeys, with a circular stair-tower projecting centrally to the west, with crowstepped gables and well supplied with shot-holes and gunloops but otherwise fairly plain. Internally is a unique arrangement in my experience, the stair-tower, which appears to rise from ground-level on the outside, herein being seen to be supported on massive corbels five feet above floor-level, presumably occasioned by the uneven site. The Fotheringham of that Ilk family, of Powrie, Tealing and Murroes, were powerful in Angus from the 14th century, and thought to have come from Hungary. Fotheringham House in Inverarity parish to the north is now demolished, but some of its panelling has been built into Murroes. Down in the den to the east is a ruinous circular doocot, also of the 16th century. The entire complex is most picturesque and sequestered.

The hamlet of Kellas, or Hole of Murroes, lies half a mile to the north on the Sweet Burn and is showing modern housing development. Another mile and a half up this burn is Gagie House, a mansion incorporating a small early 17th century fortalice on the T-plan, harled and whitewashed, with two long angle-turrets at the south gable. It has been much altered, the roof-level especially, but remains a pleasing composition. A heraldic panel to the west shows the arms of Leslie and initials *I.L.* Another panel, in the handsome Renaissance summer-house in the walled garden, has the arms of Guthrie and the date 1614. Just where the Leslies come in I am unsure. Originally Oliver lands, Gagie was bought by a son of Guthrie of that Ilk in 1610, who presumably built the house, which appears to date from that period. A grandson, marrying his cousin, acquired the main property of Guthrie Castle in the same county, and their son became Guthrie of that Ilk.

Two miles west of the kirkton is the site of Wedderburn Castle, on the bank of the Fithie Burn, in farmland near Barns of Wedderburn. This was originally a stronghold of the ancient Celtic Mormaors of Angus, from whom descend the Ogilvys and the Earls of Airlie. Later it passed to the family who took their name therefrom, the Wedderburns, who merged with the Scrymgeours, constables of Dundee and

hereditary bannermen of Scotland, from whom descends the present
James Scrymgeour-Wedderburn, 11th Earl of Dundee, *Mac Mhic
Iain*, and hereditary standard-bearer, who lives at Birkhall across the
Tay.

Powrie, pronounced Poorie, and sometimes spelt Pourie, lies a
mile farther west at the junction of the same side-road and the A928.
It is now only a farm, but once was another large castle and property.
The massive keep, of the late 15th century, is ruinous but the remains
reveal that it was a fine place, with a notable high vaulted hall on the
first floor, with large windows for its period and a very handsome
fireplace of large dimensions. There is a small vaulted chamber off,
on the same floor, which is unusual—this as well as the normal
vaulted basements below. Across the former courtyard and quite
separate is another and later range of building, still entire although
only used for farm storage, dating from the 17th century, two-
storeyed only, with a large circular conical-roofed tower at the north-
west angle and with shot-holes. The workmanship here is excellent,
revealing Renaissance features, with carved and pilastered windows,
one dated 1604. There is a large vaulted oven in the foot of the
round tower, and a great arched kitchen fireplace at the other, east,
end. This used to be called Wester Powrie—Wedderburn was Easter
Powrie—and was granted to the laird of Ogilvy about 1170, remaining with that ancient family until acquired by Thomas Fotheringham
in 1412. Alexander Fotheringham of Powrie fought at Sheriffmuir
for the Old Pretender, was taken prisoner, but managed to escape in
Edinburgh. The incident is described by the Countess of Panmure.
"Last week Poorie made his escape from his Lodgings in ye Canon-
gate, having got liberty to come out of my lord Winton's house to
take a course of Physick; so he had onlie sentries on him . . ." Powrie
Castle was destroyed by the Scrymgeours of Dudhope in 1492, and
the present older building was presumably erected thereafter on the
same site. The English at Broughty Castle in 1547 "spoiled and
burnt at pleasure . . . the rest of the town of Dundee and the Castle
of Wester Powrie with the village adjacent", says Pitscottie, who
apparently evaluated Dundee and Powrie Castle more or less
equally. There is now no village adjacent. At the road-junction near
by is a fine bronze war memorial, unveiled by the Queen Mother, to
the 4th and 5th, Dundee and Angus battalions, of the Black Watch.

Returning down the Fithie Water, the hamlet of Burnside of
Duntrune lies two miles eastwards, and just to the south of it is the
ancient estate of Ballumbie. This was formerly a parish of its own.
The mansion-house is now a hotel; and close by stands the ruin of its
former castle, now incorporated in a Victorian stableyard. Only the
east and some of the south sides of the castle remain, on its strong site
above the ravine of the Fithie, but this flank is tall and extensive
enough to reveal that the castle has been a fine one. It was originally a seat of the powerful Anglo-Norman family of Lovell; but these
remains do not date from that early period, being apparently of the
15th and 16th centuries, a courtyard castle with flanking-towers,

Letham. The Dunnichen Stone, an early-type Pictish symbol-stone with double-disc and Z-rod, and mirror-and-comb symbols below a highly unusual "flower-pot" design

Montrose. The Great Basin, the mouth of the South Esk and Scurdyness light-house. Inchbrayock, or Rossie Island, is clearly seen with its two bridges

with wide-splayed gunloops, small windows and heraldry. Traditionally Catherine Douglas, the famous Barlass who used her arm to bar the door against the assassins of James I at Perth, married one of the Lovells and lived here.

The last of the castles of this interesting parish is Pitkerro, a mile south-east of Ballumbie, in its estate, and still occupied. It has been much altered and modernised but the nucleus is a small fortalice of the late 16th century, long and narrow, only two storeys in height, like Murroes and the later part of Powrie, with a circular stair-tower projecting on the east side. The angle-turret crowning the south-west gable is a renewal, but the tiny stair-turret in the re-entrant, giving access to the gabled watch-chamber of the stair-tower is original, and supported on a little squinch, an interesting feature. Pitkerro was owned in 1534 by John Durham, second son of Durham of Grange of Monifieth. His grandson Sir James was knighted by Charles I; and his grandson Sir Alexander was colonel of his own regiment in the Civil War and Lord Lyon King of Arms.

Few parishes of this size can show so much interest and antiquity as Murroes. It is to be hoped that the continuing spread of Dundee does not engulf it. One last note; the Rev. Robert Edwards, Episcopalean minister of Murroes in 1678, was sufficiently interested in all this antiquity to write and publish a *History of Angus*—but elected to do so in pure and elegant Latin. It must, even then, have restricted its circulation.

Newtyle. This is a rather unusual place, a large village, almost a small town, which was planned rather than grew naturally. In 1832, with the railway being built from Dundee to Blairgowrie, 15 acres on the gentle north-facing slopes of the Sidlaws in Strathmore, was allotted by the Lord Wharncliffe of Belmont Castle, Meigle, to erect a village community on a regular plan, the houses to be let on 99-year leases, to contain a population of some 500, mainly railway-builders and workers—an early and attractive example of enlightened development. There was a small parish here long before that, and this new development was near the old kirkton thereof; but naturally such influx changed the character of Newtyle, or Newtyld as it was formerly called. The village has grown still further since then, but retained its neat but spacious and pleasing atmosphere, a place of wide vistas. It is approached from the south, through the Sidlaws, by the pass known as the Glack of Newtyle, from which splendid views of Strathmore burst upon the eye—*glac* being Gaelic for a defile.

The village stands fairly centrally in the parish, dominated by the large Gothic-style parish church which dates only from 1872, although it had predecessors of 1767 and earlier. In the graveyard are many ancient stones, some of the 17th century. There was also a United Presbyterian church, converted into a public hall, and a Free church likewise. There is a fine modern school.

To the south of the village, guarding the northern mouth of the

Glack, is Hatton Castle, now ruinous beside a farmhouse, but interesting and entire to the wall-head. It was built in 1575 by Laurence, Lord Oliphant, a commodious Z-planned fortalice, with square towers projecting, liberally provided with gunloops and shot-holes. The hall, on the first floor, was large, measuring 35 by 18 feet, and the workmanship throughout excellent. Robert the Bruce granted these lands to a daughter of his greatest friend, the Good Sir James Douglas, and she married Walter de Oliphant, justiciar. The property passed to the Hallyburtons of Pitcur in the next parish, in 1627. It was garrisoned for the Covenant in 1645, but Montrose took it. Strangely enough, there was another castle just to the south of this, called Balcraig, presumably a predecessor; but of this nothing remains. Some urns were dug up here last century.

A little west of the village is Bannatyne House, now an institution but formerly another old mansion dating from the 17th century; but so much "improved" in the Victorian era that few original features survive. And at Auchtertyre, almost a mile farther west still, formerly a hamlet and now a large farm, is another link with Montrose. The site is here of a smallish square encampment, where the marquis's troops spent a few nights, with the Crew Well adjoining. South of the farmhouse is the site of a souterrain, or weem, of early Pictish days. At the next farm northwards, Newbigging almost on the Perthshire border, was once a sizeable village, in 1840 with 60 houses and 230 people; now there are only two or three buildings. There were other hamlets likewise, in the parish, and their names, Chapel of Keillor and Templeton, indicate one-time places of worship.

Directly to the south of Templeton rises Kinpurney Hill (1134 feet), with its square tower, formerly an observatory, on top, commanding most extensive views. The names are confusing here. It is sometimes spelled Kilpurnie. Yet the large modern mansion and estate of Kinpurnie Castle lies nearly three miles away, on the west side of the village, at the foot of Newtyle and Keillor Hills. Near there, at the roadside, though just over the parish boundary in Kettins, is the interesting Pictish symbol-stone monolith described under that parish. A field, called Chester-park, on the high ground of Keillor is traditionally said to have been the site of a Roman camp—possibly a signal-station for the large camp at Lintrose in Kettins, four miles to the west.

Panbride, Panmure and Muirdrum. Panbride is a small coast parish, with only a kirkton and mansion of the name; Panmure is a large and ancient estate, formerly an earldom of the Maule family; and Muirdrum is a crossroads village, inland, on the main A92 road. All are situated about 10 miles east of Dundee.

Panbride, though modest today, is a very ancient place. The name comes from Bridget or Bride, a Celtic saint. Of the Celtic period here I have no details, but the barony of Panbride was given to John de Morham or Malherbe by William the Lion about 1214, and this John confirmed the king's gift of the church of Panbride to Arbroath

Abbey. The parish church stands on a slight ridge half a mile inland from the coast, on a side-road, manse and school near by. It was an ancient building, remodelled in 1681 and 1775, and rebuilt in cruciform Gothic style in 1851. Its east end is of the 17th century, and contains the burial-vault of the Earls of Panmure; and sundry old stones are incorporated in the walling, including dormer pediments with coronets and initials, and heraldic achievements. Iron jougs hang, oddly enough in a glass case, near by. The interior is bright, with some excellent coloured heraldic wood-carvings of the Maule-Ramsay family. There is also a little museum of interesting local items, such as early books, Bibles and church furniture. Outside is a louping-on stane, for horse-mounting. There are old gravestones in the churchyard. Across the road is a commodious old manse.

Half a mile east of the kirkton is the former milling hamlet of Craigmill, in the pleasant, craggy, green den of the Monikie Burn, the stream crossed by a small but substantial old single-arched bridge, angled. Seaward of this, but separated from the shore by the main railway-line, is the whitewashed mansion of Panbride, not particularly ancient of appearance but of long lineage. The ancestors of the famous Hector Boece, or Boetius, the Aberdeen scholar and historian, held the barony for several generations. He was born here.

The fishing-village of East Haven, now only a hamlet but expanding again with modern housing, was formerly larger. It too lies behind the railway, with a bridge under giving access to the boat-shore and haven amongst the skerries. A disused airfield lies to the east. West Haven, one and a half miles to the west, was part of this parish but has been absorbed in Carnoustie burgh. It was always larger than East. Inland from West Haven two miles, where the A930 crosses the A92, is Muirdrum, a post-office village and once a landed property in the barony of Downie, belonging to the Lindsays and Erskines. At its east end, where the road crosses shallow Battie's Den, is Panlathy Mill, attractively situated. The reason for the Pan prefixes hereabouts is not clear.

Panmure estate lies to west and north, flanking the den-like valley of the Monikie Burn, a large and important property. The great 17th century mansion, almost rebuilt by Bryce in 1852, has been wholly demolished; but the estate is still well cared for and remained in the possession of the Maule-Ramsay Earls of Dalhousie until recent years. Sir Peter de Maule acquired the lands as early as 1224, and his 13th descendant was created Lord Maule of Brechin and Earl of Panmure in 1646. The titles were forfeited by the 4th Earl for his share in the Rising of 1715, the Maules always being staunch supporters of the Stewarts. Harry Maule, son of the 3rd Earl, was deputy Lord Lyon King of Arms, and one of the most effective leaders of that Rising—much more so than his brother-in-law, the Earl of Mar. He and his brother, the 4th Earl, were outlawed after Sheriffmuir, escaped to Holland and never returned to Scotland. Handsome heraldic gates to the estate have never been opened since

297

that earl passed through them. Eventually an Irish barony was created for Harry's second son, as Lord Panmure, and this title merged later into the earldom of Dalhousie. The foundations of the old Maule castle are still to be seen within the estate, on the east bank of the den. The gardens of the later mansion were famous. To the north of the great wooded property are the tall hilltop "Live and Let Live" Monument and also the Camus Cross—but these are described under Monikie, in which parish they stand.

Rescobie, Restenneth and Balgavies. This interesting district due east of Forfar comprises the headwaters of the Lunan Water which flows into Lunan Bay at Red Head, a dozen miles to the east. Rescobie is an oddly shaped parish and a loch; Restenneth an ancient ruined priory and former moss, now drained; and Balgavies an old estate and another loch. There is a third loch called Fithie, attractive but smaller, near Restenneth. Dominating the parish is the lofty spine of Turin and Pitscandly Hills.

Rescobie Loch, a mile long and half that broad, lies four miles east of Forfar, with fairly flat and reedy shores. Once there was an artificial island, or crannog, at the west end, the site of a castle or refuge. Another castle is said to have been sited at the whitewashed farm of Drimmie, above the north shore, in which King Edgar is alleged to have grimly murdered his uncle, the usurping King Donald Bane, in 1097. Rescobie was a royal hunting-forest.

The church of the parish, now conjoined with Guthrie, stands on a knoll near the loch-head, and dates from 1820, typically plain but bright within. But the site is old, the bell dates from 1620, and there are many ancient stones in the graveyard, the oldest 1616. A highly interesting stone lies at the east gable, no gravestone this. It stood formerly in the open area immediately to the north, now a tarmacadamed playground for the village school, which itself is now closed. This was the site of the barony court of Rescobie, and where was held annually St. Troddan's Fair—which Fair was later removed to Forfar, and sometimes called St. Trodlins. This massive recumbent stone has a scooped hollow, almost like a small font. It is thought that this was the measure to be filled with grain, for the laird, as part of the price paid by each contributor to the Fair—for these events were much-prized baronial revenue-producers. Covered by the tarmac in the playground is the site of St. Troddan's Well. The name is a corruption of St. Triduana, patron saint of the parish, who is buried at St. Triduana's Chapel, Restalrig, Leith. A lovely woman who had taken up the cause of the Church, she it was who, pursued in love by some notable because of her fine eyes, plucked them out and sent them to him so that she might continue her labours in peace.

Amongst the marshy flats between Rescobie and Fithie Lochs is the old estate of Reswallie—the Res prefix hereabouts is a corruption of Ross, a headland. Reswallie belonged originally to the Church lands of Restenneth Priory, and came at the Reformation to Sir Richard Preston of Craigmillar, near Edinburgh, a friend of James

VI. Thereafter in 1643 the property passed to the Hunters of near-by Burnside and then to the Doigs, prominent in Dundee. Burnside estate lies a mile to the south, and some 350 feet higher, on a shoulder of Dunnichen Hill. It is quite a historic place and used to be called the barony of Dodd. Indeed Fithie used to be known as Loch Dodd; and there is still a farm of Mid Dod. The Hunter family were domiciled here from very early times, and claimed that their name was given them by Malcolm Canmore. They remained in possession until comparatively recent times. The mansion is set most attractively in a hilly and wooded site, and was rebuilt about 1800. But there is a 17th century doocot near by and an interesting circular meat-larder islanded in a little courtyard behind the house.

On the other side of the valley, a mile west of Rescobie Church, on the skirts of Pitscandly Hill, is the farm of Wemyss. This, of course, is from the Gaelic *uamh*, meaning cave. But the place is well-named, for when the railway was being built—now disused—a weem or Pictish souterrain was uncovered here, with a quern for grinding grain. Oddly enough there was another place called Wemyss two miles to the east, on what is now West Mains of Turin, where the Lindays had a castle. Presumably this hill of Pitscandly and Turin was dotted with caves. Certainly it was an important area in very early days, for on the top of Turin Hill (825 feet) is the site of a Pictish fort called Kemp's Castle, a very extensive fortress perched on the rocky escarpment. And at the west or Pitscandly end is a lesser fort, an outlier, known as Rob's Reed. There were once no fewer than five quarries working on Turin Hill.

Not far below Rob's Reed is the substantial whitewashed 18th century mansion of Pitscandly. It was for long a Lindsay property. Near by at Blackgate, a cluster of cottages on the B9134 road, are two enormous standing-stones, nine feet and seven feet high and six and four feet wide, sited 20 yards apart in the steading. Presumably they were part of a circle, for a third stone is said to have been removed. Locally these stones are reputed to be associated with a battle fought between Picts and Scots about 836, when Feredith, king of Picts, was slain. But almost certainly they were connected with worship long before that.

Restenneth Priory stands picturesquely to the north of the B9133 road, above marshy land—indeed it was originally an island in a loch—two miles west of Rescobie Church and less from the centre of Forfar. This notable monastic institution was one of the most venerable in the land; for here, in A.D. 710 St. Boniface baptised into Christianity King Nechtan of the Picts. Nechtan asked Ceolfrid of Northumbria for masons from the Saxon monastery at Monkwearmouth, to help him build a church "in the Roman manner"—probably as a battle abbey, to celebrate the great victory of Nechtansmere. The tower of Restenneth, except for the late medieval steeple, is mainly of the 11th century; but the lowest portion is older, and may well represent the porch of Nechtan's 8th century church—which would make it probably *the* oldest in Scotland. At any rate, it was a foundation of the Celtic Church. Fortunately the Augustinian canons, to whom David I gave Restenneth, on the Romanisation of the Church, were usually very respectful to the memorials of the Celtic polity, and here they allowed the Pictish tower to remain, while building a 13th century choir and nave to east and west of it. All is now roofless, but maintained in good order by the Department of the Environment. There are a piscina and sedilia in the south wall of the choir, and many recumbent gravestones, including one with an inscribed cross and another commemorating many generations of the Hunters of Burnside or Dodd. Inset in the north wall is a stone with the initials *D.B.* Could this refer to Cardinal David Beaton, who had personal connections with the priory? Restenneth's history is resounding—but not for recounting here. After the Reformation it served for some time as the parish church for Forfar. The place is a pleasure to visit—spoiled a little only by the constant noise of a large quarry near by. At time of writing, an ambitious building of stone is being erected close to the priory.

Balgavies Loch lies half a mile east of Rescobie Loch, in the chain of the Lunan Water, and is slightly deeper though smaller and even more attractive. Balgavies estate—pronounced Balguise—just to the north, formerly had a castle of the Lindsays, which James VI destroyed on his way south after the Battle of Glenlivet in 1595. Fragments of the vaulting remain a few hundred yards north-west of the present whitewashed mansion, which itself is not very old. To the south is a lean-to-type doocot of the 17th century.

The area surrounding Balgavies is scenically very pleasing. There is a flat standing-stone, five feet by four, in a field near the roadside at Westerton here, not marked on the Ordnance map.

Ruthven. There are a number of Ruthvens in Scotland—pronounced Rivven—the best known of which is near Perth. The Ruthven here described is a tiny parish of only some 2000 acres at the west end of Strathmore, in Angus, close to the Perthshire border and only 20 miles from the other; and since its postal address is "by Meigle, Perthshire", confusion inevitably arises. It is safe to say that few outside this district have ever heard of this Ruthven, for there is no real village. Nevertheless it is a most interesting entity, with many features.

It lies in the wide lower vale of the Isla, three miles east of Alyth. Its centre is Bridge of Ruthven, a small cluster of houses at the west end of the two bridges, the modern single-arch carrying the A926 Kirriemuir road across the deep trough of the Isla; and alongside it to the north, but some 20 feet lower, the ancient one, two-arched, narrow and originally parapetless, mentioned by Franke in 1658. A little way downstream is the large farm and former milling hamlet of Brigton, also taking its name from this bridge. Attractively if rather inconveniently sited amongst green braes farther *up*stream, away from the road, are the parish church and former manse. At first glance this church looks typically Victorian and uninteresting, however picturesque the riverside setting; but this is a mistaken impression. Small, built in 1857, and not very attractive inside or out, it is nevertheless a place to visit. It replaces a typical long, low, pre-Reformation chapel, a little painting of which hangs inside. Built into the west gable are two highly interesting smallish ancient stones. Both are crosses, one a fairly typical Celtic or Pictish design; the other an unusual if less pleasing crudely incised crucifix with pointed arms. Notable are the modern wrought-iron gates to the new section of the graveyard, which are attractively ornamented with representations of the first cross. There is still another interesting ancient stone here, an early medieval coffin-slab five feet long, built in as lintel to the doorway of the former minister's barn, displaying a long-shafted cross, a two-handed knight's sword and a hunting-horn. There are some old gravestones in the kirkyard, one of which is intriguing in that it appears to be only half a stone, the inscription to one William Kandow, schoolmaster, who died 1798, adding cryptically that the other half of the stone is in Guthrie churchyard! This does not end the interest of this little church; for near the head of the kirk-path which climbs towards the main road and the bridge is the site of a weem, or souterrain, an underground refuge of Pictish times or earlier. It was opened and ransacked in 1842. Lastly, the church bell here is unusual in being a ship's bell, dated 1735, from the warship *Enterprise*. In the 12th century Ruthven was a vicarage of the abbey of Arbroath, dedicated to St. Moluag, like Alyth, its privileges specially confirmed by the Pope in 1219. It had a large glebe of 22 acres.

There was a large castle at Ruthven in early times, belonging to the Earls of Crawford, not far from their Inverqueich Castle in Alyth parish upstream. It passed to the Crichton family in the 15th century, who held it for many generations, until in 1744 Ogilvy of Coul bought the estate. This is situated over a mile downstream from the bridge. Most accounts say that the castle was swept away when the present large red-stone mansion was built in the 18th century; but this is not quite true. A semi-circular flanking-tower, apparently of the 16th century, remains at the head of the walled garden to the north-west of the mansion, having a vaulted basement which has been used as an ice-house, furnished with three wide-splayed gun-loops and a tiny arrow-slit window. The castle occupied a strong position on a spine above a ravine. Near by is a mound called the Gallows Hill and a field, the Hangman's Acres. In 1496 Sir Adam Crichton had a charter of Ruthven from the Earl of Crawford.

Ruthven was a great place for mills, seven flanking the Isla in a quarter-mile. One still extant is being converted into an interesting house.

St. Vigeans. Although its village is all but swallowed up by Arbroath, the parish of St. Vigeans is both large (13,000 acres) and highly interesting. The parish areas of the two places are notably mixed up, and it is probably sensible to describe under St. Vigeans the country area west of the Brothock Water's pronounced valley, and under Arbroath that to the east and north.

St. Vigeans village and remarkable church lie a mile and a half due north of Arbroath, the latter crowning a 40-foot, high and steep natural green mound, with the village cottages clustering around the foot and the Brothock running close by, spanned by a picturesque double-arched bridge, all highly attractive. It is said to derive its name from the Columban missionary St. Fechin, abbot of Fobhar in Ireland, said to have died at Grange of Conon near by in 664—the same who gave his name to Ecclefechan. This was Latinised by the later Romish Church to St. Vigianus. The parish, at any rate, was a seat of the Celtic Church, one of the oldest in Scotland, and important before the great abbey of Arbroath was ever thought of; indeed it included all Arbroath once. The church, of warm red sandstone, is of suitably ancient construction, although nothing Celtic is now evident. As it stands, the building dates from about 1100, added to and modernised at various periods. The oldest part, with the north aisle and east gable, is of this period, and was about 60 feet by 26. In 1242, when the church was rededicated by the Romish Bishop de Bernham of St. Andrews, the west wall of the nave was added and consecration crosses are to be seen at the roots of the arches at the east and west ends, internally. There was a second consecration in 1485, by which date the south aisle and clerestory windows had been built. The tower was erected between these two dates, though its upper works have been renewed; but the door is of 1485. The last monkish priest lived on a floor of this tower, and is said to have been frightened therefrom by the Devil in the shape of a rat! It took all sorts to make a Reformation. The entire building was reconditioned in 1872, with certain new features, as at the chancel and north aisle. The effect is very fine. There is a monument to Sir Peter Young, tutor to James VI, who became laird of Aldbar in Aberlemno. There is an old font on a later pedestal, a sculptured cross at the south-east door, and two more consecration crosses outside near the east gable. Also a collection of 18th century pewter vessels.

St. Vigeans Church was famous for its Pictish stones. These have been removed to a cottage-museum of the Department of the Environment just below the kirk-mound with its surrounding graveyard. There are no fewer than 32 of them, including fragments, and they make a most exciting collection. The most renowned is that called the Drosten Stone, for this is one of the few Pictish stones actually to have an inscription. The script is thought to be of the 9th century, and the language unknown—but it has been accepted that the words include the names Drosten, Uoret and Forcus, Pictish names rendered into Gaelic. There was more than one Drosten king of Picts. It is a typical cross-slab, with a finely decorated cross flanked by an angel and some very odd animals biting each other's tails. And on the other side are some splendid representations of hunting scenes, with stag and tusked boar, an archer firing realistically at the latter; also an osprey or sea-eagle eating a fish, a bear, a hind suckling a calf, an unknown horned beast, and the usual crescent, mirror-and-comb, and double-disc and Z-rod symbols. Another slab with wheel-cross has on its back two seated ecclesiastics each with a book—which gives the lie to those who aver that the Picts had no written language—and two tough-looking characters with staffs. There is no space here to detail the other stones, but one somewhat damaged cross-slab had a most elaborately decorated cross of quite wonderful workmanship, flanked by St. John being martyred head-down in a pot of oil, Saints Paul and Anthony facing each other, and a naked man with his tongue sticking out, apparently cutting the throat of a bull. The collection should be visited by all with any feeling for Scotland's remote past.

Whether St. Fechin actually died hereabouts, or in Ireland as some aver, his chapel's site, where he is claimed to have ministered for 33 years, is still to be seen at Grange of Conon farm four miles to the north-west. There are foundations in trees beside the farm cottages, and St. Vigean's Well, a spring, still gushes out strongly near by. On the adjoining farm of West Grange, at the head of the brae north-westwards near Cairnconon, is a Pictish weem or souterrain in the field south of the road. Unmarked on the map, it is not hard to find, near a pylon, its mouth temporarily blocked with stones. It is possible to peer down into the underground storehouse.

Nearer St. Vigeans village is the former great R.N.A.S. airfield, H.M.S. *Condor*, now a Royal Marine establishment. It covers many acres, and has large housing quarters, its continuance meaning much to Arbroath. Between it and the Brothock's course is the very handsome restored 18th century Letham House, in an isolated position, containing the vaulted basement nucleus of an earlier fortalice, no doubt erected immediately after the Reformation, for this was all Church land. This house is not to be confused with Letham Grange, two miles to the north, a later mansion erected by a former laird who took the name from here. There are many Lethams in Scotland. An early linen-weaving mill was established near by in 1793, long abandoned. A mile north of *Condor*, on the A933, is the crossroads village of Gowanbank, or Colliston, with two churches. A small side-road to the north leads to Colliston Castle, above the Brothock, a most interesting 16th century fortalice on the Z-plan, still occupied and maintained, with several unusual features. It was much altered in the 17th century and later, and the parapet and rounds are modern. There are two circular towers at opposite ends of the four-storey main block, one corbelled out to provide a gabled watch-chamber, with conical-roofed turret. There are many gunloops and shot-holes. Cardinal Beaton gave a charter of Colliston to John Guthrie in 1542, and the Guthrie and Falconer arms, dated 1556, appear over the original doorway. A chamber is still called Beaton's Room.

Stracathro. Today Stracathro means to most a large hospital just off the A94, three miles north of Brechin, and little more. But fine as this establishment is, Stracathro means a great deal more. It is, in fact, a parish of 5500 acres, and was once two parishes, before Dunlappie was included in 1618. It has no village of the name, or any village at all. But it has a resounding history and many interesting features. The name is strange, and uncertain of origin. Assuming the prefix to be strath, one naturally looks for the river-name to follow. But the streams involved here are the Cruick Water and the West Water. These are notably non-Gaelic names, and it may be that one or other was differently called once, there being a suggestion that Cathroc was an old name for the Cruick. The two famous hills so prominent to the north-west, the White and Brown Caterthuns, have rather a similar sounding name. Be that as it may, one derivation we can confidently dismiss is that put forward by a one-time local authority who claimed that when the Roman general Agricola reached the river here, he ordered his legions to "Strike a' through!"—with a nice touch of the Doric.

The Romans however *were* here and their camp is still marked on the Ordnance Survey map, at the Brechin boundary a mile south of the parish church—although it requires the eye of faith to discern it now. It was given the name of War Dykes, and was reputed to measure 1900 by 1300 feet, and to quarter 12,000 of Agricola's legionaries.

The parish church stands in a pleasant but isolated position off a side-road four miles north of Brechin, and dates from 1799, being fairly plain. But an earlier church on the site, and dedicated to St. Brule, with a Braul's Well in the vicinity, was the scene of one of the most dramatic episodes in Scottish history. For here Edward I staged the humiliating interlude when he summoned the captive King John Baliol to his presence, and publicly stripped him of all the trappings of royalty in the most boorish fashion. Admittedly Baliol was his own puppet appointment; but he was the lawfully crowned king of Scots, and Edward's behaviour that day was that of a bully, despite his claim to be the First Knight of Christendom. The Wars of Independence stemmed from that scene at Stracathro. Why the English king, who was staying at Brechin Castle, chose this small church for the performance, is something of a mystery.

There are many old tombstones in the graveyard, including some that may be of particular interest. These are very long, nine feet, approximately coffin-shaped, and of soft red sandstone. Two still lie in position, completely weatherworn; three are on edge, lying beside the north gable of the church, but too heavy to be moved without aid. One is said to bear the carving of "three Danish generals"—usually a mistaken reference to Pictish ecclesiastics. It would be interesting to have these properly examined. The church interior is bright, with renewed woodwork and a small gallery.

Just south of the church and school is the farm of Ballownie, where there is a burial-cairn called Lousyhillock, at a bend in the road, grown with beeches.

Stracathro House, formerly a large Georgian mansion which once belonged to Sir James Campbell, father of Sir Henry Campbell-

Bannerman, the prime minister, is now the large general hospital, in extensive grounds half a mile east of the church. And twice as far south is the site of the Battle of Brechin, fought in 1452 between the Lindsays under the fearsome Tiger Earl of Crawford and the Earl of Huntly, with great bloodshed and a Lindsay defeat. Huntlyhill farm here commemorates the event. The Hare Cairn said to mark the spot was here long before the 15th century, however, with a stone cist discovered in it. West again, a mile beyond the Roman camp, is the mansion of Newtonmill and the farm of Newton. There are innumerable Newtons in Scotland; but this is the one which gave title to the Lord Newton of Session, whose famous portrait by Raeburn is much reproduced. The still more renowned Lord Boyd Orr of Brechin lived there in a delightful 18th century house.

Over a mile to the north, on the B966 to Edzell, where this crosses the West Water by a high old bridge, lies the pretty crossroads hamlet of Inchbare. Across the water is the former parish of Dunlappie, where, at Auchenreoch, was fought in 1130 another famous battle, when David I defeated his rebellious kinsman, Angus Mormaor of Moray. Dunlappie itself, now a farming estate with a modern mansion and a fine walled garden, was once a barony as well as a parish. Indeed the lands are claimed to have the oldest recorded history in Angus, traditionally granted by Malcolm III to MacDuff, Earl of Fife, who slew MacBeth. They remained with the Earls of Fife until exchanged for Balbirnie in Fife. Thereafter they passed through many hands. The castle of the property was called Poolbrigs, of which no trace remains. The former church also has gone, even the stones of the graveyard removed.

The mansion of Lundie Castle, which stands prominently on the side of Lundie Hill to the north, is modern.

Tannadice, Memus and Glen Ogil. Tannadice is one of those large foothill parishes of the Braes of Angus, (21,000 acres or 60 square miles) in undulating pastoral country with fine open views of the mountains; Memus is an isolated hamlet; and Glen Ogil, to the north, is one of the shorter Angus glens, which would be more aptly named Glen Noran, for down it flows the Noran Water, renowned in song. The centre of the parish lies some six miles north of Forfar.

The kirkton of Tannadice is a rather picturesque village with a slightly decayed aspect, clustered around a small den, on a slope north of the South Esk. The parish church is somewhat detached to the south, at the riverside, and dates from 1846, replacing a pre-Reformation chapel which was a rectory of St. Andrews Cathedral, the old font of which is preserved in the vestibule. The kirk's interior is bright. There are many old stones in the graveyard, but unfortunately the Pictish sculptured-stone which used to be here has disappeared. The village, rather untidily quaint, is provided with post-office and school. The schoolmaster who was appointed in 1824 was sternly informed that there must be no cock-fighting permitted in the schoolroom under any pretext.

There are hamlets in the parish, at Murthill two miles to the south-east, and at Memus three miles north-west. The former has a large modern mill of the Angus Milling Company, processing grains and animal feeding stuffs, with the Justinhaugh Hotel near by. Memus, with its strange name, is a small road-junction and burnside community, with school, hall, caravan-park and Free church dated 1843 with one lonely marble gravestone lost under a bush. Between Tannadice and Memus are two ancient earthworks, somewhat hard to distinguish now, at Baldoukie and Derachie farms. Between Murthill and Memus, in a bend of the South Esk, is the Ogilvy estate of Inshewan, with a mansion of 1828 replacing a former castle on a rock; and the Castle-hill of Auchleuchrie is not far away, only fosse and earthworks remaining.

Strangely enough there was another castle flanking this very castellated river just about a mile farther up, the Castle of Quiech, where the Quiech Burn comes in from Glenquiech. When it is remembered that Inverquharity Castle and Cortachy Castle farther adorn the same riverside one and two miles up respectively, it will be recognised that this must have been a lively area. Quiech sat on a precipitous rock above the river, looking down into a yawning abyss, and was a seat of the Earls of Buchan, the Comyns.

The upper part of the parish is very high, reaching mountain status at Hill of Glansie (2383 feet), Dog Hillock (2369 feet)—something of an understatement—and Mount Sned (2030 feet). Glen Ogil, the upper valley of the Noran Water, is entered between the flanking hills of White Top (854 feet) to the west, and Deuchar (970 feet) to the east, with the Noran forming the picturesquely named Falls of Drumly Harry between. At the 650-foot contour on White Top is a standing-stone. Glen Ogil is not long, and rises quickly. From the entrance, at Milton, the public road probes it only for two miles—although other roads branch off. In half a mile is Easter Ogil estate, with a modern mansion replacing another old castle. Wester Ogil is only a little higher, and also once had a castle, allegedly called Cossens, a Lyon place. Near here opens due westwards a side-road leading past the long, narrow Den of Ogil Reservoir to Glenquiech, behind White Top, also a former Lyon property. As was Glen Ogil itself, which comprises the main northwards basin of the Noran. Its mansion is hidden down in the wooded glen at the foot of a tree-girt loch, the public road stopping at Redheugh, a hamlet on the higher ground. The Noran rises high on Mount Sned, four miles on. Directly above Redheugh rears the prominent St. Arnold's Seat (1615 feet) sometimes called St. Ennans, with an ancient burial-cairn on top, from which prospects are magnificent, even to Edinburgh and the Lothian hills.

Half a mile south of Redheugh another side-road strikes eastwards, contouring the hillsides to Fern, by Auchnacree.

Tealing. The small parish of Tealing lying five miles north of Dundee, on the Sidlaw foothills slopes immediately below the tall

T.V. mast and other modernistic structures on the top of Craigowl and Balluderon Hills, contains no real village but four or five scattered hamlets. It is an ancient place, however, of much interest—even though a disused airfield occupies much of its southern area, scarcely an asset. Prehistoric remains are notable. In historic times the Maxwell family somehow gained these lands, presumably by marriage, far from their native Dumfriesshire, and have left traces, their Tealing House later passing to the Scrymgeour family of more local origin. The parish church is interesting in that it was the last charge of the Rev. John Glass before his deposition from the Church of Scotland in 1728 to found the Glassite sect.

The Kirkton and church stand fairly centrally in the parish. The building dates only from 1806 and is plain to the point of starkness without, standing in an old burial-ground with a great many ancient stones. A large recumbent slab at the east gable commemorates the Maxwell lairdship; and against the south front is a later and ornate memorial to the Scrymgeour Fotheringhams of Powrie. The hamlet around the church is now very decayed, though picturesque, with many formerly attractive thatched cottages empty and falling into ruin. So near Dundee, it is strange that these have not been saved and modernised.

Half a mile to the east is the dispersed community of Balgray, where lies Tealing House, now a fairly plain mid-18th century mansion amongst old trees. Near by, in fact in its home-farm steading, is a fine example of 16th century dovecote, larger than usual, crow-stepped-gabled, with stone slates, its stone nest-boxes still intact. The door lintel and south-east skew-putt are carved with the Maxwell arms and monogram of Sir David Maxwell and his wife, who built it in 1595.

A little to the west, amongst a field of raspberry canes, is an excavated and preserved souterrain, earth-house, or weem—the Gaelic word for cave—crescent-shaped, about 60 feet long by seven wide and seven deep. Now the slabbing of its roof is uncovered to reveal the stone walling and paving. These underground storehouses and refuges were fairly prevalent in this area, built about the 2nd century A.D. by the Picts. Clearly they were not intended for dwelling in, their somewhat rude workmanship contrasting strongly with the splendid stone carvings and clearly quite advanced civilisation enshrined in the many symbol-stones and cross-slabs of the area, of only a century or two later. This relic, like the doocot, is now under the care of the Department of the Environment.

Some way to the west, a side-road goes off to the north to the hill-farms of Prieston and this continues on as a track through the Sidlaws, reaching 1118 feet, and into Glen Ogilvie, and so to Strathmore near Glamis.

About a mile still farther west, in an open field to the north of the road, unseen from it, is an interesting stone-circle. There are four components, only that to the north-west upright, and this is unusual in having rough carvings consisting of five circles or cup-marks within a frame, four of them so placed so that they might conceivably have been intended to form a cross. The north-east stone has a socket-hole in the centre.

The Martin Stone, a mile to the south-west, lies just within this parish although it is convenient to describe it under Strathmartine, to which it gives name. It is a typical Celtic cross-slab with carvings and symbols, in a field near Balkello farm. North of it, the former hamlet of Old Balkello, now only a small farm, crowns a low rise below the main summit ridge of Balluderon Hill, whereon are ancient cairns. A large quarry now eats into this hillside.

KINCARDINESHIRE, OR THE MEARNS

As counties go, this is a modest one, with a population of only 48,000 and an area of 242,000 acres, containing no town larger than Stonehaven with its 4500 people. Nevertheless, there are 13 counties with fewer inhabitants, in Scotland, and 12 with smaller area. It is therefore very much the little brother of the great counties of Aberdeenshire and Angus, its neighbours in this volume, with only 19 civil parishes as against 85 in Aberdeenshire and 55 in Angus.

For all that, it has a stirring history; for neither of its neighbours can claim the same royal and governmental status which Kincardine once enjoyed, when its formerly great castle, of that name, was the seat of the early kings of Scots. This large establishment was not just a summer palace or hunting-lodge, but a major seat of authority for the monarchs, from the time of Malcolm I (he was slain at Fetteresso, in the county, in A.D. 954) until the time of Robert II (1388) although it had been waning in royal popularity for a period by then. But at the height of its power it was the centre of rule. It is interesting and significant that not only Malcolm, but Kenneth II and Duncan II were also slain near by, at Fettercairn and Mondynes respectively. Perhaps this fatality record may have had something to do with Kincardine's decline in popularity; and it is extraordinary that not even a trace of the quite substantial town, which grew up around the royal castle, now remains—although its mercat cross now stands at Fettercairn. Probably, without its royal link, there would never have been a county of Kincardine, or the Mearns; for most of it seems to be an obvious extension of Angus, and the northern part, of Aberdeenshire.

There are at least seven other Kincardines in Scotland, the name meaning merely the head of the copse-wood. It is interesting in having this alternative name of the Mearns, just as ancient. There are doubts as to the derivation of this. Some say that, just as Angus was called after Aeneas, brother of Kenneth II, so the Mearns was called after another brother called Mearnia. Others declare that it comes from *An Mhaoirne*, meaning the stewartry—as does Mearns in Renfrewshire, it being a territory governed by a royal steward. Still another school would have it merely a corruption of the moors, there being much moorland here. Be that as it may, it has long been the preferred local name—as typified by the proverb "I can dae fat I dow; the men o' the Mearns can dae nae mair." Meaning, of course, that the Mearns-men were a notably effective lot. Incidentally, the county was never called Mearns-shire.

Like Angus, Kincardineshire divides readily into four fairly distinct sections—a coastal strip, nearly all cliff-girt, fairly quickly rising to a long spine of high ground; the famed and fertile Howe of the Mearns, lying beyond, measuring approximately 16 miles by five; the Grampian mountain area to west and north, comprising about 90,000 acres, with Mount Battock (2555 feet) the highest point; and the north-facing Deeside area, which seems to turn its back on the rest and to belong to the Aberdeenshire polity. Indeed the north-eastern end of this is practically suburban Aberdeen, waging a constant battle against absorption.

Stonehaven, the county town, is a pleasant burgh set in a picturesque position on a deep bay between lofty headlands. It superseded Kincardine in the 17th century as county centre—but is hardly central. Inverbervie, 10 miles to the south, a modest place though a royal burgh, lies at the mouth of the attractive valley of the Bervie Water, with a population of only 1000—though the adjacent fishing-village of Gourdon boosts the size of the community. This is on the A92 Aberdeen highway. Laurencekirk, on the main A94 inland road, seven miles to the south-west, is a small town without burgh status. Banchory, far from all the others amongst the pine-woods of Deeside, is the third burgh, a famed holiday resort, of 2000 population. St. Cyrus, Johnshaven, Fettercairn and Auchenblae are only large villages, with Marykirk, Luthermuir, Drumlithie, Muchalls, Portlethen, Cove and others, smaller places.

Kincardineshire, like its neighbours, is noted for its fine castles and ancient estates, such as Arbuthnott—still the home of one of the oldest families in the land—Dunnottar, Crathes, Muchalls, Glenbervie, Fiddes, Thornton, Balbegno, Allardyce, and so on. There are many prehistoric sites, stone-circles especially, that at Aquhorthies being particularly notable, like the Ogham-inscribed standing-stone at Auquhollie and the Roman camp at Raedykes near by. Arbuthnott pre-Reformation church is justly renowned—and has become better-known of late, like other parts of this area, by featuring in the T.V. serial based on Lewis Grassic Gibbon's *Sunset Song*. The coastline is one of the most dramatic in Scotland, almost 30 miles of fierce cliffs, deep inlets, caves and thrusting skerries, dotted with tiny fishing-havens often hidden under frowning precipices.

Kincardineshire is all too apt to be hurried through, on the way to Aberdeen and points north, by way of the main A92 and A94 roads and the exciting Cairn o' Mount and Slug roads to Deeside. This is unfortunate, for it is a county well worth lingering in.

Arbuthnott. This is a name which has meant much in the North-East down the ages, although it is only a rural parish with no real village. But the family which takes its name from here is one of the oldest in Scotland, and has always taken a leading part in affairs. The present Viscount of Arbuthnott is prominent in conservation affairs, and sits on the Countryside Commission. The family has been settled here since the 12th century, of Norman extraction, having come here from Swinton in Berwickshire. It is interesting to note that the Swintons of that Ilk, the other stem of the family, are still at Swinton, likewise.

Arbuthnott House. The drawing-room—note the particularly fine plaster ceiling of about 1660 and the pine panelling

Benholm. Brotherton House, now Lathallen Boys' School,
with typical Mearns landscape

Arbuthnott parish extends to almost 10,000 acres, lying west and
north of Inverbervie, stretching from near the main A94 highway
almost to the sea, mostly a territory of green swelling hills and deep
dens. The parish church is justly famous as one of the finest ancient
churches in the land, made familiar to millions, at least by sight, as
the "Kirk of Kinraddie" in the television film of *Sunset Song*. It stands
in a delightful setting deep in a green den half a mile south of the
house, in its old graveyard, a pre-Reformation building of highly
unusual design dedicated to the Pictish St. Ternan. There was an
early Celtic Church establishment here; but the present building's
chancel, at the eastern end, was consecrated by that busy prelate,
Bishop de Bernham of St. Andrews, in 1242. There is a Norman
arch at the entrance to the Lady Chapel, now called the Arbuthnott
aisle, projecting southwards, which appears to be older than 1242.
This aisle was reconstructed in 1500. Its stair-tower and the bell-
tower are extraordinarily fine examples of late 15th century architecture, with strong castellated influence, corbelling and lancet
windows. The main body of the church is typically long and narrow,
but higher than usual. It was restored in the mid-19th century, and
again, after a fire, in 1890. The interior is most pleasing, especially
the vaulted Arbuthnott aisle, with its cobbled floor and crypt
beneath. Here there are a holy-water stoup and an aumbry for the
Elements; also a 13th century recumbent effigy of Hugo le Blond
Arbuthnott, over a 16th century heraldic tomb. This aisle is really
something of a tower, with a second storey above, as priest's room, a
turnpike stair giving access, and a squint-hole for the priest to peer
down into the chapel, unseen. There are also window-seats in
stone, as in castles of the period. In the main church, the chancel is
lit by five lancet windows, and there is a memorial plaque to
Alexander Arbuthnott, who was the first Protestant minister after
the Reformation. This was the famous individual who became first
Protestant principal of King's College, Aberdeen, and Moderator.
The renowned Missal of Arbuthnott, containing drawings of St.
Ternan, within oaken boards, and the 15th century Psalter, are no
longer at Arbuthnott. In the kirkyard are a great many ancient
gravestones. The former manse near by is now dower-house for the
estate.

Arbuthnott House is fully as interesting as the church. It is one of
those buildings which has grown steadily with the generations, so
that the overall impression is not of any one or two periods. There
has been a house on the strong defensive site for 800 years, but no
work earlier than the 15th century remains visible. Hugh Arbuthnott
built a typical square keep here in 1420, and his grandson completed
it as a courtyard castle with curtain-walls, flanking-towers and lean-
to buildings by the end of that century. Each generation added to or
renewed, but the great mass of the present mansion is late 17th
century, with a Georgian centre to the front. However, the courtyard itself, and parts of the enclosing walls and flanking-towers,
remain at the back, sloping down the steep defensive peninsula

between the ravines of two burns. Here, at the extreme north-east corner, is the most entire portion of early work, a late 16th century flanking-tower with crowstepped gables, slit windows, and a very unusual pair of shot-holes under one window, kidney-shaped. The range immediately to the west is a century older, but its roof-level has been altered and original aspect destroyed. It is vaulted, and there are external stone slop-drain spouts from the kitchen premises. The foundations of the keep remain in the lower storeys of the other, south side of the courtyard, now incorporated in later work. The walls here are thick and the original windows have been small; and there is a wide-arched fireplace and oven.

There is no space here to describe the excellences of the great house, with its many features of panelling, fine 17th century plaster ceilings, stairways, portraits, arms and armour. The mansion is open to the public at specified times, and should be visited. Some indication of the antiquity of the family can be gauged when it is realised that Sir Robert, who was created 1st Viscount in 1644, was 14th in descent; and that the present Viscount is the 16th. Nor is this the whole story, for the first Swinton came from Berwickshire to marry the Oliphant heiress, the Oliphants having been here from the 11th century.

Near the mansion, to the north, the ravine is crossed by a handsome bridge of 1821. This drive leads up to the village of Arbuthnott, or hamlet, which is not at the kirkton but on higher ground to the north.

Two miles down the same deep, winding valley of the Bervie Water stands the castle of Allardyce, now a farmhouse, another highly interesting and picturesque L-planned fortalice, which gives the impression of belonging all to one period, the late 16th century; but each of the wings has, in fact, been extended a century later. The tall whitewashed building is most notable for the extraordinary intricacy and prominence of its label corbelling supporting the stair-turret in the re-entrant angle, the upper portion of which forms a most pleasing turreted watch-chamber. A pend is slapped through the main-block basement near by, into the courtyard, the basement being vaulted. The name has been spelt variously as Aberdash, Allerdas, Alrethes and Ardes, the family thereof being known as Allardyce of that Ilk. The last Allardyce heiress carried the property to her husband, Barclay of Urie, at the end of the 18th century; and the last of the line was Captain Barclay-Allardyce, the famous pedestrian, who died in 1854.

The other ancient estate in the parish is Kair, four miles to the west, where for long a family named Sibbald were lairds. The mansion here is comparatively modern—of 1820. Near by is the site of a Roman camp. The farms surrounding have rather amusing names—Oldcake, Deep, Alpitty and Knap of Lawhardie. On Craighead farm, a mile north of Allardyce, there are two standing-stones on the high ground, one triangular amongst scattered pines on the ridge, and the other eight feet broad by six high, in the middle of a field near by. Burial-cairns crown eminences at Montgoldrum and Hillhead, north of Arbuthnott House. In the Hog's Hole, a former peat-bog, were found in the 19th century the remains of prehistoric red deer with enormous antlers; also stone axes and the metal head of a battleaxe.

Banchory. The burgh of Banchory, "capital of Lower Deeside", is situated 18 miles west of Aberdeen, but in Kincardineshire, and is a deservedly well-known holiday resort and tourist centre. Its parish is known as Banchory-Ternan, to distinguish it from Banchory-Devenick 14 miles to the east, and is large—of 20,000 acres—on both sides of Dee, picturesque, heavily wooded and with much high ground, the three summits of the Hill of Fare being included, at 1500 feet.

The little town, population 2000, stands where the River Feugh comes in from the south-west to join Dee, at a hub of roads, with the A943, the B974 and the A980 joining the A93 North Deeside highway. So Banchory's High Street is busy with traffic. It is the shopping-centre for a large area, and very adequately supplied. Most of its development has been on the higher ground to the north of the highway, where the district of Arbeadie was feud out in the early 19th century. Many are the hotels, guest-houses and the like. The clean silvery granite masonry is an asset as are the trees everywhere—though not in the main street. Most of Deeside is heavily wooded, but the Banchory area particularly so—indeed the pine-woods are one of the magnets which draw large numbers of visitors.

Despite the 19th century development—and it is still expanding—Banchory is an old place. St. Ternan, a Celtic missionary of noble Mearns stock, is thought to have founded a religious colony here in the mid-5th century; his bell, known as the Ronnecht Bell, is famed, and was unearthed during road-making. By 1324 a charter describes Banchory as a burgh of barony under the laird of Leys. The mercat cross of this stood near the present East Church, but has been removed to the wooded Burnett Park, west of the town. It is a simple, tall octagonal shaft, seven feet high, minus a finial.

The oldest portion of the town was the kirkton at the east end, where the kirkyard of St. Ternan's lies, near the riverside, though the old church is now gone. An unusual two-storeyed circular mort-house, to foil body-snatchers, stands in the yard and here is the old bell of the former kirk, Dutch-cast and dated 1664. There is many old table-stones, and the Douglas aisle of 1775. This was the year when the pre-Reformation church was rebuilt; then in 1824 it was removed across the road, to become the present East Church. The former manse is now a board-residence and built into its roadside walling is an ancient, small, Pictish wheel-cross stone 18 inches by 12. Built in at the other side of the road are slabs from a stone cist found near by.

Banchory Academy is a senior secondary school for the entire

Deeside district, in very modern and extensive premises. The Burnett Arms Hotel, on the main street, is an attractive old gabled hostelry. There is also an old Douglas Arms, somewhat smaller, named for a rival lairdly house. Banchory Lodge itself is now a large hotel in fine grounds near the river, offering fishing, shooting and first-class accommodation. Tor-na-Coille, another large mansion-hotel in eight acres to the west, adds riding and ski-ing to its lures. There are many others. The town has three parks—the Burnett aforementioned, most pleasing amongst birch-woods above the road to the west; nearer the town the handsome War Memorial Park and monument; and close to the town centre the old Bellfield Park and the King George Fifth Memorial Field, with recreational facilities. A plaque to the famous Scottish violinist J. Scott Skinner, a native here, adorns the wall of a High Street house. The Glen o' Dee Hospital, a large convalescent establishment for Aberdeen Infirmary, stands on high ground behind the town. At Banchory is a highly unusual local industry, a lavender-farm and lavender-water distillery and factory, Dee Lavender being renowned. Visitors are welcomed.

The parish and surroundings of Banchory are full of interest and attraction. Pride of place should probably be allotted to Crathes Castle and gardens, the great Burnett establishment completed in 1596, and one of the finest castles in the land. The Burnetts are still there, although the building is now gifted to the nation and in the care of the National Trust for Scotland. It lies over two miles east of Banchory in a large wooded estate under the Hill of Fare, surrounded by magnificent gardens which are a feature in themselves. The Burnetts, in the person of Alexander Burnard, were granted these lands by the Bruce in 1323, so they have had a long innings. Their original castle is thought to have stood on an artificial island in the former Loch of Leys, which lay on the higher ground to the north of Banchory, and though quite drained is commemorated by such names as Lochton of Leys and Lochhead. No signs of this early building remain. The present great house is substantially a massive six-storeyed tower of the 16th century, oblong, with small wing, enhanced with angle-turrets, circular and squared, and with an unusual stair-turret projecting from a gable, squared off to form a clock-tower and crenellated look-out platform. There is an interesting machicolated projection-cum-dormer-window sited high above the old doorway in the re-entrant angle, for the casting-down of missiles upon unwelcome visitors. A disastrous fire fairly recently destroyed a later wing, but happily the main tower was not affected. Amongst the precious relics is the Horn of Leys, of jewelled ivory, said to have been presented by Robert Bruce. The Burnetts, needless to say, have taken prominent part in Scots history.

At the western entrance to the estate, near Mill of Crathes, is a concentration of bridges, road and rail; and not very readily discovered amongst these is an old packhorse bridge, humped, with a single arch. In the cottage garden of Milton, closer to the Dee, lying loose and giving the appearance of neglect, is a small ancient Celtic wheel-cross stone, which should be preserved. There is rumour of another here somewhere.

North of Lochton of Leys is the great Hill of Fare, a multi-summit range with wooded slopes. Here, in 1562, was fought the famous Battle of Corrichie, when Mary Queen of Scots, at the urging of her half-brother Moray, made her only expedition into northern Scotland to bring down the power of the Gordons. At this great contest fell the Gordon chief, the 4th Earl of Huntly, dying of apoplexy in his armour; his dashing son, Sir John Gordon of Findlater, self-styled suitor of the queen, was executed in Mary's presence at Aberdeen. The queen watched the battle from a natural granite seat, still known as the Queen's Chair, on the hillside; and her Well is not far off. It was indicative of the enormous power of the Gordons that the national power had to be mobilised to reduce it. A monument commemorates the battle, a tall monolith at the roadside on the B977.

On the hill's southern slopes are two interesting buildings. Raemoir, a former Innes estate, lies two miles north of Banchory, the mansion now a hotel. Adjoining is a fine example of a type of laird's-house found only in the North-East, the hall-house, not fortified like a castle, and dating from just after the fortified period, late 17th century. Raemoir is particularly pleasing and well preserved, still being used as accommodation for the hotel, an E-planned gabled building, modest but delightful. The other house dates, strangely enough, from the same period, but is vastly different in character. This is Cluny Crichton Castle, standing on a spur of hillside above the A980, a mile to the west, in a field. It is a very late example of fortified house, of 1666, L-planned with a square stairtower in the re-entrant, now ruinous but with the main features surviving. There are two empty panel-spaces above the doorway and two gunloops guarding it, but no basement vaulting and the walling comparatively thin. The prospects are wide and beautiful. The castle was built by George Crichton of Cluny, a cadet of Frendraught who was married to the daughter of Sir Robert Douglas of Tillquhillie near by, a Royalist commander. Crichton's grandson left no issue when he died and the estate passed to the Douglases.

Tillquhillie lies nearly five miles to the south in this large parish, in the hillsides over the Dee. It is no longer a residence of the Douglases, who live in a modern mansion on the lower ground. Used only for farm purposes, which is a pity, it is an excellent and imposing example of the tall though fairly plain Scots fortalice of the late 16th century, on the Z-plan. It is four storeys in height, with rounded angles corbelled out to the square to permit gabled roofing. The doorway, with heraldry over, is in a circular tower in the re-entrant, and the walls are liberally supplied with shot-holes, the basement being vaulted. Tillquhillie was Church land, coming to David Douglas, a son of Lochleven, after the Reformation shake-up; his son John built the castle in 1576. Here his prominent but notorious kinsman, Douglas, the Regent Morton, hid incognito for some time as James the Grieve when things got too hot for him elsewhere.

This southern part of the parish is reached by two bridges from Banchory, over Dee and Feuch. The latter is well known as an attraction, an 18th century three-arched bridge with recesses for walkers, high and narrow above the rapids of the rushing rock-lined torrent. Alongside is now the rather ugly metal footbridge for the many visitors who come to admire the falls and watch for the leaping salmon. On the Banchory side is an old whitewashed tollhouse, prettily placed. All this area is richly forested. A B-road, 974, strikes south-west into the hills up Feuchside, but this is described under Strachan. Near the mouth of it is the wooded hill called Scolty (982 feet) with a monument on top to commemorate General William Burnett of Banchory Lodge, a Napoleonic Wars' celebrity. The views from here are magnificent. The hilly area to the south-east is rich in archaeological remains. At West Mulloch, on high ground a mile south of Tillquhillie, there is a fine cairn of five uprights and smaller stones in an inner circle. Another similar one stands on Eslie farm to the south-west, and in the planted forest on Mulloch Hill, near Garrol, and only 100 yards from the road and gate, is a handsome three-ringed stone-circle of eight uprights and one recumbent, picturesque amongst the trees, called Nine Stanes, well worth visiting amongst the heather and pine-clad hills and valleys.

West of Banchory there is also much of interest. The fine 18-hole golf course with its very modern club-house, stretches along the Dee on the north bank, the scenery lovely. At the hamlet of Invercannie, houses old and new, is an ancient two-arched bridge and a large modern water-works. The embankments of Cairnton are readily seen from the road, a proto-historic fort or encampment, sometimes said to be Roman but more probably Pictish. The beech avenue leading to Cairnton House is very fine, as indeed is all the magnificent woodland. In this area are the estates of Inchmarlo, Inverey and Glassel. Inverey used to belong to a friend of Sir Walter Scott, called Skene; and in a room here part of *Marmion* is reputed to have been written. Glassel House gardens are open to the public at stated times.

Banchory, then, has a great deal to offer the discerning visitor, making an excellent centre for touring much farther afield. Banchory Agricultural Show is held each July; and the Scottish Music Festival is organised by the Banchory Strathspey and Reel Society each April. Caravan-sites are available at the Recreation grounds, Banchory Lodge, and the Silver Ladies up Feuchside. The Nature Conservancy has a research centre here.

Banchory-Devenick and Cults. Place-names can be very confusing, and this lower Deeside parish is not to be confused with the mid-Deeside burgh of Banchory Ternan, much better known; and this Cults, the part of the parish north of Dee and almost a suburb of Aberdeen, is not to be confused with Cults in Fife. It is a fairly large parish of 10,000 acres, with no real village, east of Maryculter and west of Nigg. It has a high bare moorland area of small farms to the south declining to a lower belt, wooded, with estates, at the riverside, and a highly populous area across the Dee flanking the A93 North Deeside road, rising to more high ground beyond.

The parish church stands at the riverside on the South Deeside road, the A943, almost opposite Cults, dating from 1822 and typically plain but attractively set, on the site of an earlier building dedicated to St. Devenick who was buried here. The bell dates from 1597. There are many old table-stones in the kirkyard, and mort-safes to foil body-snatchers. The former Free church, now known as St. Devenick's on the Hill, stands on higher ground not far away, also with a kirkyard, with modern extension, at a picturesque tree-clad burnside. It is not now used for worship. The graveyard contains the mausoleum of the Stewarts of Banchory House.

Banchory-Devenick is an ancient estate. The Durwards had a motte-and-bailey castle here, its site still pointed out in the wooded policies. It passed to the Meldrums, the Gordons and others, till in 1743 it was bought by Alexander Thomson, advocate, whose descendant is the present Mrs. Stewart here. In 1872 the Thomsons sold to John Stewart, comb-manufacturer, whose son Sir David was provost of Aberdeen, and whose great-grandson is the present laird. The mansion is fairly modern, and Prince Albert stayed in it in 1859. Built into the walling of the large walled garden are certain Pictish stones, one or more of which may have come from near Dunnottar. One shows a fish, another a crescent with triangle, and another the double-disc and Z-rod. There is also one in the rockery beside the house with mirror-and-comb symbols.

The old and famous Bridge of Dee is in this parish, although now to all intents swallowed up in Aberdeen. Considerably farther upstream, above the church, is the almost as well-known suspension bridge of St. Devenick's, known locally as The Shakin' Briggie, its length 305 feet. Not far away is the old estate of Ardoe, its mansion now a hotel.

To cross the river by car it is necessary to go three miles farther, to the Maryculter area, and over to Milltimber, then to turn east again. Milltimber is in Peterculter parish of Aberdeenshire, but is now more or less a high-class city residential suburb—as indeed are Murtle and Bieldside also, flanking this A93 highway en route to Cults. Here are the great Tor na Dee Hospital, formerly a famous sanatorium and before that a hydropathic establishment; and the Rudolf Steiner School. Murtle was once an old barony, with a handsome Grecian mansion of the Gordons down near the river. The Murtle Burn flows down through a tree-lined den, its old meal-mill in process of conversion into a hotel.

Cults is now wholly suburban along the roadside, with shopping-area and many fine villas. But climb a little way to the north, and it is remarkable how rural and very attractive the district remains, with Scots pines and birch-scrub and even heather growing less than a mile from the busy streets. There is also plantation forestry. Cults has a wooded den dropping steeply to the riverside haughs. There are rose-nurseries here, and the Sunnyside establishment breeds Palomino ponies. Two miles north of the river, and 400 feet higher, the Countesswells estate remains secluded amongst woodlands, with a modest but attractive late 17th century mansion with central gablet and first-floor entrance. This high area used to be notable for its peat-mosses, now drained and planted. The woodland estate of Dalhebity lies to the south, and at Hillhead, to the south of this and not far above the west end of Cults, is an ancient burial-cairn hidden amongst whins and scattered trees.

Benholm and Johnshaven. Benholm is one of the coastal parishes lying between Montrose and Stonehaven, on the rocky seaboard of Kincardine, a small parish of 5500 acres, with the large village of Johnshaven but little else in the way of a community.

The kirkton stands on the brink of a very attractive den, a quarter-mile west of the main road (A92), and is altogether most picturesque, with a mill and dam deep in the valley-floor, and the parish church and large whitewashed manse above in old trees. The church replaces a pre-Reformation chapel taken down in 1832, and is plain but quite pleasing. The kirkyard is interesting, with a great many old stones, some of the 17th century, and one much earlier, a man-shaped grave-slab with crude crucifixion scene and skull. In the manse garden, steeply below, is a slender, tall, conical-roofed doocot. There is a school close by, all on the lip of the wooded ravine. Also here is the large seed-potato warehouse establishment of Nether Benholm, proudly displaying its Royal Appointment coat-of-arms, an unlikely item to come across in such a place.

Almost a mile to the north, at another den, is Benholm Castle—now ruinous—an imposing keep of the 15th century in a strong position, square on plan rising four storeys to a crenellated parapet with open rounds, with the stairhead ending in a gabled caphouse and watch-chamber of somewhat later date. The basement is vaulted, and the hall on the first floor has a great fireplace and windows with typical stone seats. Attached is a more modern mansion now more ruinous than the castle. Benholm was a seat of the Keiths, kin to the Earls Marischal, of near-by Dunnottar Castle, although said to have been built by an Ogilvie. In 1618 James Keith of Benholm, with his father George, Earl Marischal, had to find caution before the Privy Council for inciting one Andro Barclay and others to assault Robert Falconer. Five years later Benholm was the scene of a famous theft of jewellery by the earl's widowed countess.

There is a farm of Stone of Benholm almost as far *south* of the kirkton, but no standing- or symbol-stone remains. There is however a single standing-stone at Boghead, on a green hillside a farther mile southwards; and there are burial-cairns on Kenshot and Philla Hills at the north-west boundary of the parish.

On the main road a mile south of the kirkton is Brotherton. This was an ancient estate, seat of a family of that Ilk, with a castle which

318

is replaced by a large 19th century Scottish Baronial mansion and is now the well-known Lathallan School. It is down below the road near the shore where Brotherton Den cuts its way through the raised beach. This is a notable area for dens.

Immediately south of Brotherton is Johnshaven, a typical large fishing-village strung out in terraces for fully a mile along the rocky coast, rather attractive, with its houses and cottages dotted down haphazard as the knobbly terrain allows, to give odd little squares, lanes and groupings. The harbour is good and maintained, used still for fishing—though not on the scale of the 1880s when there were 60 boats. Salmon-netting and lobster-fishing and processing are carried out. There is a former Free church. In mid-village is a peculiar round tower reputed to have been a malt-store in the days when there was brewing established here—although it is an odd shape and size for this. There was once a sail-factory also. A coast-guard look-out station still stands guard to the south. Johnshaven was notorious in the old days for the activities of the press gangs. At the north end is a caravan-site, beside the rock-ribbed beach, where a rough track leads along the coast to the tiny isolated group of houses called Haughs of Benholm at the mouth of the Benholm Den.

Johnshaven has a distinct resemblance to neighbouring Gourdon, three miles to the north in Bervie parish.

Dunnottar. Dunnottar is a famous name in Scotland; firstly on account of its great ruined castle, centre of so many stirring scenes; and secondly because of its links with the long lost Scots Regalia. But it is also a parish of some 8000 acres, with some splendid cliff scenery; it contains the oldest part of the burgh of Stonehaven; and comprises some typical Mearns countryside.

The castle, so well known in picture if not in fact, magnificently crowns a huge isolated stack of rock jutting into the sea about a mile south of Stonehaven. Separated from the mainland by a deep chasm, it covers an area of over four acres, with a number of separate buildings, its sheer precipices acting as a curtain-wall to enclose them. Strangely enough, perhaps the oldest of these was ecclesiastical, not military, for here was once the parish church of the district, with its graveyard which still survives. It must have co-existed with the castle, for there were fortifications here from a very early period, even from Pictish times. This church was responsible for a considerable furore in 1394. Bruce had given these lands to his supporter Keith, the Knight Marischal. And in that year his successor, Sir William Keith, seems to have built further fortifications on the consecrated ground—by which he offended the Church Militant sufficiently to be excommunicated. The excommunication was in due course lifted by the Pope, from Rome, on payment of recompense and agreement to build a new kirk in a more convenient part of the parish.

The present extensive remains belong to various periods, with the oldest portion the tall and massive keep of the early 15th century, of five storeys with parapet and walk. The gatehouse is particularly interesting. Known as Benholm's Lodging, it is approached by a steep narrow path and defended by no fewer than three tiers of wide gunloops, the gateway of five and a half feet being the only other aperture in a solid wall of masonry 35 feet high, barring a deep cleft in the rock. How horses got up here is a mystery—but there are stable ranges amongst the many buildings, barracks and subsidiary accommodation. There is an enormous well. The castle was restored by Viscount Cowdray, of Dunecht.

The history of Dunnottar would fill volumes. It was the ancient capital of the Mearns. Bruidhe, king of the Northern Picts laid siege to it in 681. King Donald was slain here by the Danes in 900. Edward I put a garrison in it in 1296, and Wallace retook it allegedly with the slaying of 4000 Englishmen—which even for Wallace seems a trifle much. Edward III had it back again in 1334. Montrose besieged it in turn, but could not take it, in 1645. In 1650 the 7th Keith, Earl Marischal entertained Charles II here. It was only the following year that Cromwell overran Scotland and the regalia, crown, sceptre and sword of state, were deposited here for safe keeping—indicative of the reputation of the place. But Cromwell had plenty of time, and managed to starve out the garrison. Before that, however, the famous rescue of the regalia took place, more fully described under Kinneff, to which place it was taken by the minister's wife thereof. From 1685 Dunnottar was shamefully used as a state prison for Covenanters who offended the new Episcopal government. Here 167 men and women were barbarously confined in a small cell, still known as the Whigs' Vault, where nine died. In desperation, 25 managed to get out of a narrow window to attempt the descent of the beetling cliff. Two fell to their deaths, and the others, recaptured, were terribly tortured by Keith of Whiterigs, the governor—all in the name of religion.

An echo of this ghastly deed resounds at the present parish churchyard of Dunnottar, two miles to the west in the Carron valley, where Sir William Keith had set up St. Bridget's Church to replace that on the rock. Here is a simple gravestone on which are inscribed the names of nine prisoners who died in that shocking affair. It is interesting to note that when Sir Walter Scott visited here in 1793 the sight of one Robert Paterson cleaning the memorial gave him the idea and character of *Old Mortality*.

The present parish church is large and internally attractive. Rebuildings of the original took place in 1593, 1782 and in modern times. Inside, on the vestibule's east wall, is a stone commemorating the preservation of the regalia, dated 1663. On the communion-table is a large and antique hourglass for timing the sermon, from the older church. There are many old gravestones in the kirkyard. Separate from the church stands the handsome Marischal aisle, restored by Aberdeen University in 1913, in memory of the 5th Earl Marischal who founded Marischal College there. The single-storeyed crowstepped-gabled building dates from 1582, that date, with an empty panel-space appearing over the moulded doorway, plus a shield with the Keith arms and initials *G.K.* Inside there are a number of relics, including heraldic stones and old fonts.

Still another location in the parish has links with the regalia. The scanty remains of the Old House of Barras stand some four miles to the south. This was the home of Sir George Ogilvy, son of Ogilvy of Lumgair near by, who was Dunnottar's governor during Cromwell's siege. For his part in the rescue of the regalia, Charles II created him baronet of Barras. When the old garden wall was removed some time ago, the sword-belt of the sword of state was found beneath—evidently left behind in the dramatic rescue, buried here for security and forgotten. Barras is now a farm.

Near by, to the north, is the farm of Law of Lumgair, with Loch of Lumgair now little more than a bog. On the summit of the law, amongst rioting brambles is what is called a Pictish kiln; some prefer to identify it as the remains of a broch. It may well be a souterrain. Excavation is called for.

The restored castle of Fiddes lies two miles west of Barras, over the ridge; a quite delightful L-shaped fortalice of the 16th century, vaulted, with an unusual stair-tower ending in an open parapeted roof, angle-turrets and steep gables. There are a number of other unusual features. Fiddes was an Arbuthnott house, and we read that Sir Robert Arbuthnott of that Ilk recovered the lands of Fiddes in the late 15th century after they had been alienated for 200 years. In 1654 Andrew, second son of another Sir Robert, is designated as of Fiddes, and is said to "have died in the flower of his age of that disease his father died, and in likelihood had propagated in him". He had, however, many children, and his second son sold Fiddes. It was lovingly restored comparatively recently from a derelict state.

A mile north of Fiddes, on the other side of the A92, is the farm of Clochnahill. From here Robert Burns' father, William Burness, left for the south in the mid-18th century, to settle in Ayrshire. The Burness or Burnhouse family had lived in the Mearns for some time, but are thought originally to have come from Taynuilt in Argyll. *Tigh-an-allt* means House on the Burn. A memorial cairn is erected at the side of the main road here, gifted by an American descendant, William Coull Anderson, of Florida.

Back on the coast four miles to the east is the deserted cliff-top fishing-village of Crawton, now only a farm, with a stony beach far below, highly inconvenient for the fishermen. Adjoining is the narrow deep inlet of Trollachy, with a large burn falling into it over the cliffhead in dramatic fashion. This is altogether a dramatic, tortured and caverned coast, of course. Near by, the highest portion of the cliffs is called Fowlsheugh, 200 feet high and a noted haunt of sea-birds. One of the caverns is really a natural arch through a promontory, 150 yards long and wide enough to take a boat.

Durris. Durris is one of those large hilly Deeside parishes which seem to belong rather to Aberdeenshire than to the Mearns.

Although it runs to 15,000 acres, there is no real village, the major part being heather hills or the planted woodlands of Durris Forest. There is however a fairly fertile lowland strip along the riverside to the north.

Durris Castle was famous in history as a large and important stronghold, the seat of the Frasers, part of the great Comyn lands granted by Bruce to his supporter and brother-in-law Sir Alexander Fraser, high chamberlain. The Frasers retained possession until an heiress carried the lands out of the family in the late 17th century, meantime having made a large impact on the Scottish scene. The original castle of the Comyns, no doubt of the clay-covered timber variety, crowned a ditched motte or earthen mound near the riverside, still called the Castle Hill, just east of the kirkton. But the Frasers erected a great stone-built quadrangular fortalice with flanking-towers, on higher ground a mile to the east, where now stands Durris House. This in turn has gone, save for the extraordinary range of underground vaults, large and intercommunicating, such as the author has seen nowhere else. Above these rises the simple L-shaped 17th century laird's-house tower, with large modern mansion attached. The tower is unusual, and may once have boasted a parapet-walk. It has a very rudimentary angle-turret and a gabled and crowstepped watch-tower, but there have been great alterations—partly, no doubt, as a result of Montrose's burning of the castle in 1645, the Frasers being strong for the Covenant. The estate formerly comprehended the entire parish.

The parish church stands down near the riverside, below the South Deeside road (A943) and the Kirkton hamlet, reached by a picturesque wooded lane flanking the ravine of the Burn of Sheoch. The church is large and plain, dating from 1822, standing in an attractively-sited extensive kirkyard amongst old trees, its former manse near by no less than a mansion. Beside the church stand the remains of its predecessor, long used as the Durris estate burial-ground. Although much altered and roofless, interesting features survive. The skew-putts of its gables remain, and are dated 1587 on that to the north-west and 1681 to the north-east, with the initials D.A.F. Internally, on the north wall, is a very fine heraldic panel showing the Fraser arms, with the helm notably large and the shield slung slantwise, flanked by the initials T.F., probably of late 16th century date. Another inscribed panel, almost indecipherable, is on the east gable, and a massive iron mort-safe lies within. There are a number of old gravestones. Durris was formerly a chapelry of the Knights Templar.

Just above the small Kirkton is Mill of Durris, prettily situated in the den of the Sheoch Burn, though no longer functioning as a mill. This major burn rises high in the hills in Strachan parish and often runs in high spate. It enters Durris in the Blairdryne area, skirting the northern slopes of Craigmonearn (1245 feet) and its associated summits of Mongour and Craigbeg, where the lofty new television booster-mast soars. This ridge is the boundary with Fetteresso parish and its forests, to the south. In this area is the remotely sited Red Beard's Well, a medicinal spring named after a blackmailing free-booter who allegedly occupied a cave near by. A mile north of Blairdryne is a stone-circle on an eminence above Cairnfaulds farm, with four uprights and an altar-like recumbent. A good example of consumption-dyke for utilising stones cleared from the fields is close by. The small Crossroads hamlet and school lie on the Slug Road, the A957, crossing the hills from Stonehaven to Banchory—the word coming from the Gaelic *slochd*, meaning a throat or pass—a renowned highway. Just west of this Crossroads is the forested hill of Cairnshee, where there is a large burial-cairn.

Durris Forest, now Commission woodlands, covers a vast area of the parish farther east; and in its centre, near the pleasantly-situated former farm of Monthammock, is another stone-circle, hidden in Clune Wood.

Fettercairn, Kincardine and Strathfinella. It comes as a surprise to many who do not know the area to learn that Kincardine is not really an actual town or village or even a hamlet, despite giving its name to a whole county. On the face of it, this should be the county town of Kincardineshire, or the Mearns; but in fact it is no more than the crumbling site of an old castle, not even a farm. Fettercairn is the large village two miles to the south-west; and Strathfinella is a romantic and beautiful glen to the north, at the start of the famous Cairn o' Mount road to Deeside.

Kincardine was never a true town, but rather the associated community of a great royal castle, with burgh of regality status. It stretched westwards from the present farm of Castleton for over half a mile but has long since disappeared. The county seat was removed to Stonehaven in 1600. Kincardine was the victim of pacification and centralisation—for its site was wholly strategic, and when this ceased to matter and royalty preferred more central residence, it declined. At an early date, however, it was highly important, for this Cairn o' Mount pass was the key to the North-East. Kincardine Castle itself was only the successor of the earlier Pictish fortress now called Green Castle, then known as Dunfothir, or Fotherdun—a name perpetuated in Fordoun and moved four miles to the north-east. The earthworks of Dunfothir are still sited on an abrupt cliff in the jaws of Glen Sough, the western approach to Strathfinella, opposite Goskiehill farm. The Annals of Ulster record sieges of Dunfothir in 681 and 694, the Northumbrians assailing the Picts. But in stone-castle-building days it was found more convenient to build a large palace-type fortress a mile to the south-east at *Ceann-chortean*, the end of the cultivated land, Kincardine. It is not quite clear just when the move was made. Here it was that Kenneth II, eleventh in order from Kenneth MacAlpin, uniter of Picts and Scots, was murdered in 994, allegedly by Finella, daughter of the Mormaor of Angus and wife of the Mormaor of the Mearns, over the death of her son Cruthlint. Finella gave her name to the strath and also to the den on the coast, near St. Cyrus, where she was eventually hunted down and slain. The royal castle of Kincardine rose on a mound in the lower ground, and appears to have been a typical courtyard-type castle, not earlier than the 12th or 13th century. There are still extensive foundations and remains of masonry and earthworks, 134 feet square, with round gatehouse-towers projecting to the south, plus moat and former drawbridge. It is badly neglected, and for such an important place, shamefully. The fields around it still bear names like King's Park, Chancellor's Park, Dean's, Lorimer's, Archer's and Palfreyman's crofts—the only relics of a large and important community. The Cross of the Regality is now at Fettercairn. No history of Kincardine Castle is possible here. It seems to have been abandoned in the 16th century, Mary Queen of Scots being the last monarch to use it, on her expedition to demolish the power of Gordon. There is the site of a chapel dedicated to St. Catherine of Sienna near by.

Fettercairn is a parish, large village and former burgh of barony at a road-junction on the northern edge of the Howe, the name being merely a hardening of Fother-cairn. Like Edzell in Angus, not far away, it is now entered through a red-stone archway from the south, this one commemorating Queen Victoria's visit in 1861. Near by there is a fairly large hotel, the Ramsay Arms, where the queen stayed the night incognito—and wrote about it in her journal. Fettercairn has a wide central square, in which rises the mercat cross from Kincardine, its octagonal shaft having received a finial and sundial of 1670, with the Earl of Middleton's coronet and initials. Also marked thereon is the standard ell measurement. The parish church, quite large and with a steeple, stands on a slight mound to the east and dates from 1864, but has a 16th century vault. There are many old tombstones in the kirkyard. The school is very modern and bright. To the north-west, at Nethermill, is the Fettercairn Distillery, founded 1824.

Fettercairn House lies in a large estate to the east, its mansion, long, low and attractive, built in 1666 with later additions, nothing castellated. It is the seat of Lord Clifton, an English peerage, the lands having been heired in the female line from the Stuart-Forbes baronets. They had bought them in 1777, after the forfeiture of the 2nd Earl of Middleton, son of the notorious Civil Wars general (1610–73) the Middletons having held them for five centuries.

An equal distance on the other side of Fettercairn is Balbegno Castle, a most interesting example of 16th century fortalice, with later farmhouse attached, the old part now practically unused. It is an unusual version of the L-plan, tall and with a former partial parapet and open rounds, these built up in the late 16th century to form a gabled watch-chamber with oversailing roofs. Both basement and Great Hall on first floor are vaulted, the latter with splendid rib-vaulting, painted in tempera with the heraldry of many of Scotland's principal families. There is much external carved heraldry also; and the watch-chamber has panels inscribed *I.WOD* and *E.*

IRVEIN 1569. There is a gabled doocot. Balbegno was granted by James IV in 1498 to Andrew Wood of Over Blairton, the family having been hereditary constables of Kincardine Castle. Five generations of Woods followed, and then Balbegno was sold to the Middletons. In 1624 David Wood was ordered by the Privy Council not to molest William Wishart, minister of Fettercairn; however in the same breath they ordered William Wishart not to molest David Wood! The last Wood laird made a compact with Earl Middleton that whoever died first would communicate to the survivor something of what conditions were like where he went. Wood fell in battle, and in due course appeared to captured Middleton in the Tower of London. But his description of the hereafter lacks precision:

> *Plumashes above, Gramashes below,*
> *It's no wonder to see how the world doth go!*

Almost across the road from Balbegno is the vitrified fort of Green Cairn, on an eminence, with inner and outer ramparts and ditch, sometimes declared to be Finella's stronghold. It is strange to be so near Green Castle.

Strathfinella Hill rises 1358 feet two miles north of Kincardine, and there is a burial-mound near the summit called Smart's Cairn, in woodland. The strath itself, a westwards extension of Drum-tochty Glen, is picturesque. At its head is Loch Sough, a long, narrow and rather attractive stretch of water. Then follows the steep descent of little Glen Sough towards Clattering Bridge, with Glen-sough farm now an experimental station of the Hill Farming Research Organisation. At Clattering Bridge, deep in the gut of the valley, the Cairn o' Mount road strikes off steeply northwards on its exciting way a dozen miles to Strachan and on to Banchory—one of the first roads to get blocked by snow each winter. Its summit, at 1475 feet, is a magnificent viewpoint. Gradients reach one in five and a half. Half-way the road dips sharply to the pleasantly wooded Glen Dye, crossing that Water by an old bridge of 1680. The great Montrose used this route, tough as it is, in his swift campaigns.

South-west of Clattering Bridge is the interesting feature known as the Deer Dyke, a great earthen embankment stretching for miles over the hills, to curve southwards again and enclose a large area as a royal hunting-preserve. The western end of it runs down to low ground again near Fasque, a large estate with a mansion built by the Ramsays of Balmain in 1809, replacing an earlier castle. They had held the property since 1510; but it was bought by Sir John Gladstone in 1828, whose fourth son was the famous William Ewart Gladstone, prime minister. Close to the mansion is the small Episcopal church of Fasque, still used. There is a loch of 20 acres here.

Fetteresso. This very large parish of 27,000 acres contains most of the town of Stonehaven, and also the area of Muchalls, both noted separately. But even deducting these portions, the remainder is full of interest and variety. From the consistently cliff-girt and savage coast it stretches inland over ever-rising ground to the Grampian outliers at over 1000 feet, where the great Fetteresso Forest spreads itself over thousands of acres. So the parish comprises coastal fishing and holiday communities, urban development, agricultural lands, upland pastures and the empty heather hills.

Taking its name from a former important castle, ruined church and tiny hamlet, in the trough of the Carron Water a mile west of Stonehaven, it was part of the vast Comyn lands granted by Robert the Bruce to his friend and brother-in-law Sir Alexander Fraser, high chamberlain of Scotland. His heiress daughter carried the lands to her husband, Sir William Keith, the Knight Marischal, with whose family they remained for long. Dunnottar Castle, just to the south, was their headquarters.

The castle of Fetteresso was largely demolished in recent years and only fragments remain. It was burned by Montrose in 1645, and much altered and extended in the 19th century by the Duffs who had acquired it. The old church is at least entire to the wall-head though long deserted, standing on a mound in its ancient and crowded graveyard. It was dedicated to St. Caran—possibly where the river's name is derived—in 1246, but nothing so old as that survives. A stone in the east gable depicts a rampant lion and engrailed cross, with the initials *I.M.* and *A.?*. An old font is built, oddly, into the west wall, where there is also a built-up doorway dated 1720. The church was curtailed in length at that period, but even so is 94 feet long by only 19 wide. Internally there is a large heraldic panel to the Fullarton family, dated 1602, with Latin inscription; and also a holy-water stoup. The hamlet of Kirkton of Fetteresso here, is attractive by its riverside. Near by to the east is the grassy, tree-clad mound of Malcolm's Mount, where King Malcolm I (A.D. 942–54) is said to have died. Possibly it was the site of an early royal dun or castle.

The old church's more modern successor stands within the burgh of Stonehaven, on the high ground, a large and interesting building of unusual shape, said to have been built in the same style as Colonel Duff's castle enlargement, a weird architectural hybrid, but attractive. Internally it is quite fine, with a horseshoe-shaped gallery and seating for 1100. There are many interesting features. The back of the minister's chair, behind the communion-table, came from the pulpit of the early church, a panel with the initials *M.I.M.* and *P.F.* and the date 1682. There are communion-plates and -beakers of pewter dated 1768, and an ancient Breeches Bible of 1596—so called because in the third chapter of Genesis, Adam and Eve are said to have made themselves *breeches* of fig-leaves instead of the more usual aprons. There is also a collection of communion-tokens two of which are of brass and said to be almost unique. Recently a notable addition has been made to the church complex, consisting of a fine hall with concert facilities, a library and offices,

Dunnottar Castle, former seat of the Keiths, Earls Marischal

Glenbervie. Drumlithie bell-tower

made possible by a generous bequest and the efforts of the congregation. The new structure blends in very well with the odd architecture of the parent building.

Not much more than a mile to the north-east, on the coast, are the
ruined church of St. Mary of the Storms, at Cowie, the site of the
former royal burgh of Cowie, and the present-day Stonehaven
suburb of that name. But these are better dealt with under Stonehaven.

The Cowie Water, larger than the Carron, comes in near by, and
less than two miles up this wider valley is the former great estate of
Ury, latterly the seat of the Bairds, Viscounts Stonehaven, but from
1647 the lairdship of the prominent family of Barclay who had been
settled in the Mearns from the 12th century and were of the same
stock as the Berkeleys of England. Barclay of Ury, well known for
his *Apology for the Quakers*, was laird here, dying in 1690. The
family burial-ground, on a timber-covered mound half a mile north
of the derelict mansion-house, is named The Houff, a name also
used for the Old Town burial-ground at Dundee. Houff means
simply a place, or haunt, and most often refers to a public-house. Its
use here has its own wry humour. The Hays of Erroll had Ury
before the Barclays.

Still in the Cowie Water valley, but now high amongst the
Fetteresso Forest foothills, and quite hard to find, is the old mansion
of Mergie, known locally as the Stanehoose o' Mergie, standing
picturesquely in woodland under the Hill of Three Stones. This
little-known laird's-house of the 17th century, with possibly a still
earlier nucleus, was originally the mansion of a large estate. In
1590 the 10th Earl of Angus conveyed to his youngest son, Robert
Douglas, the Stonehouse of Mergie with the fortalice thereof. The
building is typically tall and fairly plain, with a stair-turret projecting above first-floor level in the centre of the north front. The roof
has been lowered.

Five miles to the north-east, still on high ground towards the
middle of the parish, amongst a pleasant welter of small rolling hills
and relics of the Caledonian Forest, is an area which ought to be
very well known indeed—and which in many another country
would be a renowned tourist attraction. This is Raedykes, covering
an area of something over a square mile, a splendid complex of prehistoric and Roman remains, totally unexploited, neglected on hill-
farming land, yet comparatively accessible. There are a large
Roman camp, early burial ring-cairns and stone-circles, and a
notable standing stone with Ogham characters.

The Roman camp is easternmost, on the farm of Broomhill,
unusually shaped with 400-yard ramparts and ditches, that to the
north particularly well preserved, the ditch lined with masonry. At
the north-east angle is the remains of a watch-tower, required here
to complete an otherwise magnificent field of view. In the centre, at
the highest point, is a cairn, with another outside the camp, to the
north. Tentative excavations at this site some years ago unearthed

Y

relics including Roman swords and a chariot-wheel and axle. There is a wide flat area to the east, suitable for games and races.

Half a mile west of the camp, across a shallow corrie of the hill on the farm of West Raedykes, is the site of a British camp on an outlying ridge. A most notable feature of this ridge is the series of at least five stone-circles, which are in fact ring-cairns, consisting of upright monoliths plus walls of small stones encircling hollowed burial-chambers, stone-lined. These are all very close together, and highly interesting. Scattered around amongst the gorse and heather are many other sites, all crying aloud for excavation. Still farther to the west, half a mile, on the farm of Nether Auqhuollie and easily seen from the road, is a single monolith about seven feet high with a series of ogham markings at its eastern corner, making it a highly important monument. Most obviously all this area had been a significant settlement in prehistoric times, on a strong defensive site with magnificent prospects. Properly uncovered and displayed it could, and should, be a superlative attraction for visitors from far and near. This is one of the most likely sites for the famous Battle of Mons Graupius.

Eastwards about three miles, on the low heather ridge of Kempstone Hill, are two modest-sized standing-stones about 200 yards apart where local legend has it that, at the Battle of Megray, a casualty ran from one to the other after his head had been cut off. There is an overgrown burial-cairn a short distance to the east. The Battle of Megray, really only a skirmish, took place in 1639 between Montrose, then in command of the Covenanting army of the North-East, and a royalist force under the young Gordon Lord Aboyne, in which Montrose won. The Megray district lies south-east of Kempstone Hill, stretching for over a mile to a deep ravine near the coast just north of Cowie and Stonehaven, threaded by the main A92 highway.

Another burial-cairn, clearly seen, stands just south of a side-road at the farm of Cantlayhills on the north side of Kempstone Hill.

Findon and Portlethen. This north-eastern corner of Kincardineshire lies north of Muchalls and south of the Dee and of the Dee-mouth parish of Nigg, a somewhat bare area of inland moorland flanked by a dramatic cliff-girt coastline, and threaded by the busy A92 highway to Aberdeen. Most of it used to be part of the large parish of Banchory-Devenick, which is described separately, but this area of Portlethen and Findon was constituted a *quod sacra* parish of its own in 1856 and in consequence, took away the main population of Banchory-Devenick, which is concentrated along this coastal area, in the three fishing-villages of Portlethen, Findon and Downies. A more modern community has also grown up about a mile inland, at Portlethen Station, on the edge of the Moss of that name, where there is a small factory and a church, not very beautiful and sitting prominently on a treeless knoll in its crowded graveyard. This started as a private pre-Reformation chapel, became a chapel-of-ease for this part of Banchory-Devenick parish—five miles away from the parish church on Deeside—and rather looked down upon, apparently, by the main congregation, for the parish minister announced in 1785 that its pulpit "was occupied by any strolling preacher who chose to hold forth to the people". Obviously time it grew up to be its own parish.

Portlethen itself is a typical cliff-top fishing-village, now in process of being taken over by Aberdeen commuters, with new houses springing up and old cottages restored. Downies, a mile to the south, is similar though smaller. The coast between is rocky and spectacular, with no road touching it. Half-way along is a small promontory called Through Gang Point, which name speaks for itself.

Findon lies an equal distance to the north and is notable as the original home of Findon or Finnan haddocks. It stands back a little from the cliff-tops, now a mixture of old and new housing, the old cottages having their fish-curing apartments. All these little communities are exceedingly exposed and treeless, though with fine prospects—sufficient to form in the mind of Sir Walter Scott the grim Drumthwacket Moor of his *Legend of Montrose*. Their wind-blown situations however by no means discourage Aberdeen folk who wish to live well away from the city.

Inland a couple of miles, on the high farmlands west of Portlethen Moss, is a remarkable group of stone-circles on outlying portions of the Kincausie estate, in Banchory-Devenick. At Aquhorthies there are two about 500 yards apart, that nearer the farm to the east, with four uprights, two very large, with recumbents describing an extensive circle. Its neighbour to the west is very fine indeed, with no fewer than 12 upright monoliths. Here a stone coffin was once unearthed. To the north, on the farm of Cairnwell, is another circle, lost in plantations; and farther along this same side-road, just below the farm of Auchlee, is a single leaning standing-stone in the field, seven feet high. Still farther north, on the Findon-Maryculter road, near a group of radio-masts and beside the farm of Craighead, is another smaller circle, of four uprights. This monument has been cared for, its circumference wall neatly built up. Together these prehistoric relics make a noteworthy archaeological complex.

Fordoun, Auchenblae and Drumtochty. By any standards, this is an important area in Scotland's story, so close to Old Kincardine, seat of the early kings. Fordoun is a huge parish of 27,000 acres, with Auchenblae its kirkton and largest community; and Drumtochty is a hill, a glen, a large forest and an estate, all lying in the Grampian foothills near the head of the Howe of the Mearns.

At the original Fordoun itself, four miles north-west of Laurencekirk—whence came the 14th century Scottish chronicler John of Fordoun, whose *Scotichronicon* is often quoted—there is now little to be seen. No village is here, and the tall whitewashed late 17th century mansion beside the ancient moat is now a farmhouse. Yet Mary

Queen of Scots erected Fotherdun into "a burgh of barony for ever" in 1554. However, the kirkton, for some reason called Auchenblae, is only a mile to the north in the narrowing deep valley of the Luther Water, a picturesque place very much climbing a hill, and sizeable as Mearns villages go. At the foot of the hill, by the waterside, is an old mill, now disused, and near by a pleasant old bridge, at present closed to traffic. This carried the access to the parish church on top of the high wooded bank, which meantime has to be reached by roundabout means. It is a famous church, the successor of St. Palladius' Chapel, with interesting features and associations. The present building is large, Gothic and not notably attractive, but bright within, dating only from 1829; its small predecessor stands roofless in the kirkyard, neglected, with an arched recess flanked by piscina and aumbry, and a rather gruesome underground vault in the floor, with bones lying around. There is also an ancient wooden coffin, now empty. This was sometimes called the Mother-Church of the Mearns, and it is believed that St. Ternan, a Mearns noble turned missionary, brought St. Palladius' bones and relics here from Ireland and founded this Celtic Church cell in the senior saint's name. Palladius was appointed bishop by Pope Celestine in 430 and seems to have functioned in Ireland. The present chapel dates from 1244 when it was romanised by Bishop de Bernham of St. Andrews, along with St. Vigeans and others. And like St. Vigeans it has a fine Pictish cross-slab, now set into the wall at the back of the present church, rather unusual in having four circular holes marking the cavities of the wheel-cross arms, but with the usual Celtic decoration—horsemen, and double-disc and Z-rod symbols. It is a pity that it is impossible to see the reverse side. In 1893 Alexander Hutcheson, of Broughty Ferry, claimed to have discovered on the edge of this stone an ogham inscription which read either *OEIDERNOIN* or *PIDARNOIN*—unfortunately meaningless to us today. In the kirkyard there is an unusual pillar memorial, with encircling inscription, to George Wishart the Protestant martyr, who was born at near-by Pitarrow in 1513. In the manse is a rather fine old desk left to the parish ministers, and originally installed in the flagship of Admiral Sir James Wishart, of the same family, who died in 1729. And in rough ground and shrubbery below the manse garden is St. Palladius' Well, circular, stone-lined and eight feet deep to the water. The church-bell is said to be the heaviest in the county, weighing half a ton. Opposite the church entrance is a former large old coaching inn, where Robert Burns is said to have passed a night.

Auchenblae village on its steep hill is almost a little town, with postal, banking and other public services, and formerly a flax-spinning mill; also a renowned fair for cattle, sheep and horses called Paldy Fair, after Palladius. This was held on high ground on the side of Herscha Hill, over a mile to the north, now ploughed field, at the mouth of little Glen Farquhar. At a stone-circle on Herscha Hill was found one of the small knobbed stone balls the Picts seem to have been fond of, which is now in the Museum of Antiquities, Edinburgh.

Glen Farquhar is pretty, on a miniature scale, and now thickly wooded, its mansion a School of Forestry. There was a Glenfarquhar Castle, a property of the Falconers of Halkerton, down near the Mains farm, but this has gone. To the north, in the foothills, are the contiguous farms of Tipperty and Chapelton, where the site of a chapel to the Virgin, in a green field, and the spring of St. Mary's Well, now no more than a ditch, may be pointed out. The entire area is very saintly, for south-west of Glenfarquhar the larger glen of Drumtochty opens, with more ecclesiastical links. It is all densely wooded and very picturesque, threaded by the Luther Water—a name to disturb the said saints—running eventually into the romantic Strathfinella—dealt with under Fettercairn. At this Drumtochty end is the modern Episcopal church of St. Palladius, at the roadside but within the estate of Drumtochty Castle, a quite large building, rather ornate for its setting, and still in use, with a few gravestones surrounding. The castle is now a boys' school, a great Gothic castellated pile built on the shelf of the wooded hillside at great expense, the architect being the famous Gillespie Graham. It incorporates the older mansion of Woodstock at the rear, though of this little is evident. Drumtochty was the original name, and to this it has reverted. In the Luther haughland are playing-fields for the pupils. To the west, still in the woodlands, the Friars' Glen and Priest's Wells are said to mark the site of a former Carmelite friary. The double glen of Drumtochty and Finella is a noted beauty spot. Behind, the land rises steeply to the heather hills which flank the Cairn o' Mount pass, quickly reaching 1500 feet and more.

The southern side of Fordoun parish is less interesting scenically, in the flats of the Howe, but here are old and famous estates. Pitarrow, of the Wisharts, or Wisehearts, lies in the open levels a mile south, now a large farm. The old castle was demolished in 1802, but its walled garden still remains, to the north, with bee-skep recesses. Built into the farmhouse walls are three stones dated 1599 and 1679, with heraldry; and there is a square doocot falling into ruin. Johan Wishard, chivaler, of Pitarrow was a signatory of the Ragman Roll in 1296, and the Wisharts took a prominent part in Scotland's story for centuries. Over a mile to the north-east, at the main A94, is the modern roadside village of Fordoun Station, not very interesting or attractive, with an inn. Main-road users, who pass this place and believe that they have seen the Fordoun which has meant so much to Scotland, have my sympathy.

North again is the large disused wartime airfield area; and beyond it, halfway back to Auchenblae, is Monboddo, now a farming estate, with many bulbfields, the mansion abandoned and derelict. This is a pity, for one wing of it is the small simple early 17th century laird's-house of the Irvines and Burnetts, a three-storey oblong block with angle-turrets and dormers, its kitchen provided with an enormous arched fireplace. A heraldic panel of Irvine impaling

Douglas arms, dated 1635, decorates the west gable. This ancient house could and should be saved, with the great Victorian additions removed. The Irvines who presumably built it did not stay long, and it passed to the Burnetts. Here in 1714 was born the famous judge James Burnett, Lord Monboddo, who anticipated the Darwinian theory, believing that men were but monkeys whose tails had worn off by constant sitting. Dr. Johnson visited the judge here in 1773.

Garvock. This is a rural Mearns parish without a village, but of quite large extent (8000 acres) lying on the north-eastern flank of the Howe, between Laurencekirk and Bervie, of mainly high and moorland ground, apt enough to its name, which means rough marshland. The long Hill of Garvock, rising behind Laurencekirk to 914 feet for over four miles, though no spectacular ridge, is the most prominent feature. The area was at one time a hunting-ground of the Earls Marischal.

Oddly enough, Garvock's most renowned claim to fame is the boiling of the Sheriff of Kincardine here, in 1420. After James I, in an outburst of irritation, had declared of John Melville of Glenbervie, the sheriff, "sorrow gin the Sheriff were sodden and supped in broo!"—much as an English king asked "who will rid me of this turbulent priest?"—five local lairds, who no doubt had their own reasons for irritation with Melville, decided that they had royal warrant for making away with him. These were Barclay of Mathers, Arbuthnott of that Ilk, Middleton of that Ilk, Falconer of Halkerton and Graham of Morphie. At a hunting-party on Garvock Hill, they slew the sheriff and then allegedly boiled him in a great cauldron in Brownies' or Fairy's Hollow, thereafter gleefully supping the soup—at least, according to Sir Walter Scott and others, although this may be a picturesque exaggeration. At any rate, the obnoxious sheriff was disposed of—and to some advantage in that, in subsequent penitence, Arbuthnott endowed a chapel at Drumlithie with a priest to say prayers daily—for Melville's soul, not his own! The scene of this happening, known as the Sheriff's Kettle, is pointed out at the junction of Brownieleys farm-road with the minor public road three and a half miles west of Inverbervie, the spot now planted with conifers—though this is certainly not the top of Garvock Hill.

The parish church stands high in an isolated position on the east slopes of the hill two miles east of Laurencekirk, and was built in 1778, replacing a very early pre-Reformation chapel of St. James, which in 1282 the famous Hugh le Blond Arbuthnott granted to the abbey of Arbroath. In 1296, "William, Vicaire del Eglise de Garvock" signed the Ragman Roll at Berwick. There is a stone set at the foot of the north gable, from the earlier church, dated 1678. The building is plain and small, situated on the edge of a whin-clad den, with an older belfry and, unusually, an old clock below. There are many old gravestones in the yard, including an ancient one incised with a simple cross and other weatherworn markings, two feet high, presumably of Celtic Church period. In the garden of the former manse near by is a stone mask, and the finial of a carved cross. A St. James' Well is said to be in the vicinity, but this could not be discovered. An annual St. James' Fair used to be held here—one wonders where the customers came from—and there are the small St. James' Lochs half a mile higher, to the north.

There are sundry burial-cairns on crests of Garvock Hill and elsewhere in the parish, seeming to indicate that, long ago, it was a more populous area. The Tower of Johnston marked on the O.S. map is modern.

Glenbervie, Drumlithie and Mondynes. Although a large parish of 15,000 acres, once called Over Bervie to distinguish it from Inverbervie at the coast, Glenbervie is a very modest one as regards population, for much of the area is hillside and moorland, reaching westwards high into the Grampians. Its kirkton lies seven miles south-west of Stonehaven, off the main road. Drumlithie is its only real village, lying a mile eastwards.

This is pleasant countryside, with wide variations of scenery, from the rolling farmlands of Mondynes to the green valley of the Bervie Water, from the crofting slopes of the Brae of Glenbervie and the forested heights of Fetteresso Forest to the great heather hills beyond. It was long a territory of a branch of the Douglas family, cadets of the Earls of Angus, who gained it by marriage in the late 15th century. One of the long line of Douglas lairds was the compiler of the famous Douglas *Peerage and Baronetage of Scotland*. Before the Douglases, the Melvilles held the barony from the 12th century; and it was one of these, John, Sheriff of Kincardine, who made himself sufficiently unpopular to be boiled and supped as broth by five local lairds— see Garvock. Glenbervie House stands near the kirkton, a mile north of the main A94 road, a large castellated and whitewashed mansion, compound of ancient and modern, retaining much of the early courtyard-type castle including two great round flanking-towers and also a 17th century gable. Unfortunately the pseudo-baronial upper works and roofline have changed the aspect of the house, but there are still gunloops, an iron yett, slit windows and vaulted basements. A square 18th century doocot stands near the roadside.

The parish church is a large Gothic building of 1826, somewhat isolated, at a side-road junction. The old church and kirkyard, with the manse, lie on the wooded banks of the Bervie a little to the south, at the back of the mansion, a sequestered spot. The church is now an ivy-clad ruin, containing the very handsome tomb of the Douglases. There are many old gravestones in the kirkyard, including that, given a canopy in 1968, of the ancestors of Robert Burns, who farmed in this area.

It is rather strange that the large parish's only village should be but a mile away, and yet not at the castle and kirkton. Drumlithie is a most attractive old-world community, quite large, set back from even the side-road, with intriguing lanes and haphazard groupings. Rising above all is an unusual tall and slender circular tower, like the Round Tower of Brechin in miniature. This is a bell-tower, with weathercock, erected in 1770 to control the hours of labour of the weaving community. The bell is still rung at New Year and for the weddings of natives. There is an Episcopal church of 1863, with the bishop's arms and a few gravestones—which is unusual. There is a plain little kirk at the end of the village, also a school. Drumlithie is well worth a visit.

Mondynes is really in Fordoun parish, but being much nearer Glenbervie, is conveniently dealt with here. It was a very important barony once, granted by William the Lion to his new abbey of Arbroath in 1178. Here it was that King Duncan II was slain in 1095 by Malpedir, or MacPender, Mormaor of the Mearns. A knobbly standing-stone on a green mound at the farm of Mains, west of the main road and railway, is alleged to mark the spot where the king fell and there is a local belief that it should be kept whitewashed; but it is called the Court Stane, and is probably an ordinary prehistoric standing-stone used to mark the judicial hill of the barony. There is no village of Mondynes, but the farms of Mains, East, West, Bridge of, Mill of, and Castleton. This last was the site of the barony's castle, Malpedir's seat, of which nothing remains; it was important, on the Knock Hill behind the present attractive 18th century farmhouse. Glenbervie Castle no doubt succeeded it. In the farmhouse garden are two unusual stone troughs, carved with ploughs and the initials *I.L.E.B.*, and *A.M.M.S.* and the date *1672*. Bulb-fields, daffodil and tulip, are a feature hereabouts.

Four miles north of this area are the long green foothill slopes of Brae of Glenbervie, with small croft-type farms giving a Highland aspect, the great planted hills of Fetteresso Forest rising behind, and a small school catering for the community. There are a large number of wells sited on the upper slopes here—Clerks, Downs, Cold, Luncheon, Maxie and Monluth. Their significance escapes me. At Bloomfield farm, near Glenbervie, the novelist Lewis Grassic Gibbon spent most of his boyhood.

Inverbervie and Gourdon. Although only a small town of less than 1000 souls, and hardly an exciting or beautiful community, this is a very ancient royal burgh with an interesting background. It lies where the Bervie Water enters Bervie Bay, between the two headlands of Doolie Ness and Bervie Brow, or Craig David, mid-way between Montrose and Stonehaven, on the A92 coast road, with its own small parish of Bervie behind. Although it claims to have obtained its burgh status from Alexander II, who had his royal castle at Kincardine seven miles inland, it became a *royal* burgh rather by accident. Bruce's young son, David II, was sent to France to escape capture by the English after Bruce's death; eventually returning to Scotland aged 18, in 1341, with his young wife Joanna, his ship was harried by the English fleet and driven out of course by storms, to make landfall here at Bervie Brow—which is why its alternative name is Craig David. In gratitude for his deliverance, and for the hospitality he received at near-by Inverbervie, he created it a royal burgh with privileges. This charter was renewed in 1598 by James VI.

There is little that is ancient of appearance, or particularly interesting about Inverbervie today, its long main King Street threaded by the busy highway. But there is quite a lot for the visitor to see. In an open square at the north end, near the large and 80-foot-high bridge over the glen of the Bervie Water, stands the 14-foot-high mercat cross on a plinth of seven steps, with a plain shaft surmounted by a ball-finial, which seems to have been renewed. There are a few old but not ancient houses. Down the hill a little from King Street, on a grassy knoll is the neglected single gable of the old kirk in an overgrown graveyard, all sadly abandoned. The modern parish church of 1837 is a large, Gothic-style building with a square tower 100 feet high. There was a more ambitious ecclesiastical establishment here once, a Carmelite friary, which stood near the bridge, and after which the pool of Friars' Dubs is named. Many graves were found hereabouts. There was also once an ancient Town House of 1569, rebuilt 1720, containing a notorious small vaulted pit known as the Black Hole, for malefactors. It has a bell dated 1792 which rang the hours for the presumably clockless citizens, at 6 and 9 a.m., and 2 and 9 p.m.—after which decent folk should have been in bed. The bell is all that remains of the Town House, and now hangs on a wooden frame outside the Town Chamberlain's office in Church Street.

Inverbervie had a reputation for pioneering flax-milling. Indeed it claims to have had the first machine for spinning linen yarn in all Scotland, set up on the Haugh of Bervie in 1788. Later there were four other flax- and tow-mills, making linen and sail-cloth, as well as woollen and sacking mills. There is still a mill working here spinning linen from flax; and also a flock-mill.

Gourdon, the port of Inverbervie, lies fully a mile to the south round the headland of Doolie Ness, really a separate community although included in the municipality. It is a busy, bustling fishing-place, only a little smaller than Inverbervie, with its own jute-mill, a large fish-curing establishment and other industry. At the pier-head is a public barometer of somewhat antiquated appearance, in memory of Lieutenant William Farquhar, R.N., drowned far away from this rockbound coast, in the China Sea last century. Much grain used to be shipped from here from the Mearns farmlands, with many granaries required to store it. Once, 108 boats fished from this port. Gourdon is not a beautiful place, any more than is Inverbervie, but it has a lively air. On the ridge of hill immediately behind, at 447 feet, is Long Cairn, a prehistoric burial-mound.

Between Inverbervie and Gourdon stands Hallgreen Castle, above the shore, a quite large late 16th century fortalice added to in later times. The old part is L-shaped, with typical angle-turrets, dormer-windows and gunloops without, and vaulted basements within. It was built by the Rait family, one of whom was captain of the guard to James IV. Another and still more interesting castle is that of Allardyce, set picturesquely within a bend of the deep valley of the Bervie Water two miles north-west of the town. It dates from around the same period and is notable for the splendid elaboration of its label-corbelling on stair- and angle-turrets. Like most such buildings it has stood within a curtain-walled courtyard; but it is unusual in that the access to this was by a vaulted pend slapped through the basement of the main block. With its tall, whitewashed walls, steep roofs and turrets, it is highly attractive, and now a farmhouse. There was a family of Allardyce of that Ilk, the name spelt often in odd ways, such as Abberdash and Alrethes, to one of whom Robert Bruce gave a charter. Cromwell nominated one of them as a justice for Kincardineshire, as "Thomas Ardes". An heiress carried the property to the Barclays of Urie in the 18th century. The famous pedestrian, Captain Barclay-Allardyce, was the last of this family.

Another notable Inverbervie native was Hercules Linton, born in 1836, designer of the famous sailing-vessel *Cutty Sark*, winner of ocean races. It was only 30 years before his birth, during the Napoleonic Wars, that a blockading French sloop-of-war pursued merchant ships into Bervie Bay, and Provost Hudson and a band of volunteers prepared to defend the burgh, marching one section to the beach, where they fired off muskets at the ship in brave style, the other section marching to Hallgreen Castle. It is to be feared that the latter were the more effective, for seeing them heading for what looked like a fortress, and fearing cannon-fire, the Frenchmen fled.

There is still another castle in the vicinity, Benholm Tower two miles to the south-west, but in Benholm parish and better described thereunder. A mile north of Allardyce, on the farm of Craighead, two standing-stones top a low ridge above the B967. One is very large and unusually rectangular, six feet high and eight broad, in the middle of a field; the other to the west, stands amongst scattered pines and is smaller and triangular. Two miles to the south, on a side-road near the oddly named farm of Dendoldrum, is the quarry of Three Wells. Where and what the wells were is uncertain; but the quarry supplied the handsome stone slates for many a fine house, including Muchalls Castle.

Kinneff and Catterline. That this small and remote parish of some 6000 acres on the wild seaboard of Kincardineshire should ever have featured notably in Scotland's story might seem improbable, but in the troubled 17th century it did, thanks to the valour and initiative of one woman, an indomitable minister's wife. Cromwell had over-run Scotland, and for safe keeping the Honours, that is the Scots regalia, had been deposited in the strong castle of Dunnottar seven miles to the north. Almost impregnable as was the castle, its defenders' stomachs were less so, and the garrison was eventually forced to surrender by starvation. Before that happened, and the country's symbols of sovereignty fell into the enemy hands, Mrs. Christian Grainger, wife of the Reverend James Grainger of Kinneff, played her undying role in history. She was friendly with the wife of George Ogilvy, the lieutenant-governor of Dunnottar, and she presented herself one day before Major-General Morgan, Cromwell's commander besieging the castle, requesting his permission to visit Mrs. Ogilvy—since she was sure that English gentlemen did not make war on women. Gaining entry, with Mrs. Ogilvy's aid she pushed Scotland's crown up under her skirts and wrapped the sceptre and sword of state in lint, to look like a distaff, and with her female servant carrying these, made her presumably very awkward exit. It is said that General Morgan actually and gallantly aided the lady on to her horse. Either he was not a very observant man, or he was quite dazzled by Mrs. Grainger's charms; for she must have looked a great deal more pregnant than when she had arrived. At any rate, she got the regalia safely back to Kinneff, where she and her husband put it all underneath their box-bed; but later, for security's sake, buried it beneath the pulpit in the church one night —the subject of a famous and dramatic painting. In due course, at the Restoration, the precious relics were handed over to Charles II.

The rewards for this piece of romantic initiative were oddly out of proportion. The Graingers were granted 2000 merks—quite a sum for a country minister, no doubt, but paltry for the service rendered. Ogilvy of Barras, the governor, was given a baronetcy, so that his wife became Lady Ogilvy; and, of all things, Sir John Keith, a brother of the Earl Marischal, owner of Dunnottar, whose only connection with the affair was that he had accepted custody of the Honours in the first place, but had smuggled himself out of the castle at an early stage of the siege to go to the king for aid, and was captured and imprisoned, was created Earl of Kintore, with a pension.

It is sad today to find Kinneff Church so comparatively neglected. Admittedly it is still entire, and open to visitors, though not regularly used as a church, the parish now being combined with Arbuthnott. But all is very shabby and with an air of disuse—though the Visitors' Book shows a great many callers still. This should be a cherished and magnetic place of pilgrimage for tourists. It is attractively situated, in a den of the cliff-girt shoreline, three miles north of Inverbervie, but the village or kirkton has been deserted and the large manse is now a private house. The parish was united with Catterline to the north in 1709, and today the population is there and at the inland village of Roadside of Kinneff, where there is a modern church. What is now the old church, though on the site of the original, was a reconstruction of 1738. Internally there are fine mural monuments to George Ogilvy and the Graingers. Also to Mr. Grainger's successors in the ministry. This last reveals a quite remarkable situation in the Scots Kirk, for the Reverend James Honeyman, a brother of the Episcopal Bishop of Orkney, was himself succeeded first by his own son, then his grandson, then his great-grandson in Kinneff, covering a ministry of 118 years.

At the rock-bound coast, a short distance to the east, is the site of

Kinneff Castle, once allegedly a royal seat, now represented by only a fragment of masonry. The castle was garrisoned by the English during the English occupation in the Edward Baliol period of David II's minority, and coins of that time have been unearthed here. Oddly enough, on similar promontories, each at only a few hundred yards distance to the north, were three other castles, Cadden, Whistleberry and Adam's. Why they were so close together is a mystery. All are gone now, though Whistleberry lasted longest, and was still there in 1633 at least. It is now a farm. Gone also is the early cell of St. Artny, sometimes called St. Arnold's, said to have stood between the church and the castle of Kinneff, where now are farm-steading buildings connected with the manse.

Catterline lies about three miles to the north, also on the coast, a cliff-top fishing-village, somewhat scattered but picturesque, with a small harbour below and the isolated stack of Forley Craig rising offshore. Near by to the south is the lighthouse on Todhead Point. The Den of Catterline lies, rather strangely, parallel with the coast and to the west of the little ridge on which stands the village, with the Catterline Burn running through. The northernmost section of this den is most attractive, with a good waterfall, but not very accessible. On the west bank of it, near the roadside, is the site of St. Catherine's Chapel and its old graveyard. This belonged to the abbey of Arbroath in pre-Reformation times, and later became the parish church, until united with Kinneff in 1709. There is nothing left of the chapel but its ogee-shaped aumbry built into the eastern wall, with a very ancient incised cross above it; but the kirkyard is kept in good order, and there are some old stones. Not far away, across valley and bridge, is the modern Episcopal church of St. Philip's, unusual in also having a graveyard.

The united parish is not large, but contains a few items of interest. Near the modern village of Roadside of Kinneff, on the main A92 road, is the farm of Temple—which indicates lands formerly belonging to the Knights Templar, or of St. John. St. John's Hill too rises in the vicinity; and a mile to the north-west is another farm called Chapel of Barras, where once was a chapel of the Order. Near this, and easily seen from the road, is a prehistoric burial-cairn on the hilltop. And on another low hilltop still farther to the north-west, on the farm of Cotbank of Barras, is a stone-circle of smallish recumbent stones with a central burial depression—really a ring-cairn. This ancient relic contrasts vividly with the radar listening-towers on the summit of the next hill westwards. Old Barras House, where Governor Ogilvy had his home, is two miles to the north-east, but in Dunnottar parish—which see.

To the south of Kinneff rises the bold headland of Bervie Brow (451 feet) or Craig David, so called to commemorate the landing here of 18-year-old King David II, Bruce's son, returning from exile to take up his throne, and bringing his French wife Joanna, in 1341. Harried by English ships, and storm-driven also, he at last made land here; and in gratitude founded a chapel on the spot, and granted a charter as a royal burgh to the little town of Inverbervie a mile to the south. The chapel is now gone, but there is another prehistoric burial-cairn on the top of Bervie Brow which can be identified.

Laurencekirk. The large village or small town of Laurencekirk lining the main A94, in the level Howe of the Mearns 10 miles north of Brechin, is familiar to travellers by road northwards to Aberdeen. It is a strung-out place whose mile-long main street is too narrow for the heavy traffic, which is no fault of Laurencekirk's. It is a comparatively modern place, having been founded and laid out in 1765 by one of those worthy Scots law lords, Francis Garden of Troup, in Banffshire, who took the judicial title of Lord Gardenstone, having bought the estate of Johnston here. He not only built Laurencekirk but gave it its name, for previously the parish had been called Conveth. A large farm just north of the village is still called Mains of Conveth. Laurencekirk was created a burgh of barony in 1779, but never became a true burgh. It is also a parish of 5600 acres. It is architecturally and scenically unremarkable, but not unpleasing, especially to the east, back from the main road, where it reaches farther than appears at first glance. In this part is the old-established Episcopal church, also built by Lord Gardenstone.

The parish church, on the site of the kirkton of Conveth, is at the north end of the village, built in 1804 and enlarged 1819. Plain externally, with belfry and clock, it is large and quite attractive within, with a side-chapel furnished with woodwork from the old Free church and an L-shaped gallery on only two sides, quite unusual. The old church on the site, dedicated to St. Lawrence, was built in 1626, some of its stones being used in the new. There are many old gravestones, not a few propped up against the east wall of the church, one dated 1695. Still in position is one to the Stiven family, who founded the snuffbox-factory for which Laurencekirk is famed. Opposite the church is the Gardenstone Arms Hotel, a former inn, and the St. Lawrence's Village Hall of 1866 adjoins to the south, with the auction marts for the cattle sales near by. Mid-way along the main street is the Masons' Lodge, built 1779, freemasonry being strong in this neighbourhood. There is a small park at the southern end of the High Street. Linen weaving, once very important at Laurencekirk, is now no more; but one of the last exponents has started a small weaving establishment at Luthermuir, a village in Marykirk parish to the south-west.

Lord Gardenstone's estate of Johnston, with its comparatively modern mansion, lies to the east on the slopes of Hill of Garvock which flanks the Howe for almost five miles on this side, rising to 914 feet. Up there, on the high ground, are the St. James' Lochs. The hilltop tower of Johnston is modern, but the Cairn of Shiels on the northernmost summit of the range is ancient.

In the old days it was not Johnston's lairdship that was important hereabouts, but that of Halkerton, now only a large farm, a mile north-west of Laurencekirk. This was the barony and burgh of barony, of the royal falconers connected with the great royal castle of Kincardine, four miles away, given to them by David I. In time they took the name of Falconer of Hawkerton or Halkerton, and in 1647 became Lords Falconer thereof. Their large castle was sited in the wood to the north of the farm, presumably defended by moats and marshland. Near here was fought a skirmish between Montrose and Sir John Hurry in 1645. Nothing now remains of the castle save some green banks widespread. The Falconers, however, survive in the person of the Earl of Kintore, the 6th lord marrying the Keith heiress and their son, the 7th succeeding his grandfather as 5th Earl of Kintore, adopting the name of Keith-Falconer. The near-by estate of Inglismaldie Castle, in Marykirk parish, remained with the family until recent years.

Another farm with a "noble" history is that of Middleton, or Middleton of Conveth, lying a mile to the east. This was the original home of the Middletons of that Ilk, from William the Lion's time. A son of this house attained prominence in the person of the notoriously evil-living General John Middleton of Caldhame, who fought against Montrose—the latter's troops were said to have slain his father at his fireside at Middleton—distinguished himself at the Battle of Worcester, and was created Earl of Middleton by Charles II, a fierce and cruel man whose orgies would make present-day depravities look pale. To get him out of the way, Charles eventually sent him to Tangier as governor. Caldhame, or Caddam, itself is now also a farm in Marykirk.

Thornton Castle is also in Marykirk parish, but being much nearer Laurencekirk is more conveniently described here, set two miles to the west, islanded in the wide plain of the Howe. It is a fairly small but most interesting late 15th or early 16th century fortalice, with more modern mansion attached, L-shaped, rising four storeys to a crenellated parapet with open rounds and a garret storey above. A curiosity is the way the parapet-walk is corbelled out as a half-round to give passage round a free-standing chimneystack on the east. Lower additions of various later dates extend north and east, and a round flanking-tower for the courtyard projects to the north-east, decorated with a heraldic panel with the Strachan arms, dated 1531. The basement is vaulted and the hall panelled, with traces of tempera painting behind it. Originally there were Thorntons of that Ilk but an heiress carried the property to Sir James Strathauchin or Strachan in 1309. The Strachans retained possession for 13 generations. Another heiress carried it to Forbes of Newton. The last Strachan laird, curiously, became parish minister of Keith, Banffshire, and was deposed for non-conformity in 1690:

> The beltit Knicht o' Thornton an' Laird o' Pittendreich,
> An' Master James Strachan, the Minister o' Keith.

Thornton passed through various hands, including those of Lord Gardenstone, until it came to another Thornton, Sir Thomas, town clerk of Dundee, in 1893. The present laird is Sir Colin Thornton-Kemsley, baronet.

Thomas Ruddiman the famous grammarian was schoolmaster at Laurencekirk—or rather, Conveth—from 1695 to 1700.

Maryculter. Maria Cultura is alleged to be the ancient name of this North Kincardineshire Deeside parish of about 8000 acres—although the Gaelic *cuil-tir*, meaning the back land, is more likely in fact. Lying immediately south of its opposite number, Peterculter in Aberdeenshire, and only six miles south-west of the centre of Aberdeen, it is a curiously slantwise rural area, sloping from around the 500-foot contour down to less than 100 feet along the Dee, in a couple of miles. There is no village other than the tiny kirkton hamlet, but many old estates and much woodland. The busy A943 South Deeside road threads the parish on the north.

The kirkton and parish church are remotely set a mile up from the river, on a small side-road, a few cottages and a large manse flanking a pleasantly sited kirkyard amongst old trees. The grey-washed church dates from 1782, so it is old without being ancient, and is cruciform in shape nevertheless, replacing an early edifice down on the low ground. Internally it is pleasing, galleried on three sides and fitted with some antique box-pews complete with their own tables. The former bell, dated 1786 and now cracked, stands in the yard to the south. There are no particularly old stones here.

The church's predecessor, now revealing little more than foundations and fragments of walling, in a high-walled old burial-ground, lies near the Dee a mile to the north-west, in the grounds of what is now called Templars' Park, behind the former manse and steading. It was the 13th century Chapel of St. Mary, from which the parish takes its name, having been built by the Knights Templar who were granted these lands, a large estate of about 8500 acres, by William the Lion in 1187. The only remaining feature is a piscina or holy-water stoup. There are many old gravestones here; but the most interesting have been removed to the West Church of St. Nicholas, Aberdeen—two finely carved recumbent effigies, of, it is thought, Gilbert Menzies of Maryculter and his wife Marjory Chalmers, dating from about 1543, the knight in armour with the Hospitallers' cross at throat. The Knights Templar, abolished by papal decree in 1312, were succeeded by the Knights Hospitallers of St. John; and these survived in Scotland until the Reformation when, like other Catholic Orders, they were dissolved. But the Venerable Order of St. John of Jerusalem in the British Realm in due course made a come-back, and today there is a plaque over the gateway to this old kirkyard commemorating the Knights' connection with the property, 1225–1925. As at other Hospitaller establishments, the Knights had a herb-garden, on the site of the walled garden of Maryculter House, where medicinal plants were grown—notably, of course, the St. John's wort. Near the chapel is a large hollow in the grassy ground known as the Thunder Hole, alleged to have been

341

supernaturally made by the descent of a thunderbolt to strike down an erring preceptor and justify Sir Godfrey Wedderburn, accused of unsuitable ongoings with a Saracen lady. A less dramatic reason for the hollow, the geologists declare, would be the melting of underground ice. Wedderburn and the Saracen lady were buried near the attractive Corbie Linn, a "kelpie-haunted spot" where the Crynoch Burn comes to join Dee, just to the west.

Templars' Park is now a highly interesting Boy Scouts' camping-ground and training-centre, with splendid facilities for nature-study, woodcraft, sports and so on for the Aberdeen Association. It was opened by Lord Baden-Powell himself in 1936. The former manse, an excellent building of late 17th and early 18th century date, although with much earlier foundations, has been restored as Warden's House and clubrooms. The large downstairs apartment is now a hall, and given a medieval stone arched fireplace from a demolished property at 38 Castle Street, Aberdeen. The belfry on the house is modern. Outside is a plaque celebrating Lord Baden-Powell's opening, and adding a nice touch "in gratitude to Fenton Wyness" who was then County Convener. This is the Aberdeen writer who did so much to bring about this excellent project.

Templars' Park was formerly the home-park of Maryculter House, and this mansion, now a hotel, adjoins to the west. It is an extensive building belonging to the 18th and 19th centuries; but the old Ha' Hoose still stands at the south-west corner, a modest, three-storeyed, T-planned building which appears to date from the later 17th century. There are, however, much earlier foundations, indeed barrel-vaulted basements, for here was the Preceptor's House of the Hospitallers. On the wing gable is a panel with the initials of William Menzies and Margaret Urquhart, of about 1747, and also heraldry of the later Gordons. The Menzies were a branch of the Pitfodels Castle family across the Dee, who gained the lands just prior to the Reformation.

East of Maryculter estate is that of Kincausie, a large property extending far southwards, the grey granite mansion of which, standing on a shelf in woodland overlooking the river, incorporates an early tower-house—though this is now hard to perceive externally. The Irvines of Drum also acquired these lands from the Knights just before the Reformation, and their descendants, Irvine-Fortesques, are still the lairds. The Den of Kincausie is famous for its botanical wealth, the Corbie-pot area being notable.

Still farther east is another well-known estate, Blairs. This is the Roman Catholic College of St. Mary, for training for the priesthood. The property was gifted to the Church by the last Menzies of Pitfodels and the college opened in 1829. The chapel has a fine crown-steeple. There is a famous library and many treasures, including splendid portraits of Mary Queen of Scots and Cardinal Beaton.

Auchlunies is another very old estate, to the south on the higher ground, until recently long in the hands of the family of Duguid, a name that has meant much in the North-East in the past.

St. Cyrus. The old kirkyard beneath the cliffs

Stonehaven, the county town of Kincardineshire. The harbour, with the headland of Dunnacaer and Dunnottar Castle in the background

Marykirk and Luthermuir. Marykirk is a rural parish of 10,000 acres, situated at the very southern edge of the Mearns, on the North Esk six miles north-west of Montrose. The small village here was known as Aberluthnott until 1721; and indeed the present parish church notice-board still calls it that. It was also called Maringtown in certain old records. Luthermuir also had alternative names, sometimes being called Luthra, and likewise Feus of Caldhame. It is a large village situated out in the levels of the Howe three miles to the north-west, near the great Forest of Inglismaldie.

Marykirk is a pleasant little place, clustered fairly unspoiled around its church and inn, with part of the old mercat cross still standing in a small garden between them. The present church dates only from 1806, and is typically plain, but two fragments of a former building remain in the kirkyard: the 17th century Thornton aisle and an older ivy-covered vault, probably a transept. These two parts are detached, but close to each other. The latter has a skew bearing the Barclay arms (of Balmakewan Newton, Conveth, etc.), the initial *I.B.* and the date 1653; but the fabric itself seems much older than this. The interior is inaccessible, and many stones are piled around. The Thornton aisle is in somewhat better shape, although still neglected, with a lintel dated 1615 and initials *A.S.*, for Strachan, thereof. Within is a handsome heraldic tomb of the Strachans. Later Forbes and Fullarton lairds are also buried herein. The original church of St. Mary here was consecrated by the famous Bishop de Bernham in 1242. The bell of the church, though recast in 1826, is old, and was cracked by a stone thrown by one of Cumberland's soldiery in 1746.

Below the village is Mary Mill, by a burnside, and near by is a four-arch bridge of 1813 carrying the A937 over the Esk, with a former toll-house on the opposite, Angus, side. There are a number of lairdships on the higher ground to the east: Kirktonhill, Balmanno and Balmaleedie. The first, with a modern tower on the skyline, belonged to a branch of the Tailzeours of Borrowfield, Montrose, its mansion rebuilt in 1800, one of the family having made a fortune in Jamaica. Balmanno House dates from the same period, built by the Auchinleck family, and has the ancient St. John's Well, with healing reputation, in the policies. Balmaleedie was a Barclay property, the laird of Balmaleedie in 1680 having the right to burial in the east aisle of Aberluthnott Kirk—aforementioned; over 20 generations of Barclays, stemming from the Mathers line, having dwelt in the parish. At the farm of Hospitalshiels two miles north-east was a hospice of the Arbroath Abbey monks; the name of Spittalmyre, near by, also applying.

Luthermuir is a very obviously "planted" village, with regular rectangular planning, feud out by local lairds as a weaving community in the early 19th century, its population once reaching 1000. Today it is still a sizeable place of cottage rows, gardens and wide streets, with its own school and *quod sacra* church. For a place with a great forest so near, a few trees would improve the amenity. Recently

z

a Mr. Taylor, last of the Laurencekirk weavers, has set up a small hand-weaving establishment in his back-garden here, with four looms—an admirable venture turning out linen napkins and table-cloths of high quality. It is reported that a Russian admiral, captain of the Tsar's yacht at the turn of the century, declared with pride that his ancestors had come from Luthermuir. Not far to the north-east lies the former estate of Caldhame or Caddam, now a farm. There was a castle, another Barclay establishment, and three dormer pediments therefrom are built into a steading wall at the roadside, with heraldry, the date 1571, and the initials *A.B.* and *I.S.* and *I.B.* Caldhame passed to the Middletons of Laurencekirk parish, and the notorious General John Middleton, later Earl of Middleton, was laird here in the mid-17th century. The bridge of Caldhame was built in 1782 by the then laird, George Keith, in remorse, it is said, for the execution of an aristocratic-named Randal Courtney who had robbed his house.

The next farm is Hatton, with much of interest, a pleasing E-shaped mansion of the late 17th century, with walled garden and some good Memel pine panelling within. Near by is an unusual double doocot of the 17th century. Behind the steading, lost in a plantation, is the site of a stone-circle, only one recumbent large monolith, six feet by two, remaining. Hatton was originally a Mont-gomerie house—although how this Ayrshire family came here is not clear. It is said that the Montgomerie lairdship ended with two spendthrift brothers who decamped leaving debts, one to France and one to Ireland. Not so long ago a gentleman from France named Montgomerie came looking for clues to locate the Irish branch, believing such might link him with Field-Marshal Viscount Mont-gomery—who certainly came from Ireland, of Scots ancestry, of a baronet family of 1808. The Arbuthnotts succeeded the Mont-gomeries, and remained here until early this century.

The Inglismaldie planted forest, covering a great acreage, is very prominent to south and west, with attractive roads through its quiet glades. Hidden away within it, to the south, is Inglismaldie Castle, still occupied and in good order, a most interesting late 16th century tower-house on the L-plan to which a large later mansion has been added. The south front shows the old part clearly, with three angle-turrets in a row at fourth-floor level, rather unusual. The interior has been much altered to link up with the extensions, but the basement is still vaulted and there is a wide and handsome turnpike stair and some good carved woodwork. A chapel to the east has been con-verted to kitchen premises. This was the origin of the establishment, for the name was Eglis-Maldie, or the Church of St. Magdalen. At the Reformation the church lands went to the Livingstones of Duni-pace, who built the castle presumably. In 1635 it passed to Sir John Carnegie, brother of the 1st Earl of Southesk, who himself was later raised to the peerage as Earl of Ethie. Later he changed his title to Earl of Northesk and Baron Rosehill and Inglismaldie. Rosehill is near by, with the remains of an Episcopal chapel and parsonage, where Bishop John Skinner, son of the author of 'Tullochgorum', was consecrated in 1782. The Falconers of Halkerton gained Inglismaldie from the Carnegies. There is a Witch Hillock lost amongst the pines of the forest near by.

Balmakewan estate, with the scanty remains of an old castle near the early 19th century mansion, lies to the south-east, with two 18th century square doocots at the steading. The well-known North Water Bridge, ancient though widened, a former toll-bridge at the border of Angus and Kincardineshire, is near by. It is now superseded by a modern structure to carry the busy A94. The old one was built by the famous John Erskine of Dun, after a dream. Markets used to be held here.

Muchalls, Newtonhill and Skateraw. This is the northern portion of the great parish of Fetteresso, quite populous along the coast, threaded by the busy A92 highway to Aberdeen, but largely empty and lofty moorland within. Muchalls is famous for its fine castle, set on high ground amongst wind-blown trees about a mile back from the road, a handsome and interesting fortalice dating mainly from the early 17th century, but containing a much earlier nucleus. It is an E-planned building with a central courtyard in which is an old well, reached through a defensive gateway with shot-holes in a curtain-wall. Externally, the tall harled walls, angle-turrets, crowstepped gables and steep roofing are typical of the period; but internally, the groined vaulting of the basement chambers is less usual, and the decorative, heraldic plaster ceilings of the Great Hall and other first-floor apartments are quite magnificent, perhaps the finest in Scotland. The original Muchalls was Fraser property, that family having gained great possessions in this part of the country by Robert the Bruce's favour towards his supporter and brother-in-law Sir Alexander Fraser, great chamberlain. It is to be feared that the Frasers had deteriorated somewhat by the end of their tenure at Muchalls, for we read that Andrew Fraser, heir to Muchalls, was summoned before the Privy Council for an unprovoked attack on Bannerman of Elsick near by, and his father had to find caution for the great sum of 5000 merks. The Council seems to have been particularly upset, declaring: "such ane feckles and unworthy cause as hes not been heard of in ony country subject to law and justice, to wit because the said Alex Bannerman simply and ignorantly took a place before Fraser at the ingoing of a door." This was in 1614; and by 1619 the Burnetts of Leys were in possession of Muchalls, and most of the splendour of the present building is to their credit. It is privately owned, but open to visitors by arrangement.

Muchalls village, more properly the Seatown of Muchalls, lies on the coast a mile to the east. It is a pleasant place, now incorporating the fishing-village and harbour of Stranathro. Like other villages along this coast, it has become a favoured housing area for people working in Aberdeen, less than a dozen miles away, and a great many of the old fishers' cottages are attractively restored. There is a large hotel. The cliff scenery here is quite remarkable, as dramatic as anywhere along this spectacular seaboard, with high fierce headlands, split and tortured stacks, caverns and deep cauldron-like bays. The quite large Muchalls Burn plunges to the sea out of a great hole in the cliff-face, in a notable waterfall. There are exciting footpaths. Fairs used to be held at Muchalls.

South of Muchalls Castle half a mile is the picturesque little hamlet of Bridge of Muchalls, over the aforementioned Burn. The dual-carriageway main road now by-passes this pleasant backwater. An equal distance north of the castle is the sequestered Episcopal church of St. Ternan. This is now a rather dull building, but it has a long and stirring history; for it is the successor of no less than four others sited at the castle, the earliest dated 1624. This was very much an Episcopal area in the old troubled days of religious controversy; and it was from here that the minister was imprisoned in Stonehaven Tolbooth, yet managed to continue to baptise his faithful parishioners' children through the iron-barred window—as portrayed in the famous picture. On still higher ground, indeed bleakly so, and two miles inland to the west, is the *quod sacra* established church of Cookney, sharing its hilltop site with school and farm, a necessary convenience for kirk worshippers when the parish church of Fetteresso is so far away; but one would have imagined a more convenient site might have been selected—though admittedly it is a highly kenspeckle house of God, with splendid views. Its predecessor is interesting, known as the Sod Kirk—although, in fact, little known now, in the locality. It is also remotely sited in trees in a field on the farm of Chapelton, just north of Elsick House. It now consists only of overgrown walling less than three feet high, measuring some 30 by 12 feet, the turf roof having long fallen in. There is one recumbent gravestone still to be seen and no doubt many more lie beneath the rioting weeds. It dates from 1760, and shows to what a low ebb Presbyterianism had sunk hereabouts at that time.

Elsick House near by is now the home of the Duke of Fife, but was formerly the seat of the Bannerman baronets thereof, a title created in 1682 by Charles II for "consistent loyalty during the Rebellion, and the heavy calamities suffered therefor". The Bannermans were hereditary banner-bearers to the king. Elsick House is a comparatively modest mansion, but pleasing, with a 17th century nucleus.

Three miles to the west, across the wide, whin-dotted moorland of the Red Moss, is the estate of Netherley, its Georgian mansion now a hotel. The woodlands hereabouts display the efforts of former proprietors to improve an otherwise somewhat bare countryside. It is criss-crossed by a network of small roads and dotted with small farms. Not far to the west rise the foothills of the mountains. The B979 road from Stonehaven to the Dee bridge, near Peterculter, passes Netherley. At Reinchall road-fork here, in the wood behind the little shop, is the Grey Stone of Reinchall, actually three stones, seemingly the remains of a circle, with a very long recumbent.

Near Cammachmore, a hamlet with an inn on the main A92 on the northern rim of the parish, is another *quod sacra* established church, Bourtreebush, plain and small, less prominently but more conveniently placed than Cookney. And a mile to the south-east is the conjoined village of Newtonhill and Skateraw, another and quite large commuter-developed fishing-community, with a pier and harbour in a deep bay of the cliffs, where skin-diving and other sea sports are popular. Along with the other fishing-villages of this neighbourhood, the smoke-curing of Findon haddocks was once carried out in most of the cottages. Findon itself is only a mile or two to the north in the next parish.

Nigg, Torry and Cove. This is the strangest corner of Kincardineshire, quite different from the rest, tucked away into the peninsula that culminates in Girdle Ness, between the Dee and Nigg Bay, all its aspects today making it seem part of Aberdeen. Indeed Torry is now not only a suburb but part of the city municipality. Nigg or *niuc* means nook, so the parish is well-named.

The prominent headland which forms the south horn of the Aberdeen harbour area, Girdle Ness, with its 130-foot lighthouse built in 1831 by Robert Stevenson, grandfather of R.L.S., rather dominates the Nigg area. Here, the long and fierce cliff-bound seaboard which has prevailed all the way from St. Cyrus, suddenly ends at the lesser promontory of Greg Ness; and the deep, mile-wide sandy bay of Nigg, formerly Sanctus Fitticus, opens with Girdle Ness at the other extremity. It has always been a place for habitation, with this amphitheatre of low ground, and the mouth of the Dee so close—as witness the three great burial-cairns which top the central spine of low hills, the Cat, Baron's and Tullos Cairns. Down in the hollow itself, at the head of the bay, is the ruined pre-Reformation church of St. Fittack's. Fitticus was a saintly hermit of the 7th century, sometimes called by the Celtic name Futac, thought to be of royal birth. The roofless ruin sits within its walled graveyard, with the vast Torry housing schemes encroaching close, all doors and windows save one built up, a lepers' squint, and a belfry dated 1704. This church used to belong to the abbey of Arbroath—and in the haugh beyond the golf course, which crowns the intervening ridge facing across to Aberdeen harbour, was the abbot's own house, the ruins long known as Abbot's Walls.

Just north of Girdle Ness is a little exposed bay, called Greyhope, which was the scene of the wreck of the whaling-ship *Oscar* in 1813 with the loss of 55 lives. The view northwards from the coast-road which climbs Greg Ness and Doonies Hill is exceedingly fine, over the wide spread of Aberdeen and up the Buchan coast sands for many miles.

The present parish church of Nigg was built two miles to the south, in 1829, and is a large and rather fine granite building standing on high ground and seen from far afield. The A956 passes the graveyard. Between it and its predecessor lie the modern industrial estates of East and West Tullos and Craigieshaw. All the area hereabouts has been swallowed by the ever-spreading city, Torry to the north and Kincorth to the west—where the old Bridge of Dee, site of Montrose's battle, crosses the river. Torry, though now a wholly modern suburb, has its history. James IV, who had his own reasons for coming this way to the sanctuary at Tain, for his reverence for the blessed "Sancto Fotino" erected the village of Torry into a free burgh of barony—a status long lapsed. This area was important for its great granite quarries in the mid-18th century, employing as many as 700 men. It was the age of street-paving, and the granite setts from here paved many a London street. Now, provision of servicing facilities for the North Sea oil-rigs is a new, drastic and somewhat controversial development, with much of old Nigg fishing-village to be swept away.

To the south of the comparatively small parish is the Loirston area, the A956 skirting the half-mile-long Loirston Loch, its waters formerly harnessed to drive a meal-mill, a bone-mill and a saw-mill. Lochs are a rarity in this area. Immediately east, half a mile, is the quite large village of Cove Bay, another cliff-top fishing community which has grown greatly of recent years. It has a most attractive harbour, this time with a good road down—by no means usual. This haven under the cliffs has utilised the rock formation as breakwater, enhanced by a massive retaining wall. Salmon cobles operate from here, as well as lobster and other inshore fishing. Part-way down the hill is an interesting establishment specialising in stone crafts, fireplaces and the like. Cove is something of a holiday resort, and there is a hotel. Near by is the rather equivocal notice: "H.M. Coastguard. Cliff Accidents. Apply Within." Some of the shore names are odd—for instance, Blow-up Nose and Colsea Yawn. Little Cove is at present fighting great Aberdeen over proposed development here also.

Inland this parish is bare and windswept—sufficiently for Scott to make it the grim Drumthwacket Moor of his *Legend of Montrose*.

St. Cyrus, Mathers and Morphie. Some places manage nicely with but one name, through a long history. Others chop and change. This coastal parish of 9000 acres, just north of Montrose and in the extreme south-east corner of the Mearns, is one of the latter. It started out as Ecclesgreig, with its largest village some distance from the present kirkton. The church and hamlet of Ecclesgreig were down on the shore, with the mansion near by. Then the large village, called Miltonhaven, was washed away by the sea, and the church removed to a higher site and called St. Cyrus; the name Ecclesgreig was adopted by a more modern estate, formerly called Criggie, more than a mile inland, while the old estate adopted the name of Kirkside. All rather confusing. But then, the geography was not static either. For the River North Esk, which now enters the sea amongst low sand-flats and dunes two miles north of Montrose, used to flow almost another couple of miles north-eastwards, to reach the sea directly under the present St. Cyrus. So that the original Ecclesgreig was on the shore at its mouth.

Mathers is an extensive district to the north of the parish, which was once a highly important barony and thanedom. Morphie, equally large, to the south-west, formerly the property of an illustrious branch of the Graham family, is now renowned for pedigree cattle.

The present village of St. Cyrus is quite large, an amalgam of the later Kirkton, Burnside hamlet and the roadside community which grew up when, in 1775, the fine bridge was built across the Esk at Kinnaber, enforcing a new line for the main north road, now the A92. This roadside part, that seen by most travellers, is not the most attractive perhaps. The kirkton lies higher, seawards, the parish church itself occupying a lofty position, its tower and steeple a landmark. The first church up here was built in 1631 by Sir Alexander Straton, of Lauriston near by, in memory of a dead son buried here on the cliff-top, small but with some architectural pretensions. This later became the Lauriston burial-vault. The present church is plain and large, dating from 1785, rebuilt and enlarged in 1854. There are few very old gravestones here, the one beside the vault being inscribed *I.S.* and *E.O.*, for Sir Alexander's dead son and his wife Euphame Ogilvy of Clova. The village is scattered, and quite pleasing away from the main road.

The Nether Kirk, formerly Ecclesgreig, the church of Greig, is much more interesting, within a walled enclosure down below the cliffs on the raised beach at the former river-mouth. There are two ruined chapels or aisles, one older and more decayed, and many interesting stones. There is a particularly fine table-stone tomb to Arthur Straton of Kirkside, a cadet of Lauriston, and his Lyon wife, dated 1646, showing a ruffed gentleman and his lady both pierced and united by Death's spear, a device both touching and gruesome. There is considerable good Scott of Criggie heraldry in one of the aisles; and near by is interred a general who commanded dragoons at Waterloo. Also there is the locally renowned grave of the lawyer who died for love, by name George Beattie—an unlikely event which becomes rather more acceptable when it is learned that he was also a poet, who, before he blew his brains out actually in this little graveyard, in 1823, rather got his own back on the lady who rejected him by leaving a long posthumous poem reproaching her. Near by are the whitewashed cottages of the salmon-fishing station, with its net-posts, still in use.

Kirkside House, formerly the Straton house of Ecclesgreig, stands half-way up the brae above, an interesting mansion of pleasing Georgian design, with an older nucleus, an inner door-lintel being dated 16??, with the initials *A.S.* and *E.M.* There is an 18th century doocot, and eagle gateposts to the main-road drive. Oddly enough there is a tradition of eagles appearing here on occasion, far as it is from their Grampian haunts.

The present Ecclesgreig House, formerly Criggie, is a large estate on higher ground to the north-west, its former mansion now used partly as a grain-store, and easily seen on the skyline from the A92.

The laird now has a modern house near by. For a while Criggie was called Mount Cyrus before settling for Ecclesgreig. Mill of Criggie lies beyond, at the head of the Den of Morphie.

Almost two miles north-east of this is the once great estate of Lauriston, now broken up, its castle and mansion in a sad state. The latter is only a gaunt shell; but more of the former remains, on a strong site at the edge of a steep wooded den. It has been a large courtyard-type stronghold, and two of the flanking-towers, though heightened in unsightly fashion, survive, linked by a high and interesting stretch of the original curtain-wall, topped by wall-walk and parapet, all seeming almost to grow out of the living rock. The southern tower appears to be an early 17th century building erected on the foundations of the former main vaulted keep, with a later stair-turret with conical roof. All is in bad condition. The original owners were Stirlings, succeeded by Stratons, Alexander Straton de Laurenston falling at Harlaw in 1411. The Straton lairdship ended in 1695.

East of this, stretching along the coast for almost two miles, is the district of Mathers. There is now no estate or mansion, and the ancient and famous castle called Kaim of Mathers has all but crumbled into the sea from its precarious cliff-top site, guarded by battlements—this towards the southern end. But from Nether Woodston northwards to the Benholm parish border near John-shaven are farms called West Mathers, Milton of Mathers and East Mathers, mainly where dens cut down steeply to the sea. St Cyrus is a great place for dens, with no less than six—attractive features. Den Finella, to the north, is the best known and has a high attenuated waterfall just below the road-bridge, with deep pot below. It got its name from the famous Finella, responsible for the death of Kenneth II in 994, who was caught here and slain—see the item on Strath-finella. Down at the mouth of the den, at the shore, was formerly the large village of Miltonhaven, built in the early 18th century to house lime-workers—the use of the local lime deposits for fertiliser then becoming important. Now nothing remains, all having been washed away by the tide, partly as a result of the quarrying of the limestone reef which acted as a barrier to the sea. Yet Miltonhaven was a burgh of barony, with weekly markets and fairs twice a year, the largest community of the parish. Only a lonely stony beach marks the site. Milton of Mathers, the large farm above, has an attractive hidden den reaching down towards the sea, with, at the foot, a picturesquely placed restaurant and large caravan site, with facili-ties, the restaurant having a circular and conical-roofed doocot. Near by is a boarding-kennels for dogs.

These places are all served by short side-roads from the main highway. At Bourtry Bush—bourtree meaning elder—on the A92, is an inn, now a hotel; and down from this is West Mathers, with the remnants of another fishing-haven at the foot, called Tangleha', four cottages and a boatstrand, with another old limekiln in the bank above. A reasonable view of Kaim of Mathers Castle may be had from here, though closer inspection demands a clamber along the cliffs. Only part of a smallish square tower remains, with the battlemented approach.

At Seagreens, a little to the north, are three cottages and a boat-strand, all that is left of a fishing-village. Here is still an icehouse, with brick vaulting, for the storage of the fish. Near by is a limekiln, and the site of the East Mathers lime quarry.

The next road down leads to Nether Woodston, where there is a salmon-fishing station, with one more old icehouse built into the cliff. A small caterpillar-tractor now serves to bring the catch up the steep cliff-track, instead of the pack-ponies used formerly. The coble that serves the stake-nets is also launched and beached on the boat-strand by tractor. There is an old well beside the icehouse. Here is one end of the Nature Conservancy reserve, which stretches southwards along the cliffs and shore to Kirkside.

Inland at the south end of the parish, the Morphie area is interesting. The old castle of the Grahams is gone, its site on the edge of the picturesque Den of Morphie, near the bridge carrying the side-road to Marykirk. These Grahams, chamberlains to the Earls of Montrose, were important folk and involved in national affairs. They had an odd ally. Tradition says that they were aided in the building of their castle by a water-kelpie from the Pondage Pool in the North Esk below, where there was a ferry-boat. This creature, although terrorising the neighbourhood, and described as having horns, claws and a forked tail, served the Grahams, allegedly carrying all the stones from the riverside to build the castle:

> *Sair back and sair banes,*
> *Carrying the Laird o' Morphie's stanes.*

The present Morphie, on higher ground to the north, and still owned by the Barclay-Graham family, has its own fame; for here Mr. W. L. Anderson, a notable farmer, breeds Shorthorn cattle renowned the world over. Innumerable champions for Royal and Highland Shows have come from Morphie, and been exported to America, Argentina, Australia, even the Soviet Union. In the large steading, alongside these aristocrats of the show- and sale-rings, is a doocot displaying the arms of the Barclay-Grahams, Mr. Anderson showing almost as much pride in the one as the other. There are two other famous herds in the area, at Canterland and Commieston. Stone of Morphie is another farm nearer the river with a huge mono-lith, $11\frac{1}{2}$ feet high, in the stackyard to give it its name. The Canterland district lies to the west. At Pitbeadlie, and on the crest of Canterland Hill (406 feet) is an ancient fort, with ramparts and ditches and a central cairn, set amongst Scots pines.

Altogether St. Cyrus is an intriguing parish. Not the least interesting of its attractions is the curious marriage custom whereby John Orr of Bridgeton, a local laird, in 1847 left £1000 to provide dowries annually for four brides married in the parish church—the tallest, shortest, oldest and youngest. So the minister has to quiz and measure all brides at their weddings, and part of the terms are that they must undo their hair and remove their shoes, so that nothing extraneous adds to their stature. Records are strictly kept.

Stonehaven. This is the county town of Kincardineshire, by no means central in the area but the largest community therein—though even so with a population of less than 5000. It is picturesquely situated at a break in the almost consistently cliff-lined Mearns seaboard, where two major streams enter Stonehaven Bay, the Carron and Cowie Waters, and where there is a mile-long stretch of sands, which greatly assisted in making the town a popular holiday resort. It lies 23 miles north of Montrose and 15 south of Aberdeen. Because of the steeply rising Black Hill—on which is sited the very prominent war memorial—and Downie Point to the south, making an excellent viewpoint, it is deservedly one of the most photographed prospects of the North-East.

Stanehive, to give it its local and ancient name, is nevertheless not so ancient a place as Inverbervie, nor yet a royal burgh. It only succeeded Kincardine itself as county town in 1600. But little of the town dates even from that period. Indeed there were two distinct communities here: the old town south of the Carron in Dunnottar parish, which grew up round the harbour established by the Earl Marischal, and where any relics of antiquity are to be found; and the new town across the river to the north, really in Fetteresso parish, dating from only the late 18th century, built round its spacious central square. The old became a burgh of barony, under the Marischal, in 1607; but it was not until 1889 that Stonehaven was raised to the status of police burgh, with its own provost and magistrates.

It got its name on account of the great rock called Craig-na-Caer, which rose from the sea at the very entrance of the harbour, a serious danger to shipping in bad weather until it was demolished in 1826 by the famous engineer, Robert Stevenson, R.L.S.'s grandfather, and a new sea-wall and harbour of five acres extent, with double basins, was contrived. It was as a fishery-haven that Stanehive developed in the main, though with also some coasting and foreign trade—now gone. As late as 1883 127 fishing-boats worked from here; but today it is mainly a yachting and pleasure-boating harbour. The sea-front is picturesque, with old houses, lanes and pleasant vistas. Here, on the north side, is the burgh's oldest building, the attractive red-stone, crowstepped-gabled 17th century Tolbooth and court-house, restored by the Town Council as a combined tea-room and museum, and opened by the Queen Mother in 1963. It was in this building that sundry Episcopal ministers were confined during the religious troubles of the mid-18th century. This was a notably Episcopal area, and the people continued to support and venerate their ministers in durance vile, bringing their children to be baptised from the barred window of the Tolbooth by the minister of Muchalls, as portrayed in the famous picture by the Victorian painter, George Washington Brownlow, now in the possession of the bishop of Brechin.

Near by is another old building of somewhat similar style, which might even be older, because of its moulded windows and cut-away angle at the north-east gable, now used for industrial purposes but which is well worthy of restoration and preservation. There were three wells along the sea-front, one of which, Duthie's, still stands at the end of Shorehead. Near it is a peculiar and massive pedestal sundial dated 1710, at the head of the pier steps, an odd amenity. One of the old granaries to the south has been adapted as modern visitors' shop and craft centre. There is a boat-store maintained by Aberdeen College of Education here, and Stanehive harbour is busy with small-boat enthusiasts. Each year a sea-angling festival is held.

If there is not a great deal of old Steenie, as the natives call it, left, part of the blame must be laid at the doors of the history-makers—Montrose, in 1645; General Monk in 1657; and Butcher Cumberland in 1746—this mainly because of the proximity of Dunnottar Castle and the Earls Marischal, sources of opposition. But there are some relics left, and the Town Council has built some attractive and harmonising replacements. What is known as the Old Tower, or Old Town Steeple, with its clock, a noted landmark in the High Street, dates only from 1790. At its foot is the mercat cross, where the Old Pretender was proclaimed in 1715; but this has been restored. Beside it is a public barometer, as at Gourdon, dated 1852, important for a fishing community.

Near by, at 51 High Street, is a rather fine and large early 17th century dwelling-house, with a stair-turret corbelled out centrally above first-floor level, and a pend slapped through the building, all restored as council flats. Just across the street is a smaller building, of some age and architectural merit, now in rather a poor condition.

An up-ended cannon barrel decorates the pavement at a street corner towards the west end of the old town, its purpose uncertain.

Steep, grass-grown slopes rise abruptly behind old Stanehive, limiting any expansion save across the Carron Water; hence the new town. This is reached by a bridge, now widened, across which the traffic pours and grinds day and night along the A92 on its way to Aberdeen, for there is no by-pass; indeed Stonehaven, set deep in a steep hollow of the rivers, with dangerous hills down into it on either side, is a difficult place to by-pass.

At the south-west corner of this bridge a former milestone is inserted; as is also a facsimile of the original bridge-stone of 1781, which records the arms of Barclay of Urie and the dates 1150, 1351, 1647 and 1781, commemorating other kinds of milestones in the history of the locality and the great families of Mathers, Keith and Barclay who in turn dominated it. Two 17th century tombstones behind the prison commemorate victims of the plague. They are now built into a wall.

The new town is regularly laid out around the tree-lined Market Square, with its steepled and arcaded Market House of 1827, now used for other purposes. It was all an early example of town-planning erected to the plans of Robert Barclay of Ury, of that great Quaker family, and many of the streets are named after members of his house. It is the shopping-centre for a wide area, and is a cheerful, bustling place with an air of spaciousness. The streets climb the hill behind, less steep than that backing the old town, and good substantial residential areas spread westwards on the high ground, with fine views over the sea. Here are the railway-station, and the present large and interesting parish kirk of Fetteresso (which see). The large number of hotels is notable, for this is very much a holiday town today. Over the door of a chemist's shop in Market Square is a plaque to Robert William Thomson, born here in 1822, who invented the pneumatic tyre at the age of only 23. Strange that the "father of modern transport" should have come from this small Mearns town. He was the son of a woollen-mill proprietor and an inventive genius, for he also first thought of the fountain-pen, the rotary engine, travelling-cranes and other utilities. The R. W. Thomson Memorial Run for Veteran and Vintage Vehicles was inaugurated in 1968 and occurs each June, keeping his memory green.

On the northern outskirts of the town, where the Cowie Water enters the bay and the sandy shore curves round towards Garron Point, are the principal holiday development and recreational facilities, with the promenade, the Queen Elizabeth and Cowie Parks, and a large heated open-air swimming-pool. Attractions for the youngsters include paddling-pool, trampolines, helter-skelter and so on. There are bowling- and putting-greens, a large municipal caravan-park, and other caravan and camping-sites. Just across the road is the new Commodore Motel, with 40 double bedrooms and a ballroom to hold 400. A little farther north still is the 18-hole Stonehaven Golf Course, stretching along the cliff-tops at Cowie.

Cowie is an interesting place—although less so than once it was. For, long ago, it was no less than a royal burgh with a royal castle, then a thanedom. Some vestiges of the castle still remain on a rock above the shore; but the site of the former burgh can only be traced in some foundations beside the cultivated land of Megray Hill a little way inland. Malcolm Canmore built the castle and gave the burgh its charter. Bruce gave it to his brother-in-law, Sir Alexander Fraser. Why it should all have faded so utterly is a mystery. Below the club-house of the golf course, however, the ruined kirk of Cowie still stands in its ancient graveyard, in pre-Reformation times called St. Mary's of the Storms, an evocative name. On a delightful cliff-top site, the first church here was dedicated to St. Nathalan, who died in A.D. 678, and seems to have been a wealthy Pictish noble. It was rebuilt in 1276 by Bishop William Wishart of St. Andrews. The eastern part of the building is this 13th century Early English work, the western less good and 15th century. It is a typical long low chapel, with a triple lancet window in the east gable, where there is an aumbry internally, a good doorway in the south front, and a semi-subterranean vault under the west gable. On this gable is a memorial to four members of the Stonehaven lifeboat crew who died trying to save survivors from the wrecked *Grace Darling*, of Blyth, in 1874. The graveyard is crowded, and still in use. A winding cliff-path leads southwards a few hundred yards to the scanty castle remains. The modern village of Cowie, now rather a suburb of the town, lies near the shore still farther to the south; this was known as "the laigh toun of Cowie". Here are the Cowie coastguard station and houses.

The great estate of Ury, once of the Barclays, then latterly of the Bairds, one of whom became Viscount Stonehaven, lies to the west in the green valley of the Cowie Water. The mansion is now roofless and abandoned and the estate worked as an agricultural unit. The Houff of Ury, an oddly-named private burial-ground of the Barclays, lies a mile north of the house in a tree-grown enclosure. On the southern side of the property has been built the large and very modern new Stonehaven Academy, with all facilities including its own swimming-pool. At the mouth of the Cowie Water's valley is established the Glen Ury Distillery, founded in 1824. Once there were no fewer than 32 licensed establishments in Stonehaven, which seems excessive—especially as the population at that time was around 3000. Perhaps there were extenuating circumstances. The town was once famous for the manufacture of wooden toys, tobacco-pipes, fishing-nets, as well as the more usual brewing, wool, cotton and flax-spinning, and of course the various branches of the fishing industry. Today, these have been superseded by other services which cater for increased leisure. Only memories, too, are the holy wells of St. Caran, near the distillery, and St. Ninian, near the Carron —a St. Ninian's Chapel once stood near by—and the Gallows Hill where Stanehive executions took place in the days when the Earl Marischal had the power of pit and gallows, with the usual adjunct of the Witches' Pool in the river. But one custom of even earlier days than these survives; at Hogmanay, the Fireball ceremony is still held, the swinging of burning balls on strings being a link with pagan times, when such activities were believed to ward off evil spirits. Possibly that is what the 32 licensed premises were about, also?

Strachan and Bridge of Dye. Strachan, pronounced locally Strawn, is the strath of the Water of Aven which runs into the Feugh and so to the Dee near Banchory, and at 42,000 acres is the largest parish of Kincardineshire, mainly mountain, Mount Battock (2555 feet) its highest point. The parish has much in common with the Deeside parishes of Aberdeenshire; indeed the county boundary runs along the Aven. The Water of Dye, coming in from the south, joins the Feugh at Strachan village; and Bridge of Dye is five miles up, on the Cairn o' Mount road.

This fine and scenic approach from the south, from Fettercairn in the Howe of the Mearns, makes an attractive run—save in wintery conditions when it can be appalling. The B974 road rises from 409 feet at Clattering Bridge to 1488 feet at Cairn o' Mount itself, in less than three miles, through the steep and treeless heather hills. Here there is a large former burial-cairn, the views back over the Howe and Strathmore being superb. Here too is the parish boundary of Strachan, though the village is nine miles on. In three miles is Spitalburn, now a roofless cottage beside the Dye Water, where once there was a hospice for travellers—and badly needed. Trees soften the austere landscape from now on down Glen Dye; and in another mile the river is crossed by the lofty, single-arch, humped and ancient Bridge of Dye, alleged to have been built by Sir Alexander Fraser of Durris—though such early erection seems doubtful. An Act of Parliament of 1681 permitted tolls for its upkeep, and the pillars for an iron chain across may still be seen. Here is a tiny community, with sawmill, estate gardens and forestry. Scolly's Cross lies about two miles on, with farm and former school; but what cross is referred to the writer could not discover. The famous 17th century Presbyterian divine, Andrew Cant, came of the family who owned Glen Dye.

The road forks in a mile farther, in attractive surroundings, the left fork leading down past Cuttieshillock to the road-junction on the B976 at Feughside Inn, a fair-sized hotel. At Cuttieshillock, now only a farmery, was formerly held an annual fair. The right fork winds on down Dye, past the picturesque Bridge of Bogendreip to the B976 again, at Strachan village. Queen Victoria and Prince Albert came by this road from Fettercairn in 1861, the queen writing appreciatively of it.

Strachan is a small place, pleasantly set in the open valley—not of the Aven, despite its name, but of the Feugh which the Aven has joined. The present parish church is not old, 1797 remodelled in 1837, with its graveyard across the road, a few old stones amongst the others, in the long grass. The oddly shaped hill of Clochnaben (1900 feet) dominates the valley, with its hump-like tor. There are ancient burial-cairns on the higher ground just north of the village, and above these stretches the wooded heights of the Blackhall Forest. A mile east of Strachan, off the winding side-road to Durris, is Mill of Cammie, attractively sited though somewhat decayed, the mill now a sawmill, the little bridge crossing the rocky bed of a tumbling burn which threads scrub woodland and plantations. All this area is heavily wooded. Just half a mile on eastwards, near the parish boundary with Durris, is Gellen, now only a farm but once famous as a "town" so-called, where, in 1644 a supernatural conflagration is recorded by Spalding: ". . . a fearful unnatural fire, whilk kindled of itself and burnt the bigging of the town only."

On the other side of Strachan village rises its smallish Castlehill, a natural eminence not far from the Feugh, on which was built one of the many Durward castles of Deeside.

APPENDIX

Places of special interest, some open to the public, others where access or view is usually possible, or can be arranged.

(*Indicates property in care of the Department of the Environment; † indicates property of the National Trust for Scotland.)

ABERDEENSHIRE

Aberdeen:
  Brig o' Balgownie
  King's College
  Marischal College
  Provost Ross's House
  Provost Skene's House
  Rubislaw Quarries
  St. Machar's Cathedral
  St. Nicholas' Church
  Wallace Tower
  War Memorial Tower
Auchindoir: Old Church
Braemar:
  Castle
  Crathie Church
  Linn of Dee
Chapel of Garioch: *Maiden Stone
Culsalmond: Newton House Gardens and Pictish stones
Daviot: *Loanhead Stone-circle
Drumoak: Drum Castle
Echt: *Stone-circle
Fraserburgh: Kinnaird's Head Castle Lighthouse
Huntly: *Castle
Insch: *Picardy Pictish stone
Inverurie:
  Balbithan House and Gardens
  Bass and Pictish stones
  *Kinkell Old Church
Kennethmont: †Leith-hall and Gardens
Kildrummy:
  *Castle
  Gardens
  Old Church
Kincardine O'Neil: Old Church
Lumphanan: †Craigevar Castle
Methlick: Haddo House
Newburgh: Forvie Sands Nature Reserve

Old Deer: *Abbey of Deer
Old Meldrum: Barra Castle
Rathen: *Memsie Cairn
Rhynie: Druminnor Castle
Strathdon:
    *Corgarff Castle
    *Glenbuchat Castle
Turriff: Old Church
Udny:
    †Pitmeddan Gardens
    *Tolquhon Castle

ANGUS

Aberlemno:
    Finavon Fort
    *Pictish stones
Arbroath:
    *Abbey
    *St. Vigeans Pictish Museum
Brechin:
    Cathedral and Round Tower
    Caterthun forts
Broughty Ferry: Broughty Castle
Dundee:
    Camperdown Castle
    *Claypotts House
    Dudhope Castle
    Old Steeple
Edzell:
    *Castle
    Retreat, Glen Esk
Forfar: *Restenneth Priory
Glamis:
    †Angus Folk Museum
    Castle
    *Cossans Stone
    *Eassie Church and Pictish stone
Glen Isla: Reekie Linn Waterfall
Kirriemuir:
    †Barrie's Birthplace
    Pictish stones in cemetery
Monifieth:
    *Ardestie Earth-house (weem)
    *Carlungie Earth-house (weem)
Monikie: *Auchinleck, or Affleck, Castle
Montrose: Museum
Tealing: *Earth-house (weem)

KINCARDINESHIRE

Arbuthnott:
  House
  Old Church
Banchory: †Crathes Castle
Dunnottar: Castle
Kinneff: Old Parish Church

SHORT BIBLIOGRAPHY

A Guide to Prehistoric Scotland, Richard Feachem (Batsford).
The Ancient Stones of Scotland, W. Douglas Simpson (Hale).
The Story of Scotland in Stone, Ian C. Hannah (Oliver and Boyd).
The Stones of Scotland, G. Scott-Moncrieff (Batsford).
The Picts, Isobel Henderson (Thames and Hudson).
The Problems of the Picts, F. T. Wainwright (Nelson).
Early Christian and Pictish Monuments of Scotland (H.M.S.O.).
The History of Celtic Place-names of Scotland, W. J. Watson (Black-wood).
The Historic Architecture of Scotland, J. G. Dunbar (Blackwood).
The Fortified House in Scotland, Volume 4, Nigel Tranter (Oliver and Boyd).
Castles, Houses and Gardens of Scotland, Nan Patullo (Blackwood).
Scottish Castles, W. Douglas Simpson (H.M.S.O.).
The Highland Clans, Sir Iain Moncrieffe (Barrie and Rockliff).
Royal Valley—Aberdeenshire Dee, Fenton Wyness (Reid).
City by the Grey North Sea, Fenton Wyness (Reid).
History of Scottish Farming, T. B. Franklin (Nelson).
The Drove Roads of Scotland, A. R. B. Haldane (Edinburgh University Press).
The North-East Lowlands of Scotland, J. R. Allan (Hale).
On Ski in the Cairngorms, V. A. Firsoff (Hale).
Discovering Angus and the Mearns, Duncan Fraser (Standard Press).
Scottish Mountaineering Club Guide—The Cairngorms.
New and *Third Statistical Accounts of Scotland*.
Angus or Forfarshire, A. J. Warden (Alexander).
History of Aberdeenshire, Alex. Smith (Blackwood).
Memorials of Angus and the Mearns, A. Jervis (Douglas).

INDEX

INDEX

Main localities are indicated in capitals and bold figures

387